Homer in Performance

ASHLEY AND PETER LARKIN SERIES IN GREEK AND ROMAN CULTURE

Homer in Performance

RHAPSODES, NARRATORS, AND CHARACTERS

Edited by Jonathan L. Ready and Christos C. Tsagalis

University of Texas Press *Austin*

Printed in the United States of America
First edition, 2018
First paperback printing, 2025

♾ The paper used in this book meets the minimum requirements of ANSI/NISO Z39.48-1992 (R1997) (Permanence of Paper).

LIBRARY OF CONGRESS CATALOGING-IN-PUBLICATION DATA
Names: Ready, Jonathan L., 1976–, editor. | Tsagalis, Christos, editor.
Title: Homer in performance : rhapsodes, narrators, and characters / edited by Jonathan L. Ready and Christos C. Tsagalis.
Description: First edition. | Austin : University of Texas Press, 2018. | Includes bibliographical references and index.
Identifiers: LCCN 2017051212
ISBN 978-1-4773-3361-7 (paperback)
ISBN 978-1-4773-1604-7 (PDF)
ISBN 978-1-4773-1605-4 (epub)
Subjects: LCSH: Homer—Criticism, Textual. | Epic poetry, Greek—History and criticism—Theory, etc. | Performing arts—Appreciation—Greece. | Oral interpretation of poetry. | Oral tradition—Greece.
Classification: LCC PA4037 .H77474 2018 | DDC 883/.01—dc23
LC record available at https://lccn.loc.gov/2017051212

doi:10.7560/316030

Contents

A Note on Iota Adscript and the Transliteration of Proper Nouns

We use an iota adscript, not subscript, when quoting Greek.

We follow Richmond Lattimore's spellings of the names of Homeric characters (kappa is *k*; chi is *ch*), but opt for Athen*a*, not Athen*e*. We Latinize the names of (familiar) ancient authors (Herodotus) and ancient scholars (Aristarchus, Zenodotus). We transliterate the names of historical figures (Megakles, Nikeratos, Perikles) and the names of actual places (Skepsis), although we retain the familiar spellings of certain places (Cyprus, Syracuse). All of this is aspirational, and inconsistencies likely remain.

Acknowledgments

WE THANK JIM BURR, NANCY BRYAN, LYNNE CHAPman, and the other members of the team at the University of Texas Press for their guidance in bringing this project to fruition. The two anonymous readers for the press provided excellent feedback on the initial submission. Kerri Cox Sullivan skillfully copy edited. We offer a special thanks to Noah Kaye for making the maps.

Introduction

JONATHAN L. READY AND
CHRISTOS C. TSAGALIS

THE AFRICANIST HAROLD SCHEUB DESCRIBES A SOUTH African taleteller at work (2002: 224–225):

> She has two important roles to play: as a storyteller and as the characters in the story. . . . When she creates characters, she is still in her role as storyteller. Thus: Nohatyula Miyeki as person; Nohatyula Miyeki as person, as storyteller; Nohatyula Miyeki as person, as storyteller, as character in the story.

Scheub's account recalls Plato's distinction between the epic poet's speaking in his own voice and in those of his characters and Aristotle's distinctions between the epic poet's speaking in his own voice, in that of the narrator, and in those of his characters (cf. de Jong 2004a: 1–8).

Encouraged to find this sort of analysis a matter of perennial interest, we base this volume on the following premise: audiences of Homeric epic in ancient Greece watched a flesh-and-blood person, a rhapsode, perform and watched him perform in the guises of the narrator and the characters. Our project examines these speakers: rhapsodes, narrators, and characters. Part I's contributors adopt a range of strategies to offer new perspectives on the performers of Homeric epic from the Archaic to the Imperial periods. In part II, contributors provide innovative analyses of the narrators and characters of the *Iliad* and the *Odyssey* as speakers.

To introduce these figures, we present some basic information about rhapsodes (Tsagalis), consider the Homeric poems' depictions of bards (Tsagalis), and review some salient facts about the epics' narrators and characters as speakers (Ready).[1]

RHAPSODES

The noun ῥαψωιδός means "stitcher of songs," an etymological association with ῥάβδος (staff) being linguistically untenable (Patzer 1952: 315–317; West 2011b). The term designates a reciter of poetry, such as that of Homer, Hesiod (Plato *Laws* 658d), Simonides, and Empedocles (Athenaeus 14.620c–d). Although the term is not attested before the late fifth century BCE, when it is employed in the aforementioned sense, it can hardly have been coined at such a late stage, given the long history of performance, especially of epic poetry.

We do not dismiss the view that the stitching element in the term *rhapsōidos* indicates continuous recitation, provided that "stitching" is understood as the combination either of different kinds of song, like a hymn and a song (cf. Pindar *Nemean* 2.2; schol. Pindar *Nemean* 2.1), or of the different parts of a more extended epic composition that was recited continuously (that is, by following the course of the plot) but not in its entirety. Taking into account the practicalities of any performance context, we cannot exclude the possibility that there is a middle ground between reciting episodes from the Homeric epics and performing the *Iliad* or the *Odyssey* in their entirety (see pp. 46–52 on the Panathēnaia). A rhapsode might, for example, sing bits of either of the two Homeric epics in such a manner that an audience could listen to the core of each poem but not the entire composition.

The distinction between the *aoidos* and the rhapsode should not be pressed too much, at least for the Archaic period (Gentili 1988: 6–7; P. Murray 1996: 97; González 2013: 219–290). Martin West argues for "a dual tradition from the time of Homer, sung delivery to the accompaniment of the phorminx on the one hand, recitation in speech tones on the other" (1981: 114), and he posits that "the eighth-century ἀοιδός with his phorminx and the classical rhapsode without it stand in a single line of tradition, the manner of delivery throughout being a kind of recitative that preserved the natural word accents but was (at least as long as the phorminx remained in use) pitched on definite notes" (cf. Schadewaldt 1959: 60; Herington 1985: 13). Nevertheless, our sources bring out the differences between singers and rhapsodes: the former perform at the suggestion of their host, and the latter in public competitions; the former compose and perform their own songs, while the latter's work is closely attached to the poetry of other individuals (Graziosi 2002: 30–31).

There are, moreover, passages in which the distinction between singers and rhapsodes is blurred. Barbara Graziosi sorts the relevant data into two sets: those pertaining to agonistic contexts and those in Plato's works (2002: 32–40). An oft-discussed fragment attributed to Hesiod refers to Homer and Hesiod as celebrating Apollo on Delos by "stitching song in new hymns" (ἐν νεαροῖς ὕμνοις ῥάψαντες ἀοιδήν, 357 M-W), and Pindar speaks of the Homeridai as "singers of stitched verses" (ῥαπτῶν ἐπέων ἀοιδοί, *Nemean* 2.1). Neither example bolsters the case for equating the singer-composer of epic and the rhapsode-reciter (West 2011b) nor supports the argument for an absolute dichotomy. It is a plausible hypothesis that verses like those found in fr. 357 M-W were composed in rhapsodic circles (Janko 1982: 113–115) in an attempt to create an aetiology for the first rhapsodic competition (Graziosi 2002: 34–36).

The same is the case *mutatis mutandis* with respect to the presentation of Homer as both a poet and an itinerant rhapsode in the *Certamen* (*Contest*) in which he is depicted as competing against Hesiod in Chalcis, composing the *Margites*, and rhapsodizing his poetry in various cities.[2] The case of the *Certamen* is instructive, since the rhapsodizing activity of Homer that is paired with his wide traveling and performance of his poetry is counterbalanced by the presentation of Hesiod as anchored to his native Askra, making only a short trip to Chalcis. His acclaimed victory over Homer in that place toys, among other things, with the marked opposition between geographical contiguity and distance. While in the autobiographical *sphragis* of the Nautilia section in the *Works and Days* the Hesiodic–Homeric contrast is expressed in terms of poetry, in the *Certamen* it is verbalized in terms of poets. In the former case, the grand content of the Trojan War epic tradition that is symbolically epitomized in the long sea journey of the Achaians from Aulis to Troy is counterbalanced by the more humble content of a Hesiodic hymn the premiere of which is presented in Chalcis, lying just across the Eurippos strait. In the latter case, the wide-traveling Homer is opposed to a Hesiod who is closely associated with his native town. As Graziosi has convincingly argued, even the *Certamen*'s epitaphs of Homer and Hesiod testify to the antithesis between "Hesiod's localized presence and Homer's geographical indeterminacy" (2002: 35).[3]

As far as Plato is concerned, there are cases in which he clearly draws a dividing line between the poet-composer and the rhapsode, the latter being taken here in the strict sense of a reciter of already composed epic poetry, while on a few occasions he seems not to distinguish between them. As a representative example of the former category we mention *Republic* 373b7–c1: "poets and their attendants, rhapsodes, actors, dancers, contractors, craftsmen of every kind of utensils and especially of those pertaining to women's ornaments" (ποιηταί τε καὶ τούτων ὑπηρέται, ῥαψωδοί, ὑποκριταί, χορευταί, ἐργολάβοι, σκευῶν τε παντοδαπῶν δημιουργοί, τῶν τε ἄλλων καὶ τῶν περὶ τὸν γυναικεῖον κόσμον). Rhapsodes and actors are seen as subordinate to epic poets and dramatic authors respectively. By contrast, in *Republic* 600d5–e2 Plato depicts Homer and Hesiod in rhapsodic guise, as itinerant performers of epic. It is clear that by doing so he extrapolates from the current view of his time ("you [Ion] perform as a rhapsode traveling among the Greeks" [ῥαψῳδεῖς μὲν περιιὼν τοῖς Ἕλλησι, *Ion* 541b8]), which was probably shaped under rhapsodic influence: Homer and Hesiod are not educators in the manner of the Sophists and their entourage but rhapsodes—that is, "actors of epic" (Graziosi 2002: 38).

In the dialogue *Ion*, perhaps the most famous discussion of rhapsodic activity from the fourth century BCE, Plato denigrates Homer by assimilating him to rhapsodes in the manner of the dialogue's protagonist, the rhapsode Ion, who is cast in a negative light. These tactics become obvious when Plato speaks of the four types of *mousikē* (*aulēsis*, *kitharisis*, *kitharōidia*, and *rhapsōidia*) and their inventors (Olympos, Thamyris, Orpheus, and Phemios). The presentation of Phemios, the well-known Ithakan singer, as a rhapsode (533b–c) is unique and has been interpreted as "an *ad hoc* ploy to tease Ion" (Graziosi 2002: 40n75 *contra* P. Murray 1996: 112 at 533c1). The substitution of Phemios for Homer has been explained by the fact that Homer is never explicitly said to be a rhapsode, only to be rhapsodizing his own poetry. Here again we see a deliberate anachronism. A fourth-century idea (that Phemios is a rhapsode) that probably originated in rhapsodic circles is projected back in time to the inventor of epic poetry.[4]

Leaving aside the context of rhapsodic recitations, which is the subject of chapters 1 and 3, we will briefly treat other aspects of rhapsodic performance, such as those that are internal or central and those that are external or peripheral to the recital of epic poetry.

The information we can gather from various literary and nonliterary sources regarding rhapsodic performance in the late Archaic and Classical periods describes an event imbued with certain staging features. With this term, taken wholesale from the field of performative arts, we mean to stress the fact that like any recital of poetry in front of an audience, the performance of epic entails various communicating strategies, some of which are central and some peripheral to poetry itself. By drawing a line between central and peripheral elements, we want simply to underline the fact that in the case of poetry composed to be performed various features of its staging in front of an audience are embedded in the song itself.

Some of the elements performatively exploited by rhapsodes, which would have been derived directly from epic diction itself and considered as internal or central to its recital, are the speech-initial, whole-line vocatives, such as διογενὲς Λαερτιάδη πολυμήχαν' Ὀδυσσεῦ (*Iliad* 2.173); staging formulas, such as τὸν δὲ ἰδὼν ἐνόησε ποδάρκης δῖος Ἀχιλλεύς (*Iliad* 11.599); second-person addresses, such as τὸν δὲ βαρὺ στενάχων προσέφης, Πατρόκλεες ἱππεῦ (*Iliad* 16.20); sound effects generated by assonance and various alliterative devices, such as χύντο χαμαὶ χολάδες (*Iliad* 4.526); and vocal differentiations on the basis of the content of a passage, such as a list of names or an emotionally loaded sequence.

Speech-initial, whole-line vocatives including the addressee's name are employed solely the *first* time a person is mentioned in a given scene. The next time he is addressed in the same scene, only an abbreviated address-expression is used. This strategy reflects, in our opinion, a reality of the performance. When introducing a specific character in such an emphatic manner, the rhapsode would performatively exploit his extended address so that the addressee would come in all his grandeur to the front of the listeners' mental horizon. In the formula διογενὲς Λαερτιάδη πολυμήχαν' Ὀδυσσεῦ, Odysseus is conjured in his full epic armature: as an illustrious hero, son of Laertes, much-resourceful Odysseus. Expressions such as τὸν δὲ ἰδὼν ἐνόησε pave the way for the introduction or epiphany of a new character, here ποδάρκης δῖος Ἀχιλλεύς (Bakker 1997a: 156–195). The function of the pronoun τὸν is to operate as a starting point that makes the verb ἐνόησε reenact in the present what Achilleus did in the past ("*him* when he saw he took notice"). Rhapsodes reciting this line may have made full use of the staging aspects of the diction, the more so since in this way they would enhance the mental visualization of the new (in this scene) character Achilleus in the minds of the audience. Their aim would be to exploit the dictional means at their disposal and turn the distality of the narrative into a presence at the level of the performance.

Character apostrophizing by the narrator—such as "and groaning deeply you addressed him, horseman Patroklos" (τὸν δὲ βαρὺ στενάχων προσέφης, Πατρόκλεες ἱππεῦ, *Iliad* 16.20)—has often attracted scholarly attention due to its marked difference from the usual nominative noun–epithet formulas. Leaving aside other aspects of this notoriously complicated issue (Kahane 1994: 107–113, 153–155), we would like to suggest a possible rhapsodic use of this device. In the case of *Iliad* 16.20, the narrator's voice is subsumed by that of the rhapsode who is performing the epic. Instead of staging Patroklos by introducing him to the audience through a noun–epithet nominative formula, it is the rhapsode-performer who addresses the hero. In the words of Egbert Bakker, "the direct address does not effect an epiphany, it presupposes one: Patroklos is already present in the performance for the performer to address him . . . he is a listener in the performance like ourselves" (1997a: 173). In this light, a rhapsode could take advantage of this built-in device to enhance the *enargeia* of his recital: Patroklos is here, together with the audience, and is about to speak to Achilleus.

Sound effects generated by assonance and various alliterative devices, such as χύντο χαμαὶ χολάδες (*Iliad* 4.526), are a typical feature of all forms of recited poetry. They draw attention to meaning or sometimes conjure an interpretive aspect that seems secondary or hidden. Rhapsodes would perhaps make use of this linguistic tool by stressing the pronunciation of the sounds so as to highlight a given point to the listeners. One might also reconstruct differences in the voicing of certain passages based on their content. For example, the list of Nereids (*Iliad* 18.39–49) could be recited at a different speed than the previous and ensuing narrative and speech by Thetis, two emotionally loaded passages. Rhapsodes would no doubt make sure that the accumulation of names created a specific effect so that the exotic nature of the Nereids and their number would be felt by the audience. Thetis is coming to the shore from her watery abode accompanied by her entire entourage. A series of names would flow through the rhapsode's mouth, striking the listeners with their arresting sounds. No good performer would miss such an opportunity (cf. M. Edwards 1987b: 117–123, 1991: 55–60).

As for external or peripheral elements, we focus on the rhapsodes' dress code, scenic presence, and training. According to Dionysius Thrax (excerpted from Heliodorus), when the Homeridai recited parts of the *Iliad* they wore crimson crowns or garlands that stood for bloodshed, while they preferred dark blue ones—symbolizing the color of the sea over which Odysseus wandered—when they recited from the *Odyssey* (316.15–19 Hilgard). Likewise, Eustathius (on *Iliad* 6.8 = I 9.20–25 van der Valk) reports that reciters of the *Iliad* dressed in red to recall the poem's bloodshed, and reciters of the *Odyssey* dressed in blue to evoke the purple color of the sea on which Odysseus wandered for years. This information can be associated with the Panathēnaia (Scheliha 1943: 403–404; West 2011b), given the grand occasion of the famous relay performance held there, but a hint in Eustathius's phrasing allows, alternatively, for a different setting.[5] This entire passage is prefaced by "even if rhapsodes of a later time performed Homeric poetry in a more dramatic style" (εἰ δὲ καὶ τὴν Ὁμηρικὴν ποίησιν οἱ ὕστερον ὑπεκρίνοντο δραματικώτερον), which follows a brief discussion of the theatrical practice of calling the plays *dramata* and not *grammata*. The use of ὑπεκρίνοντο recalls the Platonic references to certain histrionic features of rhapsodic recitals (*Republic* 373b7–c1; *Ion* 535e) (Graziosi 2002: 38). Eustathius then proceeds to argue that the dress code of rhapsodes performing the *Iliad* and the *Odyssey* is a chance event and a novel conception of later generations (σύμβαμα καὶ καινότερον ἐπινόημα τῶν ἐσύστερον), since even if the poet wrote in a dramatic style, he did not create a stage drama (ὁ δὲ ποιητὴς εἰ καὶ δραματικῶς ἔγραψεν, ἀλλ' οὐκ ἐδραματούργησε σκηνικῶς).

In our view, then, we cannot exclude the possibility that the specific dress code used by rhapsodes when performing the Homeric poems presupposes the influence of theater-culture and as such points to a much later phase in the history of rhapsodic performances. This is, after all, the picture we draw from the *Ion*, where more than once it is said that rhapsodes take care of their external appearance—"for that adorning your body and appearing as beautiful as possible is fitting for your art" (τὸ γὰρ ἅμα μὲν τὸ σῶμα κεκοσμῆσθαι ἀεὶ πρέπον ὑμῶν εἶναι τῆι τέχνηι καὶ ὡς καλλίστοις φαίνεσθαι, 530b6–8)—and that they are dressed "in a many-colored raiment and golden wreaths" (ἐσθῆτι ποικίληι καὶ χρυσοῖσι στεφάνοις, 535d2–3).

We do not know much about the size of audiences for rhapsodic performances. This matter has obviously to do with the particular venue that was used. The information in Plato's *Ion* (535d) is unique and as a result difficult to evaluate. Twenty thousand attendees (δισμυρίοις ἀνθρώποις) is a big number, even by modern standards, but it is not impossible given the size of ancient theaters. The capacity of the theater at Epidaurus, which was the venue for Ion's performance, is between twelve and fifteen thousand spectators: Ion's numbers are not greatly exaggerated.[6] In any case, audiences no doubt varied in size, but both public festivals and theaters (at a later phase) were chosen by the rhapsodes for epic recitals because of the crowds of people that flocked there. In the course of time, rhapsodes sought large audiences.

Rhapsodes functioned not as dull reciters of epic but as inspired interpreters of the poet's mind: "For the rhapsode must become an interpreter of the poet's thought for the listeners" (τὸν γὰρ ῥαψωιδὸν ἑρμηνέα δεῖ τοῦ ποιητοῦ τῆς διανοίας γίγνεσθαι τοῖς ἀκούουσι, *Ion* 530c3–4). In the *Ion*, this interpretive process is inscribed in the larger framework of the performance of epic, since it is acknowledged that poets are the interpreters of the gods: "that these beautiful poems are not manmade nor man's, but divinely made and the gods', and the poets are nothing other than interpreters of the gods" (ὅτι οὐκ ἀνθρώπινά ἐστιν τὰ καλὰ ταῦτα ποιήματα οὐδὲ ἀνθρώπων, ἀλλὰ θεῖα καὶ θεῶν, οἱ δὲ ποιηταὶ οὐδὲν ἀλλ' ἢ ἑρμηνῆς εἰσιν τῶν θεῶν, 534e2–4). To this extent, rhapsodes are interpreters of other interpreters, their work going back to the gods themselves with the poets as intermediaries (535a).

Rhapsodes strove to create a visual association between the content of the plot and what the audience actually saw in front of them. They therefore cried when they recited a sorrowful scene or episode, or expressed their fright (probably through some gesture) when they recited a fear-inducing scene. Ion says that the hair on his head rises when he says "something fearsome and terrible" (φοβερὸν ἢ δεινόν, *Ion* 535c7–8), but the point here is that kinesics were employed by rhapsodes in their attempts to make their recital more vivid. Their aim was to make the recital a true experience, a feast for the mind and senses, inviting the audience to share and participate in the epic plot. By partially reenacting the story they narrated, rhapsodes turned the recital into a performance. Such a feat would make them famous and guarantee them success (535e).

Rhapsodes no doubt possessed written copies of Homer. In Xenophon's *Memorabilia*, Sokrates asks Euthydemos, who has collected many of the works of celebrated poets and sophists and has a complete text of Homer in his library, whether he intends to be a rhapsode (4.2.1, 4.2.8–10). As West rightly points out, "the inference is that not many people owned a complete Homer, and that rhapsodes were more likely to than others" (2001: 20). Some rhapsodes not only recited Homeric poetry but also lectured on it. Isocrates (10.65) reports that certain Homeridai claimed that it was Helen herself who visited Homer and told him to compose an epic about the Trojan War because she wanted to make the deaths of the heroes at Troy more glorious than the lives of others (cf. Plato *Ion* 533c, 536d). We are in no position to determine what other topics the rhapsodes discussed. The sheer lack of information on this issue should make us extremely cautious with respect to pre-Alexandrian emendation on the basis of unseemliness (ἀπρέπεια) toward the gods or with respect to standard values or aesthetic principles.

SINGERS IN THE *ILIAD* AND THE *ODYSSEY*

We stress *ab ovo* the problem of treating the information found in the Homeric epics about the performance of epic poetry as historically accurate. Should we understand the picture the *Iliad* and the *Odyssey* draw with respect to performers of epic as an "authorial self-insertion" (Gainsford 2015: 85), or does it reflect real poets and performance practice? Gregory Nagy, who opts for the first alternative, has even coined a term, "diachronic skewing," a premier Homeric example of which is the singer (*aoidos*) who sings to the accompaniment of a stringed instrument, the phorminx (*Odyssey* 8.67, 73). Because the melodic aspect of the performance of Demodokos, a key singer in the *Odyssey*, and the use of a musical instrument are characteristically absent from all the extant material pertaining to the performance of epic in the Archaic and Classical periods, it seems that "the medium of 'Homer' has outgrown, as it were, the medium of Demodokos" (Nagy 2003: 42).[7] The representations of aoidic activity in the Homeric epics amount to stylized refashionings of epic performances that gainsay the reality of actual rhapsodic recitals. Both performer-depiction and performance-milieu stand in stark contrast: the singer with the phorminx yielded to the rhapsode with no musical instrument, and the public festival mainly replaced the prandial and postprandial occasion (González 2013: 87–88; Ebbott, forthcoming).

The situations we encounter on Ithaka in *Odyssey* 1 and in the Phaiakian palace in *Odyssey* 8 show singers of epic, Phemios and Demodokos, performing in the context of a banquet.[8] Recital of epic follows an established pattern in accordance with the rules of feasting: "the social part of the feast, whether business or entertainment, can begin only after the meal proper is over, the formula 'after they have been satisfied by their food and drink' serving as a clear line of demarcation between these two stages" (Finkelberg 1998: 89–90). Singers are experienced (*Odyssey* 1.337–338), and some are self-taught (*Odyssey* 22.347): Phemios's boast that he is αὐτοδίδακτος (self-taught) means he has composed all his songs on his own, not that he invented their subject matter. It also means by inference that other singers were taught by more experienced professionals (Schadewaldt 1959: 71; cf. Bonifazi 2012: 152–154; González 2013: 212–214). "Training" does not necessarily mean learning a given epic and then reperforming it: it can simply refer to the techniques of oral performance.[9] Singers are held in high esteem.[10] In the *Odyssey*, invented nomenclature mirrors the bards' social approval—Φήμιος Τερπιάδης ("Phemios, son of the Pleasing One"), Δημόδοκος ("accepted or approved by the people")—as does the declaration that the fame of an *aoidos* like Demodokos "has reached the wide sky" (κλέος οὐρανὸν εὐρὺν ἵκανε, *Odyssey* 8.74).

Singers interact with their audiences with respect to the particular songs they perform. A song can be interrupted: Alkinoös twice stops the performance of Demodokos, whose songs make Odysseus weep (*Odyssey* 8.139–140, 536–543; cf. Finkelberg 1998: 90). Members of the audience can ask the bard to sing a song they like, as Odysseus does at *Odyssey* 8.492–498. Interaction of this kind, which includes "song ordering," presupposes that these epic bards have an extended repertoire of songs and that they can sing on the spot what their audience desires: Phemios's epithet πολύφημος ("of many speeches") (*Odyssey* 22.376) highlights his ability to sing many stories (*Odyssey* 22.347–348) (cf. Ford 2011).

The case of Demodokos differs in part from that of Phemios. Two of the songs he sings (the first and the third) are well known, which means that they were sung in front of various audiences and that perhaps some members of the present audience have already heard them. Since these are clearly preexisting songs, Demodokos will try to meet the expectations of his audience as far as the veracity of his songs is concerned. By "veracity," we mean the "'accuracy' and 'comprehensiveness'" of Demodokos's telling (González 2013: 176). In a performance framework, veracity is the prime manifestation of notional fixity, which is in turn "derived from the well-known kinship between poetry and prophecy that has its most immediate expression in the bard's claim to divine inspiration" (González 2013: 177). In contrast to Phemios, who publicizes himself as a "self-taught" singer, the *Odyssey* emphasizes in a famous passage that Demodokos has been trained: "either the Muse, the child of Zeus, instructed [ἐδίδαξε] you or Apollo" (*Odyssey* 8.488).[11] The point is here not so much to draw a line between Demodokos and Phemios but to exploit the close association between the bard's entitlement to veracity of telling and divine inspiration. The verb ἐδίδαξε ("instructed") has as its subject not some human singer but the Muse or Apollo. By entertaining a choice between these two alternatives, Homeric epic virtually brings these two entities together because the latter is dubbed the "leader of the Muses" (Μουσηγέτης), as in Plato's *Laws* (653d3). The Muse and Apollo are the divine instructors, and the bard is their apprentice. He must sing κατὰ κόσμον ("aright," "duly"): his utterance must be harmonious with the way things happened. Veracity and accuracy, therefore, belong to the specialized diction of the singer's art.

But the term κόσμος in such a context acquires an even more specialized meaning: it also can be defined as "song." The expression ἵππου κόσμον ἄεισον / δουρατέου ("sing the song of the wooden horse") at *Odyssey* 8.492 clearly refers to an epic song about the sack of Troy. Its semantic association with κατὰ κόσμον ("aright") makes the term κόσμος resonate deeply with Archaic notions of epic performance. This observation is further corroborated by the use of κατὰ μοῖραν (*Odyssey* 8.496). By covertly allowing for the possibility that the bard Demodokos may have heard another report of the events in Troy, Odysseus urges him to report what happened κατὰ μοῖραν, which means that κατὰ κόσμον and κατὰ μοῖραν can (at least) be viewed from a similar perspective (González 2013: 194–196).[12]

Epic singers may perform songs that were either established and old or newer ones that had recently attracted attention and approval by audiences.[13] The songs pertaining to the "deeds of gods and men" are treated as established and well known (*Odyssey* 1.337–338), while the "painful return of the Achaians" (*Odyssey* 1.326–327) is designated as "the newest song" (*Odyssey* 1.352). Demodokos's songs seem to reflect an older set of songs (*Odyssey* 8.74) pertaining not only to the entire Trojan myth (his first [*Odyssey* 8.75–82] and third [*Odyssey* 8.499–520] songs) but also to "deeds of gods," stories referring to the divine world with a more amusing tone that caught the audience's attention (his second song [*Odyssey* 8.266–366]).

Although it is ill advised to extrapolate from the performances depicted in the *Odyssey* to the reality of rhapsodic performances, we are justified in underlining the performance of separate episodes, not entire poems.[14] That said, we offer two caveats: on the one hand, the venue of the feast, being the performance milieu, would have imposed temporal and social constraints that regulated the time and length of an epic performance; on the other hand, the medium of epic itself would have imposed narrative constraints concerning the embedding of another song. Selectivity may have been a part (not the whole) of historical reality, but we cannot decide about it on the basis of the Homeric examples. Be that as it may, audiences had no trouble following a known story, which the bard could begin from and stop at the point a member of the audience desired (*Odyssey* 8.43–45, 97–107, 254–255, 536–543). He could also switch with ease from one episode to another (*Odyssey* 8.492 [μετάβηθι], 500 [ἔνθεν ἑλών]).

The standard depiction of singers in Homer speaks in favor of their being permanently located in a royal court. Although it is explicitly stated that the *aoidos* is "summoned all over the boundless earth" (*Odyssey* 17.382–385), "it is Thamyris alone who appears as a musical free agent, moving from one local engagement, as retainer to the house of King Eurytus in Oechalia, to another" (Power 2010: 254). Phemios, Demodokos, the anonymous singer in Mycenae (*Odyssey* 3.267–271), and the anonymous singer in Sparta (*Odyssey* 4.17–18) are *not* itinerant bards. They live and perform in the royal courts of Odysseus, Alkinoös, Agamemnon, and Menelaos, and they seem to belong to the palace's permanent personnel. The *Odyssey* highlights the close association between the feast and such activities as singing, dancing, and playing the lyre. They are all designated as "'offerings of the feast' [*Odyssey* 1.152, 21.430], and the lyre is described as 'the mate of the rich banquet' [*Odyssey* 8.99], which 'the gods have made to be the companion of the feast' [*Odyssey* 17.270–271]" (Finkelberg 1998: 89).

The Homeric poems offer no examples of epic contests. Nowhere do two or more singers compete against one another. Multiple singers are present in the formal lamentation for both Hektor (*Iliad* 24.719–722) and Achilleus (*Odyssey* 24.58–62), but there is no reference to a contest. The same is the case with other pluralities of singers, such as the Achaians singing the paean (*Iliad* 1.472–474, 22.391–394), the Muses and Apollo (*Iliad* 1.601–604), Achilleus and Patroklos (*Iliad* 9.186–191),[15] the choruses of maidens singing and dancing in honor of Artemis (*Iliad* 18.182–183; *Odyssey* 6.102–108), the people depicted on the Shield of Achilleus singing the wedding-song (*Iliad* 18.493), and the Sirens (*Odyssey* 12.184–191).[16] In *Iliad* 2.594–600 the singer Thamyris boasts that he would defeat even the Muses in a song contest and is subsequently punished with paralysis and the loss of his ability to sing and play the kithara. Even in this case, the idea of a contest is not to be taken literally. It pertains to the singer's boast that he could best the Muses, who are the source of his inspiration, not to a real contest that took place in a specific location.[17] Moreover, Thamyris is a kitharode, not a rhapsode, and to this extent his punishment may covertly illustrate kitharodic–rhapsodic antagonism, seen from the rhapsodes' viewpoint (cf. Power 2010: 205–209, 250–257). The passage about Thamyris should not be taken as evidence for aoidic contests.

NARRATORS AND CHARACTERS

We turn next to the Homeric narrators and characters as speakers, excluding from the characters to be considered the poets discussed in the previous section.

The first verses of the *Iliad* and the *Odyssey* encourage us to picture a poet, yet to be inspired but capable of speaking in hexameters, as he invokes the Muse (cf. Ford 1992: 22–23). Just as the bard on Scheria, Demodokos, must wait for the Muse to rouse him (ἀνῆκεν) to sing of "the quarrel between Odysseus and Peleus's son, Achilleus" (*Odyssey* 8.73–75) and must invoke divine help, or at least seek divine favor, before he can sing of the ploy of the wooden horse and the sack of Troy (*Odyssey* 8.499) (Ford 1992: 26–27, 112; González 2013: 234; cf. Nagy 2009a: 333–334), so the *Iliad*'s yet-to-be inspired teller asks the Muse to sing of "the wrath of Achilleus" (1.1), and the *Odyssey*'s yet-to-be inspired teller asks for the Muse to tell of "the man of many turnings" (1.1). The Muse answers the call in each case, and we embark on a journey with our inspired poet. In the *Iliad* the uninspired poet occasionally reemerges: he calls upon the Muse to help him, for instance, with the lengthy Catalogue of Ships or with a list of victims (Ford 1992: 78; Minchin 2001: 161–180).

Invocation complete, the inspired poet begins to tell the tale in the guise of the narrator, and soon after we hear from the characters. Some see an "ironic distance" between poet and narrator (Rabel 1997: 8), while others challenge the applicability of the typical narratological approach that would distinguish between poet and narrator (Bakker 2009: 124). As for the narrator and characters, some posit a relationship of subordination (de Jong 2004a: 35): the narrator quotes the speeches of the characters (D. Beck 2012: 23). Another approach of equal heuristic value sees "the performer shifting from one role into another, from narrator to character" (Bakker 2009: 126–127; cf. 2013: 5). However we envision these relationships, our inspired poet impresses. Omniscient and omnipresent (S. Richardson 1990: 123; de Jong 2001: 5, 2004b: 14), he can range over the known world, presenting the thoughts, feelings, words, and deeds not just of mortals but of immortals too (Scodel 1998: 179; Graziosi and Haubold 2005: 82–84). He thereby provides a true account of the heroic past (Ford 1992: 6, 17, 46–47, 125–126; de Jong 2004b: 15; González 2013: 211), even if he misdirects the audience from time to time (J. Morrison 1992; S. Richardson 2006).

The narrator reports what the characters do. He reveals what they feel and think (S. Richardson 1990: 126–132): the phenomenon of embedded focalization, wherein the narrator "temporarily hands over focalization (but not narration) to one of the characters," gets us into their minds (de Jong 2004a: 101–148 [quotation from 101], 2004b: 14), although one is regularly left to guess what a character is thinking (Scodel 2014: 56–57, 65–74). Finally, he details what they say via—if we adopt the nonhierarchical approach according to which the poet shifts between narrator and character—indirect speech, speech mention, and free indirect speech (if we attribute the instances of free indirect speech to the narrator) (S. Richardson 1990: 70–80; D. Beck 2012). The narrator also comments on the characters and on their utterances and actions: we hear him explaining, interpreting, and judging (S. Richardson 1990: 140–166). The narrator moves between different genres: his similes constitute a subgenre (Ready 2011: 93–95), and he presents lists and catalogues (Minchin 2001: 73–99; Sammons 2010). He supplements his tale with "para-narratives," such as *Iliad* 18's description of Achilleus's shield, "a separate and clearly defined episode subsidiary to the main plot and narrated at some length and in detail" and one that is thematically resonant (Alden 2000 [quotation from 18]).

The characters chime in. Forty-five percent of the *Iliad* and sixty-seven percent of the *Odyssey* comprise the direct speech of the characters (Minchin 2007: 4n6; cf. D. Beck 2012: 23). Many characters get the chance to speak: seventy-seven in the *Iliad*, although "fewer than half of the speaking characters speak in more than one book, and almost a third are represented by a single speech" (Lowe 2000: 116). Characters soliloquize (Dentice di Accadia Ammone 2012: 287–299), but they usually converse with others both in public and in private. The *Odyssey* contains more one-on-one conversations than the *Iliad* does (D. Beck 2005: 149; cf. 2012: 132, 157, 185), whereas in its scenes of assembly, funeral games, and laments the *Iliad* includes kinds of formal group conversations never or rarely found in the *Odyssey* (D. Beck 2005: 149, 272). Whether speaking to themselves or to others, whether in public or in private, the characters frequently emerge as performers out to display their verbal skill (Martin 1989). When speaking in the guise of his characters, the poet revels in variety.

Like the narrators, characters present para-narratives (Alden 2000), catalogues (Sammons 2010), and similes (Ready 2011). We mentioned that the narrator can disclose what goes on in a character's head. So, too, do the characters attempt to read the minds of other characters (Scodel 2012, 2014: 62–64). Yet their diction exhibits more emotion and a greater subjectivity than that of the narrators (Griffin 1986; de Jong 2004b: 19–20; A. Morrison 2007: 91); their speeches contain more "non-formulaic and metrically faulty expressions, linguistic innovations and the like" (Finkelberg 2012: 93); and they use more free indirect speech, indirect speech, and speech mention (D. Beck 2012: 61, 130, 132, 188–190). One adopting the hierarchical model according to which the narrator quotes the characters would contrast the narrator's favoring of direct quotation with the characters' preference for the aforementioned kinds of speech presentation (D. Beck 2012: 23–24). The characters also quote hypothetical speeches attributed to a generic "someone" (*tis*); the narrators quote *tis*-speeches, too, but only ones understood actually to have been spoken (24, 47–56). Lastly, the characters deploy a greater range of genres or speech formats than the narrators do (or use them more frequently [cf. A. Morrison 2007: 91]). They insult one another, they issue commands and directives, and they recollect the past (Martin 1989; Parks 1990; Minchin 2007: 188–221; D. Beck 2012: 14–15). They rebuke and protest (Minchin 2007: 23–51, 145–174). They utter proverbs (Lardinois 1997, 2001b) and engage in lengthy lamentations (Tsagalis 2004; Gagliardi 2006a, 2006b). They offer "angry speeches" (Lardinois 2003). We might even hear a joke from Odysseus (*Odyssey* 11.57–58) (Ford 1992: 161).

The characters always speak in hexameters, even those who are not poets, and they always speak Greek, even those who know a different language. Other similarities among the characters emerge, as do differences in what they say and how they say it. Gods and men use the same genres of speech. For instance, speakers from both groups issue commands (Martin 1989: 47–65) and deliver rhetorical speeches that adduce "argumentation and reasons" in an effort to persuade (Knudsen 2014: 81, quotation from 43). Yet that gods take on the voice and speech of mortals (*audē*) when addressing mortals implies that among themselves gods talk differently from men (Gera 2003: 51; Heath 2005: 52–57). On top of that, gods know a distinct language. We learn the divine words for certain entities: the gods, for example, call "Xanthos" the river called "Skamandros" by men (*Iliad* 20.74) (Gera 2003: 52; Heath 2005: 56; Brouillet 2013). Moreover, whereas both gods and men can communicate nonverbally (Lateiner 1995), gods, especially Zeus, can speak by way of omens (Ready 2012b: 77–79).

Sorting the characters' speeches by the speaker's gender, one finds that in the *Iliad*, female characters utter six rebukes and twelve protests, while male characters utter twenty-nine rebukes and twenty-four protests; in the *Odyssey*, female characters utter eleven rebukes and eight protests, while male characters utter fourteen rebukes and twenty-one protests (Minchin 2007: 145–174). In both poems, women and men use directives in equal measure (219–221), but men ask information-questions in attempts to coerce whereas women ask information-questions to establish a connection (285). In the *Odyssey*, women ask more questions but engage in fewer conversations than men do (D. Beck 2012: 134). Men tell more stories: in the *Iliad*, men tell twenty-three of the twenty-six stories related by characters; in the *Odyssey*, they tell twenty of the twenty-four stories narrated by characters (Minchin 2007: 253, 265). Men build "details of time and place and technical language" into their tales (280); women do not, being more interested in "character and motivation" (286).

Finally, differences appear between the *Iliad*'s two warring sides. The Trojans prefer to praise, whereas the Achaians prefer to blame (H. Mackie 1996). On the battlefield, "Trojan speakers display a performative versatility unparalleled among their Achaean opponents": where Achaians favor verbal dueling (flyting), Trojans "perform genealogical narratives, wonder tales, or lyric poetry" (66).

As individual speakers, the characters distinguish themselves. The *Iliad*'s Helen is an epigrammatist (Elmer 2005; Tsagalis 2008: 117–118; cf. Bassi 2016: 79–83), engages in self-blame (Blondell 2010), and uses the language of lament even when not lamenting (Martin 2008; Tsagalis 2008: 115, 122). Indeed, "the speech types she uses, which range from the mournful widow's to the flyting warrior's, are transposed from their usual contexts to form locutions unique to her" (Worman 2002: 47). Helen also evinces "a concern with reputation (*kleos*) anomalous among mortal female characters in Homer" (47). In *Odyssey* 4, she, exceptionally for a female character, assumes a heroic role in her own storytelling (Minchin 2007: 277, 280), and, in interpreting an omen in *Odyssey* 15, she exhibits "the omniscience of the Muses and the narrative compass of the poet" (Worman 2002: 63).

Nestor masters the genre of recollection (Martin 1989: 106; cf. Dickson 1995) and "enjoys the distinction of delivering the most rhetorical speeches and using the most rhetorical techniques of any speaker in the *Iliad*" (Knudsen 2014: 83). Agamemnon frequently engages in "rebuke and dispute" and only once deploys the "discourse of memory" (Martin 1989: 114). Hektor has a habit of imagining what others will say in the future about the past (136). Diomedes (Martin 1989: 23–26) and Telemachos (Heath 2005: 79–118) mature as speakers. Odysseus aims for balance and proportionality "not merely in the subject matter of his speeches but also in the choice of vocabulary and images" (Worman 2002: 65): one observes "his orderly stylistic calibrations" (70). The *Odyssey* shows him manipulating the components of his speeches—"e.g., length of descriptions, diction, emphasized elements" (79)—so as to "mirror" his audience's "attitudes and outlooks" (74). Zeus in the *Iliad* and Zeus and Athena in the *Odyssey* deliver "table of contents" speeches in which they provide an outline of events to come. For instance, Zeus previews Odysseus's journey home for Hermes: Odysseus will make his way to Scheria on a raft; the Phaiakians will lavish him with gifts; and he will return to Ithaka with more wealth than he amassed at Troy (*Odyssey* 5.30–42) (de Jong 2001: 15 at 81–95; Ready 2012b: 75–76).

The *Iliad*'s Achilleus stands out. For John Heath, "Achilles learns, unlike anyone in the text, to employ his verbal skills not to augment his own authority but for personal reasons that derive from his tragic insight" (2005: 86). In particular, in recounting the story of Niobe to Priam in *Iliad* 24, he "puts his considerable linguistic skills to a novel use: the lyre-player [cf. *Iliad* 9.186–189] now creates a story to console an adversary, to make a truly human connection possible" (130). Achilleus thereby "aligns himself with [the] humanizing power of the poet himself. And vice versa, of course" (166). For his part, Richard Martin finds that "Achilles generally employs familiar formulas in new ways," that "what seem like new and innovative uses can in fact be explained as reworkings of familiar expressions paralleled elsewhere within the poem," and that "another phenomenon in Achilles' use of formulaic art" is "his expansion aesthetic" (1989: 170–171). Achilleus's modes of expansion include "internal expansion" ("one recurrent phrase is involved; added to it is a further modifying phrase"), "splitting" ("two expressions normally united are split so that other sentences can be inserted"), and "replacement" ("some elements of several formulaic lines are retained, while others are replaced by different fuller expressions") (208–209). Even when Achilleus "telescopes," condensing phrases or ideas that appear elsewhere at greater length, he does so with a view to expansion at a subsequent point (215–219). This feature of Achilleus's speaking defines not only the hero's mode of presentation but that of the poet himself: "in Achilles we hear the speech of Homer, the heroic narrator" (223); "the poet of the *Iliad* . . . must by this implication be a poet against others, out to obliterate their performances by speaking in more detail, . . . Achilles is the poet's voice and his emblem, a heroic speaker who outdoes others in style" (238).

The relationship between Odysseus and the *Odyssey* poet is more fraught. Audience members listening to his stories find Odysseus so skilled a taleteller that they compare him to an *aoidos* (*Odyssey* 11.368, 17.518–521). Indeed, like a poet (cf. *Odyssey* 1.337–339, 22.347–348; see pp. 10–11), the hero's repertoire is vast. In exchange for his hospitality, Odysseus tells Aiolos stories for a month (*Odyssey* 10.14). He talks well into the night when relating his adventures to the Phaiakians (*Odyssey* 11.373–376). Eumaios reports that Odysseus enchanted him with his tales for three days and that Odysseus has not finished telling of his sorrows (*Odyssey* 17.514–521; cf. 14.196–197). Not only, then, does Odysseus take on Demodokos as an entertainer (Ford 1992: 121), but all his tale telling "can be presented as posing a threat with its charms to the progress of the narrative" (Bakker 2013: 11). Odysseus's stories might "crowd out the poet's tale" (Bakker 2009: 135).

Still, with the exception of those who are seers and singers, the characters are not inspired by the Muse (cf. Ford 1992: 62; de Jong 2004b: 19; Bassi 2016: 89–93), a limitation manifesting itself above all in their ignorance of what the gods are up to (cf. Jörgensen 1904). Odysseus, for instance, can only recount an exchange between Helios and Zeus (*Odyssey* 12.374–388) because, he explains, "I heard these things from fair-haired Kalypso; and she said that she had heard them herself from the guide

Hermes" (*Odyssey* 12.389–390). Nestor presents a rule-proving exception with his introduction of a divine apparatus into his narration of the Achaians' returns from Troy in *Odyssey* 3 (Marks 2008: 122–126).

On occasion, the distinction between narrator and character blurs. Narratologists speak of paralepsis: "the narrator intrudes with his superior knowledge into the embedded focalization of a character" (de Jong 2001: xvi). For example, before Odysseus has told them who he is, the Phaiakians "marveled looking upon the wise son of Laertes" (*Odyssey* 8.17–18): "the narrator intrudes upon the Phaeacians' admiring embedded focalization, referring to Odysseus as 'the wise son of Laertes' (18) instead of 'the stranger,' as would have been logical from their point of view" (de Jong 2001: 193 at 17–20).

At the same time, interpreters profitably juxtapose the narrator's presentation with that of the characters. One can note "discrepancies" (Saïd 2011: 120): the soul of the suitor Amphimedon claims, for instance, that Penelope and Odysseus together plotted to get the deadly bow into Odysseus's hands (*Odyssey* 24.167–169), whereas Athena planted the idea of a bow contest in Penelope's mind (120–121). One can speak of "confrontation" (de Jong 2004a: 208): Poulydamas, for example, argues for the predicative import of an eagle dropping a snake, an event initially recounted with a different slant by the narrator (*Iliad* 12.200–229) (214–215). One can posit "a dialectal clash of perspectives" between the narrator and a speaking character (Rabel 1997: 61): when Achilleus reports his dispute with Agamemnon to Thetis in *Iliad* 1, "the poet sets the major protagonist to work against the narrator" (47).

SUMMARY OF CHAPTERS

The three previous sections introduced the three speakers that this volume takes as its subjects: rhapsode, narrator, and character. The reader will find that the following explorations of these figures head in new and unanticipated directions.

Part I has two aims. Chapters 1 through 4 offer the first panoramic presentation of rhapsodes and rhapsodic performances in the ancient Greek world from the Archaic to the Imperial periods. Even after the appearance of West's incisive "Rhapsodes at Festivals" (2010a, 2010b) and José González's magisterial *The Epic Rhapsode and His Craft: Homeric Performance in a Diachronic Perspective* (2013), we still lack a consolidated and multidisciplinary review of what rhapsodes did and where they did it. These chapters fill that gap. Contributors exploit literary, iconographic, and epigraphic sources to present the reader with a detailed history of the phenomenon of rhapsodic performance throughout antiquity. Chapters 5 and 6 shift gears to demonstrate the value of adopting a comparative approach to the performance of Homeric poetry. They thus continue the tradition inaugurated by Albert Lord's *The Singer of Tales* (2000 [1960]) and its juxtaposition of the performers and performance of Bosniac oral epic and Homeric poetry.

In chapter 1 ("Performance Contexts for Rhapsodic Recitals in the Archaic and Classical Periods"), Christos Tsagalis examines the performance of Homeric epic in various public contexts in the Archaic and Classical periods. After a discussion of *hors concours* epic performances at symposia and epic contests in funeral games, Tsagalis provides an exhaustive analysis of epic performances in public festivals. This chapter offers ample evidence for the wide diffusion, authority, and persistence of Homeric epic until the end of the Classical period.

Sheramy Bundrick looks at the iconographical evidence for rhapsodic performances in chapter 2 ("Reading Rhapsodes on Athenian Vases"). Although textual sources suggest the importance of *rhapsōidia* at the Panathenaic festival, Athenian vase painters did not represent these Homeric performers as frequently as they did athletes or musicians. Bundrick focuses on five black- and red-figured vases that likely feature the rhapsodic contest. Chronologically, they fall at strategic points—during the sixth century BCE, just after Hipparchos's supposed reforms, and during the fifth century, when Periklean changes to the *mousikoi agōnes* were bearing fruit—and demonstrate the ongoing relevance and popularity of the event. Bundrick also suggests that *rhapsōidia*—rather than oratory, as has often been alleged—inspired a unique scene depicting Odysseus and Aias, with Odysseus making his case to receive Achilleus's armor.

In chapter 3 ("Performance Contexts for Rhapsodic Recitals in the Hellenistic Period"), Christos Tsagalis examines the evidence for rhapsodic performances during the Hellenistic period. After surveying the material pertaining to rhapsodic recitals in theaters and gymnasia, Tsagalis maps the performances of epic poetry in festivals, considers the role of the centers around which these performances evolved, and sets the relevant material against the backdrop of what we know about epic performances in the Archaic and Classical periods. From this vantage point, a new picture can be drawn. This is a period in which rhapsodes cease to operate as free agents. Instead they belong to groups of professional artists and demonstrate increased mobility, as rhapsodic competitions take place at major festivals and all over the Greek world: Boeotia (Akraiphia, Orchomenos, Oropos, Tanagra, Thebes, Thespiai), Delos, Delphi, Euboea, Keos, and Rhodes. Rhapsodic performances become livelier under the increasing influence of dramatic performances, and the content of epic performances changes, now including both early or traditional epic and new compositions. Finally, in major festivals epic poets and rhapsodes compete in separate categories and receive different prizes.

In chapter 4 ("Rhapsodes and Rhapsodic Contests in the Imperial Period"), Anne Gangloff surveys literary and epigraphic sources, laying out the parameters within which rhapsodes continued to broadcast Homeric myth as well as the contexts of their performances in the Imperial period. She explores the distribution of these artists in space and time to identify their cultural and social functions and to explain the noticeable decrease in their number. Gangloff argues that in the Imperial era rhapsodes had lost the educational role belonging to them in the Classical period. Under Roman rule the *Iliad* and to a lesser extent the *Odyssey* became textbooks used in schools and faced increasing competition from actors, poets, and orators as well as cultural products, such as inscriptions, statues, and coins.

Chapter 5 ("Formed on the Festival Stage: Plot and Characterization in the *Iliad* as a Competitive Collaborative Process") uses cross-cultural comparanda and internal evidence to reconstruct an early stage in the development of the Iliadic tradition, before the eighth century BCE. Mary Bachvarova argues that when the epic was performed at festival competitions in the Troad, it was common practice for bards to be judged on their performance of single episodes. Later, when bards were pushed to collaborate to create a coherent narrative, as claimed for the Panathenaic regulation, they would find a way to repurpose the best episode from their repertoire by moving it to a new place or applying it to different characters. Bards could also play a capping game, as it were, taking the narrative in a new direction and recharacterizing what the previous bard had performed. This technique appears in the treatment of Hektor, who is presented from different points of view that go back to bards' different local allegiances.

Olga Levaniouk searches for overlooked performers of epic and modes of epic performance in chapter 6 ("Did Sappho and Homer Ever Meet? Comparative Perspectives on Homeric Singers"). A comparative approach, she argues, gives us reason to suspect that in ancient Greece women performed epics or epic-like songs, such as Sappho 44. Levaniouk reviews an intriguing overlap evidenced in northern Russia and Turkic central Asia: women who sing laments and wedding songs can be among the most creative composers of epic, and innovations made by such singers may appear in mainstream epic. This analysis questions the prevalent view of Homeric interdiscursivity as something created entirely by the rhapsodes, who evoke various genres of songs in their performances. This model, Levaniouk argues, is not wrong, but reductive. A comparative perspective reveals that other paths also lead to interdiscursivity in Homeric poetry.

The seven chapters in part II showcase new research on the Homeric narrators and characters as speakers. The contributors offer new applications of some enduring approaches to the epics: narratology, cognitive linguistics, and performance theory feature prominently.

To provide a transition from part I's discussion of rhapsodes, we start part II with a discussion of an essential item in the performer's compositional toolkit: the formula. In chapter 7 ("Odysseus Polyonymous"), Deborah Beck seeks to reset the study of the formula by exploring the nominative and vocative name–epithet formulaic systems for Odysseus. Because these formulas appear in the *Iliad*, the *Odyssey*, and Odysseus's own speeches, they provide a strong test case for the idea that all formulas have the potential to be meaningful at any given time. Beck enables us to move beyond the false dichotomy between metrical utility and thematic efficacy: even the most repetitive parts of the formulaic system sometimes function in thematically resonant ways.

While Beck works with both narrator text and character text, Anna Bonifazi queries that and other distinctions in chapter 8's ("Embedded Focalization and Free Indirect Speech in Homer as Viewpoint Blending") analysis of what precisely we are given access to when the narrator or a character speaks. Bonifazi explores the nature and manifestations of viewpoint expressions in third-person as well as in character discourse in Homeric epic. She illuminates the matter of viewpoint by presenting a cognitive reading of passages that previous scholarship has treated under the rubrics of embedded focalization and free indirect speech. The cognitive notion of viewpoint blending points to the integration in the minds of performers and audience members of multiple perspectives and multiple voices at these moments—a crucial point that previous scholarship has missed. This component of Homeric narration is in line with the intersubjective quality of the epic genre. Bonifazi's textual analyses focus primarily on the linguistic cues for viewpoint blending on the micro level of phrases and clauses, but she also argues for applying her model to longer passages and to other components of Homeric epic, such as similes and epithets.

The next two chapters look at the evolution of characters into proficient speakers. In chapter 9 ("Speech Training and the Mastery of Context: Thoas the Aetolian and the Practice of *Muthoi*"), Joel Christensen examines the introduction of Thoas the Aetolian (*Iliad* 15.283–284) and additional Homeric evidence alongside other material from ancient Greece and modern oral cultures to outline assumptions about the education of a public speaker. After establishing a pattern of separate stages in a youth's training in speech (observation, imitation, and practice), he offers an interpretation of Thoas as an authoritative figure and speaker. Christensen argues that the Homeric epics dramatize the education of public speakers and that in the *Iliad* this process has political valence in that it contributes to the perseverance of the Achaian coalition.

In chapter 10 ("Diomedes as Audience and Speaker in the *Iliad*"), James O'Maley explores how Diomedes learns to be a doer of deeds and speaker of words. Diomedes's role in the *Iliad* is tied to his function as an audience to stories about the deeds of his father, Tydeus. These deeds are used by characters in the poem (notably Agamemnon in book 4 and Athena in book 5) to spur Diomedes into emulating his father's prowess in competitive endeavors like open warfare, athletic competition, and the ambush. But Diomedes also surpasses his father's characterization in one important element. Rather than being an ineffective speaker but formidable actor, Diomedes shows himself to be as good as his father in action and much better in speech, and in so doing he demonstrates his keen attention to stories told by other characters in the poem.

Whereas Christensen and O'Maley look to the development of Homeric speakers, Lorenzo Garcia analyzes the bravura performance of one of the *Iliad*'s heroes in chapter 11 ("Hektor, the Marginal Hero: Performance Theory and the Homeric Monologue"). This chapter considers Hektor's monologue at 22.98–130 as a verbal performance that characterizes Hektor and reflects the representation of heroism in the *Iliad*. From a sociological perspective informed by the work of George Mead and Lonnie Athens, Garcia argues that Homeric monologues present a hero defining himself through negotiation with the system of expectations, values, and judgments of his community. In his monologue Hektor faces social pressures at odds with his impulse not to fight Achilleus. In a moment of despair, he rejects his social roles altogether and expresses his vulnerability in a poetic image reminiscent of non-epic song performances.

To supplement Garcia's take on Homeric speechifying from a sociological perspective, Jonathan Ready turns in chapter 12 ("Performance, Oral Texts, and Entextualization in Homeric Epic") to linguistic anthropology's refinement of earlier research on performance: oral performers aim to entextualize, to create oral texts that last. Observing that the Homeric poets depict a world in which oral utterances endure, Ready studies the strategies of entextualization represented in the characters' performances in the epics. He first scrutinizes two of Zeus's speeches to show how performers stitch together via formal devices utterances meant for repetition. He then attends to how performers quote previous utterances and deploy generically distinct segments, attach utterances to objects, and explicate paradigmatic stories. This analysis of characters' speeches and other indications in the epics of an interest in entextualization suggest that the Homeric poet himself looks to entextualize, to fashion an oral text, when performing.

Chapter 13 ("Homer's Rivals? Internal Narrators in the *Iliad*") provides a final perspective on the speech of the characters. Adrian Kelly argues that Homer reinforces his narrative with a constant parallel commentary on that narrative delivered by his characters. This commentary flows naturally from the progression of the story, but it deflects our attention away from the truth-value of the poet's version of events by providing a frequently inaccurate rendering of those events. Disjunctions of this sort are explained by the limitations or partiality in the character's knowledge—precisely the kind of information famously lacking about the poet himself. From events small and large, over distances near and far, Homer's internal rivals establish the authority of the omniscient, distanced bard.

THIS VOLUME, THEN, ASSEMBLES A ROSTER OF SCHOLARS with a diverse set of skills. No one Homerist is able to employ all the tools on display here, hence the need for a collaborative effort. We hope this interdisciplinary breadth will make for a book greater than the sum of its parts and will engage not only Homerists but also researchers in other areas of classical studies.

NOTES

1. In this introduction all translations are our own unless otherwise noted.

2. "Some, however, say that they flourished at the same time, so as actually to compete with each other after meeting up at Aulis in Boeotia. For after composing the *Margites*, they say, Homer went round from town to town reciting" (τινὲς δὲ συνακμάσαι φασὶν αὐτοὺς ὥστε καὶ ἀγωνίσασθαι / ὁμόσε ἐν Αὐλίδι τῆς Βοιωτίας, ποιήσαντα γὰρ τὸν Μαργίτην / Ὅμηρον περιέρχεσθαι κατὰ πόλιν ῥαψωιδοῦντα, 55–57); "from there he arrived in Corinth, and recited his poems. Receiving much honor there, he arrived in Argos, and spoke these verses

from the *Iliad*" (ἐκεῖθεν δὲ παραγενόμενος εἰς Κόρινθον ἐρραψώιδει τὰ / ποιήματα. τιμηθεὶς δὲ μεγάλως παραγίνεται εἰς Ἄργος / καὶ λέγει ἐκ τῆς Ἰλιάδος τὰ ἔπη τάδε, 286–288) (trans. West 2003a).

3. Homer: "Here the earth covers the holy head, / divine Homer who adorned the heroes" (ἐνθάδε τὴν ἱερὴν κεφαλὴν κατὰ γαῖα καλύπτει, / ἀνδρῶν ἡρώων κοσμήτορα θεῖον Ὅμηρον).

Hesiod: "Askre, rich in cornfields, is his fatherland, but after his death Minyas, the land of horse-drivers, holds the bones of Hesiod, whose glory is in the eyes of men the greatest among those who are judged for wisdom" (Ἄσκρη μὲν πατρὶς πολυλήιος, ἀλλὰ θανόντος / ὀστέα πληξίππων γῆ Μινυὰς κατέχει / Ἡσιόδου, τοῦ πλεῖστον ἐν ἀνθρώποις κλέος ἐστὶν / ἀνδρῶν κρινομένων ἐν βασάνωι σοφίης).

4. Heracleides of Pontos ([Plutarch] *De musica* 1132b) designates Phemios as an author and kitharode. Pucci takes Phemios's declaration, "and I am worthy to sing about you as about a god" (ἔοικα δέ τοι παραείδειν / ὥς τε θεῶι, *Odyssey* 22.348–349), as indicating Phemios's promise to sing the *Odyssey* (1987: 230). Earlier on, he sings the *nostos* of the Achaians ("he was singing the painful return of the Achaians from Troy that Pallas Athena enjoined upon them" [ὁ δ' Ἀχαιῶν νόστον ἄειδε / λυγρόν, ὃν ἐκ Τροίης ἐπετείλατο Παλλὰς Ἀθήνη, *Odyssey* 1.326–327]; see also [Plutarch] *De musica* 1132b: νόστον τῶν ἀπὸ Τροίας μετ' Ἀγαμέμνονος ἀνακομισθέντων ποιῆσαι ["he composed the return from Troy of those who were carried back with Agamemnon"]). See also Graziosi 2002: 40.

5. The association of this practice with the Homeridai does not turn the balance in favor of the Panathēnaia. The term "Homeridai" may here denote professional rhapsodes. Moreover, the reference to colored crowns or garlands (instead of dyed garments in Eustathius), apart from being awkward in itself (what does it mean to have a colored crown?), shows that the source—or the source of the source—from which Dionysius Thrax draws has mixed features from different phases and occasions in the evolution of rhapsodic performances: the Homeridai of Hipparchos's Panathēnaia with crowned artists and rhapsodes with dyed garments from later times.

6. Sometimes, though, a figure is shaped under the influence of a standard number designating a huge size. In Plato *Symposium* 175e6–7, we are told that Agathon's plays were performed in front of an audience of more than thirty thousand spectators (πλέον ἢ τρισμυρίοις). Any Athenian would have understood that number as being immense, since this was the total size of the Athenian citizen body; see P. Murray 1996: 122.

7. Nagy allows for reduced melody as an alternative to a total lack of melody (1990b: 17–24).

8. For a useful survey of all the Homeric passages referring to song and singers, see Grandolini 1996.

9. Differently Sealey (1957: 315–316), who takes this reference as an indication that other singers were not self-taught but recited preexisting songs. He compares the Finnish *Kalevala* in which Väinämöinen stresses his originality and claims divine inspiration: "For to sing I was created. / As an orator was

fashioned; / How, I ask not in the village, / nor I learn my songs from strangers" (XXI, 359–62, trans. W. F. Kirby).

10. *Odyssey* 1.325, 336, 346, 3.267–271, 4.17, 8.43, 62, 83, 367, 471, 479–481, 483, 487, 521, 539, 9.3–4, 17.385 (we omit from this list *Iliad* 18.604, following West's edition).

11. Another point of difference between Phemios and Demodokos pertains to the former's promise to Odysseus to recite the *Odyssey* ("and I am worthy to sing about you as about a god" [ἔοικα δέ τοι παραείδειν / ὥς τε θεῷι, *Odyssey* 22.348–349]) next to his ability to sing "cyclic" epic ("he was singing the painful return of the Achaians from Troy that Pallas Athena enjoined upon them" [ὁ δ' Ἀχαιῶν νόστον ἄειδε / λυγρόν, ὃν ἐκ Τροίης ἐπετείλατο Παλλὰς Ἀθήνη, *Odyssey* 1.326–327]) (cf. note 4). Demodokos sings only of non-Odyssean epic episodes (in book 8).

12. Various scholars have highlighted the poetological aspects of the expressions κατὰ μοῖραν / ὑπὲρ μοῖραν: Pestalozzi 1945: 40; Kullmann 1956; Fränkel 1962: 62–64; Matthews 1976; Nagy 1999a: 40, §17n2; S. Richardson 1990: 194; Janko 1992: 5–6; Currie 2006: 7; Tsagalis 2011: 226.

13. According to Finkelberg, "only a new story or song produces enchantment in the listener," whereas "the recital of a song whose content was already known to the audience" and "would have been the norm" brings delight and pleasure (1998: 93–98). González, who regards Finkelberg's interpretation as schematic, challenges this approach (2013: 190–194).

14. Later testimonies (such as Aelian *Varia historia* 13.14) about the performance of specific episodes rather than entire epics corroborate these observations; see also Slings 2000: 70.

15. We assume (partly but not solely on the basis of the semantics of δέγμενος) that Patroklos is waiting for Achilleus to finish in order to cap his song with his own responsive song. Nagy takes this as one more example of diachronic skewing in the sense of a stylized representation of relay performance of epic of the kind familiar from the Panathēnaia in sixth-century Athens (2003: 43–45).

16. Excluded from this list are references to and examples of solo performances, such as Hektor referring to an old martial dance (*Iliad* 7.241), a singer depicted on the shield of Achilleus playing the phorminx and singing the Linos song (*Iliad* 18.570) (see Ready, this volume, p. 350n3), a singer depicted on the shield of Achilleus singing to a chorus of boys and girls dancing a circular dance (*Iliad* 18.590–605), Kalypso singing while weaving (*Odyssey* 5.61), and Circe singing while weaving (*Odyssey* 10.221).

17. On Thamyris, see Kirk 1985: 216; Grandolini 1996: 48–50; Brügger, Stoevesandt, and Visser 2010: 192; Tsagalis 2012: 202–208. P. Wilson argues that the semantics of the name Θάμυρις (see Hesychius θ 90 [II 306 Latte]: θάμυρις· πανήγυρις, σύνοδος, ἢ πυκνότης τινῶν. καὶ ὁδοὺς θαμυρὰς τὰς λεωφόρους. ἔστι δὲ καὶ κύριον ὄνομα; θ 91 [306 Latte]: θαμυρίζει· ἀθροίζει, συνάγει ["*thamuris*: assembly, gathering, or the frequency of certain things/people. (They call) the highways 'frequented streets.' It is also a proper name; *thamurizei*: he/she/it gathers,

assembles"]) indicate that "Thamyris" is "an ancient Aeolic name for a special form of communal gathering, for supra-local meetings at a religious centre" and that it suggests "the centripetal force of song, the gathering into union and collectivity," while the term οἴμη designates the centrifugal paths of aoidic performance (2009: 50–51).

Part I

RHAPSODES

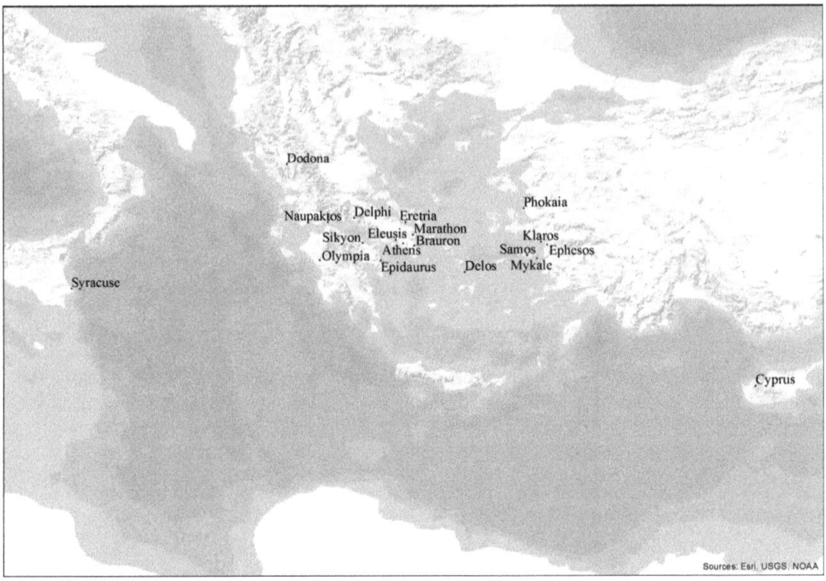

MAP I.1. *Sites of rhapsodic performance in the Archaic and Classical periods*

CHAPTER ONE

Performance Contexts for Rhapsodic Recitals in the Archaic and Classical Periods

CHRISTOS C. TSAGALIS

WHEREAS PETER GAINSFORD REVIEWS ASPECTS OF the performance of Greek epic poetry, such as pitch and melody (2015: 75–82), and José González offers a diachronic analysis of the rhapsode's craft (2013) (cf. pp. 2–8), here I present a panorama of the occasions and places of rhapsodic performances throughout the Greek world from their beginning to the end of the Classical period. For the most part, I structure this chapter by place, as Eric Csapo and Peter Wilson structure their succinct and helpful survey of reperformances of tragedy outside Athens in the fifth and fourth centuries BCE (2015). But given the fact that rhapsodic performances took place in different contexts, the classification of the relevant material should take into account this factor too. I therefore assign the material to three separate categories of increasing importance: *hors concours* performance; funeral games; and public festivals, by far the most common venue for the recitation of epic poetry and suitable for displaying its often agonistic character. Within each context, I then sort the data by geographical location. It will frequently be necessary to distinguish within a specific region, such as Asia Minor, the various sites where rhapsodic recitals were held.

We are in a position to identify from the sources available a variety of performance milieux and venues as well as the names, approximate dates, origins, and performance contexts of a dozen rhapsodes, of whom only one antedates the fifth century BCE (see appendix 1.1). Map 1.1 shows the locations of these venues and allows readers to see for themselves to what extent the performance of epic was diffused all over the Greek world.

HORS CONCOURS PERFORMANCE

Epic was recited in *hors concours*—noncompetitive—performances. In recent years some scholars have argued in favor of the symposium as a possible milieu for noncompetitive rhapsodic recitals of Homeric epic. Since this claim has been connected even with the raison d'être of at least one of the two monumental epics, I begin with some thoughts on the Homeric poems and then proceed to the case of Hesiodic epic, for which a similar claim has been made.

Oliver Taplin argues that "the *Iliad* was created to be performed through three successive nights in the banqueting-hall of a lord" (1992: 39), with the same suggestion being applied to the *Odyssey*, although within the time frame of two consecutive nights (30–31). For Taplin the picture given by the *Odyssey* reflects historical reality at the time of the composition of the Homeric epics. Taking the Homeric *aoidos* singing at the *dais* and the rhapsode reciting in the symposium as belonging to a single line of tradition, Oswyn Murray envisions the performance of the *Odyssey* as "a series of separate but doubtless consecutive banquets": "the narrative itself is structured as a series of 'cantos,' in which each canto presents an episode which is suited to be told within the context of a single banquet" (2008: 167). As for the *Iliad*, he postulates that it was designed for a more public performance, such as a festival.

These are rich but speculative arguments. To begin with, one should not conflate the Homeric *dais* and the aristocratic symposium of the Archaic period. Murray rightly draws attention to the "greater exclusivity and sense of separateness achieved with the reclining banquet" in contrast to the seated banquet as depicted in Homeric epic (2008: 162) as well as to the radical decrease of the audience's size given the restrictions of what Birgitta Bergquist coins "the dynamics of sympotic space" (1990)—that is, the limited number of couches that could be placed within the *andrōn*. Moreover, to accept these reconstructions, we have to think exclusively of the performance of *selected* episodes of the Homeric epics. Yet the main problem with this line of thought is that if rhapsodic recitals took place in the aristocratic symposia of the Archaic period, it must be explained why our sources are silent about them, whereas they shower us with information concerning lyric and elegiac poetry at the symposium. Murray offers no ancient testimony in support of his claim that the rhapsode is "rediscovered in the grand tyrannical *symposion* of the late archaic age" (2008: 163). The silence of ancient authors with respect to the inclusion of epic poetry in that phase of the banquet when the *logos sympotikos* assumes the form of a contest is noteworthy and has not been explained by the adherents of the theory of epic "sympotic" recitals.[1]

We can safely say that epics could have formed part of the general musical display that demonstrated the symposiarch's status as well as his desire to entertain his guests. When Xenophon's Nikeratos says, "I listen to rhapsodes [recite Homeric poetry] almost daily" (*Symposium* 3.6), this must be an indication of more intimate performances, not public festivals (P. Murray 1996: 20).[2] What would be the nature of these daily intimate performances? The symposium can hardly be ruled out. The fact that Nikeratos's father made him learn the entire contents of the *Iliad* and the *Odyssey* by heart so that he could recite them (Xenophon *Symposium* 3.5–6) supports the designation of the symposium as *one* of the intimate occasions in which Homeric epic was recited, since the point is that there were occasions in which Nikeratos could show off his ability to sing whatever part of Homer his listeners wished to hear. The more sumptuous a banquet, the greater the opportunity for the host to show off.

Regarding Hesiod, I will discuss the *Theogony*'s agonistic performance context in the section devoted to funeral games. As for the *Works and Days*, its segmental internal organization has been recently interpreted as amounting to a *syllogē* in the manner of the poetry of Phocylides or the *Theognidea* (Aloni 2017). I am skeptical about this proposal, but it does alert us to the generic adaptability of a semi-didactic hybrid like the *Works and Days*. I also have reservations concerning the suggestion that the symposium was the performance context for this kind of wisdom poetry (Irwin 2005; Aloni 2010; Koning 2010). In any case, what we gain from such proposed scenarios is a chance to reconsider the generic identity of certain epics and to suggest that their generic fluidity may be relevant to the widening of their performance scope, at least from the local to the regional level. After all, the extended mythical first part of the *Works and Days* covertly points to the effort to connect agricultural and seafaring instructions to beliefs about mortals' condition and relationship to the gods. Put differently, this is an attempt to reach a larger audience.

We are faced with similar problems when we try to examine potential scenarios for the performance context of the [Hesiodic] *Catalogue of Women*. Some of the epic's women had their own hero cults, such as Chloris in Argos and Alkmene in various places (Rutherford 2000: 88). Yet the poem's dearth of material with respect to the theme of death renders an association between the epic's performance and a heroic cult rather unlikely. One might imagine audiences of women and girls, but the analogy offered by Sapphic and Alcmanic lyric should not be pressed. The notion of an exclusively female audience for the *Catalogue* can, in my view, be safely put aside. The same applies *mutatis mutandis* to the symposium (see Irwin 2005).[3]

Audience response is an underestimated factor as far as performance context is concerned. But it represents an important aspect of any performance venue, the more so since concerns about the kind of audience a poem would be addressed to may have conditioned a whole series of choices pertaining to the poem's structure and content. In fact, some of the *Catalogue*'s features may have been shaped with an eye to the epic's performance. Take, for example, the poem's size, which I would not hesitate to call "impressive," since we would not expect a catalogue poem to be so long. Given that size in this case means comprehensiveness, we can recognize that the poem's scope reflects an effort to encompass an enormous amount of mythical material, stretching from the beginnings of the Greek world to the end of the race of heroes. The epic's scope would make it suitable for performance in various places, since there would hardly be any Greek who would not find in the epic genealogies of the *Catalogue* his own mythical ancestors. Another feature of the *Catalogue* that may have been shaped with an eye to audience response is the initial invocation of the Muses, who are called to assist the poet in relating the sexual unions between gods and mortal women.

By anchoring the abovementioned theme to the traditional device of invoking the Muses in the proem, the poet of the *Catalogue* telescoped the epic's content so as to have it operate as a continuation of the *Theogony*, which also contains multiple lists that become quite pronounced as the poem approaches its end. The *Catalogue* and the *Theogony* would have also formed, if only notionally, a sort of small Hesiodic cycle, albeit in the form of a pair of epics. Perhaps the existence of a longer poem of the same scope, the *Megalai Ehoiai*, is indicative of a general tendency to couple the *Theogony* with a poem that would take the world's story to the end of the race of heroes. This time though, and in marked contrast to the Epic Cycle, the poetic means to this end would be the catalogue.[4] Also aimed at gaining the audience's approval is the rapidity with which the *Catalogue* unfolds. The rhapsode performing this epic would be able to reach quickly the various genealogical trees of the Greeks and thereby cater to various ethnic groups. Furthermore, such a detailed, panoramic presentation of the entire Greek world no doubt allowed audiences to link past and present in an emotionally fulfilling way. Extended genealogies gave depth to their family lines, and depth meant authority and pride. By reaching far back in time genealogies made it possible for personal memory to meet collective memory, and the new mixture would link the heroic age with the Archaic world. Place names, proper names of mortals and immortals, family trees—all these features created an intricate mosaic (Minchin 2001: 90–92).

Nevertheless, the rather monotonous marshaling of names, reinforced by extensive parataxis and reiterated diction, was a challenge to the poem's success. Keeping the audience's attention was no easy task. Even more than is the case with Homeric epic, a renewal of the poem's beginning was needed. In this light, the reuse of a traditional attention-getting device such as the invocation to the Muses before the beginning of the fifth book should come as no surprise (Cingano 2005: 122).[5] The authority of divine inspiration goes hand in hand with the inherent exigencies of rhapsodic recital, and perhaps it was employed to introduce a part of the epic that could be separated from the rest. Who would not like to have heard on its own a presentation that started with the catalogue of Helen's suitors and proceeded to the end of the heroic race?

Leaving behind the putative association of epic poetry with the symposium, I look to Athenaeus's discussion of the lavish organization of wedding ceremonies organized by Alexander the Great at Susa in 324 BCE. Rhapsodic recitals were included among the musical performances (12.538e–539a [III 187.16–188.8 Kaibel]):

> ἐπὶ πέντε δὲ ἡμέρας ἐπετελέσθησαν οἱ γάμοι, καὶ ἐλειτούργησαν πάνυ πολλοὶ καὶ βαρβάρων καὶ Ἑλλήνων, καὶ οἱ ἀπὸ τῆς Ἰνδικῆς θαυματοποιοὶ ἦσαν διαπρέποντες . . .[6] Σκύμνος Ταραντῖνος καὶ Φιλιστίδης Συρακόσιος Ἡράκλειτός τε ὁ Μυτιληναῖος· μεθ' οὓς ἐπεδείξατο ῥαψωιδὸς Ἄλεξις Ταραντῖνος. παρῆλθον δὲ καὶ ψιλοκιθαρισταὶ Κρατῖνος Μηθυμναῖος, Ἀριστώνυμος Ἀθηναῖος, Ἀθηνόδωρος Τήιος· ἐκιθαρώιδησαν δὲ Ἡράκλειτός τε ὁ Ταραντῖνος καὶ Ἀριστοκράτης ὁ Θηβαῖος. αὐλωιδοὶ δὲ παρῆλθον Διονύσιος ὁ Ἡρακλεώτης, Ὑπέρβολος Κυζικηνός· παρῆλθον δὲ καὶ αὐληταί, οἳ πρῶτον τὸ Πυθικὸν ηὔλησαν, εἶθ' ἑξῆς μετὰ τῶν χορῶν, Τιμόθεος, Φρύνιχος, Καφισίας, Διόφαντος, ἔτι δὲ Εὔιος ὁ Χαλκιδεύς. καὶ ἔκτοτε οἱ πρότερον καλούμενοι Διονυσοκόλακες Ἀλεξανδροκόλακες ἐκλήθησαν διὰ τὰς τῶν δώρων ὑπερβολάς, ἐφ' οἷς καὶ ἥσθη ὁ Ἀλέξανδρος. ὑπεκρίθησαν δὲ τραγωιδοὶ μὲν Θεσσαλὸς καὶ Ἀθηνόδωρος καὶ Ἀριστόκριτος, κωμωιδοὶ δὲ Λύκων καὶ Φορμίων καὶ Ἀρίστων. παρῆν δὲ καὶ Φασίμηλος ὁ ψάλτης. οἱ δὲ πεμφθέντες, φησί, στέφανοι ὑπὸ τῶν πρεσβευτῶν καὶ τῶν λοιπῶν ταλάντων ἦσαν μυρίων πεντακισχιλίων.

The marriage-celebrations went on for five days, and enormous numbers of barbarians and Greeks performed: the Indian magicians were outstanding. . . . Scymnus of Tarentum, Philistides of

> Syracuse, and Heracleitus of Mytilene; after them, the rhapsode Alexis of Tarentum put on a show. The *psilokitharistai* Cratinus of Methymna, Aristonymus of Athens, and Athenodorus of Teos also appeared; and Heracleitus of Tarentum and Aristocrates of Thebes played the lyre and sang. The aulodes Dionysius of Heracleia and Hyperbolus of Cyzicus were also there, as were the pipe-players Timotheus, Phrynichus, Caphisias, and Diophantus, along with Euius of Chalcis; they first played the Pythian piece and then performed immediately afterward with their choruses. From then on the individuals previously referred to as *Dionusokolakes* [cf. Aristotle *Rhetoric* 1405a23–25; González 2013: 446] were known as *Alexandrokolakes* ["Alexander flatterers"], because of the extravagance of the gifts made to the performers Alexander enjoyed. The tragic actors Thessalus, Athenodorus, and Aristocritus gave performances, as did the comic actors Lycon, Phormio, and Ariston. The harp-player Phasimelus was also there. The garlands sent by the ambassadors and the other guests, says (Chares), were worth 15,000 talents. (trans. Olson 2010)

Athenaeus's source is the tenth book of *Ἱστορίαι περὶ Ἀλέξάνδρου* by Chares of Mytilene. Chares, a member of Alexander's court, was responsible for introducing strangers to the king during his expedition to Asia.

This report does not tell us what precisely a performer of a given genre performed or the order of presentation of the performers, and one might compare to this narrative agonistic lists from various festivals of the Hellenistic era, which likewise do not designate what specific piece a performer presented but almost always mention the victors in the same order, by category of performance (Pallone 1984: 157–158; West 2010a: 7–10). Table 1.1 lays out this analogy in a schematic manner. Perhaps Chares, Athenaeus's source, had access as a member of Alexander's entourage to some inscribed record created to commemorate this event. If so, it is a reasonable assumption that even if the actual rhapsodic recitals had not taken the form of a contest—despite Alexander's fondness for musical competitions[7]—the way it was described by Chares reflected conventions pertaining to regularly held and/or formalized contests (cf. chapter 3).

FUNERAL GAMES

The funeral games for Pelias included a poetic contest (ἀγὼν ποιήματος) organized by Akastos, which Sibyl won (Plutarch *Quaestiones*

TABLE 1.1. THE ORDER OF VICTORS IN ATHENAEUS'S REPORT DESCRIBING EVENTS OF 324 BCE AND IN A HELLENISTIC INSCRIPTION PERTAINING TO THE *AMPHIARAIA AND RHŌMAIA*

Athenaeus's Report (Describing events of 324 BCE)	*IG* VII 419 = *EO* 526 (*Amphiaraia and Rhōmaia* at Oropos, 1st cent. BCE)
	σαλπιστής: Θεόφραστος Ἀσκληπιάδου Αἰγινήτης
	κῆρυξ: Γλαυκίας Σωσάνδρου Θηβαῖος
	ἐνκωμίωι λογικῶι: Μόσχος Ἀναξ{ξ}ίππου Προυσιεύς
	ἐνκωμίωι ἐπικῶι: Ἀμινίας Δημοκλέους Θηβαῖος
θαυματοποιοί: Σκύμνος Ταραντῖνος καὶ Φιλιστίδης Συρακόσιος Ἡράκλειτός τε ὁ Μυτιληναῖος	
	ἐπῶν ποιητάς: Ἀμινίας Δημοκλέους Θηβαῖος
ῥαψωιδὸς Ἄλεξις Ταραντῖνος	**ῥαψωιδός:** Εἰέρων Ἀριστοβούλου Θηβαῖος
	αὐλητάς: Νίκων Εὐωνυμοδώρου Θηβαῖος
ψιλοκιθαρισταὶ Κρατῖνος Μηθυμναῖος, Ἀριστώνυμος Ἀθηναῖος, Ἀθηνόδωρος Τήιος	**κιθαριστής:** Μητρόδωρος Διονυσίου Νικομηδεύς
ἐκιθαρώιδησαν δὲ Ἡράκλειτός τε ὁ Ταραντῖνος καὶ Ἀριστοκράτης ὁ Θηβαῖος	**κιθαρωιδός:** Δημήτριος Δημητρίου Καλχηδόνιος
	σατύρων ποιητής: Κάλιππος Κάλλωνος Θηβαῖος
αὐλωιδοὶ δὲ παρῆλθον Διονύσιος ὁ Ἡρακλεώτης, Ὑπέρβολος Κυζικηνός	
παρῆλθον δὲ καὶ αὐληταί, οἳ πρῶτον τὸ Πυθικὸν ηὔλησαν, εἶθ' ἑξῆς μετὰ τῶν χορῶν, Τιμόθεος, Φρύνιχος, Καφισίας, Διόφαντος, ἔτι δὲ Εὔιος ὁ Χαλκιδεύς	
ὑπεκρίθησαν δὲ **τραγωιδοὶ** μὲν Θεσσαλὸς καὶ Ἀθηνόδωρος καὶ Ἀριστόκριτος	**ποιητὴς τραγωιδιῶν:** Λυσίστρατος Μνασέου Χαλκιδεύς
	ὑποκριτής: Γλαυκίας Σωσάνδρου Θηβαῖος

(continued)

TABLE 1.1. (*CONTINUED*)

Athenaeus's Report (Describing events of 324 BCE)	*IG* VII 419 = *EO* 526 (*Amphiaraia and Rhōmaia* at Oropos, 1st cent. BCE)
κωμωιδοὶ δὲ Λύκων καὶ Φορμίων καὶ Ἀρίστων	**ποιητὴς κωμωιδιῶν:** Ἀρίστων Χιόνου Θηβαῖος
	ὑποκριτής: [Κ]αλλίστρατος Ἐξακέστου Θηβαῖος
	[τραγωι]δί[α]ν παλαιάν: .... ιος
παρῆν δὲ καὶ Φασίμηλος ὁ ψάλτης	

convivales 675a). According to Hyginus (*Fabulae* 273), Olympos won in the aulos contest, Orpheus in the kithara, and Linos and Eumolpos as singers who accompanied the two instrumentalists (West 2010a: 1).[8] This event belongs to the realm of myth, but that musical contests took place during funeral games need not be a fiction. Hesiod's *Works and Days* is yet more suggestive about rhapsodic performance at funeral games.

In a famous autobiographical passage with rich poetological overtones (646–659), Hesiod tells us about his short journey from Aulis in Boeotia to Chalcis, his performance of a hymn (the *Theogony*?) at the funeral games held for Amphidamas, his victory, and his dedication of his prize (a tripod) to the Helikonian Muses, who taught him the art of song (654–659):

> ἔνθα δ' ἐγὼν ἐπ' ἄεθλα δαΐφρονος Ἀμφιδάμαντος
> Χαλκίδα [τ'] εἰσεπέρησα· τὰ δὲ προπεφραδμένα πολλὰ
> ἄεθλ' ἔθεσαν παῖδες μεγαλήτορες· ἔνθα μέ φημι
> ὕμνωι νικήσαντα φέρειν τρίποδ' ὠτώεντα.
> τὸν μὲν ἐγὼ Μούσηισ' Ἑλικωνιάδεσσ' ἀνέθηκα
> ἔνθα με τὸ πρῶτον λιγυρῆς ἐπέβησαν ἀοιδῆς.

> There I myself crossed over into Chalcis for the games of valorous Amphidamas—that great-hearted man's sons had announced and established many prizes—and there, I declare, I gained victory with a hymn, and carried off a tripod with handles. This I dedicated to the Helikonian Muses, where they first set me upon a path of clear-sounding song. (trans. Most 2006)

This example refers to a poetic contest and to a prize-winning poet. Presumably other poets took part in a contest organized within the framework of the funeral games in honor of Amphidamas. Although Hesiod uses this bit of autobiography to praise himself, we should not dismiss it all as a fabrication. Sumptuous funeral games may have included both athletic and musical contests, including competitions in epic.[9] After all, they provided a suitable agonistic milieu, as is the case with athletic contests held within the framework of funerals.[10]

PUBLIC FESTIVALS

The rise of the polis created a new context for the performance and dissemination of Archaic epic and Homeric poetry in particular. The singer's audience grew considerably in both size and range, and people of different classes gained access to the medium of epic poetry. The new socioeconomic framework within which epic performances were now placed invited and perhaps even intensified rivalry. Itinerant rhapsodes began to compete with each other in performing their own compositions as well as those from a standard repertoire of poems composed by others (West 1981: 125).[11] In fact, the term ῥαψῳδία may well reflect poetry that is "stitched" (ῥάπτειν + ᾠδή), and it (together with its cognates) may have been "either formed or disseminated in connection with poetic competitions" (Ford 1988: 306).[12]

Rhapsodic performances included both recital of one's own compositions and recital of episodes from famous epic poetry or other stichic verse, such as Hesiodic (fr. dub. 357 M-W; Plato *Republic* 600d, *Ion* 531a1–2, 531c2, 532a5–6, *Laws* 658d; Isocrates *Panathenaicus* 18, 33) and Phocylidean gnomic hexameter poetry (West 1981: 125). Such competitions spanned most of the Greek world, and they firmly attest the growing popularity in the Archaic period of rhapsodic performances of dactylic hexameter poetry, especially but not solely Homeric epic (Patzer 1952: 324). By the end of the fifth and certainly in the fourth century, the rhapsodic repertoire had expanded. We hear of Simonides of Zakynthos reciting Archilochus (Plato *Ion* 531a1–2, 531c2, 532a5–6; Athenaeus 14.620c–d), although Archilochus may well have been included in rhapsodic contests as early as the late Archaic or early Classical period, since Heraclitus tells us that "Archilochus"—that is, the rhapsodes who recite his poetry—should be beaten with a stick and banned from contests (D-K 22 B 42 *apud* Diogenes Laertius 9.1). We hear of the rhapsode Mnasion reciting Simonides's iambics and of the rhapsode Kleomenes reciting Empedocles's hexameters (Athenaeus 14.620c–d), perhaps at the Olympic Games (Diogenes Laertius 8.63.6).[13]

As to the forms of rhapsodic competition, it has been argued that there were at least three distinct modes of rhapsodic performance (Collins 2001a: 132–137): (a) stitching; (b) inserting new verses into Homer's poems; and (c) other improvisational techniques (hexameter exchanges of questions and answers of a gnomic or philosophical nature[14]; completing verse couplets, or capping; recitation of passages). We are in no position to ascertain which of these modes were employed in which festivals, but there is a case to be made that some of them were practiced in the late Archaic period and others in the Classical era.

Asia Minor

Epic poetry was widely diffused and performed in the coastal Greek cities of Asia Minor. Homeric poetry in particular must have been at the forefront of rhapsodic recitals as early as the Archaic period. For Ionians, in particular, Homeric epic was at the heart of their religious festivals, since it occupied a special place in the shaping of their collective identity.

KLAROS The *Homeric Hymn to Artemis* (*Homeric Hymn* 9) refers to the goddess driving her chariot through Ionia from the river Meles via Smyrna to Apollo's shrine at Klaros. This short hymn may have been recited at the famous sanctuary in Klaros in the context of a musical contest associated with the festival in honor of the siblings Artemis and Apollo (Baumeister 1860: 344; K. O. Müller 1875: 121–122; Reisch 1885: 3). The first lines (9.1–6) of the hymn point in this direction.

EPHESOS/MYKALE: PANIONIA Thucydides provides our earliest piece of information about the Ephesia, which he mentions in conjunction with the Delia (3.103–104).

> ἦν δέ ποτε καὶ τὸ πάλαι μεγάλη ξύνοδος ἐς τὴν Δῆλον τῶν Ἰώνων τε καὶ περικτιόνων νησιωτῶν· ξύν τε γὰρ γυναιξὶ καὶ παισὶν ἐθεώρουν, *ὥσπερ νῦν ἐς τὰ Ἐφέσια Ἴωνες*, καὶ ἀγὼν ἐποιεῖτο αὐτόθι καὶ γυμνικὸς καὶ μουσικός, χορούς τε ἀνῆγον αἱ πόλεις.

> There had been also in the distant past a great gathering of the Ionians and neighboring islanders at Delos. They used to come there to the festival with their wives and children, *just as the Ionians now*

> *go to the festival at Ephesos*, and they used to hold contests there in athletics, poetry, and music, each city producing its own chorus. (trans. Warner 1972 [adapted])

Thucydides's reference to the Ephesia of his time (424 BCE) makes it likely that the comparison with the older festival of the Delia pertains to not only the gathering of all Ionians but also the content of the festival itself. What happened in the Delia in the past probably happened in the Ephesia of 424 BCE: it also included "contests in athletics, poetry, and music," and "each city produced its own chorus."

What, then, about the Panionia? This was an old festival celebrated at Mykale until its replacement by the Ephesia in the 490s BCE, when the Persians crushed the Ionian Revolt. The Ephesia, which must have had the same content as the Delia as far as musical contests were concerned, may well have taken over all kinds of events from the Panionia. The Panionia was associated with the Panionion cult center at Mykale, where Ionians celebrated Poseidon Helikonios. This must have been a grand occasion for them, given the status of this festival for their collective consciousness. The cult of Poseidon Helikonios (see Herodotus 1.148) may have reminded the Ionians of their ancestors' war against Melia (the Meliac War), the acquisition of its territory, and the use of a common shrine of the same god that existed there before the war (Wade-Gery 1952: 2–6).

Since the *Iliad* explicitly refers in a simile to the sacrifice of a bull in honor of "the Helikonian lord" (*Iliad* 20.403–405), it has been thought that it was recited at the Panionia festival in the Archaic period. After all, this was the festival of the Panionian League and as such a likely context for the rhapsodic performance of Homeric poetry, including but not limited to the *Iliad* and the *Odyssey*.[15] At that time Homer was regarded as the author of other epics too, including the *Thebais* and the *Epigonoi*, as references in the works of Pausanias and Herodotus as well as in the *Certamen* (the narrative of an imagined poetical contest between Homer and Hesiod) make clear.

According to Pausanias (9.9.5), Callinus attributed the *Thebais* to Homer. Given the dating of Callinus to the middle of the seventh century BCE and his Ephesian origin, two conclusions emerge. First, Callinus (and many others, as Pausanias says) considered Homer the poet of the *Thebais* almost a hundred years before the time of Peisistratos. This view must have prevailed also in the sixth century, as Herodotus's reference to the *Thebais* by means of the phrase τῶν Ὁμηρείων ἐπῶν εἵνεκα ("because of the Homeric poems") shows (5.67) (see pp. 50, 60–62). Second, Callinus's attribution of the *Thebais* to Homer must reflect not his personal opinion but a belief widespread during his lifetime in Ephesos, his native city. The best context for the circulation of such a view would have been the festival of the Panionia held in honor of Poseidon Helikonios.

With respect to the *Epigonoi*, Herodotus's reference to this epic as Homeric (4.32), an attribution about which the historian is anything but certain, indicates not only that Herodotus knew from other sources that the *Epigonoi* was considered Homeric but also that this attribution must go back to the Archaic period. In fact, since the *Thebais* and the *Epigonoi* form a thematic pair, their attribution to Homer must have happened around the same time.[16] Since we know that Callinus attributed the *Thebais* to Homer, then the same may apply to the *Epigonoi*, and if that holds true, then the attribution of Theban epic to Homer must have been connected to a specific context, such as an early festival. In my view, the festival of the Panionia is a legitimate candidate.

The *Homeric Hymn to Poseidon* (*Homeric Hymn* 22) praises the god as lord of both Helikon and Aigai in Achaia in the northern Peloponnese. Some scholars conjectured that "Helikon" here is an error for "Helike"—since Helike and Aigai in Achaia are attested together as places sacred to Poseidon (*Iliad* 8.203)—and suggested that the Panionia was the context for which this hymn was composed.[17] This scenario remains likely irrespective of whether the epithet "Helikonios" is to be derived from Mount Helikon in Boeotia (Aristarchus) or from the city of Helike in Achaia (most other ancient authorities).[18] The confusion over the etymology of "Helikonios" is a separate issue from the fact that one way or the other the Ionians had brought the cult of Poseidon Helikonios to Asia Minor after their migration, perhaps after passing through Athens (Herodotus 1.148; Strabo 8.7.2, 14.1.20; Pausanias 7.24.5–6).

As to the particularities of epic performance at the Panionia, various theories have been proposed. One of the most recent is that it spanned a twelve-day period, each day seeing the performance of what now are four books of the *Iliad* and the *Odyssey*.[19] The fact that the Panionian League included twelve cities may have been a crucial factor for the regulation of these performances, which must have involved a number of singers (Frame 2009: 551–620). Others, who also see in the Panionia a suitable venue for epic performances, do not associate them with the aforementioned theory about the formation and shaping of the Homeric epics (West 2011a: 20).

PHOKAIA The existence of the epic *Phokais* and of two Phokaian poets, Thestorides ([Herodotus], *Vita Homeri* 16 West: as author of the *Phokais*) and Prodicus (Pausanias 4.33.7: as author of the *Minyas*),[20] indicates poetic activity at Phokaia at some period, probably before the Phokaians' evacuation of the city in 540 BCE to avoid subjugation to the Persians (Herodotus 1.164–168; Strabo 6.1.1). The *Phokais* might have dealt with the foundation legend of Phokaia or with more recent historical events in the manner of Mimnermus's elegiac *Smyrneis*. We cannot rule out the possibility that it was recited in Phokaia. However, the *Phokais*, like perhaps the Koan *Meropis*, might be a pseudo-archaic poem created in the Hellenistic age (West [*per litteras*]), and the poet Thestorides nothing more than a fiction. The matter seems impossible to decide on the basis of the information available.

Attica

All the information that has come down to us with respect to rhapsodic performances in the rest of Attica outside of Athens should be treated with caution. It is unlikely that rhapsodic performances took place *solely* during the Panathēnaia in Athens and that recitals did not occur elsewhere in Attica. Still, the ancient evidence presents a blurry picture.

APATOURIA A speech by Kritias in Plato's *Timaeus* provides the sole bit of information about rhapsodic performances at the festival of the Apatouria (21b1–7):

> ἡ δὲ Κουρεῶτις ἡμῖν οὖσα ἐτύγχανεν Ἀπατουρίων. τὸ δὴ τῆς ἑορτῆς σύνηθες ἑκάστοτε καὶ τότε συνέβη τοῖς παισίν· ἆθλα γὰρ ἡμῖν οἱ πατέρες ἔθεσαν ῥαψῳδίας. πολλῶν μὲν οὖν δὴ καὶ πολλὰ ἐλέχθη ποιητῶν ποιήματα, ἅτε δὲ νέα κατ' ἐκεῖνον τὸν χρόνον ὄντα τὰ Σόλωνος πολλοὶ τῶν παίδων ᾔσαμεν.
>
> Now the day was that day of the Apatouria which is called the Registration of Youth, at which, according to custom, our parents gave prizes for recitations, and many poems of many poets were recited by us boys, and many of us sang the poems of Solon, since they were new at that time. (trans. Jowett [adapted])

Although the text speaks only of rhapsodic contests and not of their content, the "many poems of many poets" are likely to have included some epic and possibly Homer (West 2010a: 7). The Pseudo-Herodotean *Life of Homer* (*Vita Homeri* 2.29–31) discusses at length Homer's participation (συνεορτάσοντα) in the Apatouria festival that took place on Samos. His invitation by clansmen, his presence there during a sacrifice to the Kourotrophos, his reclining and eating together with clansmen in a feast—all these features are remarkably similar to the situation we encounter in the passage from Plato's *Timaeus*.

The date of the event described by Kritias must be placed in the fifth century, but both the festival and the rhapsodic performances are much older. This assumption is corroborated by the fact that Kritias compares Solon's poetry with that of Homer and Hesiod, calling Solon's poems "new at that time." His phrasing implies that Solon's poetry would be recited in the old Apatouria, since it had not yet fallen out of fashion. Since Solon predates the specific Apatouria to which Plato's text seems to refer, the meaning of "new" for Solon's poems is "new at this festival." This interpretation suggests that at least some of the "many poems of many poets" that were included in these rhapsodic recitals were not new, that they had been regularly performed in the Apatouria for some time so as not to be considered "newcomers" to the festival. Their regular performance would mean that they remained in fashion. Of course, in this case we are talking about recitals not by professional rhapsodes but by youths, who recited poetry as part of a contest that accompanied the third phase of the Apatouria, the Koureotis, the whole festival marking the transition of Athenian youths from their family proper to their phratry. This line of interpretation is consistent with the fact that Athenian youths were educated in Homeric poetry as part of their upbringing, and so the inclusion of Homeric epic in the contests of the Apatouria is to be expected.

BRAURONIA I begin with an entry from Hesychius's *Lexicon* (β 1067 [I 344–345 Latte]):

> Βραυρωνίοις· τὴν Ἰλιάδα ᾖδον ῥαψωιδοὶ ἐν Βραυρῶνι τῆς Ἀττικῆς. καὶ Βραυρώνια ἑορτὴ Ἀρτέμιδι Βραυρωνίαι ἄγεται καὶ θύεται αἴξ.
>
> *Brauroniois*: Rhapsodes used to sing the *Iliad* at Brauron in Attica. The festival Brauronia is celebrated in honor of Artemis at Brauron and a goat is sacrificed.

We cannot extrapolate from Hesychius's entry that rhapsodic contests at the Panathēnaia originated at this location in rural Attica just because it was Peisistratos's hometown (*pace* Kern 1897 and Zschietzschmann 1931: 59). J. A. Davison states, "There is nothing in Hesychius' words to show when the Brauronian practice originated or the source from which it was derived, what form it took, how long it went on, or what influence it exerted (if any)" (1958: 29). He also draws attention to the danger of making the exact opposite assumption—that Hipparchos established rhapsodic contests at Brauron to create the impression that the Panathenaic contests originated in Brauron.

Still, Hesychius's entry has its value. It is indisputable that Brauron was Peisistratos's hometown, and it is indisputable that tyrants, and especially the Peisistratidai, were eager to manipulate certain facts in order to promote their own interests (cf. Herodotus 1.60). I would not be surprised if some new piece of evidence reveals that, after the introduction of rhapsodic contests at the Panathēnaia, the Peisistratidai introduced rhapsodic contests in Brauron in order to show that what happened at the Panathēnaia had already happened in their hometown of Brauron. Let us not forget that Peisistratos aimed at strengthening the links between his hometown of Brauron and the city of Athens. The establishment of a Brauronion, a sanctuary on the Acropolis in the sixth century BCE, where Artemis Epipyrgidia had been honored since the Bronze Age (Simon 1969: 158, 1983: 83; Travlos 1971: 124–125), is in keeping with such a political strategy. In this light, one cannot exclude the possibility that Peisistratos or his sons had undertaken a similar activity with respect to the rhapsodic recitals at Brauron.

That said, no currently available evidence supports this theory. In fact, it is odd that the Hesychian entry does not mention the association of Peisistratos with rhapsodes in his Attic hometown (Shapiro 1993: 103, 106n41; cf. Hamilton 1989b: 459n18, 460n23). The entry does not specify who established rhapsodic performances in Brauron, when this individual did so, and if there was any connection with the Panathēnaia. Why, then, are scholars willing to speculate about a link with the Peisistratidai? Just because Brauron was Peisistratos's hometown and because the Peisistratidai are so closely connected with the introduction of rhapsodic contests at the Panathēnaia? But if the Hesychian entry originated in a source reflecting Peisistratid interests, then it would have included some reference to the Peisistratidai themselves. Since the entry contains no such hint, it seems to me unlikely that either the entry itself or its source is forged. Forgery happens for a reason, and as the entry stands there is no reason to consider it forged. One cannot rule out that the Peisistratidai invented such stories, but that scenario would require a new piece of evidence (beyond the Hesychian entry) that mentions the Peisistratidai.

Other components of the entry lead in the same direction. That Hesychius speaks solely of the *Iliad* militates against the notion that the entry depends on a source forged by the Peisistratidai. The Peisistratidai belonged to the deme of Philaidai ([Plato] *Hipparchus* 228b; Plutarch *Solon* 10.4) and traced their origins to Pylos and Peisistratos, the son of Nestor the Neleid (Herodotus 5.65; Diogenes Laertius 1.53). On a mid-seventh-century relief *pithos* from Pikermi (close to Brauron in north-eastern Attica), the name Antilochos appears next to a warrior figure. Given that "its date . . . is unusually early for a Trojan subject" and that Antilochos is "a relatively minor figure in the epic" (Shapiro 1983: 89–90), the possibility arises of rhapsodic performances of the *Iliad* at Brauron, although Alan Shapiro interprets the presence of Antilochos as a sign of Peisistratid interest in the family's Neleid origins (Antilochos being the grandson of Neleus). As far as I can see, a Peisistratid forgery would make more sense if the Hesychian entry mentioned either the *Odyssey* alone or the *Odyssey* together with the *Iliad*.

The Peisistratid connection aside (Scheliha 1987: 49), the Hesychian entry points toward the rhapsodic performance of the *Iliad* at the festival of the Brauronia.[21] Given that this was an annual festival, held on a larger scale every four years (Aristotle *Athenaion Politeia* [*Ath. Pol.*] 54.7), and that the entry does not specify an episode or episodes from the *Iliad* performed during the Brauronia, Martin West speculates that the entire *Iliad* may have been recited "on these bigger occasions" every four years (2010a: 6).

ELEUSIS The *Homeric Hymn to Demeter* (*Homeric Hymn* 2) is so closely associated with Eleusis and the foundation of the Eleusinian Mysteries that it was likely composed for recitation at the games held there three years out of every four (K. Müller 1875: 121, 127; N. Richardson 1974: 12; West 2003b: 8). The hymn belongs to the Archaic period, probably the first half of the sixth century BCE (N. Richardson 1974: 5–11; Janko 1982: 183; H. Foley 1994: 29–39; West 2003b: 9). That it does not mention Athens or any Athenian has made some scholars opt for a date before Peisistratos (Allen, Halliday, and Sikes 1936: 114, 126). We would then need to postulate an establishment of the games a whole century earlier than their first attestation around 500 BCE (*IG* I^2 5) (Deubner 1969: 91; N. Richardson 1974: 42).

A more difficult question pertains to the performance context of the hymn to Demeter found in *P.Berol.* 13044 (*HymnDemPBerol*). Bruno Currie (2012: 184–209, 2016: 79–104) argues that the *HymnDemPBerol* is a direct source for the *Homeric Hymn to Demeter*, which would mean that the audience of the latter was familiar with the former, that is, with the earlier version of Persephone's rape, so as to be able to appreciate the allusion of the *Homeric Hymn to Demeter* to the *HymnDemPBerol.* What then would the performance context of the *HymnDemPBerol* have been? Eleusis is, in my view, a legitimate possibility, since all the attested hymns to Demeter are in one way or another linked to Attica. Indeed, according to Pausanias (1.22.7, 4.1.5, 9.27.2, 9.30.12), the *genos* of the Lykomidai at Phyle in Athens used in their mystery cult the hymns to Demeter by Musaeus, Pamphos, and Orpheus (Currie 2012: 190n46).

HEPHAISTIA The *Homeric Hymn to Hephaistos* (*Homeric Hymn* 20) refers to the cooperation of Hephaistos and Athena, who teach "splendid crafts to mankind on earth" (20.2–3). These two gods are often mentioned together in Athenian myth and cult: their close association, a purely Attic phenomenon, can be best seen in their sitting next to each other in the groupings of the Twelve Gods on the Parthenon frieze, as well as in the setting of a statue of Athena Hephaistia next to the statue of Hephaistos in the temple built in his honor close to the Athenian Agora (Parke 1977: 92–93).

The hymn may have originated at an Athenian festival,[22] and the Attic Hephaistia around the second half of the fifth century BCE is a reasonable candidate (West 2003b: 18).[23] The idea of the evolution of human civilization emerged in the sixth century (Asius fr. 8 *GEF*; *Phoronis* frr. 1–2 *GEF*) but reached its heyday in the fifth due to the teaching of the sophist Protagoras. Another candidate is the Attic festival of the Chalkeia, celebrated on the last day of Pyanepsion (mid-October). This old festival was dedicated to both Hephaistos and Athena, the former being the god of smiths (χαλκεῖς) (Allen, Halliday, and Sikes 1936: 410; Deubner 1969: 35–36; Parke 1977: 92–93).

MARATHON In the eighteenth century, scholars such as G. E. Groddeck (1786: 48) and C. D. Ilgen (1796: 590) argued that the *Homeric Hymn to Herakles* (*Homeric Hymn* 15) was recited as an *exordium* to an epic about Herakles. They had in mind something like the *Herakleia* of Pisander of Kamiros and an epic with the same title by Panyassis of Halikarnassos. The failure to find any context for such a recital worked decisively against this theory. When scholars began to realize the importance of the performance context, another suggestion was put forward—that the *Homeric Hymn to Herakles* was recited at the festival held at Marathon in Herakles's honor every four years (Baumeister 1860: 348; West 2003b: 18), although some label this thesis "a mere supposition"

(Allen, Halliday, and Sikes 1936: 396). It was in Athens that Herakles received divine honors for the first time in the fifth century BCE (Euripides *Herakles* 1330–1337; Diodorus Siculus 4.39; Pausanias 1.15.3, 1.32.4).

There were other festivals for Herakles in Attica, among which the one in Kynosarges must have been especially important (Deubner 1969: 226). These festivals at Marathon and Kynosarges in honor of Herakles stand out. Herodotus stresses that after the Battle of Marathon, the Athenian army hastened from the Herakleion at Marathon to the Herakleion of Kynosarges in order to protect Athens from the Persian fleet, sailing at full speed after its defeat at Marathon (6.116). The way Herodotus links the two Herakleia shows their symbolic importance for the Athenians. The Athenian collective consciousness associated the sanctuaries of Herakles with Athens' mythical history, since, after his liberation from Hades by Herakles, Theseus renamed as Herakleia all but four of his own sanctuaries that were until then called Theseia (Plutarch *Theseus* 35). In the end, the festival at Marathon seems the most likely site for a performance of the hymn, since we know from Pindar (*Olympian* 9.89–90, 13.110) that the event included athletic contests (Deubner 1969: 227).[24]

PANATHĒNAIA The best-known context for rhapsodic performances in the Archaic and Classical periods is the Panathēnaia—that is, the Greater Panathēnaia—in Athens. Recitals of epic poetry by rhapsodes may have begun with the festival's reorganization in 566 BCE. Although the festival took place before the sixth century BCE (*Iliad* 2.550–551; Davison 1958: 25), it was expanded and embellished during the 566 boom by the addition of new contests.[25]

Eusebius, our single source, speaks only of an ἀγὼν γυμνικός (a gymnastic contest): *agon gymnicus, quem Panathenaeon vocant, actus* (Eusebius *Chronicon* = Jerome 102a–b Helm). Yet other contests could have been included even at this early stage, the more so since equestrian races may have existed even before the gymnastic contest was introduced to the Panathēnaia in 566 BCE. After all, Eusebius is interested in telling us not which contests were included at the early Panathēnaia, but only when the ἀγὼν γυμνικός was first introduced. On the basis of Panathenaic amphorae bearing the inscription ΤΟΝ ΑΘΕΝΕΘΕΝ ΑΘΛΟΝ and the impressive increase in the representation on Attic vases of epic themes during the same period, scholars have suspected that a crucial change occurred in Athens with respect to the performance of epic poetry by rhapsodes.[26] This cardinal event was probably the transformation of the older festival into a large-scale spectacle that included rhapsodes, kitharodes, aulodes, and auletes[27] competing for prizes in 566 BCE.

As for who led the process of expanding and embellishing the Panathenaic festival, Peisistratos has his rivals. The fact that the Panathēnaia (in their expanded form) were established in the archonship of Hippokleides (Marcellinus *Vita Thucydidis* 2–4 = *FGrH* 3 F 2) makes the Philaidai reasonable candidates. A less likely but still legitimate candidate is Lykourgos, the head of the Plainsmen around 560 BCE (Herodotus 1.59). Peisistratos's status and impact work in his favor, even if he first rose to power five years (561/0 BCE) after the reorganization of the Panathēnaia in 566 BCE. In an effort to bypass this problem, Shapiro imagines that "Pisistratus later promoted and laid down rules for competitions which had been introduced shortly before he came to power" (1989: 20; cf. Ziehen 1949: 459).

The content of early rhapsodic contests at the Panathēnaia is not known, but it seems a fair assumption that the work of Homer was included. In this period Homer was regarded as the poet of a variety of epic poems, among which the *Iliad* and the *Odyssey* were only the ones that would always be attributed to him. The performance of Homeric epic at the Panathēnaia, then, included but went beyond the *Iliad* and the *Odyssey*. This supposition accounts for the remarkable growth of representations on vases of episodes from the Trojan War during this period, which stands in sharp contrast to the paucity of depictions on vases of Iliadic and Odyssean episodes (Friis Johansen 1967). The festival likely saw rhapsodic performances of (what we label as) cyclic epic (Theban and Trojan) as well as of the *Iliad* and the *Odyssey*.[28]

Although the pairing of Theban and Trojan epic at the early Panathēnaia reorganized by Peisistratos in 566 BCE may strike one as odd, multiple factors could have prompted such a political and cultural agenda. According to Aristotle's *Athenaion Politeia* (17.3–4), Peisistratos had friendly relations with Argos because he was married to the Argive Timonassa, daughter of Gorgilos.[29] Timonassa was previously the wife of Archinos from Ambrakia who belonged to the Kypselidai. With this Timonassa, Peisistratos had two more sons, Iophon and Hegesistratos, nicknamed Thettalos.[30] Aristotle says that this marriage was the reason for Peisistratos's friendship with the Argives, a friendship evidenced in the support one thousand Argives led by Hegesistratos (Thettalos) offered Peisistratos at the Battle of Pallene.[31] Aristotle also finds that the pro-Argive sentiments of Peisistratos and his family explain the Spartans' eagerness to restore democracy and overthrow the Peisistratidai (*Ath. Pol.* 19.4). Peisistratos, then, had every reason to endorse the recital of Theban epic at the Panathēnaia, since it highlighted Argos and the Argives. After all, the opposite had already been done in Sikyon, where Kleisthenes's anti-Argive policy made him ban all rhapsodic performances of Theban and Trojan epic because of the Argives' prominent role in both (see pp. 60–62).

That Peisistratos used poetry for the promotion of his political agenda is well known. The Neleidai from whom Peisistratos's family came were descendants of Nestor, the only survivor from Herakles's legendary attack on Pylos. According to Herodotus (5.65), the Peisistratidai were Pylians and Neleidai, and Peisistratos was named after the son of Nestor. Herodotus adds that two of the early Athenian kings (Kodros and Melanthos)[32] were descendants of the Neleidai. Here we find strong evidence that the recital of the *Odyssey* at the Panathēnaia would be in accord with the mythical past of Peisistratos's family, thus functioning as a bridge between his claim to power and the authority of Homer, whose poetry had begun to operate on a political, or rather cultural-political, level too.

Relevant as well is that after Peisistratos's first exile the Alkmeonid Megakles called Peisistratos back to Athens (around 545 BCE), offering him the hand of his daughter. The marriage did not last, since Peisistratos did not want to get that close to the Alkmeonidai, but Megakles's helping Peisistratos had larger political implications. The tyrant Kleisthenes of Sikyon, the same one whose anti-Argive sentiment manifested itself in the banishment of Theban and Trojan epic from his city, married his daughter Agariste to none other than the Alkmeonid Megakles. In this light, the Alkmeonidai aimed at having it both ways, creating strong ties to both anti-Argive Sikyon and pro-Argive Peisistratid Athens. If we add that the Alkmeonidai, too, as Pausanias reports (2.18.8–9), came from one of the two branches of the Neleid family[33] that settled in Athens (the other being the Paionidai) and that their ultimate ancestor was Alkmeon, son of Amphiaraos,[34] father and son being involved in the first—unsuccessful—and the second—successful—Argive expeditions against Thebes, respectively, it is a fair assumption that the Alkmeonidai who played a key role in Athens also had reasons to endorse Theban epic.

Apart from their interest in promoting ties with Argos, the Peisistratidai emphasized their links to Boeotian Thebes and in particular to the sanctuary of Apollo Ptoios in Akraiphia as a response to Alkmeonid interest in Delphi. Whereas there is no record of Peisistratid activity at Delphi, the Alkmeonidai were constantly involved with the sanctuary. When the Alkmeonidai had to abandon Athens, they went to Phokis. Megakles participated in the First Sacred War against Krisa, and Alkmeon served as an envoy to Delphi for Kroisos in the sixth century

BCE. After the destruction of Apollo's temple in 548 BCE, the Alkmeonidai paid for its reconstruction, sparing no expense to make the temple more lavish than before. All these events show that there was little, if any, room for Peisistratid activity in Delphi.

The Peisistratidai then turned their attention to other sanctuaries of Apollo, among them that of Apollo Ptoios in Boeotia and the sanctuary of Apollo Pythios, which they themselves founded in Athens.[35] Shapiro shows that the Peisistratidai supported non-Delphic sanctuaries in order "to mitigate the influence of the Alcmeonids in Delphi" (1989: 52; cf. Larson 2000: 211n77). So, Peisistratid activity in Ptoon had a political aim, as was the case with everything the Peisistratidai did. We are lucky to possess a dedication by Hipparchos to Apollo Ptoios (probably erected before 519 BCE), inscribed on a simple base of local Boeotian stone. More revealing is an earlier dedication (*IG* I^3 1469) at the same sanctuary of Apollo Ptoios by Alkmeonides son of Alkmeon, brother of the Alkmeonid Megakles, and one of the key figures of this famous family during this period. Scholars have interpreted the Peisistratid dedication as an effort to balance the Alkmeonid offering and to counter Alkmeonid interest and active involvement in Delphi.

I will pass over for the moment other aspects of Peisistratid involvement with sanctuaries of Apollo, but I point here to the signs of building activity by the Peisistratidai in the sanctuary of Apollo Ptoios—in fact they may have built a temple and a treasury there (Winter 1993: 223)—which would testify to their special interest not simply in Apolline cult but in Apolline cult in Boeotia. Peisistratid connections to this area, which was under the control of Thebes, are further witnessed by the fact that Peisistratos received financial support from the Thebans for his final return to Athens (Herodotus 1.61; Aristotle *Ath. Pol.* 15.2). All in all, the sponsoring of Theban epic (the *Thebais* and the *Epigonoi* featuring the victories of Thebes and Argos respectively) provided the Peisistratidai with a unique opportunity to stress the mythical importance of both these great cities in Boeotia and the Argolid (Larson 2000: 208–219).[36]

At the early Panathēnaia rhapsodes performed only portions of Homer (and perhaps other epic poetry) within the framework of a contest. Hipparchos, the culture-oriented son of Peisistratos, gave a further boost to rhapsodic performances by organizing a serial performance of the *Iliad* and the *Odyssey* after 522 BCE, even if we are in the dark as to whether these two epics were recited from beginning to end.[37] Certain scholars maintain that the "Panathenaic Rule"—or "Panathenaic Regulation"—functioned as the bottleneck for the ensuing narrowing of the range of epics assigned to Homer. This bottleneck only gradually led to the separation of the *Iliad* and the *Odyssey* from the rest of cyclic epic until their final and exclusive attribution to Homer (Nagy 2001). Hipparchos may have initiated this process, but he did not bring it to completion: much later Herodotus (5.67) seems to employ the term Ὁμήρεια ἔπεα for both the *Thebais* and the *Iliad* (Shapiro 1992: 73). The existence of dozens of sixth-century black- and early red-figured vases showing musical performances in a Panathenaic setting proves the existence of *mousikoi agōnes* at the early Panathēnaia, long before Perikles's assumed introduction of musical contests in the fifth century. This case can serve as an analogue for the case of Hipparchos, who may have done (with respect to the older contests) what Perikles probably did later on—namely, reorganize the musical contests by adding or reshaping certain events and dropping others (cf. Shapiro 1992: 57).[38]

As to the extent of the epic material presented at the early Panathēnaia, various clues indicate the recital of self-contained episodes instead of entire epics. According to Aelian (*Varia historia* 13.14) "rhapsodes of old" (οἱ παλαιοί) performed previously selected (πρότερον διηιρημένα) episodes from Homeric poetry, like the Πατρόκλεια ("the Patroklos episode"), the Λύτρα ("the Ransom"), the ἆθλα ἐπὶ Πατρόκλωι ("the [funeral] games in honor of Patroklos"), the Ἀλκίνου ἀπολόγους (Κυκλώπειαν καὶ Νέκυιαν καὶ τὰ τῆς Κίρκης) ("the stories told by Odysseus to Alkinoös [the Cyclops story and the visit to the House of the Dead and the Circe episode]"), and the Νίπτρα ("the episode of washing Odysseus's feet"). Vase paintings suggest the same thing: as early as 580 BCE the painter Sophilos seems to have been familiar with the designations of epic episodes, since he used the title Πατρόκλου ἆθλα ("the [funeral] games in honor of Patroklos") in a vase painting (Shapiro 1993: 103).

The audience's familiarity with cyclic epic would have eased the transition from one episode to the next. This episodic performance of epic poetry resembles cyclic or syntagmatic iconographical representations in which different images appear next to each other according to narrative sequence. These images "share a connection . . . but they illustrate separate actions, with a narrative gap between" (Burgess 2004: 10). The same phenomenon applies *mutatis mutandis* to the rhapsodic recitals of episodes from epics based on a stable skeleton of myth with a fixed narrative sequence.[39]

A turning point with respect to rhapsodic recitals at the Panathēnaia came in 522 BCE, when Peisistratos's elder son Hipparchos, designated by Aristotle as φιλόμουσος (*Ath. Pol.* 18.1), "brought the Homeric epics to this land [scil. Athens] and compelled the rhapsodes at the Panathēnaia to go through them in sequence by relay, just as they do even nowadays" (καὶ τὰ Ὁμήρου ἔπη πρῶτος ἐκόμισεν εἰς τὴν γῆν ταυτηνί, καὶ ἠνάγκασε τοὺς ῥαψῳδοὺς Παναθηναίοις ἐξ ὑπολήψεως ἐφεξῆς αὐτὰ διιέναι, ὥσπερ νῦν ἔτι οἵδε ποιοῦσιν, [Plato] *Hipparchus* 228b7–c1). But what exactly did Hipparchos bring (ἐκόμισεν) to Athens? It seems to me unlikely that he brought a written copy of a full-blown version of the *Iliad* and the *Odyssey* (Merkelbach 1952) and that some official supervised the relay-recitations,[40] ensuring that rhapsodes abided by the new rules and followed this written copy.[41] Such a scenario would require rehearsals, organized supervision, and a number of other practicalities.[42] According to another interpretation, Hipparchos brought the Homeridai to Athens and "arranged for a complete performance of the poems of Homer" (West 1999: 382). This suggestion accords with his practice of inviting and bringing to Athens famous poets of his time, like Anacreon and Simonides (cf. Slings 2000: 60–66), but difficulties concerning the time needed for a complete performance of the entire *Iliad* and *Odyssey* remain.

The recital of the entire *Iliad* and *Odyssey* may have taken 26.9 and 20.7 hours respectively, if James Notopoulos's (1964: 4–7) calculation of the recital speed of modern Cretan and Cypriot singers can be accurately applied to ancient rhapsodic performance (cf. Jensen 1980: 46–50; Thornton 1984: 47–48; Taplin 1992: 27). West—a staunch supporter of the assertion that a complete recital of both Homeric epics took place at the Panathēnaia after Hipparchos's reorganization of the festival—builds an argument on (perhaps) too many assumptions (2001: 19n47): (1) that the division of each epic into twenty-four rhapsodies reflects the recitation units assigned to the entire group of rhapsodes reciting each poem; (2) that the Panathēnaia lasted four days (for ancient sources, see West 2001: 19n47); (3) that the recitations took place over all four days; (4) that the *Iliad* and the *Odyssey* ran concurrently, with six rhapsodies of each per day (meaning that the same individual could not attend both performances from beginning to end), or were squeezed into two days apiece (which would mean around thirteen hours of recital of the *Iliad* per day and around ten of the *Odyssey* per day!). This second solution does not solve the problem of the exact meaning of the phrase τὰ Ὁμήρου ἔπη used in the *Hipparchus*. Do "the verses of Homer" refer to all the poetry attributed to Homer or only to the *Iliad* and the *Odyssey*? Scholars have leaned heavily on this expression, but it does not cover the range of epic recited at the Panathēnaia.

The passage tells us only what Hipparchos did for the first time (πρῶτος), not what happened in the rhapsodic contests at the Panathēnaia. It also explains that the Panathenaic Rule reformed a practice according to which only some favored episodes were recited and those in a random order, with each rhapsode singing whatever episode he wanted, irrespective of what the previous rhapsode had done.[43] Another relevant and equally puzzling passage reports that a law required rhapsodes at the Panathēnaia to recite only "the verses of Homer" (Lycurgus *Against Leocrates* 102). Again, it is unclear whether only the *Iliad* and the *Odyssey* are meant, especially since the law described belongs to the Athenian past (οἱ πατέρες . . . ὥστε νόμον ἔθεντο).[44]

In 446 or 442 BCE, Perikles implemented further changes to the rhapsodic recitals of epic at the Panathēnaia, in tandem with a broader reshaping of the festival's musical contests. This information comes from a much-debated passage from Plutarch (*Pericles* 13.9–11). Davison interpreted Plutarch's phrasing πρῶτον ἐψηφίσατο (13.11) as meaning that a decree was passed for the first time according to which musical contests would be held at the Panathēnaia (1958: 33–36). Given that earlier festivals were the sites of musical contests, Perikles's initiative makes sense only if we postulate that musical contests had been interrupted at some point in the fifth century. But no evidence for an interruption exists. The absence of musical scenes on sixth-century prize amphorae stems from the fact that the prize at these competitions was not olive oil (Zschietzschmann 1931: 58). Likewise, the building of a spectacular venue, the Odeion, where the contests would now take place (Shapiro 1989: 41) does not imply that rhapsodes and kitharodes had lacked a place to compete in the past: Hesychius refers to "a place where rhapsodes and kitharodes used to compete before the theater was built" (τόπος ἐν ὧι πρὶν τὸ θέατρον κατασκευασθῆναι οἱ ῥαψωιδοὶ καὶ οἱ κιθαρωιδοὶ ἠγωνίζοντο, ω 39 [IV 257 Hansen-Cunningham]). The purported passing of a decree by Perikles does not mean that the musical contests had ceased for some time. The information about the building of the Odeion and the holding of the musical performances there after the assembly approved Perikles's proposal may be correct, as may be Plutarch's discussion of the election of ἀθλοθέται (judges awarding the prizes) to supervise the musical competitions, among whom Perikles may have featured. Most likely, Perikles gave a boost to musical performances by creating an impressive venue for them and by introducing "new contests in music by awarding prizes in certain categories for the first time" (Shapiro 1989: 41). Plutarch's phrasing leaves much to be desired. We cannot trust his story that Perikles thought of building the Odeion when he saw himself depicted in Cratinus's *Thracian Women* with the Odeion on his head (fr. 73 K.-A.). Equally mistaken is Plutarch's attribution to Perikles of the introduction of the musical contests at the Panathēnaia (*pace* West 2010a: 4).

OTHER OCCASIONS IN ATTICA The *Homeric Hymn to the Earth Mother of All* (*Homeric Hymn* 30) seems to be associated with the cult of Magna Mater in Phrygia and may have been recited by rhapsodes in various cities in Asia Minor (K. Müller 1875: 122). Since the poem provides no indications of place or date, it is hard to specify the cities in which it was performed.

Hesychius refers to the festival of the Galaxia in Athens: "a festival <in Athens for the mother of the gods> in which they boil the *galaxias*; it is barley-made porridge in milk" (ἑορτὴ <Ἀθήνησι μητρὶ θεῶν ἀγομένη> ἐν ἧι ἕψουσι γαλαξίαν· ἔστι δὲ πόλτος κρίθινος ἐν γάλακτι, γ 80 [I 360 Latte]). The only inscription (*IG*^{2} 1011.13) we possess referring to the Galaxia is an honorary decree dated to 106/5 BCE, but if the festival was celebrated before the Hellenistic period, it could have provided a context for the recital of this hymn.

The endings of *Homeric Hymn to the Sun* and *Homeric Hymn to the Moon* (*Homeric Hymns* 31 and 32) show that they probably functioned as preludes to epics about famous heroes (Baumeister 1860: 366, 368). Filippo Càssola rightly stresses that only these two Homeric hymns end not with a promise for a future song but with a specific reference to the function of the hymns as preludes "a un racconto epico, o ad una serie di racconti epici" (1975: 440; cf. Zanetto 2006: 312).[45] A single poet may have composed these two hymns, although Càssola (1975: 440), opting for a late Classical or even Hellenistic date, advises caution and argues that the similarities between the two hymns may only be due to their belonging to the same rhapsodic school (1975: 440).

Their performance context remains unknown. West suggests an Attic venue on the basis of the reference to the Moon's daughter Pandie (32.15), who features in an Attic genealogy (Apollodorus *FGrH* 244 F 162 [Henrichs 1975: 13n40]) as "the wife of Antiochus, the eponymous hero of the Antiochid *phylē*" (2003b: 19).[46] Some ancient sources refer to the Attic festival of the Pandia, held during the month of Elaphebolion, immediately after the City Dionysia (Photius π 137 [III 150 Theodoridis]; *EM* 651.21–24 [Gaisford]; Poll. I, 37).[47] This festival of Zeus would have been a good place to perform the *Hymn to the Moon*, with its reference to Pandia's father, Zeus (32.14).

Cyprus

Performances of epic poetry must have taken place on Cyprus as early as the Archaic period. After all, a major cyclic epic, the *Cypria*, is associated with the island. The second and shorter *Homeric Hymn to Aphrodite* (*Homeric Hymn* 6) self-reflexively refers to its own performance at a competition (lines 19–21)[48]:

> Χαῖρ' ἑλικοβλέφαρε γλυκυμείλιχε, *δὸς δ' ἐν ἀγῶνι*
> *νίκην τῷδε φέρεσθαι*, ἐμὴν δ' ἔντυνον ἀοιδήν.
> αὐτὰρ ἐγὼ καὶ σεῖο καὶ ἄλλης μνήσομ' ἀοιδῆς.
>
> I salute you, sweet-and-gentle-one of curling lashes: *grant me victory in this competition*, and order my singing. And I will take heed both for you and for other singing. (trans. West 2003b)

We can perhaps be more specific by thinking of Old Paphos as the particular venue for the performance of this hymn, since it was in that place that men and women from various cities gathered to celebrate and honor Aphrodite on an annual basis. The hymn may have functioned as a prelude to the performance of an epic poem (Martin 2000: 410–411; West 2010a: 1–2).

Similar suggestions have been made for another *Homeric Hymn to Aphrodite* (*Homeric Hymn* 10), since it refers to Cyprus and Salamis and requests that Aphrodite grant the poet "beautiful singing" (3–5):

> Χαῖρε θεὰ Σαλαμῖνος ἐϋκτιμένης μεδέουσα
> πάσης τε Κύπρου· *δὸς δ' ἱμερόεσσαν ἀοιδήν.*
> αὐτὰρ ἐγὼ καὶ σεῖο καὶ ἄλλης μνήσομ' ἀοιδῆς.
>
> I salute you, goddess, queen of well-cultivated Salamis
> and of all Cyprus: *grant me beautiful singing.*
> And I will take heed both for you and for other singing.

Some scholars thought that rhapsodes at Salamis on Cyprus recited both of these hymns to Aphrodite (*Homeric Hymns* 6 and 10) (Baumeister 1860: 355; K. Müller 1875: 121; Reisch 1885: 3), but West's suggestion of a performance of hymn 6 at Old Paphos is a legitimate possibility.

Delos

Regarding the festival of the Delia held on Delos in the Archaic period, we possess information from (a) the *Homeric Hymn to Apollo* (lines 146–178, especially 146–150),[49] (b) Thucydides (3.104), and (c) a spurious Hesiodic fragment quoted by Philochorus (*FGrH* 328 F 212;

[Hesiod] fr. 357 M-W *apud* schol. Pindar *Nemean* 2.1d [III 31 Drachmann]).[50] Combining these three sources, scholars have argued that Peisistratos saw to the purification of Delos and the reestablishment of the festival at which the poetry of Homer was performed in order to demonstrate that he possessed the real Homer, given to him by the Homeridai, a group of Chian rhapsodes claiming descent from Homer himself. Peisistratos's attempt to link Homer the Ionian to Athens was a carefully planned political move, and an effective one at that.

The same is the case with the tyrant Polykrates of Samos, who also features with respect to Delos in the aforementioned passage of Thucydides (3.104). Polykrates's effort to create a Samian maritime empire in the Aegean passed through Delos. In a masterly symbolic move, he chained the nearby island of Rheneia to Delos and organized an event involving the combination of two festivals, the Delia and the Pythia, to be celebrated on Delos. This combination of the Delia and Pythia festivals into a single event bears a striking similarity to the combination of a Delian part and a Pythian part in the *Homeric Hymn to Apollo* that was performed at the Delia.

Special mention must be made of Cynaethus, a Chian poet credited by some scholars with the composition of a Delian hymn in honor of Apollo. This hymn was to be recited at a Delian festival attended by Ionians from various regions.[51] The hymn does not duplicate the Delian section of the *Homeric Hymn to Apollo* as we have it but shares with it certain verses. When Polykrates "announced that he was going to celebrate a combined Delian and Pythian festival on Delos in honour of Apollo," in 523/2 BCE, Cynaethus may have produced for this occasion "a combined Delian-Pythian hymn by conflating the older Pythian hymn with his own Delian one" (West 2003b: 11). He would have made several changes to the two preexisting hymns so that they fit together in a single, unified composition.[52]

Delphi

The first Pythian Games of 586 BCE may have been the context for the recital of the Pythian hymn to Apollo, at a point before Cynaethus combined it with the Delian hymn to the same god (West 2003b: 10–11). The games would have been a suitable occasion for its recital, since the hymn refers to central Greece and the events that followed the First Sacred War, when the Delphic sanctuary was freed from Krisa's control after Krisa was destroyed (591/0 BCE) by the Amphictyonic League. The Pythian hymn describes Apollo's journey to Pytho through central Greece, his building of the temple and killing of the serpent, his subsequent journey around the Peloponnese to Krisa, and the institution of his cult there. The earlier version of the Pythian hymn, which must not have been very different from the one preserved, may well have been performed in the Pythian Games of 586 BCE.[53]

Dodona

Rhapsodic recitals must have taken place at the sanctuary of Dodona in northwestern Greece during the Classical period. We possess two tripods, one of which was dedicated (*à la* Hesiod) to the sanctuary. It bears the inscription "Terpsikles the rhapsode dedicated [me] to Zeus Naios" (Τερψικλῆς τῶι Δὶ Ναΐωι ῥαψωιδὸς ἀνέθηκε, *GDI* 5786) and has been dated to the fourth century BCE (*SEG* 46.2312; González 2013: 497). The dedication of a tripod to Zeus accompanied by the designation of the dedicatee not only by his name but also by his profession hints at the reason behind the dedication. Terpsikles may have taken part in rhapsodic recitals at Dodona, hence his dedication of a tripod. This interpretation is further supported by the fact that Terpsikles, whose rare name is an indication that he may have come from a family of rhapsodes (West 2010a: 7), recalls Phemios, who is called Terpiades in the *Odyssey* (22.330).

With respect to another tripod, bearing the inscription Κλέαρχος Διομέδοντος ῥαψωιδὸς μ' ἀνέθ<η>κε, Louis Robert suggests that, despite its unknown provenance and its equally uncertain connection to Olympia, it comes from Dodona (1936b: 39). Like the Terpsikles inscription, it includes both the dedicatee's name and his profession. If Robert's suggestion is correct, then we can assume that both inscriptions point to rhapsodic performances at Dodona.

Eretria

A fourth-century decree dating to around 340 BCE institutes musical contests at the Artemisia in Eretria in Euboia (*IG* XII.9 189.15–21). The contests would begin four days before the end of the month of Anthesterion and would involve rhapsodes, aulos-players, kitharists, kitharodes, and parodists. All the participants in the contests were expected to perform a prosodion (processional song) before the sacrifice and to wear the same clothes at that stage that they would wear during the contest.

The prizes for rhapsodes were 120 drachmas for the first, 30 drachmas for the second, and 20 drachmas for the third. Since the same inscription determines the prizes for kitharists (110 drachmas for the first, 70 for the second, and 55 for the third), kitharodes (200 for the first, 150 for the second, and 100 for the third), and parodists (50 drachmas for the first, 10 for the second, and no third place prize), we can draw some conclusions concerning the status of rhapsodes in this festival. A comparison of the prizes given for the first, second, and third places in these three contests shows that kitharists and kitharodes were more esteemed than rhapsodes, of whom the winner of the first prize received considerably more money than the other two, but still not as much as the first kitharist and kitharode. West observes that the best rhapsode received almost the same amount of money as the third-best kitharode (2010a: 6). Only the prizes given to parodists were smaller than those given to rhapsodes.

The decree's meticulous concern for the daily needs of the contestants, the existence of a preliminary trial (προαγών), the stress on compliance with certain rules, the breaking of which would incur a penalty from the chief magistrates of the city, and the participation of all the competitors in the procession before the sacrifice—all these details testify to the festival's elaborate organization and, perhaps, to its attracting a considerable number of competitors for the musical contests.

Naupaktos

The existence of the epic entitled *Ναυπάκτια* or *Ναυπακτι(α)κά* implies the performance of epic poetry in Naupaktos in the Archaic period. Given that the title does not refer to the epic's content, it is likely that this poem "was current in the Naupactus area or believed to originate from there" (West 2003a: 33; cf. Marckscheffel 1840: 257). The currency of this epic in the area of Naupaktos would entail a special link with this region, but such a connection must be dissociated from the origin of its poet.

Following Charon of Lampsakos (*FGrH* 262 F 4), Pausanias attributed the poem to a certain Karkinos from Naupaktos, against all other authorities (unknown to us) who assign it to a Milesian (10.38.11). Pausanias's opposition to the widespread view about the epic's Milesian author is based on the disjunction between the poem's content and its title. This kind of reasoning—since the poem is called *Naupaktia*, its author must be a Naupaktian, not a Milesian—misses the mark, for we do not have any other example of a poem named after the provenance of its author. In truth, epics are identified by their popularity in a specific region (*Cypria*, *Phokais*) (West 1999: 365) and are usually "transmitted without an author's name, from naïve interest in their contents: it was the scholars who looked for the 'poet,' only to resign themselves to uncertainty" (Burkert 1972b: 75 [trans. West 1999: 365–366]).

We are therefore left with the possibility that the *Ναυπάκτια* or *Ναυπακτι(α)κά* was composed and/or systematically performed in the area of Naupaktos. Since we know of a flourishing epic tradition in western Greece, and given Pausanias's reference to the poem's special association with women, George Huxley suggested that this epic "was well suited to recitation at a festival of Ariadne" (1969: 69).[54] This reconstruction relies on a theory of the existence of a genealogical school of epic poetry active in the region of Naupaktos (Trowbridge and Oldfather 1935: col. 1984; Huxley 1969: 69; V. Matthews 1977: 189n4). Huxley's suggestion is pure speculation, but this school may very well have existed, perhaps competing against one in Orchomenos in Boeotia: both cities claimed to have in their territory the grave of the greatest representative of genealogical epic in the Archaic period, Hesiod himself (Mazon 1928: xiii; Schwartz 1960: 504). The inhabitants of the city of Thespiai in Boeotia argued that Orchomenos's claim that Hesiod's body was brought back to Orchomenos was not accurate and that the poet's body remained hidden at the precinct of Zeus Nemeios in western Lokris (Plutarch *Banquet of the Seven Sages* 19 [162c–e]; cf. Nagy 2009b: 305). According to Jacques Schwartz, a real rivalry must have existed between Chalcis and Naupaktos, the former having been the place in which Hesiod emerged victorious against Homer (1960: 503–504). With respect to our inquiry, it is likely that in this case we have traces of a performance context for early genealogical poetry in which the *Ναυπάκτια* or *Ναυπακτι(α)κά* would have had its proper place.[55]

Peloponnese

Performance of epic poetry in the Peloponnese must have been fairly widespread in the Archaic and Classical periods. The existence of the *Danais* and the *Phoronis*, two epics centered on the region of Argos, is noteworthy, especially if they promoted an Argive viewpoint—the *Danais* offering a new home for the Danaidai, and the *Phoronis* highlighting the preeminent position of Phoroneus and Argos in the history of human civilization. We know of rhapsodic performances at Epidaurus, Olympia, and Sikyon.

EPIDAURUS We have two pieces of information with respect to rhapsodic recitals at Epidaurus. The first pertains to the *Homeric Hymn to Asklēpios* (*Homeric Hymn* 16), which August Matthiae (1800: 95) suggested was composed for the festival of the Asklēpieia held at Epidaurus. More cautiously, one may imagine the Asklēpieia to have been a venue for the hymn's performance (Epidaurus being the major cult center for Asklēpios), irrespective of whether it was composed for this festival. After all, Asklēpios was honored in other places too, such as Akragas, Athens, and Kos, and nothing in the hymn itself suggests a specific association with the games at Epidaurus.[56]

An argument in favor of a performance in Epidaurus requires attending to external factors. Themistios's victory in boxing and the *pankration* proves the existence of athletic contests at the Asklēpieia in Epidaurus as early as 530 BCE (Pindar *Nemean* 5.52–53). The games held there were of Panhellenic importance and scope, since they were called ἱεροί (sacred) like the Olympian, the Pythian, the Isthmian, and the Nemean Games (schol. Pindar *Nemean* 5.96 [III 100 Drachmann]) and the judges of the contests were called Hellanodikai (*IG* IV^2 1, n. 98).

As for musical contests, they must have been introduced at Epidaurus toward the end of the fifth century BCE. That timing would explain Sokrates's astonishment at hearing that the rhapsode Ion had gone to Epidaurus to compete in reciting epic: "The Epidaurians do not host a contest of rhapsodes, do they?" (Μῶν καὶ ῥαψωιδῶν ἀγῶνα τιθέασι τῶι θεῶι οἱ Ἐπιδαύριοι; *Ion* 530a5–6) (Edelstein 1945: 210). The performance of tragedies and comedies there in the Classical period prompts the same conclusion. According to Aelian, the tragic poet Aristarchus of Tegea, an older contemporary of Euripides, wrote and dedicated (which probably means "presented") a play with the same name as the god (fr. 101 *apud Su* ε 3893 [I 352 Adler]). The comic poet Theopompus, a contemporary of Aristophanes, also likely dedicated a comedy to the god (*Su* θ 171 [II 697–698 Adler]). Both poets wished to thank Asklēpios for curing them. Finally, Philippe-Ernest Legrand suggested that the Greek original for Plautus's *Curculio* (*The Weevil*) was written and performed at Epidaurus (1905). In light of the sustained and broad range of musical contests held at Epidaurus, the performance of the hymn at the celebration of the Asklēpieia becomes probable (Edelstein 1945: 211).

Plato's *Ion* presents a much more straightforward case. In this dialogue, the wandering rhapsode Ion of Ephesos, who earns part of his income from the prizes he gains in rhapsodic contests (535e4–6), has just won first prize by reciting Homer at the festival of the Asklēpieia held in Epidaurus. Ion informs us that he has come to Athens to compete in its much more glamorous and esteemed festival, the Panathēnaia. Pindar testifies to the presence of athletic contests at the festival in honor of Asklēpios in Epidaurus much earlier than Plato's *Ion* (*Nemean* 3.84, 5.52;

Isthmian 8.68), but we are in no position to ascertain whether musical contests were held there as early as the mid-fifth century BCE (Edelstein 1945: 208–211; P. Murray 1996: 99).[57]

OLYMPIA Olympia was a likely venue for the performance of the *Homeric Hymn to Hermes* (*Homeric Hymn* 4). The sacrificial procedures carried out by Hermes upon killing two stolen cows by the Alpheios River recall the sacrifices to the Twelve Gods at Olympia. One of the six altars at Olympia was dedicated to Apollo and Hermes, the two main gods of the hymn (West 2003b: 13–14; Faulkner 2008: 3).[58]

Diodorus Siculus refers to a group of first-class rhapsodes sent by Dionysios I of Syracuse to Olympia (together with several *tethrippa*) in 388 BCE (14.109) (P. Murray 1996: 20; West 2010a: 6–7). A huge crowd gathered to listen to their performance, since these particular rhapsodes were famous for their vocal skills. But as soon as they started reciting Dionysios's poems, the audience began to laugh at them. This anecdote reveals the following: first, that rhapsodes could perform outside the regular program, which does not seem to have included rhapsodic contests per se; second, that a good voice (εὐφωνία) could attract large crowds, since even the performance of the best poetry would fall flat if the rhapsode lacked this attribute; and third, that content mattered more than a good voice, since Dionysios became a laughing stock because of the low quality of the poems performed. This last point shows that on this particular occasion the rhapsodes did not perform Homer, Hesiod, or Archilochus, which Plato's *Ion* included in their standard repertoire (531a1–2, 531c2, 535a5–6). Indeed, the designation of the poems performed as Διονυσίου τὰ ποιήματα suggests that the rhapsodes recited Dionysios's own compositions.

SIKYON The third case in point is the city of Sikyon in the northeastern part of the Peloponnese and close to the cities of Corinth and Argos.[59] The key political figure here is the tyrant Kleisthenes, who ruled Sikyon from 600 until 560 BCE. According to Herodotus (5.67), while at war with Argos, Kleisthenes undertook two initiatives to downplay the importance of what he considered to be Argive propaganda or Argive influence in Sikyon. On the one hand (τοῦτο μέν), he put an end to the rhapsodic contests taking place in Sikyon "because of the Homeric poems" (τῶν Ὁμηρείων ἐπῶν εἵνεκα), "since the Argives and Argos were the main themes of the songs" (ὅτι Ἀργεῖοί τε καὶ Ἄργος τὰ πολλὰ πάντα ὑμνέαται). On the other hand (τοῦτο δέ), Kleisthenes desired to cast out of the land the shrine of the hero standing in the agora of the Sikyonians, that is, of Adrastos son of Talaos, an Argive.

According to an argument first put forward by George Grote (1869: 129–130) and developed more fully by Ettore Cingano (1985; 2004: 75–76), Herodotus tells us that Kleisthenes banned the performance of Theban epic because it too often mentioned the Argives and that he replaced the cult of Adrastos, the leader of the Argive army against Thebes, with the cult of the Theban hero Melanippos, responsible for the killing of the Argive hero Tydeus. The *Thebais* included this last mythical episode (fr. 9 *PEG* 1 = 5 *EGF* = 9* *GEF*) and also referred to the special connection between Adrastos and Sikyon, since Adrastos had fled there after his dispute with Amphiaraos, who had killed Adrastos's father, Talaos (fr. 7* *GEF*).

Several arguments prove that Herodotus refers here to both Theban and Trojan epic.[60] I will draw attention to one that merits special recognition. The two measures undertaken by Kleisthenes to downplay the Argive element in Sikyon are interrelated.[61] The banishment of the rhapsodic contests of Theban epic and the replacement of Adrastos's shrine by that of Melanippos work toward the same political goal. In addition to these measures, which stemmed from anti-Argive feeling in Sikyon during the war against Argos, Kleisthenes implemented a third measure aiming at erasing all traces of pro-Dorian sentiment in Sikyon: he changed the names of the Dorian tribes so that they did not have the same names in Sikyon and Argos. He called his own tribe "leaders of the people" (Ἀρχέλαοι), while naming the other Dorian tribes after three different animals (Ὑᾶται, Ὀνεᾶται, Χοιρεᾶται [Swinites, Assites, Porkites]). Herodotus refers to this third measure immediately after the other two prompted by the war with Argos (5.68). He thus delineates a whole set of political measures implemented by Kleisthenes in his attempt to suppress the Argive and pro-Dorian element in Sikyon.

It is within the framework of these anti-Argive and anti-Dorian politics of Kleisthenes that we should interpret the tyrant's decision to marry his daughter Agariste to the Athenian Megakles, a notable member of the powerful family of the Alkmeonidai. Herodotus offers a detailed presentation of the contest for her hand with suitors coming from various areas of Greece and beyond (Italy) to woo Agariste (6.126–131). In a context endowed with rich Homeric overtones, the favorite Hippokleides of Athens loses, and Megakles emerges the unexpected victor, much as Menelaos unexpectedly won Helen's hand. The marriage of Megakles to Agariste made the Alkmeonidai famous all over Greece (καὶ οὕτω Ἀλκμεωνίδαι ἐβώσθησαν ἀνὰ τὴν Ἑλλάδα) (6.131). What Herodotus does not tell us is that, behind the inset narrative of the wooing of Agariste, Hippokleides's self-ridicule and failure, and Megakles's victory, lies Kleisthenes's systematic advancement of his anti-Dorian political agenda. Such a marriage, strengthening the ties between Sikyon and Athens, was a well-planned political maneuver.[62] Kleisthenes aimed at nothing less than bringing Sikyon closer to Athens.

Samos

The *Homeric Hymn to Hera* (*Homeric Hymn* 12) may have been composed for the Heraia or some other festival in Hera's honor on Samos. The same or a similar venue (again on Samos) may have seen performances of the *Homeric Hymn to Hermes* (*Homeric Hymn* 18). West observes that the rare epithet "giver of joy" (χαριδῶτα, 12) attributed to Hermes is also applied by Plutarch (*Aetia graeca et romana* 303d) to Hermes in the context of a Samian festival (2003b: 18).[63]

Rhapsodic or rhapsodic-like contests took place at the festival of the Heraia on Samos at least in the Classical period (Herington 1985: 165). Plutarch describes the event (*Lysander* 18.4):

> Σάμιοι δὲ τὰ παρ' αὐτοῖς Ἡραῖα Λυσάνδρεια καλεῖν ἐψηφίσαντο. τῶν δὲ ποιητῶν Χοιρίλον μὲν ἀεὶ περὶ αὐτὸν εἶχεν ὡς κοσμήσοντα τὰς πράξεις διὰ ποιητικῆς, Ἀντιλόχωι δὲ ποιήσαντι μετρίους τινὰς εἰς αὐτὸν στίχους ἡσθεὶς ἔδωκε πλήσας ἀργυρίου τὸν πῖλον. Ἀντιμάχου δὲ τοῦ Κολοφωνίου καὶ Νικηράτου τινὸς Ἡρακλεώτου ποιήμασι Λυσάνδρεια διαγωνισαμένων ἐπ' αὐτοῦ τὸν Νικήρατον ἐστεφάνωσεν, ὁ δὲ Ἀντίμαχος ἀχθεσθεὶς ἠφάνισε τὸ ποίημα.

> The Samians, too, voted that their festival of Hera should be called Lysandreia. And the poet Choerilus was always kept in his retinue to adorn his achievements with verse; while with Antilochus, who composed some verses in his honor, he was so pleased that he filled his cap with silver and gave it to him. And when Antimachus of Kolophon and a certain Niceratus of Herakleia competed with one another at the Lysandreia in poems celebrating his achievements, he awarded the crown to Niceratus, and Antimachus, in vexation, suppressed his poem.

This passage informs us that rhapsodic contests of some kind were held at the Samian Lysandreia, a festival that replaced the older Heraia after the battle at Aigos Potamoi (405 BCE). Since Lysander appears to have been the judge at this festival, his death in 395 BCE provides a *terminus ante quem* for dating the contest between Antimachus and Niceratus. Choerilus was a Samian, whom Lysander admired and kept by his side, hoping the Samian poet would praise him in one of his compositions. Although Choerilus composed historical epic—he wrote an epic poem called *Persica* or *Perseis* about the Persian Wars—he never devoted a single verse to Lysander. Conversely, when the epic and elegiac poet Antimachus of Kolophon and a certain Niceratus from Herakleia competed by composing poems (epic?) in honor of Lysander at the Lysandreia, the Spartan general garlanded Niceratus. This story shows that at the Lysandreia performers recited new poems in the context of a poetic competition and that these poems had a common topic, in this case Lysander himself. It is not possible to ascertain whether these rhapsodic contests (with different epics altogether) were carried over to the Lysandreia from the earlier festival of the Heraia. In light of the performance of hymnic poetry at the Heraia, I would neither exclude nor endorse this possibility.

Syracuse

According to the historian Hippostratus, the rhapsode Cynaethus from Chios, an eminent Homerid, first recited the Homeric epics in Syracuse (*FGrH* 568 F 5 *apud* schol. Pindar *Nemean* 2.1d [III 30 Drachmann]):

> Ὁμηρίδας ἔλεγον τὸ μὲν ἀρχαῖον τοὺς ἀπὸ τοῦ Ὁμήρου γένους, οἳ καὶ τὴν ποίησιν αὐτοῦ ἐκ διαδοχῆς ἦιδον· μετὰ δὲ ταῦτα καὶ οἱ ῥαψωιδοὶ οὐκέτι τὸ γένος εἰς Ὅμηρον ἀνάγοντες. ἐπιφανεῖς δὲ ἐγένοντο οἱ περὶ Κύναιθον, οὕς φασι πολλὰ τῶν ἐπῶν ποιήσαντας ἐμβαλεῖν εἰς τὴν Ὁμήρου ποίησιν. ἦν δὲ ὁ Κύναιθος τὸ γένος Χῖος, ὃς καὶ τῶν ἐπιγραφομένων Ὁμήρου ποιημάτων τὸν εἰς Ἀπόλλωνα γεγραφὼς ὕμνον ἀνατέθεικεν αὐτῶι. οὗτος οὖν ὁ Κύναιθος πρῶτος ἐν Συρακούσαις ἐρραψώιδησε τὰ Ὁμήρου ἔπη κατὰ την ξθ´ Ὀλυμπιάδα, ὡς Ἱππόστρατός φησιν.
>
> "Homeridai" was the name given anciently to the members of Homer's family, who also sang his poetry in succession. But later it was also given to the rhapsodes, who no longer traced their descent back to Homer. Particularly prominent were Cynaethus and his school, who, they say, composed many of the verses and inserted them into Homer's work. This Cynaethus came from a Chian family, and, of the poems that bear Homer's name, it was he who wrote the *Hymn to Apollo* and laid it to his credit. And this Cynaethus was the first to recite Homer's poems at Syracuse, in the 69th Olympiad (= 504/1 BCE), as Hippostratus says. (trans. West 1999: 368)

The performance is dated to the sixty-ninth Olympiad (504–501 BCE). Given that dating by Olympiads is also attested in F 4 and that Hippostratus may have taken this practice from the historian Timaeus of Tauromenium (*FGrH* 362 F 5, p. 595 [commentary]), I do not see any special reason to doubt the authenticity of this information. As to the precise date of Cynaethus's performance, Hippostratus may have consulted a list of victors in a rhapsodic competition that featured Cynaethus first. The date would be consistent with the contemporary practice of keeping victor lists for tragedy and dithyramb in Athens. Felix Jacoby (*FGrH* 362 F 5, p. 596 [commentary]) objects with respect to the dating of this contest in Syracuse that the numbering by Olympiads could not have been reported by tradition, especially since we know nothing about official victor lists for games taking place in Syracuse. Moreover, it is unlikely that specific dates were available for local Sicilian poets. Conversely, West argues that Hippostratus drew this information from the association of Cynaethus's performance "with some other event that yielded a synchronism with the tyranny of Cleander of Gela, which began in 505" (1999: 368). West reminds us that Gela's and Syracuse's histories would soon be intertwined and that a statue in Gela bearing the inscription "I am the s[tat]ue of [K]ynaithos the son of Epochos" (ϙ]υναιθο εμι το α[γαλ]μα το Επoχο) may designate the rhapsode Cynaethus, since this name is quite rare (1999: 368). The matter is not easy to decide, but I am rather inclined to accept West's suggestion, since the existence of a contest in Syracuse is independent of a performance by Cynaethus there. Since the scholion does not refer to a contest, we do not need to look (necessarily) for victor lists. After all, Cynaethus must have acquired enough fame (at least after the performance of the *Homeric Hymn to Apollo* on Delos in 523/2 BCE., which the scholion mentions immediately before his recital in Syracuse) to receive an official invitation to recite Homeric poetry at Syracuse. Perhaps his performance, if a success, paved the way for more sustained and organized musical activity in the city under the patronage of Hiero some years later (477–466 BCE).

Varia

Clearchus of Soloi reports that rhapsodes performed Homeric hymns or poems of the same type at a Dionysiac festival that had died out (fr. 91a Wehrli *apud* Athenaeus 7.275b). We are not told the name of the city in which it was held, but we are informed that more than one rhapsode participated in an actual recital honoring one or more gods

(West 2010a: 6). The presence of a series of rhapsodes may indicate that different hymns were performed.

Equally inconclusive is the sole piece of evidence for rhapsodic recitals on Crete, in Sparta, and in the Dorian-inhabited part of Libya provided by Maximus of Tyre: "For late did Sparta turn to rhapsodizing, late also did Crete, and late too the Dorian race living in Libya" (ὀψὲ μὲν γὰρ Σπάρτη ῥαψωιδεῖ, ὀψὲ δὲ καὶ Κρήτη, ὀψὲ δὲ καὶ τὸ Δωρικὸν ἐν Λιβύηι γένος, 17.5 [Trapp]) (Herington 1985: 175). We know neither when rhapsodic recitals were introduced in these Doric-speaking areas nor the contexts in which the rhapsodes performed. It is pointless to speculate, especially since the extant information about the festival of the Karneia at Sparta speaks exclusively of other musical contests without any reference to rhapsodic performances. Yet the wide range of musical contests held in Sparta starting in the Archaic period renders the possibility of a complete absence of rhapsodic recitals less probable, if not remote.

Likewise, although we know of the epic poetry of the Cretan Epimenides, we lack evidence for the performance of his poetry in his native land. The same situation obtains when it comes to Kyrene in Libya. Although we are aware of an Archaic epic, the *Telegony* written by Eugammon of Kyrene, there is not even a single hint about its recital there. Nevertheless, we could easily imagine such a scenario: the poem alludes to King Arkesilaos II of Kyrene when it has Odysseus sire two sons with Penelope, Telemachos and Arkesilaos (Eustathius *Od.* 1796.35 = II 117.17–21 Stallbaum).

The *Homeric Hymn to Dionysus* (*Homeric Hymn* 26) ends with a prayer in which the god is asked to grant to humans that they come to his festival in happiness in due time again and again for many years to come. This ending suits the context of an annual festival held in honor of Dionysos. The sole geographical reference in this short hymn is to Mount Nysa, mentioned as Dionysos's birthplace, as it is in hymn 1 to the same god. West rightly questions whether the reference to Mount Nysa should be treated as an indication of the provenance of this hymn (2003b: 2). Augustus Baumeister entertained the possibility that hymn 26 was recited at the Dionysia in Brauron (1860: 360) on the basis of *Su* β 521 (I 493 Adler)

Β ρ α υ ρ ώ ν: τόπος τῆς Ἀττικῆς, ἐν ὧι τὰ Διονύσια ἤγοντο

Brauron: a place in Attica, in which the Dionysia were held.

Yet Dionysia were celebrated in various places, and there is no hint whatsoever that the hymn bears a specific connection with Brauron.

CONCLUSION

The overall picture of rhapsodic recitals in the Archaic and Classical periods can be summarized as follows.

1. The main venue for rhapsodic performances was the public festival. This preference arises from various factors: (a) The time frame of several days allowed rhapsodes to recite extended parts of epic poems. (b) Massive attendance played a role, since it attracted professional rhapsodes, who would be able to perform their art in front of large audiences. (c) This was the ideal venue for an agonistic context, since different rhapsodes tried to show their skill in a place where they could win acclaim and recognition.

The information we possess with respect to other venues is limited. The case of the symposium is certainly a legitimate possibility, but it has to be approached with caution. Perhaps we should not be speaking of rhapsodic recitals but of the use of epic verses or short passages at that phase of the banquet when the *logos sympotikos* assumed the form of a contest. Another public occasion that probably included, though to a limited extent, rhapsodic recitals with an agonistic tinge was the funeral, when it took the form of a lavish, grand-scale event that included athletic contests and musical performances.

2. Rhapsodes performed throughout the Greek world: Asia Minor (Klaros, Ephesos, Mykale, Phokaia), Attica (Athens, Brauron, Eleusis, Marathon), the Aegean (Delos, Samos), Cyprus, central and northern Greece (Delphi, Dodona, Eretria, Naupaktos), the Peloponnese (Epidaurus, Olympia, Sikyon), and Syracuse. This diffusion testifies to a great interest in epic poetry. Itinerant rhapsodes flocked to the festivals held in these places and recited epic. This was the standard picture on a local, regional, and panhellenic level.

3. Tyrants tried to promote their political image and agenda by banning (Kleisthenes in Sikyon), endorsing and aggrandizing (Hipparchos at the Panathēnaia), or lavishly financing (Dionysios I at Olympia) rhapsodic recitals either at home or abroad. This aspect of the recital of epic poetry was undoubtedly conditioned by the principal performance venue, the public festival, where attendance by large audiences offered the perfect opportunity for increasing one's political capital.

APPENDIX 1.1. RHAPSODES IN THE ARCHAIC AND CLASSICAL PERIODS

Reference	*Name*[a]	*Place of Origin*	*Place of Performance*	*Occasion*	*Date*
Stephanis 127	Ἄλεξις	Tarentum	Susa	Alexander's wedding	324 BCE
Plato's *Ion*	Ἴων	Ephesos	Epidaurus	Festival of Asklēpios	4th cent. BCE
Stephanis 1445	Κλεομένης		Olympia	Olympic Games	5th–4th cent. BCE
Schol. Pindar *Nemean* 2.1c/e	Κύναιθος	Chios	(1) Delos (2) Syracuse	(1) Festival for Apollo	6th cent. BCE
Stephanis 1721	Μνασίων			Epideixis	5th–3rd cent. BCE[b]
Stephanis 1817	Νικήρατος		Herakleia (?)	Rhapsodic contest	5th cent. BCE
Stephanis 2141	Πράτυς			Rhapsodic contest	5th cent. BCE
Diodorus Siculus 14.109	Ῥαψῳδοὶ Διονυσίου (tyrant of Syracuse)	Syracuse	Olympia	Epideixis	4th cent. BCE
Stephanis 2281	Σιμωνίδης	Zakynthos	Athens	Recital in the theater	4th–early 3rd cent. BCE
Stephanis 2355	Σωσίστρατος				4th cent. BCE (?)
Stephanis 2402	Τερψικλῆς		Dodona		4th cent. BCE
Stephanis 2786	]στρατος	Sikyon			366–338 BCE or 329/8 BCE

[a]The order of the rhapsodes' names is alphabetized according to the Greek alphabet. Despite discussing Hesiod's case in the main text of this chapter, I have decided not to include him in the list of rhapsodes proper. The same goes for Empedocles, who was not a rhapsode.

[b]Given the uncertain date for Mnasion, I include him both in this appendix and in the one pertaining to rhapsodes of the Hellenistic period in chapter 3. The fifth–third centuries BCE range is determined by the fact that this rhapsode recited Simonides's iambs (late sixth–early fifth centuries BCE) and is mentioned by the third-century BCE grammarian Lysanias in the first book of his work *On Iambic Poets*. See González 2013: 496.

NOTES

1. This is typical, for example, with otherwise first-rate work on the symposium such as that of Pellizer (1990) and Rösler (1990).

2. All translations are my own unless otherwise noted.

3. Cf. the criticism of Fletcher (2006) and Aloni (2017).

4. More speculative is the suggestion that the *Megala Erga* (if a separate poem) contained agriculturally oriented instructions of the sort we find in the farming section of the Hesiodic *Works and Days*. If so, the parallel circulation of thematically related epics of the Hesiodic type may have been more prevalent than we think.

5. On the function of invocations in Homeric and Hesiodic epic, see Minton 1962.

6. A part of the Greek text is missing. Kaibel notes in the critical apparatus (III p. 187), "haec sic fere ordinanda καὶ ἦσαν διαπρέποντες οἱ ἀπὸ τῆς Ἰνδικῆς θαυματοποιοί, <τῶν δὲ Ἑλλήνων> Σκύμνος κτλ, cf. Aelian 25 de Timotheo tibicine; cf. XIII p. 565a."

7. See Plutarch's description of Alexander's musical taste (*Alexander* 4.11.4–5): "At any rate, though he instituted very many contests, not only for tragic poets and players on the flute and players on the lyre, but also for rhapsodists, as well as for hunting of every sort and for fighting with staves, he took no interest in offering prizes either for boxing or for the pancratium" (trans. Perrin 1967).

8. According to Eumelus's *Korinthiaka* (fr. *22 *GEF*), musical contests were also held at the first Isthmian Games, and Orpheus won the kitharodic contest.

9. I disagree with Power, who entertains the possibility that the contest in the funeral games of Amphidamas in Chalcis was "lyric in nature" (2010: 429). The autobiographical filtering of the entire *sphragis* in the *Nautilia* section of the *Works and Days* is based on a comparison between Hesiodic and Homeric epic (Tsagalis 2006: 105–113, 2007: 269–290, 2009b: 151–157).

10. On the agonistic context and the performance of epic, see Gainsford's useful remarks (2015: 84–85). He stresses the importance of a "direct, more personal style of competition," drawing attention to the contests between Homer and Hesiod (*Certamen*) and Lesches and Arktinos (Phanias fr. 33 Wehrli), with Hesiod and Lesches being victorious, and to the attacks on Homer by Syagros and on Hesiod by Kerkops (Diogenes Laertius 2.46). Poetic duels like those between the seers Mopsos and Kalchas ([Hesiod] *Melampodia* fr. 214 M-W) or Thamyris and the Muses (*Iliad* 2.599–600) should also be taken into account.

11. Ford thinks that other forms of stichic verse, like the sort of elegies performed at dinner parties, were also included in rhapsodic performances in the Classical period (1988: 306). Cf. Gentili 1988: 156.

12. Patzer's view—that only epic poets were called rhapsodes, since they strung together one dactylic hexameter verse after the other (1952)—is true as far as the stringing of verses is concerned. The same principle also applies to other unmelodic verse, not sung, such as elegy and iambus.

13. Diogenes tells us that Empedocles recited his poetry on his own (ἀλλὰ καὶ αὐτὸς ἐρραψῴδει τὰ ἑαυτοῦ, 9.18). See also West 2011b.

14. This would have been in keeping with the tendency to recite Hesiod and Phocylides in addition to Homer in the Archaic period: see West 1978: 164n3 (Chamaileon fr. 28 Wehrli [Athenaeus 14.620c]), 1981: 125.

15. W. Müller (1836: 28n2), Mazon (1942: 217), and von der Mühll (1952: 307) hold that the poet of the *Iliad* had taken part or observed a bull sacrifice at the Panionia festival. West agrees and adds that "he [the poet of the *Iliad*] had very likely captivated crowds there with his recitals" (2011a: 20).

16. The *Certamen* credits Homer with the authorship of both the *Thebais* and the *Epigonoi*. Apart from the equal length (seven thousand verses) of both poems and the first verse of each that is cited in the *Certamen*, we learn that Homer began to recite "his" Theban epics while wandering (περιερχόμενος) after his defeat in the contest against Hesiod. According to the *Certamen*, Homer is the author only of Theban and Trojan epic, and in the latter case of only the *Iliad* and the *Odyssey*. He is not credited, as happens in other sources, with the composition of other cyclic and hymnic poetry, such as the *Cypria*, the *Aithiopis*, the *Ilias parva*, the *Nostoi*, or the *Hymn to Apollo*. The date of the *Certamen* is late, but there is general agreement that it rests on much earlier material. The tradition on which the *Certamen* ultimately draws must have presented Homer as the author of Theban and Trojan epic.

17. Differently, Baumeister 1860: 357–358 (with earlier bibliography), who argued that the Boeotian Helikon is meant here (on the basis of Hegesinous fr. 1 *GEF* and Homeric epigram 6.2). Several scholars agree with Baumeister: Allen, Halliday, and Sikes (1936: 413–414); Càssola (1975: 578–579); Zanetto (2006: 306). West follows the conjecture of Martinus 1605 (2003b: 18).

18. The attestation of a handful of Boeotian place names (Mykale recalling Mykalessos, Thebes under Mykale, Kadme instead of Priene, etc.) around the altar of Poseidon Helikonios at the Panionion prompted Wade-Gery to argue that Poseidon's epithet Helikonios derived from Mount Helikon in Boeotia (1952: 64n16). For the Boeotian origin of the epithet Helikonios, see Aristarchus (schol. D *Iliad* 5.422 [247.42–45]), who argued against the association of the epithet Helikonios applied to Poseidon with the Achaian city of Helike, claiming that (a) if an Achaian connection existed, then we would expect the epithet Ἑλικήϊος, not Ἑλικώνιος, which comes from Ἑλικών in Boeotia, and (b) the entirety of Boeotia was sacred to Poseidon (ἡ Βοιωτία ὅλη ἱερὰ Ποσειδῶνος), a not very strong argument given that the entirety of the Peloponnese was also sacred to Poseidon (τὸ παλαιὸν τὴν Πελοπόννησον οἰκητήριον γεγονέναι Ποσειδῶνος, καὶ τὴν χώραν ταύτην ὥσπερ ἱερὰν τοῦ Ποσειδῶνος νομίζεσθαι, καὶ τὸ σύνολον πάσας τὰς ἐν Πελοποννήσωι πόλεις μάλιστα τῶν ἀθανάτων τὸν θεὸν τιμᾶν τοῦτον, ["(because they thought) that in the days of old the Peloponnese was the habitat of Poseidon, and that this land is considered to be sacred to Poseidon, and that the sum of all the cities in the Peloponnese honor this god most of the immortals"], Diodorus Siculus 15.49.4). Differently, schol. AbT

Iliad 8.203b–c (Erbse) and schol. bT *Iliad* 20.404b–c, which derive "Helikonios" from "Helike," a city of Poseidon in the Peloponnese, and identify Aigai, which appears together with Helike in this Homeric verse, with an island close to Euboia. See Prinz 1979: 343–345. Nevertheless, most ancient authorites tried to explain the formation "Helikonios" as coming from the genitive plural of Ἑλίκη (Ἑλικῶν), like ἀνέμη (ἀνεμῶν) > ἀνεμώνιος: see *GG* 3.2, p. 879.9 (Lentz); Eustathius *Il.* 1214.27 = IV 427 van der Valk; *Et. Guid.* 550.16; *Et. Magn.* 387.38. Wade-Gery also maintained that the Ionians inhabited Boeotia at a very early date, before moving to Attica, where they founded a shrine of Poseidon Helikonios on the summit of Agrai on the hill Ardettos (see Cleidemus *FGrH* 323 F 1; also Wade-Gery 1952: 64n17). It is possible that when they led an organized colonial expedition to Asia Minor they did the same thing with the shrine of Poseidon at Mount Mykale (Wade-Gery 1952: 5).

19. On the four-book segments, see Davison 1965; differently, Thornton (1984: 18 and n. 46), who believes that the *Iliad* was performed "during three consecutive nights, or at a later stage days, each performance lasting about nine hours" either in the festival of Apollo on Delos or in the Panionia at Mykale.

20. See also Clement of Alexandria *Stromata* (*Miscellanies*) 1.21.131.3; Plutarch *De Pythiae oraculis* 25, p. 407b; *Su* o 658 (III 565.20–1 Adler).

21. After all, Brauron and Thorikos were the two minor centers in Attica at the expense of which Athens grew during the sixth century (Boersma 2000: 52).

22. Baumeister (1860: 356) refers to "Athenian games" (*ludis Atheniensibus*) without further specification.

23. Cf. the arguments of Càssola (1975: 374), who does not refute the possibility of an Athenian performance context but observes that Hephaistos and Athena constituted a pair in the canon of the Twelve Gods and that "the poet could have cited Athena in a celebration dedicated only to Hephaistus."

24. See Shapiro 1992: 57, referring to a local festival at Marathon in which musical contests were held. A red-figured pelike (in Bulgaria) shows a victorious kithara player surrounded by four Νίκαι, each representing the festival whose name is inscribed above her: Panathēnaia, Marathon, Nemea, and Isthmia.

25. This growth of the Panathēnaia must have been triggered both by the influence of the Olympic festival and by the political aspirations of Peisistratos. The expansion of the Panathēnaia must, on a secondary level, be seen within the larger context of the establishment of Panhellenic games throughout Greece during the same period (Pythia 586 BCE, Isthmia 582 BCE, Nemea 573 BCE). See Shapiro 1989: 19.

26. The relation between iconography and epic poems is a hotly debated question. Lowenstam (1992, 1993, 1997, 2008) and Shapiro (1983, 1992, 1993) illuminate the ways iconographical representations and epic communicate with each other.

27. See West 1992: 338, following Davison 1958: 37, 42 and 1962. See also Shapiro 1992, 1993 and the prize list (*IG* II^2 2311) for the events at the Panathēnaia of ca. 380 BCE.

28. For an analogous situation, see the analysis regarding Sikyon (pp. 60–62). Cf. Cingano 1985, 2004; Shapiro 1993: 103; Burgess 2001: 129.

29. For the close ties between Argos and Peisistratos and his family, see also Forrest 1981: "That the Hippias-group and the Peisistratos-group were somehow related is put beyond doubt by the name which one fourth-century Hippias and one fourth-century Peisistratos gave to their sons. Given what we know of the Athenian family's ties with Argos, Argeios Peisistratou (*IG* XI 598) and Argeios Hippiou (*SEG* 19.580) are no accident."

30. Hippias and Hipparchos were Peisistratos's sons from his first wife (Aristotle *Ath. Pol.* 17.3).

31. It is not clear when this marriage took place. According to Aristotle (*Ath. Pol.* 17.4), some argued that it happened when Peisistratos was first exiled (ἐκπεσόντα τὸ πρῶτον), whereas others say that it took place while he was in power (κατέχοντα τὴν ἀρχήν).

32. For Melanthos's descent from Neleus, see also Hellanicus *FGrH* 4 F 125.

33. There were three Neleid branches that fled from Messenia after Herakles sacked Pylos.

34. On Amphiaraos, see Krauskopf 1981; on possible elements in the *Thebais* that appear on vases, see Torres Guerra 1995: 272–316.

35. For a discussion of Peisistratid activity in Boeotia and the Peisistratid nexus of Athenian–Boeotian interests, see Larson 2014: 420–426.

36. We can also look for internal Peisistratean links to Theban epic. Poseidon's metamorphosis into a horse and his mating with Erinys and subsequent siring of Arion, Adrastos's horse—to which Adrastos owes his salvation in the first Argive expedition against Thebes—is such a case. The association of the Peisistratidai with Poseidon was strong. Neleus was the son of Poseidon, whose depiction (together with Athena) in the work of such celebrated artists as Exekias and the Amasis Painter points to the old cults of Poseidon Hippios and Athena Hippia on Kolonos Hippios (Shapiro 1983: 91). In the *Odyssey* (3.4–61), Telemachos and the disguised Athena arrive at Pylos, offer sacrifices to Poseidon, and are welcomed by Nestor's son Peisistratos, whom Athena admires (3.36–53). Shapiro speculates that the Neleidai "brought the cult of Poseidon with them from Pylos to Attica at the end of the Bronze Age" and highlights the "coincidence" between, on the one hand, Poseidon's equine associations and Nestor's horsemanship (Γερήνιος ἱππότα Νέστωρ) and, on the other hand, the equine (ἱππο-) first part of the names of Peisistratos's two most well-known sons (Ἱππίας, Ἵππαρχος) (1983: 92–93). Pausanias adduces the *Thebais* (fr. 11 *GEF*) and the *Iliad* (23.346–347) as evidence that Poseidon is the father of Arion, Adrastos's horse (8.25–27). This pairing of the *Thebais* and the *Iliad* with respect to Poseidon's siring of Arion shows how these epics could be used to promote or highlight the role of Poseidon. What has escaped attention is that Nestor, emphatically called "Neleian" in this particular context, utters these lines in the *Iliad*. This case indicates that the connection between Poseidon, the Neleidai, and Peisistratos's family could appear in both Theban and Trojan epic.

The early Panathēnaia may well have been a possible context for the pairing of Theban and Trojan epic, next to other cyclic Trojan epic.

37. For two different views, see West 1992: 340 (supporting the relay performance of the entire epics) and Burgess 2004: 11–16. For a balanced appraisal of this issue, see Ford 1997.

38. A Panathenaic amphora by the Kleophrades Painter (dated shortly after 500 BCE) is inscribed with what seems to be the beginning of a hexameter (ὧδε ποτ' ἐν Τίρυνθι; cf. *Iliad* 2.559), providing a parallel for the required lengthening of the first syllable of Τίρυνθι. According to Davison (1958: 37n22) and Shapiro (1998: 95–96), the fact that this half-verse does not come from the *Iliad* or the *Odyssey* renders the possibility of the Kleophrades amphora depicting a rhapsodic contest at the Panathēnaia remote, if not impossible, given the dating of the vase. Herington argues (1985: 14–15) that this half-verse came from an epic poem about Tydeus or Diomedes, given their connection to Tiryns, or one about Herakles, who is regularly associated in myth with Tiryns. Shapiro suggests that we should leave the Kleophrades amphora out of the discussion of rhapsodic performance at the early Panathēnaia, especially because the two sides of this amphora (1998: figs. 21–22, pp. 96–97) may belong to the same scene and because the figure holding a staff on a *bēma*, whom others have labeled a rhapsode, is really an aulode, as the flute player on the other side suggests. Cf. Bundrick, this volume, p. 95n10.

39. Cf. Fantuzzi and Tsagalis (2015: 15): "The existence of an earlier stage or phase during which the Epic Cycle represented a connected whole of epic traditions facilitated the filling-in of narrative gaps by means of a mythologically oriented *pars pro toto* principle."

40. See Diogenes Laertius 1.57: τά τε Ὁμήρου ἐξ ὑποβολῆς γέγραφε ῥαψῳδεῖσθαι, οἷον ὅπου ὁ πρῶτος ἔληξεν, ἐκεῖθεν ἄρχεσθαι τὸν ἐχόμενον ("He [Solon] wrote a law that Homer's works should be recited by rhapsodes, so that wherever the first stopped, from that point the next [rhapsode] should begin").

41. Nagy (1996a: 65–112) adduces various arguments against the idea of a standard written text; see also Slings 2000: 68–69; Graziosi 2002: 221.

42. One such practicality concerns prizes for rhapsodes, on which see *IG* II^2 2311 = *SIG* III 1055 (dated to 380 BCE) and the comments of West (2010a: 3–4) and Rotstein (2012: 102–106).

43. See also Sealey 1957: 349, who aptly notes that the relay performance of the Homeric epics makes sense only if the poems had not been reduced to writing.

44. Differently, Slings 2000: 68, who takes the reference to Homer as designating the poet only of the *Iliad* and the *Odyssey* and seems to accept that the law mentioned by Lycurgus is genuine.

45. Gelzer argues that these two hymns are not preludes to epic poems but astral hymns dedicated to gods of the universe and to be interpreted allegorically (1987:166).

46. Others have suggested an association with the Pandionid *phylē* through

Pandion: K. Müller 1875 (1841): 123; Hermann 1846: §59, 5; Deubner 1969: 176–177 (on the basis of Demosthenes 21.8); Parke 1977: 136.

47. See also the designation of the Moon as πανδία (Allen, Halliday, and Sikes 1936: 435).

48. Baumeister 1860: 355; K. Müller 1875: 121; Reisch 1885: 3; West 2003b: 16.

49. "But it is in Delos, Phoibos, that your heart most delights, where the Ionians with trailing robes assemble with their children and wives on your avenue, and when they have seated the gathering they think of you and entertain you with boxing, dancing, and singing" (trans. West 2003b) (ἀλλὰ σὺ Δήλωι Φοῖβε μάλιστ' ἐπιτέρπεαι ἦτορ, / ἔνθα τοι ἑλκεχίτωνες Ἰάονες ἠγερέθονται / αὐτοῖς σὺν παίδεσσι καὶ αἰδοίηις ἀλόχοισιν. / οἱ δέ σε πυγμαχίηι τε καὶ ὀρχηθμῶι καὶ ἀοιδῆι / μνησάμενοι τέρπουσιν ὅταν στήσωνται ἀγῶνα, 146–150).

50. "In Delos, back then at the very beginning, I and Homer, singers, / sang-and-danced, stitching together a song in new *humnoi*, / making Phoebus Apollo the subject of our song, the one with the golden weapon, the one born of Leto" (trans. Nagy 2010: 71) (ἐν Δήλωι τότε πρῶτον ἐγὼ καὶ Ὅμηρος ἀοιδοὶ / μέλπομεν, ἐν νεαροῖς ὕμνοις ῥάψαντες ἀοιδήν, / Φοῖβον Ἀπόλλωνα χρυσάορον, ὃν τέκε Λητώ).

51. See Burkert 1979: 52–62; Janko 1982: 112–115, 200, 228–231; West 2003b: 11–12; N. Richardson 2010: 13–14.

52. Differently, Aloni (1989: 35–68, 117–124), who suggests that there was a second version of the Pythian hymn compiled by the Peisistratidai. For a useful survey of various arguments, see Clay 1997: 501–502.

53. See Allen, Halliday, and Sikes 1936: 199–200, who observe that the Pythian hymn was written before 586 BCE, when the Pythian Games were established, since verses 264–271 show that chariot races had not yet been instituted.

54. Huxley's suggestion is based on Lérat 1952: 167–169, who argued in favor of a cult of Ariadne in western Lokris.

55. Debiasi suggests a different line of interpretation (2003). He argues that the *Naupaktia* may have taken its name from the building of the Argo, just as the city of Naupaktos had been named "from the ship-building that was carried out at that place, whether it was the Herakleidai who built their fleet there or, according to Ephorus, the Lokrians who had made ships there earlier on" (ἀπὸ τῆς ναυπηγίας τῆς ἐκεῖ γενομένης, εἴτε τῶν Ἡρακλειδῶν ἐκεῖ ναυπηγησαμένων τὸν στόλον, εἴθ'—ὥς φησιν Ἔφορος [*FGrH* 70 F 121]—Λοκρῶν πρότερον παρασκευασάντων, Strabo 9.4.7). This explanation would require that an epic was named *Naupaktia* because it referred to the building of the ship *Argo*, although the building of this ship took place at Pagasai, which had been named in its own turn ἀπὸ τῆς ναυπηγίας τῆς Ἀργοῦς (Strabo 9.15). Moreover, if it were the case that the title of the epic referred to the building of the *Argo*, it would not follow that the city of Naupaktos was named after the epic. The city has no connection with it. But Charon's evidence (*FGrH* 262 F 4) tends to confirm the assumption that the epic was connected with the city.

56. In Athens, the festival in honor of Asklēpios was called Epidauria (Pau-

sanias 2.26.9; Philostratus *Vita Apollonii* 4.18) (Roscher, *Lexikon* I.1: 631; Edelstein 1945: 195–199; West 2003b: 18). In later times, games in honor of Asklēpios were held at festivals in the following places: Ankyra, Kalymna, Karpathos, Carthage, Kyzicos, Ephesos, Lampsakos, Laodikeia, Nikaia, Pergamon, Prousias, Soloi, Rhodiopolis, Termessos, Thyateira, and Tyros (Nilsson 1906: 413).

57. Plato's *Ion* is particularly useful with respect to the performances given by rhapsodes: they stand on a platform (535e2) wearing impressive clothes and golden garlands (530b6–8, 535d2–5), deliver their verses with "a certain incantatory quality, above the level of ordinary colloquial utterance but well below the level of song" (Herington 1985: 13), and resemble to some extent actors (532d6–7) as they impersonate their characters, although outright imitation must have been, as Aristotle had argued (*Poetics* 26), more restrained in the case of rhapsodic performance (Herington 1985: 12–13). See pp. 6–8 in the introduction.

58. For alternatives pertaining to the origin of the poet of this hymn and the place of its composition (not of its performance), see Càssola 1975: 174. West also draws attention to lines 124–126, in which Hermes spreads out the hides of the cows on a rugged rock, "as even now in after time they remain long-lasting through the ages in a fused mass," arguing that the poet has in mind some "rock formation that looked like a pair of spread hides" (2003b: 14; his translation).

59. Sikyon was a city with a rich musical tradition. We know of a Lysander of Sikyon who excelled in ψιλὴ κιθάρισις (solo—lit. "bare"—lyre-playing) and is dated around the beginning of the fifth century. He is thought to have been responsible for several improvements in the performance of solo lyre-playing without the accompaniment of song (West 1992: 69). ψιλὴ κιθάρισις was invented by Aristonikos of Argos and was introduced at the Pythia in 558 BCE (Menaichmus *FGrH* 131 F 5; Pausanias 10.7.7). Given that Kleisthenes of Sikyon organized a Pythia festival in Sikyon too (schol. Pindar *Nemean* 9, title [III 149 Drachmann]), it is not unthinkable that it contained solo lyre-playing (among other events), thus contesting Argive *kitharisis*. After all, the Sikyonian monopteros at Delphi depicting Orpheus standing next to a kithara-holding Philammon exemplifies another effort by Kleisthenes to create a bridge between the kitharodic traditions of Delphi and Sikyon. See Power 2004, 2010: 275–276. Another Sikyonian musical VIP was the late sixth-century Epigonos, after whom a kind of zither was named (ἐπιγόνειον), as well as a school of harmonic theorists (West 1992: 78–79).

60. One indirect piece of evidence pertains to Theban epic. A century after Kleisthenes's banishment of Theban epic from Sikyon, the cult of Adrastos was restored in an effort to invigorate Sikyon's political ties with the other Dorians of the Peloponnese among whom Argos played a key role. A specific poetic rendering of Theban myth drawing heavily on the *Thebais* reinforced the oligarchic Dorian-oriented sentiment in the city: namely, Pindar's *Nemean* 9, in which Pindar assigned the foundation of the Sikyonian Pythia not to the anti-Dorian Kleisthenes but to Adrastos, the symbol of pro-Dorian sentiment

in Sikyon (Hubbard 1992; Athanassaki 2009: 178–183). Chromios's (the ode's *laudandus*) decision to take part in the local games at Sikyon, after winning at the much more prestigious Panhellenic games at Nemea, reflected a joint effort by Chromios and Hiero of Syracuse to strengthen their ties with the Peloponnesian Dorians. Such a political initiative was in tune with the fact that Hiero had already drawn from the Peloponnese no less than half of the ten thousand colonists who settled in Sicilian Aetna (Diodorus Siculus 11.49.1). In support of the view that Herodotus refers to Trojan epic as well, see *Certamen* 17 (West) in which Homer, reciting certain lines from the *Iliad* (2.559–568ab), delights Argive officials by praising their city and race. The Argives honor him with various gifts, among which are daily, monthly, and yearly sacrifices to him in Argos and every five years on Chios. The aforementioned verses recited by Homer mention the Argive heroes who participated in the Trojan War. For Argos and Homer, see Graziosi 2002: 153–154. Kleisthenes's measure would not make any sense unless both Theban and Trojan epic were associated in the minds of the citizens of Sikyon (and, of course, more widely) with Argos and the Argives.

61. Torres Guerra suggests that the *Thebais* was performed in the festival of the Nemea, Nemea being an area with a strong Argive element (2012: 520–528). He adds that the episode of the strife between Amphiaraos and Lykourgos that gained in prominence from 570/560 BCE onwards (see Krauskopff 1981) and was widespread in the Peloponnese (it is attested both in Sparta and Olympia; see Krauskopff 1981: nos. 32, 33) may have featured in the *Thebais*. What is particularly relevant to our inquiry is the anti-Kleisthenic, pro-Argive sentiment in Nemea and the city of Kleonai that controlled Nemea. If this scenario obtains, then a date for the performance of the *Thebais* after 573 BCE, when the Nemean Games became a Panhellenic festival, seems plausible.

62. On traces of an attempt to affiliate Sikyon with Athens in the early sixth century BCE, see Hesiod (*Catalogue* fr. 224 M-W), who makes Sikyon son of Erechtheus, and Asius (fr. 11 *PEG* 1 = *EGF* = *GEF*), who makes him the son of the Erechtheid Metion (West 1985: 107, 2002b: 122).

63. Ilgen took verse 12 as an interpolation by a rhapsode (1796: 589) and was followed by Baumeister (1860: 349). Allen, Halliday, and Sikes (1936), Càssola (1975), and Zanetto (2006) keep verse 12. West (2003b) omits verses 10–11 and keeps 12.

CHAPTER TWO

Reading Rhapsodes on Athenian Vases

SHERAMY D. BUNDRICK

THE POPULARITY OF THE RHAPSODIC CONTEST AT the festival of the Greater Panathēnaia cannot be doubted. Literary sources make this clear: Plato's *Ion*, set in the late fifth century BCE, features as Sokrates's foil a young and successful rhapsode who has newly arrived in Athens after competing in a festival at Epidauros. Although critical of the rhapsode's art, the dialogue nonetheless conveys *rhapsōidia*'s prominence. The admittedly scanty evidence suggests the contest became part of the Panathenaic program much earlier in the festival's existence, perhaps close to its alleged foundation (more likely, reorganization) in 566/5 BCE, while significant reforms are thought to have taken place later in the sixth century under the initiative of Peisistratos's son Hipparchos (Tsagalis, this volume, pp. 46–52). For much if not all of the Panathēnaia's history, then, *rhapsōidia* joined other musical contests (*mousikoi agōnes*) for kithara and aulos and shared in their prestige. Like the kithara and aulos players, rhapsodic victors received valuable prizes, the first-place rhapsode perhaps earning a gold *stephanos*.[1] *Ion* shows that rhapsodes came to Athens from across the Greek world to participate in this contest.

Despite the high visibility of rhapsodes at the Panathēnaia, a paradox exists in respect to their depiction on Athenian figured vases, otherwise a useful source of information about festival events. Among scenes of musical contests involving aulos or kithara (Kotsidu 1991; Shapiro 1992; Bundrick 2005: 160–174), and certainly compared to scenes of athletic competition, images of rhapsodes are nearly nonexistent. Inscribed prize amphorae holding Athena's sacred olive oil and bearing images of both the goddess and the event for which the prize was being awarded were granted to victors in the athletic and equestrian contests (Bentz 1998),

FIG. 2.1. *Athenian calyx krater with kitharodic contest. In the manner of the Peleus Painter, ca. 440 BCE. London, British Museum E 460. Photo © The Trustees of the British Museum/Art Resource, NY.*

which accounts for the large number of representations of events like the *stadion* (sprinting footrace) and *tethrippon* (four-horse chariot race). However, Panathenaic prize amphorae were not given to winners of the *mousikoi agōnes*, who as just noted received other types of prizes.[2] Images of aulos and kithara contests do survive on vases of other shapes, presumably because of their popularity, and we can assume for these at least some inspiration from the Panathenaic festival. On a calyx krater in the manner of the Peleus Painter from ca. 440 BCE (fig. 2.1), a kitharode mounts a *bēma* (platform) in preparation for his performance.[3] A figure likely to be an *athlothetēs* (judge) sits to right and an unidentified female spectator to left, while two winged Nikai assure the viewer that the kitharode will prevail.

Rhapsodes did not attract the attention of Athenian vase painters to the same degree as instrument players did, and modern scholars have had to mine the corpus of surviving pottery to find them. Alan Shapiro advocated a trio of sixth-century vases as showing the contest in action (see figs. 2.2–2.5) (1993), while the present author added a recently discovered, fifth-century vase to the series (see fig. 2.6) and proposed reconsideration of another that had often been identified as oratory rather than *rhapsōidia* (see fig. 2.7) (2015).[4] This chapter collects all the black- and red-figured Athenian vases that, based on certain criteria, likely feature the contest. Chronologically, they fall at strategic points during the history of the Panathenaic festival and offer a view into contemporary attitudes toward the event. In addition to the five vases that seem to represent the *agōn* in a straightforward way, I reconsider a unique black-figured pelike depicting Odysseus and Aias, on which Odysseus is making his case for being given Achilleus's armor (see fig. 2.8).[5] Although some scholars have asserted that this scene was inspired by contemporary oratory, I propose that it was inspired by *rhapsōidia*. Finally, I speculate on why rhapsodes were shown on vases so rarely, despite the popularity of their art in Athens.

IN SEARCH OF *RHAPSŌIDIA*

The challenge of identifying rhapsodes on Athenian figured pottery arises from the iconography itself. Competitors in other *mousikoi agōnes* hold instruments, like the kitharode in the calyx krater mentioned earlier (fig. 2.1), or, in the case of singers in the aulodic contest, appear alongside aulos players. Similarly, athletes are easily recognized, if not by the paraphernalia of their events then by their frequent nudity. Rhapsodes lack such obvious attributes, and one is forced to recognize them by what is *not* present as much as by what *is*. Even the five scenes classified here as depictions of *rhapsōidia* form a rather heterogeneous group.

A key element that unites all five scenes and seems essential to identifying the setting as an *agōn*—as opposed to simply a conversation—is the presence of an audience, which is visually set apart from a figure who seems to be a performer. On the three black-figured vases (figs. 2.2, 2.4, 2.5), the spectators are all bearded males and represent elite members of the community, in keeping with a tendency to showcase such characters in sixth-century Athenian iconography (cf. Stansbury-O'Donnell 2006: 128–186). The seated positions of some figures and the staff-wielding postures affected by others imply power and privilege: indeed, the staff itself, whether associated with a seated or a standing man, designates a "privileged citizen about town" (Stansbury-O'Donnell 2006: 142).

On the earliest amphora, from ca. 540 BCE (fig. 2.2), both spectators are seated upon stools, and both are elaborately garbed in a way that

FIG. 2.2. *Athenian pseudo-Panathenaic amphora with rhapsodic contest. Ca. 540 BCE. Liverpool, World Museum 56.19.18. Photo: National Museums Liverpool.*

challenges the prominence of the (apparent) performer between them. The one to right sniffs a flower in a pose also adopted by some listeners in contemporary scenes of musical contests.[6] On a slightly later amphora, from ca. 520 BCE (fig. 2.4), the two standing spectators appear more engaged in the performance, the one to left gesturing as if in response. His forked staff differs from the more typical walking stick and may mark him as an official involved in the *agōn* rather than a casual listener. The man at right, meanwhile, leans upon his staff with one hand back at his hip, a stance almost deceptively casual in its studied elegance. The third vase, a contemporary black-figured pelike (fig. 2.5), includes

FIG. 2.3. *Athenian pseudo-Panathenaic amphora with Athena Promachos. Ca. 520 BCE. Oldenburg, Stadtmuseum XII.8250.2. Photo: Stadtmuseum Oldenburg, A. Gradetchliev.*

FIG. 2.4. *Reverse of figure 2.3 with rhapsodic contest. Oldenburg, Stadtmuseum XII.8250.2. Photo: Stadtmuseum Oldenburg, A. Gradetchliev.*

one seated and one standing spectator: here, the seated listener stretches out a hand toward the performer, a more profound sign of engagement than in the earlier scenes. The standing man at left, accompanied by a dog that perhaps indicates his status, also gazes intently at the performer.

A red-figured calyx krater by the Pantoxena Painter from ca. 440 BCE (fig. 2.6) differs from the sixth-century vases in the composition of the depicted audience and helps cement the identification of these other scenes as *rhapsōidia* precisely by doing so. Instead of Athenian elites at their leisure framing the central figure, a pair of Nikai swoop into the scene to guarantee his victory, one carrying a fillet and the other a wreath (Bundrick 2015: fig. 3).[7] Their appearance confirms that this is not only a performance but an actual contest, and since the performer in question lacks either a musical instrument (compare fig. 2.1) or an accompanist carrying an instrument—as would be the case with an aulodic contest featuring a singer and aulos player (Vos 1986; Shapiro 1992: 60–61; Bundrick 2005: 170–171)—he must by default be a rhapsode. By extension, the seated figure on the *klismos* to right must be a judge—like comparable figures in the *kitharōidia* scene (fig. 2.1) and in depictions of other *mousikoi agōnes*—while the beardless figure to left is also best identified as a judge. The latter's slightly foliate staff recalls those of other judges in athletic and musical contest scenes of the period and represents a subtler version of the forked staff held by officials in prior images (as possibly in fig. 2.4) (Bundrick 2015: 9–10).

The *bēma* that the rhapsode ascends on the Pantoxena Painter's krater (fig. 2.6)—and that appears on two of the scenes already discussed (figs. 2.4 and 2.5)—visually sets him apart from the audience while also ensuring his identification. The only publication of this krater prior to the present author's 2015 article suggested the victorious youth might be an athlete (Rizzo 2004). However, one finds a *bēma* only in scenes of (or otherwise evoking) *mousikoi agōnes*, never in scenes related to gymnic competition, even when a participant in the latter is receiving a prize

FIG. 2.5. *Athenian pelike with rhapsodic contest. Ca. 520 BCE. Dunedin, Otago Museum E48.226. Photo: Otago Museum, Dunedin, New Zealand.*

FIG. 2.6. *Athenian calyx krater with rhapsodic contest. The Pantoxena Painter, ca. 440 BCE. Tarquinia, Museo Nazionale Tarquiniense 137262. Photo © MiBACT–Soprintendenza Archeologia, Belle Arti e Paesaggio per l'Area Metropolitana di Roma, la Provincia di Viterbo e l'Etruria Meridionale.*

(cf. Bundrick 2015: 10–11). Again, by default, he must be a rhapsode, and the presence of a *bēma* helps secure other scenes as *rhapsōidia*, too. The Pantoxena Painter's rhapsode mounts the *bēma* in advance of the performance (compare the kitharode in fig. 2.1), while in other instances the performance is already in progress (figs. 2.4 and 2.5). A *bēma* can have one step, two, or even three on Athenian vases, the painter's choice likely driven by compositional needs more than any desire for documentary accuracy. That the Pantoxena Painter's rhapsode is climbing the *bēma* leaves room for two steps, for instance, while the shape of the pelike in figure 2.5 permits only one level, with the performer standing upon it. The constraints of space on a pot never allow a performer to tower over his listeners, but one is nonetheless reminded of Plato's *Ion*, where the rhapsode describes his effect upon audiences: "I look down time to time from the *bēma* and see them weeping and gazing up at me fearfully, sharing the astonishment of what is being said" (535e1–3, trans. R. Allen [1996: 15]).

FIG. 2.7. *Athenian amphora with possible rhapsodic contest. The Harrow Painter, ca. 480 BCE. Paris, Musée du Louvre G222. Photo © RMN-Grand Palais/Art Resource, NY.*

On the red-figured amphora attributed to the Harrow Painter (fig. 2.7), the inclusion of a *bēma* supports the identification of the figure as a rhapsode, although, as noted earlier, some scholars have described him as an orator.[8] He is wrapped in a carefully draped but unembellished himation, with his right hand held close to his chest and enveloped in the folds, and his open mouth indicates that he is speaking. The painter's somewhat awkward choice of a three-stepped *bēma* means that the rhapsode is considerably smaller in scale than the man watching him, who leans upon a staff like one of the spectators on the Oldenburg amphora (fig. 2.4). The speaking figure does resemble fourth-century and Hellenistic statues of orators, such as, for example, the well-known portrait type of the orator Aeschines.[9] This identification, however, is complicated by the fact that Attic vases generally do not depict political activities such as those associated with the lawcourts or assembly. Moreover, the *rhētores*—who were both famous and infamous—did not become ubiquitous in the Athenian lawcourts until later in the fifth century, after the reforms of Ephialtes in 462 BCE (Arthurs 1994; Worthington 2007). Dating as it does to ca. 480 BCE, the Harrow Painter's vase would seem to be too early. One may also note the fragmentary inscription on the top step of the *bēma*, the last three letters of the word *kalos* ("beautiful"). A similar inscription appears on the *bēma* in two musical contest scenes, where it celebrates the performance and almost transforms the performer into a statue.[10] Indeed, were it not for his open mouth, the viewer might suspect the Harrow Painter's figure *is* a statue.

The nearly identical costume of the Pantoxena Painter's rhapsode (fig. 2.6) also helps confirm that the Harrow Painter portrays a rhapsode, for no orator would be depicted with judges and Nikai in an *agōn*. Instead, the garments of both these men resemble those seen in some images of aulodic contest, where the singer of the pair stands wrapped in his himation as the aulos player pipes along.[11] In each instance, the himation gives an impression of *sōphrosynē* (moderation) and even *aidos* (modesty). The contrast with the *skeuai* (costume or ensemble) of rhapsodes as described in Plato's *Ion* is significant, for Sokrates says the performers are "decked out in many-colored [*poikilēi*] clothing and crowned with gold" (535d2–3, trans. R. Allen [1996: 15]). This characterization may or may not be exaggerated to suit Plato's agenda on rhapsodes, but it does recall the depiction of some kitharodes on vases and the description of their *skeuai* elsewhere (Power 2010: 251). The Pantoxena Painter's rhapsode wears a wreath and is about to receive another, but otherwise there is no hint of luxury. Perhaps this restraint on the vase painter's part was intentional: to link the rhapsode to Athenian ideals of *isonomia* as expressed through the plain citizen's himation and perhaps even to render him an embodiment of the *archaia paideia*, the "old" educational system that celebrated Homer and advocated the memorization and recitation of epic poetry by schoolboys (Bundrick 2015: 18–24). Schoolboys, too, can appear on Attic vases in this costume and pose.[12] The painted rhapsode becomes, to use Gregory Nagy's phrase, a "virtual Athenian" (2010: 11) even though, as *Ion* suggests, many competitors were from other Greek cities and were not Athenian.

The costumes and poses of the rhapsodes on the three black-figured vases (figs. 2.2, 2.4, 2.5) are quite different and indicative of sixth-century customs. They wear chiton and himation, as was typical of the day, in a loosely draped style that permitted animated performance. The garments of the performer on the Liverpool amphora (fig. 2.2) are highlighted in added paint, while the rhapsode on the Oldenburg amphora (fig. 2.4) wears a grand wreath mirrored by one of his listeners. The hooked staff held by this rhapsode raises questions. For a long time, scholars believed the word "rhapsode" to be derived from *rhabdos*, or staff, and to reference a particular type of staff wielded by the performers. In more recent scholarship, however, the word *rhapsōidia* is said to derive from *rhaptein*, "to sew" or "to stitch," with the metaphorical meaning of stitching a song or poem together (Ford 1988: 300; Shapiro 1992: 72; Collins 2001b: 12–13; West 2010a: 2).[13] It is possible that some rhapsodes did carry some kind of distinctive staff and that this vase painter has depicted it, but its absence in all but one of the other scenes—it appears in figure 2.2, although not hooked—means that it cannot be considered a definitive attribute.

The absence of a *bēma* on the Liverpool amphora (fig. 2.2)—the only vase in the group missing this feature—might suggest that no *agōn* is being shown here at all but that instead we have a friendly conversation between elite peers. In this case, the vase's shape would contribute to the identification of the scene as *rhapsōidia* (Shapiro 1993: 98–101). Both this amphora and the one in Oldenburg (figs. 2.3, 2.4) are of the type known as pseudo-Panathenaic, meaning that with their form and the depiction of Athena Promachos on their obverses (fig. 2.3) they mimic Panathenaic prize amphorae that held sacred olive oil and were awarded to athletes. They lack, however, the formal inscription ΤΟΝ ΑΘΕΝΕΘΕΝ ΑΘΛΟΝ ("from the games at Athens") that would designate a prize vase (Tsagalis, this volume, p. 46). Because pseudo-Panathenaics typically included festival events on their reverses, as did prize amphorae, it seems likely that these two examples show rhapsodes, even though rhapsodes did not receive olive oil as prizes (Shapiro 1993). As noted at the beginning of this chapter, what is *not* present is important: no musical instruments, no athletic equipment, and no athletic nudity to suggest any of the other Panathenaic *agōnes*.

HEROIC RHAPSODES?

Some or all of the following iconographic elements, then, might be incorporated into a scene of *rhapsōidia*: an audience, a *bēma*, a performer lacking attributes that would otherwise identify him as a musician or athlete, and/or the performer being shown in the act of speaking. Using these same criteria, we can revisit a sixth scene that is mythological in subject but may nonetheless evoke the rhapsodic *agōn*: a black-figured pelike said to be "near" the Rycroft Painter (meaning near his style, although perhaps not by the same hand) and dating from ca. 500 BCE (fig. 2.8).[14] This scene is noteworthy in Athenian vase painting as the ear-

FIG. 2.8. *Athenian pelike with scene of Odysseus and Aias. Near the Rycroft Painter, ca. 500 BCE. Naples, Museo Archeologico Nazionale 81083 (H3358). Drawing after* Annali dell'Instituto di Corrispondenza Archeologica *(1865), plate F.*

liest known image of the contest between Aias and Odysseus for the arms of Achilleus, the *hoplōn krisis*. The identification of both heroes by inscription and the prominence of armor in the scene confirm the subject. Despite its impact on later events, namely the suicide of Aias, the *hoplōn krisis* is not common on Athenian vases and otherwise appears on a group of red-figured cups that cluster in the first quarter of the fifth century.[15] In all those examples, the emphasis is on the vote of the Greeks to determine the armor's ownership. For instance, on a cup signed by Douris as painter, Athena watches as a succession of men come forward to lay pebbles in piles.[16] The larger pile to left is surely Odysseus's, and Odysseus himself may be the figure at far left reacting with surprise and delight (D. Williams 1980: 139). The cup's opposite side shows a fight breaking out over the heap of Achilleus's armor, presumably before the vote, while its interior shows the story's coda, in which Odysseus gives the armor to Achilleus's son, Neoptolemos. The cups are close in time to mentions of the *hoplōn krisis* in Pindar (*Nemean* 7.23–30, 8.21–32) but have no iconographic relationship to those poems. They may or may not have any relationship to Aeschylus's lost play *Hoplōn krisis*, the first of an apparent trilogy, which exists today only in a handful of fragments (*TrGF* 3, frr. 174–178; Sommerstein 2008: 175–179) and, like the cups, cannot be dated precisely. In highlighting the process of voting with pebbles (*psēphoi*), the cups may be celebrating the nascent Athenian democracy most of all (cf. Spivey 1994).

The black-figured pelike instead—and uniquely—presents a moment before the vote in which Aias and Odysseus attempt through speeches to convince their compatriots of their respective worthiness (fig. 2.8). Judging from the surviving fragments, the heroes likewise gave speeches in Aeschylus's *Hoplōn krisis*, but the pelike verifies that this episode existed earlier in mythological tradition (cf. D. Williams 1980: 141; Hedreen 2001: 109n63). Whether the vase relates to a lost literary source, however, must remain a mystery.[17] Odysseus, wrapped in his himation, with his right hand concealed beneath the fabric, stands upon a single-stepped *bēma*. He is at attention, holding a spear in his left hand, and his lips are parted as if speaking (compare the performer in fig. 2.7). To right stands Aias, similarly dressed in a himation and leaning upon his spear like an elite spectator (cf. figs. 2.4, 2.5, 2.7), one hand resting on his hip in a posture of either impatience or exaggerated nonchalance. Between the two men looms the outsized panoply of Achilleus, the unmistakable reminder of the *agōn*'s purpose. The painter has provided no iconographic clues to indicate who will be victorious, except perhaps Odysseus's visual prominence on the *bēma*, but the viewer already knows who will win the day.

In some previous scholarship on the Naples pelike, Odysseus's pose and garments have been compared to those of orators, much like the Harrow Painter's amphora discussed earlier (fig. 2.7) (Ghedini 2009: 50–51).[18] To depict Odysseus in the guise of an orator, it is argued, emphasizes the persuasive power of his speech. And yet, as we have seen, the *rhētores* were not a force at the time of the Harrow Painter's amphora, let alone the Rycroft Painter's pelike, which dates two or three decades earlier. Given the discussion throughout this chapter—with particular attention to both the Harrow Painter's amphora and the Pantoxena Painter's calyx krater (fig. 2.6)—perhaps it is more appropriate to see Odysseus in the guise of a rhapsode, proclaiming his own deeds in the style of a late sixth-century Panathenaic competitor. The "Odysseus" and "Aias" inscriptions placed as though issuing from the heroes' mouths add a self-referential effect. The viewer is reminded that their story, and all the Trojan War adventures, were the rhapsode's particular domain.

I do not propose that the *hoplōn krisis* episode formed part of the specific repertoire of rhapsodes at the Panathenaic festival, for there is no way of knowing that, and given vase painters' capacity for invention when it came to Trojan/Homeric subjects (Lowenstam 1992), it need not be the case. Rather, I suggest that this vase painter had seen rhapsodic contests in action, and when he imagined his two heroes competing with words, he imagined them in similar fashion. One may compare a series of black-figured vases dating from ca. 530 BCE until the end of the sixth century that depict the hero Herakles as a kitharode, in many cases mounting or standing upon a *bēma* as if participating in an *agōn*.[19] In no surviving myth does Herakles perform in such a way—on the contrary, he murdered his music teacher, Linos—and yet vase painters characterized him as a Panathenaic competitor, surely a reference to the increasing popularity of *mousikoi agōnes* in Athens.

RHAPSODIC IMAGERY IN CONTEXT

Even if one includes the *hoplōn krisis* pelike in the corpus of scenes that depict or otherwise reference the rhapsodic contest at the Panathenaic festival, this is still a sample of only six vases, far fewer than representations of other *mousikoi agōnes*. In evaluating how they might inform our knowledge of *rhapsōidia*, one must bear in mind that the intention of Athenian vase painters was not to represent life around them in a documentary or visually accurate way. We have seen this already with the garments of the Pantoxena Painter's rhapsode (fig. 2.6), which contrast with those described for the rhapsode in Plato's *Ion* (Tsagalis, this volume, p. 7). Both the painter and Plato likely had agendas behind their characterization of rhapsodic costume. Even so, the vases provide key evidence for the contest, given the paucity of epigraphic and textual sources for *rhapsōidia* in the period they cover, from the mid-sixth to slightly later than the mid-fifth centuries. Because the timing of the six vases falls at important points in the festival's history, I shall now consider them in chronological order and within that larger framework.

The earliest of the six, the pseudo-Panathenaic amphora in Liverpool from ca. 540 BCE (fig. 2.2), is one of a series of prize and imitation amphorae that could be interpreted as evidence for the earliest *agōnes* of the Greater Panathēnaia, traditionally held to have been either established or reorganized as a penteteric festival in 566/5 BCE (Neils 2007; Tsagalis, this volume, pp. 46–47). Archaeological evidence, including the construction of both a new temple on the Acropolis (the so-called

Bluebeard Temple) and a new ramp leading up the hill, as well as the apparent establishment of the cult of Athena Nike on the Acropolis bastion, supports the contention of increased ritual activity even though secure epigraphic testimony for the festival's genesis is lacking (cf. Shear 2001: 671–676; Neils 2007: 41–42; Paga 2012: 180–181). The shapes of the amphorae, the inscriptions in the case of the prize amphorae, and the distinctive iconography of the obverses on both the prize and imitation versions seal an association of these vases with the Panathēnaia. The obverse of the Liverpool amphora (not pictured), where Athena Promachos stands between a pair of columns surmounted by panthers, is consistent with the rest of the group, and, as we have seen, this image coupled with the pseudo-Panathenaic shape helps confirm the reverse scene as *rhapsōidia*.

About thirty pseudo-Panathenaic amphorae, including the Liverpool vase, date from before ca. 530 BCE, making them valuable source material for the earliest games (Neils 2007). A number of different events are featured on these vases, including footraces, chariot races, and wrestling. In addition to the Liverpool amphora's implying the early inclusion of *rhapsōidia* in the festival, three pseudo-Panathenaic amphorae attest to the appearance of aulodic contests, and it is likely that *kitharōidia* ranked among early events, too.[20] The early Panathēnaia seems to have been a well-rounded festival along the lines of the older games at Olympia and Delphi (Neils 2007: 46–47).[21] *Mousikoi agōnes* were not part of the festival at Olympia, but the Pythian Games at Delphi had been reorganized to include aulos contests and contests for kitharodes ca. 586 BCE (Pausanias 10.7.2–5; cf. Bundrick 2005: 7).[22] An *agōn* for kitharists, an instrumental performance without sung accompaniment, was added to the Pythian roster in 558 BCE (Bundrick 2005: 8). It is likely that the Panathenaic program was intended to rival those of the more venerable Panhellenic festivals, and it seems that Athenian administrators of the festival believed *mousikoi agōnes*, including *rhapsōidia*, to play an important role from the beginning.[23]

The Liverpool amphora (fig. 2.2) features only the three figures of performer and spectators and does not include any hint of setting. All three of the contemporary pseudo-Panathenaic amphorae with aulodic contests, however, show their performers standing on a *bēma*, two of them single-stepped and more table-like, the third double-stepped and emphasized with added white paint.[24] Perhaps early rhapsodic contests similarly made use of a *bēma*, in which case the painter of the Liverpool amphora has omitted it for compositional reasons, to make the performer more visually prominent. In all three of the aulodic contest scenes, the performers have been depicted much smaller in scale than the audience, to compensate for each *bēma*'s height. Unfortunately, it remains unknown where any of the Panathenaic *mousikoi agōnes*, or indeed most of the festival events, were held during the first century or more of their existence. Scholarship on the Classical Athenian Agora—the area northwest of the Acropolis that served as the city's primary agora from at least the early fifth century BCE onward—suggests that the Panathenaic Way was either first laid out or was developed from an earlier road around the time of the festival's alleged establishment/reorganization in 566/5 BCE (Shear 2001: 677–679). It is likely the *mousikoi agōnes* were held outdoors here, perhaps with a *bēma* for the performers and wooden bleachers or other seating for spectators, although one cannot rule out the possibility of temporary buildings.[25]

The next three vases in the sequence of rhapsodic images (including the *hoplōn krisis* pelike, figs. 2.3–2.5, 2.8) fall in the last two decades of the sixth century, that is, after the alleged and apparently significant reforms of Peisistratos's son, Hipparchos (cf. Shapiro 1993; Shear 2001: 366–368). Exactly what Hipparchos did and when remain open questions (cf. Tsagalis, this volume, pp. 49–51). His alterations to the rhapsodic *agōn* may have been carried out as early as the 530s while Peisistratos was still alive (Shear 2001: 367), or after Peisistratos's death, perhaps at the Greater Panathēnaia celebrated by Hipparchos himself in 522 BCE (West 1999: 382). All the sources describing his activities are much later in date, namely the pseudo-Platonic dialogue *Hipparchus*, which claims that he was "the first to bring over to this land [Athens] the poetic utterances of Homer, and he forced the rhapsodes of the Panathenaia to go through these utterances in sequence, by relay, just as they do even nowadays" (228b–c, trans. Nagy 2002: 9–10).[26] Since *rhapsōidia* seems to have already existed as a Panathenaic *agōn*, this statement has been interpreted by some to mean that Hipparchos played a role in bringing authoritative versions of the Homeric *Iliad* and *Odyssey* to Athens from Ionia.[27] It also details the organization of the contest, although how it unfolded remains unclear: seemingly rhapsodes followed one after another, perhaps proclaiming parts of a prescribed text in sequence, perhaps each performing his own selection (cf. Nagy 2010: 22; West 2010a: 3; Bundrick 2015: 13n52). In any case, recent scholarship has stressed the capability of rhapsodes to embellish the Homeric passages. Instead of a fixed recitation that sounded the same each performance, we should imagine something more flexible, even improvisational in nature (cf. Collins 2001a, 2001b).

Although one should take the changing artistic styles of the later sixth century into account, it may not be coincidental that both the Oldenburg amphora (fig. 2.4) and the Dunedin pelike (fig. 2.5) convey such a dynamic performance. We have already noted the outstretched hand of one spectator in each instance, meant to indicate his engagement and reaction, and the slightly upturned head and open mouth of the rhapsode on the Dunedin pelike. The *bēma* clearly distinguishes performer from audience and enhances the performer's status, and the rhapsode on the Oldenburg amphora has a distinctive staff. Even if it is risky to see the effects of Hipparchos's reforms directly on the vases, the appearance of these scenes at this point in time—together with a surge in images of aulos and kithara players in a contest setting—nonetheless recalls the growing status of the Panathenaic festival and Athens's ambitions to be a cultural leader (cf. Bundrick 2005: 160–164, 2015: 16–17).

Dating from the fifth century and, more specifically, after the Persian Wars, the two remaining vases (figs. 2.6, 2.7) serve as a chronological bridge between the sixth-century scenes and fourth-century textual sources such as Plato's *Ion*. The Pantoxena Painter's krater (fig. 2.6) is of particular interest because its date of ca. 440 BCE (or slightly later) places it during the time of Perikles and thus another key period in Athenian cultural life (Bundrick 2015: 17). Plutarch's later biography of Perikles claims that he invented the Panathenaic *mousikoi agōnes*: "Perikles, seeking acclaim, decreed first that a contest in *mousikē* be held at the Panathēnaia, and when he had himself been chosen as *athlothetēs* he prescribed how they should compete in piping, singing, and playing the kithara. Then and thereafter they used to watch the *mousikoi agōnes* in the Odeion" (13.11, trans. Miller 1997: 222). Although Plutarch does not mention the rhapsodic contest, the phrase *mousikoi agōnes* implies that it was included.[28] However, in attributing the foundation of the *mousikoi agōnes* to Perikles, he must be mistaken, for the iconography of surviving vases testifies to the long history of these contests. Scholars instead believe that Perikles reorganized existing *agōnes*, perhaps by adding or removing events, changing the prizes, the rules, and/or their oversight (Shapiro 1992: 57; Shear 2001: 356–358; Bundrick 2005: 171; Power 2010: 427).[29] Evidence suggests he was elected to the *athlothetai* in advance of the 446/5 BCE Greater Panathēnaia, an act that perhaps inspired these reforms (Shear 2001: 543). The pseudo-Aristotelian *Constitution of the Athenians* specifies that ten *athlothetai* oversaw all the Panathenaic games, including the *mousikoi agōnes*, and arranged for their prizes (60.1–3; cf. Nagy 2002: 40–41).[30]

Plutarch's second observation—that "then and thereafter they used to watch the *mousikoi agōnes* in the Odeion"—is more plausible from archaeological and other perspectives. Indeed, the remains of the curious hypostyle hall on the southeastern slope of the Acropolis—identified by most scholars with Perikles despite its contradictory attribution by Vitruvius to Themistokles—represent the earliest surviving site we have for the performance of the contests.[31] The Odeion must have been built in the 440s or 430s, given its mention in later fifth-century texts. Some scholars have tended toward the latter date while others increasingly favor a date closer to the Greater Panathēnaia of 446/5.[32] Although not completely excavated, its current reconstructed plan meshes well with Plutarch's description of the Odeion as being "arranged internally with many rows of seats and many columns and [having] a roof which sloped down from a single peak" (*Pericles* 13.9, trans. Camp [2001: 101]). Whether it had external walls or just a roof is unclear, although the possibility that it was open on the sides has gained traction in recent years and helps resolve questions of lighting and other matters (cf. Miller 1997: 229). How seating was arranged and how visible performers would have been, given the nine or ten rows of interior columns, are also still debatable issues. Given that the Pantoxena Painter's krater dates to ca. 440 BCE or a little after—absolute dating of Athenian vases being impossible—it is reasonable to imagine the rhapsode and his *bēma* being inside the Odeion (Bundrick 2015: 17) (fig. 2.6). We cannot be sure, however, whether there really would have been a *bēma* inside, or whether the painter has adopted iconographic convention.[33] A *bēma* would certainly have helped with any visibility issues arising from the apparent forest of columns.

Even though the Pantoxena Painter's krater remains the only identified rhapsodic scene from this period, images of contests related to the kithara and aulos abound, the uptick in their numbers perhaps attributable to an increase in popularity of the *mousikoi agōnes* during this time (Shapiro 1992; Bundrick 2005: 169–174, 2015: 25). Perikles's reforms and the new Odeion surely reignited interest in the contests, and one may also note the many musical innovations of the second half of the fifth century, the so-called New Music (LeVen 2014). The Pantoxena Painter's scene echoes contemporary images of other *mousikoi agōnes* through the inclusion of Nikai and judges who must be the *athlothetai* (compare fig. 2.1). Prize-granting Nikai first appear in musical contest scenes around midcentury (Bundrick 2005: 168; cf. Kotsidu 1991: 104–129), while the visual prominence of *athlothetai* may reflect greater responsibilities in festival administration given to this group (see p. 97n30). Likewise consistent with fifth-century iconography is the rhapsode's beardlessness, which probably does not indicate an age younger than eighteen but instead conceptualizes an ideal of youthfulness (Bundrick 2015: 18). Men from their late teens upward would have competed together in this contest, making either a beardless or bearded performer plausible. One finds the same alternation in other images of *mousikoi agōnes* (cf. Power 2010: 484–485).[34] The Pantoxena Painter's rhapsode does depart from most kithara and aulos players in the matter of his costume, a plain himation as opposed to the elaborate and often patterned garments frequently seen for musicians. Perhaps this was the painter's way of signaling the very traditional nature of this contest (Bundrick 2015: 18–24). One otherwise sees no difference between *rhapsōidia* and *kitharōidia* or other of the *mousikoi agōnes* as presented on the vases, even though kitharodes may have received more valuable prizes and in general may have been considered more prestigious performers.[35] The Pantoxena Painter's krater supports the idea that rhapsodes were still respected in the mid-fifth century, even at a time of great cultural change.

CONCLUSIONS

We return to the paradox outlined at the beginning of this chapter: if rhapsodes and *rhapsōidia* had been respected in Athens since their introduction to the Panathēnaia, why did sixth- and fifth-century vase painters depict them so rarely? Granted, the accidents of survival play a role. Until the discovery of the Pantoxena Painter's krater in the early 2000s and its identification as a rhapsodic scene by the present author in 2015, no images of rhapsodes survived from the Periklean period, and more vases with rhapsodic imagery may yet be uncovered. Even so, the current corpus of *mousikoi agōnes* scenes implies greater attention to performers of the kithara and aulos.

The answer may lie not with a question of prestige for the rhapsode and his art, but one of practicality for the vase painters. Compared to performers with musical instruments or athletes with their equipment and movement in space, rhapsodes were more challenging to portray and simply may not have been as interesting to painters. The excitement of the primarily verbal and aural art of the rhapsode would have been difficult to convey in a way that was easily recognizable and visually appealing, whereas scenes of musicians and athletes were more straightforward in presentation. This may have been a particular consideration given that much Athenian figured pottery was exported to places like Magna Graecia, Sicily, and Etruria, where rhapsodic contests may not have existed but musicians and athletes flourished, and musical and athletic imagery in general was very popular. Indeed, of the six vases discussed here as referencing *rhapsōidia*, none has a documented provenance in Athens or Attica, and four come from Italy. The Etruscan owner of the Pantoxena Painter's krater in Tarquinia (fig. 2.6), for instance, may not have interpreted the scene as a rhapsodic contest but as something else altogether (Bundrick 2015: 26–27). Despite the modern characterization of Athenian vase painters as fine artists, they were businessmen first and foremost, with products to sell. Rhapsodes may have brought audiences to the Odeion and other Athenian venues, but they may not have attracted traders or other customers to a potter's workshop.

NOTES

Many thanks to Jonathan Ready and Christos Tsagalis for the invitation to contribute to this volume and for their guidance as I prepared my chapter; thanks as well to the anonymous referees. Any errors that remain are my own. For assistance with photographs and permissions, many thanks to Alessia Argento and Massimiliano Piemonte (Soprintendenza Archeologia, Belle Arti e Paesaggio per l'Area Metropolitana di Roma, la Provincia di Viterbo e l'Etruria Meridionale); Franziska Boegehold (Stadtmuseum Oldenburg); Anne Harlow (Otago Museum); Nathan Pendlebury and Andrew Jackson (National Museums Liverpool); Robbi Siegel (Art Resource, New York); and Keely Heuer for eleventh-hour help with figure 2.8.

1. An early fourth-century inscription (*IG* II^2 2311) lists prizes for some of the Panathenaic *agōnes* for kithara and aulos. Three fragmentary lines, including one mentioning a first-place *stephanos* prize, are thought by some scholars to have originally referenced *rhapsōidia* (Neils 1992b: 15–16; Rotstein 2012: 103–106).

2. One surviving Panathenaic prize amphora with a kitharodic contest remains an unexplained anomaly: St. Petersburg, Hermitage 17794, from Tanais: *ABV* 410.2; BAPD 303118; Kotsidu 1991: 295, cat. no. P17.

3. London, British Museum E 460 (fig. 2.1), from Gela: *ARV*^{2} 1041.2; BAPD 213525; Bundrick 2005: 169, fig. 99.

4. The vases:

a) black-figured pseudo-Panathenaic amphora (fig. 2.2), Liverpool, World Museum 56.19.18: BAPD 43332; Shapiro 1993: 98–102, figs. 26–27;
b) black-figured pseudo-Panathenaic amphora (figs. 2.3–2.4), Oldenburg, Stadtmuseum XII.8250.2, from Orvieto: BAPD 4662; Shapiro 1993: 98, 100, fig. 25;
c) black-figured pelike (fig. 2.5), Dunedin, Otago Museum E48.226: BAPD 302889;

d) red-figured calyx krater attributed to the Pantoxena Painter (fig. 2.6), Tarquinia, Museo Nazionale Tarquiniense 137262, from Tarquinia: Rizzo 2004; Bundrick 2015: figs. 1–3;
e) red-figured amphora attributed to the Harrow Painter (fig. 2.7), Paris, Musée du Louvre G222, from Etruria: *ARV*[2] 272.7; BAPD 202843.

5. Naples, Museo Archeologico Nazionale 81083 (H3358), from Capua: *ABV* 338.3, 694; BAPD 301859; *LIMC* 1: 316, cat. no. 80, *s.v.* "Aias I"; Baggio 2006; *Vasi antichi* 2009: 46–47.

6. For example, a pseudo-Panathenaic amphora with aulodic contest attributed to the Princeton Painter, New York, Metropolitan Museum of Art 1989.281.89: BAPD 42104; Neils 1992a: 155, cat. no. 18.

7. An inscription above the youth's head can perhaps be reconstructed as "Pantoxena Korinthoi Kale" ("Pantoxena is beautiful to Korinthos") and does not designate or describe the rhapsode (Bundrick 2015: 3–6).

8. Orator: Shapiro 1993: 97, describing the scene as "problematical" although "this man looks more like an orator"; P. Zanker 1995: 45; Mitchell 2009: 172; Ghedini 2009: 51. Rhapsode: Vos 1986: 122; Padgett 1989: 162–163, cat. no. H7 ("probably a rhapsode"); Kotsidu 1991: 306, cat. no. V46; Bundrick 2015: 24–25.

9. For example, a Roman copy of a lost Greek original in the Museo Archeologico Nazionale of Naples: P. Zanker 1995: 46, fig. 26.

10. The two vases:

a) red-figured pelike by the Pan Painter with kitharode, New York, Solow Art and Architecture Foundation: BAPD 2460; Bundrick 2005: 167, fig. 98;
b) red-figured amphora attributed to the Kleophrades Painter likely showing an aulodic contest, London, British Museum E 270: *ARV*[2] 183.15, 1632; BAPD 201668; Shapiro 1993: 96, fig. 21. The figure on this latter amphora has sometimes been identified as a rhapsode, but Shapiro convincingly argued that he should be read together with the aulos player on the other side and that therefore an aulodic *agōn* is in progress.

11. For example, a red-figured pelike attributed to the Painter of Oxford 529, London, British Museum E 354, from Kameiros (Rhodes): *ARV*[2] 1119.5; BAPD 214813; Bundrick 2015: fig. 7; and more generally for comparanda, Vos 1986: 130, cat. nos. 46–49, 51–52.

12. For example, a red-figured cup by Douris, Berlin, Antikensammlung F2285, from Cerveteri: *ARV*[2] 426, 431.48, 1653, 1701; BAPD 205092; Bundrick 2005: 2–3, figs. 1–2.

13. This explanation of *rhapsōidia* comes from one of the scholia to Pindar *Nemean* 2.1–3, whereas another of the scholia claims that the term derives from *rhabdos* (schol. *Nemean* 2.1c 29–30, cited in Collins 2001b: 13). The word "rhap-

sode" is first attested in the fifth century, for example, in Herodotus 5.67.1 and Sophocles *Oedipus Tyrannos* 391 (Ford 1988: 300; West 2010a: 2–3; González 2013: 399–416).

14. See note 5 for bibliographic references concerning this vase. Baggio does mention a resemblance between this scene and rhapsodic imagery discussed in Shapiro 1993 but does not press the point (2006: 95).

15. *LIMC* 1: 326–327, s.v. "Aias" I; D. Williams 1980; Spivey 1994; Hedreen 2001: 104–109, with references to specific vases.

16. Vienna, Kunsthistorisches Museum 3695: *ARV*² 429.26, 1653; BAPD 205070; D. Williams 1980: pls. 33.8, 34.1–2.

17. D. Williams links both the pelike and the group of red-figured cups to an increased interest in Salamis and its hero Aias after Athenian acquisition of that island (1980: 143–144).

18. Cf. Baggio 2006: 94, although he emphasizes that oratory was considered a useful skill for all educated men, not just for the *rhētores* of the lawcourts.

19. For example, a black-figured amphora attributed to the Leagros Group, Worcester Art Museum 1966.63: BAPD 1986; Bundrick 2005: 161, fig. 95. For these scenes generally, see Schauenberg 1979; Kotsidu 1991: 113–114; Shapiro 1992: 70; Bundrick 2005: 160–161, 2015: 11, 16–17 (with further references at 16n71); Power 2010: 285–293.

20. The three amphorae:

a) unattributed pseudo-Panathenaic amphora from ca. 550–540 BCE, London, British Museum B 141: BAPD 4092; Shapiro 1992: 62, fig. 40;
b) pseudo-Panathenaic amphora by the Princeton Painter from ca. 540 BCE, cited in note 6;
c) pseudo-Panathenaic amphora from ca. 540 BCE, Austin, Jack S. Blanton Museum of Art 1980.32 (ex Castle Ashby): BAPD 25; Neils 1992a: 155, cat. no. 17.

For early images of aulos and kithara players as evocative of the earliest Panathenaic versions of these events, see Shapiro 1992: 61–70; cf. Shear 2001: 354–356.

21. Another nineteen early prize amphorae attest the festival games, but because these were apparently not used as prizes for *mousikoi agōnes*, none of those events appear.

22. The contest for kitharodes at Delphi may have predated this reorganization. Pausanias notes that the aulodic contest was removed from the program only four years later because the performances were believed too "elegiac." Evidence for rhapsodic contests at Delphi does not come until the Hellenistic period, as part of the Amphictyonic Sōtēria and Aetolian Sōtēria (West 2010a: 8; Tsagalis, this volume, pp. 112–115).

23. The rhapsodic contest of the Panathēnaia is not the earliest attested; Herodotus mentions an *agōn* at Sikyon in the early sixth century (5.67.1; West 2010a: 2–3; Tsagalis, this volume, pp. 60–62).

24. Table-like *bēma*: the vases in London and New York (notes 6, 20); double-stepped: the vase in Austin (note 20).

25. Shear notes the closure of two wells along the Panathenaic Way ca. 550 BCE (wells Q13:5 and S21:2) and suggests that "the need for additional space is perhaps to be connected with the introduction of the musical games which are first attested between 550 and 540 BCE" (2001: 678).

26. Cf. discussion of the so-called Panathenaic Regulation or Panathenaic Rule of performance in Nagy 2010: 21–23.

27. Shapiro takes the statement as historical fact (1992: 72–73), whereas Nagy suggests caution (2002: 13).

28. Rhapsodic contests being held in the Odeion: Boyd 1994: 112–113 (noting that the Pnyx is also a possibility); West 2010a: 4.

29. Shear suggests, "The relevant decree was probably passed sometime after the penteteric festival of 450/49 and well before the celebration of 446/5 BCE" (2001: 358).

30. Shear notes that these officials are first attested by this name in sources dating to ca. 446 BCE (2001: 455–463). Perikles may therefore have been among the first elected. Shear argues that at some point the *athlothetai* gained greater control over the Panathēnaia as compared to other officials, such as the *hieropoioi*.

31. Vitruvius 5.9.1 for a Themistoklean attribution, accepted in Davison 1958 and Kotsidu 1991: 144. For a Periklean date and further discussion, see Miller 1997: 218–242; Hurwit 1999: 216–217; Mosconi 2000; Shear 2001: 769–772; Bundrick 2005: 172, 2015: 17; Power 2010: 545–549.

32. For the question of dating, see Miller 1997: 221–223 (leaning toward a date in the 430s and indeed independent of Perikles's reorganization of the *mousikoi agōnes*); Shear 2001: 770 (favoring the 446/5 Panathēnaia as the "impetus for the project"); Wallace 2004: 264 (the 440s); Power 2010: 495 (favoring a date around 446/5).

33. A few vases postdating the Odeion's construction include columns in scenes of *mousikoi agōnes*: for example, a red-figured bell krater by the Kadmos Painter with aulodic contest and Ionic column, Oxford, Ashmolean Museum 1960.1220: BAPD 215713; Bundrick 2005: 171, fig. 100. Once again, however, we cannot be certain the painters intended to represent the Odeion exactly and so cannot use the vases as evidence for its reconstruction.

34. The rhapsode's shorter height compared to the judges is explained compositionally by the three-line *kalos* inscription above his head (see note 7) and the prizes held aloft by the Nikai.

35. For prizes and prestige among the *mousikoi agōnes*, see Rotstein 2012; cf. Power 2010: 150–157 for possible rivalry between kitharodes and rhapsodes.

CHAPTER THREE

Performance Contexts for Rhapsodic Recitals in the Hellenistic Period

CHRISTOS C. TSAGALIS

GREEK EPIC POETRY CONTINUED TO BE RECITED DURing the Hellenistic period both in the same type of venues as in the Archaic and Classical periods and in new ones. For this period, however, a slightly different picture emerges as far as performances are concerned. A clear distinction can be drawn between agonistic and non-agonistic epic, the former recited in festivals and theaters and the latter in multifarious contexts, such as symposia and weddings. The scant literary evidence is at times helpful in regard to identifying the kind of epic poetry performed, whereas the abundant epigraphic testimonia are silent about the content of the epics. True, Homeric poetry may have by this time become more the object of reading than recitation, but it was still performed in competitive and noncompetitive contexts.

Victor lists from festivals, and to a lesser extent lists of participants in the Sōtēria at Delphi, are the most important source of relevant information for the Hellenistic period. They testify to the different kinds of epic poetry performed: the ἐγκώμιον ἐπικόν (a eulogy in hexameters combining features of the ancient lyric encomium with newer elements from the encomium in prose) and new epic poetry (Pallone 1984: 163).[1] In a similar vein, performers of epic include not only the traditional rhapsode but also the poets themselves, who could at times recite their own poetry, as well as the Homēristai (Ὁμηρισταί), who represent a more dramatic phase in the performance of epic poetry in the theaters (Collins 2001a: 152; González 2013: 466). From the information available, we can glean forty-six occasions of rhapsodic performance, of which we often (but not always) know the names of the rhapsodes themselves (see

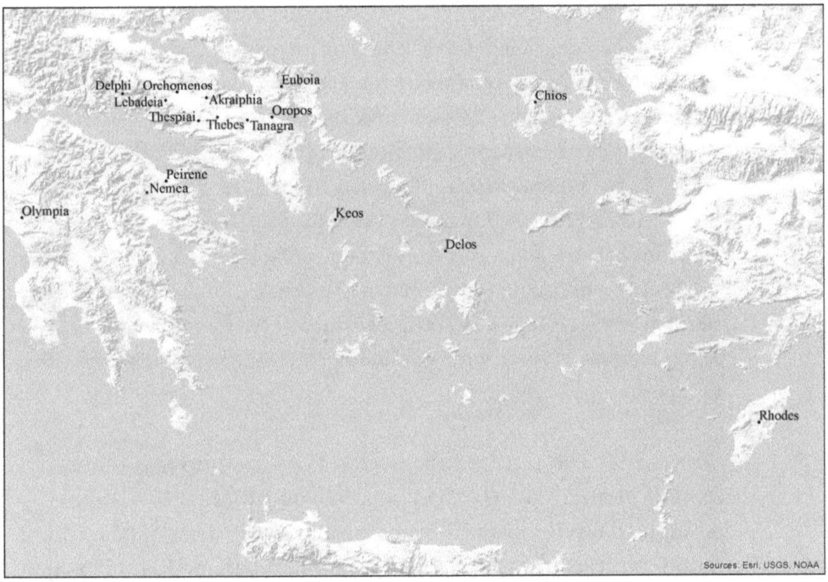

MAP 3.1. *Sites of rhapsodic performance in the Hellenistic period*

appendix 3.1 at the end of this chapter). Please consult map 3.1 for places mentioned in this chapter.

THEATERS

Rhapsodic performance in the theater is mainly a feature of the Hellenistic (and Imperial) periods, but it began in the late fourth century BCE under Demetrios of Phaleron, ruler of Athens from 317 to 307. The source of this information is Athenaeus, who makes some interesting remarks on the so-called Homēristai (Ὁμηρισταί) (14.620a–d [III 367.8–368.5 Kaibel]):

> Οὐκ ἀπελείποντο δὲ ἡμῶν τῶν συμποσίων οὐδὲ ῥαψωιδοί· ἔχαιρε γὰρ τοῖς Ὁμήρου ὁ Λαρήνσιος ὡς ἄλλος οὐδεὶς εἷς, ὡς λῆρον ἀποφαίνειν Κάσανδρον τὸν Μακεδονίας βασιλεύσαντα, περὶ οὗ φησι Καρύστιος ἐν Ἱστορικοῖς Ὑπομνήμασιν ὅτι οὕτως φιλόμηρος ὡς διὰ στόματος ἔχειν τῶν ἐπῶν τὰ πολλά· καὶ Ἰλιὰς ἦν αὐτῶι καὶ Ὀδυσσεία ἰδίως γεγραμμέναι. ὅτι δ' ἐκαλοῦντο οἱ ῥαψωιδοὶ καὶ Ὁμηρισταὶ Ἀριστοκλῆς εἴρηκεν ἐν τῶι περὶ Χορῶν. τοὺς δὲ νῦν Ὁμηριστὰς ὀνομαζομένους πρῶτος εἰς

τὰ θέατρα παρήγαγε Δημήτριος ὁ Φαληρεύς. Χαμαιλέων δὲ ἐν τῶι περὶ Στησιχόρου καὶ μελωιδηθῆναί φησιν οὐ μόνον τὰ Ὁμήρου, ἀλλὰ καὶ τὰ Ἡσιόδου καὶ Ἀρχιλόχου, ἔτι δὲ Μιμνέρμου καὶ Φωκυλίδου. Κλέαρχος δ᾽ ἐν τῶι προτέρωι περὶ Γρίφων 'τὰ Ἀρχιλόχου, φησίν, [ὁ] Σιμωνίδης ὁ Ζακύνθιος ἐν τοῖς θεάτροις ἐπὶ δίφρου καθήμενος ἐραψῴδει.' Λυσανίας δ᾽ ἐν τῶι πρώτωι περὶ Ἰαμβοποιῶν Μνασίωνα τὸν ῥαψωιδὸν λέγει ἐν ταῖς δείξεσι τῶν Σιμωνίδου τινὰς ἰάμβων ὑποκρίνεσθαι. τοὺς δ᾽ Ἐμπεδοκλέους Καθαρμοὺς ἐραψώιδησεν Ὀλυμπίασι Κλεομένης ὁ ῥαψωιδός, ὥς φησιν Δικαίαρχος ἐν τῶι Ὀλυμπικῶι. Ἰάσων δ᾽ ἐν τρίτωι περὶ τῶν Ἀλεξάνδρου Ἱερῶν ἐν Ἀλεξανδρείαι φησὶν ἐν τῶι μεγάλωι θεάτρωι ὑποκρίνασθαι Ἡγησίαν τὸν κωμωιδὸν τὰ Ἡσιόδου, Ἑρμόφαντον δὲ τὰ Ὁμήρου.

Our parties also featured rhapsodes. For Larensius was more fond of Homer's poetry than anyone you can imagine—fond enough to render insignificant Cassander, the king of Macedon, who Carystius in his *Historical Commentaries* [fr. 8, *FHG* iv.358] claims liked Homer so much that he routinely recited long passages from the poems. Cassander also owned an *Iliad* and an *Odyssey* that had been privately copied for him. Aristocles in his *On Choruses* [fr. 10, *FHG* iv.331] reports that rhapsodes were also referred to as Homēristai. The first person to introduce the individuals known today as Homēristai into the theaters was Demetrius of Phaleron [fr. 33 Wehrli = fr. 55A Fortenbaugh-Schütrumpf]. According to Chamaeleon in his *On Stesichorus* [fr. 28 Wehrli], it was not just Homer's poems that were recited, but also those of Hesiod and Archilochus, and of Mimnermus and Phocylides as well. Clearchus says in book I of *On Riddles* [fr. 92 Wehrli]: Simonides of Zacynthus used to recite Archilochus' poems in the theaters while seated on a stool. Lysanias in book I of *On Iambic Poets* reports that the rhapsode Mnasion gave public performances in which he acted out some of Simonides' iambs. The rhapsode Cleomenes recited Empedocles' *Purifications* [31 A 12 D-K] at Olympia, according to Dichaearchus in his *History of Olympia* [fr. 87 Wehrli = fr. 85 Mirhady]. Iason in book III of *On Alexander's Offerings* [*FGrH* 632 F 1] claims that the comic actor Hegesias performed Hesiod's poems in the large theater in Alexandria, and that Hermophantus performed Homer's. (trans. Olson)

According to Athenaeus, whose source is Aristocles's *Περὶ χορῶν*, the Homēristai had performed Homeric epic in the theater at Athens since the time of Demetrios of Phaleron. They differed from rhapsodes like Ion, who competed in festivals, probably in their more dramatic and expressive performance of Homeric poetry. The Homēristai may represent a further phase in the evolution of rhapsodic performances of Homer, far removed from the restrained rhapsodic recitals of the Archaic and Early Classical periods. The Homēristai embody a more developed theatricalization of rhapsodic performance (Nagy 1996b: 161–162; Collins 2001a: 152–153). In fact, Athenaeus's use of the term "present-day Homēristai" (οἱ νῦν Ὁμηρισταί) makes sense only if there were "old-time Homēristai," who can be none other than the rhapsodes, as Aristocles would have it in his work *On Choruses*.[2]

It is a mistake to think that it was *solely* the new theatrical setting that led rhapsodes to perform Homeric epic in a dramatic fashion. The setting no doubt intensified these histrionic components, but it did not create them. After all, Ion, who competes in a festival at Epidaurus, incorporates dramatic elements when performing. Perhaps Demetrios of Phaleron, who was acquainted with the progressive introduction of dramatic features by rhapsodes themselves in their recitals, decided to go one step farther and bring them to the theater, where audiences could watch them perform in even greater numbers. At this point the influence of the theatrical venue, in which different actors/performers acted out the words of various types of texts (Hesiod, Archilochus's iambs, Mimnermus, Phocylides, Simonides's iambs, Empedocles, tragedy, comedy), would have made the performances of rhapsodes even more dramatic.

Athenaeus informs us that, apart from in Athens, the Homēristai acted out (ὑποκρίνασθαι) Hesiod and Homer in the great theater of Alexandria. Here, too, the wide variety of poetry performed in the theater must have had a significant influence on the performance of Homeric poetry. That the comedians Hegesias and Hermophantos performed Hesiod and Homer, respectively, in Alexandria reflects an additional phase in the theatricalization of Homeric performance (Collins 2001a: 153).[3]

In the Hellenistic period the Homēristai signed contracts with the people who hired them to act out Homer (Husson 1993; Collins 2001a: 154–155).[4] These legal documents determined the fees to be paid to the Homēristai and indicate that they sometimes performed with mimes, the Homēristai reciting Homer while the mimes emphasized the actions described therein. To be more specific, we may postulate that the Homēristai acted out scenes from Homer, while the mimes further intensified the presentation by not using speech at all. Although the papyri detailing these contracts do not designate the content of the performances, Homer must have been included among other, more recent compositions, otherwise the name Homēristai would have been an empty shell (González 2013: 449n57), especially at a time when extreme specialization was the norm (465).

The venue of these performances may have been public, to judge from the existence of contracts and the competitive context.[5] At least one papyrus refers to "a poetic contest" (ἀγὼν ποιητῶν, *P.Oslo* III 189.19 [text 2 in Husson 1993]). It is not clear whether the performances of the Homēristai in private venues (like dinner parties) also took place during the Hellenistic period, since the relevant sources belong to the Imperial period (West 2010a: 5n12).

GYMNASIA

Dating to the second century BCE (Stephanis 1708) or first half of the first century BCE (West 2010a: 10), a victor list from Chios (*IChios* 57.10 = *SIG* III 959.9 = *GDI* 5660) pertains to musical and athletic games held at the gymnasium on the island (see Boeckh on *CIG* 2214; also *SIG* III 959). A certain Miltiades son of Dionysios from Chios won the rhapsodic contest. The majority of the contests recorded in this inscription are athletic. The competitors sacrificed to the Muses because they were engaged in musical contests and to Herakles as the regular protector and patron of gymnasia and palestrae (*SIG* III 959.6: ἔθυσαν ταῖς τε Μούσαις καὶ τῶι Ἡρακλεῖ). The musical competitions, placed before the athletic ones on the victor list, are the *psalmos* (playing a stringed musical instrument with the fingers), the rhapsodic contest, and the *kitharismos* (playing the box-lyre with a plectrum [West 1992: 51]). The purpose of these contests was to demonstrate that the youths of Chios excelled in music and sport (*SIG* III 959, n. 2; cf. *SIG* II 578.32, 717.42, 717.96).

FESTIVALS

The standard venue for rhapsodic recitals during the Hellenistic period was a festival that hosted musical contests. Even a cursory look at the available data shows that in this context Boeotia looms large. This region of mainland Greece hosted numerous festivals: the Ptōia and the trieteric Sōtēria in Akraiphia, the Basileia in Lebadeia, the Charitēsia in Orchomenos, the Amphiaraia and Rhōmaia in Oropos, the Sarapieia in Tanagra, the Rhōmaia in Thebes, and the Mouseia in Thespiai. Rhapsodic recitals were also held in Amarynthos, Delos, Delphi, Keos, and Rhodes.

I include in this catalogue only cases in which the inscriptional record specifically refers to a recital by a rhapsode. Festivals are presented in alphabetical order (English alphabet) of the places in which they were held. I start with Boeotian festivals under the general heading "Boeotia."

Boeotia

AKRAIPHIA: THE PTŌIA AND TRIETERIC SŌTĒRIA We first hear about musical contests at the festival of the Ptōia, celebrated in honor of Apollo, in the context of their reorganization in 228–226 BCE, although this reorganization may have consisted of the introduction of musical contests (Schachter 1981: 70–71). The relevant victor list contains seven entries: a trumpeter, a herald, a rhapsode, an epic poet, an aulete, a kitharist, and a kitharode. Four of them come from Boeotia, Thespiai being best represented among the victors. The others are an Ephesian, a Sikyonian, and an Athenian. The geographical distribution of the winners shows that the festival attracted professionals from different parts of the Greek world, even from across the Aegean. Boeotians predominated, and understandably so, since the festival of the Ptōia took place in Boeotia, where there was a branch of the Peloponnesian guild of *technitai Dionysou*. Indeed, most winners of festivals held in Boeotia "were primarily citizens of Boiotian cities or of cities near Boiotia (Athens, Chalkis, Opous)" (Chaniotis 2010: 260).

One victor in the rhapsodic competition in this pentaeteric Ptōia was Agathon son of Damas from Thespiai (Stephanis 24), who prevailed at some point between the end of the second and the beginning of the first century BCE. In the extant victor list he is mentioned immediately before Χρύσιππος Ἀρίστωνος Ἀκραιφιεύς, who won the prize as the best ἐπῶν ποιητής. This Chrysippos was competing on home ground, since the Ptōia was celebrated in Akraiphia. Rhapsodes rarely won on their home turf, inscriptions indicate. There are only four cases (in the Hellenistic period) in which a rhapsode won in a contest taking place in his home town: Habron son of Philoxenos from Thebes and Aeimnastos son of Euphraios from Thebes both won the rhapsodic contest at the Theban Rhōmaia[6]; Miltiades son of Dionysios from Chios (West 2010a: 9) won the first prize in the musical games held in the gymnasium on Chios (see p. 102); and Boukattes son of Glaukos from Tanagra won as a rhapsode at the Sarapieia (see pp. 108–109).

Another rhapsode who won at the pentaeteric Ptōia was Archias son of Soteridas from Thebes (Stephanis 441). The archon of Akraiphia, when Archias won, was Kaphisotimos, who is probably the same person as the father of Polyxenos from Akraiphia who won with an ἐγκώμιον λογικόν (an encomium in prose) in the trieteric Sōtēria held also in Akraiphia in the first century BCE after the defeat of Mithridates VI of Pontos by Sulla in the First Mithridatic War.[7] This Kaphisotimos may also have been the brother of a certain Lysitheos (see *Leb.* 11A.19 in Manieri 2009: 157), delegate of the city of Akraiphia to the festival of the Basileia in Lebadeia (Manieri 2009: 111, 132).[8] In these trieteric Sōtēria a rhapsodic contest was held but the name of the victorious rhapsode does not survive on the stone. In *IG* VII 2727, this rhapsode is mentioned immediately after the epic poet Protogenes son of Protarchos from Thespiai.

THE BASILEIA IN LEBADEIA Dated to around the middle of the second century BCE, an agonistic inscription containing a victor list shows that the festival of the Basileia in Lebadeia in Boeotia included rhapsodic recitals (*SEG* 3.368 = Manieri *Leb.* 9 [2009: 153–154]). We can infer that the contest mentioned in this list was organized by the Boeotian confederacy, since all victors from Boeotia are designated by the ethnic **Βοιώτιος** and not by the name of their city of origin (Manieri 2009: 154). The name of the rhapsode who won in the contest does not survive on the stone (Stephanis 2919); we know only that he came from Boeotia. It has been suggested that the victorious herald from the city of Pyramos in Antiocheia (whose name does not survive in the inscription) was the rhapsode Zenodotos son of Sopatros from Antiocheia (Stephanis 1024), who won the rhapsodic competition at the Mouseia in Thespiai at some point between 210 and 203 BCE (*IG* VII 1762.5 = *IThesp* 163 = *Thes.* 18 [Manieri 2009: 376–378]). This should come as no surprise, since rhapsodes had strong voices and could also excel in a contest of heralds. Moreover, all these artists belonged to guilds of professionals who traveled around and at times competed in more than one event in a musical context (Aneziri 2009: 218–220; see table 3.1).

THE CHARITĒSIA IN ORCHOMENOS Although the cult of the Charites at Orchomenos was an ancient one and may have involved dancing in the goddesses' honor, musical contests were introduced, according to the epigraphical evidence, only in the first century BCE. This development must be connected to the policy of Sulla, who sought to regain the support of the Boeotians after his victory against Mithridates VI of Pontos. The musical competitions were thus added to the preexisting celebrations in honor of the Charites, just as additions were made to the Sōtēria in Akraiphia and the Erōtid(e)ia in Thespiai (Manieri 2009: 180–181). The musical contests of the Charitēsia display prosopographical af-

TABLE 3.1. INSTANCES OF RHAPSODES COMPETING IN MORE THAN ONE TYPE OF CONTEST

Stephanis 2174	(χορευτής), [αὐλωι]δός, [ῥαψωι]δός
Stephanis 1146, 1368, 1913	(ᾠιδός), (τραγικὸς συναγωνιστής), ῥαψωιδός
Stephanis 908	(κωμικὸς ὑποκριτής), (ῥαψωιδός)
Stephanis 1055	κωμωιδός, (ῥαψωιδός)
Stephanis 1979	[ποιη]τής, μελοποιός, ῥαψ[ωιδός], θεολόγος
Stephanis 822	κῆρυξ, [τραγ]ωιδός, κωμικός, ῥαψωιδός
Stephanis 54, 955, 956	κῆρυξ, ῥαψωιδός

Note: Information derived from Chaniotis 1990 and González 2013: 486–487. I follow with slight modifications the practice used in González 2013: 486nn36–37: parentheses indicate that the relevant term has been inferred from the context; underlining indicates uncertainty; and the roman font shows that the inference is certain.

finities with the musical contests at Oropos, Thespiai, and Akraiphia, since various artists appear in the victor lists of more than one of these festivals during the same period. The same holds true for rhapsodes: one won in both Oropos and Orchomenos, and another in Orchomenos and Amarynthos in Euboia.

Kraton son of Kleon from Thebes (Stephanis 1502) won the rhapsodic contest at both the Charitēsia in Orchomenos (*IG* VII 3195.11–12 = Manieri *Orc.* 23 [2009: 199–200]) and the festival of the Amphiaraia and Rhōmaia held in Oropos (*IG* VII 418.7 = *EO* 524 [pp. 426–427] = Manieri *Oro.* 18 [2009: 246–248]). In the relevant victor list he is mentioned immediately after the poet Mestor son of Mestor from Phokaia (Stephanis 1686), who is also recorded as a poet above the rhapsode Theodotos son of Pythion from Athens (Stephanis 1146) in another victor list from the festival of the Mouseia in Thespiai (*IG* VII 1760.17 = *IThesp* 172 = Manieri *Thes.* 33 [2009: 402–404]).[9] In contrast to *IG* VII 3196 and VII 3197, this victor list does not include the victors in the festival of the Homolōia, which was also held in Orchomenos. In this light, it is fair to argue that *IG* VII 3195 refers only to the *agōn* of the Charitēsia that preceded the contests mentioned in *IG* VII 3196 and VII 3197. This older *agōn*, which included thymelic competitions between tragic and comic poets, either represented the renewal of a preexisting contest or was simply added to the ancient display in honor of the Charites. The use of the Boeotian dialect would contribute to the consecration of the solemnity of the new contest, almost like a rebirth of the ancient Agriōnia, the relevant inscriptions of which had always used the local dialect (Manieri 2009: 206; cf. González 2013: 512).

Another rhapsode who won at the Charitēsia in Orchomenos around the beginning of the first century BCE was Mentor son of Apollodoros from Herakleia (Stephanis 1667; *IG* VII 3196 = Manieri *Orc.* 24 [2009: 200–202]), although we do not know which Herakleia: Angelos Chaniotis proposes the one in Thessaly (2010: 260n14). This individual may have been the same Mentor who won a contest for rhapsodes held in Amarynthos in Euboia (*IG* XII.9 139.10). In contrast to the victor list recording Kraton's victory in the rhapsodic recital, this inscription is *not* marked by its "archaizing Boiotian orthography" (West 2010a: 9).[10] Moreover, and against what seems to have been common practice, the rhapsode's name precedes that of the poet. The same is the case with another victor list from Orchomenos, in which the Athenian Noumenios son of Noumenios (Stephanis 1893) is mentioned before the epic poet Aminias son of Demokles from Thebes (*IG* VII 3197 = Manieri *Orc.* 25 [2009: 202–207]).

OROPOS: THE AMPHIARAIA AND RHŌMAIA The establishment of musical contests at the festival in honor of the hero Amphiaraos dates at least from the fourth century BCE (see Manieri 2009: 211–218). We have a victor list from the Megala Amphiaraia in which after the initial formula ([οἵδε ἐνίκων Ἀμφιαράϊα] ̣τὰ μεγάλ[α]) comes a list of musical contests with the names of the winners (*IG* VII 414 = *EO* 520). Unfortunately, the part of the inscription immediately after the initial formula is missing, with the result that we are not sure whether a rhapsodic contest was included. But since the rest of the list mentions the poet of a prosodion, the boy kitharist, the boy aulode, the adult kitharist, the adult aulode, the aulete, the kitharode, and the sophist, we may ask what else could have been recorded between the initial formula οἵδε ἐνίκων Ἀμφιαράϊα] ̣τὰ μεγάλ[α] and the surviving list. On the basis of the extant victor lists in musical contests held at various festivals during the late Classical and Hellenistic periods, we may postulate that epic poetry would have been mentioned. We are in no position to decide whether it would have been new epic poetry, an epic encomium, or rhapsodic recital (West 2010a: 9).

All the information pertaining to rhapsodic recitals in Oropos belongs to a later reorganization of the festival in honor of Amphiaraos after Sulla's victory in the First Mithridatic War, when the Megala Amphiaraia was renamed the Amphiaraia and Rhōmaia. I list the contests included in the five Amphiaraia and Rhōmaia festivals for which we possess epigraphical records and highlight the relevant information about the winning rhapsodes:

EO 521 = Manieri *Oro.* 15 (2009: 241–243): trumpeter, herald, encomium for the god in prose, epic encomium, ἐπῶν ἱερὸς ῥαψωιδός (Biottos son of Menelaos from Chalkis [Stephanis 524; González 2013: 508 no. 44]), α[ὐ]λητῷ[ν ἱ]ερός and kitharist, kitharode.

IG VII 416 = *EO* 523 = Manieri *Oro.* 16 (2009: 243–245): trumpeter, herald, encomium in prose, epic encomium, rhapsode (Artemon son of Isidotos from Athens [Stephanis 422; González 2013: 508 no. 42]), epic poet, aulete, kitharist, kitharode, satyr-poet, tragic actor, comic actor, tragic poet, comic poet, epinicion.

IG VII 418 = *EO* 524 = Manieri *Oro.* 18 (2009: 246–248): encomium in prose, epic encomium, rhapsode (Kraton son of Kleon from Thebes [Stephanis 1502; González 2013: 511 no. 50] who won also at the Charitēsia in Orchomenos in the early first BCE), epic poet, aulete, kitharist, kitharode, tragic actor, comic actor, satyr-poet, actor, tragic poet, comic poet.

IG VII 419 = *EO* 526 = Manieri *Oro.* 19 (2009: 248–250): trumpeter, herald, encomium in prose, epic encomium, epic poet, rhapsode (Eieron son of Aristoboulos from Thebes [Stephanis 820; González 2103: 509 no. 46]), aulete, kitharist, kitharode, satyr-poet, tragic poet, actor, comic poet, actor, old tragedy.

IG VII 420 = *EO* 528 = Manieri *Oro.* 20 (2009: 250–251): trumpeter, herald, encomium in prose, epic encomium, epic poet, rhapsode (Theophanes son of Sokrates from Thebes [Stephanis 1186; González 2013: 510–511 no. 48]), aulete, kitharist, kitharode, satyr-poet, actor of old tragedy, actor of old comedy, poet of new tragedy, actor, poet of new comedy, actor.

The range of musical contests and the wide distribution of the places of origin of the various contestants show that the Amphiaraia and Rhōmaia was a festival celebrated on a grand scale.[11]

THE SARAPIEIA IN TANAGRA The Sarapieia held in the city of Tanagra, situated in the southeast corner of Boeotia, was the only festival dedicated to the Egyptian god Sarapis that included musical contests.[12] The cult of Sarapis, often together with the cult of Isis, became widespread in the Greek world starting in the third century BCE. From the agonistic inscription recording the participation of two rhapsodes in the musical contests held in Tanagra, we learn that Sarapis and Isis were honored together with other gods: [εἰς τὴ]ν θυσίαν τῶι Σαράπιδι καὶ τῆι

Ἴσιδι καὶ τοῖς ἄλλοις θεοῖς (*IG* VII 540.48). In Athens there was a sanctuary dedicated to Sarapis on the Acropolis (Pausanias 1.18.4) as well as an association active as early as the middle of the third century BCE that was responsible for Sarapis's cult, the Sarapiastai (*IG* II^2 1292). Sarapis's cult was also in Boeotia. Apart from Tanagra, we know that the cities of Cheroneia, Koroneia, Kope, Orchomenos, Thebes, and Thespiai had all welcomed Sarapis's cult (Manieri 2009: 263).[13]

The musical contests in Tanagra took place every five years, during the month of Homolōios (Roller 1989: 114), and attracted artists from the entire Greek world, from Asia Minor to Italy. At least twenty-three competitors are named: the Athenians won eight prizes, and the Boeotians (including four Tanagrans) nine (Roller 1989: 114). The Athenians were probably members of the guild of *technitai Dionysou* (Διονυσιακοὶ τεχνῖται) who had also participated in the fourth Pythais in Delphi (Manieri 2009: 273). Although an association of Sarapiastai is not mentioned in the extant victory list in which the two rhapsodes appear, it is likely that such an association dealt with the logistics of the festival and the musical contests. In fact, the family of the rhapsode Boukattes, a Tanagran local, seems to have been responsible for the organization and supervision of the festival and the contests. According to *IG* VII 541–543 (see Manieri *Tan.* 2 [2009: 268–277]; *SEG* 19.335, 25.501), the *agōnothetēs* named Glaukos and the president of the commission named Kaphisias were the sons of Boukattes (I), the city archon and priest of Sarapis. The rhapsode Boukattes (II) and the satyric poet Alexandros must have been the sons of the *agōnothetēs* Glaukos, that is, grandsons of Boukattes (I).[14]

Apart from Boukattes (II), *IG* VII 540.25 offers us the name of another rhapsode, Aristodikos son of Demokrates from Opous, who won the second prize in the rhapsodic competition. The values of the prizes offered to the first and second victor in each category of the musical contests reveal that the rhapsode, and by extension the rhapsodic contest itself, belonged to the category that received the lowest prizes.[15] The following lists of prizes in this contest indicate the different statuses of the various winners (cf. Manieri 2009: 265):

1. aulete, kitharode, ancient tragedy, epinician: first prize = 168¾ drachmas; second prize = 50 drachmas;
2. tragic poet, comic poet, epic poet, kitharist, ancient comedy: first prize = 135 drachmas; second prize = 50 drachmas for the tragic poet and 40 drachmas for the epic poet, the kitharist, and the ancient comedy;
3. aulode: first prize = 112¾ drachmas; second prize = 40 drachmas;

4. rhapsode, poet of satyrical drama, trumpeter, herald, actor of new tragedy and comedy: first prize = 101¼ drachmas; second prize = 40 drachmas only for the rhapsode and the poet of satyrical drama.

According to this list, Boukattes son of Glaukos received 101¼ drachmas for his victory in the rhapsodic contest, while Aristodikos son of Demokrates, who was second in the same contest, got only 40 drachmas.

THE RHŌMAIA IN THEBES As many as three musical contests were held in Thebes during the late Hellenistic period: the Agriōnia, the Herakleia, and the Rhōmaia. Only one surviving victor list pertains undoubtedly to the Rhōmaia (*SEG* 54.516 = Manieri *Theb.* 31 [2009: 299–301]). The founding of the Rhōmaia occurred after L. Mummius's victory over the Greeks and the destruction of Corinth (146 BCE), hence the naming of the new games after Rome.[16] The victor list shows that Theban victors dominated the Rhōmaia. The victorious rhapsode is Habron son of Philoxenos from Thebes (Stephanis 12), who also won at the festival of the Mouseia in Thespiai (*IThesp* 171 = Manieri *Thes.* 31 [2009: 399–400]; cf. Roesch 1982: 494; Knoepfler 2004: 1260). Only the victorious trumpeter is from Delphi. The same is the case for *IG* VII 2448 (Stephanis 54 = Manieri Theb. 10 [2009: 302–303]), another victor list from Thebes, in which we hear about a certain Aeimnastos son of Euphraios from Thebes, who won the rhapsodic contest (and also the heraldic *agōn*).[17] On the basis of this Theban dominance (with the exception of an Aeginetan trumpeter), the Theban Rhōmaia becomes a more plausible candidate than the Agriōnia for this inscription, too, despite the fact that the inscription as we have it contains no specific information about the festival to which it pertains (Knoepfler 2004: 1262–1263; Manieri 2009: 303). Moreover, the order in which the victors are recorded is the same with one exception: in the inscription in which Aeimnastos appears, the rhapsode's name is given before that of the epic poet, while in the inscription in which Habron appears, he is mentioned after the epic poet (West 2010a: 9).

Denis Knoepfler (2004: 1271) and Alessandra Manieri (2009: 37–38, 287–288, 301) interpret the Theban dominance in these two victor lists from the Theban Rhōmaia as the result of the conflict between different groups of artists. They postulate a local, Boeotian guild that defected, so to speak, from the mother-guild of Dionysiac artists of the Isthmus and Nemea, one of the three main guilds of οἱ περὶ τὸν Διόνυσον τεχνῖται during the Hellenistic period (the other two being the Athenian guild and that of Ionia and the Hellespont).[18] This schism would explain why the Thebans who belonged to the local guild of Theban artists take precedence in both victor lists. Their proposal can only remain speculative in the absence of lists of contestants in the Theban Rhōmaia. If we had those lists, we could check whether Thebans dominated the ranks of contestants just as they dominated the victor lists (Manieri 2009: 301; Chaniotis 2010: 260nn14–15).[19]

THE MOUSEIA IN THESPIAI Albert Schachter leaves open the possibility that "an agon of some sort may have been celebrated in honor of the Muses of Helikon as early as the fifth century B.C." (1986: 163), but the earliest secure piece of information about the inclusion of a musical contest in the festival of the Mouseia in Thespiai dates to the middle of the third century BCE (*SEG* 15.320). At that stage the musical contests likely consisted of competitions in dithyramb, tragedy, and comedy (Feyel 1942: 115; Schachter 1986: 163). Rhapsodic contests, together with contests of epic poets, auletai, aulodes, kitharistai, and kitharodes, were added during a major reorganization of the Mouseia at some point between 217 and 205 BCE.[20] The Mouseia was one of the most important festivals in the Hellenistic (and Imperial) period, attracting professional artists from all three main guilds of Διονύσου τεχνῖται (Manieri 2009: 315).

We know of four rhapsodes who won the first prize at the Mouseia. The earliest among them is Zenodotos son of Sopatros from Antiocheia in Kilikia[21] (Stephanis 1024; see *IG* VII 1762 = *IThesp* 163), who probably took part in the reorganized games at some point between 210 and 172 BCE. Zenodotos is immediately preceded in the victor list by a certain Heliodoros son of Heliodoros who comes from the same Antiocheia. It is possible that these two victors belonged to the guild of Dionysian artists of Ionia and the Hellespont and had traveled all the way to Thespiai to participate in the reorganized Mouseia that had just started to include contests for epic poets and rhapsodes.[22]

Another victorious rhapsode is recorded in *IThesp* 170.22 (= Manieri *Thes.* 30 [2009: 397–399]), which dates between 118 and 112 BCE. Only the ending –ος survives on the stone, but given that both his father's name and the city of his origin are identical with Εἴρανος Φρυνίδου Ταναγραῖος (Stephanis 822; González 2013: 505–506), who had won as a comic actor at the Amphiaraia and Rhōmaia in Oropos (*IG* VII 416.26 = *EO* 523.26 = Manieri *Oro.* 16 [2009: 244]), scholars have restored [Εἴραν]ος in *IThesp* 170.22. In addition to his success as a rhapsode and a comic actor, Eiranos also won at the Ptōia in Akraiphia (*BCH* 44 [1920]: 261 = Manieri *Acr.* 14 [2009: 107]) in the heraldic competition, in two other contests (neither surviving on the stone) (*IG* VII

542.1 = Manieri *Tan.* 3.1 [2009: 277]), and as a tragic actor (*IG* VII 543.1–4 = Manieri *Tan.* 4.1–4 [2009: 278]). He also prevailed at the Sarapieia in Tanagra.[23] In contrast to the victor list discussed earlier, only local Boeotians appear in this inscription: three Thespians, two Tanagrans, and one Theban. The sequence in the victor list is the following: poet of prosodion, trumpeter, herald, epic poet, rhapsode, auletes, [aulode]. A fair number of these victors are also known from other victor lists: the epic poet Demokles son of Ameinias from Thebes also won the contest of epic encomia in Oropos (Manieri *Oro.* 16) and prevailed as epic poet in Thebes (Manieri *Theb.* 10). He may well be the father of Ameinias, who won double victories at the Charitēsia in Orchomenos as epic poet and poet of a satyr-drama (Manieri *Orc.* 25) and at the Amphiaraia and Rhōmaia in Oropos (Manieri *Or.* 19) with a new epic poem and an epic encomium (Manieri 2009: 399).

Habron son of Philoxenos from Thebes (Stephanis 12) appears as winner of the rhapsodic recital in another victor list (*IThesp* 171 = Manieri *Thes.* 31 [2009: 399–400]). He is the same Habron who had won (shortly after 118 BCE?) a rhapsodic contest at the Theban Rhōmaia. The sequence of victors in this list is the same (poet of prosodion, trumpeter, herald, epic poet, rhapsode, auletes, aulode) as in *IThesp* 170, but the winners are not all Boeotians (as in *IThesp* 170). Thespians dominate (three overall), but there is an Argive trumpeter (Praxokles), a Theban rhapsode (Habron), and even a Pamphylian aulode (Polyxenos).

The same sequence of winners is also observed in *IThesp* 172 (Manieri *Thes.* 33 [2009: 402–404]), although this time the victor list records, after the aulode, a kitharist, a kitharode, a poet of satyr-drama, and two actors, one of old tragedy and one of old comedy. The victorious rhapsode, Theodotos son of Pythion from Athens, also participated in the fourth Pythais in Delphi, in which he competed as both a rhapsode and a tragic actor (Manieri 2009: 404; González 2013: 510 no. 47). Most of the victors mentioned in this list pertaining to the musical contest of the Mouseia in Thespiai are also known from other victor lists, mainly from Boeotia. The epic poet Mestor son of Mestor from Phokaia, who is mentioned immediately before the rhapsode Theodotos, also won as an epic poet in Orchomenos (Manieri *Orc.* 23) and with an epic encomium in Oropos (Manieri *Oro.* 18).

Delos

Two rhapsodes are recorded in a list of artists (*IG* XI.2 105.27–28) from Delos dated to 284 BCE. The inscription is not a victor list but belongs to the *tabulae archontum* (Robert 1936a: 244; Sifakis 1967:

19). It records the *chorēgoi* for the Apollonia and for the Dionysia for boys and then proceeds with a list of those artists who performed non-competitively in honor of Apollo (οἵδε ἐπεδείξαντο τῶι θεῶι ἐπὶ Ἀριστοκρίτου ἄρχοντος). The list comprises tragic and comic actors, an aulete, kitharodes, a psaltes, a kitharist, and the two rhapsodes who (contrary to the usual practice in victory lists) are placed at the end of the catalogue. The listing of the homelands of the participants shows that Delos attracted artists from all over the Greek world (Megara, Chalcis, Athens, Sinope, Thebes, Ambrakia, Methymna, Argos, and Thessaly). The two rhapsodes are Archelas from Thessaly (Stephanis 435; González 2013: 498 no. 15) and Glaukos from Athens (Stephanis 549; González 2013: 499 no. 16). In sharp contrast to the *chorēgoi*, who are only recorded by their patronymics, the artists are mentioned by their proper name followed by their ethnic; this is because the *chorēgoi* were citizens of Delos and metics, whereas none of the artists comes from Delos.[24] We do not know whether Archelas and Glaukos participated in the actual contest, although it is reasonable to assume so. At any rate, they recited *hors concours* epic poetry at Delos, probably of traditional content (see p. 128n32[4]).

Delphi

THE AMPHICTYONIC SŌTĒRIA The festival of the Sōtēria was established in Delphi in commemoration of the salvation of the Delphic oracle and Greece in general from the invasion of the Gauls (279/8 BCE). In the case of the Amphictyonic Sōtēria, we are fortunate to possess not only victor lists but also catalogues of contestants (Sifakis 1967: 63). The latter aid the reconstruction of musical contests in the Hellenistic period, given that they furnish information that victor lists by definition exclude. In the case of rhapsodic activity, we can now see how large the actual contest was and how many artists and rhapsodes took part. In two inscriptions the formula is "the following competed" (ἠγωνίσαντο δὲ οἵδε, *SEG* 1.187a; *SEG* 18.230), and in several others "the following competed in the contest at the Sōtēria" (οἵδε ἠγωνίσαντο τὸν ἀγῶνα τῶν Σωτηρίων, *SEG* 18.235; *GDI* 2563, 2564, 2565, 2566).

I list here in alphabetical order the rhapsodes who took part in the Amphictyonic Sōtēria. This list is taken from Martin West's article (2010a: 8) with the addition of Aristomenes son of Aristomenes (*GDI* 2565).

1. Ἀγαθῖνος Κριτοδήμο[υ Σικ]υώνιος (Stephanis 18); *GDI* 2565 = Nachtergael 1977: 420 no. 9, line 9 (258/7 or 254/3 BCE)

2. Ἀρισταγό[ρας] (Stephanis 306); *SEG* 1.187a = Nachtergael 1977: 408 no. 3, line 5 (ca. 265–258 BCE)
3. Ἀριστείδης Ἀρίστωνος [. . .]ς (Stephanis 318); *GDI* 2565 = Nachtergael 1977: 420 no. 9, line 10 (258/7 or 254/3 BCE)
4. Ἀριστομένης Ἀριστομένου [. . .]ιος (Stephanis 362); *GDI* 2565 = Nachtergael 1977: 420 no. 9, line 11 (258/7 or 254/3 BCE)
5. [Εὐθ]ύδημος Χάρητος Ἀθηναῖος (Stephanis 948); *GDI* 2566 = Nachtergael 1977: 423 no. 10, lines 9–10 (257/6 or 253/2 BCE)
6. Καλλίας Ἀρχετίμου Συρακ[όσιος] (Stephanis 1325); *SEG* 18.230 = Nachtergael 1977: 409 no. 4, line 13 (ca. 265–258 BCE)
7. Κλειτόριος Ἀριστείδου Ἀρκάς (Stephanis 1429); *SEG* 18.230 = Nachtergael 1977: 409 no. 4, line 12; *GDI* 2563 = Nachtergael 1977: 413 no. 7, line 11; *GDI* 2564 = Nachtergael 1977: 416 no. 8, line 10; *GDI* 2566 = Nachtergael 1977: 423 no. 10, lines 8–9 (ca. 265–252 BCE)
8. Πολύμνηστος Ἀλεξάνδρου Ἀρκάς (Stephanis 2106); *GDI* 2563 = Nachtergael 1977: 413 no. 7, line 10 (260/59 or 256/5 BCE)
9. [. . 4–5 . .]ν Θρασωνίδου Σινωπεύς (Stephanis 2729); *GDI* 2564 = Nachtergael 1977: 416 no. 7, line 11 (259/8 or 255/4 BCE)
10. . . .]ράτης Καλλιφ [. . . (Stephanis 2762); *SEG* 18.235 = Nachtergael 1977: 411 no. 5, line 11 (262/1 or 258/7 BCE)
11. [. . .]ς Ἀθηναῖος (Stephanis 2886); *SEG* 18.235 = Nachtergael 1977: 411 no. 5, line 12 (262/1 or 258/7 BCE)

On the basis of this list of rhapsodes who participated in the Amphictyonic Sōtēria, we can make the following observations.

1. The maximum number of rhapsodes taking part in the same contest is three, but regularly the competition is between two. One observes that the same reference appears under more than one name, meaning that these rhapsodes competed in the same contest in the Amphictyonic Sōtēria.

2. In sharp contrast to the musical contests held in Boeotia, at the Amphictyonic Sōtēria in Delphi there was no contest involving the presentation of new epic poems. In the extant inscriptional material no ποιητὴς ἐπῶν is ever mentioned. Rhapsodes, usually recorded in victor lists after the ποιητὴς ἐπῶν, are here placed first in the lists of participants.

3. A certain Kleitorios son of Aristeides from Arkadia was a frequent competitor in the Amphictyonic Sōtēria at Delphi. In a short span, he

participated no less than four times (*SEG* 18.230; *GDI* 2563, 2564, 2566), not three (*pace* West [2010a: 8]): he appears first among the competing rhapsodes three times and second once.

4. The geographical range of participants in the rhapsodic contest of the Amphictyonic Sōtēria covers Arkadia, Athens, Sikyon, and distant places to the east and west, like Sinope and Syracuse.

THE AETOLIAN SŌTĒRIA The Amphictyonic Sōtēria did not last for long. The Aetolians, who had occupied Delphi since the beginning of the third century BCE, reorganized the festival in an attempt to turn it into a Panhellenic event under their control. They changed its periodicity from annual to quadrennial, added athletic contests to the musical ones, and introduced Zeus Soter to be honored along with Apollo. By asking the Greek cities to recognize the musical contests as *isopythian* and the athletic one as *isonemean*, they turned the Sōtēria into a *stephanitēs agōn*, which was typical for all Panhellenic games (Sifakis 1967: 64). The program of the Aetolian Sōtēria basically followed the program of the older Amphictyonic Sōtēria that it replaced (Sifakis 1967: 83; Nachtergael 1977: 359).

As I did for the Amphictyonic Sōtēria, I offer a list of the victors in the rhapsodic contests in alphabetical order (cf. González 2013: 499–504). West provides a similar list in chronological order (2010a: 8). The formulaic heading before the commemoration of the winners is now "the following were victorious" (οἵδε ἐνίκων, *FD* III 4.125), or "the following were victorious at the Sōtēria" (οἵδε ἐνίκων τὰ Σωτήρια, *SEG* 2.260.2, 260.5, 260.6; *FD* III 4.126, 127, 128):

1. Εὐρύβιος Λυκίσκου Μεγαλοπολίτης (Stephanis 982); *SEG* 2.260 = Nachtergael 1977: 479 no. 63, line 6 (225/4 BCE); *FD* III 4.125 = Nachtergael 1977: 480 no. 64, line 6 (221/20 BCE)
2. Νικίας (*vacat*) (Stephanis 1820); *FD* III 4.126 = Nachtergael 1977: 481 no. 65, line 7 (217/16 BCE)
3. Π[. . . (Stephanis 1971); *SEG* 2.260 = Nachtergael 1977: 476 no. 59, line 6 (241/40 BCE)
4. Σίμακ?]ος Σατύρου Ἀργεῖος (Stephanis 2273); *SEG* 2.260 = Nachtergael 1977: 478 no. 62, line 5 (229/28 BCE)
5. Φιλοκράτης Λυσίππου Ἀργεῖος (Stephanis 2530); *FD* III 4.127 = Nachtergael 1977: 482 no. 66, line 7 (213/12 or 205/4 BCE)
6. ỊΑΛΛΗΣ (*vacat*) (Stephanis 2979); *FD* III 4.128 = Nachtergael 1977: 483 no. 68, line 6 (209/8 or 205/4 BCE)

On the basis of these victor lists of rhapsodes who participated in the Amphictyonic Sōtēria, we can make the following observations:

1. As far as rhapsodic contests are concerned, it seems that no change was introduced in the Aetolian Sōtēria. According to the usual practice in victor lists of artists competing in festivals during the Hellenistic period, only the first victor is mentioned. A partial exception comes in *IG* VII 540.25 from the Sarapieia in Tanagra, the first part of which is a victor list. The name of the rhapsode who was second in the rhapsodic competition is not given in the actual victor list but later on, when the exact prizes are recorded (see p. 108).

2. A certain Eurybios son of Lykiskos from Megalopolis carried two successive victories in the rhapsodic contest in 225/24 and 221/20 BCE.[25]

3. With respect to the geographical range of the winners, all our admittedly scant information refers to Peloponnesian victors, an Argive (Simakos) and a Megalopolitan (Eurybios).

THE PYTHAIS[26] An inscription shows that three rhapsodes belonging to the Athenian guild of Dionysiac artists participated in the fourth Pythais of 98/97 BCE and recited epic poetry (*FD* III 2.48.31).[27] They are Kallon son of Kallon (Stephanis 1368; González 2013: 511 no. 49), Theodotos son of Pythion (Stephanis 1146; González 2013: 510 no. 47), and Xenophantos son of Eumachos (Stephanis 1913; González 2013: 513 no. 53). Of these three, Theodotos, who is also known from his victory in the rhapsodic contest at the festival of the Mouseia in Thespiai (after 85 BCE) (*IG* VII 1760.17 = *IThesp* 172 = Manieri *Thes.* 33 [2009: 402–404]), did not function only as a rhapsode in the fourth Pythais. He was also a member (*FD* III 2.48.26) of a group of artists, "the ones who will sing the paians and the chorus" (τοὺς ἀισομένου[ς] τούς τε παιᾶνας καὶ τὸν χορὸν, *FD* III 2.48.20), and, together with the other two aforementioned rhapsodes, Kallon and Xenophantos, he belonged to another group of artists, "the ones who competed with them . . ." (τοὺς τούτοις συναγωνιξαμένους Κάλ[λ]ων<α> Κάλλωνος, Θεόδοτον Πυθίωνος, Φιλόνικο<ν> Ἕρμωνος, Νίκωνα Ἀριστίωνος, Ξενόφαντον Εὐμάχου, *FD* III 2.48.37–38).

In the list of Athenian artists of Dionysos who took part in the fourth Pythais, the three rhapsodes are recorded after the three epic poets, in accordance with the general practice that we find in lists of participants and victor lists.

Euboia

The only information we have with respect to a rhapsodic contest held in Euboia is based on Adolf Wilhelm's restoration of the text of a victor list recording the names of victors at the games held in Amarynthos around the beginning of the first century BCE.[28] The relevant text (*IG* XII.9 139) runs as follows:

ἀγαθῆι τύχηι· ἐπὶ πολε[μάρχου]
Θεοκλέους τοῦ Ξένω[νος]
  δημαρχούντων
[Φ]ιλοφάνου τοῦ Ἀρισ— —]
Σωστράτου τοῦ Ἀριστ [— — —]
  οἵδε ἐνίκων·
  ἐπῶν ποητή[ς]
Δημόδοτος Ἡρακλείτ[ου]
  <ῥ>α[ψωιδός]
[Μ]έντω[ρ Ἀπολλοδότου]
  [Ἡρακλεώτης].

If Wilhelm's supplement is correct, then this Mentor son of Apollodoros (González 2013: 512–513 no. 51)—Wilhelm's "Apollodotos" (1905, on *IG* XII.9 139.10) is clearly wrong—from Herakleia may be the same Mentor son of Apollodoros from Herakleia (Stephanis 1667), who prevailed during this period in the rhapsodic contest at the festival of the Charitēsia in Orchomenos (*IG* VII 3196 = Manieri *Orc.* 24 [2009: 200–202]; see p. 106 under "Charitēsia").

In comparison with other victor lists, it must be noted that after the formula οἵδε ἐνίκων introducing the contests and the respective victors, the first contest recorded is that in epic poetry, after which the rhapsodic contest is immediately mentioned. There is no reference to a contest of trumpeters and heralds, which is often placed at the top of the victor list. The epic poet Demodotos son of Herakleitos is not accompanied by his place of origin, and no other contest is recorded.

Keos

An unnamed rhapsode is mentioned in an early third-century BCE decree from the city of Koresia on the island of Keos in the Cyclades (*IG* XII.5 647.35 = *SIG* III 958). The decree makes provisions for the winners of athletic games accompanying a local festival. The πρόβουλοι are responsible for establishing the athletic contest, electing the γυμνασίαρχος, and providing the prizes. The games involve archery and javelin contests for men and boys. The prizes differ with respect to age category: the men will be awarded weaponry, the boys a portion of meat. It is at this point that we learn that a rhapsode will also get a portion of meat. The decree declares that the names of the winners of the contests should be written on a white tablet (regularly used for public purposes) by the γραμματεύς and also, if allowed by the law, inscribed on a *stele* to be erected in the sanctuary (*IG* XII.5 647.40–42: ἀναγράφειν δὲ εἰς λεύκωμα ἑξῆς τοὺς ἀεὶ νικῶντας τὸγ γρα<μ>-|ματέα· ἂν δὲ δόξει ὁ νόμος, ἀναγράψαι εἰς στήλην καὶ στῆσαι | εἰς τὸ τέμενος).

No mention is made of a rhapsodic contest, and yet the rhapsode will get the same award as the boys who win the archery and javelin contests. West suggests that the rhapsode was present "to lend a suitably heroic colour to the martial contests" (2010a: 7). We might note the resemblance between this decree and a victor list from Chios (*IChios* 57 = *SIG* III 959 = *GDI* 5660) in which a musical contest of stringed instruments and a rhapsodic competition precede the athletic contests taking place at the gymnasium, although in the inscription from Keos no provision is made for musical *agōnes*.

Rhodes

A rhapsode called [Ni]komed[es] (Stephanis 1858; González 2013: 503 no. 25) is mentioned in a third-century BCE victor list pertaining to the festival of the Megala Erethimia held in honor of Apollo Erethimios on Rhodes (*BCH* 99 [1975]: 102 face B.1, col. I.4–5). We are in no position to tell whether this [Ni]komed[es] was a Rhodian or from some other place, since the patronymic or ethnic that followed his name on the stone has been lost: Rhodians are mentioned by their name and patronymic, and others by their names and ethnic.

The rhapsode is recorded first in the list, even before the trumpeter and the herald, who are here mentioned only after two kitharists and two aulodes (one a boy contestant, and the other an adult male contestant) and immediately before the victors in the athletic contests. As on the victor list from Chios that combines musical and athletic contests (see the previous section), there is no epic poet or any other poet recorded in the list. The contests, musical and athletic alike, seem to have attracted participants from all over the Greek world: an Opountian and a Koan (musical contests), two Lokrians, four Milesians, a Samian, an Ephesian, and an Alabandian (a city of Karia or Phrygia).

CONCLUSION

We can draw the following picture of rhapsodic performances in the Hellenistic period.

1. Rhapsodes do not operate as free agents but tend to belong to guilds of artists. We know that there were three large guilds of *technitai Dionysou* during the Hellenistic period: an Athenian guild, one of the Isthmus and Nemea, and one of Ionia and the Hellespont. Rhapsodic professionalism did not, of course, start in the Hellenistic period, but it certainly acquired a new form. In fact, we may postulate a situation in which the polis organizing a given festival would assign professional administrators the duty of providing whatever was needed for the staging of the festival. The state officials would have been in contact with the representatives of the guilds of Dionysiac artists and not with performers individually (González 2013: 479). Various honorific decrees testify to the granting to artists of the right of *proxenia*, *ateleia*, and the like (González 2013: 480).

2. Mobility increases. We find rhapsodes (and artists at large) participating in more than one festival and at venues far away from their place of origin. The competition would involve two or three rhapsodes. Mobility was, no doubt, enhanced by professionalism and motivated by the new conditions prevailing in the Hellenistic world, such as the increased flow of money, and by the privileges given to artists by those who organized the actual festivals.

3. Rhapsodic competitions take place at all major festivals and all over the Greek world: Boeotia (Akraiphia, Orchomenos, Oropos, Tanagra, Thebes, Thespiai), Delos, Delphi, Euboia, Keos, and Rhodes. Coupling this feature with the fact that new epic compositions were recited at all major festivals, we can see that epic poetry survived and flourished in an agonistic context but also in a way that must have been distinct from the production of Alexandrian literary epic (Pallone 1984: 159).

4. Under the influence of dramatic performances, rhapsodes intensified their attempts to make their recitals livelier for the audience. Again, as Plato's *Ion* informs us, this phenomenon was at work already in the fourth century BCE, but it became more pronounced during Hellenistic times. Although acting out parts of epic is traditionally assigned to the Homēristai, I am inclined to attribute some aspects of this practice, which of course may have varied in intensity, to professional rhapsodes as well.

5. The content of epic recitals must have undergone serious changes

after the Classical period. Although Athenaeus reports that Homer, Hesiod, and Phocylides were recited by rhapsodes in the theaters (14.620a–d [III 367.8–368.5 Kaibel]), there is no extant source, literary or epigraphic, designating what rhapsodes actually recited in festivals during the Hellenistic period. In the extant victory lists, rhapsodes are often preceded (and less often followed) by epic poets (ἐπῶν ποιηταί), who wrote new epic poems with which they competed.[29]

In this light, there are three alternatives. First, epic poets recited their new poems, while rhapsodes recited traditional epic (Homer, Hesiod, etc.), and separate prizes were awarded because the two contests were different (Fantuzzi 1988: xxxvi; González 2013: 488–499).[30] Second, rhapsodes recited solely new epic poems, but two prizes were awarded, one for best poem and one for best rhapsode (West 2010a: 7).[31] This scenario seems unlikely, since there are cases in which rhapsodes performed in the absence of contests for epic poets. For instance, the lists of participants at the Amphictyonic Sōtēria at Delphi include the names of the various competing rhapsodes but not of epic poets.[32] It would have been odd if rhapsodes performed new epic poems written for this occasion in the absence not only of the poet himself but of an actual contest in which this poet competed. Third, rhapsodes recited both new epic poems and traditional epic. Two possibilities arise: (a) the rhapsode whose name is recorded in a victor list is the one who recited the new epic poem that won the competition or (b) the rhapsode who won the competition of rhapsodic recital is not the same as the rhapsode who recited the epic poem that was awarded the first prize.

We should recall that victor lists regularly record the first victor.[33] González draws attention to the order in which epic poet and rhapsode appear in the victor lists. He argues that when the name of the epic poet follows that of the rhapsode in the victor list, the rhapsode did not perform the poetry of the epic poet (2013: 508 no. 45, 509n124, 511 no. 48, 512 no. 51). Since, for example, in a victor list from the Amphiaraia and Rhōmaia held in Oropos (*IG* VII 420) the tragic and comic poets are recorded before the tragic and comic actor, it is likely that the same order would have been followed in the case of epic poet and rhapsode should the former have recited the poetry of the latter. But since the rhapsode precedes the epic poet, the rhapsode probably did not recite the poetry of the epic poet. I am inclined to endorse this argument.

But does it mean that when the rhapsode followed the epic poet he recited the latter's new epic poetry? González suggests that there are cases in which the rhapsode may have still recited traditional epic. In *EO* 523, Demokles son of Ameinias from Thebes appears under the category of epic encomium and is the same person who won as epic poet in *IThesp* 170. This shows, apart from the "close relationship between epic encomiast and epic poet," that "the rhapsode at Thespiai would have performed not a new composition but one from the traditional repertoire" (González 2013: 505). In *EO* 526, Aminias[34] (*sic*, not Ameinias) son of Demokles from Thebes won both as an epic encomiast and an epic poet: he must have recited his new epic, just as he performed the epic encomium. The rhapsode Eieron son of Aristoboulos from Thebes who follows in the list recited traditional epic (González 2013: 509). *EO* 521 is particularly interesting, since after the epic encomiast, but before the rhapsode, no award for the epic poet is recorded, although the list contains an entry for such an event (González 2013: 509n124).

Another argument in support of González's claim pertains to the mechanics involved in having a rhapsode perform a new epic poem composed for performance in a given festival. Here the similarity with but also the difference from actors is worth considering. Both rhapsodes and actors as performers must have been familiar with the text they would perform. It is unthinkable that rhapsodes and actors would read for the first time the new epic or drama at the actual festival. To argue that rhapsodes would perform new epic poems, one must accept that rhapsodes, like actors, would have been presented with a written copy beforehand. This means that the epic poet would have been in touch with the guild of artists to which the rhapsode belonged and that some sort of agreement would have been reached for the recital of the poet's new epic. In the case of drama, which requires a lengthy process of production, it is easier to picture such a scenario. Perhaps sometimes this was also the case with epic poetry.[35]

Unfortunately, the only instance of the same person being both poet and rhapsode dates from the second century CE and so falls outside this chapter's purview. Still, it is indicative of what may have happened on certain occasions: an epic poet could also be a rhapsode. This poet-rhapsode was Πόπλιος Αἴλιος Πομπηϊανὸς Παίων (Stephanis 1979), who is recorded in the famous inscription on the Colossus of Memnon (*IK* 11.1 no. 22, lines 1–6):

> Ε]ἰσηγησαμένου Ποπλίου Αἰλίου Πομπη[ϊανοῦ]
> Παίονος Σιδήτου καὶ Ταρσέ[ως] καὶ Ῥοδίο[υ,]
> [ποιη]τοῦ πλειστονείκου, μελοποιοῦ καὶ ῥαψ[ωιδοῦ]
> [θε]οῦ Ἁδριανοῦ θεολόγου ναῶν τῶν ἐν Π[εργάμωι,]
> [ἀγ]ωνοθέτου ἀποδεδειγμένου τῶν Σεβ[αστῶν]
> Πυθίων

> On the proposal of P. Aelius Pompeianus Paion of Side, Tarsos, and Rhodes, winner of many poetry contests, lyric poet and rhapsode of the god Hadrian, *theologos* of the temples of Pergamon, appointed *agōnothetēs* of contests of the Sebasta Pythia.

Perhaps the designation θεοῦ Ἀδριανοῦ immediately following the title of rhapsode was needed to differentiate this Παίων from other rhapsodes reciting Homer.[36] This particular rhapsode was known as "the new Homer" (νέου Ὁμήρου, *ISide* 70).[37]

I think we should be satisfied with the most economical scenario: when only rhapsodes are mentioned, they are likely to have recited traditional (meaning not new) epic. As for the coexistence of new epic poets and rhapsodes in the same victor list, it is possible that while rhapsodes continued to perform traditional epic, the new epic poets made their appearance as performers-composers (in the manner of Hesiod in the Archaic period or Antimachus of Kolophon [Plutarch *Lysander* 18.4] in the Classical period) and recited their new compositions either in agonistic or epideictic contexts (cf. González 2013: 489).

6. As for the length of these rhapsodic recitals, if we accept that rhapsodes in most cases performed traditional epic (that is, Homer, Hesiod), then we can be sure that they recited selected parts from these well-known poems. The same may have been the case with new epic poems. Of course, one is entitled to ask what the meaning would be of reciting sections of an epic poem that nobody had heard or read before. Yet anthologized performances, if I may employ this term, of new epics could have made sense to the audience, since they were of a traditional form and based on either mythology or local history (cf. Fantuzzi 1988: xxxvi). Perhaps we should allow for the possibility that epic poets submitted, independently of the performance, a complete written text to be judged by the κριταί.

APPENDIX 3.1. RHAPSODES IN THE HELLENISTIC PERIOD

Reference	*Name*	*Place of Origin*	*Place of Performance*	*Occasion*	*Date*
Stephanis 12	Ἄβρων Φιλοξένου	Thebes	(1) Thebes (2) Thespiai	(1) Festival of the Rhōmaia (2) Festival of the Mouseia	(1) ca. 120 BCE (2) ca. 110–90 BCE
Stephanis 18	Ἀγαθῖνος Κριτοδήμο[υ	Sikyon	Delphi	Festival of Amphictyonic Sōtēria	257/6 or 254/3 BCE
Stephanis 34	Ἀγάθων Δαμᾶ	Thespiai	Akraiphia	Festival of Ptōia	2nd–1st ca. BCE
Stephanis 54	Ἀείμναστος E[ὐφ]ραίου	Thebes	Thebes	Festival of the Agriōnia (?) or Rhōmaia (?)	late 2nd–early 1st cent. BCE
Stephanis 306	Ἀρισταγό[ρας]		Delphi	Festival of the Amphictyonic Sōtēria	265–258 BCE
Stephanis 318	Ἀριστείδης Ἀρίστωνος [. . .]ς		Delphi	Festival of the Amphictyonic Sōtēria	258/7 or 254/3 BCE
Stephanis 335	Ἀριστόδικος Δημοκράτους	Opous	Tanagra	Festival of the Sarapieia	90–80 BCE
Stephanis 362	Ἀριστομένης Ἀριστομένου [. . .]ιος[a]		Delphi	Festival of the Amphictyonic Sōtēria	258/7 or 254/3 BCE
Stephanis 422	Ἀρτέμων Ἰσιδότου	Athens	Oropos	Festival of Amphiaraia and Rhōmaia	after the First Mithridatic War
Stephanis 435	Ἀρχέλας	Thessaly	Delos	Epideixis	284 BCE

(*continued*)

APPENDIX 3.1. (*CONTINUED*)

Stephanis 441	Ἀρχίας Σωτηρίδου	Thebes	Akraiphia	Festival of Ptōia	1st cent. BCE
Stephanis 524	Βίοττος [Μ]ε[ν]ελάου	Chalcis	Oropos	Festival of Amphiaraia and Rhōmaia	after the First Mithridatic War
Stephanis 533	Βουκάττης Γλαύκου	Tanagra	Tanagra	Festival of the Sarapieia	90–80 BCE
Stephanis 549	Γλαῦκος	Athens	Delos	Epideixis	284 BCE
Stephanis 820	Εἱέρων Ἀριστοβούλου	Thebes	Oropos	Festival of Amphiaraia and Rhōmaia	after the First Mithridatic War
Stephanis 822	[Εἴραν]ος Φρυνίδου	Tanagra	Thespiai	Festival of the Mouseia	118–112 or 110–90 BCE
Stephanis 908	Ἑρμόφαντος		Alexandria	Theater	Middle 3rd cent. BCE
Stephanis 948	Εὐθύδημος Χάρητος	Athens	Delphi	Festival of the Amphictyonic Sōtēria	257/6 or 253/2 BCE
Stephanis 982	Εὐρύβιος Λυκίσκου (bis)	Megalopolis	Delphi	Festival of the Aetolian Sōtēria	225/4 and 221/0 BCE
Stephanis 1024	Ζηνόδοτος Σωπάτρου	Antiocheia	Thespiai	Festival of the Mouseia	210–203 BCE
Stephanis 1055	Ἡγησίας		Alexandria	Theater	Middle 3rd cent. BCE
Stephanis 1146	Θεόδοτος Πυθίωνος	Athens	(1) Delphi (2) Thespiai	(1) 4th Athenian Pythais (2) Festival of the Mouseia	(1) 97 BCE (2) after 85 BCE
Stephanis 1186	Θεοφάνης Σωκράτου	Thebes	Oropos	Festival of Amphiaraia and Rhōmaia	after the First Mithridatic War
Stephanis 1325	Καλλίας Ἀρχετίμου	Syracuse	Delphi	Festival of the Amphictyonic Sōtēria	265–258 BCE
Stephanis 1368	Κάλλων Κάλλωνος	Athens	Delphi	4th Athenian Pythais	97 BCE

(*continued*)

Reference	*Name*	*Place of Origin*	*Place of Performance*	*Occasion*	*Date*
Stephanis 1429	Κλειτόριος Ἀριστείδου (four times)	Arcadia	Delphi	Festival of the Amphictyonic Sōtēria	265–259; 260/59 or 256/5; 259/8 or 255/4; 257/6 or 253/2 BCE
Stephanis 1502	Κράτων Κλέωνος	Thebes	(1) Oropos (2) Orchomenos	(1) Festival of Amphiaraia and Rhōmaia (2) Charitēsia	(1) after the First Mithridatic War (2) early 1st cent. BCE
Stephanis 1667	Μέντωρ Ἀπολλοδώρου	Herakleia	(1) Orchomenos (2) Amarynthos	(1) Festival of Charitēsia (2) Contest of rhapsodes	(1) beginning of 1st cent. BCE (2) beginning of 1st cent. BCE
Stephanis 1708	Μιλτιάδης Διονυσίου	Chios	Chios	Musical and athletic games in the gymnasium	2nd cent. BCE
Stephanis 1721	Μνασίων			Epideixis	5th–3rd cent. BCE[b]
Stephanis 1820	Νικίας		Delphi	Festival of the Aetolian Sōtēria	217/6 BCE
Stephanis 1858	Νικομήδης		Rhodes	Festival of the Megala Erethimia	3rd cent. BCE
Stephanis 1893	Νουμήνιος Νουμηνίου	Athens	Orchomenos	Festival of the Charitēsia	Beginning of 1st cent. BCE
Stephanis 1913	Ξενόφαντος Εὐμάχου	Athens	Delphi	4th Athenian Pythais	97 BCE
Stephanis 1971	Π[-]		Delphi	Festival of the Aetolian Sōtēria	241/0 BCE
Stephanis 2106	Πολύμνηστος Ἀλεξάνδρου	Arkadia	Delphi	Festival of the Amphictyonic Sōtēria	260/59 or 56/5 BCE

(*continued*)

Stephanis 2174	Πυθοκλῆς Ἀριστάρχου	Hermione	Nemea or Peirene or Delphi or Olympia or Boeotia[c]	Festivals with musical contests	3rd cent. BCE
Stephanis 2273	Σίμακ?]ος Σατύρου	Argos	Delphi	Festival of the Aetolian Sōtēria	229/8 BCE
Stephanis 2530	Φιλοκράτης Λυσίππου	Argos	Delphi	Festival of the Aetolian Sōtēria	Last decade of the 3rd cent. BCE
Stephanis 2729	[. . $^{4-5}$ . .]ν Θρασωνίδου	Sinope	Delphi	Festival of the Amphictyonic Sōtēria	259/8 or 255/4 BCE
Stephanis 2762	]ράτης Καλλίφ[		Delphi	Festival of the Amphictyonic Sōtēria	ca. 260 BCE
Stephanis 2886	]ς	Athens		Festival of the Amphictyonic Sōtēria	ca. 260 BCE
Stephanis 2919	ΙΑΛΛΗΣ		Delphi	Festival of the Aetolian Sōtēria	end of 3rd cent. BCE
Stephanis 2979	[Βοι]ώτιος	Boeotia	Lebadeia	Festival of the Basileia	ca. middle of the 2nd cent. BCE
IG VII 2727	[-]		Akraiphia	Festival of the trieteric Sōtēria	1st cent. BCE
IG XII.5 647	[-]	Keos (Coresia)			beginning 3rd cent. BCE

Note: The order of the rhapsodes' names is alphabetical (Greek alphabet).

[a]There is also a tragic poet Aristomenes son of Aristomenes from Athens (*TrGF* 1, 145), who participated in the fourth Pythais of the Athenians in Delphi in 97 BCE. It must be noted that these two figures share many common features (first name, father's name, and association with musical contests in Delphi).

[b]Given Mnasion's uncertain date, I have decided to include him in the appendices of rhapsodes provided here and in chapter 1. The fifth- to third-century BCE range is determined by the fact that this rhapsode recited Simonides's iambs (late six–early fifth century BCE) and is mentioned by the third-century BCE grammarian Lysanias in the first book of his work *On Iambic Poets*.

[c]See Nachtergael 1977: 319, 321, 429–430; González 2013: 503 no. 28.

NOTES

1. González claims that it is impossible to know whether the dividing line between the epic encomium and the new epic poems recited in the Hellenistic period was that the former pertained to individuals and the latter to deities or cities (2013: 490–491).

2. See González 2013: 449–451 and 451n62 with bibliography on the Homēristai.

3. On Hegesias and Hermophantos, see González 2013: 499, 502.

4. For payments received by the Homēristai, see González 2013: 458, 460, 463.

5. González is right to claim that even if the verb ἀγωνίζεσθαι (as Robert 1983: 184 argues) need not have indicated a typical competition between various contestants, it could hardly have been completely non-agonistic: a single performer would have aimed at gaining the favor of the audience (2013: 459–460).

6. With respect to the victory of Aeimnastos, I follow Knoepfler's suggestion that the relevant festival was the Rhōmaia (2004: 1262–1264); see also González 2013: 504–505.

7. The contests may have been interrupted by the war and then reorganized after the reaffirmation of Roman supremacy in Boeotia; see Manieri 2009: 131–132.

8. Manieri calls Polyxenos a *poeta epico* (2009: 111), but this is clearly a mistake, since in the relevant inscription (*IG* VII 2727) he is a victor with an ἐγκώμιον λογικόν. In fact, he is immediately followed in the same victor list by a certain Protogenes son of Protarchos from Thespiai, who won the first prize as an epic poet (and also as comic and epinician poet, according to the same victor list).

9. For this Mestor in other victor lists, see González 2013: 510.

10. The use of the Boeotian dialect in *IG* VII 3195 (the victor list recording Kraton the rhapsode) has been interpreted in various ways by different scholars: see Manieri 2009: 205–206 with the relevant bibliography.

11. Apart from Boeotians, the contestants in the musical *agōnes* at the Amphiaraia and Rhōmaia came from Neapolis, Echinos, Skarpheia, Miletos (*EO* 523), Taras (2), Myrine in Aiolis (*EO* 524), Aegina, Proussa, Nikomedeia, Kalchedon, Chalcis (*EO* 526), Tarsos (2), Chalcis, Amphipolis, Mallos, Trallis, Syracuse, and Opous (*EO* 528).

12. There is no extant information concerning musical contests at the Sarapieia of Amorgos and Mythemna on Lesbos.

13. Manieri suggests that the introduction of the cult of Sarapis in Boeotia indicates the friendly relations between Boeotia and Egypt in the third century BCE. Both Orchomenos (*IG* VII 3166) and Tanagra (*IG* VII 507) issued *proxeny* decrees for Sosibios, the highest magistrate of Ptolemy IV.

14. For the family tree of Boukattes, see Calvet and Roesch 1966: 331; cf. Stephanis 533; González 2013: 508–509.

15. The sponsor Charilaos provided the funds for the organization of the

Sarapieia, prizes included (Schachter 1981: 203–204n1 [*SEG* 31.496]; Roller 1989: 114).

16. Knoepfler dates the only victor list that undoubtedly comes from the Theban Rhōmaia to shortly after 118 BCE on the basis of the "defection" of Theban artists from the guild of artists from the Isthmus and Nemea (2004: 1277).

17. On the same person winning as both herald and rhapsode, see p. 104 on the Basileia held in Lebadeia.

18. See Aneziri 2009: 218–220; also *SEG* 54.516.

19. We know of only two rhapsodes who were not Boeotians (Zenodotos from Antiocheia on Pyramos and Mentor from Herakleia [in Thessaly?]) who won rhapsodic contests at Boeotian festivals.

20. See Schachter 1986: 164–165 (who follows Feyel) and the detailed analysis of Manieri (2009: 315–326) for the Hellenistic period.

21. From Pyramos (ἀπὸ Πυράμου). Notice that the immediately preceding victor in the victor list also comes from Antiocheia; Manieri says that only the place name Antiocheia (without further specification) is mentioned in the case of Heliodoros, although the text she prints clearly has Ἀντιοχεὺς ἀπὸ Πυράμου (see also *IThesp* 163) for both the epic poet Heliodoros and the rhapsode Zenodotos (2009: 378). Thinking that in the case of Heliodoros the Syrian Antiocheia is meant, Manieri considers the possibility (following Bonnet 2001: 57) of some sort of link with the Seleukidai of Syria. West rightly asserts that these two Asian Greeks "must have come to Thespiai in partnership" (2010a: 8).

22. West draws attention to the fact that a number of victor lists from the Mouseia at Thespiai record epic poets but no rhapsodes (*IThesp* 161, 164, 165, 174) (2010a: 8).

23. We do not know in which contest he was victorious. Unsure of the restoration [Εἴραν]ος, West observes that given that (i) in the same inscription from Oropos we have a clear example of two brothers being mentioned, one (Artemon son of Isidotos from Athens) a rhapsode and the other (Straton son of Isidotos from Athens) a comic actor, and (ii) in *IG* VII 540 we find Boukattes son of Glaukos from Tanagra as rhapsode and his brother Alexandros as poet of satyr-drama, it is likely that the victorious rhapsode recorded in *IThesp* 170.22 is the brother of the comic poet Εἴρανος Φρυνίδου Ταναγραῖος, who won at Oropos (2010a: 9n20).

24. There is a kitharode named Philodamos (*IG* XI,2 105.24) whose place of origin is not recorded. Was he a Delian, or did the stonecutter simply not know where he came from?

25. For problems with the quadrennial periodicity of the Aetolian Sōtēria, see Sifakis 1967: 69–70.

26. Since my study concerns only rhapsodic recitals, I have not included references to epic poets winning in festivals when no rhapsode is mentioned. I exclude, then, Sosikles from Koroneia, who won at the Pythian Games in Delphi (Plutarch *Quaestiones convivales* 2.4.1), and the poetess Aristomache from Ery-

thraia, who won twice at the Isthmian Games and dedicated a golden book in the Sikyonian Treasury in Delphi (Plutarch *Quaestiones convivales* 5.2); see Pallone 1984: 162–163.

27. For the Athenians' Pythais to Delphi, see Sifakis 1967: 86–88, 90–92 (on the fourth Pythais).

28. This victor list may pertain to the festival of the Tamyneia (Kourouniotis 1899: 141) or the Artemisia (Knoepfler 1988: 388n26) in honor of Artemis Amarysia. According to Pausanias, this festival was transplanted to the deme of Athmonia in Attica (again in honor of Artemis) and celebrated there in no less splendor (1.31.5). Strabo, who testifies to the magnificence of this festival, reports that he had seen in the temple of Artemis Amarynthia a column with an inscription recording that in the past the Eretrians celebrated the festival in majestic grandeur: the processions comprised 3,000 hoplites, 600 horsemen, and 60 chariots (10.448).

29. In general, the order in which different victors and contests are recorded in victor lists corresponds to the order in which the relevant contests took place at the festival. Chaniotis (*per litteras electronicas*) draws my attention to the fact that kitharodes (who received bigger prizes than rhapsodes) are recorded in the middle or end of victor lists (but not at the beginning), which may in itself indicate that kitharodic contests had pride of place at the festival.

30. The rhapsode Ion emphasizes that it was his performance that earned him the victory crown, not the poetry of Homer itself (Plato *Ion* 530d7–8).

31. Pallone leaves the question open (1984: 161–162).

32. For cases in which a rhapsode is recorded without any mention of an epic poet, consider the previously discussed items:

(1) The inscription from Chios reporting that Miltiades son of Dionysios from Chios won the rhapsodic contest (see p. 102). The absence of any reference to the performance of a new epic poem—an absence understandable in the venue of a gymnasium frequented by παῖδες, ἔφηβοι, and νέοι—suggests that the young Miltiades sang traditional epic.

(2) The decree from the city of Koresia on the island of Keos in the Cyclades mentioning an unnamed rhapsode (see pp. 116–117). The decree makes provisions for the winners of athletic games accompanying a local festival.

(3) The victor list pertaining to the festival of the Megala Erethimia in honor of Apollo Erethimios on Rhodes mentioning a rhapsode named [Ni]komed[es] (see p. 117). The name of the rhapsode appears first in the victor list and is not preceded or followed by that of an epic poet.

(4) Archelas from Thessaly and Glaukos from Athens, who recited at Delos *hors concours* (ἐπεδείξαντο) epic poetry (see pp. 111–112). On Demokles son of Ameinias from Thebes, see p. 120.

33. Even if we had both the lists of participants in the actual contest and the victor lists, we would not know who recited which epic.

34. This Aminias must have been a rather gifted poet, since he is also listed as ἐπῶν ποιητής and ποιητὴς σατύρων in a victor list (*IG* VII 3197.10 and 25) from the Charetēsia in Orchomenos (beginning of first century BCE).

35. The content of these new epic poems was of the traditional type, whether mythological or reflecting local history: see Ziegler's list of *epopoioi* (1988: lvii–lxxxviii); Fantuzzi 1988: xxxvi; González 2013: 488n40.

36. Gangloff (this volume, pp. 144–146) surveys various interpretive scenarios. She endorses removing the comma after Ἁδριανοῦ and rendering Paion the *theologos* of the god Hadrian in the temples of Pergamon.

37. See Chaniotis (forthcoming): "By analogy with expressions such as ὑμνωιδοὶ θεοῦ Σεβαστοῦ καὶ θεᾶς Ῥώμης, ὑμνωιδὸς Θεοῦ Αὐγούστου, and ὑμνωιδὸς Θεοῦ Ἁδριανοῦ, we should read μελοποιὸς καὶ ῥαψωιδὸς Θεοῦ Ἁδριανοῦ and separate this function from that of a theologos serving in the temple of the imperial cult in Pergamon. As a μελοποιὸς καὶ ῥαψωιδὸς Θεοῦ Ἁδριανοῦ, Paion composed melic and epic poems that had the deified Hadrian as their subject—not poems to be recited to Hadrian. Hadrian's hunting exploits, and possibly also his relationship to the deified Antinoos, which could easily be assimilated to that of the epic heroes Achilleus and Patroklos, offered suitable subject matter for such poems, with which Paion could have earned the designation 'New Homer.' Paion's activity as a rhapsode of Hadrian is comparable to that of ποιηταὶ εἰς τὸν αὐτοκράτορα in Thespiai."

CHAPTER FOUR

Rhapsodes and Rhapsodic Contests in the Imperial Period

ANNE GANGLOFF

MELIC POETS SANG TO THE ACCOMPANIMENT OF AN instrument. By contrast, traditional rhapsodes, although occasionally accompanied by a musician, specialized in the vocal performance of poetic texts that could be "sung" without musical accompaniment (West 1981: 113–115; Ford 1988). From early on, they were associated with the epics of Homer and were notable conduits for Homeric poems, as Plato's *Ion* attests.[1] Inscriptions show that they actively took part in contests (Pallone 1984; West 2010a), although Plato describes them in the *Laws* as being mostly popular with old men (658d). This trend was perhaps the result of a cultural change over time, as the *Iliad* and the *Odyssey* became cornerstones of school education and written texts appeared in more and more private libraries from the end of the fifth century BCE (Burkert 1987: 57; Chaniotis 2010; West 2010a: 6). The decline in the popularity of rhapsodes might also be due to the fact that in Athens Homer's works served as a foundation for the heroic and civic ideal that had been left badly shaken by the Peloponnesian War (Isocrates *Panegyricus* 159). Still, Chares of Mytilene mentioned the rhapsodes at the marriage of Alexander the Great at Susa in 324 BCE (*Stories of Alexander* 10 = *FGrH* 125 F 4; Athenaeus 12.538e), and Hellenistic kings, following in Alexander's footsteps, had rhapsodes participate in their feasts, where they had a laudatory function (Plutarch *Alexander* 4.11; *Quaestiones convivales* 736E–F). By engaging rhapsodes, these kings aligned themselves with the Homeric kings, whose feasts were accompanied by *aoidoi*.

In the Imperial period, according to literary sources in which the association between rhapsodes and epic is almost automatic (Lucian *Zeus the Tragedian* 20, *Charon* 7; Athenaeus 14.620a), rhapsodes still performed epic poems, most notably those of Homer and, to a lesser extent, those of Hesiod, but their numbers appear to have decreased considerably. In his book on stage performers (1988), Ioannis E. Stephanis records eleven for that time, out of a total of sixty-two across all periods, but I have elsewhere suggested dismissing one of the eleven attestations, that of Erato, friend of Plutarch, who is described as a *lurōidos*, one who specializes in lyre playing and singing (= Stephanis 881) (Gangloff 2010: 52–53). By contrast, Stephanis lists forty-six rhapsodes for the Hellenistic period (among which four attributions are questionable). Other evidence tells the same story: among the artistic representations of performers from the Imperial period, none can be definitively identified as a rhapsode, as Christophe Vendries has pointed out to me (pers. comm.). In the literature of Imperial Greece, Plutarch, Lucian, and Athenaeus use the terms *rhapsōidoi*, *rhapsōideō*, and *rhapsōidia*, often in a stylized or figurative manner, without reference to contemporary entertainments. These terms do not appear in Pseudo-Plutarch's treatise *On Music*.

In this chapter, I try to make sense of the dwindling number of rhapsodes. I first offer an inventory of all the traces of their activity that remain in epigraphic and literary texts: a challenge arises in picking out these artists from among those called "Homerists." I then examine the participation of rhapsodes in contests and their distribution in space and time in order to determine the cultural and social functions fulfilled by these artists and to understand why their numbers decreased so notably, even though rhapsodic performances appear to have initially emerged in an agonistic setting (Ford 1988: 306). Many of the places mentioned in this chapter can be found on map 4.1.

A PROBLEM OF IDENTIFICATION: RHAPSODES OR HOMERISTS?

The term "rhapsode" appears in nine inscriptions from the Imperial era:

1. An epitaph from Argos, dating to the second or third century CE, erected by Aurelius Apollonides, priest to Zeus Sabazios, in memory of several individuals, including a rhapsode who lived thirty years (*SEG* 31.312; *IG* IV 649; Stephanis 2082; González 2013: no. 61):

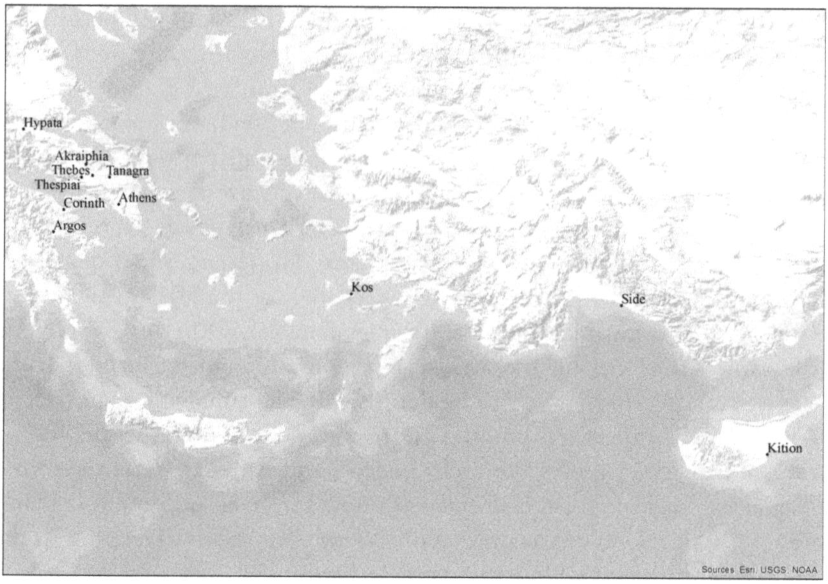

MAP 4.1. *Rhapsodes' homelands and sites of rhapsodic performance in the Imperial period*

Αὐ[ρ(ήλιος)] Ἀπολλωνίδης,
[ἱερεὺς] Διὸς Σεβαζείου, τὸ μνῆμα
[κατεσκ]εύασεν ζῶν. Πο. Ἀπολλωνίδ<α> <Δ>ίων· χαίρε[τε].
[— —]ιον, ζήσας ἡλικία[ς] ἔτεσι τριάντα δύω. Πολείταρ[χε]
vacat
[— — —]α ῥαψωιδέ, χαῖρε, ζήσας ἔτη λʹ.

Au[r(elius)] Apollonides
[Priest] to Zeus Sabazios, built this grave
while alive. P. Apollonides, Dion, farewell.
[—]ion, having lived thirty-two years. Poleitarchos
[—], rhapsode, farewell, having lived thirty years.
(my translation)

2. The honorary decree for Aelius Alkibiades of Nysa by the Dionysiac *technitai* of Ephesus dating from the reign of Hadrian (*IK* 11.1 no. 22; Stephanis 1979; Robert 1938)
3.–9. Seven inscriptions regarding the Mouseia contests in Thespiai and the Ptōia of Akraiphia, dating from between the end of the first century and the beginning of the third century CE (three of which relate to the same artist).

3. *BCH* 44 (1920): 262 no. 12 (Roesch 1982: 226 no. 5; Stephanis 2846; Manieri 2009: 122; González 2013: no. 57; Akraiphia, end of first or beginning of second century)
4. *IThesp* 178.18 (*IG* VII 1773; Stephanis 993; Manieri 2009: 412–414; González 2013: no. 58; Thespiai, ca. 150–160)
5. *IThesp* 177.29–30 (Stephanis 2859; Manieri 2009: 414–416; González 2013: no. 63; Thespiai, ca. 150–160 or after 169 CE)
6. *IG* VII 4151.4–6 (Roesch 1982: 227 no. 7; Stephanis 956; Manieri 2009: 123–125; González 2013: no. 60; Akraiphia, end of second or beginning of third century, before 212)
7. *BCH* 27 (1903): 297, col. A line 10 (Roesch 1982: 227 no. 9; Stephanis 955; Manieri 2009: 126–128; González 2013: no. 64; Larymna, 212/213, see Strasser 2002: 112–124)
8. *IThesp* 180.16–17 (*IG* VII 1776; Stephanis 955; Manieri 2009: 422–423; González 2013: no. 64; Mount Helikon, 212/213, see Strasser 2002: 112–124)
9. *IG* VII 2726.1 (Stephanis 955; González 2013: no. 64; village of Sengena, near Akraiphia, after 212)

I set aside two inscriptions of the Imperial era in which the way the term *rhapsōidos* has been rendered is questionable:

> *ISALAMIS* 64 (Salamis of Cyprus, third or fifth century CE):
>
> [— — — —]χίας *vacat*
> [— — — —]ν ἐχούσης
> [— — ῥα]ψῳδι̣ *vacat*
> [— — — — — — — —]
>
> *IG* IV 682.9 (Hermione, Roman imperial period):
>
> [ἀλλ ὅσα ῥαψωι(?)]δός τε καὶ ἐγ κυκλίοισ{ο}ι χοροῖσιν.

Two other epitaphs that do not contain the term "rhapsode" pose interpretative difficulties. The first comes from Kition, Cyprus, and most likely dates from the second or third century CE, according to the letterforms (Yon 2004: no. 2083, fig. 32; *GVI* 1305; Stephanis 1405; González 2013: no. 59). The deceased specialized in Homeric poems, and the epigram borrows from the vocabulary of Homer:

> Μὴ σπεύσῃς, ὦ ξεῖνε, παρελθέμεν,
> ἀλλά με, βαιὸν / στῆθι, μάθῃς

Κιλικᾶν ἔξοχον ἠιθέων /
ὅς ποθ' ὁμηρείαισι μετέπρεπον
ἐν σελίδεσσιν / δεικνὺς ἡρώων
ἠνορέην προτέρων *vacat* / εἰ δὲ
πάτρην ζητεῖς, Κίτιον μάθε,
πεντάκι δ' ὀκτὼ / Μοῖρά μ' ἐτῶν
ζωῆς νόσφισεν ἧιδε τάφωι.

Do not walk past quickly, stranger, but rather stop awhile
to learn about me, Kilikas, superior among young men;
I once distinguished myself in Homer's books
by showing the courage of heroes past.
If you are looking for my homeland, then know it is Kition;
at the age of five times eight years Fate
took me off the path of life and brought me to this grave.
(my translation)

Some have imagined Kilikas to be a teacher, and others, a rhapsode.[2] The answer to this question depends on the sense of δείκνυμι, which could refer to being a teacher or to being an artist, but in this instance context does not help us to determine which meaning is the right one. Furthermore, δείκνυμι might also apply to the performance of an actor specializing in the interpretation of Homeric poetry, a Homerist.[3]

The second, equally ambiguous, epitaph was found in Athens and dates to the first or second century CE (Kaibel 101; *IG* II^{2} 9145; *GVI* 1332; Stephanis 1782; González 2013: no. 56):

Ὄντως δίζηαι,
ξένε φίλτατε, τίς
πόθεν εἰμί; / Κῶ<ς> μέν
μοι πατρίς ἐστιν, ἐγ[ὼ]
δ' ὄνομα Νεικομήδη[ς], /
Μουσάων θεράπων
ἄιδων <θ>υμέλαισιν Ὁ-
μηρο<ν>, / δόξαις ἐνγε-
λάσας περίκειμαι νή-
δυμον ὕπνον.

Do you really wish to know, very dear stranger,
who I am and whence I come?
Kos is my homeland, my name is Nikomedes,

servant of the Muses,
I sang Homer's poems in the theater;
after having enjoyed many successes,
I now lie in sweet sleep.

(my translation)

Georg Kaibel suggested that Nikomedes was a Homerist, meaning an actor (1965:34). He cited a passage from *The Adventures of Leucippe and Clitophon* by Achilles Tatius that describes this type of artist (3.20–21). Despite the fact that this assumption is also to be found in *IG* II^2 9145, uncertainty over the identification of Nikomedes as a rhapsode or a Homerist/actor remains.

These two examples illustrate the problem of defining the Homēristai, a term which seems to have been used only rarely, since it occurs a mere sixteen times in extant literary sources, inscriptions, and papyri:

1. Aristocles, *On Choruses* (*apud* Athenaeus 14.620b)
2. Petronius 59
3. Artemidorus 4.2
4. Athenaeus 14.620b
5. *Philoxenus-Glossary*, *CGL* II, p. 22, lines 40–42, Goetz = *CGL* VI, p. 108 *s.v. Atellanus*
6. Dositheus, *Hermeneumata Pseudodositheana*, *CGL* III, p. 172, line 46 and p. 240, line 7
7. Diomedes Grammaticus = *GrL*, I, p. 484, 12–16 Keil
8. Eustathius 4.970 van der Valk
9. *P.Oxy.* III 519, fr. A, line 4 (second century CE, Oxyrhynchus)
10. *P.Oxy.* VII 1050, line 26 (second or third century CE, Oxyrhynchus)
11. *P.Oslo* III 189, verso, line 12 (third century CE, Oxyrhynchus)
12. and 13. Papyrus SB IV 7336, lines 26 and 29 (third century CE, Oxyrhynchus)
14. *P.Oxy.* VII 1025, line 8 (third century CE, Arsinoe at Fayum)
15. Roueché 1993: 18 (before end of third century CE, Aphrodisias in Caria)
16. *AE* 1982: 754 (Heger 1980, after Hadrian's time?, Virunum).

Five other sources, although not employing the word Homēristēs, relate to dramatic performers specializing in the recitation of Homeric poems. In addition to the two inscriptions cited previously (Yon 2004: no.

2083; Kaibel 101), there is also the funerary epigram for Cyrus of Lampsakos, found in Pompeiopolis, Paphlagonia. It dates back to the Imperial period and concerns two theatrical actors who specialized in Homeric texts (Marek 1993: 144 no. 28, photo in table 43, and 63–65; *SEG* 43.920; *Steinepigramme* II 10/05/04). As noted earlier, Achilles Tatius in *The Adventures of Leucippe and Clitophon* mentions a traveling actor who recited Homeric poems in theaters and who was equipped to play the battle scenes (3.20–21). Finally, *P.Bodl.* I 143, line 3 includes, in a list of expenditures from Fayum dated to the first half of the fourth century CE, the "Homeric allowances," or perhaps "allowances for Homeric actors," paid to the actors for their speeches by a man named Soukidas (Tedeschi 2002: 135).

Most of these data originate from Egypt or Asia Minor and almost all date to the Imperial period, between the reign of Nero and the first half of the fourth century CE. They describe Homerists as traveling artists who performed at private banquets or public feasts or in theaters. They were part of the *akroamata*, professional artists who originally performed at *panēgyreis* in non-agonistic settings (*hors concours*). Audiences appreciated their representations of Homeric battle scenes, and some Homerists even carried special equipment, including swords, spears, and shields (Petronius 59; Artemidorus 4.2; Achilles Tatius 3.20–21; Roueché 1993: 18). They developed a histrionic style of presentation in their movements and recitations. This theatrical aspect was also present in the art of the ancient rhapsodes, whose acting abilities were acknowledged as early as the fourth century BCE (Plato *Ion* 532d, 535b–e, 536a; *Republic* 395a; Alcidamas *Sophists* 14; Aristotle *Rhetoric* 1403b22; Diodorus Siculus 14.109.1–2; West 2010a: 9). However, because of their highly theatrical style, a number of Homerists are identified in our sources as actors or are associated with actors or mimes (Petronius 59; Artemidorus 4.2; Achilles Tatius 3.20; *Philoxenus-Glossary*, *CGL* II, p. 22, lines 40–42, Goetz = *CGL* VI, p. 108 *s.v. Atellanus*; Dositheus, *Hermeneumata Pseudodositheana*, *CGL* III, p. 172, line 46 and p. 240, 7; Roueché 1993: 18; *P.Oxy.* VII 1025, line 8).

Athenaeus attests to the relationship, but also possible confusion, between rhapsodes and Homerists. During "dinner-table talk" about the *akroamata*, the conversation focuses on rhapsodes, since P. Livius Larensius, the Roman official hosting the banquet, has a keen interest in Homer (14.620a–d, trans. Olson):

> Our parties also featured rhapsodes. For Larensius was more fond of Homer's poetry than anyone you can imagine—fond enough to

> render insignificant Cassander, the king of Macedon, who Carystius in his *Historical Commentaries* claims liked Homer so much that he routinely recited long passages from the poems. Cassander also owned an *Iliad* and an *Odyssey* that had been privately copied for him. Aristocles in his *On Choruses* reports that rhapsodes were also referred to as Homēristai. The first person to introduce the individuals known today as Homēristai into the theaters was Demetrius of Phaleron. According to Chamaeleon in his *On Stesichoros*, it was not just Homer's poems that were recited, but also those of Hesiod and Archilochus, and of Mimnermus and Phocylides as well. Clearchus says in Book I of *On Riddles*: Simonides of Zacynthus used to recite Archilochus' poems in the theaters while seated on a stool. Lysanias in Book I of *On Iambic Poets* reports that the rhapsode Mnasion gave public performances in which he acted out some of Simonides' iambs. The rhapsode Cleomenes recited Empedocles' *Purifications* at Olympia, according to Dicaearchus in his *History of Olympia*. Iason in Book III of *On Alexander's Offerings* claims that the comic actor Hegesias performed Hesiod's poems in the large theater in Alexandria, and that Hermophantus performed Homer's.

The following information can be extracted from this passage.

1. At the time of Aristocles the musicologist, whom historians place approximately at the end of the second century BCE (Wentzel 1895), rhapsodes were referred to as Homēristai, undoubtedly owing to the fact that they were highly specialized in their knowledge of Homeric poems. This link is confirmed by later authors, namely Diomedes Grammaticus in the fourth century CE: "Because those who formerly recited parts of Homeric poems in front of theatrical audiences and who were called, due to Homer, Homerists, used a staff, that is, a rod" (*Quod olim partes Homerici carminis in theatralibus circulis cum baculo, id est virga, pronuntiabant qui ab eodem Homero dicti Homeristae, GrL* vol. I, p. 484, 12–16 Keil; cf. Eustathius [4.970 van der Valk], who probably took his inspiration from Athenaeus).

2. Rhapsodes, "who today are called Homēristai," were first introduced into theaters by Demetrios of Phaleron, the statesman who reformed Athenian drama in the last quarter of the fourth century BCE. In my view, this indicates that at the time of that reform rhapsodes were not yet referred to as Homēristai, as this term does not occur in any sources before the end of the second century BCE, when it was used by

Aristocles.[4] Johannes Frei suggested that Demetrios was the first to bring rhapsodes into the theater *orchēstra*, whereas before that time they would recite near the altars or on the steps of temples (1900: 11–13). His interpretation is based on the first example in the list of artists given by Athenaeus: Simonides of Zakynthos recited (ἐραψώιδει) Archilochus in theaters while seated on a stool (he was not, therefore, a Homerist/actor), according to Clearchus, a contemporary of Demetrios of Phaleron and a Peripatetic and student of Aristotle, born before 340 BCE. It appears likely that Simonides of Zakynthos was one of the first rhapsodes to perform on a theatrical stage (Stephanis 2281). Frei examines the reform initiated by Demetrios from the broader perspective of the development of theater construction in the fourth century BCE, linking this reform with the emergence of the term θυμελικοί to refer to musical contests. Θυμέλη, which used to describe the altar at the center of the *orchēstra*, later came to denote the *orchēstra* itself.[5]

3. The performers listed as examples tend to corroborate the statements by Aristocles and Chamaeleon of Herakleia Pontika (a grammarian and Peripatetic who lived at the end of the fourth or beginning of the third century BCE) about the reform introduced by Demetrios regarding rhapsodes and about the relative variety in the rhapsodes' repertoire at the end of the fourth and into the third century BCE, despite the fact that they specialized in Homeric poems. The last example is particularly interesting since it describes actors at the theater in Alexandria performing passages from Homer and, most likely, Hesiod, not the manuscripts' "Herodotus" (Meineke 1867: 297). The first, Hegesias, is a comic actor, while the specialty of the second, Hermophantos, is not mentioned. However, he is probably the first Homerist/actor that we know of, although the term "Homēristēs" is not used to describe him. These actors' performances were an extension of the rhapsodes' acts. They unfortunately cannot be dated with certainty, nor can the source that mentions them. The latter might be Jason of Nysa, grandson, pupil, and successor to Posidonius at the school of Rhodes sometime after the middle of the first century BCE (Jacoby 1916),[6] but we may also be dealing with another, unidentified Jason.

This passage from Athenaeus highlights the link between rhapsodes and those actors specializing in the performance of Homeric poems: it demonstrates that during the Imperial period, both kinds of performers (rhapsodes and actors) were referred to as Homēristai, which suggests that the category was broader than modern studies on the Homerists have indicated. Several sources give no information as to the nature of each Homerist's performance (*P.Oxy.* VII, 1050; *P.Bodl.* I 143; *AE* 1982: 754). In papyrus SB IV 7336, line 26, he may even be a pantomime, since he appears before a "dancer's choreographer" (?) and a reader, Sarapas. *P.Oslo* III 189 mentions a celebration during which a demonstration (ἀπόδειξις) by Homerists is organized alongside a poetry contest, reminiscent of the association between epic poets (that is, authors of traditional epics) and rhapsodes in the contests of continental Greece.[7] It is highly likely that the third or second century BCE saw the emergence of a category of artists whose members would have fundamentally defined themselves, as etymology suggests, as specializing in Homeric poems, at the very time that the monopoly over the dramatic interpretation of these texts was increasingly slipping out of the rhapsodes' grasp. Under this assumption, it is difficult to determine the number of rhapsodes in the Imperial period, especially if one considers that many professional artists had diversified their skill set in order to make a living from their art (Chaniotis 1990).[8]

There is no confusion, however, as regards contests, since the term *rhapsōidos* was always used in the list of victors. It may be ventured that in the agonistic setting rhapsodes remained truer to tradition than when they performed in theaters or during festivals, since the format of competitions (which could vary) was defined by local regulations.[9]

RHAPSODES AND CONTESTS

As already observed by Frei, rhapsodes, just like epic poets, gradually disappeared from contests (1900: 28). During the Classical and Hellenistic periods, rhapsodes and epic poets appeared in about twenty musical contests in continental Greece (Tsagalis, this volume, chapters 1 and 3).[10] In the Imperial era, only two contests, located in Boeotia, included performances by rhapsodes: the Mouseia of Thespiai, dedicated to the Muses of Mount Helikon, and the Ptōia of Akraiphia, in honor of Apollo Ptōios.

Generally speaking, during this period far fewer contests were organized in continental Greece than in Asia Minor, but they too seem to have peaked at approximately the same time—the second or first half of the third century CE—to judge from the large corpus of epigraphic documentation that survives. Contests seem to have continued through the middle of the third century when economic conditions allowed, but documentary sources for them have disappeared (Robert 1984: I.40; Spawforth 1989: 193–197; Vendries 1999: 270–271, 281–282): we mostly have information on athletic competitions in the late period (Gutsfeld 2013; Remijsen 2015). The Mouseia and Ptōia were part of this general trend and offer evidence on rhapsodes, in particular as regards the second century and the early third century. The Mouseia festival was organized by the Thespians in the temple of the Muses, located in the Valley of Helikon (Roux 1954; Schachter 1986: 147–153; C. Müller 1996). It had acquired great prestige after it was reorganized at the end of the third century BCE: it was penteteric (occurring every fifth year), thymelic (musical), dramatic (for actors), at least partly stephanitic (winners received wreaths), and isopythic (with the same status as the Pythian contest). In the course of the first two centuries of the empire, the contest was modernized in order to highlight its role in the Imperial cult, which could lend the festival greater prestige. Starting from about 20 CE, the program included encomium contests in honor of Iulia Sebasta (that is, Livia, the name given to her after the death of Augustus), assimilated with Mnemosyne, mother of the nine Helikonian Muses, and in honor of Roman benefactors (*AE* 1973: 494; *Teiresias* 6 (1976): E.76.48; Roesch 1982: 181 no. 2).[11] Plutarch states that in his time the contest remained penteteric and was well known (*Amatorius* 748E; cf. Pausanias 9.31.3). The Ptōia, which were reorganized at the end of the second century BCE, were thymelic, penteteric, and stephanitic, but lost much of their luster during the empire, and Plutarch mentions how deserted the temple of Apollo Ptōios had become (*De defectu oraculorum* 414A).

Festivals were discontinued as the empire entered its first years, most likely for economic reasons. Over the course of the first century CE, they were organized again sporadically by local patrons, before being reinstated at the end of the first or the beginning of the second century. Ptōia contests were then celebrated on a more regular basis from the end of the second century onward. At the beginning of the third century, the contests became, at least in part, thematic (winners got cash prizes), although it is difficult to understand why this change occurred.[12]

The lists of victors at the Mouseia and Ptōia show that rhapsodes were among the first to compete, according to a conventional sequence: first came the so-called introductory contest involving herald and trumpeter (in no set order); there followed, if they were included in the program, the poet, the rhapsode, and the aulete, who began the section of the contest dedicated to instrumental music. The rhapsode shared with the poet—especially the epic poet—the same function: that of magnifying and enhancing the object of their song (cf. Lucian *Zeus the Tragedian* 6.12). But in the Imperial period the poetry contest was sometimes not part of the program: the catalogues in *IG* VII 4151 and *IThesp* 180 do not include any. In the two catalogues of victors at the Mouseia dating from the second half of the second century (*IThesp* 178; 177), the poetry contest is coupled with a prose encomium contest, the event in each case sticking to the same sequence of performers: poet *prosodiou*, herald, trumpeter, encomiographer for the emperor, encomiographer for the Muses, poet for the emperor, poet for the Muses, rhapsode, pythaule, etc. Since Hesiod was honored in Thespiai, where a bronze statue had been erected in the agora, and in the temple of the Muses at Mount Helikon as the founder of the cult of the Muses, it is likely that the rhapsodes competing in the Mouseia recited excerpts from his poems rather than Homer's.[13] Two victors, Cornelius Eukarpos of Argos and M. Aurelius Eukairos of Tanagra, won a double victory at the Ptōia in both the herald and the rhapsode categories (*IG* VII 4151; 2726), a feat attributable to the fact that these two types of performance required an excellent voice. Pollux attests to the vocal qualities that heralds—responsible for announcing the contests, candidates, and winners, and especially well attested during the Roman period (Crowther 1994)—were expected to demonstrate (4.94). The rhapsode, too, was judged on the quality of his voice (West 2010a: 7, 9). In discussing the poems of the tyrant Dionysios, who asked the leading rhapsodes of his time to recite at the *panēgyris* of the Olympic contests, Diodorus underscores the audience's admiration for the *euphōnia* of the performers (*hypokritōn*) (14.109.1–2). These double victories may also highlight how difficult it was to enlist a significant number of competitors in the Ptōia by the end of the second century and throughout the third century CE.

The position of the rhapsode in the overall program and his relationship with the poet and the herald are indicative of his minor role in these competitions, as herald and trumpeter were the least prestigious categories of the contests (Crowther 1994: 135–155), with the encomiographer and poet warranting only a bit more consideration. Examining the prizes mentioned in the agonistic catalogues from Oinoanda in Lykia and Aphrodisias in Karia during the Imperial period, Michael Wörrle derives a hierarchy in which the encomiographer and the poet come just after the trumpeter and the herald, but win only half or less of the prize money awarded to the comic actor, the tragic actor, and the kitharode. This ranking seems to have emerged in the Hellenistic era, since it appeared at the beginning of the first century CE in connection with the Sarapieia at Tanagra (Wörrle 1988: 234–236). In essence, it was already implied in what Plato had to say about the taste of his contemporaries in the *Laws*, which dates from the middle of the fourth century BCE: adult audiences had a preference for tragic and comic actors, while rhapsodes had fallen out of favor (658d).

This shift appears at the Mouseia, too, for which two catalogues of victors for the same festival that took place at the end of the third century BCE have survived (*IThesp* 161 and 163, ca. 209 BCE; Manieri 2009: 374–378; Schachter 2010–2011: 52). Both contain the five stephanitic disciplines (epic poet, aulete, aulode, kitharist, and kitharode), but the second adds to the list of thymelic victors the herald or trumpeter, the rhapsode, and the epinikion poet. At a time when the contests were being reorganized, these additional disciplines were most likely nonstephanitic (Schachter 2010–2011: 36–38; Slater 2010: 274) and less prestigious than the others. The table of prizes awarded at the Eretrian Artemisia toward 340 BCE points in the same direction (*IG* XII.9 189.15–20): the three prizes for rhapsodes amounted to 120, 30, and 20 drachmas; to 110, 70, and 55 drachmas for kitharists; and 200, 150, and 100 drachmas for kitharodes (West 2010a: 6; Tsagalis, this volume, pp. 56–57). It is probable that rhapsodes came to be left out of contests in the Imperial period because of their lesser position. Plutarch (*Quaestiones convivales* 514C) and Lucian (*Menippos* 4.17) sometimes use the verb ῥαψωιδέω pejoratively, underscoring the repetitive and tiresome nature of the special style of recitation adopted by the rhapsodes—rhythmic, monotonous, and unmelodious—and implying that the genre had fallen out of favor with both the public at large and a number of *pepaideumenoi*.

The victors among the rhapsodes came from Boeotia, the Peloponnese, and Thessaly. One performer, known only by his patronymic (son of Philokrates), was Theban (*BCH* 44 [1920]: 262 no. 12). The last rhapsode for whom information remains, M. Aurelius Eukairos of Tanagra, was a two-time victor at the Ptōia (including a double victory in both the herald and rhapsode categories). He also won first place at the Mouseia, very close in time to his double victory at the Ptōia, sometime after 212 CE (*BCH* 27 [1903]: 297; *IThesp* 180; *IG* VII 2726; Strasser 2002: 112–124). Two other artists came from Corinth and Argos: Eutuchianos of Corinth and Cornelius Eukarpos of Argos (*IThesp* 178; *IG* VII 4151). An epitaph dating from the second or third century in honor of a rhapsode was found in Argos (*IG* IV 649). Another victor, whose name has been lost, came from Hypata in Thessaly (*IThesp* 177). So, whereas the Ptōia had only a local reach, the Mouseia attracted performers in all disciplines from the entire Greek world.

According to available records, the agonistic art of the rhapsodes appears to have constituted a specialization that was, in the Imperial era, specific to continental Greece, particularly Boeotia, and perhaps linked to the cult of the Muses and that of Apollo. The role of rhapsodes in worship seems to have been, initially at least, broader. In a corrupt passage, Athenaeus mentions a feast that no longer existed by the end of the fourth century BCE, during which rhapsodes would visit each deity and honor it by singing (7.275d). This role may have become more limited during the Hellenistic period, owing to the rhapsodes' repertoire, which mostly comprised epic poetry. In any event, the bulk of the evidence that we have for rhapsodic activity in the last two centuries BCE comes from the contests that took place in Boeotia (the Rhōmaia of Thebes, the Amphiaraia-Rhōmaia of Oropos, the Sōtēria and the Ptōia of Akraiphia, the Charitēsia of Orchomenos, the Sarapieia of Tanagra, and the Mouseia of Thespiai) (West 2010a: 8), and virtually all the other inscriptions collected by Martin West for the Hellenistic period refer to performances dedicated to Apollo (2010a: 7–8):

1. *IG* XI.2 105 (Delos, 284 BCE)
2. *BCH* 99 (1975): 102 fr. B (Rhodes, contest in honor of Apollo Erethimios, third century BCE)
3. *SEG* 1.187a; 18.230; 18.235; *GDI* 2563–2566 (Delphi, yearly Amphictyonic Sōtēria contests between ca. 262 and 252 BCE)
4. *SEG* 2.260.2, 2.260.5, 2.260.6; *FD* III 4.125, 4.126, 4.127, 4.128 (Delphi, penteteric Aetolian Sōtēria contests between ca. 244 and 207 BCE)

Furthermore, most rhapsodes who took part in contests in the second and first century BCE were from Boeotia (four from Thebes, one from Tanagra, one from Thespiai: six out of a total of fourteen) and Athens, which, under the Peisistratidai, had organized the Panathēnaia, the contest most closely associated with the recitation of Homeric poems (five rhapsodes out of fourteen) (cf. West 2010a: 3–5, 12). Dio Chrysostom underscores the importance of rhapsodes in Athenian education in Sokrates's time.[14]

Rhapsodes also came from cities that had a strong and long-standing relationship with the figures of Homer and Hesiod. I mentioned that Hesiod was honored in the temple of the Muses at Mount Helikon and in Thespiai. It is likely that there were two rhapsodes identified at Argos because the city still boasted a special relationship with Homer, even in the Imperial period: the *Iliad* refers to the king of Argos at one time as

Agamemnon (*Iliad* 1.30)[15] and at another time as Diomedes (*Iliad* 2.559–568).[16] The city housed a cult to Homer, as attested by two texts dating to the second or early third century CE (cf. Kimmel-Clauzet 2013: 207–209). According to the *Contest of Homer and Hesiod* (*Certamen*), the Argives initiated a civic cult to Homer, to give thanks for having been celebrated in book 2 of the *Iliad* (17–18, ed. Colonna). According to Aelian's *Varia historia*, the Argives associated Homer and Apollo in their sacrifices (9.15). Argos had a long-standing tradition of epic singers. Already in the Archaic period, it appears that a special category of these singers, the *arnōidoi*, sang any portion of the Homeric epics they wanted, in any order they wanted, as part of contests where the first prize was a lamb (*arnos*) (schol. Pindar *Nemean* 2.1d = Dionysios of Argos [between the fourth and third centuries BCE] *FGrH* 308 F 21).[17] Agamemnon is also presented as the king of "wealthy Corinth" in the Catalogue of Ships (*Iliad* 2.570–576), and perhaps a reason Corinth continued to produce rhapsodes is that it was attached to its highly prestigious mythical past. Argos, Cyprus—the island where the epitaph to Kilikas of Kition, a specialist in Homeric texts, was found—and Athens competed for the honor of being Homer's birthplace (*Greek Anthology* 16.295–298; Aulus Gellius 3.11.6; Pausanias 10.24.3 [on Cyprus's pretensions]).

We do not know in which non-agonistic contexts rhapsodes performed during the Imperial period. If we dismiss Erato, the musician friend of Plutarch who appears in the *Symposiacs* (645D, 736D), the only other reference to the presence of rhapsodes at banquets is given by Athenaeus (14.620a), but it is ambiguous: does οὐκ ἀπελείποντο δὲ ἡμῶν τῶν συμποσίων οὐδὲ ῥαψωιδοί mean that rhapsodes were physically present at Larensius's banquets, or that they were present only in the diners' conversation?

One interesting case that can provide insight into the context of the performances is that of Paion, from the Pamphylian city of Side in Asia Minor. We are well informed about the poet thanks to Louis Robert (1980: 10–20; cf. Bowie 1990: 65–66; Fein 1994: 118–126). Paion traveled to Thebes in Egypt, and two epigrams he composed, one in his own name and the other for Mettius—who was probably a Roman official who may have been his patron at one time—were to be found on the Colossus of Memnon. Paion was probably part of Mettius's retinue during the latter's visit to the Memnon. Since the first century CE, and most notably since Hadrian had traveled to Egypt in 130, the statue had become a tourist destination for soldiers, officials, and scholars. One Mettius Modestus may have been governor of Pamphylia around 130–131 (Eck 1983: 169, 171n415), but nothing in Paion's epigrams indicates that Paion and Mettius had accompanied Hadrian on his visit to the

Memnon (*pace* Robert 1980: 19–20). Around 142, Paion is mentioned in a decree by the *technitai* of Ephesos, who voted on his proposal to honor the benefactor Alkibiades of Nysa (Robert 1938; *IK* 11.1 no. 22, lines 1–6):

> Ε]ἰσηγησαμένου Ποπλίου Αἰλίου Πομπη[ϊανοῦ]
> Παίονος Σιδήτου καὶ Ταρσέ[ως] καὶ Ῥοδίο[υ,]
> [ποιη]τοῦ πλειστονείκου, μελοποιοῦ καὶ ῥαψ[ωιδοῦ]
> [θε]οῦ Ἁδριανοῦ θεολόγου ναῶν τῶν ἐν Π[εργάμωι,]
> [ἀγ]ωνοθέτου ἀποδεδειγμένου τῶν Σεβ[αστῶν]
> Πυθίων

> On the proposal of P. Aelius Pompeianus Paion of Side, Tarsos, and Rhodes, winner of many poetry contests, lyric poet and rhapsode, *theologos* of the god Hadrian in the temples of Pergamon, appointed *agōnothetēs* of contests of the Sebasta Pythia.
>
> (my translation)

Paion was a brilliant and renowned professional poet, who had achieved some degree of fame. He was a Roman citizen, most likely thanks to Hadrian, as the name Aelius and the *praenomen* Publius suggest. He was also a dignitary of the Imperial cult in Pergamon and, more precisely, was the θεολόγος attached to the temples of the Augusti, a title meaning "he who celebrates the deity." *Theologoi* were required to praise the gods and invoke them in their prose (Robert 1943: 185). Finally, Paion is described as having two specializations in poetry: "lyric poet and rhapsode."

This text can be interpreted in several ways. According to Robert, Paion was part of Hadrian's entourage and composed and/or recited for him lyric poems and the Homeric poems (1980: 17). Hermann Wankel understands the noun θεός preceding the name of the emperor to indicate that Paion served the Imperial cult as a rhapsode and lyric poet: he translates, "Komponist und Rhapsode (im Kult) des vergöttlichten Hadrian" (*IK* 11.1, p. 138). Paion could also glorify the emperor in those contests that were closely associated with the Imperial cult.[18] During the reign of Trajan, the *technitai* guilds had been reorganized into one universal synod under the dual patronage of Dionysos and the emperors. But the decree may be interpreted in a third way, as Simone Follet has suggested to me (pers. comm.): by removing the comma following Ἁδριανοῦ in line 4, one could take Paion as the θεολόγος of the god Hadrian at the temples of the Augusti in Pergamon. This interpretation is to be preferred to that of "rhapsode of the god Hadrian," a phrase not attested anywhere else.

In any case, even though the inscription emphasizes Paion's many victories, the secondary role of the poetic and rhapsodic contests makes it unlikely that they would have sufficed to bring him the renown implied in his being a citizen of multiple cities and in his role as θεολόγος and ἀγωνοθέτης. It is more likely that his success came from being under Hadrian's protection. Nor do we know much about Paion's rhapsodic performances, especially whether he recited his poems *hors concours*, as was customary at that time among the best poets and orators. That Paion produced hexametric poems is suggested by the title of "new Homer" bestowed upon him in a decree from Side in honor of his son (*ISide* 107, line 11).[19] Perhaps he even recited his own compositions, not those of Homer and other poets, particularly when not engaged in a contest. Paion's specialties are in line with what we know to have been Hadrian's tastes in literature, especially poetry. The emperor was attracted both by the archaic style—and I believe that rhapsodes practiced their art in this manner—and by the precursors of the *poetae novelli*, who cultivated metrical variety and followed popular trends (J.-W. Beck 2015). Indeed he brought under his protection Mesomedes of Crete, a lyric poet of greater renown than Paion, who had written, among other works, an encomium to Antinous (Fein 1994: 26, 47–60; cf. Bélis 2003; Whitmarsh 2004). There is also an obvious relationship between the rhapsodes' traditional activity and the glorification by the Greek city-states of their archaic and mythical roots, a movement institutionalized in 131–132 CE when the Panhellenion was established. A number of factors, then, came together to explain why, on account of Paion, the art of the rhapsodes briefly came back in fashion.

One wonders how other rhapsodes, whose names survive only in catalogues and in epitaphs, made a living. A partial answer may be found in the case of M. Aurelius Eukairos of Tanagra. He appears to have been a professional performer and boasted at least two specializations, that of rhapsode and that of herald. As Homerists, it is possible that a number of artists who shared the same repertoire, sound, and interpretative strategies developed several specialties—that is, as rhapsodes, tragic or comic actors, and mimes or pantomimes—which would have enabled them to live from their art.[20]

CONCLUSION

The art of the rhapsodes at the time of the early Roman Empire appears to have been an archaizing trend, the term "rhapsode" disappearing altogether by late antiquity, with the exception of its use by Diomedes Grammaticus. Although the specificity of Boeotian records may introduce a bias, sources seem to agree that rhapsodes' agonistic activity was by then limited to two penteteric contests in Boeotia—the Mouseia and the Ptōia—and their role in worship reduced to honoring the Muses of Mount Helikon, Apollo, and the emperors. The tradition of the rhapsodes seems to have mostly been preserved by those cities in continental Greece that were closely associated with Homer and the Homeric poems, such as Argos and Corinth, or with Hesiod, like Thespiai. In a way, the presence of rhapsodes confirmed the fact that these links were old. The lack of documentary sources may distort the picture, but no records exist as regards Athenian rhapsodes in the Imperial period, even though they had been one of Athens' specialties since the end of the Archaic era. The very term "rhapsode" is only to be found in agonistic catalogues and appears to have been rarely used. Perhaps it was subsumed under the more general category of "Homerist." Rhapsodes were reduced to a minor branch of Homeric performers. In order to survive, they had to diversify their skill set and perform as heralds, poets, actors, or dancers.

By the Imperial era, although literary sources still use the label "Homeric" when referring to them, rhapsodes had become a secondary conduit for Homer's poetry. They lost their educational role in the Classical period, when the *Iliad* and to a lesser extent the *Odyssey* became textbooks used in schools and when their other traditional functions—recounting a glorious historical past and praising a city-state or an aristocrat—faced competition from many other sources: actors, poets, and orators as well as inscriptions, statues, and coins. At the time of the early Roman empire, Homeric performances had essentially become the prerogative of other Homerists—actors, mimes, and pantomimes, who came to be included in official performances and contests in the second century CE, so popular had they become—and naturally of sophists, who energetically exploited Homeric myths and poems.

NOTES

I wish to extend my heartfelt thanks to Jean-Yves Strasser, Jonathan Ready, and Christos Tsagalis for reviewing my chapter and sharing some helpful comments and to Christophe Vendries for his suggestions. Many thanks also to my translator, Odile Montpetit.

1. Burkert comments on the link between rhapsodes and Homer: "It is clear that this name [Homer] is the trademark on which the rhapsodes were professionally dependent; no wonder they were engaged in Homeric propaganda" (1987: 49).

2. Sykutris identified Kilikas as a teacher whose epitaph was composed by a

pupil (1928; followed by Oziol in Yon 2004: 279). Tsopanakis constructs lines 3 and 4 as follows: K. μετέπρεπε δεικνὺς ἠνορέην προτέρων ἡρώων ἐν ὁμηρείαις σελίδεσσιν (1984: 398 no. 31). For reasons having to do with the coherence of both verse and line, it does not seem logical to separate ἐν ὁμηρείαις σελίδεσσιν from δεικνύς. However, as observed by Sykutris, the language used in the epigram seems constrained, and so the position of the phrase ἐν ὁμηρείαις σελίδεσσιν, in my view, seems less crucial than the meaning of δεικνύς. The name Kilikas is attested in Cyprus: Fraser, Matthews, Osborne et al. 1987: 255.

3. On Homerists/actors, see Husson 1993; Nagy 1996b: 158–186; Hillgruber 2000; Garelli-François 2000: 504–506; González 2013: 447–465.

4. *Contra* Nagy 1996b: 158–186, according to whom the term "Homerist" emerged in connection with the reform introduced by Demetrios of Phaleron, who set up a body of artists specializing in Homer and henceforth having a more professional status supervised by the state. Homerists in the Imperial period would have been their distant descendants.

5. In the *skēnikoi*, or "dramatic" contests, actors would perform from the *skēnē*.

6. This is assuming that these examples are not drawn from Aristocles's *On Choruses* (end of the second century BCE). Relying on a list of victors at the Sōtēria of Delphi and at the Lēnaia, Bonaria suggests situating the actors sometime in the middle of the third century BCE (1965), but this too is highly speculative, in particular as regards Hermophantos (Stephanis 908), who was identified as a comic actor who won the Lēnaia around 250 BCE (Capps 1900: 134–135). It must be recalled that Athenaeus does not specify that Hermophantos was a comic actor.

7. On this subject and the opposition between traditional epics and Callimachean aesthetics, see Pallone 1984.

8. By having more than one specialty, performers could meet the requirements of several categories and thus make a living, but it was rare for musicians taking part in sacred festivals to combine specialties, given the high standards required.

9. For a discussion of creative improvisation in rhapsodic performance, see Collins 2001a.

10. Pallone 1984: 160–161: in the fifth and fourth centuries BCE, there are references to an epic poet at the Lysandreia of Samos, to "epic-rhapsodic" contests at the Asklēpeia of Epidaurus, the Panathēnaia of Athens, and the Naia of Dodona, to rhapsodes taking part in contests at the Artemisia of Eretria, and to performances by rhapsodes at Olympia; in the third century BCE: presence of rhapsodes at the Sōtēria of Delphi; in the second century BCE: presence of rhapsodes and epic poets at the Sōtēria of Delphi; between the third and first centuries BCE: presence of rhapsodes and epic poets at the Mouseia of Thespiai; between the second and first centuries BCE: presence of rhapsodes and epic poets at the Ptōia of Akraiphia; from the end of the second to the beginning of the first century BCE: reference to epic poets at the Sarapieia of Tanagra; from the end of the second to the beginning of the first century BCE:

reference to rhapsodes and epic poets at the Agriōnia of Thebes; between the second and first centuries BCE: presence of mostly Athenian epic poets and rhapsodes at the festival in honor of Pythian Apollo at Delphi; first century BCE: presence of epic poets and rhapsodes at the Amphiaraia of Oropos and at the Charitēsia of Orchomenos. See also Chaniotis 2010: 259–262, who adds the Megala Erethimia in Rhodes (third century BCE), the Artemisia in Amarynthos (first century BCE), the Basileia of Lebadeia (second century BCE), the Rhōmaia of Oropos and Thebes (late second and first century BCE).

11. On how the Mouseia evolved and were organized, see Jamot 1895: 363–366; Feyel 1942: 88–132; Roesch 1965: 225–229; Schachter 1986: 163–179, 2010–2011: 29–47; Knoepfler 1996.

12. On the Ptōia, see Holleaux 1890: 59–64, 200–203; Feyel 1942: 133–147; Lauffer 1959; Schachter 1981: 70–73 *s.v.* "Apollo Ptōios"; Roesch 1982: 225–243. On references to a prize (*thema*) in agonistic catalogues, see *BCH* 14 (1890): 190–191, no. 21, line 15 (before 212); *BCH* 27 (1903): 297–299, col. A, lines 11–12 (shortly after 212). On prizes awarded at contests, see Slater 2010 (esp. 274–275 on the Mouseia).

13. Thespiai was located five miles east of Askra, birthplace of Hesiod (in ruins in the second century [Pausanias 9.29.2]). On the honoring of Hesiod: *IG* VII 4240 (stele dedicated to the Muses honoring Hesiod, Thespiai, end of the third century BCE); *IG* VII 1785 (stone marker for a religious association dedicated to the Hesodian Muses[?], Μωσά[ων τ]ῶν Εἰσιοδείων, Thespiai); Pausanias 9.27.5, 30.2–3, 31.3–5; Calame 1996: 43–56; Beaulieu 2004: 103–117; Kimmel-Clauzet 2013: 218–223.

14. Dio Chrysostom *Orationes* 13.17: "Will not a much more ridiculous society be made by these teachers of your children of whom I speak—I mean the gymnastic masters, the cithara players, and the schoolmasters, including the rhapsodists and the actors?" (trans. Cohoon). Cf. Lucian *Anacharsis* 21, in which Solon describes the education of adolescents in Athens: "As they progress, we recite [ῥαψωιδοῦμεν] for them sayings of wise men, deeds of olden times, and helpful fictions, which we have adorned with metre that they remember them better. Hearing of certain feats of arms and famous exploits, little by little they grow covetous and are incited to imitate them, in order that they too may be sung and admired by men of after time. Both Hesiod and Homer have composed much poetry of that sort for us" (trans. Harmon). See also Isocrates *Panegyricus* 159. Plutarch mentions, in relation to Kimon's time, an inscription on a herm in the Stoa of Hermes in Athens that referred to the encomium for Menestheus, king of Athens, in the Catalogue of Ships (*Iliad* 2.552–554), as a result of which he formulates an overall judgment on the value of Athenians (*Cimon* 7.6).

15. Cf. Dio Chrysostom *Orationes* 7.119: "Nor shall the poor become harpers or flute-players contending for victory in the theatres, even if we shall offend certain distinguished cities by so doing, cities such as Smyrna or Chios, for example, and, of course, Argos too, for not permitting the glory of Homer and Agamemnon to be magnified, at least as far as we can help it" (trans. Cohoon).

16. On the partition of the Argolid between Agamemnon and Diomedes

and the latter's presence in Argos, see Burkert 1998: 51–53. On the importance of Diomedes in Argos in the fifth century BCE, see Pindar *Nemean* 10.7. See also Herodotus 5.67 on the ban on rhapsodic performances at Sikyon at the beginning of the sixth century BCE, because rhapsodes singing *Homereia epea* were praising Argos, which was at war with Sikyon.

17. On the Homeric tradition in Argos, see Burkert 1972a: 189–194, 1998: 56–58.

18. I mentioned that in the Imperial period the Mouseia included encomia and poetry contests celebrating Livia or the emperor. In the second half of the second century, an agonistic catalogue refers to them as "Traiana Hadriana Sebasta Mouseia" (*IThesp* 177), and soon after 212, they are described as "Kaisareia Sebasta Mouseia" (*IThesp* 180). See also the "Ptōia (kai) Kaisareia" (*IG* VII 2712, after 212).

19. Paion is also qualified as a *philokaisar*, thus underscoring his relationship—personal or tied to his role in the imperial cult—with the imperial house (Robert 1980: 13).

20. *P.Oxy.* III 519 states the payment of a Homerist who performed at a celebration in Oxyrhynchus in the second century CE. The salary he received was quite high, 448 drachmas, which is a little less than the mime (496 drachmas), but much more than the dancer (between 100 and 200 drachmas).

CHAPTER FIVE

Formed on the Festival Stage: Plot and Characterization in the Iliad *as a Competitive Collaborative Process*

MARY R. BACHVAROVA

OVER A HUNDRED YEARS AGO, WALTER LEAF BEGAN the "Prolegomena" of his commentary to the *Iliad* with the observation, "It is impossible to approach either the textual criticism or the exegesis of Homer without some theory as to the way in which the *Iliad* and *Odyssey* reached their present form" (1900: xiii). Martin West's recent addition to the scholarly conversation on the origin of the Homeric poems, *The Making of the Iliad: Disquisition and Analytical Commentary* (2011a), follows through on this premise in detail, dissecting the *Iliad* line by line with the presumption that it was the product of a single poet ("P") who rethought, reshaped, and expanded his text as he wrote it by reworking and adding lines and episodes. In this chapter I take a different approach: I argue that the repurposing of episodes, the diversions off the straight narrative path, and the nuanced characterization of the heroes on both sides of the conflict—all of which have exercised generations of critics of the *Iliad* before West—cater to an aesthetic originating in a festival setting in which bards competed by performing one after another discrete episodes and which I localize in time and space to the pre-eighth-century BCE Troad.[1]

I refer here not merely to the practice of composition in performance but to competitive collaboration in which multiple bards compete at a festival, each performing different episodes from the same epic tradition, but not necessarily in a fixed order. They may choose to perform an episode for which they are famous or to respond to the previous bard's performance, and they are free to reorient the viewpoint of the narration to fit their own perspective and local allegiance. They thus create a ver-

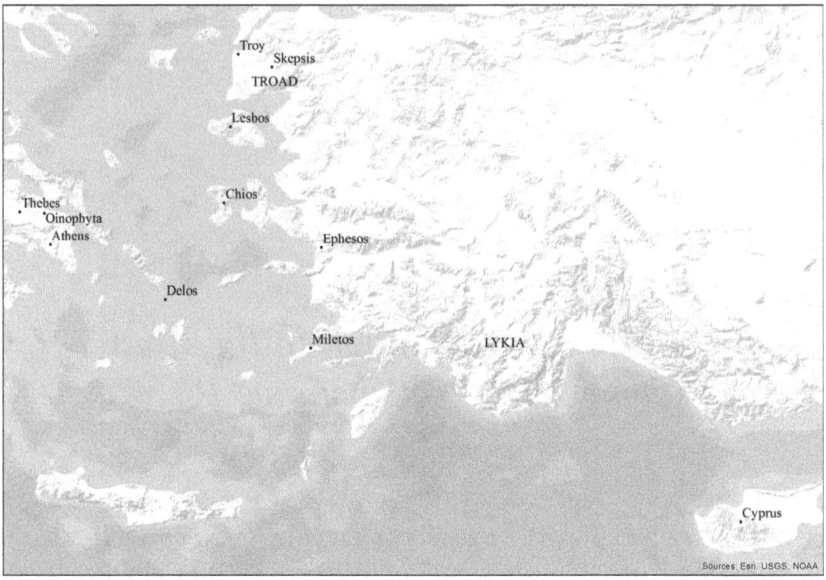

MAP 5.1. *The Iron Age Aegean*

sion of the narrative that lacks the internal cohesion modern readers expect from a story, but has great richness of texture. I first discuss ethnographic evidence from central Asia for performing discrete episodes from an epic tradition in festival settings and then the evidence from ancient Greek texts for similar performances. Afterward I move on to explaining some episodes in the *Iliad* in light of an aesthetic that derives from the appreciation of serial performances of episodes in a single epic tradition by multiple bards, and I suggest we can see the impact of a festival regulation of the type that ancient authorities attributed to the Panathēnaia in respect to the *Iliad*. I next argue that a bardic version of the sympotic practice of capping—picking up and completing a discourse unit left incomplete by the previous performer—also played a role in early epic performances. Finally, I suggest that the characterization and recharacterization of Hektor presented in the *Iliad* originated as the natural by-product of the various allegiances of bards performing in the Troad before the story of the fall of Troy dominated the festival stage of the Panionia. The *Iliad* makes stylized use of an established technique to deepen our sympathies for the Trojan hero while maintaining a certain distance on his suffering.

EPISODIC PERFORMANCES OF EPICS: ETHNOGRAPHIC PARALLELS

By looking for a modern counterpart to a monumental "Homer" imagined as a single bard able to produce via composition in performance a text of many thousands of lines, ethnographers have biased the comparative data that Homerists in turn have used to reconstruct the original performance context shaping the oral tradition out of which the extant Homeric epics emerged. The best bard has been defined as the one who could produce the longest, most comprehensive version of the epic in question, even though some scholars have acknowledged the difficulty of performing epics of the length of the *Iliad* and the *Odyssey* from end to end (Jensen 1980: 33–40; Ford 1997: 83–89). For instance, Minna Skafte Jensen provides examples of lengthy written epics that are products of scholars aggregating traditional material (1980: 33), and she notes several situations in which singers were pushed to produce the longest, most "complete" version possible and found it a daunting task (2011: 281–294), while Dwight Reynolds, when describing his procedure for recording the Arabic epic *Sirat Bani Hilal*, states, "Although in living memory no poet of al-Bakātūsh had ever undertaken to sing the epic from 'beginning to end,' I initiated my fieldwork by requesting a poet to do so" (1995: 19).

However, modern ethnographic parallels from central Asia for Homeric performances suggest that performances of an entire epic by a single bard were not the norm—nor was performance of the entire epic end to end by a series of bards participating in a festival—and that each bard's performance would not have taken many hours. With regard to Turkmen epic performances, for example, the norm is often performance of single episodes (Kurbanova 2000: 123). Daniel Prior notes about the performance of the Kyrgyz *Manas* epic in the 1930s, "It was a time-consuming labor for a bard to keep his whole epic repertoire up to date with the changing tastes of audiences and patrons. Short episodes were easier to keep in trim, and the effort saved could be expended on playing for virtuosity" (2000: 35). That bards could be associated with specific episodes is indicated by Reynold's comment about performers of *Sirat Bani Hilal*: "One interesting aspect shared by both coffeehouses and patronage circuits is that audiences in particular locales apparently often ask the visiting poet for the same episode, year after year—perhaps owing to the pleasure of knowing and anticipating the story, perhaps owing to an association built up between certain poets and certain tales" (1995: 116).

To be sure, modern audiences of traditional epic value sheer quantity. The length of the Kyrgyz epic *Manas* is a point of pride, as is that of the inner Asian *Gesar Ling*.[2] Moreover, a traveling bard dependent on local hospitality may wish to leave his audience in suspense at the end of one night's performance to ensure they will come back for more, a gambit attempted by Odysseus at the Phaiakian court: he tries to break off his story, pleading the need to sleep, but accepts his audience's urging to continue (*Odyssey* 11.330–332, 379–384). Such a strategy could create the expectation of episodes being performed in order.

However, there is another way of performing an oral epic: in a competitive festival setting, different bards might contribute different episodes—not the entire epic—when competing for a prize or simply to produce the best version possible, with each contributing what he is best known for. I saw this type of performance on television in Kyrgyzstan in the summer of 1995 as part of the celebration of the one-thousandth anniversary of *Manas*, yet I have found only brief mentions of it in the scholarly literature (Thompson et al. 2006: 182; van der Heide 2015: 130). Competitive performance of sections of *Manas* has been a long-standing tradition, part of the competitive ethos endemic to the nomadic cultures of central Asia (van der Heide 2015: 159, references omitted):

> The Soviet Union organised Manas competitions, where many Manaschïs were brought together to recite and be judged by a jury. Before the Soviet Union, the concept of competition was not unknown to poets and improvisers. In a so-called *aitïsh*, poets challenged each other to outwit one another in sharp and smart improvisations. In a Manas *aitïsh*, one Manaschï started a recital, that was followed up by another and if present, yet another.

Such contests have remained important in the formation and reputation of *manaschïlar*, although modern competitions lack the same level of improvisation that had allowed a *manaschï* to respond to the previous performers (van der Heide 2015: 160):

> The Manaschï competitions of the Soviet era were quite different from the old *aitïsh*, however. When I asked Talantaalï Bakchiev if this kind of competitions [*sic*] actually fitted the Manas, he said that the modern version was not right (*tuura emes*). In the new form, every narrator prepares their own piece beforehand, unlike at the old *aitïsh*, when recitals arose from interaction between participating Manaschïs.

Whereas these Kyrgyz performances tend to have a competitive component, according to the Kalmyk bard Nyamin Mandzhaiev the performance of the Kalmyk national epic *Džangar* is more of a collaborative enterprise. Recently deceased in his nineties, Mandzhaiev was a well-known *džangarči* and remembered the pre-Soviet era. According to him, *džangarčnr* would each perform their signature pieces at festivals, and in that way they would achieve the best performance possible of the entire epic.[3]

EPISODIC PERFORMANCE OF HEXAMETRIC NARRATIVES IN FESTIVAL SETTINGS

The evidence from the hexametric texts in the Homeric dialect indicates not only the existence of a competitive context but that bards' performances were relatively short and episodic (Tsagalis, this volume, p. 50). Outside of the two monumental epics attributed to Homer, the scale of hexametric narratives is much smaller. Hesiod's *Works and Days* and *Theogony* comprise respectively 826 and 1,013 lines. Homeric hymns, which introduced another performance by asking for the support of a particular divinity, were not so long as to require a subsequent epic performance, which we would expect to be proportionately longer than the introductory hymn, to reach monumental length.[4] Among the longer examples, the *Homeric Hymn to Aphrodite* (*Homeric Hymn* 6) has fewer than 300 lines; the hymns to Hermes (*Homeric Hymn* 4) and Demeter (*Homeric Hymn* 2) each have fewer than 600 lines. The *Homeric Hymn to Apollo* (*Homeric Hymn* 3), which appears to combine what were originally two separate hymns to the Delian and the Pythian variants of Apollo (Tsagalis, this volume, p. 55) and thus presents one possible result of a collaborative performance stitching together a song (schol. Pindar *Nemean* 2.1d = Philochorus *FGrH* 328 F 212, Hesiod fr. 297 Most), is still fewer than 600 lines long.

Rhapsodic performance was serial or sequenced (schol. D *Iliad* 1.604 [van Thiel]; Collins 2004: 169–175; González 2013: 383–392), although scholars have interpreted "serially" differently, some arguing that the serial performance did not necessarily follow the order of the narrative (Collins 2004: 193n4, 200–201), others that the storyline was continued from where the previous singer left off (Nagy 1996b: 71–73; González 2013: 372–375). However, Hellenistic scholars referred to another type of competition in which each of the competitors, called *arnōidoi* ("singers for a lamb"), sang whatever piece they wanted (schol. Pindar *Nemean*

2.1d = Dionysius of Argos *FGrH* 308 F 2), indicating that a bardic competition did not necessarily follow the sequencing rule. Rather than sing pieces that built a larger, coherently structured song, each bard could choose his favorite episode, as seen in the capping game between Homer and Hesiod in *Vita* 1 West (*Certamen*), which ends with each reciting "the most beautiful of his own poems."[5] Hesiod provides a section of the *Works and Days* (383–392) and Homer some bits from the *Iliad* (13.126–133, 339–344; *Vita* 1.12).[6] The following discussion excavates traces of this second type of performance in the *Iliad*.

TRACES OF EPISODIC PERFORMANCE IN THE *ILIAD*

As Plato points out (*Ion* 535b1–c3), some episodes or passages of the *Odyssey* and the *Iliad* are more thrilling (Odysseus revealing himself to the suitors before he slaughters them) or moving (the laments of Andromache, Hekabe, and Priam). Even if in a festival competition bards were expected at least nominally to pick up where the last left off, they likely would have manipulated the narrative so that they could perform what they considered their best piece or what would most please the audience. The Panathenaic regulation attributed to Hipparchos (Tsagalis, this volume, pp. 49–52), which "forced the rhapsodes in the Panathēnaia to go through them [the Homeric epics] in relay, in order [*ex hupolēpseōs ephexēs*]" ([Plato] *Hipparchus* 228b8–9, see Nagy 2002: 9–15, 42–47), suggests that episodic performances were at that point considered a problem in need of rectification. Perhaps a new aesthetic had developed in Athens, seen in the exclusively Attic performance genre of tragedy (note Phrynichus's early sixth-century date), which demanded a new kind of cause-and-effect coherence and thus replaced the older aesthetic that I argue remains evident in the *Iliad*. Furthermore, if a written text needed to be made in the time of the Peisistratidai to cross-check the rhapsodes (Jensen 1980: 128–158, 2011: 295–328), then presumably they were working hard to circumvent the rule.

Moreover, what does "in order" mean with respect to a genre in which, of the only two extant representatives, both start *in medias res*, and one allows Odysseus to tell over the course of four books a much earlier set of episodes, while the other tells of not the beginning, middle, and end of the ten-year Trojan War but a mere few days of battle? What does "in order" mean for a genre whose two representatives are built out of episodes that are not necessarily connected? As Aristotle says (*Poetics* 1455b),

> In dramas the episodes [*epeisodia*] are brief, while it is by means of them that epic is made long. For the story [*logos*] of the *Odyssey* is not long; someone is away from home many years and pursued closely by Poseidon and is on his own. Furthermore, the situation at home is such that his goods are being devastated by suitors and his son is plotted against, but he himself arrives after a stormy journey, and having brought about a recognition, saves himself and kills his enemies. So this is the core of the story [*to idion*], while the rest is episodes.

What Aristotle saw in the *Odyssey*—the use of extraneous episodes to create an interplay between retardation and forward movement of the plot—critics have held up as one of the great achievements of the Iliadic narrative (Kirk 1962: 337–354). In the late 1800s and early 1900s, however, Analysts worked to separate out layers of accretions and even to excise material they deemed later interpolations into Homer's genuine text (West 2011a: 51–62). Even among Analysts, what is the core of the epic and what is a later addition have not been universally agreed upon. For example, Ulrich von Wilamowitz-Moellendorff saw books 12–15 as the original layer, with 12.199–289, 430–471, 13.39–154, 802–837, and book 14 being the "Hektorgedichte" (1920: 232–235, 514–515, 591), while West considers books 1, 2, 11, and 16 to be the "primary layer" (2011a). Some critics argue that a single poet added the episodes to his work, either inspired to create a work of monumental size in the one-off effort of dictating for posterity or, as West has argued, by revising his written work over time, a process easy for a modern author using a word processor, but more difficult, he admits, for a man editing the written text either by means of dictating to an amanuensis or by annotating a papyrus scroll that was then recopied by a scribe (West 2011a: 14).[7] Some Analysts imagined the piecing together of different layers, possibly extolling different heroes, such as Achilleus, Diomedes, or Hektor (von Wilamowitz-Moellendorff 1920), while for West the most efficient telling of the story was the first intent of "P" and secondary embellishments deepened the meaning and effect as P rethought his oeuvre in the making (2011a). Others have accepted the obvious digressions (other than the *Doloneia* of book 10) as genuine and have argued that the apparent inconsistencies were a hallmark of oral composition in performance.

What has not been recognized is that the positive aesthetic valuation of including set pieces in the narrative that are not necessary to move the plot forward comes out of the performance of episodes of the *Iliad* by poets in a festival setting, a collaborative enterprise that created a sum that was more than its parts, as Aristotle appositely said (*Metaphysics* 1045a), and whose parts did not need to cohere with the logical tightness Aristotle found so compelling in the plotting of the best tragedies. When it was his turn to perform, a bard could still insert an episode that, while not furthering the plot, did not conflict with the overall trajectory, as with the *Doloneia*. Or, if he were ordered to keep to the timeline set by the previous performer, the bard could jump forward or back by embedding a story told by an intradiegetic narrator, as in books 9–12 of the *Odyssey*. Or, he could adapt a storyline to a different set of characters, such as the sequence used for the duel between Memnon and Achilleus, which in the *Iliad* has been attached to the sequence of duels between Patroklos and Sarpedon, and then Hektor and Patroklos, as a way of incorporating an evidently popular plot sequence that the audience would have recognized as belonging to a later episode in the Trojan War. Certainly both the death of Memnon and duels involving Patroklos were made up of traditional motifs, but the avoidance of mentioning Memnon seems purposeful and shows the *Iliad*'s awareness of the Memnon story (M. Edwards 1991: 18–19, 316; Kullmann 2015; Davies 2016: 3–24). The conclusion to be drawn is that the audience too would have been aware of and appreciated the clever recasting of an episode for which Memnon was known.

Or, perhaps the bard would recast a set piece to fit a different place in the narrative timeline, as Prior speculated about one version of *Manas* (2000: 20):

> Sagïmbay thought out the arrangement of episodes, and started from the beginning: Manas's Birth. Four years later he had barely finished the final episode, the Great Campaign to China, before sickness made him quit. His version of *Semetey*, on which he had earned his name, did not make it onto paper. Or did it—? In the Great Campaign episode, Sagïmbay narrates a dramatic river-crossing scene using language closely paralleling that of other bards' narrations of a similar river-crossing scene in *Semetey*. Did Sagïmbay try to memorialize a bit of his famous *Semetey* by interpolating it into his last *Manas*-sessions, knowing that the time had run out?

Such recasting could explain the oddities of book 3 of the *Iliad*, which reads as an epyllion recounting the early days of the war on the Skamandrian plain, telling of a single combat between Paris and Menelaos aborted by Aphrodite before her protégé could be killed and thus setting the stage for a protracted siege (Jamison 1994: 5–7; West 2011a: 127–128). It portrays as recent events the failed embassy of Agamemnon and Odysseus that led the Achaians to the walls of Troy in the first place as well as the judgment of Paris, which was the ultimate cause of Helen's departure from Menelaos's palace. It brings Helen to the walls of Troy to display her beauty to the Trojan elders, who act as if they have never seen her before, and to have her answer Priam's questions about the identity of the warriors on the opposing side, although he should have long since figured out who they are. The *Iliad*, then, shows the effect of the kind of regulation claimed for the Panathēnaia, or at least of the aesthetics that would arise from such a regulation.

The number of scenes that could be explained as episodes included in our *Iliad* because they were crowd pleasers, whether or not they furthered the action, just as they would have been at a festival where multiple bards performed their most successful pieces, is easily multiplied. The duel between Aias and Hektor in book 7 is one example. Whereas Leaf saw the duel in book 7 as a later addition (1900: 296–297), Geoffrey Kirk shows that a "copy–model" relationship is not supportable; each draws on a type scene (1978; cf. 1990: 230–231). West, however, sees the episode as a pedestrian reworking of the duel in book 3 and the meeting between Glaukos and Diomedes in book 6 and suggests P must have selected Aias as Hektor's opponent because no one else could be (2011a: 189, 191, 194). All ignore the popularity of the confrontation in Archaic art (Burgess 2001: 54–55, 67; González 2013: 49–52). As mentioned earlier, the *Doloneia* has been singled out as an interpolation that is forgotten as soon as book 10 ends, but it has been rehabilitated as a representative of a traditional "nocturnal ambush" storyline (Dué and Ebbott 2010). In other words, the *Doloneia* was a popular set piece embedded in the Greek bardic tradition, rather than a late invention.

Of course, evidence from Greek epic that could provide us with such traditional scenes for comparison is scanty, but cognate Old Indic literature and the Near Eastern epic traditions with which the bards responsible for the Homeric tradition were in close contact in Anatolia and Cyprus (Bachvarova 2016) give us further comparanda for key episodes that were included as old favorites, although not furthering the basic plot of the *Iliad*. For example, the digression in book 3 allowed for the incorporation of an episode with roots in the Greco-Anatolian epic tradition going back prior to the Iliadic story itself. Stephanie Jamison shows that the *teichoskopia*, the oath-swearing ceremony for the truce that allowed for the single combat, and the duel itself represent a connected set of events with parallels to the wife-napping of Draupadi in the *Maha-*

bharata (1994). The narration thus both retains an old narrative sequence and contains "a number of set-piece ideas which occur separately and with a different purpose elsewhere" (M. Edwards 1987a: 56–57). Jamison concludes, they "belong to an inherited Indo-European narrative pattern that has its roots in a particular societal institution—the fine line between legal and illegal abduction in the typology of Indo-European marriage" (1994: 16).

In book 5 the narrative shifts to Diomedes's *aristeia*, which allows not only for the glorification of an Argive hero who must have had some independent importance and then was pulled into the Trojan War storyline (Burgess 2001: 84–85) along with the incorporation of motifs that could otherwise have been attached to Achilleus (Kullmann 1960: 85–89; Lang 1995: 154–156) but also for the introduction of an old and popular Near Eastern episode, the narrative sequence of a goddess insulted by a hero who then returns to her parents to complain. It is first attested in the Sumerian *Gilgamesh and the Bull of Heaven* (written down around 1900 BCE) and was incorporated into the Akkadian *Epic of Gilgamesh*, there linked to the goddess of sex and war Ishtar. The storyline was also attached to the Ugaritic goddess Anat in *Aqhat* (Burkert 1992: 96–99; West 1997: 361–362). While in the Near Eastern epics the goddess gets her way, in the *Iliad* Aphrodite, after failing to rescue Aineias from Diomedes, is mocked with pointed comments by Zeus and Athena, who has taken on the warrior side of the Mesopotamian goddess, drawing attention to the change in the narrative required because Aphrodite was allowed to assimilate only Ishtar's sexual side (Bachvarova 2016: 325–326).

Similarly, in book 14, the seduction of Zeus episode—which follows a sequence also found in the *Homeric Hymn to Aphrodite*—has strong parallels both with early second-millennium Sumerian stories about Inanna dressing and ornamenting herself to play the innocent maiden for her bridegroom (West 1997: 203–205, 382–384) and with the seduction episode in the Hurro-Hittite *Song of Hedammu* in which Anzili, the sister of the Storm-God, beautifies herself to seduce and put to sleep the Storm-God's rival, the sea-snake Hedammu, son of the Sea-God (see Bachvarova in López-Ruiz 2017: 165–167). In the *Iliad* Hera, both wife and sister to Zeus, seduces and puts to sleep the Greek storm-god so that the Greek sea-god Poseidon can aid the Achaians. In order to do so, she tricks Aphrodite with a lying tale to obtain her magical girdle (Burkert 1992: 91–93; West 1997: 147). As with the episode in which Diomedes wounds Aphrodite, the reworking of the inherited material seems pointed, exactly what Mark Griffith has shown we should expect to come out of the competitive ethos endemic in the poetic performances of ancient Greece: "rivalry with one's peers and—especially—

predecessors, in the form of allusion, reworking and improvement . . . operates as a keen stimulus to refinement and innovation, and can often take the form of a kind of obligatory 'parricide'" (1990: 191).

The realization that such reworking conforms to the aesthetic standards of an audience used to performances of various episodes from the epic tradition by multiple bards in competition with each other allows us to recast the Neoanalytic approach to the Homeric texts, "the method of explaining sections of the *Iliad* as semi-rigid adaptations of motifs taken over from older epic contexts; and, increasingly broadly, the examination of the relationship of the content of the *Iliad* . . . to the epic tradition as a whole" (Kullmann 2015: 112). The adaptations can be seen as an outgrowth of competitive exploitation at the level of episodes of traditional referentiality. Michael Nagler has shown that the repeated use and reworking of formulas, motifs, and type scenes were not simply mechanical by-products of composition in performance but allowed for deep resonances to be felt by competent audience members who found their expectations confirmed, challenged, or confounded and were acutely sensitive to minor deviations in wording (1974: esp. 62–63). As John Miles Foley frames it, "Formulas and themes . . . not only contain information and determine the perception or reception of the whole. The fixity of the relationship between metonyms and their inherent meanings is a measure of the wonderfully fertile prescriptiveness of traditional structures as cognitive categories" (1991: 60).

Analogously, the recasting of episodes was more than an attempt to squeeze in a known sequence out of its normal place. When the Diomedes and Aphrodite episode was first recast to fit a Greek goddess, or the seduction of Zeus storyline was pulled out of the theogonic tradition into the story of the fall of Troy, the original audience who knew the earlier version could appreciate the recasting. Similarly, an audience who recognized an episode as being displaced from its original location in the Trojan War storyline would appreciate the joke, as it were. I suggest that repurposing episodes was already a well-appreciated practice even before bards were expected to conform relatively closely to the narrative thread in order to give the festival audience a coherent telling of at least a section of the overall plot.

CAPPING AMONG BARDS IN COMPETITIVE COLLABORATIVE PERFORMANCES OF EPIC

Derek Collins compares the rhapsodic picking up of the epic narrative "by cue" (*ex hupobolēs*, Diogenes Laertius 1.57 = Dieuchidas of Megara *FGrH* 485 F 6) to the improvisatory capping game of sympotic *skolia* that Homer and Hesiod play in the *Certamen* (2004: 84–98, 194–199). The *skolion* is one example of "overtly confrontational and antithetical forms of composition" (Griffith 1990: 192) in which a line of poetry offered by one contestant is finished in such a way as to change the direction of its meaning, similar to one type of Turkic *aitïsh* contest (Collins 2001a: 145–146). Capping is not attested until a later period, but it seems the Homeric audience was accustomed to such games, appreciating the retardations and changes in plot direction that distinguish the *Iliad*. This ethos of responding to and topping the previous speaker appears in the battlefield boasting of Iliadic warriors (Martin 1989: 67–88; Griffith 1990: 192; Parks 1990), and Richard Martin posits that the competitive exchanges of the characters within the *Iliad* match the competition among bards to present the most authoritative version of the *Iliad* (1989: 238). For him, the bard's product is an entire epic, the longer the better (Martin 1989: 220–230, 238–239). I would argue, rather, that the competitive back and forth among characters mimics the serial performance in festivals in which each bard responds to and attempts to top the previous performer.

The narration tends to call attention to the changes in direction and the need to divert from a dead end, such as a major character dying before his time or the sacking of Troy before its time, through the use of a contrafactual statement (for example, *Iliad* 7.104–106, 21.516–517; see N. Richardson 1993: 97). Or, the narration will move to the divine plane, where the gods might argue about the course of action, or Zeus assert his right to control the plot: "Just as the will of Zeus is thematically the 'plot' of the poem, so also, from a compositional point of view, Zeus is a figure who can be invoked by the poet at any time to re-infuse poetic order into the story" (Nimis 1999: 74). When the gods themselves serve as spectators commenting on how the narrative twists and turns and sparring over what direction it should go in, they draw attention to the fact that it does deviate in clever and unexpected ways. For example, after the *Iliad* establishes the traditional storyline of an angered, withdrawn hero who causes suffering to his followers (Nagy 1999a: 72–83; M. Lord 1994), the close of book 1 changes the narrative direction with a discussion among the gods. At the beginning of book 2 Zeus uses the expedient of sending a lying dream to Agamemnon promising him success in order to get the Achaians onto the battlefield, which also allows for the opportunity to include what looks like a set piece culminating in the humiliation of Thersites in the assembly (Davies 2016: 50–55 on possible parallels with the *Aethiopis*). Book 3 again opens with the council of the gods, and, as noted earlier, it incorporates another set piece by resituating it from the beginning stages of the war, while in book 4 Zeus *qua* bard notes that the storyline is difficult to continue effectively since what would be expected now is the return of Helen (4.13–19). This not only displeases Hera but also would be admitting defeat to the preceding bard. Zeus manages to find a way to pivot in a new direction by having Pandarus break the truce, and now the bard has a chance to show off his battle descriptions.

Similarly, in book 8 the Trojans and Hektor are given the upper hand only reluctantly, as it were, despite the fact that the Achaians must be in dire peril to motivate the embassy to Achilleus in book 9. It has been argued that the gods' many interventions repeatedly delaying or diverting the will of Zeus show the bard's ambivalence about allowing the foes of the Achaians to succeed (Nimis 1999: 73–74).[8] I contend that we see here the aesthetic of diverting or reorienting a narrative, which originated in the practice of capping in relay festival performances, exploited in a sophisticated manner to illustrate the conflict in trajectory at the heart of a plot that blends two points of view and subordinates Hektor's storyline to Achilleus.

LOCAL ALLEGIANCES AND THE RECHARACTERIZATION OF HEKTOR

In the *Iliad*, despite the insistence his branch of the Dardanid lineage will come to an end, Hektor occupies much more of the audience's attention than Aineias, and he vies for center stage with Achilleus. While Achilleus is named in the first line of the *Iliad*, Hektor is named in its final line and is the only hero whose name appears in every book (Robertson 1968; J. Scott 1921: 217, 218). It is true that critical opinions have been divided with regard to whether Hektor was always part of the Iliadic storyline. One view is that Homer invented him so as to transfer the Memnon storyline to the *Iliad* (see Burgess 2001: 64). For West, Hektor was added to give Achilleus a rival; he is not an organic part of the story (2011a: 45). H. T. Wade-Gery proposed that the historical figure Hektor of Chios was the inspiration for the introduction of a Hektor into Homer's *Iliad* (1952: 6–7). John Scott considered Hektor to be a substitute for Paris as leader of the Trojans (1921: 226–227, 231–232). Jonathan Burgess, however, has effectively argued for his role as Troy's defender before Homer's *Iliad*: "The *Iliad* is noticeably casual in its first references to him (1.242; 2.802, 807, 816), and supporters of the argument for Homeric invention never quite manage to explain this away" (2001: 64). Moreover, as Martin observes, "that there are two 'creative' heroes at the pinnacle of the *Iliad*'s stylistic hierarchy lends unusual resonance to the poem, giving it the complexity of musical counterpoint" (1989: 131). Indeed, many scholars have found Hektor more sympathetic than Achilleus. For James Redfield the *Iliad* told "The Tragedy of Hector" (1994), and Seth Schein has argued that "the laments and burial of Hektor . . . constitute a triumph, not of Hektor himself . . . but of the civilized values of Troy: though defeated and destroyed militarily, they have the last word poetically" (1984: 186). That Hektor could be used to exemplify the *polis* ethos beginning to develop in the eighth century (Scully 1990: 116–127; Raaflaub 1993) must have been a major reason the point of view sympathetic to the defeated Trojans could remain in the text, but it was not the origin of his story nor of Greek interest in him as a character.

I believe that in an early, pre-Panionic stage of the Homeric tradition about the fall of Troy, the audience had an active interest in the ruling house of Troy, presumably because contemporary local dynasties considered themselves to have descended from legendary Dardanidai: the various audience members were each invested in different heroes. For this reason bards affiliated with different cities or patronized by different dynasties chose to perform versions of events in which a particular local hero was most prominent, and one of the natural results of this was the narrative complexity and "counterpoint" that Martin describes, as each bard gave due glory on the battlefield to his chosen hero. We can see the remnants of this competition in chance remarks by characters, but it is Hektor who has won the battle among the Anatolian heroes, and it is in his characterization that we can get a sense of how competing bards could have presented competing points of view on the heroes they were supporting, capping and recharacterizing earlier depictions that took a different perspective. The complex depiction of Hektor's character could have arisen as a natural result of the bards' competitive collaboration in telling episodes from the story of the fall of Troy.

Whereas many scholars have focused on the eighth century BCE as crucial in shaping the Homeric *Iliad*, arguing that Panhellenic performance settings caused bards to deemphasize local lore and allegiances (Nagy 1990a: 43–47; González 2013: 236–244), I consider an earlier period and a different setting than the interstate sanctuaries that begin to appear in the archaeological record in the eighth century (Rutherford 2013: 37–40) to be decisive for the portrayal of Hektor as an important and complex character in the *Iliad*. I look to the time after a

Greek epic about the fall of Troy first came into being—which I would place around 1160–1050 BCE—and before the putative Panionic stage, no later than the end of the eighth century BCE, when the story about the fall of Troy at the hands of the Achaians became the focus of performances at the Panionia. I have argued that the lower limit for the window within which a narrative about Troy first entered Greek epic is set by the appearance of contraction in the Greek language because the formula *Iliou proparoithe(n)* requires the name of the city to be scanned as four syllables, without contraction of the genitive ending. The upper limit is based on the conventional dates for the Trojan War, plus ninety years, representing the three generations of historical memory. That is, I make the assumption that the legend of the fall of Troy does not refer to an actual historical destruction, and therefore the tale cannot have come into existence until the interval within which historical memory operates had elapsed (Bachvarova 2016: 400–402, 458–464).[9]

Competition for control of the Troad is well attested for the seventh century in the Greek sources, including Herodotus (5.94) and Strabo (13.25, 35, 38–42, 52–55), and local polities interested in claiming to be the rightful heirs of Troy attached themselves to the sons of either Aineias or Hektor (Bachvarova 2016: 409–414, 436–445; cf. Nagy 1999a: 142–217, 321–324). But I would assert that competition over control of the Troad had been ongoing for some centuries, motivating claims by Greek dynasties of kinship with the Dardanidai. I suggest that as soon as Iron Age Greeks were settling in the Troad—certainly by the Protogeometric period, beginning around 1050 BCE—they had reason to make use of a shared yet contested legendary history that explained contemporary Greco-Anatolian relations and justified occupation of the strategic site of Troy: first Greeks competing with Anatolians (Bachvarova 2016: 361–373, 402–415, 429–431) and then Aeolians competing with Ionians. The latter stage left its traces on the Homeric dialect, with its mixing of Aeolic forms into an archaizing form of East Ionic (Bachvarova 2016: 372–373, 409–417, 429–438; cf. Horrocks 1997; Jones 2011a, 2011b). Ionian bards perhaps achieved sufficient superiority over Greek bards performing in other dialects to silence all other epic traditions telling of the fall of Troy during the period when the story about the city's destruction dominated the epic performances at the Panionic festival, which must have existed before ca. 700 BCE, when the Meliac War occurred among members of the Ionian Dodecapolis (Frame 2009: 541–549).

More than fifty years ago Wade-Gery argued that the Panionia would have provided a formative setting for the *Iliad* (1952: 14–16; cf. Högemann 2000: 191–193; Nagy 2010: 214, 224–232, 320–321; Tsagalis, this volume, pp. 38–40). Douglas Frame has more recently made a detailed argument for the Panionia as a crucial venue for bards performing the *Iliad*, suggesting that our monumental *Iliad* grew out of that collaborative performance setting, with different bards contributing to the final whole (2009: 557–563). He imagines twelve poets, one from each of the cities making up the Ionian Dodecapolis, contributing three books each of the *Iliad* or the *Odyssey*. Additionally, Frame places the Panionia originally at Miletus (2009: 17–18, 515–647). While I agree that the Panionia was first celebrated at Miletus (Bachvarova 2016: 413–415, 438–445, 448–449), the *Iliad* we have does not extensively cater to Milesian interests. The Lykians Sarpedon and Glaukos, whose appearance would flatter the aristocracy of Miletus (Bachvarova 2015, 2016: 438–439; cf. Bryce 2006: 146–147), do not dominate most sections of the *Iliad* in the way that Hektor does. Yet the sympathetic portrayal of Hektor and his grief-stricken father, as opposed to a Hektor whose primary function is the chief opponent of the Greeks, appears mostly in books 6, 22, and 24. And, as William Merritt Sale has shown, formulas, especially those in the nominative, referring to the Trojans are rare and not frequently repeated (1989, 1994): he attributes this to a reworking of their characterization to frame them in a more positive light (cf. Bachvarova 2016: 432–448).[10]

The portrayal we have, therefore, of Hektor suggests that he was embedded in an already extant Greek tradition about the fall of Troy, and earlier than Sarpedon and the Glaukidai were, and that our *Iliad* is the product of a tradition that at that early stage was open to differing points of view on the Trojans presented by bards with allegiances to local dynasties. At that point a version sympathetic to the Trojans was combined with the Greek-centric version featuring Achilleus and his Achaian companions. The interest in Hektor as a fictional ancestor of a Greek dynasty makes more sense for epics about Troy performed primarily within a festival circuit confined to the relevant region of Anatolia, not as far east as Miletus. I have suggested that the relevant festival circuit was one in which Apollo was the chief honoree (Bachvarova 2016: 449–452)—in part because Apollo plays an important role generally in the epic, and in part because much of book 1 reads as a hymn to Sminthian Apollo, who was worshiped on Tenedos (Faraone 2016). One possibility is the festival circuit that would have existed within the Aeolian Dodecapolis (Herodotus 1.149; Strabo 13.35).

There are hints in the *Iliad* that Hektor and Achilleus had been "competing for the spotlight," to use Jonathan Ready's phrasing (2011: 222–260), in the epic tradition before the *Iliad* approached its final form, supporting my contention that we can see the vestiges of a performance context in which at least some audience members on some occasions considered themselves to be descended from the Dardanid dynasty (Bachvarova 2016: 432–438). Later sources (Lycophron *Alexandra* 265; schol. Lycophron 258, 265 = Stesichorus 224 *PMG*; schol. A *Iliad* 3.314 [Erbse] = Ibycus 295 *PMG*) oddly name Apollo, not Priam, as Hektor's father (Scully 1990: 59–60; Burgess 2001: 65). While this could be nothing more than an attempt to explain why Apollo is so invested in Hektor in Homer's *Iliad*, the repeated insistence that he is *not* the son of a god in the *Iliad*—as in Poseidon's sarcastic remark at 13.54 (cf. Nagy 1999a: 148–149, with a slightly different interpretation)—suggests the Homeric tradition was aware of the alternate parentage for Hektor. The comments are doing more than contrasting him with the greater hero Achilleus and Hektor's Dardanid cousin Aineias: they are pointedly denying a tradition that would put him on the same level.

Moreover, Hektor likely rivaled Aineias as the link to the legendary ruling house in the Troad well before the seventh century. It has long been acknowledged that a dynasty in the Troad must have claimed descent from Aineias, the Dardanid whom the *Iliad* treats as the one survivor (*Iliad* 20.302–308; cf. *Homeric Hymn to Aphrodite* 196–197).[11] Strabo's discussion of the claims of the house of Skepsis in the Troad (13.1.52–53) seems to reveal a desire on the part of the Aineidai to eliminate a claim to autochthony promulgated by Hektor's fictional descendants. According to the geographer, Skepsis was moved to its current location from higher up on Mount Ida by Hektor's son Skamandrios and Aineias's son Askanios. But, in Demetrios of Skepsis's version of events, Strabo says, the Aineidai alone founded the new town. Strabo opposes these stories to the versions of Aineias's fate that have him emigrating to Italy. Dionysus of Halicarnassus also calls attention to Homer's apparent knowledge of a dynasty in Phrygia descending from Aineias (1.53.5).[12] There is one hint, in the persona of Hektor of Chios, whom Wade-Gery dates to 800 (1952: 6–9), that by the eighth century there was an advantage to creating a connection to the Dardanidai through a link to Hektor himself (Bachvarova 2016: 435–436). But the *Iliad* denies any claims of a dynasty connecting itself to Hektor by giving his son two names, Astyanax and Skamandrios, even stopping to explain them as if drawing attention to its own version of events in which this son bearing two names is fated to die and bring Hektor's line to an end (6.401–403), as opposed to the versions in which Skamandrios and Astyanax were considered to be different sons of Hektor (schol. Euripides *Andromache* 224) (Bachvarova 2016: 412; cf. Nagy 2010: 203–204).

The ongoing conflict in the real world between dynasties that connected themselves to two different branches of the Dardanid house may be mirrored in the *Iliad* by the conflict between Aineias and Priam, touched on by the narrator in an allusion to an otherwise unknown backstory in which Aineias is angry at Priam because he gives him no honor at all (13.460–461). Strabo says that according to later historians this *dusmeneia* was what allowed Aineias to survive the war (but how exactly he does not say) (13.1.53). Achilleus too may refer to the competition when he mocks Aineias before they duel for his futile desire to be honored by Priam above his own sons (20.179–181). Poseidon in his prophecy about the fate of Aineias asserts that Zeus hates the race of Priam (20.293–308),[13] and the genealogy Aineias recites to Achilleus makes clear that he does not belong to the branch that could be blamed for Troy's fall, neither Priam's nor his father Laomedon's (20.213–240), whose sins were refusing to compensate Apollo and Poseidon for building the "holy walls" of Troy (21.440–452) and insulting Herakles (5.640–643, 648–651) (Fehling 1991: 7–12). Rather, Aineias traces his lineage back to the founder of Dardania, not Troy. This episode, which includes the references to earlier meetings between the two, has been considered an interpolation possibly derived from a lost epic *Aineis* (Heitsch 1965, 1968) or evidence that the *Homeric Hymn to Aphrodite* and the *Iliad* were authored by the same poet (Reinhardt 1961: 507–521), but I, like Nagy (1999a: 268–275), prefer to see it as evidence of a variant local tradition in which Aineias was the chief defender of Troy.

Just as the obvious diversions in the narration are stylizations of the changes in narrative direction that would arise when the epic performance changed hands, so alternations in the portrayal of Hektor follow a pattern set by the changes in point of view that would have resulted as bards with different allegiances attempted to elicit the audience's sympathy for various heroes, responding to or recharacterizing a previous bard's portrayal of a particular character. As Ready has shown, drawing on Leonard Muellner's principle that "each move is meant to top the next one, which it also includes and betters" (1996: 87), the verbal competition within the *Iliad* extends even to the "competitive dynamics" of sequences of similes, in which subsequent similes "reuse and recharacterize" a previous simile (2011: 99). Ready also shows that a character can "reuse elements from the narrator's earlier image(s) and/or recharacterize an actor or set of actors" (2011: 87–107, quotation from 157). Whereas Ready, since he analyses the Homeric text synchronically, focuses on sequencing across the text, I am interested in both the synchronic and the diachronic dimensions. I am thinking in terms of a bard picking up a narrative from the previous performer and taking it in a new direction of his own choosing, perhaps recharacterizing by linking episodes in a novel way or reusing a well-known episode in a novel way, but in my recasting of the notion of traditional referentiality I am also envisioning bards responding to earlier versions by subsuming and recharacterizing them (cf. Griffith 1990: 192–193).

As I will show, in the first six books a contrast between the Achaians' point of view on Hektor and the audience's is set up by giving the audience information about Hektor that pushes them to feel sympathy for him. However, once that sympathy is established, a pointed recharacterization of Hektor's role over the course of the next fourteen books renders him not the hero of his own story but a tool to enhance the prestige of Achilleus. Again, an internal point of view is contrasted with that of the external audience, but here it is Hektor who lacks full information, whereas the audience is continually reminded of it. Hektor's conviction that Zeus supports him is shown to be delusional, although the audience is kept in the dark about how much success Hektor will be allowed to have. From book 16 onward Hektor's death and funeral compete with that of Patroklos, with the final three books switching back and forth between commemoration of Hektor and commemoration of Patroklos, books 23 and 24 reframing in turn the point of the narrative.

The first few books of the *Iliad* give tragic depth and richness to Hektor's character as protector of his city. It is as if the narration, by the way it unfolds, presents, then corrects, the Greek-centric point of view, with book 1 and most of book 2 focusing on the Achaians' experience of the war and showing Hektor from their perspective as the foremost warrior of the Trojans, a man-slayer (*androphonoio*) (Whallon 1979; Stoevesandt 2004: 227). We gain access for the first time to the Trojans' perspective when Zeus sends Iris in the guise of Hektor's younger brother Polites with a message warning them that the Achaians are massed to attack. Again, the persona of Hektor "of glittering helm" (*koruthaiolos*),[14] "son of Priam" (2.816–817),[15] is that of a warrior first and foremost, in contrast to his father, whom Iris dismisses as an "old man [to whom] endless words are dear, as if it were a time of peace" (2.796–797), before turning expressly to Hektor (2.802–803). Hektor's dynastic connection legitimizes his position as the Trojans' military leader, but the city is Priam's to rule, not Hektor's. And his lineage is contrasted with the divine lineage of Aineias, son of Aphrodite, who is leader of the Dardanidai as the head of its junior line (2.819–821). Foremost warrior that he is, Hektor nevertheless remains inferior to his cousin and subordinate to his father.

Book 3 opens with the telling contrast of Paris showing off in the front line until he sees Menelaos, at which point he is seized with fear and retreats into the crowd of Trojans. After Hektor rebukes him for his cowardice, Paris responds by commenting on his persona as preeminent warrior, "Always your heart is untiring like an axe, . . . your thoughts in your chest cannot be frightened," but he snidely points out that he could hardly refuse the gifts of Aphrodite (3.15–66). In other words, Paris too has the special favor of the same goddess who bore Aineias, unlike Hektor. At this point Paris offers to return the goods he took from Menelaos but not Helen herself, and it becomes obvious to the audience that Hektor has no power over his brother, no ability to halt the inexorable destruction of his city and his line. This was such a problem for Herodotus that he insisted Helen was not actually at Troy, for in that case Priam would have returned her (2.120) (J. Scott 1921: 228–229).

Already the first three books enable the audience to understand Hektor's character differently than his Achaian foes do. Yes, he takes second place to Achilleus as a warrior, but he is more than a warrior: he is a son and brother. He is trapped in a role that he must carry out even though it will lead to the end of his life and of all that gives his life meaning, and his acceptance of his fate is in telling contrast to Achilleus, whose aggrieved withdrawal from the battlefield brings suffering on his people and leads to the death of his closest friend. Hektor's story may have been subsumed and subordinated by Achilleus's story, but the melded storyline as presented to us so far asserts Hektor's depth of character and moral superiority to Achilleus.

At the end of book 4, right before the narrative narrows its focus to Diomedes in book 5, we get a last portrait of the battle as a whole. Apollo, watching the battle from the walls of Troy, is indignant (*nemesēse*) at the Argives' advance. Like the audience and the Achaians, the god is privy to the information that Achilleus has withdrawn from battle, and he takes the opportunity to shout the news to the Anatolian host (4.507–513). Athena responds by going into the crowd of fighters to rally the Achaians. If the gods serve as an internal audience directing the reactions of the external human audience, surely we should connect the different allegiances they feel at this moment to the different allegiances of various audience members.

Zeus puts a stop to the gods' interference, and the Achaians assert their "natural superiority" at the beginning of book 6 (West 2011a: 173), no longer giving quarter to the enemy or pausing to despoil their bodies. "Now the Trojans, defeated by their lack of stalwartness at the hands of the war-loving Achaians, would have gone back into Ilium" (6.73–74) if Helenos had not advised Hektor to go into the city to bid his mother to make an offering to Athena. The illogic here of the chief warrior of the Trojans abandoning the field at such a juncture to order the completion of a ritual that does not have the intended effect—Athena will reject it—is glaring. West explains it as allowing for Paris to be returned to the battlefield, after having been swept off by Aphrodite (2011a: 174). Kirk suggests, "In all this the singer is plainly determined to get Hektor back into Troy; the organizing of prayers is a subsidiary mechanism, not without a certain importance in itself, but it is the great scenes with Hekabe, Paris and Andromakhe that must have been his main narrative aim" (1990: 163). The sequence of meetings ends with Hektor bidding farewell to Andromache for the last time, a moving scene that appealed to the tastes of Homer's later Hellenistic readers, as shown by the positive comments here of the bT scholion at 6.467 (Kirk 1990: 223). Using traditional motifs to new ends (Kirk 1990: 18–21, 219–228), this scene develops Hektor's sympathetic characterization as a man with conflicting roles to play (Redfield 1994: 123–124), committed as he is to defending his city, his family, and his lineage, even in the knowledge that it is futile.

The point that the more sympathetic and balanced characterization of Hektor should eclipse the one-sided image held by the Achaians within the story is made throughout the scene by the choice of location and epithets. The meeting of Hektor and Andromache is at the Skaian Gate, before which Hektor will later be killed (West 2011a: 183) and which marks the boundary between his roles of father and husband and of protector of the city even at the expense of his family. Attention is brought both to the meaning of Hektor's own name ("holder," Nagy 1999a: 146–147; Scully 1990: 59–60) and to the effect that his role has on his family (including its impending extirpation) when the narrator explains that, while "Hektor called his son Skamandrios, the others called him Astyanax [leader of the city], for Hektor alone protected Ilium" (6.402–404). The helmet of Hektor *koruthaiolos* frightens Astyanax, causing him to burst into tears, so Hektor removes it and only picks it up again when he leaves to resume his role as warrior (6.466–495). Once Andromache has set off for "the well-situated home of man-killing Hektor" (6.498) to lament him with her maidservants although he is not yet dead (6.499–500), Hektor meets up with Paris, carefree and prancing like a racehorse, and once again shoulders the burden put upon him by his feckless brother.

At this point the Achaians build a wall around their camp, turning the battle into one between two nearby cities, a traditional plotline of Greek epic (Hainsworth 1993: 329, 344), and turning Hektor from a defender into an attacker. This again reads like the opening of the war, with the absence of Achilleus a good excuse. It gives Hektor a chance not only to shine as a preeminent warrior but also to exceed his allotted role (Nagy 1999a: 147). From now on the narrator undercuts Hektor's glory by reminding the audience of its temporary nature. Just as Achilleus can receive due honor only when his people are being defeated, Hektor, dear to Zeus as he is (see p. 177n17), can be victorious only as long as Zeus chooses to give him *kudos*—a fact of which the human characters are aware.[16] But only the external audience knows in addition that Hektor's *kudos* is meant to enhance Achilleus's importance, and we do not know how far that *kudos* will extend. As James Morrison points out, "A coherent set of predictions . . . suggests that the [Achaians'] ships will not be successfully defended. . . . As the narrator highlights the importance of defending the ships, the audience seizes upon predictions regarding the extent of the damage Hector will inflict before he is driven back" (1992: 76). Thus, certainty over Hektor's eventual fate does not mean certainty over the Achaians' fate.

Here we have a key example of capping over the course of repeated performances of the same episodes, subsuming and recharacterizing the earlier versions. In this case they are traditional episodes possibly originating in a version of the epic tradition that allowed Hektor to receive unalloyed glory. This version could have been performed in his honor for audience members who considered themselves to be descendants of the house of Troy as long as the episode stood alone, or even in a festival setting along with other episodes so long as it was not necessary to subordinate them to a single coherent storyline in which Achilleus was the preeminent warrior.

Whereas earlier we saw that Hektor was humanized in contradiction to the one-sided view of the Achaians internal to the narrative and therefore to that of audience members or bards invested in the Achaian point of view, now we see Hektor put in his place in contradiction to the bards and audience members invested in him. But Hektor himself acts as if he does not realize that his storyline has been capped. He is buoyed by his success and confident in the support of Zeus so far, unaware of what we the audience have been told by the narrator, that this is not about him, but about Achilleus—this is not his story, but Achilleus's story. His descent begins in book 12 (Redfield 1994: 144–159). Near the beginning (12.45–46), Hektor, looking for a place to cross the ditch in his chariot in front of the Achaian wall, resembles a lion or boar, whose "glorious heart [*kudalimon kēr*] does not feel dread or fear, and his bravery [*agēnoriē*] kills him." At this point, Poulydamas advises Hektor not to cross with the horse teams, and Hektor agrees. But the next time he advises Hektor, with regard to a portent, both he and the narrator anticipate Hektor's rejection, the narrator labeling the Trojan prince *thrasus* ("[over]bold") and Poulydamas opening with, "Hektor, always somehow you rebuke me in assemblies, although I am advising the right things" (12.210–212). Unsurprisingly, then, Hektor repudiates his advice, asserting, "Let us trust in the plan of great Zeus" (12.241). His pig-headedness has struck earlier Homeric scholars (schol. bT *Iliad* 22.91; J. Scott 1921: 216), but we can see it in a sympathetic light, wrong as it is, given everything we have been told about Hektor being nothing more than a plaything of the gods, his temporary achievement of *kudos* only a way to give *kudos* to Achilleus in the end, and also given the intimate scenes within Troy where we could admire his determination to do what he must even at the expense of all he holds dear. We understand why he might be seduced by the fantasy that the destruction of his city and his line is not so certain.

In book 15, in a scene that seems to rework a version of events belonging to when the Achaians first landed at Troy and Hektor killed Protesilaos (2.701), Hektor, able to seize the prow of Protesilaos's ship because Zeus is pushing him forward, calls out to the Trojans to bring fire: "Now Zeus has given a day worth all to us, to seize the ships, which coming here against the will of the gods placed on us many pains, because of the baseness of the elders who restrained me when I wished to fight at the prows of the ships and blocked the host. But, even if then wide-seeing Zeus injured our minds, now he himself urges and enjoins" (15.719–725). How wrong he is! This is the event that will cause Patroklos to be drawn into the fight, and Zeus has already summarized the action to follow: Patroklos will be killed by Hektor, many warriors will be killed, including his son Sarpedon, and then Achilleus will kill Hektor. From that point on the Achaians will drive forward again from the ships "until they take steep Ilium through the plans of Athena" (15.64–71).

The shift of Zeus's favor in battle away from Hektor, now that Zeus has fulfilled his promise to Thetis, is marked at 16.169 by the narrator's transfer of the epithet "dear to Zeus," which had been used four times for Hektor, to Achilleus.[17] And, when Hektor dares to put on Achilleus's divinely made armor, Zeus even addresses him directly, informing him that now he deserves the death that is so near to him (17.198–208). Unfortunately for Hektor, only we can hear Zeus. Again, during the battle over Patroklos's body when Hektor attempts to drive off Achilleus's immortal horses, who are standing stock still, "like a grave marker on a tomb" (17.434–435), Zeus promises them he will not allow Hektor to mount behind them, commenting on the innate wretchedness of mortals, their griefs and excesses, and he restates that his support will extend only so far as the end of that day (17.441–455). Perhaps the horses are to be imagined as being able to hear him, but we are again the primary audience for Zeus's words. And again Hektor is excluded.

In book 18 Achilleus prepares to reenter the fray to seek revenge for the death of Patroklos. Hektor remains in the position of knowing less than the internal audience of the gods and the bard's human audience. We watch him make the fateful decision that we know will be the immediate cause of his death: rejecting Poulydamas's advice in assembly to retreat within Troy's walls for the night and arguing that the glory bestowed on him by Zeus extends to driving the Achaians into the sea (18.293–294). The Trojans applaud his speech, "foolish, for Pallas Athena had taken their wits from them, and they approved of Hektor, who counseled badly, and no one did Poulydamas, who advised well" (18.311–313). The narrative switches away from Hektor, and we hear Achilleus's words, his promise not to bury Patroklos until he brings Hektor's armor and head, along with twelve Trojans whose throats he will slit before his pyre. Until then captive Trojan women will lament for his companion (18.333–342). Achilleus by returning to the battlefield has seized the narrative spotlight from Hektor, and he dominates the next three books. The question now is whether Achilleus will be able to break free of the preordained plot, as laid out by Zeus to Hera in book 15, and sack Troy before its time (N. Richardson 1993: 52).

At long last in book 22 we witness the culminating duel of the *Iliad*, in which the preeminent champions of each side face each other, the result of which is not in doubt. Our sympathy has been pulled to Achilleus's side through the portrayal of his intense grief at the death of his beloved companion, and we have been awed by his prowess in battle, but now the threads of Hektor's sympathetic portrayal are picked up from book 6.[18] We see his parents begging him not to face Achilleus, bringing to the fore again Hektor's double bind: the conflict between his duty to his city and his duty to his family. Now he is shown as repudiating both in his desire to present a good image of himself to future audiences—to us: "Now my fate is upon me. Would that I die not without a struggle nor without glory, but doing something great to be remembered by those who will exist in the future" (22.303–305). Hektor, like Achilleus, is aware of his future fate as a hero (Nagy 1999a: 148–150; Bakker 1997a: 165–166), and the final books switch back and forth between the heroization of Patroklos and Hektor.

Hektor had requested that if Achilleus should be the one to win their duel, he return his body, as Hektor would Achilleus's. At that point Achilleus rejected his request in the strongest of terms (22.258–272), and now he goes on to attempt to defile his body, to cause it to disintegrate to nothing, by dragging it behind his chariot (22.395–404, 23.14–21). In this way Achilleus would eliminate the possibility of hero worship for his rival. Book 23 is devoted to the funeral and games for Patroklos, setting him up as a hero to be worshiped (Nagy 1999a: 115–117). The narrative could have ended here, but another book remains in which Zeus shows himself to be committed to Hektor's receiving his due, condemning Achilleus's actions as earlier he had condemned Hektor for daring to wear Achilleus's armor and reiterating how dear the pious Hektor is to him (24.66–70, 113–115). It is made clear to us that now our sympathy should be with Hektor again. The portrayal of Priam's grief is as moving as that of Achilleus's, and Hektor receives a burial that matches quite precisely that of Patroklos (24.782–799). They are on an even plane as heroes in death, and the last emotion we sympathize with is the Trojans' suffering caused by the loss of "horse-taming Hektor."

CONCLUSION

Whereas Leaf looked to the explication of the final stage of the epic that produced the *Iliad* as key to its exegesis, I do not assert that our *Iliad* must be the result of a scribe or scribes taking down a competitive collaborative performance by multiple bards playing a capping game. Rather, much that has puzzled or tantalized critics over the centuries can be referred to a fairly early stage in the epic tradition, when serial episodic performance of the epic in festival competitions created an aesthetic that provides a convincing explanation for two distinct phenomena: first, for what is considered to be great in the text, such as the sympathetic portrayal of the Trojans—the audience expects dueling points of view from the regional performers—and the ebb and flow of the plot, each of which are ways to respond via recharacterizing to an earlier performance of a rival bard at the festival; and second, for the tolerance of elements that grate on the sensibilities of careful readers, such as the repeated type scenes—for example, the duel between Menelaos and Paris and the duel between Aias and Hektor—and the supposedly clumsy repurposing of episodes originally placed elsewhere: the whole point is for the audience to appreciate the ingenious refitting. We gain a new understanding and appreciation of the traditional techniques of Homeric bards when we move beyond just accepting these as flaws we can overlook and instead appreciate them as recognized tools in their compositional toolkit.

NOTES

1. For some of the places mentioned in this chapter, see map 5.1.

2. However, the famous version of the Kyrgyz epic *Manas* published by Wilhelm Radloff appears to be a conglomeration of performances by five different bards (Hatto 1990: 601–602).

3. Pers. comm., G. D. S. Anderson. Dr. Anderson (Living Tongues Institute for Endangered Languages) and Prof. K. D. Harrison (Swarthmore College) brought Mandzhaiev to the United States in the summer of 2013 to participate in the Smithsonian Folklife Festival.

4. I do not agree with Muellner that the *Theogony* should be considered a *prooimion* of the *Iliad* (1996: 52–54). It begins by praising Zeus (its own *prooimion*) and then moves into a genealogical text with similarities to the Hesiodic *Catalogue of Women*.

5. Unless otherwise noted, all translations are my own.

6. This background illuminates an additional comment in the scholia to Pindar *Nemean* 2.1: "Some say that, since the poetry of Homer had not been brought together under one thing, and since it was otherwise scattered and separated into parts [*merē*], whenever they would sing it rhapsodically [*rhapsōideō*] they would do something similar to sequencing or sewing, making it into one thing" (trans. Collins [2001a: 133, adapted]). See González 2013: 78 with earlier references and Nagy 1996b: 78–79 with further ancient sources referring to the idea of a text made up of originally "scattered" parts. Scodel, however, argues that many of the episodes of the *Iliad* and the *Odyssey* cannot stand on their own without reference to the *Iliad* or the *Odyssey* that we have, rather than the broader Trojan cycle (2002a: 48–49).

7. See the critique of González (2013: 68–70).

8. Nimis's overall argument, that the inconsistencies in Zeus's predictions in book 8 reflect the poetic process of working out the plot while performing the epic, is incompatible with J. Morrison's explanation of the lack of match between prediction and action as a purposeful misdirection of the audience by a poet in control of the plot (1992). My own view of the prehistory of the text is not compatible with either analysis.

9. If we do wish to connect the legend with a historical destruction, then that would add twenty years to the window, assuming we choose the destruction of Troy VIIa, fixed at 1180 BCE. See Bryce 2006: 64–67. On the question of the historicity of the Trojan War, see most recently Rose 2014: 40–42.

10. Stoevesandt critiques Sale's methodology, arriving at the conclusion that "Sales These muß . . . in den Bereich der Spekulation verwiesen werden" (2004: 29–38, quotation from 38).

11. See Reinhardt 1961: 450–453, 507–521; M. Edwards 1991: 298–301; Faulkner 2008: 4–10; West 2011a: 26.

12. For ancient discussions of Aineias's fate, see M. Edwards 1991: 300–301.

13. The speech in fact contradicts what the god stated earlier, that he holds Priam and his city close to his heart because of his consistent piety (4.44–49). One way to explain this inconsistency is to see the breaking of the truce by the Trojans as provoking Zeus's anger (4.157–168) (schol. bT *Iliad* 20.306). Others solve the problem by athetizing the verses. See M. Edwards 1991: 325–326.

14. This epithet is applied frequently and almost exclusively to Hektor when his name is in the nominative (one time for Ares). In the accusative, his name receives the epithet *khalkokorustēn* ("bronze-helmeted") eight times; it is applied once to Sarpedon. See Page 1959: 249–250 on the epithets.

15. Hektor is frequently labeled with his patronymic, but Paris only once (6.512).

16. 17.565 (Agamemnon speaking to Athena in the guise of Phoenix), 19.204 (Achilleus speaking to Agamemnon), 8.216, 11.300, 12.174, 255, 437, 13.347–348, 14.364, 15.327 (Apollo bestows it), 595, 602–606, 644, 16.730, 18.456 (Thetis to Hephaistos, attributing it to Apollo), 19.414 (the horse Xanthos to Achilleus). That this is a zero-sum game is shown by Agamemnon's petulant complaint to Zeus when it seems that Hektor will set fire to the Achaian ships: "Indeed, by leading astray by this *atē* someone of the arrogant kings (on our side) have you also stripped him of great *kudos*?" (8.236–237). There would have been great *kudos* for the Achaians because Hektor, "beloved of Zeus," did not realize that they were succeeding on the left flank with the determined help of Poseidon, working at cross-purposes to Zeus, but at that moment Hektor leapt into the Achaian camp where the walls were low (13.674–680). Achilleus prays to Zeus when he sends out Patroklos to give him *kudos*, "so that Hektor will know that our attendant knows how to fight alone" (16.241–244). As Apollo abandons Hektor to his death, Athena encourages Achilleus to carry off great *kudos* by slaying him (22.216–218), and Achilleus so boasts after carrying out the deed (22.393). Achilleus, like Hektor, pushes it too far when he continues to abuse Hektor's body while the gods become more and more offended. Zeus sends Thetis down to persuade her son to leave off, stating that he has given Achilleus *kudos* for nine full days, against the gods' wishes, but now he must return the body (24.107–116).

17. *Dii philos* used for Hektor at 6.318, 8.493, 10.49, 13.674; Achilleus at 1.74 (Kalchas speaking before assembly), 16.169, 18.203, 22.216 (Athena speaking in the duel between Hektor and Achilleus), 24.472; Pyleus at 2.628 (Catalogue of Ships); Phoenix at 9.169 (Agamemnon speaking, arranging the embassy to Achilleus); Odysseus at 10.527 (return from the Trojans' camp); Patroklos at 11.611 (Achilleus speaking, sending him to Nestor).

18. On the connections between books 6 and 22, see Schadewaldt 1965: 226–229; Kirk 1990: 210, 214; N. Richardson 1993: 108.

CHAPTER SIX

Did Sappho and Homer Ever Meet? Comparative Perspectives on Homeric Singers

OLGA LEVANIOUK

SINCE THE PUBLICATION OF ALBERT LORD'S *SINGER OF Tales*, the search for comparative insights into Homeric poetry has widened, and the comparative method has been used to test hypotheses, change perspectives, and suggest new possibilities.[1] My goal here falls into the latter category: to offer some suggestions about performers of epic in ancient Greece that cannot be proven but seem reasonable in light of evidence from other traditions. Rather than focus on rhapsodes, I will look at the variability in individual performance styles typical of modern oral traditions and speculate about the non-rhapsodic female singers who may have sung epic poetry in ancient Greece. I suggest that such performances existed and affected the formation of Homeric texts.

Much work has been done on the interdiscursivity of Homer, above all on the ways the Homeric epic incorporates and refracts the traditional genre of lament.[2] Drawing on Margaret Alexiou's diachronic study and Aida Vidan's analysis of women's songs from the Milman Parry Collection of Oral Literature, Casey Dué shows that "the *Iliad* and the *Odyssey* are infused with voices of lament at every point" and "those voices are primarily the voices of women" (2006: 39). The same can be said for other genres: didactic poetry, choral lyric, and wedding songs can all be heard behind Homeric hexameters and are woven into the fabric of the epic (Martin 1984, 1989: 86–88; Karanika 2013). The question I would like to pose in this connection is this: what is the performative ecology that supports such rich interdiscursivity?

The simplest model is to imagine rhapsodes who hear different songs and incorporate them into epic, but evidence from other traditions suggests something more complex. Both in northern Russia and in Turkic traditions of central Asia, women who sing laments and wedding songs also sing epic, employing distinct styles and techniques based on their mastery of women's songs. These styles and techniques are used for epic composition in general, not only for evoking laments or weddings, and frequently involve the introduction of new episodes. The individual styles (idiolects) of such singers can be picked up by subsequent generations of performers.

The fact that there were no female rhapsodes at the Panathēnaia does not mean that there were no female performers of epic in Greece. If we were to look only at the most prevalent forms of epic performances in central Asia, we would conclude that men performed epic poetry at festivals. Upon closer inspection, however, it becomes clear that women take part in song contests (*aytïs*), perform epic poetry in private settings, and play a role in the perpetuation of epic (Zhirmunsky 1962: 257–258). There is evidence that in Greece rhapsodic performances of Homer coexisted with other distinct but closely related modes of performance on Homeric themes (Power 2010: 250–257). Furthermore, there is evidence for near-epic songs by women, such as are also attested in other traditions. It is therefore possible to imagine behind the Homeric texts performers straddling different modes and styles. The evidence from other traditions can give us some ideas about where to look for them and what we may be missing.

NEAR-EPIC PERFORMANCES BY WOMEN

The key piece of evidence for the diversity of epic-like performances in Greece is our one example of a near-epic song by a woman: Sappho fragment 44. It is an isolated survival, but considering the state of the preservation of our evidence, there is no reason to assume that this song represents a unique event in Greek song culture (though its recording in writing may be so). Sappho 44 describes the wedding of Hektor and Andromache in meter cognate to Homeric hexameter and in phraseology cognate to Homeric diction. Gregory Nagy characterizes this poem as "an example of epic as refracted in women's song-making traditions" and compares it to a performance encountered by Joyce Flueckiger in her fieldwork in Chhattisgarh, India (1996: 170). It is worth revisiting here what Flueckiger observed.

The epic in question is performed in several regions and by several groups. The Ahir caste of Uttar Pradesh refer to the epic as *Lorik-Candā* and sponsor its performances at various festivals and at village or town fairs. In these public settings the epic is performed exclusively by male singers. The Ahirs also invite singers to perform at weddings and at the birth of children, where women are present (Flueckiger 1989: 36–37). In Chhattisgarh, the epic is called *Candainī*, and it is here that Flueckiger observed the following: "One night as I was recording an elderly Gond (tribal) woman singing a variety of narrative songs, she began singing about the wedding of the epic heroine and her first husband. But the woman did not consider this to be Candainī singing" (1989: 40). While the narrative content corresponded to *Candainī*, the performer deployed a distinct *rāg* "tune" and style. Commenting on the similarity of the Gond woman's song and Sappho 44, Nagy observes: "We find a striking ancient Greek parallel in Sappho fragment 44" (1996a: 57). In the case of *Candainī*, the Gond woman's performance was not unique: Flueckiger heard other women singing segments of epic narrative but identifying these performances with another genre. She also notes that the situation has recently begun to change: some female performers have performed the *Candainī gīt* professionally in a "male" style accompanied by male musicians. These singers gained popularity because of their unusual position as professional and public female performers (1996: 146). Importantly, Flueckiger observed a correlation between the performative ecology and the thematics of the epic: in Chattisgarh, where women perform songs on epic themes, there is also a noticeable focus on women *within* the *Candainī* epic as performed by men (11, 146–147).

Among the singers of epic song in northern Russia there is no difference in meter and melody between male and female performers, and yet, as we will see, there are sometimes differences in style and content. For example, Pavel Rybnikov reports that he had difficulty in persuading one of his singers to sing *Ivan Godinov* because it was a "woman's epic" (*babya starina*). Men do know these songs, but perform them without enthusiasm, whereas women, according to Rybnikov, perform these songs with special care (1989: 62).

Differences in content are also apparent in the Telugu *Ramayana* songs studied by Velcheru Rao (1991). These are songs performed by Brahmin women, often at weddings or family celebrations, that dwell on the subjects absent from the public performances of the epic, such as Sita's pregnancy, childbirth, relations with parents-in-law, and ceremonies for averting the evil eye from a baby. The songs often express attitudes uncharacteristic of the men's *Ramayana* performances—for example, that a firstborn daughter brings luck to the family (Rao 1991: 122). Women who sing these songs also attend public *Ramayana* performances by men and draw no explicit contrast between the two ways of performing the epic (117).

In her work on women's songs collected by Parry and Lord, Vidan points out that women's songs in Bosnia, performed at weddings and female gatherings, share traditional expressions, blocks of verses, and themes with the epic tradition (2003: 22). She reports cases of women whose fathers were singers of epic and who claimed that they were able to sing epics (19). Russian evidence, to which I will return, provides multiple examples of epic songs transmitted through women in families of singers.

In Bosnia the main distinction between men's and women's songs is the musical accompaniment, a situation reminiscent of what Flueckiger described with regard to the *Candainī* epic in Chhattisgarh. In both cases there were some singers able to perform these songs both with musical accompaniment and without it. Especially interesting are Vidan's observations regarding Kate Murat (née Palunko), who sang epic songs with a distinctly feminine outlook, provoking some scholarly disagreement on the question of whether such songs constitute "heroic epic," given their "insufficiently pronounced martial spirit" (2003: 16).

How, then, should we imagine the relationship of Sappho 44 to epic? Aeolic and specifically Lesbian forms that are part of Homeric diction testify to the well-recognized role of Lesbos in the evolution of Homeric poetry (West 2002a; Cassio 2005: 12–19; Nagy 2011), and Timothy Power argues convincingly that the "epic patrimony of Archaic Lesbos," the Aeolic epic tradition that existed on Lesbos from at least the tenth century BCE, was inherited both by Ionian rhapsodes and by Lesbian kitharodes, all of whom would perform their accounts of Trojan myth at Lesbian festivals (2010: 259–260). Sappho would have been familiar both with Homeric hexameters and with the living Lesbian epic tradition, which would have featured songs for the kithara in lyric meters, including perhaps meters that reflect engagement with rhapsodic hexameters, such as the dactylically expanded glyconics of Sappho's poem (Power 2010: 260–261, 378–394). Would the rhapsodes, for their part, be familiar with songs such as Sappho 44?

Creative engagement with Trojan myth could hardly have been a one-way street,[3] and there were certainly occasions when women's songs and performances of epic by men came into contact. Weddings are a case in point: these are celebrations where women typically sing and which may last for many days, gather large crowds, and demand lavish spending—suitable conditions for epic performances featuring the same kitharodes and rhapsodes that performed at festivals. Sappho 44 could have been performed at weddings, events that are both private and public, individual and collective.[4]

The possibility of festival performance should also not be excluded, and indeed these two types of occasion are not incompatible. Evidence has been accumulating for the performance of Sappho's songs at the interpolis sanctuary of Hera, Zeus, and Dionysus in Messon, Lesbos, which emerges as a location for women's choral performances both in Alcaeus and in Sappho (Nagy 2016). In the newly supplemented version of Sappho 17, the speaking persona refers to a festival, in which both women and girls take part, being celebrated in the precinct of Hera. Nagy argues that this festival is taking place at Messon and that the beauty contests and choral performances of Lesbian women mentioned in Alcaeus 130b are part of the same festival (2016: 471–475). The aetiology of the festival is narrated in Sappho 17, and, crucially, this aetiology has to do with a Trojan myth: the festival was celebrated for the first time by the Atreidai as they tried to find their way home back from Troy. Perhaps Sappho 44 was also performed at Hera's festival. A song about the heroes of the Trojan myth would not be out of place at a festival founded by the Atreidai, nor would a wedding song at a festival of Hera, the goddess of weddings and marriage.

There are dictional links between Sappho 44 and the two poems that refer to the festival, Sappho 17 and Alcaeus 130b, and these have to do with the crowds, the sounds of the festival, and the singing and ritual shouts of women. The crowd of girls and women in Sappho 17 ([ὄ]χλος . . . παρθέ[νων . . . γ]υναίκων, 17.13–14) is described in terms virtually identical to Sappho 44.14–15: ὄχλος / γυναίκων τ' ἄμα παρθενίκα[ν]. In Alcaeus 130b, the Lesbian women fill the sanctuary with the "divine sound of women, of the annual sacred ululation" (Alcaeus 130b.34–35). The ululation of the Lesbian women may be mentioned in Sappho 17, if ολ[in line 16 is to be restored as ὀλολύσδην (Neri 2014: 19), and it is certainly mentioned in Sappho 44.31: "and women cried out, all the older ones" (γύναικες δ' ἐλέλυσδον ὄσαι προγενέστερα[ι). Alcaeus's "divine echo" is also present in Sappho 44.25 (ἄχω θεσπεσία) and also at the beginning of the line, recalling the Homeric ἠχῆι θεσπεσίηι (e.g., *Iliad* 23.213), which occurs at line beginnings. In Sappho the expression refers to the choral song of the girls, accompanied by aulos and castanets (44.24–27). Sappho 44 overflows with sensory detail evocative of both weddings and festivals: crowds on the move, people everywhere in the street, wagons and chariots, music, song, the din of voices, the smells of myrrh and frankincense. Even the fact that Andromache arrives by sea (44.7) would fit the festival context, since Hera on Lesbos is especially concerned with sea voyages (Nagy 2016: 472–473).

Choral performances by women and girls are singled out in connection with Messon both in Sappho and in Alcaeus, and so it seems that women and their songs played a dominant role in Hera's festival. In that regard the festival is similar to a wedding and would constitute a possible occasion for the performance of near-epic songs by women, such as Sappho 44.

It is noteworthy that not only the marriage but also the wedding of Hektor and Andromache is mentioned in the *Iliad*. Andromache is Hektor's "wife of many gifts" (ἄλοχος πολύδωρος) at *Iliad* 6.394 and 22.88, an epithet that may refer to the richness of her dowry, something that is lavishly described in Sappho 44 (8–10) as consisting of golden coils and chains, silver cups, ivory, and something purple, probably robes or fabrics. Andromache's native city and her father, from whose house she sails to Troy in Sappho 44, are mentioned practically every time Andromache appears in the *Iliad*, most expansively in *Iliad* 6, where the focus is precisely on the fact that the daughter of Eëtion from Hypoplakian Thebes is married to Hektor (τοῦ περ δὴ θυγάτηρ ἔχεθ' Ἕκτορι χαλκοκορυστῇ, 6.398). The very day of the wedding is famously mentioned at *Iliad* 22.467–472: as Andromache faints, she loses the headdress, including her veil (κρήδεμνον), that Aphrodite gave her on the day when Hektor led her from the house of Eëtion. In other words, the wedding voyage of Andromache from her father's house to that of Hektor, the subject of Sappho 44, features in Andromache's two main Iliadic scenes, her last meeting with Hektor, in *Iliad* 6, and her witnessing of Hektor's death, in *Iliad* 22. Could the Iliadic Andromache be a refraction of women's songs on Lesbos? It is plausible that the echoes of Andromache's wedding in Homer are there not simply because Andromache is Hektor's wife but also because there were women's songs about her wedding to Hektor, such as Sappho 44. It is likely that Sappho 44 is the only surviving instance of a larger phenomenon and that such women's songs ranged in character from lyric to epic.

In what follows, I argue that performances of epic by women who are experts in laments and wedding songs can have a lasting impact on the epic tradition.

DIVERSITY WITHIN TRADITION

In search of women's influence on epic, I will discuss two traditions. First, I turn to the performers of epic in the extreme north of Russia, primarily around Lake Onega. These performances offer models for thinking about flexibility and fixity, the individuality of performers, and women among the singers of epic songs. Second, I look to Kyrgyz,

Kazakh, and Uzbek oral epics, focusing on competitive performances by men and women and their impact on epic poetry.

I begin with the northern Russian evidence because the fieldwork records available from this region are particularly suited for the study of individual styles. The evidence from this region provides a concrete example of how within the same tradition, the same period, and the same region, some singers faithfully reproduce the songs they learned from their teachers, while others produce new songs and greatly vary their performances. Women who are masters of lament are often among the second group. The singers of the first type often trace their songs to a famous regional singer who lived several generations before them. The singers of the second type typically cannot name a source for their songs or name multiple ones. The interaction between these different modes of composition in performance provides examples of evolution within tradition.

The epic songs of northern Russia are known as *byliny* or *stariny* (singular: *bylina*, *starina*) and were sung primarily on the shores of Lake Onega and Lake Ladoga and in the White Sea region. The existence of these songs occasioned a transformation in the study of Russian folklore in the middle of the nineteenth century, when Rybnikov discovered in the remote Olonets region an "Iceland of Russian epic" (Razumova 1989: 5).[5] Rybnikov's fieldwork was soon followed by that of Aleksandr Gilferding, who, in addition to discovering new singers and songs, was able to collect *stariny* from the same singers as Rybnikov (Gilferding 1894–1900). Aleksandr Grigoriev and Nikolai Onchukov in the last years of the nineteenth century and in the early part of the twentieth, as well as Soviet researchers who embarked on recording expeditions between 1926 and 1935, widened the scope of documentation. In many cases they were able to collect from children and grandchildren of Rybnikov's singers (Grigoriev 2002, 2003; Onchukov 1904; Astakhova 1938, 1951). The assembled evidence makes it possible to study particular singers together with their students and descendants.

What emerges from this fieldwork is the importance of the individual talents of each performer and their profound impact on the tradition. Some singers combine masterful performance with great stability of their texts. Most often, this happens in families. For example, one of the best singers recorded by Rybnikov in the 1860s, Trofim Ryabinin, passed on his art to his son, Ivan Ryabinin, who sung *stariny* inherited from his father almost without changes, except for occasional additions that made his performances slightly longer. The single largest recorded deviation of Ivan Ryabinin from his father's wording was the addition of two extra lines in the description of Vol'ga's departure with his host of fighters (Astakhova 1938: 71). The other changes are for the most part slight alterations of wording within the line ("he had an uncle" versus "there was his uncle") or changes in the order of elements while the wording remains exactly the same (Astakhova 1938: 71).

The same songs were recorded also from the grandson and great-grandson of Trofim Ryabinin, and there were no significant changes, primarily some additional repetitions. Comparing the texts recorded from Trofim Ryabinin with those of his heir in the fourth generation, Anna Astakhova writes of the "astonishing stability" of the Ryabinin family tradition (1938: 74). This stability, it is important to note, is not based on lack of ability to recompose in performance. In the repertoire of Pyotr Ryabinin-Andreev (Trofim's great-grandson) there are songs where he skips some episodes sung by his great-grandfather and adds some by borrowing from other *stariny.* This kind of recombination is, of course, typical of oral epic cross-culturally (Rybnikov 1989: 80). On the whole, however, singers such as those in the Ryabinin family so faithfully preserve their versions of each *starina* that some can be traced back to particular singers of the eighteenth century and most to local schools of the seventeenth century.[6]

Women participate in such near-exact transmission as much as men do. In the nineteenth and twentieth centuries, the telling of *stariny* was not an exclusively male domain, and some female singers were well known, although the famous singers of the eighteenth century are, to my knowledge, all male and only men traveled from place to place to sing their songs when free from agricultural labor (Rybnikov 1989: 50–52).[7] Women's performances, therefore, were more local and received less publicity than men's, but they were not different in quality. One of the best singers recorded in the 1920s, Egor Surikov, learned his *stariny* from his mother, who had been recorded by Gilferding in the 1870s. Surikov's texts were remarkably close to those of his mother (Astakhova 1938: 74).

The second type of *stariny* teller comes closest to the kind of singer Lord describes in the *Singer of Tales* (2000 [1960]: 30–67) and Wilhelm Radloff in his studies of Turkic performers (1870: xvi–xvii). When learning a *bylina,* this kind of singer learns initially only the overall plot and then, by using typical scenes and descriptions and creating connections between them, fleshes out his or her own text. Once created, these idiolectal texts remain generally stable and often become more and more polished. Nastasya Bogdanova developed a distinctly idiolectal text of "Dobrynya and Alyosha" and thereafter did not significantly alter it with reperformance, but continued to add detail and deepen the psychology of the characters by, for example, enlarging on a scene in which Dobrynya parts with his wife (in the 1932 version as compared to that of 1926) (Astakhova 1938: 77). Although some of Bogdanova's *stariny* can be traced to the same source as Surikova's, they tend to be much longer (her *Dunai* is 473 verses in comparison with Surikova's 270), mostly due to character development and extended dialogues (Astakhova 1938: 77–79). Singers who create stable idiolectal texts often have clear individual styles. Bogdanova's songs are distinguished by psychologically rich dialogues, while those of Maksim Antonov, for instance, feature ornate and expanded descriptions of heroes, their horses, and ships. Antonov made such descriptions into something of a signature by, for example, repeating his striking depiction of Ilya Muromets as the hero sets out on each new journey, so that the vision of Ilya becomes in Astakhova's words the "dominant visual image" of the song, as in these verses from *Ilya Muromets's Travels* 3–5: "His head is white, his beard is grey, falling over his white chest, spreading like smooth pearls" (Astakhova 1938: 82, 181).

The difference between singers who tend to be faithful to their models and singers who do not lies partly in their personal inclinations and attitude to variation. A singer intent on faithful performance, if he or she forgets an episode, tends to omit it, being more concerned about "getting it wrong" or "falsifying" the tale than truncating the song (Astakhova 1938: 75, 80–81). Others have a different attitude. Gilferding, for example, characterized one of the singers, Andrei Sorokin, as "cavalier" in this regard. When Gilferding pointed out that Sorokin used to sing a certain episode differently, Sorokin replied: "What does it matter? I can do it one way or the other way—as you like" (Gilferding 1894: 26–27).

There are also singers who vary their *stariny* in a manner different from Antonov and Bogdanova. These singers begin by learning the plot of a *starina*, but do not gradually develop their own, idiolectal but stable, texts. They change their song significantly every time they perform it, freely using their arsenal of plots, episodes, scenes, and expressions. An example is a famous singer known as Shegolyonok, whose style was studied on the basis of fourteen *byliny*, ten of which were recorded multiple times. Nikolai Vasiliev comments that his versions of the same *bylina* differ so much that one could take them for songs of two different singers (1907: 170–196). His changes do not tend in the same direction, like those of Antonov and Bogdanova, and can happen at any level, from new episodes and hybrid plots to completely different verbal expressions. A fascinating case is Marfa Kryukova, daughter of the famous singer Agrafena Kryukova, who both greatly extended her songs (one of her *stariny*, *Garves*, grew to be 2,164 verses long) and knew more than a hundred of them (according to Astakhova, the usual number for a good singer is between twenty and forty) (Astakhova 1939: 177). Kryukova never repeated a *starina* exactly as before, but freely used her huge arsenal of episodes, motifs, and traditional expressions to compose a new version in each performance. Her versions, while fully traditional in the sense that they are composed of traditional elements, are also strikingly different from all other known versions of the same songs, including those of her mother. Kryukova almost never assigned her songs to a single source, but named at least two: for example, "from my mother and grandfather Ganya," or "from many locals and some passers-by" (Astakhova 1939: 178–179). Most of her songs did come from her own family, but it seems that in her youth, Kryukova would use every opportunity to hear *stariny* (for instance, spending time with the fishermen as they mended their nets and sang) and always asked passers-by for stories. The unusual *starina* about Garves was created in this latter way, when a foreigner (a "German" according to locals, but most foreigners would have been so called) arrived in Kryukova's village on some, as she thought, "learned" business. He told her the story about Garves and other knights, which, over the years, grew in her performances into a long song. It was recorded from her twice, and while the later version exactly replicated the plot of the earlier version, there is not a single verse in the two versions that is literally the same (Astakhova 1939: 180–181).

Even Kryukova, however, never altered the main turns of the plot and the characteristics of the protagonists. This can be explained by the singers' conviction that the *stariny* represent historical truth and are handed down by a reliable tradition. Ivan Ryabinin, when he traveled to Moscow to perform his *stariny* and was questioned by a listener doubtful of their veracity, replied, "Of course these songs are true. Otherwise, why sing them?" (Chicherov 1982: 17). Researchers mention that once in a while someone among the listeners would express doubt about the truthfulness of a *starina*. This skepticism was generally met with indignation by the rest of the group, who insisted on the distinction between a fairy tale (an entertaining fiction) and a *starina* (a true story about the past) (Chicherov 1982: 16–17).[8]

FROM IDIOLECT TO TRADITION

The generational studies of singers and their students in the north of Russia show how an individual singer's idiolect can impact the tradition. Rybnikov, for example, observed how a lament sung by a young woman from Pudozh for her cousin was immediately picked up by other women and became widely known. An exceptional lament became a traditional song. Like the best epic singers, the best lamenters leave their imprint on the tradition (Rybnikov 1989: 78, 1991: 115–117). If an epic singer who creates stable idiolectal texts has among his or her students singers such as Ivan Ryabinin, a brilliant performer capable of recreating his models almost exactly, then what used to be an idiolectal feature, such as a striking description of Ilya's white hair or a dramatic dialogue, will cease to be idiolectal and become initially a local feature of a particular family or school of singers and with time potentially even a pan-traditional element.

Turkic evidence provides interesting examples of this process. Victor Zhirmunsky, for example, notes that in Uzbekistan particular variants of a given epic song (*dastan*) long remain associated with the name of their creators and that these names are transmitted by the oral tradition along with the songs themselves. Even parts of the epics, single episodes or descriptions, can bear the *sphragis* of their creator. For example, the grotesque depictions of the Kalmyk warriors in some versions of the *Alpamïš* are said to stem from the mid-nineteenth-century singer Amin-baxšï, who excelled at such descriptions (Zhirmunsky 1962: 438). Of course, each poet would alter Amin-baxšï's words in the process of creating his poetic idiolect, and yet something that belonged to Amin-baxšï's individual style became part of the shared language of the tradition and part of the "grammar" that the next generations of singers acquired.

In contrast to modern oral traditions, when it comes to Homer we largely lack the ability to track the development of the epic historically and can only reconstruct its diachrony based on the texts that survive. Nevertheless, it is possible that the presence of idiolects is detectable in Homer. In her study of Homeric constructions ("learned pairings of form and function" [2014: 4]), Chiara Bozzone observes that individual language (I-Language, in her terminology) can be idiosyncratic enough that "we may sometimes catch a glimpse of individuality" in specific parts of the Homeric epics (78–79). Bozzone's case in point is a half-line construction for the verb προσέειπε, which she generalizes as follows (79):

$$[(\smile)\ \smile -\ ]_{\text{Obj./Subj.Pr}}\ \text{προσέειπεν}\ [\smile - \times]_{\text{Obj./Subj.NP}}\ (5\times)$$

Odyssey 16.166 provides an example: στῆ δὲ πάροιθ' αὐτῆς. τὸν δὲ προσέειπεν Ἀθήνη ("he stood before her. And Athena spoke to him"). The construction is limited to several consecutive books, *Odyssey* 14–17. The fact that this construction is rare, that it is localized to one stretch of narrative, that it admits some variation (the subject can come before or after the verb), and that elsewhere προσέειπε occurs in different, and very rigid, constructions—all these factors suggest that this construction was a "local experiment of an individual poet" (81) or, it may be added on the basis of comparanda, of a local family or school of poets. There are also several isolated constructions in *Iliad* 23, which could suggest that it was "created by a different I-Language," though, as Bozzone herself admits, much work needs to be done to move from anecdotal observations to anything approaching a proof (81–83).

Should the use of idiolectal constructions be sufficient for us to say that we can hear a voice of an individual singer in *Odyssey* 14–17 or *Iliad* 23? We are far from being able to answer such a question, but the evidence of other traditions suggests that the presence of individual voices within an oral epic is to be expected (cf. Ready 2012a: 72) and that these voices do not have to belong to the very latest stage of the poem's evolution or only to its dominant performers.

LAMENTERS AS PERFORMERS OF EPIC

In the northern Russian material, some of the most remarkable idiolectal texts belong to lamenters who perform epic. Bogdanova, mentioned earlier, is typical. It is no accident that Bogdanova was also a great master of laments, a genre of song that resists stability. If a *starina* can be sung in the same way again and again, laments have to be adjusted to their occasion. A performer of lament was expected to tell the story of the deceased and his or her circumstances of death and to voice the traditionally conceived thoughts and feelings of the family. Russian laments are dialogic: whether the lamenter sings in her own voice or as one of the women related to the dead, she addresses, in turn, the deceased and those assembled at the funeral. When singing epic songs, a master lamenter would typically be inclined to flesh them out with dialogic scenes of deeply felt dramatic emotions. Bogdanova, for example, used her skills as a lamenter not only to represent laments within *stariny* but more generally to create dialogue and enhance descriptions of emotion.

Several researchers who work on the *stariny* remark that the skills of lamenters influenced their way of performing epic songs. Three features are typically mentioned: first, great creativity in variation; second, greater attention to emotion and psychological motivation; and third, an increased tendency toward interdiscursivity. An example is Anna Pashkova, whose two versions of *Djuk* show all the signs of a lamenter performing epic, including the introduction of unusual motifs and scenes (for instance, the hero's mother asking the hero to pray and eat before departing), an ability to manipulate elements at different levels (plots, motifs, expressions, constructions) and combine them smoothly into a text, and the fact that some of the variation occurs on the basis of non-epic songs (Chernyaeva 1981: 21–29).

Some striking examples of lament merging into epic are provided by a gifted lamenter, Irina Fedosova, who reperformed her laments for collectors, primarily Eppidifor Barsov, starting in the 1860s and continuing through the 1890s.[9] Many researchers, beginning with Barsov himself, note the "epic" character of Fedosova's laments and even call them "*byliny* laments" because of the large number of expressions and constructions that are typical of *byliny* (Chistova and Chistov 1997: 480). As Aleksandr Veselovsky notes (1873), this is a case of two cognate traditional genres developing in constant contact.[10] It would be equally correct to call Fedosova's *byliny* "lament *byliny*" because of the lament techniques used in them. I highlight not just the epic diction of Fedosova's laments but the way she expands her laments in reperformance. Just as she can use her skills as lamenter in composing epic, so she can also expand her laments, turning them in effect into epic songs.

Funeral laments reflect the circumstances of the death and include descriptions of the life that preceded it (the bride of the dead soldier was waiting for him; the wife and children of a dead husband used to live safely and affluently when he was alive). Fedosova turned these descriptions into extended epic-like narratives. For example, she begins her lament for a man killed by lightning with a striking divine prologue reminiscent of the dialogue between Zeus and Helios at *Odyssey* 12.354–391 and between Zeus and Poseidon at *Odyssey* 13.125–145. The prophet Ilya (Elijah) complains to God about a farmer, who is working on Ilya's day (something forbidden by superstition) and not going to church, and threatens to bring on a storm and strike the offending farmer with lightning. God responds by saying "Whatever you want Ilya—you do as you will!" (*Плач об убитом громом-молнией* [*Lament for a man killed by lightning*] 16, Chistova and Chistov 1997: 202). There follows an extended description of the storm, during which farmers take shelter in their houses and pray, except for one who decides to wait out the storm under a tree. Next is a moving scene in which the storm passes and the wife of the farmer realizes that her husband is missing, runs to look for him, first sees his horse standing alone, and finally sees a tree "split into splinters, bent to the ground" and next to it her "trusty head" (her husband) prostrate on the ground, "his white chest pierced with that arrow, his spirited heart torn by lightning, his white arms thrown wide" (*Плач об убитом громом-молнией* [*Lament for a man killed by lightning*] 101–103, Chistova and Chistov 1997: 204). Only beginning with line 119 does Fedosova switch from her narrative to address the widow in the second person. In effect, Fedosova develops her lament into a narrative song similar to epic.

It comes as no surprise, then, that, although Fedosova's fame derived from her laments, she also sang epic songs. Her laments follow all the conventions of tradition, and yet they are undoubtedly extraordinary and were seen as such by all who heard her, from her fellow villagers, who started inviting her to perform laments when she was only thirteen years old, to admiring audiences in Saint Petersburg and Moscow, where, possibly already in her nineties, she performed in 1895 and 1896.[11] The audiences were mesmerized, and Fedosova received much publicity in the press (Chistov 1997: 428; Andreev and Vinogradov 1937: 21–22). The size of Fedosova's laments is exceptional: one of the laments in Barsov's collection, the bride's lament upon her betrothal, is 1,074 lines long and is answered by the mother's lament, 514 lines in length (Chistov and Chistova 1997: 277–312). She achieves this expansion by freely and creatively using the traditional diction of lament and *bylina* to paint scenes and develop plots that are absent or expressed only briefly in shorter laments. Fedosova's songs provide examples of laments merging into epics and of lament techniques being used for epic singing.

The result is epic poetry infused with lament, but the process whereby this happens is not what we might expect. Instead of an epic singer who knows laments and uses them in his songs, we find a lamenter singing epic and developing her laments into an epic-like form.

I have pointed to examples in South Slavic and Telugu traditions of women's songs that were epic or near-epic but had a distinct feminine outlook. In the case of northern Russia too researchers detect a feminine outlook in women's performance, such as a tendency to enlarge psychologically potent scenes—like a hero's parting from his wife, a mother's complaint, or joy at a hero's return—and an attention to everyday details and scenes, such as describing how a mother gives food and clothing to her heroic son as he sets off from home. The epic songs of lamenters do not necessarily describe or even evoke laments: rather, they use lament-derived techniques to tell an epic tale. The lament-derived skills and techniques of epic performers can have an impact on non-lament scenes in an epic tradition, such as scenes of family life and dialogues.

The question for Homerists is whether such evidence is in any way applicable to Homer. The role of lament in Homer remains the prime example of interdiscursivity with women's songs. The Homeric poems evoked for their audience the laments that both the singer and the listeners heard at funerals. It has been suggested that women's laments were crucial for the development of the epic (Murnaghan 1999; Nagy 1999b; Sultan 1999; Dué 2006). As Nagy comments on *Odyssey* 24.58–64, wherein the Muses sing a *thrēnos* at Achilleus's funeral, "the lamentation by the Muses is what propels the imperishable glory of Achilles, as sung in both epic and lyric" (2013: 101). The laments by Andromache, Hekabe, Briseis, and Helen in the *Iliad* are not only laments of women for their husbands and sons but, as Dué puts it, "prototypical laments for heroes," who, from the point of view of the ancient audiences, continue to be lamented in epics at seasonally recurring festivals (2006: 43). We do not, then, underestimate the role of lament in the evolution of epic, but we might underestimate the role of lamenters, of women who might have influenced epic in broader and more varied ways than is usually envisaged, not only by being overheard by the male performers of epic but by performing epic songs of their own.

EPIC AND LAMENT IN TURKIC TRADITIONS

Turkic evidence offers striking parallels to the Homeric vision of epic's origins in lament. Nienke van der Heide reports that during her fieldwork in Kyrgyzstan she was "told on a number of occasions that the *Manas* epic started off as just one song: the mourning song (*košok*) that Manas's singer Ïrchï-uul composed after Manas's death. This song was passed on to the next generations, and built upon by other singers, until it reached the size that it has today" (2008: 102). An alternative version of the origins of *Manas*, also derived from the oral tradition itself, is that the first performer of the epic was the legendary poet Toktogul, about whom it is said that not only people but birds, animals, rivers, and mountains listened to his song (104). Toktogul, like Ïrchï-uul, is said to have created the epos out of "weeping songs" (Musaev 1994: 115; van der Heide 2008: 103).

Quite apart from the actual origins of epic, the idea that epic stems from lament might be sustained by singers' own practices and processes whereby laments acquire the features of epic. Researchers who study Kyrgyz *košok* note that the traditional phrases, movements, gestures, and vocal qualities that are used in *košok* are to be found in oral epics (Pritchard 2011: 168–169). In Kyrgyzstan there is a distinction between a ritual and private *košok* at a loved one's funeral and a public *košok*, which evokes personal grief at a safer distance and focuses on praise and commemoration of the dead. This distinction mirrors the one Alexiou detected in Homer and archaic usage between a *goos*, performed by the family and expressing their personal grief, and a *thrēnos*, a mourning song performed by professional singers (2002 [1974]: 11–12, 102–103). In the Kyrgyz funeral yurt, laments gradually emerge from sobbing and may dissolve into it at any point when a woman can no longer sustain the expected melodic and verbal patterns (Pritchard 2011: 180). A mourner is joined by other performers, lamenting in turns and simultaneously, each woman with her own words. Maureen Pritchard records a person from the Talas region commenting that "*košok* is dialogue" (2011: 180). All of these features of the *košok* are, of course, shared by Greek laments. Pritchard notes that it is impossible to capture these polyphonic performances in written texts, and women are generally unable to reperform their *košok* upon request, the exception being the professional mourners, who can put forth a "dry" performance, refraining from emotional involvement (181).

There is also a different kind of *košok*, one that is sung to the accompaniment of the *komuz* and now performed primarily by men. These *košok* are subdued and restrained, and although the singer may use a tight or wavering voice, he will not choke, blur his articulation, or collapse sobbing. Although most of Pritchard's informers called this genre *košok*, there is a more technical term for it, *joktoo*. These songs are performed in public (they may even be aired on television), often during a ritual that marks the fortieth day after death, commemorating the deceased and offering praise and consolation. The notional transition from lament to epic is visibly enacted in this transition from funeral *košok* to the longer, more epic, and calmer *joktoo*. Today, *joktoo* is performed primarily by *aqïns*, that is, epic singers, but Radloff recorded a "memorial lament" (*joktoo*) performed by a daughter for her father, Čokčoloy, that overlapped with epic in prosody and diction and compared the deceased to epic heroes (Hatto 1983: 186, 192). Here too we have an example of an epic song performed by a female lamenter and of lament merging into epic. How, then, should we imagine the "weeping songs" out of which Toktogul creates the first *Manas*? Perhaps not only as funeral laments but as epic songs performed by women lamenters. According to Nina Smirnova, while men generally sing *joktoo* among the Kyrgyz, women performed such laments among the Kazakh, and specifically the daughter of the deceased was expected to sing praises for her father and recall his life in her laments (1967: 146).

SONG CONTESTS BETWEEN MEN AND WOMEN: MODERN EVIDENCE

It is probably fair to say that no other mode of discourse by women has a more profound influence on epic than the lament (esp. Caraveli 1986; Holst-Warhaft 1992). There is evidence to suggest, however, that weddings also provided an occasion for public or semi-public performances by women, and in some cultures, including ancient Greece, they were also occasions for performing laments (Seaford 1987: 114–115; Lardinois 2001a: 83–85). Weddings constitute occasions for performances both of epic by male singers and of women's epic songs, and they are also frequently the subject of such songs. The *Candainī* epic is performed at weddings, and the wedding of the heroine was the subject of one Gond woman's song recorded by Flueckiger. Telugu *Ramayana* songs are performed at weddings, and the wedding of Rama and Sita is one of their major subjects. Rao remarks that it is seen "through women's eyes" and that "every detail relating to women's roles in the ceremony is carefully described, even the saris the women wear" (1991: 121). Sappho 44, with its descriptions of the finery and jewelry that Andromache brings and of the actions of maidens and women who go to meet her, fits the same pattern.

Russian, Turkic, and, as far as we can judge, ancient Greek weddings also feature(d) competitive singing by men and women, and in all these traditions echoes of such songs find their way into epics. This, then, is another context in which to look for non-rhapsodic performers of epic and for a complex performative ecology to undergird Homeric interdiscursivity.

Since the subject is too large to tackle fully here, I will consider just one type of performance—song contests between men and women. Kazakh tradition makes a good starting point, since it is rich in varieties of song contests (*aytïs*), including *aytïs* between girls and boys and *aytïs* between singers (*aqïns*). The former kind often appears in descriptions of weddings. Its simplest form is a joking and teasing duel between girls and boys in four-line stanzas. In such contests girls assert their superiority and disparage men, while the boys claim the opposite but also jokingly speak to the girls of their love (Winner 1958: 29–34; Smirnova 1967: 91–101).[12]

A common variety of wedding song in the form of a male–female dialogue is the so-called *džar-džar* song, in which every line ends with the refrain "*džar-džar*." At Kazakh weddings, these songs can be sung by two choruses. The boys sing in a lighthearted manner and tell the bride not to postpone her farewells to her family and home: she will have to abandon her former life and adapt herself to a new household. The stanzas of the girls are described by Thomas Winner as "mournful" and express fear of the future, the sadness of parting from home and friends, and the loss of freedom in marriage (1958: 37; cf. Smirnova 1967: 134–139).

A cognate genre in Uzbek is known as *yor-yor.* When it was performed as part of the Uzbek wedding ritual, this song was not dialogic. Rather, it was performed by a chorus of women as they welcomed and saw off the bride. There is, however, another wedding genre, *ulan*, which is dialogic—it is a contest in song and wit between representatives of the bride's and the groom's parties. In the Uzbek epic *Alpāmïš*, there is an extended scene of *ulan* performances. After a long absence, Alpāmïš returns home in the nick of time to prevent his wife's marriage to the usurper Ultan. Disguised as an old servant Qultai, Alpāmïš arrives at the start of the wedding festivities and competes in *ulans* first with Ultan's mother (Mirzaev, Abdurakhimov, and Mirbaldaeva 1999: lines 13,035–13,105) and then with his own wife, now Ultan's bride, Barčin (lines 13,105–13,210), winning both contests. Apart from the general, and much remarked upon, similarity of the plot to the *Odyssey* (Germain 1954: 11–54; A. Lord 1991: 211–244; Grossardt 2006: 33–37; S. West 2012: 538–539), there are many more specific parallels that could be drawn between the *ulan* contest of Alpāmïš and Barčin and the dialogues of Penelope and Odysseus in the *Odyssey*, especially their conversation in *Odyssey* 19 (Levaniouk 2011: 229–246, forthcoming). For example, Barčin is overcome by emotion and remarks that Qultai's voice is just like that of Alpāmïš (Mirzaev, Abdurakhimov, and Mirbaldaeva 1999: lines 13,118–13,120); she explains, in song, that she is remarrying to prevent the death of her and Alpāmïš's son (lines 13,131–13,135); and Alpāmïš-Qultai sings of his tearful wanderings away from home (lines 13,144–13,145) and refuses to take off his hat when Barčin asks him to (lines 13,143, 13,146).

My purpose here, however, is not to compare the two scenes, but rather to comment on the way a wedding performance is incorporated into the epic. The *yor-yor* and *ulan* songs are not quoted in the *Alpāmïš* in the way they would be actually performed at a wedding. Rather, the meter and rhythm of *yor-yor,* in combination with the dialogic form of *ulan*, is used to evoke an occasion and create a musical background for the scene of Alpāmïš's encounter with Barčin.

In discussing the music of the *Alpāmïš*, Faizulla Karomatli notes that the dialogue in the *Alpāmïš* represents a hybrid form: it is dialogic, like *ulan*, and uses four-line stanzas with refrain, like *yor-yor* (1999: 58–59). Further, according to Karomatli, *yor-yor* is no longer performed in its ritual function in those regions where *Alpāmïš* is performed, while *ulan* is used only sporadically (59–60). Yet practically every recording of the *Alpāmïš* features this wedding dialogue, and in each audio recording it is sung to a wedding melody, although the melody varies depending on the school and personal proclivities of each singer. The evocation of the wedding song is present even in the *Alpāmïš* of Yorlakab-baxši, a representative of the "single melody" mode of performance, which tends to "quote" sparingly from other genres of song (59).

In the *Alpāmïš*, the wedding song contest with its melodic signature became a stable part of the epic tradition and apparently took on a life of its own, independent of the actual synchronic wedding ritual in which such hybrid songs, or even their separate components, are no longer performed. The tradition of song contest in the setting of the wedding left its imprint on the epic in the form of the dialogue between Alpāmïš and Barčin. Alpāmïš and Barčin can have the kind of conversation they have in the epic in part because of the prominence of male–female song contests in Turkic song culture. Such competitive performances seem to have declined in Uzbekistan, but they had already become part of the epic tradition.

Moreover, being refracted in epic is not the only way a song contest can become textualized. In contrast to ephemeral *aytïs* that cease to exist with the end of a performance, there are also traditional ones, in effect songs about the famous *aytïs* of old, which are performed by a single singer taking the roles of both contestants. One such *aytïs* re-creates a mid-nineteenth-century contest between a male singer, Birdžan (1834–1897), and a female singer, Sara (1878–1916) (Karataev 1968: 335–336). This is an *aytïs* between singers, and yet it also has features of the wedding *aytïs* between girls and boys.

Aware of Sara's fame and her victories against other singers, Birdžan arrives for a contest with her shortly before her marriage—she is already betrothed. As is typical of an *aytïs* between epic singers (*aqïns*), each contestant praises his or her own clan and disparages the clan of the other, but Sara also boasts of her beauty, described in an idealized and traditional way. Both describe their poetic art in hyperbolic terms (words are "intricate ornaments etched on gold and silver," "glowing silks of Samarkand," "flame that cannot be extinguished by a whole river") and ridicule the art of their opponent (Karataev 1968: 335). The main theme of this particular *aytïs*, however, is the position of women. It is as a man and a woman that Birdžan and Sara clash on the questions of morals, customs, wealth, fortune, and happiness. This theme is also decisive for the outcome of the *aytïs*: Sara loses because she is a woman. Birdžan reminds Sara that she is betrothed to a man who is by everyone's consent not her equal and that she has no choice. Birdžan asks if he could take a look at Sara's future husband and if she is indeed as proud of her family as she claims to be. Sara gives up, responding with a stanza about the bitter lot of woman, "who cannot be in charge even of her own person." Interestingly, although Sara loses, the *aytïs* concludes with Birdžan's praise for her (Karataev 1968: 336).

Versions of this *aytïs* have been expanded to tell the story of Sara's life: Sara may lose the contest, but she emerges as the main hero of the song. In terms of its dynamics, the *aytïs* of Birdžan and Sara is reminiscent of male–female song contests, both monodic and choral, sung at weddings. Such songs seem at first to be balanced and symmetrical, and yet in the end the focus is on the girl, who will always ultimately lose because she will have to marry.

In the Turkic examples, there is a correspondence between the ecology of performances outside of the epic and the epic itself. The prominence of song contests between men and women corresponds to the importance of the *ulan*-like dialogue between Alpāmïš and Barčin in the Uzbek *Alpāmïš* and the existence of the Kazakh *aytïs* of Birdžan and Sara as a traditional song. The existence of male–female contests involving such famous epic singers as Birdžan presupposes the existence of female singers able to compete at this level. There are multiple examples of such competitions, including those of Suyumbay and Kunbala and Sayadil and Maysa (Karataev 1968: 324–326). Especially interesting is the *aytïs* of Bozdak and Akbala, which is part of a poem about the doomed love of the two protagonists (Radloff 1870).

SONG CONTESTS BETWEEN MEN AND WOMEN: ANCIENT GREECE

The wedding *aytïs* has parallels in Greece. The genre is reminiscent of the Greek *oaristus*, as exemplified by Pseudo-Theocritus 27, an exchange of one-liners where a boy asks a girl to marry him, is mercilessly teased, responds in kind, and in the end, as always, wins (Levaniouk 2011: 85–91). A choral version of such a duel is dramatized in Catullus 62, which plays both with Sappho's songs and with wedding songs directly (Bowra 1961: 219–221; Seaford 1987: 114–115). Echoes of agonistic songs sung at weddings are present in Aeschylus's *Suppliants*, where a female chorus sings in a dialogue with a male one. Richard Seaford has argued that traces of such wedding songs are also to be seen in Sappho 27, in a fragment of the Danaid trilogy in which both boys and girls sing on the morning after the wedding night (fr. 43 Radt), and in the Hesiodic *Shield* 276–284, where choruses of both boys and girls sing in a wedding procession (1987: 114–115).[13]

There is also evidence from Greece of poetic contests outside of the wedding. One example is the legendary competition between Corinna and Pindar (won by Corinna). Pausanias, in reporting on the depiction of Corinna with a victory ribbon in the gymnasion of Tanagra, adds that she might have won because she was the most beautiful of the women of her time (9.22.3). In an anecdote reported by Plutarch, Corinna instructs Pindar in using myth in his poetry and then laughs at his effort (*On the Glory of the Athenians* 348a)—an attitude reminiscent of the Turkic *aytïs*.

Even more similar to the *aytïs* between Birdžan and Sara is a dialogue in song between Sappho and Alcaeus, quoted by Aristotle (*Rhetoric* 1.1367a), in which Alcaeus appears to make a sexual advance while Sappho fends him off. The sparring in song of Alcaeus and Sappho, like that of Birdžan and Sara, became a song in its own right. As Nagy puts it (2007: 228, emphasis in original),

> a process of recomposition-in-performance could recreate not only the given composition itself but also the identity of the composer credited with speaking as the "I" in the notionally original composition. The voice of the composer could even be replaced by the voice of a performer other than the notionally original composer. In short, a *reperformed composer* could become a *recomposed performer.*

As the *aytïs* of Birdžan and Sara continued to be reperformed on various occasions, Birdžan and Sara also become what Nagy has termed "recomposed performers." Nagy argues that the notional composer of the song about Sappho and Alcaeus is Alcaeus, and that too can be paralleled in the Kazakh *aytïs* tradition: the composition of the traditional *aytïs* is ascribed to one of the original participants—in the Kazakh case, the loser of the contest.

Outside of Homer, then, there are traces in other ancient Greek sources of performances and performers resembling what we find in the Turkic evidence. There is also plentiful evidence within the epic itself. I have argued elsewhere that the dialogue between Odysseus and Penelope in *Odyssey* 19 should be seen as a contest between two masterful singers (Levaniouk 2011: 291, 303–304). This contest happens in a pre-wedding atmosphere on the eve of the bow contest and is contextualized by wedding-related themes and diction (229–246, 271–279, 316–322; cf. Levaniouk, forthcoming). We do not know whether wedding music could be heard in the voices of the rhapsodes as they performed these scenes, but the use of wedding diction in itself can be seen as having a similar effect, evoking, in Flueckiger's words, "the interpretive frame" of the wedding (1996: 30).

Another contest takes place between Helen and Menelaos in the *Odyssey* (4.235–289), performed before an audience at a feast. Following Helen's story about Odysseus's secret mission to Troy, Menelaos offers his own account, in which instead of a Helen who sees through Odysseus's tricks and longs for home we see a Helen who would have undermined the Achaian stratagem had not Odysseus recognized her deception. Although the immediate context of these performances is recollection of Odysseus's Trojan deeds for the sake of Telemachos, their larger context is a wedding, since a double wedding is being celebrated at the palace as Telemachos arrives (*Odyssey* 4.3–7).

The dialogue between Odysseus and Nausikaa at *Odyssey* 6.85–197, a scene long recognized as imbued with wedding poetics (N. Austin 1991; Karanika 2014: 55–68), can also be seen as a song contest. As Andromache Karanika shows, Odysseus responds with a competitive performance to Nausikaa's previous song. Nausikaa sings a hymn to Artemis (as indicated, Karanika argues, by the structural similarities of her performance and the *Homeric Hymn to Artemis*), and Odysseus complements her performance by comparing Nausikaa first to Artemis and then to the palm by Apollo's altar on Delos.

Karanika observes that "it is the same kind of competition that we find in the *Contest of Homer and Hesiod*, in which Homer allegedly attends a festival in Delos and composes a poem" (2014: 62). The *Contest of Homer and Hesiod* is in fact remarkably close in structure, techniques, and even overall setting to a Kazakh *aytïs*. In the song contest of Nausikaa and Odysseus, the wedding theme may be strong and the agonistic notes muted, but the capping style of Odysseus's response is nevertheless reminiscent of a song contest. Moreover, in alluding to Delos, the exchange of songs between Odysseus and Nausikaa evokes the festival on Delos in the *Homeric Hymn to Apollo*, so that Nausikaa, with her *khoros* of girls, emerges as a figure structurally parallel to the Delian maidens, while Odysseus takes on the role of an itinerant rhapsode, the "blind man from Chios" of the hymn (166–176) (Karanika 2014: 63–65).[14] The exchange of performances between the chorus of the Delian maidens and the blind man of Chios consists of mutual praise, but the symmetrical nature of these envisioned performances and their focus on artistic excellence is implicitly agonistic. The Delian maidens are depicted as singing a hymn for Apollo, Leto, and Artemis and then transitioning to singing the "men and women of old" (*Homeric Hymn to Apollo* 158–161). In this, they give us a "glimpse of interaction between epic and lyric poetry," as Karanika puts it (2014: 65), but also perhaps a glimpse of female and non-rhapsodic performers of epic poetry.[15]

Just as in the *Odyssey* the origins of epic can be envisaged as a lament for Achilleus sung by the Muses, so these origins can be envisaged as a wedding song. In Pindar's *Pythian* 3.88–95 and *Nemean* 5.23–72, the Muses sing at the wedding of Peleus and Thetis. In *Nemean* 5, as Apollo plays the phorminx, they sing of the past, telling the story that leads to this very wedding: "first of all they sing, leading off from Zeus, holy Thetis and Peleus" (αἱ δὲ πρώτιστον μὲν ὕμνησαν Διὸς ἀρχόμεναι σεμνὰν Θέτιν/ Πηλέα θ', 25–26). Interestingly, they sing a *humnos* beginning with Zeus, just as the Homeridai begin with a *prooimion* to Zeus in *Nemean* 2.1–3.[16] The performance of the Muses in *Nemean* 5, just like the performance of the Delian maidens in the *Homeric Hymn to Apollo*, seems to be a choral performance that develops into epic.[17] The wedding of Peleus and Thetis is an epic theme that was, according to Proclus, placed at the beginning of the *Cypria*. In *Nemean* 5 the same theme is sung by the Muses, but their song is reminiscent of Sappho 44 in its mixed epic and wedding thematics. The focus is not on the beginnings of the Trojan War but on the tales of love and jealousy that lead to the wedding: the "Potiphar's wife" plot with Hippolyta in the role of the wife and Peleus as her slandered object of desire, Zeus's decision to reward Peleus with a perfect Nereid bride, and the marriage arrangements between the kinsmen Zeus and Poseidon.

CONCLUSION

In northern Russian epic songs, in Turkic epic, and in Indian traditions, rich interdiscursivity within epic correlates to a rich ecology outside of epic of performances by both male and female performers with a variety of personal styles. This evidence suggests the possibility that what lies behind Homeric interdiscursivity is not simply an evocation of different genres, whereby a rhapsode absorbs women's songs and echoes them. Another model would be a complex ecology that includes not only laments but also epic songs by masters of laments who use their mastery to alter the epic tradition in distinct ways.

Such an ecology would also include song competitions between men and women, epic performances at weddings, and epic performances by women with a focus on weddings. Women who sing laments and wedding songs can be among the most creative singers of epic, and they can use their skills to create their own versions of epic songs. It is possible that women in Greece sang Homer and that their poetic idiolects entered the tradition and may thus be present in our texts.

NOTES

1. It would be impossible to provide here a comprehensive list of recent comparative work on Homer. Some of the most relevant examples include: Martin 1984, 1989; J. M. Foley 1991, 1995, 2002; Nagy 1995; Danek 1998; Minchin 2001; Scodel 2002a; Dué 2006; de Vet 2008; Ready 2012a.

2. Alexiou 2002 [1974] is the classic on this subject. On laments in Homer, see Holst-Warhaft 1992; Murnaghan 1999; Sultan 1999; Dué 2002, 2006; Tsagalis 2004.

3. See Aloni 1986 and Dué 2002: 59–60 for discussion of Iliadic refractions of Lesbian traditions.

4. See Pernigotti 2001 for the idea that an interplay of individual and collective perspectives is present in Sappho 44 and that both are suitable for multiple occasions.

5. On Rybnikov's work, see Razumova 1989: 9–43.

6. Chicherov discusses the "schools" with distinct differences in repertoire (1982). For example, the Elustafiev school tended toward warlike heroic songs and the school of Konon toward songs with more peaceful themes (77–78).

7. Noteworthy are cases of traveling craftsmen who also sing epic songs. For example, Rybnikov mentions two tailors who went from place to place offering their services; both were excellent singers (1989: 50, 62).

8. See Reichl 1992: 125 on the same attitude and the same distinction in the Turkic evidence.

9. Barsov first published his collections of northern Russian laments in three volumes, which appeared in 1872, 1882, and 1885. An expanded edition with commentaries appeared in 1997 (Chistova and Chistov 1997). This edition includes an article on Barsov, his work, and the influence of his collection on the subsequent study of laments (Chistov 1997).

10. On Veselovsky's article, which anticipated the work of Mahler and Vinogradov on the traditional phraseology of laments, see Chistov 1990, 1997: 439, 481.

11. Fedosova did not know in what year she was born, and in press reports

dating between 1895 and 1899 her age ranges from seventy to ninety-eight (!) years old (Chistov 1997: 420).

12. On audience involvement in *aytïs* performances, see Reichl 1992: 77–78.

13. See also Swift 2006: 127–129 on hymeneal motifs in Euripides's *Hippolytus*.

14. On Homer ("the blind man from Chios") in the *Homeric Hymn to Apollo* and his interactions with the Delian maidens, see Nagy 2015: 188–200. On this passage and "the sequence of topics" sung by the Delian maidens, see Ford 1992: 45–46.

15. Nagy argues that the Homeric Hymns are morphologically older than the Homeric epics and that they are *prooimia*, which allow subsequent *metabasis* to epic (2010: 79–102).

16. On the beginning of *Nemean* 2, see Nagy 2010: 105–106, 353–360; on the scholia, see Nagy 2010: 65–69.

17. On choral performance merging into epic, see Nagy 2010: 93–102. Ford describes the song of the Muses in *Nemean* 5 as "heroic song" and compares it to the song of the Delian maidens (1992: 46).

Part II

NARRATORS AND CHARACTERS

CHAPTER SEVEN

Odysseus Polyonymous

DEBORAH BECK

HOMERIC FORMULAS GIVE VOICE TO HOMERIC SPEECH in several senses at once. The rhapsode depends on them to tell his (or her) poetic tale, and thus formulas as a group offer a glimpse of a conversation between the human performers and the audiences who would have listened to the Homeric epics and other poems like them. Within the Homeric poems, we find several types of speakers of the art language I once heard described as "Homer-ese." Different formulas appear, and are used in different ways, in the narrative in the *Odyssey* as compared to that of the *Iliad*. Similarly, the personalities of individual characters emerge partly through variations in the formulas that they utter, both within a given poem (cf. Martin 1989) and between the two Homeric epics. The "Homeric formula" cannot be fully understood unless the norms and patterns of *all* of these different speakers are taken into account. Whoever the speaker, a key feature of formulas is that in some contexts, and in some speeches, they play a key role in the telling of an affecting and memorable story; in others, they move the plot from point A to point B. Being able to make sense of the different ways that formulas "speak" in different contexts—different poems, different speakers, different metrical environments, different kinds of storytelling—is one of the defining features of an audience's experience of Homeric poetry, whether the poem comes from an ancient rhapsode or a modern printed translation.

Formulas associated with Odysseus provide a rich case study for understanding how formulas are used by the full range of Homeric speakers: he is the only character whose formulas are well attested in the *Iliad*, the *Odyssey*, and also his own speeches. Whereas Jenny Strauss Clay surveys the several epithets with a prefix *polu-* that modify Odysseus (1983: 29–34), this chapter casts a wider net. It constructs a formulaic system for Odysseus by grouping the formulas for him in three related sets: first, the most common nominative name-epithet formulas characteristic of (but not limited to) speech introductory verses in narrator text, then the full-verse vocative formulas used by characters who address Odysseus, and finally the epithets that Odysseus uses to refer to himself in his own speeches. As these Odysseus formulas will reveal, even the most formulaic and repetitive parts of the formulaic system are compatible both with the basic parameters of Milman Parry's definition of "formula" and with remarkable aesthetic force and individual creativity.

The starting point of formulaic studies for the last fifty years has generally been Parry's definition of a formula as "an expression regularly used, under the same metrical conditions, to express an essential idea" (1987: 13). This definition has been both the linchpin and the bane of Homeric studies since scholars began in the 1960s to grapple seriously with Parry's arguments. Every word in it has been the subject of vigorous and prolonged debates, most of which rage to the present day. How regular is "regular"? What about expressions that for various reasons seem like they might be formulas but appear only a handful of times, or just once? What constitutes "the same metrical conditions"? Or, to ask the same question a different way, what exactly do we mean by "context"? Perhaps most problematic, Parry's notion of "essential idea" came to be seen, and justly so, as much too broad and unsubtle, and it is on this aspect of the formula that the majority of work in recent decades has concentrated.

While our lack of agreement on a single, uncontroversial definition of "formula" cannot be ignored, settling this issue should not be the *sine qua non* of formulaic studies. After the primarily structural work of the 1960s explored the flexibility of the various components of formulas, subsequent research demonstrated that the use of traditional repeated language such as formulas still leaves plenty of room for individual artistic creativity (Russo 1997). In certain contexts, at least, these formulas have been shown to possess the kind of aesthetic meaning and significance that Parry's work had initially seemed to rule out. Recent studies have proposed the concept of "interformularity" as a way to approach allusions between the two Homeric poems within an oral compositional framework (Bakker 2013). Other recent work has suggested that Homeric characters understand epithets as meaningful words (Elmer 2015).

The question of whether a formulaic epithet has a contextually relevant "meaning" has tended to be answered with either "yes" or "no."

The most frequent and regular noun–epithet formulas (those typical of speech introductions) are almost universally assigned to the "no" column. For instance, in a study that elsewhere presents compelling analyses of the rich and sophisticated meanings conveyed by traditional language, John Miles Foley says that nominative epithets for Odysseus depend "not on the immediate narrative context but on the metrical situation" (1999: 206), and he classifies speech introductory formulas as "traditional punctuation" (221). Elsewhere, I have argued that speech introductions belong in the "yes" column (D. Beck 1999, 2005).

This chapter, by contrast, proposes that we abandon the "yes/no" approach to the question of meaning in formulaic language: in formulas, as in any kind of language, meaning exists on a spectrum. The meaning of a given speech introductory formula may be the same as its propositional content—"Odysseus answered him"—or its specific wording may play a central role in telling the story in a particular scene. These are not mutually exclusive when we regard meaning not as an "either/or" choice but as an "oscillation" between these two possibilities that arises from an "artfully controlled process" (Machacek 1994: 335). Similarly, the dichotomy in explaining the choice of a particular formula as determined by either meaning or metrical factors is a false one. We do not conceive of ordinary spoken language as a function of either meaning *or* grammar. Rather, when people speak, they effortlessly construct utterances that are both meaningful and grammatical. Given that a Homeric poet "was, as it were, a native speaker of the language 'Epic'" (Kahane 1997: 261), it seems likely that he would do the same thing.[1]

At the definitional level, we can move beyond several unproductive "either/or" dilemmas to improve our understanding of how formulaic systems work, if we take into account various dimensions of formulas that Parry's definition does not consider but are nonetheless compatible with his basic approach. The most important of these is what we mean by "contextual responsiveness," and indeed what we mean by "context." The relationship between "context" and "formula" has been not only the subject of the majority of the post-Parry work on formulas but also the basis for arguments that reject Parry's approach entirely, on the grounds that an oral poem would be unable to avoid jarring or inappropriate phrasing as successfully as the Homeric poems seem to. For instance, Harmut Erbse assumes that aesthetically effective or complex language cannot be traditional or formulaic (1994; cf. Shive 1987). However, as the nominative and vocative formulaic system for Odysseus makes clear, even the most repetitive and "formulaic" formulas can and do reflect contextually specific qualities of the ongoing story. These may include the emotions that the main narrator describes or the feelings of characters about people and events that they refer to.

But the fact that formulas *can* have a meaningful expressive dimension does not imply that they either *must* or *always* mean something significant in a given context. Indeed, once we look out for it, we notice a similar kind of fluidity about which aspects of the context will affect what a particular instance of a formula means (or does not mean). This presents an engaging challenge for an attentive audience in that a formula that had no particular significance the last time it was used, or even the last ten times it was used, may at any moment take center stage in the narrative and demand the audience's attention: drawing on and adapting Wolfgang Iser's reader-oriented approach (1974), Foley envisions an audience of oral poetry capable of noting such shifts (1991: esp. chapter 2). For instance, the distinction between generic epithets, which modify many characters, and unique epithets specific to one character is not hard and fast across every kind of context. To take just one example, the epithet πεπνυμένος ("thoughtful, shrewd") is unique to Telemachos in the *Odyssey*, but generic in the *Iliad* (Heath 2001).

Narrative level, too, defines the "context" of a Homeric formula. Important studies of formulas have marginalized formulas in characters' speeches by overstating both the differences between formulas in character speech and those in narrator text (Martin 1997a) and the rarity of formulas in character speech (N. Austin 1975: esp. 48–53). In fact, the various expressions that we call "Homeric formulas" play a key role in character speech as well as narrator text, and a view of formulas that takes narrator text as the norm or the baseline will result in an impoverished understanding of the Homeric language of formula. As we will see, formulas in character speech constitute a system of their own that both overlaps with and differs from the formulaic system in narrator text. A study of the formulas for Odysseus as they are used by all these various speakers creates a vibrant and nuanced picture of formulas in which both individual formulas and formulas as a larger group operate on a spectrum of meaning that varies according to different kinds of contexts, including the narrative level, the individual speaker, and the metrical shape of the formula.

NOMINATIVE FORMULAS: ΠΟΛΥΜΗΤΙΣ, ΠΟΛΥΤΛΑΣ, ΔΙΟΣ

The most common epithet for Odysseus, πολύμητις ("of many plans"), to a great extent conforms to the regular and almost mechanical characteristics of "formula" put forward in Parry's work. It appears predominantly within the half-verse speech introductory formula προσέφη [occasionally μετέφη] πολύμητις Ὀδυσσεύς ("Odysseus of many plans replied"; 70 of 87 instances), almost entirely in the nominative case. The only instance of πολύμητις that is either not in the nominative or not referring to Odysseus is *Iliad* 21.355, πολυμήτιος Ἡφαίστοιο #, where Hephaistos causes the river Xanthos to catch on fire at the behest of Hera. We also find one passage that uses this formula as part of a longer, unique speech introduction containing various context-specific details (*Iliad* 1.440–441). These speech introductory formulas can include various context-specific details in the first half. The most common full-verse speech introductory formula that includes πολύμητις is τὸν (or τὴν) δ' ἀπαμειβόμενος προσέφη πολύμητις Ὀδυσσεύς ("Odysseus of many plans answered him [or her]"; 5× *Iliad*, 45× *Odyssey*), but in place of ἀπαμειβόμενος, we may find a range of metrically equivalent participles that present the speaker's emotions or intentions (ὑπόδρα ἰδών ["glaring"; *Iliad* 4.349, 14.82, 7× *Odyssey*], ἐπιμειδήσας ["smiling"; *Iliad* 10.400, *Odyssey* 22.371], δολοφρονέων ["planning trickery"; *Odyssey* 18.51, 21.274]).[2] Four *Odyssey* verses that end in προσέφη πολύμητις Ὀδυσσεύς identify the addressee in the first half (8.474, 8.486, 22.390, 23.247). These verses, unlike most other instances of this formula, introduce the first speech in a conversational exchange or a resumption of conversation after a temporary silence, rather than an immediate response to the previous speech. There are also two speech conclusions that include πολύμητις Ὀδυσσεύς (*Iliad* 10.148, *Odyssey* 20.183; cf. the speech conclusions at *Iliad* 23.709 and 755, which include the metrically distinct formula Ὀδυσεὺς πολύμητις).

Of the eleven Odysseus-related instances of πολύμητις that appear outside of speech frames, five are found in characters' references to Odysseus, and these are always characters who are speaking positively about him or are favorably disposed toward him.[3] These occur twice in the *teichoskopia* (*Iliad* 3.200 by Helen and 3.216 by Antenor), and at *Odyssey* 2.173 (Halitherses), 4.763 (Penelope, in a prayer to Athena), and 19.585 (Odysseus himself, speaking in disguise to Penelope).

Regarding the remaining six instances of πολύμητις, those in the *Iliad* differ from those in the *Odyssey*. The *Iliad* examples feature Odysseus going about his business in ways that make necessary contributions to the ongoing story but do not dwell on Odysseus in particular, such as when he helps return Chryseis to her father (1.311; cf. 3.268, 4.329, 10.488). In the *Odyssey*, by contrast, the main narrator uses πολύμητις outside of speech-framing language only in Odysseus's reunion, so to speak, with his bow at the end of book 21 and the beginning of book 22. While πολύμητις is associated with speech-related formulas in both

TABLE 7.1. INSTANCES OF πολύμητις MODIFYING ODYSSEUS IN HOMERIC EPIC

	Iliad	*Odyssey*
Speech introductions		
τὸν/τὴν δ' ἀπαμειβόμενος προσέφη (occasionally μετέφη) πολύμητις Ὀδυσσεύς	5×	45×
With contextually appropriate participle metrically equivalent to ἀπαμειβόμενος		
ὑπόδρα ἰδών	4.349, 14.82	7×
ἐπιμειδήσας	10.400	22.371
δολοφρονέων	none	18.51, 21.274
other participles	none	14.439 (# καί μιν φωνήσας), 17.453 (ἀναχωρήσας)
With named addressee	none	8.474, 8.486, 22.390, 23.247
Unique speech introduction with context-specific details	1.440–441	18.312
Speech conclusions	10.148, 23.709, 23.755	20.183
Miscellaneous instances in narrator text	1.311, 3.268, 4.329, 10.488	21.404, 22.1
Characters refer to Odysseus	3.200 (Antenor), 3.216 (Helen)	2.173 (Halitherses), 4.763 (Penelope), 19.585 (Odysseus in disguise)

Total: 18 occurrences in the *Iliad*, 68 occurrences in the *Odyssey*.

TABLE 7.2. DISTRIBUTION OF πολύμητις

	Iliad	*Odyssey*
Proportion occurring in character speech	2 of 19, 11%	3 of 68, 4%
Proportion occurring in speech frames	12 of 19, 63%	63 of 68, 93%
Proportion of speech introductions that are not τὸν/τὴν δ' ἀπαμειβόμενος προσέφη πολύμητις Ὀδυσσεύς	3 of 8, 38%	15 of 62, 24%

Note: Iliad total of 19 includes the only instance of πολύμητις modifying someone other than Odysseus, πολυμήτιος Ἡφαίστοιο [21.355].

the *Iliad* and the *Odyssey*, it performs a wider variety of narrative functions in the *Iliad* than it does in the *Odyssey*. That is, the proportion of instances in character speech in relation to the total is higher in the *Iliad* (2 of 19, as opposed to 3 of 68 in the *Odyssey*), and the proportion found in speech frames is much lower (12 of 19 versus 63 of 68). Moreover, a higher proportion of *Iliad* speech introductions featuring πολύμητις say something besides "Odysseus of many plans answered him/her" (3 of 8 *Iliad*, 15 of 62 *Odyssey*). In the *Iliad*, πολύμητις is by far the most common epithet for Odysseus in a formula that extends from the main caesura to the end of the verse. These full-verse formulas convey various kinds of information (amusement, anger), but they do not shine a narrative spotlight on Odysseus's actions and feelings. Tables 7.1 and 7.2 summarize this discussion of πολύμητις.

The *Odyssey* uses a more wide-ranging formulaic system for Odysseus than the *Iliad*, even though it draws on the same repertoire of noun–epithet formulas. On the one hand, the most common epithet πολύμητις appears in the *Odyssey* in fewer different kinds of contexts: indeed, it appears almost exclusively (63 of 68 instances) within a full-verse speech introductory formula. On the other hand, the epithet πολύτλας—which is rare in the *Iliad* (5 of 42 instances)—occurs in the *Odyssey* both in the full-verse speech introductory formula τὸν δ' ἠμείβετ' ἔπειτα πολύτλας δῖος Ὀδυσσεύς ("much-enduring godlike Odysseus then answered him") and in a number of more detailed and elaborate speech frames. In these passages, a conclusion for the previous speech and an introduction for the next speech appear in separate verses, sometimes along with additional verses containing further details that in a strict sense are not necessary for clarity. Such longer speech-framing passages often convey the types of emotions that the *Iliad* presents in briefer and less emphatic ways, such as the formula at *Iliad* 10.400: τὸν δ᾽ ἐπιμειδήσας προσέφη πολύμητις Ὀδυσσεύς ("smiling, Odysseus of many plans answered him").

In fact, πολύτλας might be seen as a different word in the *Iliad* as compared to the *Odyssey*. In the *Iliad*, Odysseus does not seem more clever when he is identified as πολύμητις than when he is called πολύτλας, nor does he seem to be suffering unusual difficulties at the two points in the *Iliad* when his speeches are introduced with formulas containing the epithet πολύτλας (9.676, 10.248). The *Odyssey*, meanwhile, uses πολύτλας full-verse speech introductory formulas in several scenes in which Odysseus's endurance, and/or the absence of clever and tricky behavior, play a key role in the episode (Beck 1999).[4] In addition to the full-verse speech introductory formula τὸν δ᾽ ἠμείβετ᾽ ἔπειτα (or αὖτε προσέειπε) πολύτλας δῖος Ὀδυσσεύς, the *Odyssey*—but not the *Iliad*—includes a number of variations, expansions, and elaborations on this full-verse introductory formula that depict various conversational details, many of which highlight Odysseus's emotions in response to speeches addressed to him.

For example, after Alkinoös promises Odysseus safe conduct home (*Odyssey* 7.309–329), the delighted Odysseus responds by praying to Zeus that all may be as Alkinoös has said (7.329–331)[5]:

> ὣς φάτο, **γήθησεν δὲ πολύτλας δῖος Ὀδυσσεύς,**
> <u>εὐχόμενος</u> δ᾽ ἄρα εἶπεν ἔπος τ᾽ ἔφατ᾽ ἔκ τ᾽ ὀνόμαζε·
> "Ζεῦ πάτερ . . ."
>
> Thus he [sc. Alkinoös] spoke, and **much-enduring godlike Odysseus smiled,**
> and he spoke out a word in <u>prayer</u> and addressed him by name:
> "Father Zeus . . ."

After 329 concludes Alkinoös's speech, the speech introduction at 330 clarifies the direction of the conversation for the audience: Odysseus responds to Alkinoös's offer by praying to Zeus rather than by replying to Alkinoös himself.[6] Although the first half-verse of a line ending προσέφη πολύμητις Ὀδυσσεύς can specify *either* the speaker's emotions *or* the identity of his addressee, more than one verse is needed in order to present several context-specific details at once. The epithet πολύμητις, unlike πολύτλας, is not found in such multiverse speech frames in either the *Iliad* or the *Odyssey*. It has a different role to play in the formulaic system for "Odysseus."

Some of the multiverse speech frames that include the noun–epithet formula πολύτλας δῖος Ὀδυσσεύς draw a vivid picture of Odysseus's interior landscape, rather than explaining concrete details like the type of speech or a change of addressee. In these cases, the audience can make sense of the story on a literal level without the information provided by an extended speech frame, but the story without these details would be a different tale. In that sense, these speech frames too play a key role in telling the story in the *Odyssey*. For instance, a verse that describes Odysseus's emotional response to a speech he has just heard may appear as a conclusion to a preceding speech: ὣς φάτο, – – – [verb of three long syllables that depicts emotion, such as ῥίγησεν "shuddered," γήθησεν "smiled"] δὲ πολύτλας δῖος Ὀδυσσεύς. This is followed by the full-verse speech-introductory formula καί μιν φωνήσας ἔπεα πτερόεντα προσηύδα ("speaking, [unnamed subject] addressed winged words to him/her"), either immediately, as at 5.171–172, or with additional detail in between the two.[7]

For example, 13.248–256 describes Odysseus's joy at learning that he has reached Ithaka at last and his instantaneous resolve to conceal his emotions.

> "τῶ τοι, ξεῖν', Ἰθάκης γε καὶ ἐς Τροίην ὄνομ' ἵκει,
> τήν περ τηλοῦ φασὶν Ἀχαιΐδος ἔμμεναι αἴης."
> ὣς φάτο, **γήθησεν δὲ πολύτλας δῖος Ὀδυσσεὺς**
> **χαίρων** ἧι γαίηι πατρωΐηι, ὥς οἱ ἔειπε
> Παλλὰς Ἀθηναίη, κούρη Διὸς αἰγιόχοιο·
> <u>καί μιν φωνήσας ἔπεα πτερόεντα προσηύδα</u>·
> οὐδ' ὅ γ' ἀληθέα εἶπε, πάλιν δ' ὅ γε λάζετο μῦθον,
> αἰὲν ἐνὶ στήθεσσι νόον πολυκερδέα νωμῶν·
> "πυνθανόμην Ἰθάκης γε καὶ ἐν Κρήτηι εὐρείηι, . . ."
>
> "Stranger, the name of Ithaka reaches even to Troy,
> which they say is far from the Achaian land."
> Thus she spoke, and **much-enduring godlike Odysseus smiled**,
> **rejoicing** in his ancestral land, as Pallas Athena
> spoke to him, the daughter of Zeus aegis-wielder.
> <u>And he addressed winged words to her.</u>
> Nor did he speak truly, but he bit back his account,
> always holding in readiness profit-oriented thoughts in his heart.
> "I used to hear about Ithaka, at least, even in wide Crete, . . ."

Such a multiverse passage brings the audience from Athena's speech to Odysseus's reply just as either of the full-verse speech introductory formulas τὴν δ' ἀπαμειβόμενος προσέφη πολύμητις Ὀδυσσεύς or τὴν δ' ἡμείβετ' ἔπειτα πολύτλας δῖος Ὀδυσσεύς would; without this extended interior view of Odysseus's thoughts and feelings, we are not privy to the lightning-speed feat of concealment and deception that Odysseus pulls off here. When he learns that he has returned to his long-desired home, a moment when we might well expect him to be overwhelmed by the joy mentioned in the passage, Odysseus instead suppresses both his emotions and his initial response to Athena's question. The extended speech frame dramatizes this process for the audience.[8] In fact, this passage draws our attention to the connection in the *Odyssey* between Odysseus's general capacity for endurance and his ability to control his emotions in particular. It may be that this connection explains why πολύτλας δῖος Ὀδυσσεύς, but not πολύμητις Ὀδυσσεύς, appears in several multiverse speech frames that describe Odysseus's emotions.

All the regular uses of πολύτλας—both full-verse formulas and the various kinds of multiverse speech frames in which the epithet is found—are in some sense *less formulaic* than the more common epithet πολύμητις. At a very concrete level, πολύτλας appears less often than πολύμητις does. A lower proportion of πολύτλας as compared to πολύμητις appears in speech introductions, and the group of speech introductions that includes πολύτλας features a wider variety of content, length, and relationship to the narrative context. Like πολύτλας, most of the epithets for Odysseus are attested in both poems, but they are used in different ways in the *Iliad* as compared to the *Odyssey*. These patterns reveal that even the most repetitive and common types of formulas have clear and precise meanings that vary in different narrative contexts: in many key respects, πολύμητις and πολύτλας are not used as they would be if they were true synonyms.

The preceding discussion of the unique epithet πολύτλας has treated the generic epithet δῖος that accompanies it as an irrelevant sidekick, but the formula δῖος Ὀδυσσεύς on its own appears more often in Homeric epic than the longer formula πολύτλας δῖος Ὀδυσσεύς. Unlike nominative formulas that include either πολύμητις or πολύτλας, approximately one-third of the occurrences of δῖος Ὀδυσσεύς appear in character speeches (5 of 18 in the *Iliad*; 13 of 41 in the *Odyssey*). Here is a common narrator text name–epithet formula for Odysseus that differs in a number of striking ways from the longer half-verse name–epithet formulas found in speech introductions. Foley argues that δῖος "designat[es] important . . . figures within Homeric epic" (1999: 215) without a clear and specific meaning or a connection to particular contexts, but, as we will see, the evidence does not bear out this claim.[9] In particular, both the proportion of δῖος Ὀδυσσεύς that appears in characters' speeches and the attitudes of characters who refer to Odysseus in this way suggest that even the most regular and "formulaic" formulas can and do have varied shades of meaning in response to their narrative contexts.

Other characters call Odysseus δῖος Ὀδυσσεύς a total of eighteen times, and in every instance, the character who is speaking is sympathetic to or praises Odysseus. In the *Iliad*, both Agamemnon and Nestor refer to Odysseus this way as they are discussing plans of various kinds that involve Odysseus (Agamemnon: 1.145, 19.141; Nestor: 9.170, 11.767), but one of the positive references to δῖος Ὀδυσσεύς comes during the *teichoskopia* from the Trojan Antenor, who might not be supposed to be among Odysseus's most fervent admirers. In fact, all three Trojans who comment on Odysseus in this part of the *teichoskopia* speak admiringly of him. Priam, wondering from the walls of Troy who Odysseus might be, remarks on his impressive physique and compares him to a ram (3.192–198). Helen identifies him both as Λαερτιάδης πολύμητις Ὀδυσσεύς (200)—the only instance in Homeric epic of the nominative case of this patronymic—and as outstanding in clever plans and tricks (201–202). Antenor reminiscences at length (202–224) about entertaining Odysseus and Menelaos as guest-friends when they visited Troy to discuss Helen (τοὺς . . . ἐξείνισσα καὶ ἐν μεγάροισι φίλησα ["I gave them hospitality and had friendly feelings for them in my halls"], 207). In the course of praising Odysseus's speaking abilities, Antenor refers to him by name five times, of which two also feature an epithet. Antenor's first reference to each of his Greek visitors includes a generic, general epithet, δῖος for Odysseus (205) and ἀρηίφιλος for Menelaos (206). This invites both the internal and the external audiences to dwell more favorably on each Greek visitor than we might have done if they were named without an epithet. When Antenor reaches the climax of his speech—a vivid and elaborate tableau of Odysseus engaged in public speaking—he introduces his star performer as follows: ἀλλ' ὅτε δὴ πολύμητις ἀναΐξειεν Ὀδυσσεύς, / στάσκεν ("But when, indeed, Odysseus of many plans would arise to speak, he used to stand," 216–217).

This rather limited sample size tells us that, although characters do not use epithets as extensively as the main narrators do, they do use them on a regular basis.[10] In many of the instances in which a character uses an epithet, it indicates some kind of positive relationship between the speaker and the character to whom he refers, and not always in places where such relationships might be expected to flourish. In fact, δῖος is not a straightforward reflection of a given speaker's positive relationship with or view of Odysseus: it may help to create that relationship for an audience. As we will see in more detail in the discussion of vocative formulas in the next section, the meanings of the most frequent and repetitive formulas in characters' speeches, as well as those found in narrator text, contribute on multiple levels to telling an effective tale.

While δῖος is generic in both the *Iliad* and the *Odyssey*, a number of other epithets are generic in one poem but not the other. This in itself implies that such formulas have different (and contextually appropriate) meanings in different narrative contexts. The concept of a "unique" epithet, which has been treated as an either/or question, in fact exists on a spectrum, where (to paraphrase George Orwell's *Animal Farm*) some epithets are more unique than others, and a given epithet may be unique in one kind of environment but generic in a different setting. For example, the "generic" epithet διογενής appears in both the *Iliad* and the *Odyssey*, mainly in the vocative but also in the nominative: in each poem, 16 of 23 instances of διογενής appear in the vocative and the rest are nominative forms.[11] But this superficial similarity conceals some key variations that highlight the range and subtlety of the formulaic system for Odysseus. First, διογενής is generic in the *Iliad* but not in the *Odyssey*, where it is used only for Odysseus, and, second, nominative forms of διογενής are not found in the *Iliad*, but they appear in characters' speeches in the *Odyssey*.[12] At the same time, the full-verse vocative for Odysseus in which διογενής most often appears, διογενὲς Λαερτιάδη πολυμήχαν' Ὀδυσσεῦ ("god-born son of Laertes, much-contriving Odysseus"; 7× *Iliad*, 15× *Odyssey*), is formulaic in both Homeric poems. As with formulas found in speech introductions in narrator text, the Homeric epics contain one set of vocative formulas that are used differently in different contexts.

VOCATIVE FORMULAS

Because systems of vocative formulas are in many respects akin to systems of nominative formulas, they offer a useful corrective to the mistaken idea that formulas are a feature of narrator text, as Norman Austin suggests (1975: 52–53). As we have seen by looking at διογενής, certain epithets associated with characters' speech resemble the more well-known nominative formulas on which most formulaic studies are based. Like an epithet in a nominative formula found in narrator text, διογενής most often appears as part of a common proper-name formula, but it may also be found in contexts that vary in both narrative content and metrical shape from the usual patterns for this epithet. Indeed, the other two epithets that make up the full-verse vocative for

Odysseus flesh out our understanding of a "system" of epithets and formulaic language that exists within characters' speeches, alongside the better-understood formulaic system found in narrator text. To a great extent, these two formulaic systems are analogous and separate, but the basic characteristics of the two systems are comparable, and some formulas (like δῖος Ὀδυσσεύς) are part of both systems. Together, these two overlapping systems make up the formulaic system of the Homeric poems. In many instances, the meanings of the various epithets in this system contribute both to their specific narrative contexts and also to conveying larger themes.[13]

Just as some formulaic epithets are found *only* in narrator text, while others make regular appearances in character speeches as well, one of the epithets in Odysseus's full-verse vocative formula is restricted to characters' speeches while the others occur from time to time in narrator text. The epithet πολυμήχανος appears in both the most common formulaic full-verse vocative for Odysseus (7× *Iliad*; 15× *Odyssey*) and in a unique apostrophe from Agamemnon in the underworld (ὄλβιε Λαέρταο πάϊ, πολυμήχαν' Ὀδυσσεῦ, *Odyssey* 24.192). The one non-vocative case use of πολυμήχανος appears in a speech by the disguised Athena, telling Telemachos that his father will soon return home ἐπεὶ πολυμήχανός ἐστιν ("since he is a man of many contrivances," *Odyssey* 1.205).

If we place this particular epithet for Odysseus alongside other words in Homeric epic that use the μηχ- root, we see that the kinds of "contrivances" that define Odysseus are a good thing in both the *Iliad* and the *Odyssey*. In the *Iliad*, the opposite of the kind of creative flexibility represented by πολυμήχανος is ἀμήχανος, with which characters evaluate something or someone as "misguided" (Hektor in rejecting Poulydamas's counsel, *Iliad* 13.726), "impervious to rational advice" (Zeus's angry rebuke of Hera for her interference in the fighting at Troy, 15.14; Patroklos's sorrowful criticisms of Achilleus at 16.29), or—for things rather than people—"not accomplished" (ἀμήχανα ἔργα, cf. ὄνειροι ἀμήχανοι, *Odyssey* 19.560; and perhaps *Odyssey* 19.363, an emotional exclamation of Eurykleia about her absent master where ἀμήχανος appears to mean "at a loss"). At *Iliad* 15.14, Zeus describes Hera as ἀμήχανε and her δόλος as κακότεχνος, a *hapax legomenon* that underlines the sense of ἀμήχανος not as lacking any contrivances whatsoever but as lacking praiseworthy or appropriate flexibility in a given situation. The only instances of ἀμήχανος that appear outside of character speech occur in contrary-to-fact conditions at *Iliad* 8.130 and 11.310, whose form and content give a subjective cast to the tale that heightens its expressive force (Louden 1993:

184). Characters in the *Iliad* use ἀμήχανος to express their frustration or to rebuke characters with whom they have a close emotional relationship, but no *thematic* similarity binds together these pragmatically consistent uses of the word, still less any connection to Odysseus in particular. Odysseus is distinguished by his formulaic epithets as "full of contrivances," but the inverse quality, ἀμήχανος, does not relate to anyone in particular.

In the *Odyssey*, however, the penchant for contrivance that defines Odysseus through the formulaic epithet πολυμήχανος also characterizes the suitors as his opponents and opposites. The opposite of πολυμήχανος in the *Odyssey* is *bad* contrivances in the person of the suitors, who are criticized both individually and collectively by Odysseus, Penelope, and Telemachos as "contriving" internal accusative objects such as κακά and ἀτάσθαλα, often in association with forms of ὕβρις.[14] Indeed, of the sixteen instances of the verb μηχανάομαι in Homeric epic, just two appear in the *Iliad* while thirteen refer to the suitors' misdeeds, predominantly from the perspective of Odysseus and his family.[15] In this way, a formulaic epithet plays a key role in depicting one of the central themes of the *Odyssey*, not because stratagems come to the fore every time Odysseus is addressed this way but because the poem uses words containing the root μηχ- *either* to refer to the admirable cleverness of Odysseus—on which so much of the poem's story depends—*or* to express negative views held by Odysseus and his family about the outrageous behavior of their main adversaries.[16]

Λαερτιάδης (son of Laertes), the last epithet that makes up the full-verse vocative formula for Odysseus, appears mainly in characters' speeches. In the *Odyssey*, where this patronymic is found both more often and in a wider range of cases and narrative contexts than in the *Iliad*, all its uses have a clear expressive force. At one level, this is not surprising, given not only that characters are more prone than the main narrators to refer to people in terms of their relationships but also that characters make more use of expressive, emotional, and/or judgmental language (Griffin 1986). Indeed, in *all* the contexts in which Λαερτιάδης appears, lively feelings related to Odysseus are in play, either in how another character feels about Odysseus or in how Odysseus feels about his own situation. At the most basic level, the vocative is itself an expressive feature of discourse.[17]

On the rare occasions when the main narrator of the *Odyssey* (never the main narrator in the *Iliad*) uses this patronymic to refer to Odysseus, the story always focuses on the emotions of either Odysseus or someone who wants him to do something. In some passages, this is literally true: ὄφρ' ἔτι μᾶλλον / δύη **ἄχος** κραδίην Λαερτιάδεω Ὀδυσῆος ("So that even more **grief** might enter the heart of Odysseus the son of Laertes," 18.348–349 = 20.286–287) refers not only to ἄχος for Odysseus but also to the desires and intentions of Athena, whose actions in both cases give rise to this purpose clause. Similarly, a repeated expression states that Athena stood beside "Odysseus the son of Laertes" in order to accomplish something (16.454–455 [purpose clause at 457–459] = 17.360–361 [purpose clause at 362–363]).

In perhaps the most dramatic instance in which the main narrator of the *Odyssey* refers to Odysseus with a patronymic, the singer Phemios is debating whether he should try to escape the general slaughter of the suitors by seeking sanctuary on the domestic altar where Λαέρτης Ὀδυσεύς τε (22.336) used to offer roasted thighs of oxen, or by supplicating Odysseus (λίσσοιτο, 337). At 22.339–341, he decides in favor of supplication:

> ὧδε δέ οἱ φρονέοντι δοάσσατο κέρδιον εἶναι,
> γούνων ἅψασθαι Λαερτιάδεω Ὀδυσῆος.
> ἦ τοι ὁ φόρμιγγα γλαφυρὴν κατέθηκε χαμᾶζε
>
> In this way it seemed the better course to him, thinking
> things over,
> to grasp hold of the knees of Odysseus son of Laertes.
> And indeed he put down his hollow lyre on the ground

This passage both depicts and conveys the emotions not only of Phemios but also of the external audience. Presenting the details of Phemios's thought process draws the audience in and engages them emotionally with the story, independent of the specific decision that Phemios is trying to make. By spelling out the steps that Phemios goes through in his decision process, the narrator casts it as a conversation in which Phemios is "talking" to himself.[18] Moreover, Phemios's plan will require him to arouse emotion in Odysseus: supplication, a form of appeal that may include the physical gesture described at 340 as well as a speech to the person whose mercy is desired, depends for its effect on forging an emotional bond between the speaker and the addressee.[19] Indeed, Phemios begins his speech to Odysseus (344–353) with emotional imperatives (αἴδεο καί μ' ἐλέησον [reverence and pity me], 344) and he concludes by invoking the support of Telemachos, whom he describes in terms of Odysseus's love for him (καί κεν Τηλέμαχος τάδε γ' εἴποι, σὸς φίλος υἱός ["and Telemachos might confirm these things, your dear son"], 350). So, both the narrative background for the speech and the content of the speech link Phemios's appeal to Odysseus's emotional bonds with both his father and his son.

Outside of this full-verse vocative formula, characters use Λαερτιάδης to refer to Odysseus's wife (5×), his companions (12.378), or his home (16.104, 18.24, 21.262). In fact, the character who most often uses the epithet Λαερτιάδης in the *Odyssey* is Odysseus himself. He uses this "Odysseus" full-verse vocative formula for himself several times during his tale to the Phaiakians in books 9–12 when narrating speeches addressed to himself, as well as during a deceptive story to Eumaios about having met "Odysseus" at Troy (14.486); he also speaks four of the five instances of the full-verse vocative formula for Penelope that includes his own name. Besides these two vocative formulas, two of the three instances of the formula ἐς μεγαρὸν Λαερτιάδεω Ὀδυσῆος appear in speeches by the disguised Odysseus (16.104, 18.24). Indeed, Odysseus's regular use of epithets to refer to himself distinguishes him from any other character.

After the full-verse vocative for Odysseus, the most common formula in which the patronymic Λαερτιάδης appears is a full-verse vocative for Penelope. She has two distinct full-verse vocatives, each of which defines her identity in relation to a significant male authority figure (cf. Beck 2005: 96–100). These vocatives complement the subjective and expressive force of periphrases that use familial relationship words—such as ἄλοχος in place of the name "Penelope"—to refer to the members of Odysseus's family (de Jong 1993). The suitors four times use the self-serving expression "daughter of Ikarios, circumspect Penelope" [κούρη Ἰκαρίοιο, περίφρων Πηνελόπεια], a manner of identifying her that bolsters their contention that she should return to her parents' house and remarry whichever of the suitors she chooses. Both κούρη, which can mean "unmarried maiden" as well as "daughter" within its larger sense of "primarily a class of *young* persons" (*LfgrE*), and Ikarios rather than Odysseus as the male relative in relation to whom Penelope's identity is established redefine this married matron as a suitable "bride" for a young man hoping to make an advantageous marriage. Many male characters are addressed with vocative formulas that include a patronymic—Odysseus himself is only one example—but for a married woman, her husband would normally succeed her father as the anchor of her identity and her social position. By addressing Penelope as a daughter rather than a wife, the suitors do their best to ignore the existence of Odysseus and his claims on Penelope.

Meanwhile, the disguised Odysseus addresses Penelope during their conversation in book 19 as ὦ γύναι αἰδοίη *Λαερτιάδεω Ὀδυσῆος* ("respected wife of *Odysseus the son of Laertes*"; 19.165, 262, 336, 583). Every word in this formula places Penelope within a different familial structure than the one the suitors evoke with their vocative: Penelope is addressed here as the wife (*LfgrE* γυνή def. 3) of a hero, whose position deserves respect from those around her.[20] Odysseus is following the general tendency of characters to address others in terms of their own relationship to the addressee (de Jong 1993: 289–291), although the oblivious Penelope does not yet realize this in book 19. I am among those who believe that Penelope does not recognize Odysseus until book 23 (cf. Emlyn-Jones 1984), although Odysseus's full-verse vocative surely contributes to Penelope's endlessly debated feelings of unease and excitement about the stranger with whom she converses in book 19. Telemachos, by way of comparison, addresses Penelope as μῆτερ or μῆτερ ἐμή.

In fact, the only character to follow Odysseus's rather than the suitors' approach to addressing Penelope is Theoklymenos, who uses the ὦ γύναι αἰδοίη Λαερτιάδεω Ὀδυσῆος vocative (17.152) to begin a solemn and forceful speech incorporating language of both prophecy (μαντεύσομαι, 154) and oath-taking (ἴστω νῦν Ζεὺς πρῶτα ["let Zeus first now know"], 155) in which he states that Odysseus is already present on Ithaka and planning evil for the suitors to pay them back for the evils they have committed (157–161). Taken together, the various elements of Theoklymenos's speech imply that Penelope's position of respect as Odysseus's wife will be restored once he defeats the suitors. Indeed, this vocative might provide indirect support for Steve Reece's argument that Theoklymenos represents a kind of narrative doublet for Odysseus (1994): Reece posits an alternative version of the Odysseus story that has left traces in our *Odyssey*, in which Odysseus meets up with Telemachos after Telemachos travels to Crete in search of news about his father, and they return to Ithaka together to punish the suitors. To sum up, only characters who want to marry Penelope address her as "daughter of Ikarios," whereas only characters who actually are married to her, or who are in the act of prophesying the return of her husband to the pining wife, address her as "wife of Odysseus."[21]

These two vocatives offer a salutary reminder that while metrical shape is not the straitjacket that Parry considered it to be, we ignore metrics at our peril when studying how different formulas that refer to the same character are used in specific narrative contexts. In the vocative case, these two formulas for Penelope are metrically identical and thus offer a clear example of two formulas that differ only semantically. However, this is not true in other cases, where we find κούρη Ἰκαρίοιο, περίφρων Πηνελόπεια, but not ὦ γύναι αἰδοίη Λαερτιάδεω Ὀδυσῆος, since the initial ὦ γύναι cannot be included in this formula in a metrically feasible way except in the vocative case. κούρη Ἰκαρίοιο, περίφρων Πηνελόπεια is found in a single dactylic hexameter not only in the vocative case but also in the nominative (identical to the vocative in form) and the dative (whose only difference from the nominative/vocative is the scansion of the dative περίφρονι as ⏑ / – ⏑ ⏑ instead of ⏑ / – – for the nominative/vocative περίφρων). And these non-vocative case forms of the "daughter of Ikarios" formula for Penelope appear not only in narrator text but also in the speeches of characters friendly to both Odysseus and Penelope, including Odysseus himself in disguise.

Striking demonstrations of the positive tone of the "daughter of Ikarios" formula in the nominative and dative cases come from a repeated expression in which Athena puts ideas into Penelope's head that strengthen her bond with Odysseus by leading either to Odysseus's increased admiration of her cleverness among the suitors (18.158–159) or to the bow contest and thus to Odysseus's triumphant return and success (21.1–2). Similarly, when the disguised Odysseus tells Eumaios at 17.561–563 that he wants to talk to the "daughter of Ikarios" about "Odysseus" (οἶδα γὰρ εὖ περὶ <u>κείνου</u> ["for I know well about <u>that man</u>"], 163), we gain renewed appreciation for the precision and subtlety of the formulaic system of characters' vocative formulas. The "daughter of Ikarios" formula for Penelope is part of the language repertoire of the disguised Odysseus, but he never uses this expression when talking directly *to* Penelope. Instead, his vocative addresses to her in their conversation in book 19 use common repeated formulas to convey that he acknowledges her status as the wife of Odysseus.

The two full-verse formulas for Penelope draw together the various features of the formulaic system, or spectrum, that we find in characters' speeches. Some formulas include language that is used only by characters: the vocative case form ὦ γύναι perforce cannot appear in narrator text, with the hypothetical exception of an apostrophe. Other expressions appear in both characters' speeches and narrator text, such as the "daughter of Ikarios" formula that appears at both narrative levels in the nominative and dative cases. Moreover, in some but not all of their occurrences, both of these formulas for Penelope play a key role in telling one of the main stories in the *Odyssey*. The usage patterns for the vocative and non-vocative cases of the "daughter of Ikarios" formula offer a powerful example of the precisely varied shades of meaning that a given formula can have in different narrative and metrical contexts. In the vocative case, where there is a metrically identical alternative, this formula is used only by the suitors, who want to address Penelope so as to make her a suitable target of their courtship. In other cases, where no formulaic alternative to "daughter of Ikarios" exists, both the main narrator and friendly characters—but not the suitors—repeatedly use this expression to talk warmly about Penelope in close proximity to either direct or indirect evocations of her love for Odysseus. That is to say, these two formulas are not synonyms, and the contexts in which they appear are strongly linked both to metrical factors and to the attitude of the speaker toward Penelope.

ODYSSEUS NARRATING

Only Odysseus repeatedly refers to himself using formulas that include both an epithet and his name. Moreover, most of the formulas with which Odysseus refers to himself are used also—or even primarily—by the main narrator.

By way of comparison, both Menelaos and Nestor recount extended narratives in which they themselves feature as characters. During such narratives, the storytelling character may mention his own name in various ways, but Menelaos and Nestor name themselves differently than the main narrator does. In Menelaos's narrative of his νόστος (*Odyssey* 4.333–592), he sometimes includes his own name as well as an epithet in the vocative case when he recounts speeches that were addressed to him (such as διοτρεφὲς ὦ Μενέλαε, 4.561), but unlike Odysseus, he never uses the full-verse vocative that the main narrator regularly presents at the beginning of characters' speeches addressed to Menelaos. Nestor, who tells a long tale about his youth at *Iliad* 11.656–803 when talking to Patroklos, mentions himself in the dative in his story (Νέστορι, 11.761). Nestor does use the vocative epithet that describes himself when other characters address him, but he uses it to describe Peleus, not himself (ἱππηλάτα Πηλεύς, 11.772).

The "Odysseus" formulas in Odysseus's speech appear in two different kinds of contexts. Most commonly, Odysseus includes vocatives addressed to himself in the speeches that he recounts in his narrative in *Odyssey* 9–12 when several of his interlocutors use the same full-verse vocative to address him as we see in speeches presented by the main narrator.[22] Odysseus also uses a shorter vocative following the bucolic diaeresis that is found only in books 9–12, φαίδιμ' Ὀδυσσεῦ.[23] These two expressions constitute a modest formulaic system specific to Odysseus himself for referring to "Odysseus" in the vocative case. As with all the formulas in character speech that we have considered so far, this one overlaps with but is not identical to formulas used by the main narrator for the same thing.

There is no apparent reason that φαίδιμ' Ὀδυσσεῦ could not be used in speeches presented by the main narrator as well. The metrically equivalent formula φαίδιμ' Ἀχιλλεῦ appears regularly (*Iliad* 9.434, 21.160, 21.583, 22.216; *Odyssey* 24.76), and in both narrator text and character speech in the *Odyssey* we find various cases of φαίδιμος υἱός. Moreover, φαίδιμ' Ὀδυσσεῦ is spoken in books 9–12 by characters who have similar attitudes to and relationships with Odysseus, and in some cases by the same individuals, as those who use the longer full-verse vocative formula for Odysseus. But the presence of a formula for Odysseus that is unique to Odysseus's own narrative, yet *not* entirely unlike the uses of the epithet φαίδιμος elsewhere in Homeric epic, gives an individual coloring to the tale Odysseus tells in books 9–12 and distinguishes his formulaic style from that of the main narrator. Neither of these vocatives contribute to Odysseus's disguise, since he begins his tale by announcing his identity to the Phaiakians: εἴμ' Ὀδυσεὺς Λαερτιάδης, ὃς πᾶσι δόλοισιν / ἀνθρώποισι μέλω ("I am Odysseus the son of Laertes, who am of interest to all men because of my clever stratagems," 9.19–20). Rather, such vocatives referring to the narrating speaker seem to be a function of an extended story that features a lot of speeches: Menelaos uses them too, although his vocatives, like the rest of his tale, are more modest in scope than Odysseus's.

Among Odysseus's many skills as a speaker, he can use formulas to disguise himself through his speech in addition to his changed appearance. This is consistent with Sheila Murnaghan's assertion that a "ringing announcement of [Odysseus's] name" is characteristic of most of the reunions in the poem (1987: 56): we may extend the idea that name and identity go together to argue that using one's own name as though it belonged to someone else is a potent kind of disguise. While he is incognito on Scheria and on Ithaka, Odysseus uses various "Odysseus" formulas to refer to himself, as well as the vocative expression discussed at the end of the previous section that identifies Penelope as "wife of Odysseus son of Laertes." In these speeches, Odysseus brings formulas into play as part of his disguise, to striking dramatic effect for both the internal addressees and the external audience. No other character uses epithets to refer to himself as though he were talking about someone else. In all of the various instances when Odysseus talks about himself in the third person, the ongoing conversations in which he makes these remarks dwell on his identity.

For example, when Odysseus asks Demodokos for a song about the Trojan Horse which "Odysseus" crafted, he refers to himself as δῖος Ὀδυσσεύς (8.494), and he uses the same formula when he seems to pass Penelope's test by describing the clothes "Odysseus" was wearing when they met in Crete twenty years before (19.225). Later in the conversation with Penelope, Odysseus urges her to delay the bow contest because πολύμητις Ὀδυσσεύς (19.585) will soon return. All of these speeches take place at points where Odysseus's disguise plays a decisive role in the story. So, Odysseus responds to Demodokos's tale about "Odysseus" and the Trojan Horse first by weeping and then, in response to questions from his hosts, by telling his own story in books 9–12. He convinces Penelope of his bona fides by describing the clothes that "Odysseus" had on when he left for Troy. In the last speech he addresses to his wife before they meet again in book 23, he gives her instructions about the bow contest, which will soon reveal his identity to the suitors (although not yet to Penelope herself) and open the way to reestablishing marital relations with Penelope.

The appearance of epithets at these moments, in such a way as to discount any possibility that the speaker himself could be the person so described, heightens the drama and excitement of the story. For the characters, these epithets seem to offer indisputable (if implicit) proof that the speaker and Odysseus are two different people, while the external audience relishes the irony of Odysseus referring to himself in the third person just when his internal interlocutor might most want to know his true identity. In all of these speeches, Odysseus uses the pose of a third-person form of speaking about himself as a disguise, not as part of a quasi-poetic presentation of his own adventures.[24]

CONCLUSIONS

These three groups of formulas (nominatives, vocatives, and the nominative and vocative formulas found in Odysseus's own speeches) constitute an overlapping set of expressions that function in broadly similar ways in a wide range of speech contexts. In all of them, individual epithets enrich the stories that are told in Homeric poetry on the level of both the events and emotions of specific scenes and the ongoing themes that shape the narrative as a whole.

Sometimes, as with the nominative epithet πολύτλας and the two vocative "synonyms" for Penelope, the meaning of a particular epithet is relevant to specific contexts in which the formula occurs. At other times, as we see with the ideas inherent in the epithet πολυμήχανος, an epithet evokes a theme that plays a key role in the narrative but may not be active in every individual scene or speech in which that epithet appears. In other words, formulas are like another language in that they have contextually significant meanings to varying extents in various contexts. As with any utterance, the fact that formulas do have the potential to mean something in a forceful and aesthetically effective way does not require that they either can or should have such a contextually dependent meaning all the time.

This view of formulas allows us to put aside a number of unproductive debates about formulas by showing that various problems that have been seen as "either/or" questions in fact make more sense in terms of "both/and." These issues include the questions of whether epithets do or do not have contextually appropriate meanings (both are possible, depending on the context) and whether a specific formula is used for metrical *or* semantic reasons (both, with one or the other having more or less relative importance depending on the context). An important corollary of these results is that our failure to arrive at an uncontroversial definition of "formula" may not matter very much, since the various axes that define formulas operate on a spectrum rather than in a binary fashion. We cannot pin all of these axes down to a specific point at the same time for any individual formula, or for a formulaic system, but this is a natural property of a definition that is based on various spectrums of possibilities. It should not be seen as a flaw in either the concept or the definition of "formula."

When we understand that even the most repetitive formulas can have contextually significant meanings, we shift the parameters for understanding the aesthetic properties of Homeric narrative. That is, if the very formulas that most scholars had all but abandoned as carriers of meaning are recognized as intricately woven not simply into the meter but into the storytelling of the Homeric poems, this should remove any doubts about whether formulas are compatible with meaning and artistry. Most formulas regularly *can* and *do* have a contextually significant meaning; no formula *always* or *must* have such meaning. Finally, this spectrum approach gives us a formulaic system that is consistent with the way actual people use language when they speak, fleshing out the picture that has been emerging in recent years of Homeric poetry as a stylized form of ordinary speech that can be understood using the same kinds of tools that we use to understand other forms of speech.

This study leaves some exciting and important questions unanswered.

Perhaps most important, how should we interpret the differences between the formulaic system for Odysseus in the *Odyssey* as compared to the *Iliad*? Are these differences a function of the two different stories told by the two poems, where Odysseus is the main character in one but not in the other, or of more fundamental differences in composition? That is beyond the scope of this paper, but a study of additional formulaic systems besides the one laid out here for Odysseus may shed new light even on the Homeric Question.

NOTES

I have learned a lot from contributing to this volume. I would like to thank Jonathan Ready and Christos Tsagalis, both for inviting me to contribute to this project and for their clear-eyed and helpful comments on preliminary drafts of my chapter. I would also like to extend my appreciation to the other authors in the volume, whose ideas have enriched my understanding of Homeric speech and narrative, and to the anonymous readers for the University of Texas Press.

1. Foley offers perhaps the most influential example of this approach to traditional oral epic, taking as one of his central premises the idea that "oral tradition works like language, only more so" (1999: 6). From a linguistically oriented vantage point, Bakker suggests that Homeric poetry be characterized not as oral poetry, but as "the stylization of ordinary speech" (1997a: 98). Other important studies that approach Homeric poetry as fundamentally a kind of speech include Martin 1989 and Minchin 2007.

2. Individual citations are given only when the total number of occurrences is less than five.

3. N. Austin discusses the positive emotional coloring of characters' references to other characters in relation to epithets and naming in particular (1975: 49–53).

4. Not every element of a formula is equally responsive to context, and verbs play the least meaningful part in various contexts. Visser argues that in battlefield killing verses, the names of the participants are more important semantically than the particular verb of killing, which is chosen mainly in order to accommodate the metrical shapes of the names (1988), and Machacek makes a similar claim with respect to the verbs in speech-introductory formulas (1994).

5. Greek quotations are taken from the Oxford editions of Monro and Allen; all translations are my own.

6. A similar conversational sequence is indicated by 23.111–112, where Penelope's circumspect words to Telemachos (105–110) receive an appreciative reply from Odysseus (113–122) rather than his son, the addressee.

7. Létoublon argues that the epithet πτερόεντα should be understood as

evoking the arrow that, once shot, cannot be recalled (1999). She bases her argument on a comprehensive survey of both Homeric evidence and modern scholarly treatments.

8. For a fuller discussion of this episode, see D. Beck 2005: 53–57.

9. More generally, Parry discusses formulas of this shape and the kinds of language that are typically found elsewhere in a verse that includes them (1987: 40–50).

10. Because N. Austin focuses mainly on how infrequently formulas appear in character speech in comparison to narrator text (1975: 48–49), rather than on how the characters use formulas on their own terms without reference to other usage patterns, he sees characters as peripheral to understanding Homeric epithets.

11. This figure includes verses with varying degrees of manuscript support, because the fact that this is a regularly occurring vocative formula for Odysseus is not materially affected by whether there are twelve or sixteen attestations in the *Odyssey*.

12. In a conversation between Telemachos and Eurykleia, each of whom calls Odysseus διογενής (2.352, 366), and in Odysseus's indirect-speech report to Penelope of his adventures (23.306).

13. Nagy provides a clear and eloquent statement of the connection between formula and theme (1999a: 1–5).

14. For an illuminating overview of the uses and meanings of ἀτασθαλ- words, including their relationship to ὕβρις, see Cairns 2012: 35–49.

15. There are two instances where μηχανάομαι is not used by members of Odysseus's family in reference to the suitors. At 20.394, the single instance of μηχανάομαι in narrator text appears in a long aside about the imminent fate of the suitors; de Jong explores the "unusually emphatic" nature of the narrator's comments here (2001: 503 at 392–394). Telemachos, distraught and unnerved by the changed appearance of Odysseus outside Eumaios's hut in *Odyssey* 16, is the only character who attributes contrivances to someone other than the suitors: οὐ γάρ πως ἂν θνητὸς ἀνὴρ τάδε μηχανόῳτο / ᾧι αὐτοῦ γε νόωι ("A mortal man would not be able to contrive these things in any way with his own mind," 16.196–197).

16. Sometimes Odysseus uses uncommon μηχ- words for hostile actions committed against him by characters other than the suitors, or for his inability to find a way to escape from a difficult situation: ἀμηχανίη (9.295, his feeling after the Cyclops eats his companions), μῆχος (12.392, 14.238, expressing regret about difficult situations for which no solution could be found), περιμηχανάομαι (14.340, an incident in one of his lying tales in which some Thesprotians plot to enslave him), and πολυμηχανίη (23.321, referring to Circe in the indirect speech in which Odysseus narrates his adventures to Penelope).

17. See Banfield 1982: 33, who also notes that direct address is restricted to direct speech.

18. Garcia (this volume) offers a complementary perspective on monologues

as involving an "internalized audience." For the involving effects for an audience of conversations in storytelling, see Tannen 1989: 9–35.

19. See D. Beck 2012: 67–68 for an overview of supplication as a speech genre.

20. According to Kahane 1997 (in which the arguments of Kahane 1994 are presented in a more concise form), the verse-final position of Odysseus's name would give heroic stature to Odysseus rather than Penelope, but it seems to me that in fact this verse not only underlines the status of both at once but also suggests that the heroic status of each depends at least somewhat on the status of the other. Using the expressions for Helen to argue that meter and position are themselves carriers of meaning, Tsagalis develops Kahane's ideas about the heroic significance of name localization (2009a).

21. Friedrich makes an analogous point about the contextual appropriateness of the different vocatives that Achilleus addresses to Agamemnon in *Iliad* 1 (2002).

22. At least five times in books 9–12, spoken by Circe (uncontroversially at 10.401 and 10.488, as well as several additional instances with varying degrees of manuscript support) and by various souls in the underworld (Agamemnon [11.405], Achilleus [11.473], and Herakles [11.617]).

23. 10.251 (Eurylochos), 11.100 (Teiresias), 11.202 (Antikleia, near the *end* of her speech [181–203]), 11.488 (Achilleus), 12.82 (Circe).

24. The bibliography on Odysseus as a narrator, and whether he should be seen as a poet or a particularly skilled character narrator, is enormous. See de Jong 2001: 221–227 for a wide variety of relevant scholarship and D. Beck 2012: 205nn19–22 for more recent studies.

CHAPTER EIGHT

Embedded Focalization and Free Indirect Speech in Homer as Viewpoint Blending

ANNA BONIFAZI

THE FUZZY BOUNDARIES OF FOCALIZATION AND FREE INDIRECT SPEECH

This chapter looks at Homeric instances of the phenomena called "embedded focalization" and "free indirect speech." The goal is to consider these two phenomena from a cognitive perspective and to interpret them as instances of viewpoint blending. I will first introduce the notion of blending (or conceptual integration), independently of the notion of viewpoint. Then I will introduce insights by Eve Sweetser regarding viewpoint markers and viewpoint configurations (2012).

Through an analysis of passages from the *Iliad* and the *Odyssey*, I will argue that a viewpoint-blending reading makes sense of the fuzzy boundaries of interpretation that such terms as "focalization" and "free indirect speech" do not and cannot clarify. With particular reference to Homeric epic, viewpoint-blending readings allow us to overcome exclusive inferences such as "*either* the viewpoint of X *or* the viewpoint of Y," for focalization, and "(just) two sources of the utterance," for free indirect speech. The language may be ambiguous enough to cause us to integrate multiple viewpoints and multiple voices in our mind. The advantage is that we do not need to search for single or dual viewpoints and voices any longer. We can see and hear the multiple people involved. The chapter ends with suggestions about further work in Homeric viewpoint blending and a nod to the intersubjective dimension of epic poetry.

Irene de Jong's narratological idea of focalization as presented in *Narrators and Focalizers: The Presentation of the Story in the Iliad* (2004a [1987]) is inspired by Mieke Bal's (1983), which differs from Gérard Genette's

(1972: 206–211).[1] For example, unlike Genette, for whom "the narrator's status does not . . . affect the point of view" (Broman 2004: 59), de Jong holds that "the story, consisting of a fabula . . . looked at from a certain, specific angle, is the result of the focalizing activity (focalization) of a focalizer" (2004a: 31). Focalization is a presupposition of narration: the primary narrator is also a focalizer. Moreover, the focalizer is not only one "who sees"[2] in the literal sense but also one who perceives, who thinks, who feels, in a word "who sees" in a broader, metaphorical sense. Since the first edition of *Narrators and Focalizers*, works on ancient Greek texts have used "focalization" as a convenient term to identify subjective perceptions of events—prototypically those of characters—independently of who verbalizes them. The general assumption is that a switch in focalization tends to correspond to a changing of the focalizing subject. One entity focalizes at a time, and it is through the eyes of an individual that certain events or states are seen/felt/thought of.

De Jong's main claims are that the primary narrator is both narrator and focalizer and that the narrator may represent characters as focalizers through stretches of text featuring "embedded focalization." Embedded focalization is said to take place when "the NF_1 [the primary narrator and focalizer] temporarily hands over focalization (but not narration) to one of the characters, who functions as F_2" (de Jong 2004a: 101). In *explicit* embedded focalization, the epic text semantically spells out someone's act of focalizing by means of verbs of perception, verbs of thinking, verbs expressing feelings, and indirect speech introduced by report clauses (102–118). In *implicit* embedded focalization (118–123), various semantic clues contained "in final clauses, (some) causal clauses and indirect (deliberative) questions" (118) are considered revealing.

A second range of Homeric instances that are relevant to the current chapter is discussed by Deborah Beck in a monograph on speech presentation in the *Iliad* and the *Odyssey* (2012). Her second chapter is devoted to evidence of "free indirect speech" (57–78; further cases are mentioned in her notes on pages 210–216). In a number of cases, the utterances cannot be attributed to a specific source because no report clause occurs, and the speech is linguistically characterized as other than direct speech. In other words, the language prompts a link to the voice of someone other than the primary narrator, even though nobody is formally taking the floor. In Homeric epic, free indirect speech appears after indirect speech or speech mention and tends to occur more in character text than in narrator text. Overall, it may express "varied intensities of emotional power" according to its location in stories (78). The second part of D. Beck's chapter focuses on "extensive uses of free indirect speech" (65).

Whose voice is represented, or whose voice is in the foreground, and how to interpret the linguistic markers that point to different sources are central issues in scholarly treatments of FIS (free indirect speech) as well as FIT (free indirect thought) and FID (free indirect discourse, including speech and thought). An exhaustive overview of the theoretical underpinnings exceeds the scope of this chapter. Here I just recall, first, an assumption that I find compatible with a blending reading and, second, the core issue of the debate "single vs. dual voice" in discussions of free indirect discourse.

The expressivity of FID resides in a balance that is negatively defined, as this quotation from Ann Banfield shows (1982: 108):

> (1) FID is neither an interpretation of the character's speech or thought, which implies an evaluating Speaker, nor a direct imitation of the quoted individual's voice; rather, the words or thoughts of the self represented retain all their expressivity without suggesting that their grammatical form was originally uttered, aloud or silently.

I will return to this idea in my conclusion to establish a connection with blending. The potentially blurred distinctions between voice of X and voice of Y constitute the topic of the "single vs. dual voice" debate. Free indirect speech can be read as a manifestation of two voices (the character's and the narrator's) or an effect achieved just by the narrator and her single voice.[3]

Debates on FID and FIST (free indirect speech and thought) mainly revolve around "either/or" interpretations and around consistent treatments of the linguistic devices that usually convey them, such as deictic markers, pronouns, and tense.[4] It is difficult to find objective and universal criteria for identifying where FID or FIST occurs and where it does not. An example attesting these difficulties is Luuk Huitink's observation about D. Beck's discussion of FIS in Homer (2013):

> (2) The syntax often leaves it unclear whether the text belongs to the main speaker or the narrator, and hence if there is speech representation at all. This contradiction—free indirect speech resembles both direct speech and narrator text—, which is admittedly also present in much other work on free indirect speech, is not resolved by Beck, so that a clear assessment of the nature of free indirect speech in Homer is still lacking.

Similar fuzzy boundaries in interpretation concern embedded focalization. At the end of the textual analyses in her chapter 4, de Jong admits that "in a number of cases . . . the boundary between primary and secondary focalization turned out to be not as clear-cut as the theory of the model 'predicts' them to be" (2004a: 123).[5]

In his cognitive narratological approach, David Herman proposes to move from focalization to a broader cognitive notion of construal that is "the common root of voice and vision" (2009: 99–109, quotation from 99).[6] Analogously, I suggest considering passages indirectly conveying someone's vision/thoughts/feelings and passages evoking someone's voice in a continuum: several parameters concur in the linguistic formulation of viewpoint; some are more oriented to inner voice or introspection, and some are more oriented to audible voices or to auditory imagery, without a clear-cut distinction (let alone opposition).[7] Above all, in line with Barbara Dancygier's cognitive approach to viewpoint, I find it useful to consider viewpoint in relation to not only a specific individual but also more comprehensive narrative strategies. To use Dancygier's words, viewpoint "may be spread over a number of different narrative spaces and tellers" (2012: 86).

I regard the fuzzy boundaries concerning focalization and free indirect speech as a resource. They invite us to ask ourselves what makes two sources of vision or voice co-present and why we cognize this. They invite us to delve more into the linguistic ambiguity of certain constructions. And they invite us to take into account multiple individuals' expressions of thoughts and speech. The idea of viewpoint blending addresses all of that and suggests emerging interpretations that are new.

Before we inquire into viewpoint as alluded to in Homeric instances of embedded focalization and free indirect speech, let us see how the idea of blending in cognitive linguistics works and how it differs from the intuitive notion of blurring.

BLENDING, OR CONCEPTUAL INTEGRATION

The process of blending, or conceptual integration (Fauconnier and Turner 2002), identifies a mental operation that "plays a pervasive role in language and communication" (Turner 2015: 211). It consists of integrating in our mind independent mental spaces and developing new meaning that is not drawn from those spaces individually.

Mental spaces are "temporary cognitive structures prompted by the use of linguistic forms" (Dancygier 2006: 5).[8] Linguistic constructions of different size and type can function as space builders. Mental spaces are abstract structures, but also *partial* structures (Dancygier and Sweetser 2014: 77), as human beings are not capable of grasping cognitive structures completely, that is, of cognizing every single component in them. Spaces relate to each other in various ways, depending on the relationships prompted by discourse. We may deal with embedded spaces, parallel spaces, hinted spaces that are linked sequentially, or form a network of spaces (Dancygier and Sweetser 2014: 80).

When we run a blend, we integrate two or more input spaces by mapping correspondences. Crucially, the resulting blend, which in turn is a mental space, has its own meaning, "elements and properties that are not available from other spaces" (Turner 2015: 213). We do not, then, just mix or blur correspondences. We process a new emergent structure and new conceptualizations.

An example from Dancygier's discussion on blending in literature may help (2006). The prologue to the book *The Future of Life* by Edward Osborne Wilson starts with the following question (2002: xi; indentation in original):

(3) Henry!
    May I call you by your Christian name?

"Henry" is Henry David Thoreau, the philosopher and writer who lived in the nineteenth century (1817–1862). Dancygier identifies a blend in this question (2006: 6–7). As we read it, we integrate the mental space prompted by the reference to Thoreau as a living person (therefore including a reference to his lifetime as well), which is input space 1, with the mental space prompted by the very beginning of *The Future of Life* by Wilson, published in 2002 (input space 2). The correspondences that we can map include the idea of addressing someone in writing and the idea that Wilson, by writing about nature and environment, relates to Thoreau's writing about nature and environment. However, what is temporally impossible in the two input spaces becomes possible in the blend: in an *ad hoc*, blended mental space (the "blended 'letter' space" [Dancygier 2006: 7]) Wilson can have a correspondence with Thoreau. This is an emergent structure that is not contained in input space 1 or in input space 2.

A further fundamental characteristic of blending is that of partial projection: "The inputs cannot be projected into the blend as wholes; rather, the structure needed for the blend is selected and then projected into the blended space" (Dancygier and Sweetser 2014: 82). In the example of E. O. Wilson and Thoreau, in order to process the blend we do not map correspondences about the physical aspect of the two individuals or about the number of works that they respectively wrote.

Since Gilles Fauconnier and Mark Turner presented the idea, blending and conceptual integration have been applied in many different scholarly fields, including literary criticism.[9] Felix Budelmann and Pauline LeVen offer a recent application of the idea of blending to ancient Greek literature (2014). The authors propose a reading of Timotheus's complex and sometimes puzzling figurative language in terms of a systematic poetics of blending. Most of the examples of blending quoted by Fauconnier and Turner show that conceptual integration is an everyday basic mental operation, something that we perform unconsciously. Timotheus's linguistic choices, Budelmann and LeVen point out, reveal something different: "He does not simply *draw on* our minds' capacity for blending, but he *stimulates* it to the highest degree" (2014: 198, emphasis in original). The blends resulting from this specific type of poetry come from a deliberate strategy: to make available to the audience networks of images to be processed (and enjoyed) together.

I will offer three blending interpretations regarding Homeric epic. They range over different sizes of linguistic constructions. The first example relies on a general example mentioned by Turner in *The Literary Mind*, that is, the blend constituted by talking animals (1996: 57). One input space includes animals that stand and/or eat and make noises, and the other space includes human beings who talk. The blend projects only part of the two input spaces—for example, the structure of talking animals does not necessarily clarify how they move their mouth, or how fast they speak. Likewise, it does not specify whether they talk while eating or while sitting. The new meaning, the new conceptual structure emerging uniquely from the blend may be seen in what talking animals could perform that human beings could not, such as exhibiting superhuman powers, or performing actions that in a real world cannot take place.

The *Iliad* provides a case in point for such a blend. Xanthos, one of Achilleus's two immortal horses, replies to the master's wish not to die like Patroklos (*Iliad* 19.408–409):

> (4) καὶ λίην σ' ἔτι νῦν γε σαώσομεν ὄβριμ' Ἀχιλλεῦ·
> ἀλλά τοι ἐγγύθεν ἦμαρ ὀλέθριον·
>
> We shall still keep you safe for this time, o hard Achilleus.
> And yet the day of your death is near.[10]

Turner remarks that "blended spaces can project structure *back* to their input spaces. Input spaces can be not only *providers* of projections to the blend, but also *receivers* of projections back from the developed blend" (1996: 60, emphasis in original). In the case of talking Xanthos, the blend, for example, projects back to the input space "animals making noises" the idea of powerful protection, while projecting back to the space "human talk" the idea of prophecy, a skill typically given to or inspired by some superhuman entity.[11] In addition, Achilleus, the primary narrator, and we as readers are able to hear the horse's voice, which is a further emerging element of the blending process. Moreover, this blend is closely connected to the intrinsic blend represented by Achilleus, a human being destined to die and a son of a god at the same time, and the blend represented by Xanthos, a regular horse, immortal being, possibly owned by Hera, and subject to the Erinyes.[12] The discussion could continue, as the passage and the implications are complex. What matters here is that by interpreting these words as reflecting at least the blend "speaking horse," we acknowledge multiple cross-mappings, and we enjoy all of them. We do not need to decide whether Xanthos's speech is more similar to that of a horse, or of a human, or of a god. The utterance is powerful to the extent that it is the result of blending.

The second example concerns a larger linguistic construction: an entire story pattern. Odysseus's visit to the land of the dead (*Odyssey* 11) functions as a blend. The input space of an adventurous journey by a living hero to a new and remarkable place where he meets several people is mapped onto the input space of an afterlife experience in which only dead people in the ghostly house of Hades can be met. This blend constitutes an emergent structure in that it invites inferences that could not be drawn from the input spaces. Odysseus's visit to the land of the dead while pursuing, as a living human being, his way home yields the truly heroic nature of Odysseus, who can survive death qua *hero*.[13] We may say that the blend of the two story patterns is further blended with the narrative skeleton of a *katabasis*, the narration of a "descent" to hell that worked as an initiation practice in the mystery cults (cf. p. 242). Listeners to descriptions of Odysseus's travel to the house of Hades would probably project some of the katabatic features in book 11 of the *Odyssey* and at the same time would enjoy the Phaiakian interruption (*Odyssey* 11.328–384), reminding them of the larger frame of the hero's *nostos* narrated at the court of the Phaiakians.

The third example is not a Homeric passage but a formulation concerning epic traditions in general: "performance arena," as used by John Miles Foley (1995). Linguistically this is a noun phrase, a small-scale construction. Traditional oral art, Foley explains, rests on three characteristics: a performance arena, where people meet and the exchange takes place; a register; and communicative economy. "Performance arena" indicates "the locus in which some specialized form of communication is uniquely licensed to take place" (8). The phrase "performance arena" maps the input space of a sand-area that is surrounded by seats and used for shows, originally including animal fight/entertainments and political debates, onto the input space of a performance of oral poetry attended by an audience. "Performance arena" highlights the importance of a public space (the oral performance as a public event) and the context of a contest (between different performers judged by an audience).

VIEWPOINT BLENDING

Eve Sweetser includes the following among the factors that determine viewpoint in language (2012: 4–6): where speakers and hearers are; when; what speakers and hearers presuppose, think, know; what speakers and hearers feel, evaluate; and all that speakers and hearers cognize about the viewpoint of others. It goes without saying that the plurality of speakers/tellers/narrators and the plurality of hearers/readers that a literary work may refer to create a complex network of viewpoints.

Furthermore, our human capability for imagining and sensing what our addressees and other people think or feel enables us to incorporate multiple viewpoints in language. This may happen on the macro level of discourse units, such as paragraphs, and on the micro level of individual sentences. An instance on the micro level is the particle ἦ, according to Ruth Scodel's investigation (2012): the communicative role of ἦ (an "emotional particle," per Samuel Bassett [1938: 102]) resides in introducing assertions or questions verifying the rightness of the speaker's inferences, or of the predictions or evaluations of the addressees. This interpretation quintessentially recognizes the cognitive human ability of mind reading and the cognitive processing of others' viewpoints.

The handling of multiple viewpoints in third-person sentences poses interesting challenges. How can we process viewpoint construal when language does not explicitly attribute words to anyone in particular? Third-person sentences are not deemed impersonal or lacking in focalization just because they are third-person-based. In line with Ronald Langacker's remarks (1990: esp. 13–15), the more a third-person sentence renders implicit the communicative setting, the more subjective the sentence is (cf. Herman 2009: 104; Sweetser 2012: 8). For example, Sweetser comments that in "Ted told Susan that he felt tired" the hearsay marker "Ted told Susan" clarifies that the responsibility for the content and the experience of feeling tired are attributed to a subject that is clearly distinct from the third person reporting all of this (2012: 6). Conversely, in "Ted felt tired" the communicative setting is not made explicit. The responsibility of the content and the experience can be attributed to the speaker as well. In other words, whoever writes this shows that she has access (or pretends to have access) to Ted's feeling of tiredness. The linguistic construction blends the character's and the writer's viewpoint.[14]

The last aspect of viewpoint that is relevant to the following textual analyses concerns its configuration beyond the vantage point of individuals. Dancygier asserts, "Viewpoint does not necessarily rely on a viewing subject, so that is it not necessarily 'someone's' point of view, but it relies crucially on a selection of an aspect of space topology which provides a filter through which the events are narrated" (2012: 61). Viewpoint can reflect an addressee's, a third party's, and the main narrator's viewpoint, but it can also be prompted and recalled by linguistic/narrative strategies that define and design a work as a whole. Dancygier offers an elaborate discussion of the establishment of viewpoint that goes beyond the representation of someone's speech or thought. Here I report an example of hers that is perhaps less complex than others. The main blend implied in Virginia Woolf's *Mrs. Dalloway* is that between the story viewpoint and subsequent ego viewpoints presented with almost no authorial transition from one to another (69–70). This is something that we readers process as a blend from different input spaces, that is, the narrative space embracing the whole story and the narrative spaces connected to the worlds of the multiple characters populating the novel.

The next subsections confine the analyses to the *Iliad* and the *Odyssey* on the micro level of sentences or clauses. In the following section I will suggest further directions for research regarding viewpoint blending in larger passages or episodes.

Embedded Focalization As Viewpoint Blending

The third-person sentences that we read in the Homeric poems are generally attributed to a *persona* (the primary narrator and primary focalizer, in de Jong's terms) or to an embodied version of "the Homeric performer," even though this embodied version is subject to conspicuous variants, diachronically at the very least. We actually confront a blend: "the Homeric performer" blends a professional identity and an unspecifiable multiplicity of actual bards and rhapsodes that metonymically represent "Homer" as they have sung or recited Homer with their voice.[15] Let us see how this blended entity of the performer prompts viewpoint blending in a few *loci* that de Jong interprets as instances of embedded focalization.

The first passage is about Hektor's stance at the beginning of the duel with Aias (*Iliad* 7.216–218).

> (5) Ἕκτορί τ' αὐτῶι θυμὸς ἐνὶ στήθεσσι πάτασσεν·
> ἀλλ' οὔ πως ἔτι εἶχεν ὑποτρέσαι οὐδ' ἀναδῦναι
> ἂψ λαῶν ἐς ὅμιλον, ἐπεὶ προκαλέσσατο χάρμηι.
>
> and for Hektor himself the heart beat hard in his breast, but he could not
> any more find means to take flight and shrink back into
> the throng of his men, since he in his pride had called him to battle.

De Jong proposes to read the ἀλλά-clause as conveying embedded focalization because the words depict Hektor's considerations (2004a: 121), and the epic narration at this point does show the narrator's access to Hektor's thoughts. However, the line preceding the ἀλλά-clause is equally, if not more, interesting. The depiction of the state of Hektor's θυμός does not sound less drawn from Hektor's feelings. Most important, αὐτῶι may work as indirect reflexive ("to Hektor himself"), implying that the primary narrator takes Hektor as the subject of consciousness. The line occurs after the representation of the Trojans being frightened by the sight of Aias (Τρῶας δὲ τρόμος αἰνὸς ὑπήλυθε γυῖα ἕκαστον ["the Trojans were taken every man in the knees with trembling and terror"], 215). The subsequent αὐτός singles out Hektor as the center—while the Trojans are the periphery—and the focal information is his epistemic and emotional state.[16]

I read the formulations of lines 216–218 (not just 217–218) as a blend. Input space 1 is prompted by the epic narration of the story, and it contains the elements "the narrator reads the mind of Hektor" and "the narrator formulates Hektor's considerations." Input space 2 is triggered by the situation within the story, and it contains the elements "Hektor is anxious" and "the reason for the anxiety is that he called Aias to battle and now he cannot withdraw himself." In the viewpoint blend, the thought of Hektor is reenacted through the voice and viewpoint of the primary narrator. This is the emergent element: the performer for a moment thinks and fears what Hektor thinks and fears, while remaining at the same time the performer of the Iliadic excerpt.

A second instance discussed by de Jong encompasses two *loci* where the robe that Hekabe is supposed to offer to Athena in the temple is said to be "the largest, the nicest, and the loveliest." Here is the text of the two passages (*Iliad* 6.269–273, 293–295):

> (6) ἀλλὰ σὺ μὲν πρὸς νηὸν Ἀθηναίης ἀγελείης
> ἔρχεο σὺν θυέεσσιν, ἀολλίσσασα γεραιάς·
> πέπλον δ', ὅς τίς τοι χαριέστατος ἠδὲ μέγιστος
> ἔστιν ἐνὶ μεγάρωι καί τοι πολὺ φίλτατος αὐτῆι,
> τὸν θὲς Ἀθηναίης ἐπὶ γούνασιν ἠϋκόμοιο.
>
> But go yourself to the temple of the spoiler Athena,
> assembling the ladies of honor, and with things to be sacrificed,
> and take a robe, which seems to you the largest and loveliest
> in the great house, and that which is far your dearest possession.
> Lay this along the knees of Athena the lovely haired.
>
> (7) τῶν ἕν' ἀειραμένη Ἑκάβη φέρε δῶρον Ἀθήνηι,
> ὃς κάλλιστος ἔην ποικίλμασιν ἠδὲ μέγιστος,
> ἀστὴρ δ' ὣς ἀπέλαμπεν· ἔκειτο δὲ νείατος ἄλλων.
>
> Hekabe lifted out one [robe] and took it as gift to Athena,
> that which was the loveliest in design and the largest,
> and shone like a star. It lay beneath the others.

De Jong includes these passages in a list of relative clauses that can be interpreted as conveying embedded focalization (2004a: 120). She specifies that in the first passage (6) the occurrence of **τοι** and of **αὐτῆι** (lines 271 and 272) make it explicit that the focalizer is Hekabe. Hektor invites his mother to bring to Athena not just any robe, but the robe that she perceives as the loveliest and largest of all. In the second passage (7), line 294 (**ὃς κάλλιστος ἔην ποικίλμασιν ἠδὲ μέγιστος** ["that which was the loveliest in design and the largest"]) closely evokes lines 271–272 in (6): **ὅς τίς τοι χαριέστατος ἠδὲ μέγιστος / ἔστιν ἐνὶ μεγάρωι καί τοι πολὺ φίλτατος αὐτῆι** ("which seems to you the largest and loveliest / in the great house, and that which is far your dearest possession").

The passages have a similar syntactical shape, but a relative clause *per se* does not perspectivize, although it may be employed to introduce perspectivized information together with other co-occurring features (see

p. 247 on the construction "relative pronoun + δή" and viewpoint). I highlight how the text in (6) lends itself to a multiple-viewpoint blending reading, while (5) includes just the blending of the narrator's voice expressing Hektor's words. If superlative forms are evaluative/affective expressions that are apt to convey embedded focalization (de Jong 2004a: 120, 143), whose focalization is expressed at lines 294–295? I propose to read a viewpoint blend given by the cross-space mapping of three input spaces: Hektor's words reported a few lines earlier; Hekabe's judgment about the nicest and biggest robe; and the narrator's expansion on the robe that eventually Hekabe chooses. Those lines encode all three perspectives. An "either/or" reading would weaken the sense of the expansion provided by the relative clause.[17]

The final example seems obvious, but it may reflect some intriguing complexity in terms of viewpoint (*Iliad* 24.327–328):

> (8) . . . φίλοι δ' ἅμα πάντες ἕποντο
> πόλλ' ὀλοφυρόμενοι ὡς εἰ θανατόνδε[18] κιόντα.
>
> . . . All kinsmen were following
> much lamenting, as if he went to his death.

De Jong comments, "Here the NF_1 through the addition of ὡς εἰ ('as if') makes clear that the interpretation of Priam's mission as suicidal is the characters'" (2004a: 121). This is certainly one of the components of the viewpoint expressed by means of ὡς εἰ θανατόνδε κιόντα ("as if he went to his death"), and it is perhaps reinforced by the semantic clue given by the verb ὀλοφύρομαι, used more than once for people mourning or sensing someone's death (see *Iliad* 8.464, 21.106, 23.75; *Odyssey* 16.22, 19.522, 22.447, 24.59). But we may add further components.

The lexical choice φίλοι can be argued to be viewpointed in that it evokes people dear to someone—Priam, in this case. Maybe the perspective of Priam is part of this third-person passage as well, judging from a few previous narrative shots: Iris reaches Priam's house, and "There she found outcry and mourning. / The sons sitting around their father inside the courtyard" (24.160–161); and Priam declares at 246 "my wish is to go sooner down to the house of the death god." Or at least it cannot be excluded. The present participle κιόντα does not help to disambiguate. In other words, Priam's viewpoint according to which he is aware that he resembles someone who is heading to the underworld may be incorporated as well. The resulting viewpoint blend features the co-occurrence of relatives and friends thinking, "It is as if Priam is going to die," and Priam thinking, "It is as if I am going to die" (the present participle κιόντα contributing to the actuality of the perception). The katabatic perspective possibly alluded to by the whole narrative of Priam's journey (C. Mackie 1999: 488–491; Herrero de Jáuregui 2011) would add a further feature: the same viewpoint blend may incorporate also the image of Priam waiting for his journey to meet Achilleus in the underworld. This Achilleus in turn is a blend of Achilleus alive in his tent and Achilleus dead in the underworld.

So far my interpretation of viewpoint blending concerned the conceptual integration of different individuals' vantage points. I argued that passages (6), (7), and (8) feature a blend of three input spaces, that is, the primary narrator's and two different characters (or group of characters) that share the same contextual frame.

Free Indirect Speech As Viewpoint Blending

Let us now select three passages from D. Beck's discussion of free indirect speech. The first passage is taken from the highly emotional moment of the Achaians' and in particular Achilleus's mourning rituals and laments over Patroklos's corpse (*Iliad* 18.343–345):

> (9) Ὣς εἰπὼν ἑτάροισιν ἐκέκλετο δῖος Ἀχιλλεὺς
> ἀμφὶ πυρὶ στῆσαι τρίποδα μέγαν, ὄφρα τάχιστα
> Πάτροκλον λούσειαν ἄπο βρότον αἱματόεντα.
>
> So speaking brilliant Achilleus gave orders to his companions
> to set a great cauldron across the fire, so that with all speed
> they could wash away the clotted blood from Patroklos.

D. Beck reads "so that with all speed / they could wash away the clotted blood from Patroklos" as a purpose clause mixing the expression of Achilleus's anxiety, through the superlative form τάχιστα ("with all speed"), and the narrator's wording: the adjective αἱματόεις ("bloody") usually occurs in the narrator's speech (2012: 213). The result, she argues, is that the free indirect speech clause "enables the narrative both to foreground the lament that precedes the preparations . . . and to give significant emotional coloring to this order" (65).

While considering the phenomenon in a cognitive perspective, let me use the terms employed by José Sanders and Gisela Redeker in a mental-space reading of free indirect discourse in a contemporary news text (1996). In (9) the *base space* is triggered by the subject who relates the events in third-person, and an *embedded space* is triggered by the imagined setting where Achilleus, the companions, the fire, and Patroklos's corpse with clotted blood are co-present (the big tripod is going to be added soon). By means of the explicit performative verb "he gave orders" (ἐκέκλετο, 343), we "hear" the voice of Achilleus while some details of these orders are reported. In Sanders and Redeker's terms, "he gave orders" is a space builder that gives us access to Achilleus's voice as he gives orders.

However, while this verb and the following infinitive construction (στῆσαι, 344) take the narrator's base space as a reference point, the ὄφρα-clause is ambiguous. On the one hand, we can attribute the specification of the purpose of the order to Achilleus in line with the preceding representation of his words: the use of the superlative evokes subjectivity (see p. 241; cf. de Jong 2004a: 143; Fludernik 1993: 227–228; D. Beck 2012: 65; see also Bonifazi, Drummen, and de Kreij 2016: II.3, §§60–61 on δή and superlatives in Homeric epic). On the other hand, the language keeps a reference to the base space through λούσειαν ("they could wash," 345), which features the third-person number and the optative mood, both typically used in *oratio obliqua*. This configuration of direct and indirect representation of Achilleus's orders suggests blending. Input space 1 is where we imagine the epic teller specifying Achilleus's purpose, and in input space 2 we imagine Achilleus specifying his own purpose. The blended space is that of the two merging voices conveying a merged viewpoint.

This example may prompt one to wonder about the difference in the genre of Greek archaic epic between free indirect speech and direct speech as far as the perception of voices is concerned. After all, in the reproduction of a character's speech, too, the voice of the narrator does not disappear. The difference is this: during the performance of direct speech, audience and performer are completely displaced into the embedded space of the speaking character(s), the shift of the deictic center being a grammatical marker of that. The voice of the characters(s) thus prevails. In the performance of free indirect speech, conversely, the displacement is ambiguous, and the perception of viewpoint is linked to both the base space and the embedded space. The voice that we hear is a blend of the two input voices.

The second passage from D. Beck's examples features free indirect speech in character speech instead of narrator text (*Odyssey* 19.296–299):

(10) τὸν δ' ἐς Δωδώνην φάτο βήμεναι, ὄφρα θεοῖο
ἐκ δρυὸς ὑψικόμοιο Διὸς βουλὴν ἐπακούσαι,
ὅππως νοστήσειε φίλην ἐς πατρίδα γαῖαν,
ἤδη δὴν ἀπεών, ἢ ἀμφαδὸν ἦε κρυφηδόν.

But he said Odysseus had gone to Dodona, to listen
to the will of Zeus, out of the holy deep-leaved oak tree,
for how he could come back to the rich countryside of Ithaka,
in secret or openly, having been by now long absent.

Odysseus in disguise tells Penelope about Odysseus's adventures and Odysseus's stay with the Thesprotians. φάτο ("he said," 296) builds an embedded space where the hero Odysseus tells of his trip to the oracle of Dodona. In turn, this embedded space is embedded in the beggar's narration to Penelope (see τὴν δ' ἀπαμειβόμενος προσέφη πολύμητις Ὀδυσσεύς ["Then resourceful Odysseus spoke in turn and answered her"], 261) and in the further space that is the base space of the epic teller performing the *Odyssey*. So, we process a blend provided by three coexisting mental spaces, the viewpoints linked to each of the three tellers and three voices. In fact, the voice of Odysseus (see φάτο, 296) is audible in the blend also at lines 298–299: the requests to the god at the oracle in Dodona are not only reported but also echoed in a sort of reperformance (ὅπως νοστήσειε φίλην ἐς πατρίδα γαῖαν, / ἤδη δὴν ἀπεών, ἢ ἀμφαδὸν ἦε κρυφηδόν ["how he could come back to the rich countryside of Ithaka, / in secret or openly, having been by now long absent"]). The same words occur at *Odyssey* 14.327–330. There we process the same type of blend, the only difference being that in the embedded space correlated to the plot of the *Odyssey* the interlocutor is Eumaios instead of Penelope.[19]

The final passage from D. Beck's selection illustrates free indirect speech once again in relation to a character speech. The character in question is Phoinix, and the speech is the long address he delivers in order to persuade Achilleus to return to his companions (*Iliad* 9.590–595):

(11) καὶ τότε δὴ Μελέαγρον ἐΰζωνος παράκοιτις
λίσσετ' ὀδυρομένη, καί οἱ κατέλεξεν ἅπαντα
κήδε', ὅσ' ἀνθρώποισι πέλει τῶν ἄστυ ἁλώῃ·
ἄνδρας μὲν κτείνουσι, πόλιν δέ τε πῦρ ἀμαθύνει,
τέκνα δέ τ' ἄλλοι ἄγουσι βαθυζώνους τε γυναῖκας.
τοῦ δ' ὠρίνετο θυμὸς ἀκούοντος κακὰ ἔργα . . .

And then at last his wife, the fair-girdled bride, supplicated
Meleagros, in tears, and rehearsed in their numbers before him
all the sorrows that come to men when their city is taken:
they kill the men, and the fire leaves the city in ashes,
and strangers lead the children away and the deep-girdled women.
And the heart, as he listened to all this evil, was stirred
within him . . .

D. Beck shows that in lines 593–594 "we are given unmediated access to" the words of Kleopatra as reported here by Phoinix (2012: 72). The present tense of the verbs κτείνουσι, ἀμαθύνει (593), and ἄγουσι (594) conveys immediacy. The following participle describing Meleagros's reaction—ἀκούοντος, 595—confirms Phoinix's intention to present part of the content of Kleopatra's plea as vividly as possible. In terms of viewpoint blending, however, an additional element should be taken into account: the double occurrence of the combination δέ τε (593, 594). τε connects to sayings, proverbs, and shared knowledge of traditions/myths/encyclopedic data in a number of contexts (Bonifazi, Drummen, and de Kreij 2016: IV.2, §§102–105; III.2, §36). I suggest that the blend includes at once the primary narrator's vantage point of the reperformance of Phoinix's words; Phoinix's viewpoint about Kleopatra's moving words; Kleopatra's emotional viewpoint while she is pleading with Meleagros; and, finally, a collective viewpoint coming from universal wisdom. What happens to cities being taken is common knowledge: men are killed, the city burns, and children and women are led away.

Let me quote a passage that supports this reading and addresses in general the question of individual/subjective viewpoint versus collective/intersubjective viewpoint (*Iliad* 18.306–309):

(12) . . . οὔ μιν ἔγωγε
φεύξομαι ἐκ πολέμοιο δυσηχέος, ἀλλὰ μάλ' ἄντην
στήσομαι, ἤ κε φέρῃσι μέγα κράτος, ἦ κε φεροίμην.
ξυνὸς Ἐνυάλιος, καί τε κτανέοντα κατέκτα.

. . . I for my part
will not run from him out of the sorrowful battle, but rather
stand fast, to see if he wins the great glory, or if I can win it.
The war god is impartial. Before now he has killed the killer.

Hektor is closing his speech to Poulydamas. He expresses his decision to stay and see whether Achilleus or he himself will win. He backs up his thought by affirming the impartiality of Ares, who can avenge a slaying by cutting down the one who slew. The Greek displays the combination καί τε, along with a wordplay around the sounds 'kt,' as Mark Edwards notes (1991: 182). While τε stresses the shared-knowledge aspect of the saying, καί introduces an illustration, a specification about ξυνὸς Ἐνυάλιος. All of this invites the reader to consider that, within this speech, Hektor not only expresses his own viewpoint but also incorporates a traditional viewpoint by possibly quoting a saying, κτανέοντα κατέκτα, with reference to Ares, and introduced by τε.

It is time to draw some conclusions. First, even if a character talks in direct speech, the space corresponding to the primary narrator while he is reperforming those words does not disappear from our mind (or from the mind of the audience listening to his voice). Second, the voice of a character blended with the voice of the performer is an element contributing to the configuration of viewpoint. Exploring focalization without voice is not enough to account for viewpoint analysis. Third, several types of viewpoint blending are represented in the *loci* that I discussed. The simplest configuration is a blend of the narrator's viewpoint and one of the character's: see (5), the primary narrator and Hektor. A parallel type is the blend of the primary narrator and a character's *voice* and viewpoint: see (9), Achilleus on Patroklos. A more complex type is the blend involving the primary narrator and two different characters or group of characters: see (6) and (7), the primary narrator, Hektor, and Hekabe; (8), the primary narrator, the kinsmen, and Priam; and (10), which adds the voice of Odysseus-Odysseus and the voice of Odysseus-in-disguise. Finally, (11) and (12) display the blend of a character's viewpoint playing the role of narrator (Phoinix in [11]) or speaking in the first person (Hektor in [12]), the viewpoint of the primary narrator reenacting the speeches, and a collective viewpoint prompted by gnomic features. (11) reflects a further viewpoint, that is, Kleopatra's. Overall, this goes beyond "either/or" alternatives. It invites the processing of multiple viewpoints at the same time.

HOMER BEYOND IMPERSONALITY AND BEYOND SINGLE-VIEWPOINT CONFIGURATIONS

One of the merits of de Jong's book (2004a) is that it dismantles, once and for all, the dogma of Homeric objectivity.[20] Analogously, one of the merits of D. Beck's work (2012) is that the occurrence of free indirect speech in Homer is brought to light. This chapter not only builds on de Jong's focalization and D. Beck's FIS approaches by adding the cognitive relevance of new meanings emerging from viewpoint blends but also aims to pave the way for a general reconsideration of viewpoint in Homeric epic, together with a suggestion about how to tackle the question of which linguistic devices prompt which viewpoint.

Before I list Homeric themes and episodes that may be the object of further studies concerning viewpoint blending—thus encompassing a macro level of analysis—I am going to mention a couple of examples still on the micro level of text. They address the subtleness and the deliberate avoidance of single-viewpoint constructions. Here is a simple case of free indirect thought that provides a viewpoint blend of the character's and the main narrator's stances (*Odyssey* 5.441–443):

> (13) ἀλλ' ὅτε δὴ ποταμοῖο κατὰ στόμα καλλιρόοιο
> ἷξε νέων, τῇι δή οἱ ἐείσατο χῶρος ἄριστος,
> λεῖος πετράων, καὶ ἐπὶ σκέπας ἦν ἀνέμοιο·
>
> [B]ut when he came, swimming along, to the mouth of
> a sweet-running river, this at least seemed to him the best place,
> being bare of rocks, and there was even shelter from the wind
> there.

The relevant wording in this case is τῇι δή οἱ ἐείσατο χῶρος ἄριστος ("this seemed to him the best place") (542). In Homer the construction "relative pronoun + δή" in third-person narration can mark an omniscience-based addition of information (*Odyssey* 2.16, 7.156, 10.115, 21.24) or the omniscience-based access to the stance of a character (*Odyssey* 13.30, 20.289). Even though δή can be called a viewpoint marker, its occurrence in this passage does not disambiguate whose viewpoint is conveyed: the narrator's access to Odysseus's evaluation is implicit enough to be assimilated to Odysseus's own evaluation.[21] Only at *Odyssey* 7.281 do the same words occur (τῇι δή μοι ἐείσατο χῶρος ἄριστος), uttered this time by Odysseus in front of Queen Arete. To conclude, the relative clause including δή in *Odyssey* 5.442 is not a straightforward case of authorial intrusion.

Another example regarding just one word is that of the non-straightforward adverbial meaning of αὐτοῦ (thirty-two occurrences in the *Iliad*; fifty-three in the *Odyssey*). The word αὐτοῦ is used in character speech as well as in narrator text. In character speech it may mean "here"/"in this very place," while in narrator text it may mean "there"/"in that very place." In previous work, I contended that the utterance of αὐτοῦ in narrator text may achieve the effect of making proximal the space or time referred to (Bonifazi 2012: 281–282). Here I add that this ambivalence may be a viewpoint ambivalence encoded in the word: "in the very place" can fit the distant vantage point "there and then" (usually attributed to the primary narrator) as well as the immediate vantage point "here and now" (usually attributed to the characters). If the lexical item is always the same, the narrator can use it to project his own "here and now" onto the "here and now" of the epic past.

Let us now consider five lines from the *Odyssey* that linguistically look like a most regular and uniform omniscient representation of what happens—even though in content they depict a quite tense moment (*Odyssey* 20.345–349):

(14) ὣς φάτο Τηλέμαχος· μνηστῆρσι δὲ Παλλὰς Ἀθήνη
ἄσβεστον γέλω ὦρσε, παρέπλαγξεν δὲ νόημα.
οἱ δ' ἤδη γναθμοῖσι γελώων ἀλλοτρίοισιν,
αἱμοφόρυκτα δὲ δὴ κρέα ἤσθιον· ὄσσε δ' ἄρα σφέων
δακρυόφιν πίμπλαντο, γόον δ' ὠΐετο θυμός.

So spoke Telemachos. In the suitors Pallas Athena
stirred up uncontrollable laughter, and addled their thinking.
Now they laughed with jaws that were no longer their own.
The meat they ate was a mess of blood, their eyes were bursting
full of tears, and their laughter sounded like lamentation.

"ὣς φάτο X" is a formulaic construction marking the switch from direct speech to third-person narration. What follows is the description/narration of what happens to the people co-present in the scene after the speech is over. Two recurrent signs of the narrator's omniscience are also displayed: the telling of divine intervention mingled with human action/reaction and the access to the inner state of the characters (see θυμός, and the verb οἴω/οἴομαι, a verb indicating a subjective view). In terms of viewpoint, some twists emerge. The mention of Pallas Athena as an agent prompts a widening of the mental space, from the human-only sphere of action to the human *and* divine sphere of action. Yet the consistency in the use of the aorist tense across lines 345 and 346 (φάτο, 345; ὦρσε, παρέπλαγξεν, 346) shows that the primary narrator has access to both perspectives and has authorial control of both spaces.

Lines 347–349 feature a shift in tense from aorist to imperfect (ἤσθιον, 348; πίμπλαντο, ὠΐετο, 349). This may correspond to a shift from an extradiegetic to an intradiegetic perspective or from an off-stage to an on-stage presence of the narrator.[22] However, two lexical items may index different aspects concerning the intradiegetic perspective in 347–349: ἤδη (347) and δ' ἄρα (348).

In the Homeric poems ἤδη occurs more in character speech than in narrator text whereas ἄρα occurs more in narrator text than in character speech.[23] With regard to Herodotus's and Thucydides's works, I interpret the communicative role of ἤδη to be the marking of firsthand experience, that is to say, the perception of someone witnessing an event from inside the situation. This perception does not necessarily regard time but may regard space or any reality that a character or the historian evaluates (Bonifazi, Drummen, and de Kreij 2016: IV.4, §§151–161).[24] In the passage in question, I read the co-occurrence of ἤδη with the imperfect tense as conveying the narrator's firsthand experience of the suitors' "carnivorous frenzy" (Bakker 2013: 94).[25] In this sense the narrator becomes an observer of the scene from within the hall—a quite different viewpoint from the cosmic one of the previous line. δή near the peculiar adjective αἱμοφόρυκτα "reeking with blood"—a *hapax legomenon*—seems to reinforce the idea of the primary narrator's stancetaking.

Conversely, at 348 ἄρα (on which see Bonifazi, Drummen, and de Kreij 2016: II.5, §§51–58) may signal the return to the previous, more distanced and more global, viewpoint of the omniscient narrator, who is able to see tears behind their laughter and foresees ominous lament from their spirit.[26] Curiously, the tense is still imperfect. Even more curiously, a comment in secondary literature hints at the possibility of further viewpoints attached to these lines. Joseph Russo wonders who sees the meat blood-defiled: "It is not clear to whom the meat appears in its bloody transformation. The scholia say only Theoklymenos sees it. More likely everyone *except* the suitors sees it. Possibly they too see it, but have no memory of it once their seizure has passed" (1992: 124, emphasis in original). In fact, the text continues with the speech of Telemachos's guest-friend Theoklymenos, who explicitly mentions the appearance of tears and the sound of wailing (*Odyssey* 20.351–357). On the whole, the third-person narration realized in these lines is a complex one, and not necessarily because of frequent switches from X's viewpoint to Y's viewpoint. The complexity may reside in the almost imperceptible incorporation of multiple viewpoints at the same time.

In a mental-space perspective, Homeric narration is a sequence of smaller and larger linguistic constructions that work as space builders. The audience deals with millions of mental spaces prompted by the epic language. Viewpoint emerges as a configuration that not only relates to single characters and their actions but also is connected to the relations between them, to what groups people represent, and to the vantage point from which comprehensive scenes are described.

This chapter has focused on the complexity of viewpoint at the micro level of individual passages and individual clauses. Viewpoint on the macro level of larger discourse units would deserve attention too. For example, D. Beck also discusses "extensive uses of free indirect speech" (2012: 65), in particular the second song of Demodokos (*Odyssey* 8.266–367) and Phoinix's speech to Achilleus (*Iliad* 9.434–605). Scott Richardson comments about Demodokos, "We lose sight of the intradiegetic singer as the extradiegetic narrator takes over the story. The signs of indirect narration disappear, and the words become the narrator's own" (1990: 85). De Jong, too, discusses Demodokos's song in terms of blurred narrative levels (2009). Over long stretches of speech, characters play the role of narrators. This tells us not only that the primary narrator and focalizer can give voice and turn into characters as secondary narrators and focalizers—to use de Jong's terms—but also that characters can turn in a viewpoint blend into primary storytellers and viewers/evaluators.

A full discussion of additional extended cases of viewpoint blending will require a separate investigation. Let me list a few possible themes and topics that I deem worth exploring: the significance of the image of the nightingale as applied to Penelope in the final part of the *Odyssey* (Levaniouk 1999) and, by analogy, other embedded animal metaphors in the two Homeric poems; several incongruous wordings in the *Odyssey* that make the linear unfolding of the plot clash with a character's knowledge and recognition abilities (Bonifazi 2012: 69–120); and the incorporation of traditional lament at different points of the *Iliad* (Alexiou 2002 [1974]; Dué 2002). Blending, even without the viewpoint component, may be underlying even the processing of mixed genres.[27] Finally, as for the relation between viewpoint and viewing subjects, we may think of the stunning versatility of the Homeric narrator when it comes to the visualization of items, single or grouped, animate or inanimate. Recent work by Alex Purves (2010), Jenny Strauss Clay (2011), and Christos Tsagalis (2012) substantiates and expands on the idea that the Homeric narrator manipulates spatial viewpoint in many ways to achieve different effects.

CONCLUSION: THE ADVANTAGES OF A VIEWPOINT-BLENDING APPROACH

Applying the idea of viewpoint blending to embedded focalization and to free indirect speech brings some advantages. It does not confine our interpretation to establishing exact boundaries and to isolating single-viewpoint passages. It allows us to see and hear—voices are an indispensable component of Homeric epic—a viewpoint configuration that takes into account multiple perspectives at the same time. The input spaces need not be just two (for example, the epic narrator's and a character's). They may also encompass what a character reports about the viewpoint of a different character. The main narrator may incorporate viewpoint markers that index a collective viewpoint of common wisdom or shared knowledge or viewpoint markers that convey the bard's explicit stance about a certain action. Crucially, we do not perceive the resulting viewpoint blend as an indistinct fusion of elements; rather we perceive all the elements of the cross-space and we enjoy the new elements emerging from the blend insofar as they emerge only in the blend.

In a way, these findings counterbalance Banfield's observation (see [1]): to a negatively defined expressivity of FID ("the words or thoughts of the self represented retain all their expressivity without suggesting that their grammatical form was originally uttered, aloud or silently"), we can oppose, by blending different input spaces, our cognitive conceptual integration of all the grammatical forms with all their different suggestions.

This chapter has also aimed to start new discussions about viewpoint in Homeric discourse in general and especially about the viewpoint interpretation of epic linguistic devices. On the one hand, it challenges the uniformity or consistency of viewpoint in third-person narration: interpretive complexity may come not so much from the recognition of boundaries or neat switches between X's viewpoint and Y's viewpoint as from the connection to further, coexisting viewpoints concerning individuals as well as groups. On the other hand, the textual analyses attest to the relevance of particles, adverbs, tense, and pronouns to the construction of viewpoint. Their significance is never absolute, never attached just to one of these features, but emerges only in connection to co-occurring features.

A final consideration concerns what I called a collective viewpoint. Similes, *gnōmai*, and formulas, for example, could be seen as narrative spaces where collective views are converging. I link collective viewpoints to an inherently intersubjective quality of the epic genre, to the telling of immanent stories that belong to communities. Consider, for instance, the frequency of the particle τε in similes (Bonifazi, Drummen, and de Kreij 2016: II.4, §§32–37; IV.2, §§54–57). If we assume that τε marks not only coordination but also shared knowledge about tradition (myths, encyclopedic knowledge, and traditional imagery), then we may read τε in similes as prompting (or contributing to the prompting of) an intersubjective viewpoint. Intersubjectivity adds to the expressivity of similes without diminishing any reference to a specific character's subjectivity or any reference to local content meanings.[28] Future work could explore how the expression of collective viewpoint relates also to formulas and epithets and how it relates to the surrounding utterances, which in turn are inevitably viewpointed utterances.

NOTES

I warmly thank Jonathan Ready and Christos Tsagalis for their invaluable advice, Cristóbal Pagán Cánovas for his important feedback, and Eve Sweetser for her vital encouragement.

1. For elaborate discussion of the differences between and a critique of both approaches, see Belfiore 2000: 48–53; Broman 2004; Herman 2009: 99–103.

2. The distinction between "who talks" and "who sees" is one of the fundamental tenets in Bal as well as in Genette. Fleischman clarifies: "When focalization changes, what changes is not the narrative voice; the angle of vision through which events in a text are filtered will always be *verbalized* by the narrator. What changes is *the perception that orients the report*" (1990: 217, emphasis in original). Nünlist stresses that "focalization," unlike point of view, "keeps the lenses through which events are seen distinct from the voice reporting those events" (2011).

3. Representative works supporting the two different views are Pascal 1977 (dual voice) and Banfield 1982 (single voice). A helpful summary of the positions can be found in Vandelanotte 2009: 245–247. See also Sanford and Emmott 2012: 189.

4. For example, a careful study of deixis and of pronouns and proper names in FIST leads Vandelanotte to distinguish between FIST and DIST (free indirect speech and thought and distancing indirect speech and thought). The former is mimetic and character-oriented, while the latter is non-mimetic and narrator-oriented (2009: 222–231).

5. On the ambiguity as to who is the focalizer in some Odyssean passages, with reference to de Jong's *Narratological Commentary on the Odyssey* (2001), see Scodel 2002b.

6. This construal consists in focal adjustment, which Langacker decomposes into selection, abstraction, and several components of perspective (figure-ground alignment; vantage point + orientation; deixis; subjectivity/objectivity) (1987). See Herman 2009: 104. On construal, see also Langacker 2015.

7. For auditory imagery, I refer the reader to Chafe's illuminating article on the covert prosody of written language (1988).

8. Mental spaces theory was originally introduced by Fauconnier (1985).

9. On the latter, see http://markturner.org/blending.html for a list of relevant publications. See also the bibliography in the 2006 special issue of *Language and Literature* devoted to blending.

10. English translations of passages from the epics are by Lattimore (1951 for the *Iliad*; 1965 for the *Odyssey*), with some modifications to spelling. The Greek text of Homeric passages comes from the *Thesaurus Linguae Graecae*.

11. Besides animals' and rivers' talk in the *Iliad*, we may think of other (and more common) talking situations representing blends—for instance, gods offering counsel to heroes by resembling human beings (as Athena-Mentes in *Odyssey* 2 and 3) and perhaps the idea of a talking god *tout court*.

12. See in particular Johnston 1992 on the connection between the horse, the goddess's indirect involvement in war, and the prophetic power of chthonic entities.

13. Stanford calls the descent to the land of the dead "customary" for great heroes, such as Gilgamesh, Orpheus, Herakles, and Theseus (1996, vol. 1: 381).

14. The choice of personal pronouns plays a pivotal role in the expression of viewpoint and in free indirect discourse; see Dancygier 2008.

15. On Homer as a metonymy and on metonymical communication in ancient Greek literary texts, see Nagy 2015.

16. See Bonifazi 2012: 137–149 for a reading of Homeric αὐτός, the pronoun, and αὐτός, the predicative adjective, as implying a center-periphery figure.

17. On the intensification of viewing in this passage, see Tsagalis 2012: 391–392.

18. I follow West's edition reporting θανατόνδε; the TLG online edition (based on T. W. Allen's text) has θάνατον δέ.

19. The participial phrase ἤδη δὴν ἀπεών occurs also one more time (*Odyssey* 13.187–189): ὁ δ' ἔγρετο δῖος Ὀδυσσεὺς / εὕδων ἐν γαίηι πατρωΐηι, οὐδέ μιν ἔγνω, / ἤδη δὴν ἀπεών· ("But now great Odysseus wakened / from sleep in his own fatherland, and he did not know it, / having been long away"). This time the source of the utterance is the primary narrator. In the next section I will say more about ἤδη as a viewpoint marker. Here I anticipate that ἤδη statements report events as firsthand experience, and this view from within the situation does not necessarily concern time. In *Odyssey* 13.187–189 it does: the primary narrator expresses a temporal viewpoint—associated with the sense of certainty (think of ἤ + δή)—that is the same as Odysseus's. In other words, the primary narrator locates himself in the situation experienced by the character in question and says ἤδη δὴν ἀπεών, "(sure), now being away for a long time." The preceding short clause οὐδέ μιν ἔγνω qualifies as a blend of the experience of Odysseus and of the experience of the narrator accessing the experience of Odysseus.

20. See de Jong 2004a: 14–15 for an overview of secondary literature assuming the objective and impersonal character of early epic narration. On page 137 the author recalls the remarks in Opelt 1978 and in Griffin 1986 that affective and evaluative words in Homer "are found exclusively in the speeches of characters." On pages 18–20 she summarizes the views of authors claiming, conversely, that subjectivity is part of Homeric third-person narration, at least sporadically. An early work that stands out in this respect is Bassett 1938 (in particular 81–113).

21. Elsewhere, I have shown that in Herodotus and in Thucydides δή marks the voice and stance of different subjects, including those of the historians and the characters (Bonifazi, Drummen, and de Kreij 2016: IV.4.5 and 4.6). Sometimes a deliberate blending of voices and stances seems to be conveyed, especially in Thucydides. Homer and Herodotus share the recurring use of δή mainly to mark narrative progression. Homeric epic features δή in constructions connected to authorial comments, such as the counterfactual νυ κε δή; see

also a rare οἷον δή uttered by the narrator at *Odyssey* 20.393–394 (οἷον δὴ τάχ' ἔμελλε θεὰ καὶ καρτερὸς ἀνὴρ / θησέμεναι): I translate "what [a dinner] the goddess and the very strong hero were about to give [to the suitors]!" I remind the reader that δή in Homer is far more frequent in direct speech than in narrator text. The frequencies for δή based on an analysis of twelve books of the *Iliad* (13–24) and twelve books of the *Odyssey* (1–12) are the following: in the *Iliad* 1.7 instances of δή per one hundred lines of narrator text and 5.1 per one hundred lines of direct speech, and in the *Odyssey* 3.8 per one hundred lines of narrator text and 4.7 per one hundred lines of direct speech.

22. See Genette 1980: 250–252 on extradiegetic vs. intradiegetic narrators and Dancygier 2012: 64–67 on offstage and onstage narrators. On the imperfect tense conveying an internal perspective in ancient Greek, see, for example, Bakker 1997b. Sweetser relates the imperfective aspect to the expression of experiential states: "[imperfective aspect] marks viewing an event from inside its temporal extent" (2012: 6).

23. ἤδη occurs only twelve times in narrator text out of ninety-nine total instances in the *Odyssey*, and only five times out of fifty-three in the *Iliad*. As for the distribution of ἄρα, the same sample of books (*Odyssey* 9, 10, 17, 18 and *Iliad* 4, 5, 6, 17) gives this percentage: 11.9% narrator text vs. 1.5% direct speech in the *Odyssey*, and 10.7% narrator text vs. 2.9% direct speech in the *Iliad*.

24. In that work I call ἤδη a stance marker. The interpretive substance does not significantly change if ἤδη is defined as a "viewpoint marker." Wakker, discussing instances in Xenophon, calls ἤδη an "evaluative particle" (2002: 10).

25. One of this chapter's anonymous readers perceptively observes that the expression γναθμοῖσι γελώων ἀλλοτρίοισιν ("with jaws as of other men") (347) may indicate blended nonverbal communication. The hysterical laugh seems to exploit multiple sources of sound.

26. De Jong takes the text and the supernatural phenomena being described as a prolepsis of the suitors' death (2001: 502).

27. See Sinding 2005 on the theoretical basis for and the concrete elements resulting from a blend of genres in Joyce's *Ulysses*.

28. For pragmatic and cognitive explorations of the concept, see Traugott and Dasher 2002; Verhagen 2005; Praetorius 2009; Sweetser 2012: 8; Sidnell, Enfield, and Kockelman 2014.

CHAPTER NINE

Speech Training and the Mastery of Context: Thoas the Aetolian and the Practice of Muthoi

JOEL P. CHRISTENSEN

IN HIS RESPONSE TO ACHILLEUS DURING THE EMBASSY in *Iliad* 9, Phoinix invokes their personal relationship and, in particular, his position as Achilleus's teacher (9.437–443):

> πῶς ἂν ἔπειτ' ἀπὸ σεῖο, φίλον τέκος, αὖθι λιποίμην
> οἶος; σοὶ δέ μ' ἔπεμπε γέρων ἱππηλάτα Πηλεὺς
> ἤματι τῶι ὅτε σ' ἐκ Φθίης Ἀγαμέμνονι πέμπε
> νήπιον, οὔ πω εἰδόθ' ὁμοιΐου πολέμοιο,
> οὐδ' ἀγορέων, ἵνα τ' ἄνδρες ἀριπρεπέες τελέθουσι.
> τοὔνεκά με προέηκε διδασκέμεναι τάδε πάντα,
> μύθων τε ῥητῆρ' ἔμεναι πρηκτῆρά τε ἔργων.[1]

> How could I be left here without you, dear child, alone? The old man and horse-trainer Peleus assigned me to you on that day when he sent you from Phthia with Agamemnon still a child, not yet educated in the ways of crushing war or assemblies where men become most prominent. He sent me for this reason: to teach you all these things, how to be a speaker of words and a doer of deeds.

Ancient commentators emphasize both the anticipation of classical rhetoric in these lines (schol. bT *Iliad* 9.443 ex 1–4 [Erbse]) and a common ground between "words" and "deeds," namely that the successful execution of either requires "good counsel" (εὐβουλία, schol. AT *Iliad* 9.443 c1). Phoinix may also reflect on the conflict between Achilleus and Agamemnon in describing the assembly as the place where men become "preeminent" (οὐδ' ἀγορέων, ἵνα τ' ἄνδρες ἀριπρεπέες τελέθουσι).

His claim that Achilleus was to learn "to be a speaker of words and a doer of deeds" (μύθων τε ῥητῆρ' ἔμεναι πρηκτῆρά τε ἔργων) makes explicit for this epic that words *and* deeds are expected from its leading men; that words, moreover, are a species of deeds;[2] and that both are acquirable through practice or, from a later perspective, education.[3]

Despite the critical importance of being a speaker of words and doer of deeds, the Homeric epics say very little directly about how one achieves excellence in either. Nevertheless, the epics do seem to share views on both the form and the content of education. In what follows, I will not attempt to reconstruct the educational system of a real world external to the Homeric epics, but instead I will use the information provided within them to isolate immanent assumptions about education and action.[4] In part, this investigation offers an object lesson on what a Homeric narrator does not tell: many aspects of the cultures that influenced the Homeric epics are occluded by the passage of time, basic narrative economy—why explain something well known?—or the aesthetics of Panhellenic leveling. (Conventions of education specific to one region or city would likely be avoided.)[5] So, in part, while the absence of specific information in Homer is telling, compressed moments provide insight into what has not been told.

Phoinix's memorable line has long been held as indicative of some larger rhetorical program. In commenting on this passage, the scholiast, who imagines that Achilleus needs to learn "rhetoric" (τὸ τῆς ῥητορικῆς ὄνομα εἰδώς), adduces other passages attesting to the discipline in Homer (schol. bT *Iliad* 9.443)[6]: Nestor's claim that it is the province of the old to advise "with counsel and speeches" (βουλῆι καὶ μύθοισι), while the young fight (*Iliad* 4.322–335); Odysseus's story that he won Achilleus's arms by a "judgment among the ships" (δικαζόμενος παρὰ νηυσί, *Odyssey* 11.545); and the brief mention of "youths striving over speeches" in the re-introduction of Thoas in *Iliad* 15 (ὁππότε κοῦροι ἐρίσσειαν περὶ μύθων, 15.284).

In this chapter I will explore the associations of Thoas's introduction in particular to sketch out how the culture(s) implied within the Homeric poems might approach training in public speech. I will focus first on how Thoas's introduction engages with the political concerns of the *Iliad* and the agonistic character of Greek culture. Next I will consider the resonance of his introduction with other educative movements in Homer, specifically that of Telemachos in the *Odyssey*. The discussion will then take a comparative turn, drawing on studies of education in literate and nonliterate societies to emphasize how the *Iliad* describes separate stages in the education of a public speaker: periods of observation, imitation, and practice with peers, followed by reinforcing responses of critique and praise. Rather than presenting a clear curriculum—which would be out of place in poetry—the epic encodes its understanding of oratorical training by offering an example of a public speaker at different stages, in the persons of Diomedes, Odysseus, and Nestor. After exploring the quality of Thoas's speech, I will conclude with brief comments on how the deployment of this pattern fits within the epic in contrasting with Trojan practices and in anticipating Achilleus's return.

ACHAIAN POLITICAL DIFFERENCE AND THE APPEARANCE OF THOAS THE AETOLIAN

Speech is critical to the *Iliad* because of its connection to politics—as Aristotle notes, language capacity makes human beings especially, if not uniquely, political (*Politics* 1253a7–19). The epic develops its political themes by contrasting language use in three communities.[7] Although Zeus's language translates into political reality on Olympos because it is backed by his physical force, even the king of the gods makes compromises to maintain stability.[8] For the Trojans, however, the political hegemony of Priam's family hampers public debate (Christensen 2015a).[9] In contrast to both the Olympians and the Trojans, the Achaians endow multiple speakers with authority. As Nestor says to Agamemnon in *Iliad* 9, a king needs good advice from whoever happens to offer it (9.69–78).[10] How exactly is it that the Achaians have (and employ) a surplus of effective advisors?

The appearance and description of Thoas the Aetolian, a relatively minor *basileus* (king), illustrate well that the Achaians allow authoritative speech to spring from multiple sources and also imply a potential reason for Achaian ability in speech, namely, cultural conventions regarding training in public speech.[11] Before Thoas speaks, the narrative authorizes him with a unique speech preface (*Iliad* 15.281–285):

Τοῖσι δ᾽ ἔπειτ᾽ ἀγόρευε Θόας, Ἀνδραίμονος υἱός,
Αἰτωλῶν ὄχ᾽ ἄριστος, ἐπιστάμενος μὲν ἄκοντι,
ἐσθλὸς δ᾽ ἐν σταδίηι· ἀγορῆι δέ ἑ παῦροι Ἀχαιῶν
νίκων, ὁππότε κοῦροι ἐρίσσειαν περὶ μύθων·
ὅ σφιν ἐϋφρονέων ἀγορήσατο καὶ μετέειπεν·

> Among them then Thoas the son of Andraimon spoke publicly: he was the best of the Aetolians in his knowledge about the spear and also fine at close combat—but in the *agorē* [assembly] few of the Achaians overcame him, whenever the young men used to strive over speeches—well-intentioned toward them, he spoke publicly and addressed them:

This introduction also uses formulaic language to enroll Thoas in an exclusive group of advisors: the phrase "well-intentioned toward them, he spoke publicly and addressed them" (ὅ σφιν ἐϋφρονέων ἀγορήσατο καὶ μετέειπεν) is reserved elsewhere for effective speakers such as Priam (*Iliad* 7.367) and Nestor (*Iliad* 1.253, 2.78, 7.326, 9.95).[12]

In addition to affirming Phoinix's emphasis on the dual spheres of speaking and doing, the contrast in Thoas's ability—best in his tribe at fighting, but surpassing *all* the Achaians in speech—asseverates that competence in one does not necessarily translate into the other: Nestor, no longer a fierce warrior, stands out for his ability to conquer everyone in the assembly ("Oh, truly, old man, you conquer all the sons of the Achaians in the assembly again!" [ἦ μὰν αὖτ' ἀγορῆι νικᾶις, γέρον, υἷας Ἀχαιῶν], *Iliad* 2.370);[13] Hektor contrasts with Poulydamas, who excels in speech just as he excels with the spear ("But the one excelled in speeches, while the other was much better at the spear" [ἀλλ' ὃ μὲν ἄρ μύθοισιν, ὃ δ' ἔγχεϊ πολλὸν ἐνίκα], *Iliad* 18.252); and Achilleus admits to his mother that, while no one surpasses him in war, others are better in the assembly ("Since I am the sort of man I am, no one of the bronze-girded Achaians [surpasses] me in war; but there are many others better in the assembly" [τοῖος ἐὼν οἷος οὔ τις Ἀχαιῶν χαλκοχιτώνων / ἐν πολέμωι· ἀγορῆι δέ τ' ἀμείνονές εἰσι καὶ ἄλλοι], *Iliad* 18.105–106).

Thoas's importance throughout the epic is rather limited: such an extensive speech introduction accords him the authority necessary for this specific moment.[14] In making the subsequent, successful intervention believable to the audience, the passage also expands upon an Iliadic movement in the use of public speakers and draws on larger cultural assumptions. In particular, the line "whenever the youths used to strive over *muthoi*" (ὁππότε κοῦροι ἐρίσσειαν περὶ μύθων, *Iliad* 15.284) has caught the attention of commentators. Richard Martin, for example, sees this passage as indicating the agonistic nature of *muthoi* (1989: 68). Hans van Wees understands it as indicating that competition occurs among groups of similar age (1996: 9).[15] Elton Barker privileges "the social acceptability of *eris*" in the epic's presentation of the institutionalization of dissent in the public sphere (2004: 110).[16] Although the suggestion is speculative, I propose that Thoas's introduction reflects a training through play in the performance of authoritative speech akin to instruction and practice in swordplay and other martial skills. Even if the reference does not correlate with what we would identify as an educational *institution*, imagining that it does so forces us in part to consider the origin of a practice critical in the development of skills prized in the (adult) heroes depicted in Homer's world.

The language and resonance of Thoas's introduction seem to set it apart from the action of the epic in which it is embedded. First, the sentence's syntax—imperfect main-clause verb and indefinite temporal clause: νίκων, ὁππότε κοῦροι ἐρίσσειαν περὶ μύθων—implies an activity that was regular and ongoing, that is, something that happened more than once. Second, the lexical force of ἐρίσσειαν generally invokes the portrayal of heroic excellence, perhaps recalling Hesiod's positive *eris* of productive competition rather than his negative strife of civil disputes and war (*Works and Days* 11–26).[17] Third, beyond general accordance with Greek agonism, the line may resonate with a formulaic background specifically marking excellence in speech. The lengthened aorist of *erizō* (ἐρίσσ–) appears four times in Homeric epic in the same metrical position: the other three occurrences describe the impossibility of anyone rivaling Odysseus in speech (οὐκ ἂν ἔπειτ' Ὀδυσῆΐ γ' ἐρίσσειε βροτὸς ἄλλος, *Iliad* 3.223), hard work (δρηστοσύνῃ οὐκ ἄν μοι ἐρίσσειε βροτὸς ἄλλος, *Odyssey* 15.321), and knowledge (οἶδ' Ὀδυσεύς, οὐδ' ἄν τις ἐρίσσειε βροτὸς ἄλλος, *Odyssey* 19.286).[18] In each case, the form's association with Odysseus—as an exemplar of Homeric values and a special talent in speech—recalls again the ideal of "being a speaker of words and doer of deeds."[19] (As I will discuss, there are also formal and mythographic connections between Odysseus and Thoas.) The formulaic argument might simply indicate a competition suspiciously well matched to the context—on the general idea of the competitive superiority of a figure like Odysseus—to valorize Thoas for this specific moment. But, as I will argue, there are interpretive advantages to positing a reference to a more regular or recognizable cultural practice.

HOW DO HEROES LEARN?

A context for youths to practice speech becomes more attractive when aligned with other Homeric presentations of speech development. So far, I have argued that Thoas's introduction is contextually relevant in establishing his authority to perform a given speech and that it resonates with cultural thematics of competition. Furthermore, the syntax of line 284 (ὁππότε κοῦροι ἐρίσσειαν περὶ μύθων) suggests Thoas's excellence and success in an ongoing process that is relevant to his current mastery if not directly formative for it. Thus, for at least some of Homer's ancient audiences the passage likely responded to cultural notions of preparation and training that we may call "education," for lack of a better term.[20] Based on Phoinix's position as a tutor, it is clear that the Homeric epics assume that teaching and learning are possible (and necessary). When it comes to one part of heroic performance—fighting—few would imagine that there was no period of acquisition and regular practice. Hektor does announce that he "has learned to be a noble man" (ἐπεὶ μάθον ἔμμεναι ἐσθλὸς, *Iliad* 6.444) but reveals nothing specific as to how he learned this.[21] The epics, however, do provide an impressionistic survey of a youth developing from being "without speech" (*nēpios*) to acknowledging and controlling speech content, form, and context.[22]

Age is associated with the (in)ability to speak in Homeric epic. Phoinix's speech from *Iliad* 9 provides us with another useful starting point. When he says Peleus "sent you from Phthia with Agamemnon still a child, not yet educated in the ways of crushing war or assemblies" (ἤματι τῶι ὅτε σ' ἐκ Φθίης Ἀγαμέμνονι πέμπε / νήπιον, οὔ πω εἰδόθ' ὁμοιΐου πολέμοιο, / οὐδ' ἀγορέων, 9.439–441), he cannot mean that Achilleus was an infant incapable of speech as the etymology of *nē–epos* ("without *epos*") might imply.[23] Instead, his use of the adjective speaks to its cultural resonance: *nēpios* does sometimes denote general immaturity, and several authors have emphasized its general connotation of ignorance (Ready 2011: 181), but Homeric usage also retains a strong association with speech. For example, when Nestor criticizes the Achaians for their public behavior in *Iliad* 2, he tells them that they "speak publicly like children, childish ones who don't have any concern for the works of war" (ὢ πόποι ἦ δὴ παισὶν ἐοικότες ἀγοράασθε / νηπιάχοις, οἷς οὔ τι μέλει πολεμήϊα ἔργα, 2.337–338). While Nestor implies that children who *do not understand words* are incapable of strategic speech, Aineias suggests that controlling speech genre and context is something *he* knows, *unlike a child*, when he warns Achilleus not to "hope to frighten me with words like some child since I myself also know clearly how to utter threats and reckless words" (μὴ δὴ ἐπέεσσί με νηπύτιον ὣς / ἔλπεο δειδίξεσθαι, ἐπεὶ σάφα οἶδα καὶ αὐτὸς / ἠμὲν κερτομίας ἠδ' αἴσυλα μυθήσασθαι, *Iliad* 20.200–202).[24]

In the *Odyssey*, Penelope worries about her son's journey because he is a "*nēpios*, unknowing of the toils [of war] and assemblies" (νήπιος, οὔτε πόνων εὖ εἰδὼς οὔτ' ἀγοράων, 4.818). A scholion glosses this line as meaning that Telemachos "is inexperienced of words and deeds" (ἄπειρος τυγχάνει ἔργων καὶ λόγων, schol. *Odyssey* 4.818a [Pontani]) and relates the sentiment to Phoinix's tutoring of Achilleus in the *Iliad*.[25] While the *Iliad* emphasizes elsewhere that it is characteristic of children not to understand correct speech or context (20.244–245), Telemachos, *contra* his mother, presents a clear example of the difference between a "child," who does not understand speech, and an adult, who does (*Odyssey* 2.312–317).[26]

> ἦ οὐχ ἅλις ὡς τὸ πάροιθεν ἐκείρετε πολλὰ καὶ ἐσθλὰ
> κτήματ' ἐμά, μνηστῆρες, ἐγὼ δ' ἔτι νήπιος ἦα;
> νῦν δ' ὅτε δὴ μέγας εἰμὶ καὶ ἄλλων μῦθον ἀκούων
> πυνθάνομαι, καὶ δή μοι ἀέξεται ἔνδοθι θυμός,
> πειρήσω, ὥς κ' ὔμμι κακὰς ἐπὶ κῆρας ἰήλω,
> ἠὲ Πύλονδ' ἐλθών, ἢ αὐτοῦ τῶιδ' ἐνὶ δήμωι.

> Isn't it enough that you wasted my many fine possessions before, when I was still just a child [νήπιος], suitors? But now, when I am big, and I have learned by listening to the speech of other men, and the heart within me grows, I will discover some way that I may visit upon you wicked fates either when I go to Pylos or here in this country.

These comments sharpen the semantics of νήπιος and help to bring the cultural associations of Thoas's introduction in the *Iliad* into relief. While Telemachos uses the adjective to describe the helpless state he was in when the suitors came to his home, he contrasts his current state with νήπιος in two ways. On the one hand, he is bigger; on the other hand, he has learned by "listening to the *muthos* of others" (ἄλλων μῦθον ἀκούων).[27] In this, Telemachos provides us with a crucial hint regarding the method and content of Homeric speech education. Learning from the speeches of others and growing beyond a νήπιος, Telemachos confirms, entails an understanding of speech contexts, contents, and use.[28] Now that Telemachos is no longer νήπιος, he has called an assembly, he has engaged in dissent, and he has formulated a plan on his own. Of course, this does not all go according to plan: Telemachos's first public speech—overly emotional and somewhat disorganized—is interrupted and ultimately ineffectual.[29] One might argue, then, that Telemachos's maturation as a speaker requires further practice and attending to the speeches of his elders—which is part of what happens in books 3 and 4 during his visits with Nestor and Menelaos.[30]

In the world and language of Homer, to recapitulate, part of becoming an adult is leaving the state of "speechlessness" (being a νήπιος) by gaining knowledge of the places and uses of speech. The knowledge to be acquired has multiple parts. A chief component is the content of speeches, as Phoinix himself declares to Achilleus: "This is the way we have learned before from the stories of heroic men" (οὕτω καὶ τῶν πρόσθεν ἐπευθόμεθα κλέα ἀνδρῶν / ἡρώων, *Iliad* 9.524–525).[31] In addition, an effective speaker is also conversant in standards of form and context—what kind of speech is appropriate to each situation. The examples of Telemachos and Achilleus imply that an understanding of speech content, form, and context was achieved at first through observation and then, in some cases, through tutelage. Thoas's speech introduction, moreover, points to the mastery of these fields through practice. Such practice may be circumstantial: "striving" over speeches likely takes place as a part of the regular operation of the Achaian army, and youths might engage in this during their real-world war experience. Yet the specification of *kouroi* may also indicate that Thoas's conquest occurred in a type of lower-stakes gaming or play.

EDUCATIONAL PARALLELS

So far, then, Homeric epic offers us two clear stages in acquiring excellence in speech: observing the speech of others and then imitating it. These basic steps and the proposed context have parallels in Greece as well as nonliterate cultures. That Thoas's imitative practice could have been part of a youthful *game* has theoretical support in modern and ancient scholarship on education. Modern educational theory has shown that role-playing and games contribute positively to education for all ages (Carnes 2014; cf. Gottschall 2012: 41).[32] This fact was not unfamiliar to ancient thinkers. Aristotle recognizes the importance of play as practice for adult activities, as is evident in the *Politics* when he prescribes play in gymnastics for physical development and later when he asserts that games should promote the imitation of the occupations taken on in later life: "For children should pretend to do all those things which are akin to their later occupations: for this reason it is necessary that children's games [τὰς παιδιὰς] are mostly imitations of things they will attend to seriously later in life" (*Politics* 1333a25–27). Plato, too, sees experience in adult activities, starting with observation and then moving into practice, as an essential pedagogical progression (*Republic* 536e6–537a11).

The cultural background assumed by Thoas's introduction and echoed elsewhere in the Homeric epics presents an adult world into which youths are initiated through observation (as with Telemachos), tutelage (as with Achilleus and Phoinix), practice in competition with coevals, and then experimentation in the adult realm.[33] This three-stage process echoes age-association groups in other parts of Archaic Greek life: choruses were split into performance groups of *paides*, *kouroi/ephēboi*, and *andres*.[34]

Such coordinated public training, regimented from a young age, offers evidence of a rudimentary type of education paralleled in other contexts as well. In particular, dining practices and aristocratic associations likely introduced and reinforced some speech practices. For instance, in the early Classical period, joining Spartan mess-halls (*syssitia*)—to which men were accepted around age twenty—involved habituation to such Laconian speech forms as, according to Aristotle, "short-talking" and "giving and taking insults" (μελετῶσι δὲ εὐθὺς ἐκ παίδων βραχυλογεῖν, εἶτα ἐμμελῶς καὶ σκώπτειν καὶ σκώπτεσθαι, fr. 611.70–71; cf. Griffith 2001: 50).[35] Derek Collins emphasizes the "value that Greek culture, and especially local Greek communities, placed on the spontaneous ability to recite or sing poetry on demand" (2004: 197). As an example of how and where this skill is developed, Collins discusses Polybius's description of the Arcadians (4.20.8–12; cf. Athenaeus 625d), who raised their children to perform "hymns and paeans in which they praise their local heroes and their gods" (ὕμνους καὶ παιᾶνας, οἷς ἕκαστοι κατὰ τὰ πάτρια τοὺς ἐπιχωρίους ἥρωας καὶ θεοὺς ὑμνοῦσι, 9). After they learned to sing, they would dance in competitive choruses and then sing in turn or succession at banquets as adults: "they sing in turn, following upon one another" (ἀνὰ μέρος ἄιδειν ἀλλήλοις προστάττοντες, 11). While Collins emphasizes the function of rivalry and shame in this context, he also recognizes the continuous and communal institution that was both a product and a producer of an Arcadian (and Greek) ideology (2004: 199–200). Homeric poetry is not ignorant of such uses of speech. In the *Homeric Hymn to Hermes* the god begins to sing "at the spur of the moment just as adolescents sling insults at one another during the feasts" (ἐξ αὐτοσχεδίης πειρώμενος, ἠΰτε κοῦροι / ἡβηταὶ θαλίῃσι παραιβόλα κερτομέουσιν, 55–56; cf. Collins 2004: 68–71).

The passage from the hymn speaks to the possibility of a cultural institution that provides training in verbal art, even one as informal as children's games. If Thoas's speech introduction hints at a cultural structure—whether an official institutionalized practice like choral performance or a more informal contingent practice such as the aristocratic banquet[36]—that supports the acquisition and practice of authoritative language, such a structure would allow younger men to experiment with conventional speech genres, mimicking and emulating the language of their elders.[37] In addition to speech *form*, such as insult, exhortation, love song, praise poem, and hymn/prayer, young speakers would practice the execution of devices shared with poets and committed in part to memory, like *paradeigmata* and *gnōmai*. Indeed, when identifying Nestor and Odysseus as effective speakers in the *Iliad*, Richard Martin notes that they both perform "from memory" (1989: 81). Wisdom literature like Hesiod's *Works and Days* or the fragmentary *Kheironos hypothekai* establishes authoritative tones through sententious repetitions and gnomic utterances.[38] Although such traditional models are important in training, they were not simply copied: using modern paroemiology as a framework, André Lardinois has argued that while the epic's most dynamic speakers use *gnōmai* in their persuasive speeches, they use them in characteristic, individualized ways (1997, 2000).

Details from other cultures are of special comparative value here. Evidence for the acquisition of such skills in nonliterate cultures has been overlooked or underemphasized in Western scholarship for many reasons, but preeminently because of biases conditioned by literacy and formalized educational institutions (Akinnaso 1992: 70–73). But studies from the last half of the twentieth century onward have shown that nonliterate cultures are perfectly capable of training their members in cognitively complex skills through apprenticeship and life structuring (Akinnaso 1992: 73–75).

Anne Salmond, for example, describes Maori children learning traditional speech by lingering around the official speaking ground, the *marae*, and watching their elders deploy proverbs, genealogical accounts, and local histories (1975).[39] Furthermore, Salmond suggests that the youths practice these methods following their elders' performances both in the *marae* itself and competitively in informal situations.

Less extensive, but still illustrative, parallels are available from Africa. Among the Igbo of Nigeria proverbs—valued in adult speeches as structural devices of both beginning and ending—are used to educate and socialize children (as authoritative utterances) and to instruct in the execution of adult speech: child proverb use is monitored and commented upon (often through more proverbs) by adults and peers (Nwachukwu-Agbada 1994). In a comparison of learning in West African *poro* training and public schools in Liberia, moreover, scholars have identified similarities in structure, methods, and content: initiates observe and imitate the skills to be learned while also participating in evaluation and performance (M. Watkins 1943; Lancy 1975, 1980; Murphy 1980; Akinnaso 1992: 74). These steps are similar to those emphasized by many scholars as essential aspects of "informal learning": particularism, contextualization, and imitation (Akinnaso 1992: 78).

Education in speech is often latent and integrated into a culture—informal learning is "embedded in everyday life" (Akinnaso 1992: 78). In the oral culture of Yorùbá society, children match recitation of game poetry with physical activity, as they engage in stylized competition and the imitation of adult behaviors. Through collective storytelling contexts, as well, children develop their intellects (by using riddles and engaging with narratives) while also absorbing moral lessons and mythological structures from the Yorùbá traditions (Akínyemí 2003: 166–171). Similarly, the oral culture of the multiple linguistic groups of hunter-gatherers of Namibia and Botswana, often referred to controversially by Westerners as San or Bushmen (Guenther 2006: 256n1), prizes skill in oratory and awards it with prestige and influence while acknowledging many different aspects of competence without having a specific course of training.[40] Community members receive, observe, and practice their models of speech as a matter of daily life, absorbing distinctions between different speech contexts and functions (Guenther 2006: 252–253). Even for ritualized speech performances like divination, the content and the style of verbal performance are marked as separate steps in the educational process.[41]

Cross-cultural comparison, then, offers some confirmation for what I have sketched out about education in public speaking from the evidence of the Homeric epics. The acquisition of the knowledge and skills pertaining to speech was plausibly based on a process that required observation, imitation, practice, and some kind of feedback loop of critique or censure.

In ancient Greece, it is the public nature of such performances that both emphasizes their importance to the community at large and underscores the ways in which communal response can dictate the form that speeches take (the feedback loop). In Plato's *Republic*, when discussing ways in which the youths are publicly corrupted, Sokrates reflects on public speaking engagements (492b5–c8):

> Whenever the masses are seated close together in the assembly, the lawcourt, the theater, the military encampment, or any other place shared for the gathering of a crowd, they will reproach [ψέγωσι] with a great uproar some of the things that are said and done, but praise [ἐπαινῶσιν] others; they do both excessively; as they shout out and applaud, the rocks and whichever place they occupy double the uproar of the reproach and praise

> [τοῦ ψόγου καὶ ἐπαίνου] in response to them. What sort of reaction do you think will overcome a youth in this sort of circumstance? Or, what sort of private education for him do you think will endure which would not be completely washed away by this sort of reproach and praise [ψόγου ἢ ἐπαίνου], even carried away through the flood to wherever this environment carries it, and that he will both say that the same things as these are noble and shameful and will prepare just as these men do and be this sort of man?

Although Sokrates denigrates the influence of public rhetorical displays, he nevertheless points to a consciousness of the potential for ways of speaking to perpetuate themselves by virtue of their effectiveness. Public approbation or censure valorizes effective manners of speaking and also allows for the introduction and dissemination of new methods. Furthermore, Sokrates's emphasis on the (negative) influence of praise (*epainos*) and censure (*psogos*) points again to the agonistic or competitive nature of early Greek speech-making.[42] As David Elmer (2013) has persuasively argued, praise and blame are constitutive parts of the development and expression of political order in the *Iliad*. As critical elements of the larger culture with a formative influence on public speech, it is only natural that praise and blame would be integrated into raising and educating the youth. And the Homeric epics do not shy away from regulating speeches to cultural norms, as when Nestor tells Diomedes that he has not reached the "*telos* of speeches" (οὐδὲ πάλιν ἐρέει· ἀτὰρ οὐ τέλος ἵκεο μύθων, *Iliad* 9.56) or Euryalos is upbraided and forced to apologize for his verbal treatment of Odysseus (*Odyssey* 8.159–185).

Although there is no direct mention of praise in Thoas's speech introduction, the *Iliad* echoes the cultural assumptions that make it possible for a man to become an effective orator and contribute to his community's leadership. Thoas, in my reading, is one instance of this process whose presentation, however brief, helps us to frame the characterization of more well-known figures. Achilleus, in all likelihood, is offered as a model of speaker who is still in the process of learning.[43] The *Iliad* also dramatizes such an educative experience through Diomedes, who appears apprenticed to older speakers like Nestor and Odysseus and seems to react to approbation and censure during the epic's story (Christensen 2009). As James O'Maley argues in this volume, Diomedes's status as a good "audience member"—or perhaps a pupil?—is part of what prepares him to act. Diomedes observes the actions and speeches of *Iliad* 1–3; he displays an understanding of speech contexts in upbraiding Sthenelos for criticism of Agamemnon in book 4 (cf. Christensen and Barker

2011; Sammons 2014); and he then practices public speech—with acclamation—in refusing Paris's offer in book 7 (7.400–404) and in criticizing Agamemnon in book 9 (9.32–49).[44] Diomedes, as others have noted, functions as a surrogate-Achilleus;[45] once he has developed as both a speaker of words and a doer of deeds, he exits the epic to make room for Achilleus's continued development. In the meantime, however, Thoas appears and presents a compressed repetition of Diomedes's education in and subsequent use of speech.

THOAS AS SPEAKER AND THOAS'S SPEECH

As discussed earlier, Thoas has limited importance in the *Iliad* even though he appears as leader of the Aetolians in book 2 (2.638).[46] His genealogy makes him, in a way, an apt substitute for Diomedes, whose father Tydeus was expelled from Aetolia by Oineus, whose own son, Meleagros, died and left Thoas in charge of the Kalydonian contingent.[47] And, indeed, in introducing Thoas, the catalogue says more about the absence of the sons of Oineus (who are dead) than it does about Thoas himself (*Iliad* 2.638–644). Like Diomedes as well, Thoas has some broader associations with Odysseus. Odysseus mentions tricking Thoas during a story in the *Odyssey* (14.462–506) (cf. Newton 1997–1998), and in the mythical tradition Odysseus is linked by at least one author with Thoas's daughter: "Odysseus went to Aetolia to Thoas the son of Andraimon and married his daughter" (Ὀδυσσέα δὲ εἰς Αἰτωλίαν πρὸς Θόαντα τὸν Ἀνδραίμονος παραγενόμενον τὴν τούτου θυγατέρα γῆμαι, Apollodorus *Epitome* 7.40).[48] The characterization of Thoas and Odysseus in the *Iliad* is similar enough that Jim Marks has called Thoas the latter's "double" (2003: 212). In this doubling, both Thoas and Odysseus function as versions of the effective speaker who uses his talents for the good of the Achaian collective in the *Iliad*. But, as I have suggested in this chapter, Diomedes, Thoas, Odysseus, and Nestor together occupy different stages in the figure's development.[49]

Let us briefly return to the passage from *Iliad* 15. Thoas's speech introduction endows him with authority within the immediate context as one who speaks publicly with good intentions.[50] Although his speech is directed primarily to the captains—the men who can actually act on his advice—its public nature is invoked twice (τοῖσι δ' ἔπειτ' ἀγόρευε, 15.281; ἀγορήσατο καὶ μετέειπεν, 15.285). What kind of speech justifies such a strong introduction? Thoas's speech divides into two parts, and its primary focus is preserving the host (15.286–300):

A "ὢ πόποι, ἦ μέγα θαῦμα τόδ' ὀφθαλμοῖσιν ὁρῶμαι,
οἷον δ' αὖτ' ἐξαῦτις ἀνέστη κῆρας ἀλύξας
Ἕκτωρ· ἦ θήν μιν μάλα ἔλπετο θυμὸς ἑκάστου
χερσὶν ὑπ' Αἴαντος θανέειν Τελαμωνιάδαο.
ἀλλά τις αὖτε θεῶν ἐρρύσατο καὶ ἐσάωσεν
Ἕκτορ', ὃ δὴ πολλῶν Δαναῶν ὑπὸ γούνατ' ἔλυσεν,
ὡς καὶ νῦν ἔσσεσθαι **ὀΐομαι**· οὐ γὰρ ἄτερ γε
Ζηνὸς ἐριγδούπου πρόμος ἵσταται ὧδε μενοινῶν.

B ἀλλ' ἄγεθ', ὡς ἂν ἐγὼν εἴπω, πειθώμεθα πάντες.
πληθὺν μὲν ποτὶ νῆας ἀνώξομεν ἀπονέεσθαι
αὐτοὶ δ', ὅσσοι ἄριστοι ἐνὶ στρατῶι εὐχόμεθ' εἶναι,
στήομεν, εἴ κεν πρῶτον ἐρύξομεν ἀντιάσαντες
δούρατ' ἀνασχόμενοι· **τὸν δ' οἴω** καὶ μεμαῶτα
θυμῶι δείσεσθαι Δαναῶν καταδῦναι ὅμιλον."

Ὣς ἔφαθ', οἳ δ' ἄρα τοῦ μάλα μὲν κλύον ἠδ' ἐπίθοντο·

"Alas, truly this is a wonder I see before my eyes, that he rises here again indeed having avoided death—Hektor; really the heart of every man was hoping he died at the hands of Aias, Telamon's son; but one of the gods has protected him and saved him again—Hektor who has loosened the knees of many Danaans, as I think will happen now too. For he does not stand there a forefighter, devising thus, apart from loud-thundering Zeus.

But come, let us all obey as I say. Let us order the multitude to return to the ships, but we ourselves, however many claim to be the best in the army, let us stand, and see if opposing him by holding out our spears, we can hold him off first: I think that he, even though he is eager, will fear in his heart to enter the throng of Danaans."

So he said and they really heard him and also obeyed.

If we accept the basic thesis that Thoas stands in part as a dramatization not only of the plurality of Achaian speakers capable of providing useful advice but also of *how* younger speakers gain this ability, then this moment—Thoas's last significant speech—should stand as the culmination of his training and an indication of the type of accomplishment such a speaker should achieve.

At first glance, this speech seems to be rather bland. But a closer reading reveals it to be both sensitive to the context and armed with rhetorical approaches used elsewhere in the epic. First, Thoas's opening lament ("Alas, truly this is a wonder I see before my eyes") echoes other moments where speakers identify a common danger or shame and preface their understanding of the situation before calling for action (cf. *Iliad* 13.99–105, 20.344–346). This constitutes a rhetorical articulation of their shared stakes while also using dramatic—as in mimetic—language, narrating how Hektor's resurgence defies his own expectations (*Iliad* 15.287–289) and attributing it (correctly) to divine intervention (15.290–291). Parenthetical mentions of Hektor's name structure the first half of the speech (A), and the collective Achaian surprise is developed through a run of correlating temporal adverbs (αὖτ' ἐξαῦτις, τις αὖτε, ὡς καὶ νῦν), situating their danger in a narrative sequence.

The vivid first section, which I suggest creates a shared articulation of their situation, terminates in a traditional line and focuses on responsive action. In the second part (B), Thoas uses what, following Lawrence Goldman, I term a "gambit" as he shifts to his concrete plan (ἀλλ' ἄγεθ', ὡς ἂν ἐγὼν εἴπω, πειθώμεθα πάντες, 15.294).[51] This gambit is associated elsewhere with authoritative speech (cf. *Iliad* 9.26, 9.704, 12.75, 14.74, 14.370, 18.297),[52] and with the exception of Agamemnon's panicked plea at *Iliad* 9.26, similar speeches are accepted without further comment by their addressees. Like other advisors in both council and assembly speeches, such as Nestor (*Iliad* 2.76–83, 2.435–441) and Antenor (*Iliad* 7.345–353), Thoas offers a series of first-person plural verbs to call for a unified response to Hektor. Within this unity, however, he differentiates between the mass of the army (πληθὺν μὲν ποτὶ νῆας ἀνώξομεν ἀπονέεσθαι, *Iliad* 15.295) and the best men (αὐτοὶ δ', ὅσσοι ἄριστοι ἐνὶ στρατῷι εὐχόμεθ' εἶναι, 15.296) to reassert the responsibility of the latter to protect the host. The form of his speech is also well matched to its content: Thoas's channeling of collective experience and use of collective language emphasizes the importance of the safety of the army as a whole.

Compared to many of Homeric epic's most striking speeches, Thoas's speech is rather straightforward and unmemorable. It is marked, however, as especially effective: Thoas's plan is granted additional authority by the immediate acceptance of his audience ("Ὣς ἔφαθ', οἱ δ' ἄρα τοῦ μάλα μὲν κλύον ἠδ' ἐπίθοντο, *Iliad* 15.300).[53] The Homeric presentation of speeches explores what language does in different contexts and with different approaches. Thoas's speech is prized in part, I suggest, because it does what it needs to with economy. He uses the *right* words at the *right* time to maximal effect. As part of epic teaching *us* about speech, this speech joins the more rhetorical and poetic speeches as an example of the range of effective speech types.

This moment also serves as the culmination of a dramatization of Thoas's development as a speaker. Although named as a captain of his people at *Iliad* 2.638, Thoas is marked as a replacement for Oineus's son Meleagros (2.641–643). In the *Iliad*'s action, he appears first as a warrior defeating an opponent (4.527–531) and then alongside Odysseus as the last named of the Achaians who stand to face Hektor (7.168) before Poseidon takes his form to exhort Idomeneus (13.216–218). After this speech, Thoas disappears from the epic, with the exception of joining the group to witness oaths between Agamemnon and Achilleus.

Thoas's development in the epic parallels Diomedes's, whose excellence in speech follows his *aristeia* (Christensen 2009; O'Maley, this volume). Whereas Diomedes receives direct comments about speech from Nestor (*Iliad* 9.53–62) followed by the feedback loop of public approbation (*Iliad* 7.403–404, 9.50–51, 9.710–711, 14.433), I submit that Thoas and Diomedes are implicitly witnesses to successes and failures in speech alongside the epic's audience(s) during the council and assembly scenes. Both Thoas and Diomedes fade from the epic *after* effective speeches that formulate plans to preserve the Achaians in a time of danger. Through the process prior to these points, the epic educates its characters and its audiences alike in its assumptions about the use of public speech in preparation for Achilleus's return. Their narrative patterns anticipate and prepare us for his return as a warrior but also for his maturation as a public speaker in books 19, 23, and 24.

CONCLUSIONS AND FURTHER CONSIDERATIONS

In this chapter I have made the case that the Homeric epics reflect a cultural consciousness of the educational steps necessary for training in speech, including stages of observation, apprenticeship, practice, and real-world execution. The introduction of Thoas, with its brief mention of youths striving over speech, is part of a discrete, impressionistic presentation of cultural attitudes about education: here, it may imply a stage of preparatory gaming, which would not have been alien to Greek culture in the Archaic period or to later theorists like Plato or Aristotle; at the very least, the line may echo the training inculcated from the process of observing and absorbing praise and blame in public contexts. Telemachos's model from the *Odyssey* and modern parallels from nonliterate cultures have served to make these arguments more plausible.

Thoas's introduction, as I anticipated at the end of the last section, is also an extension of a particular Homeric style of telling, which is to present a series of implied comparisons and contrasts rather than a direct message. Thoas's relationship to and representation of the larger Achaian polity is part of a broader Homeric program.

In addition to isolating some essential elements of the educative process, I have also suggested that the epic dramatizes different stages of this process as well in the persons of Diomedes, Odysseus, and Nestor. Certainly, the participation of these multiple figures is critical to the epic's depiction of the Achaian response to crisis. But the dangers presented by public speakers—such as Agamemnon, Thersites, and Achilleus—serve as reminders that institutional responses to threatening speech are also politically important.[54] An obvious question is how the pattern I have discussed applies to the very man Phoinix was sent to teach to be "a speaker of words and a doer of deeds." Clearly, Achilleus is a special case—*the* special case of this epic—but his use of language evolves as well, and a full version of these arguments would describe how his public speech changes after his return to the Achaians (especially in his chairmanship of the funeral games).

Perhaps less obvious, but no less important for the epic as a whole, is the place of speech among the Trojans: Hektor is paired with a single advisor, Poulydamas, described as being "his companion, born on the same night who excelled in speeches just as the other conquered with his spear" (Ἕκτορι δ' ἦεν ἑταῖρος, ἰῆι δ' ἐν νυκτὶ γένοντο, / ἀλλ' ὃ μὲν ἂρ μύθοισιν, ὃ δ' ἔγχεϊ πολλὸν ἐνίκα, *Iliad* 18.251–252).[55] Poulydamas tries to educate Hektor with a homily about the different attributes of men (*Iliad* 13.726–734):

> Ἕκτορ, ἀμήχανός ἐσσι παραρρητοῖσι πιθέσθαι.
> οὕνεκά τοι περὶ δῶκε θεὸς πολεμήϊα ἔργα,
> τοὔνεκα καὶ βουλῆι ἐθέλεις περιίδμεναι ἄλλων·
> ἀλλ' οὔ πως ἅμα πάντα δυνήσεαι αὐτὸς ἑλέσθαι.
> ἄλλωι μὲν γὰρ ἔδωκε θεὸς πολεμήϊα ἔργα,
> ἄλλωι δ' ὀρχηστύν, ἑτέρωι κίθαριν καὶ ἀοιδήν,
> ἄλλωι δ' ἐν στήθεσσι τιθεῖ νόον εὐρύοπα Ζεὺς
> ἐσθλόν, τοῦ δέ τε πολλοὶ ἐπαυρίσκοντ' ἄνθρωποι,
> καί τε πολέας ἐσάωσε, μάλιστα δὲ καὐτὸς ἀνέγνω.

> Hektor, you are impossible to persuade with words. Since the god grants for you to excel in the works of war, you also wish to be able to understand better than the rest in council but you could

> not ever claim everything for yourself at once. For god grants the works of war to one and dancing to another, and the lyre and song to another, and in another wide-browed Zeus sets a mind—a fine one because of which many men will profit, and he saves many, and he himself knows this for sure.

Here, among the Trojans, Poulydamas countermands the excellence in word and deed praised by Phoinix to Achilleus in book 9: Hektor believes, falsely, that he is "a speaker of words and a doer of deeds" and thereby makes it impossible for Poulydamas to be either.[56]

The *Iliad* shows that talent in speech, its forms, and its uses can be developed and offers a dramatization of such a process. At the same time that it shows the political advantage of having men who can deliberate and make convincing public proposals, it also emphasizes that the political atmosphere must be able to accommodate such men in order to reap these benefits. In book 1, the situation is so toxic and Agamemnon and Achilleus are so heedless of public good that they use language to bring greater ruin to their community. Hektor and the Trojans are shown to do something similar. The introduction of Thoas the Aetolian, so very brief, confirms the importance of acquiring talent in public speech, conditions audiences to see the absence of this ability or intolerance of it elsewhere, and prepares us not just to judge the speeches to come but to reflect on the effect of language throughout and outside the poem.

NOTES

Part of this paper was presented at the 2008 CAMWS Annual Meeting in Tucson, Arizona. Gratitude is due to Benjamin Sammons for a careful reading of an earlier draft and to the editors of this volume, whose patient prodding improved the original submission greatly.

1. The Homeric text used in this chapter is T. W. Allen's OCT; all translations are my own.

2. See Martin 1989 for Homeric use of language as action based on speech-act theory (cf. J. Austin 1962; Searle 1969). For speech-acts in Homer, see also Roochnik 1990; Clark 1997b; Gottesman 2008; Christensen 2010, 2015b.

3. Cf. Pseudo-Plutarch *Vita Homeri* 1736–1739: "For life is sustained by means of actions and words, and he says that he was made a teacher of the young man about both" (ἐπεὶ γὰρ ὁ βίος ἐκ πράξεων καὶ λόγων συνέστηκε, τούτων φησὶ διδάσκαλον ἑαυτὸν τοῦ νεανίσκου γεγονέναι). For Phoinix's words as "practical education," see Burrage 1947: 147. On the Homeric epics as reflective of aristocratic educational practices, see Griffith 2001: 33–36.

4. For the Homeric epics as fantasy of the past, see van Wees 1992. For education in Classical Greece, see Griffith 2001: 23–25.

5. For the synthesis of local traditions "into a unified Panhellenic model that suits most city-states but corresponds exactly to none," see Nagy 1999a: 7; cf. Rutherford 2005: 11. See Ross 2005: 301–307 for "Proto-Panhellenism" in the *Iliad*.

6. For Greek rhetoric as a "teachable skill" and for the complex character of the speeches represented in Homer, see Knudsen 2014: 38–87.

7. For these three communities, see Christensen 2009, 2015a; Elmer 2013: 86–173. For Homeric politics, see Nicolai 1983; Sale 1994; Donlan 1997, 2002; Hammer 2002; D. Wilson 2002; Barker 2004, 2009.

8. Zeus's authority is never truly in doubt (Slatkin 1991; Friedman 2001: 108). Stensgaard argues that Zeus relies on persuasion (2003: 60–65); cf. Martin 1989: 54 for Zeus as "the master of the poetics of power."

9. On Trojan politics, see H. Mackie 1996: 21–26; Barker 2009: 68–74; Elmer 2013: 132–145.

10. For this passage in the development of the Achaian response to internal conflict, see Christensen 2009.

11. For other appearances of Thoas, see pp. 267, 270, 276nn48–49; Janko 1992: 259; Newton 1997–1998: 152.

12. See Dickson 1995: 103; cf. Scodel 2002a: 70; Roisman 2005: 24–27. This full line is also applied to Poulydamas at *Iliad* 18.253.

13. For Nestor as the epic's ideal speaker, see Martin 1989: 81; Dickson 1995; H. Mackie 1996: 132. For his rhetorical skill, see Knudsen 2014: 77–79. See also Roisman 2005; Christensen 2008.

14. On speech introductions as a feature of oral composition, see M. Edwards 1970; Riggsby 1992.

15. A scholion imagines the contest among Achaians in general: κοῦροι Ἀχαιῶν ("young men of the Achaians") is a synonymous for υἷες Ἀχαιῶν ("sons of the Achaians") because "a contest of children would be strange" (ἄτοπος γὰρ ἡ τῶν παίδων ἄμιλλα, schol. *Iliad* 15.283–284 ex. 1). Κοῦροι Ἀχαιῶν (*Iliad* 3.183, 14.505, 17.758, 22.391) marks the Achaians in general; where κοῦροι stands without the ethnonym (*Iliad* 1.470, 9.86, 9.175, 12.196, 18.493), it generally indicates a younger group in subservient or auxiliary positions. For *kouroi* as referring to "institutionalized age-groups" and "young elites," see Griffith 2001: 39–40. Janko is concerned instead with the sensibility of Thoas (a middle-aged man?) competing with youths (1992: 259).

16. Barker also sees this introduction as marking the "ordinariness" of "dissent in the assembly" (2009: 65). Hogan notes the ubiquity of competition in these lines, but not any type of real world contest (1981: 32).

17. For the two *erides* in Homer, see Thalmann 2004; cf. Hamilton 1989a: 64; Nagler 1992: 79. For Thoas's appearance as a marker of the function of *eris* "in establishing or enacting hierarchies," see Thalmann 2004: 375. Greek culture was agonistic in general (Griffith 1990), and competition was likely an essential part of education.

18. Cf. *Odyssey* 4.80. Schol. AT *Iliad* 23.88 provide one more variant that may be of relevance to this line. The widely accepted text of 23.88 reads νήπιος, οὐκ ἐθέλων, ἀμφ' ἀστραγάλοισι χολωθείς ("the fool, [killed him] unwillingly, because he was angry over dice"). While this reading was preferred by Didymus, other manuscripts offered ἀμφ' ἀστραγάλῃσιν ἐρίσσας. The language of strife applies to a children's game (dice) that then spills into adult violence.

19. For Odysseus as a speaker, see Martin 1989: 62–64; Scodel 2002a: 201–209; Knudsen 2014: 83. For Odysseus and social cohesion, see Elmer 2013: 100–104.

20. There are no equivalents to modern "schools" before the fifth century BCE (D'Angour 2013: 295; cf. Burrage 1947: 147). Modern (Western) assumptions, however, about differences in education between literate and nonliterate cultures are firmly rooted in concepts of literacy and formalized institutions (Akinnaso 1992: 68–70).

21. For historical evidence of military training by age group in Archaic Greece, see Griffith 2001: 36–39. Cf. van Wees 1996 for implicit types of training in the Homeric poems. For tutelage under older men in Archaic poetry, see, for example, Theognis 1.27–30, 33–36, 305–308.

22. For continuities between the rhetorical strategies of Homeric speakers and those described by Aristotle, see Knudsen 2014. For her, Homeric rhetoric was likely "something that must be learned and consciously cultivated by habit, an ability, implying the existence of greater and lesser degrees of sophistication and success" (2014: 102).

23. For *nēpios* as "connoting immaturity in its extreme," see Petropoulos 2011: 84 who cites *Odyssey* 4.818. Elmer follows S. Edmunds 1990 in attributing an unsocialized, or antisocial sense to *nēpios*, which can mark "disconnection" from a community (2013: 140). In the case of the unlearned, it may mark a connection that was never made. For *infans* and the same associations in Latin, see Varro *De lingua latina* VI.52.

24. Aineias shortly goes on to describe women squabbling in the street (*Iliad* 20.251–255), but, although these passages do blend, the rhetorical steps are separate: Aineias switches from "foolish/immature" speech to carping (here, feminized) speech that creates strife (ἔριδας καὶ νείκεα . . . / νεικεῖν, 20.251–252) and anger (χολωσάμεναι ἔριδος, 20.253). Aineias tries to deny Achilleus's insults their efficacy—"You will not turn me from my valor with words" (ἀλκῆς δ' οὔ μ' ἐπέεσσιν ἀποτρέψεις μεμαῶτα, 20.256)—and to dismiss his ability as nonheroic, belonging to a child *or* a woman. Diomedes dismisses Paris in a similar fashion: "I don't care about this, it's as if a woman or senseless child struck me!" (οὐκ ἀλέγω, ὡς εἴ με γυνὴ βάλοι ἢ πάϊς ἄφρων, *Iliad* 11.389).

25. On Phoinix and the *Odyssey*'s Mentor as "tutors," see Griffith 2001: 34–35.

26. For ancient authors imagining Telemachos becoming an orator, see Wissman 2009: 423–425. For the educational purpose of the *Telemachy*, see Petropou-

los 2011; cf. H. Clarke 1967: 43; Heitman 2005: 58–62; Wissman 2009: 415–417. Some scholars also see this as an initiation ritual (Felson-Rubin 1994: 67–91; Thalmann 1998: 206–215).

27. Not being *nēpios* also implies understanding what is better and what is worse: "But I consider in my *thumos* and know each thing, both the noble and the worse. Previously, I was still *nēpios*" (αὐτὰρ ἐγὼ θυμῶι νοέω καὶ οἶδα ἕκαστα / ἐσθλά τε καὶ τὰ χέρεια· πάρος δ' ἔτι νήπιος ἦα, *Odyssey* 18.228–229). The speech aspect of νήπιος is not always activated in Homeric usage but is associated with limited thinking and the "thoughts of children" (Wissman 2009: 427).

28. A scholion emphasizes that someone who was raised by women would not have the opportunity to practice speeches previously: "But by necessity he was raised by women and beaten down by sorrows; he never learned the art of public speech or became many-wayed like his father" (ἀλλ' ἔδει τὸν ἐν γυναιξὶ τεθραμμένον, λύπαις τεταπεινωμένον, ῥητορειῶν οὐ πεπειραμένον οὐδεπώποτε, πολύτροπον γενέσθαι παραπλησίως τῶι πατρί, schol. *Odyssey* 1.93b). For the significance of the term *polytropos* here in communicating rhetorical skill, see Wissman 2009: 423.

29. For the qualities and (in)efficacy of Telemachos's speech, see Petropoulos 2011: 69–72. As Benjamin Sammons has suggested to me, a youth's failure in speech may be depicted by the epics as part of the learning process (with other examples including Antilochos's speech in *Iliad* 23 and Euryalos's speech in book 8 of the *Odyssey*, both of which are regulated by social norms when the speakers must apologize for their contents). Achilleus's behavior in book 1 may be put in this category.

30. On his journey to Pylos and Sparta and the importance of the effects of Nestor's and Menelaos's speeches, see Barker and Christensen 2015.

31. For the importance in education of listening and reciting Homeric poetry, see Burrage 1947: 149. Plato makes reading and reciting Homer (and other putative classics) a central part of childhood education into adolescence (D'Angour 2013: 303).

32. For play as part of education in Plato, see D'Angour 2013.

33. Apprenticeship was seen as critical among the early interpreters of Homer: the scholia to the *Odyssey* complain that Telemachos did not have a male model to guide his growth (Wissman 2009: 420–421). Burrage (1947) suggests that such tutelage would have been exceptional and that the father was usually the son's instructor, as when Nestor provides guidance on driving a chariot at *Iliad* 23.306.

34. See Griffith 2001: 44–45, 48–50 for similar age gradation in Spartan military training.

35. For practice in questioning and answering and in the use of poetry in the Spartan mess hall, see also Plutarch *Lycurgus* 18–19.

36. For the banquet as the context for "higher education" in Archaic Greece, with Spartan and Cretan *syssitia* developing into contexts for "all-around training" by the fourth century BCE, see Griffith 2001: 56–57, 67.

37. Kennedy argues that Homeric speakers *had* to learn persuasion from their elders (1963: 63). Cf. Mifsud 1997: 29.

38. See Lardinois 2003 for stylistic correspondences between Homeric speeches and Hesiod's *Works and Days*.

39. Cf. the work of Martin (1984), who suggests that poetic musing in hexameter poetry was designed for the education of rulers.

40. For the importance of storytelling and different genres of speech in these cultural groups, see Guenther 2006: 252–256.

41. In the more formal training in divination among the Yorùbá, traditional texts are memorized first through "conscious training" (specific rote memorization) and then through observing the master's performance or attending assemblies of professionals (Akinnaso 1993: 91).

42. The dichotomy between praise and blame is an ancient inheritance from Indo-European society that was also a "fundamental principle in the archaic Greek community" (Nagy 1999a: 222).

43. Duclos argues that the *Iliad* is about the education of Achilleus "through the death of his friend Patroklos, concerning the relationship between cause and effect" (1987: 57).

44. He receives yet another public acclamation after dismissing Achilleus's rejection of the embassy (*Iliad* 9.697–711). In his final significant speech of the epic, Diomedes criticizes Agamemnon again but offers a counterplan to the former's proposal of flight (*Iliad* 14.110–133). For Diomedes's steps, see Christensen 2009.

45. For Diomedes's replacement of Achilleus, see von der Mühll 1952: 195–196; Lohmann 1970: 251; Nagy 1999a: 30–31; Griffin 1980: 74; Schofield 1999: 29. For Diomedes as a Homeric innovation, see Andersen 1978; Cook 2009.

46. See note 11.

47. Diomedes is connected with Thoas as well. According to the testimony for Euripides's lost *Oineus*, Diomedes returned to Kalydon to depose Agrios (the father of Thersites). It is he who puts Andraimon, Thoas's father, in power. In this context, Thersites is cousin to Thoas and Diomedes and is a negative variation on their characterization as a dangerous and disruptive public speaker.

48. Outside the Homeric tradition, Odysseus and Thoas are paired in the *Ilias parva* and the Hesiodic *Catalogue of Women* (Marks 2003: 212–214). Thoas may have been the one to wound or mutilate Odysseus as part of his disguise to enter Troy (Gantz 1993: 641–642).

49. Marks calls Thoas and Odysseus "antithetical multiforms" when focusing on Odysseus's antagonism toward Thoas in the *Odyssey* (2003: 213). They are deployed—along with the others mentioned—in complementary roles in the *Iliad*, however.

50. Cf. note 12.

51. Studying the speech of the Huli of Papua New Guinea, Goldman calls "gambits" statements that "'gloss' propositions by indicating how that information is to be received, that is, whether the statement forwarded is an opinion,

guess, belief, or assertion, and whether it is verbal, object, person, or action-oriented" (1983: 27). Such statements, Goldman shows, are not only markers of opinion and judgment but also tend to "structure" speeches by signaling a change in topic or tone.

52. Agamemnon uses the same transitional line at *Iliad* 2.139, and, even though the result is undesired (the Achaians flee), the baldly stated plea is obeyed.

53. For an analysis of the instances of this line in the *Iliad*, see Hammer 1997: 9–12, where he connects it directly to Nestor's comments on persuasion in book 9.

54. For Thersites as a poet of blame, see Nagy 1999a: 261–264. For the importance of the institutionalizing of speech in Homer, see Barker 2004, 2009.

55. Poulydamas is the only Trojan figure apart from Priam to be valorized with the full-line speech introduction (ὅ σφιν ἐϋφρονέων ἀγορήσατο καὶ μετέειπεν, *Iliad* 18.253) that introduces Nestor, Odysseus, and Diomedes elsewhere. For the relationship between Poulydamas and Hektor, see Dickson 1995: 133–143; cf. Redfield 1975: 143–153; Elmer 2013: 137–138. For the absence of an effective council of advisors among the Trojans, see Christensen 2015a: 27–29; cf. Nicolai 1983: 10; H. Mackie 1996: 27.

56. For the structure of Trojan politics as implicated in the downfall of the city, see Christensen 2015a. On Trojan politics in general, see Sale 1994; H. Mackie 1996; Barker 2009: 68–74; Elmer 2013: 132–145.

CHAPTER TEN

Diomedes as Audience and Speaker in the Iliad

JAMES O'MALEY

THIS CHAPTER EXAMINES INTERNAL PERFORMANCE and conversational strategies, but it will do so through an examination of a character whose function as a narrator and conversationalist is inextricably linked to his role as an audience to other internal narrators. The Iliadic character Diomedes, like Telemachos in the *Odyssey*, is highlighted as the son of an outstanding father. Also like Telemachos, Diomedes is defined by his function as an audience to stories about the deeds of his father, Tydeus, so that, as Laura Slatkin puts it, "the reiterated, one might say relentless, designation of Diomedes as son of Tydeus cumulatively creates the effect of an inextricable identification of son with father" (2011: 101). Unlike the situation facing Telemachos (Martin 1993: 239–240), however, the battlefield setting of the *Iliad* affords Diomedes the opportunity to emulate the deeds of his father by fighting bravely and excelling in competitive endeavor. And for the most part Diomedes utilizes this opportunity. Tydeus's heroic feats are used by Agamemnon in book 4 and Athena in book 5 in order to spur Diomedes to emulate his father, and Diomedes proves himself adept throughout the poem in the same spheres of paternal excellence that Agamemnon's and Athena's narratives emphasize, namely open warfare, ambush, and athletic contests. He proves himself to be a good audience member, and perceives, internalizes, and acts on the messages that are imparted by the stories told to him at the beginning of his involvement in the poem.

But Diomedes's engagement with—and emulation of—his father in the context of speech and narrative does not end there. Both Tydeus and Diomedes are themselves portrayed as speakers within the poem, and their respective characterizations help us to understand further Diomedes's role in the poem and his relationship to the memory of his father. For Tydeus is portrayed as a prominent, skilled, but ultimately ineffective speaker in the stories told about him by Agamemnon and Athena: he participates in two embassies, both of which end in failure and unsuccessful attempts at persuasion. Diomedes, meanwhile, develops throughout the poem into a polished and persuasive speaker who excels at different genres of speaking.

This chapter argues that Diomedes's development as a speaker in the poem is a successful response to his father's portrayal by Athena and Agamemnon as an ineffective speaker but formidable actor. Diomedes is a persuasive speaker and a successful narrator, but he also proves himself an attentive and astute audience to other characters' narratives.

DIOMEDES AS AUDIENCE

From his earliest involvement in the *Iliad*, Diomedes is shown as a narratee. He serves as an audience not only to addresses and general speeches but also to extended paradigmatic narratives, a form that, as several scholars demonstrate (Ebbott 2010; Slatkin 2011; Sammons 2014), is of vital importance to the *Iliad* as a whole.

Diomedes first appears in the poem during Agamemnon's *Epipolēsis* (4.223–418), an episode in which Agamemnon exhorts the leaders of the Achaians to redouble their efforts and rebukes them for shirking battle (Martin 1989: 124–130; D. Beck 2005: 154–164). The culmination of this episode is Agamemnon's encounter with Diomedes and Sthenelos at 4.365–418. Agamemnon begins by asking Diomedes why he is hanging back from fighting (4.370–371) and then contrasts him unfavorably with his father, Tydeus, whom "they say. . . surpassed all others" (περὶ δ' ἄλλων φασὶ γενέσθαι, 4.375).[1] Agamemnon next presents an extended narrative of Tydeus's deeds (4.376–398), focusing on two embassies made by Tydeus, first to Mycenae, where he unsuccessfully appealed for help in a planned attack on Thebes (4.376–381), and then to Thebes itself, where he challenged and beat the Thebans in athletic contests (4.385–390) and successfully overcame an ambush that they set for him on his way home (4.391–398). Agamemnon concludes, "This was Tydeus, the Aetolian; yet he was father / to a son worse than himself at fighting, better in conclave" (τοῖος ἔην Τυδεὺς Αἰτώλιος· ἀλλὰ τὸν υἱὸν / γείνατο εἷο χέρεια μάχηι, ἀγορῆι δέ τ' ἀμείνω, 4.399–400). Agamemnon's intention here is clear. He is trying to motivate Diomedes to emulate his father's prowess, and his narrative provides a paradigm for Diomedes's own actions.

ὤ μοι, Τυδέος υἱὲ δαΐφρονος ἱπποδάμοιο,
τί πτώσσεις, τί δ' ὀπιπεύεις πολέμοιο γεφύρας;
οὐ μὲν Τυδέι γ' ὧδε φίλον πτωσκαζέμεν ἦεν,
ἀλλὰ πολὺ πρὸ φίλων ἑτάρων δηίοισι μάχεσθαι,
ὡς φάσαν οἵ μιν ἴδοντο πονεύμενον· οὐ γὰρ ἔγωγε
ἤντησ' οὐδὲ ἴδον· περὶ δ' ἄλλων φασὶ γενέσθαι.
ἤτοι μὲν γὰρ ἄτερ πολέμου εἰσῆλθε Μυκήνας
ξεῖνος ἅμ' ἀντιθέωι Πολυνείκεϊ λαὸν ἀγείρων.
οἳ δὲ τότ' ἐστρατόωνθ' ἱερὰ πρὸς τείχεα Θήβης,
καί ῥα μάλα λίσσοντο δόμεν κλειτοὺς ἐπικούρους.
οἳ δ' ἔθελον δόμεναι καὶ ἐπήινεον ὡς ἐκέλευον,
ἀλλὰ Ζεὺς ἔτρεψε παραίσια σήματα φαίνων.
οἳ δ' ἐπεὶ οὖν ᾤχοντο ἰδὲ πρὸ ὁδοῦ ἐγένοντο,
Ἀσωπὸν δ' ἵκοντο βαθύσχοινον λεχεποίην,
ἔνθ' αὖτ' ἀγγελίην ἐπὶ Τυδῆ στεῖλαν Ἀχαιοί.
αὐτὰρ ὃ βῆ, πολέας δὲ κιχήσατο Καδμείωνας
δαινυμένους κατὰ δῶμα βίης Ἐτεοκληείης.
ἔνθ' οὐδὲ ξεῖνός περ ἐὼν ἱππηλάτα Τυδεὺς
τάρβει, μοῦνος ἐὼν πολέσιν μετὰ Καδμείοισιν,
ἀλλ' ὅ γ' ἀεθλεύειν προκαλίζετο, πάντα δ' ἐνίκα
ῥηϊδίως· τοίη οἱ ἐπίρροθος ἦεν Ἀθήνη.
οἳ δὲ χολωσάμενοι Καδμεῖοι κέντορες ἵππων
ἂψ ἀναερχομένωι πυκινὸν λόχον εἷσαν ἄγοντες,
κούρους πεντήκοντα· δύω δ' ἡγήτορες ἦσαν,
Μαίων Αἱμονίδης, ἐπιείκελος ἀθανάτοισιν,
υἱός τ' Αὐτοφόνοιο μενεπτόλεμος Λυκοφόντης.
Τυδεὺς μὲν καὶ τοῖσιν ἀεικέα πότμον ἐφῆκε·
πάντας ἔπεφν', ἕνα δ' οἶον ἵει οἶκόνδε νέεσθαι·
Μαίον' ἄρα προέηκε θεῶν τεράεσσι πιθήσας.
τοῖος ἔην Τυδεὺς Αἰτώλιος· ἀλλὰ τὸν υἱὸν
γείνατο εἷο χέρεια μάχηι, ἀγορῆι δέ τ' ἀμείνω.

Ah me, son of Tydeus, that daring breaker of horses,
why are you skulking and spying out the outworks of battle?
Such was never Tydeus's way, to lurk in the background,
but to fight the enemy far ahead of his own companions.
So they say who had seen him at work, since I never saw nor
encountered him ever; but they say he surpassed all others.
Once on a time he came, but not in war, to Mycenae
with godlike Polyneikes, a guest and a friend, assembling

people, since these were attacking the sacred bastions of Thebes,
and much they entreated us to grant him renowned companions.
And our men wished to give them and were assenting to what they asked for
but Zeus turned them back, showing forth portents that crossed them.
Now as these went forward and were well on their way, and came
to the river Asopos, and the meadows of grass and deep rushes,
from there the Achaians sent Tydeus ahead with a message.
He went then and came on the Kadmeians in their numbers
feasting all about the house of mighty Eteokles.
There, stranger though he was, the driver of horses, Tydeus,
was not frightened, alone among so many Kadmeians,
but dared to try their strength with him, and bested all of them
easily, such might did Pallas Athena give him.
The Kadmeians who lash their horses, in anger compacted
an ambuscade of guile on his way home, assembling together
fifty fighting men, and for these there were two leaders,
Maion, Haimon's son, in the likeness of the immortals,
with the son of Autophonos, Lykophontes,[2] stubborn in battle.
On these men Tydeus let loose a fate that was shameful.
He killed them all, except that he let one man get home again,
letting Maion go in obedience to the god's signs.
This was Tydeus, the Aetolian; yet he was father
to a son worse than himself at fighting, better in conclave.

Agamemnon's speech is not the only time in the *Iliad* that a description of Tydeus's heroic deeds is used in an attempt to spur his son to action. In book 5 the goddess Athena tells a different version of the same story in order to motivate Diomedes, who is hanging back from attacking the god Ares (5.800–813):

ἦ ὀλίγον οἷ παῖδα ἐοικότα γείνατο Τυδεύς.
Τυδεύς τοι μικρὸς μὲν ἔην δέμας, ἀλλὰ μαχητής·
καί ῥ' ὅτε πέρ μιν ἐγὼ πολεμίζειν οὐκ εἴασκον
οὐδ' ἐκπαιφάσσειν, ὅτε τ' ἤλυθε νόσφιν Ἀχαιῶν
ἄγγελος ἐς Θήβας πολέας μετὰ Καδμείωνας·
δαίνυσθαί μιν ἄνωγον ἐνὶ μεγάροισιν ἕκηλον,
αὐτὰρ ὃ θυμὸν ἔχων ὃν καρτερὸν ὡς τὸ πάρος περ,
κούρους Καδμείων προκαλίζετο, πάντα δ' ἐνίκα

ῥηϊδίως· τοίη οἱ ἐγὼν ἐπιτάρροθος ἦα.
σοὶ δ' ἤτοι μὲν ἐγὼ παρά θ' ἵσταμαι ἠδὲ φυλάσσω,
καί σε προφρονέως κέλομαι Τρώεσσι μάχεσθαι·
ἀλλά σευ ἢ κάματος πολυάιξ γυῖα δέδυκεν,
ἤ νύ σέ που δέος ἴσχει ἀκήριον. οὐ σύ γ' ἔπειτα
Τυδέος ἔκγονός ἐσσι δαΐφρονος Οἰνεΐδαο.

Tydeus got him a son who is little enough like him,
since Tydeus was a small man for stature, but he was a fighter.
Even on that time when I would not consent to his fighting
nor drawing men's eyes, when he went by himself without the Achaians
as a messenger to Thebes among all the Kadmeians,
then I invited him to feast at his ease in their great halls;
even so, keeping that heart of strength that was always within him
he challenged the young men of the Kadmeians, and defeated all of them
easily; such a helper was I who stood then beside him.
Now beside you also I stand and ever watch over you,
and urge you to fight confidently with the Trojans.
And yet the weariness has entered your limbs from many encounters,
or else it is some poor-spirited fear that holds you. If so,
you are no issue then of the son of wise Oineus, Tydeus.

This narrative mirrors Agamemnon's story from book 4, but does not include either the failed embassy to Mycenae, or the ambush Tydeus survived on his return, instead focusing only on his victory in athletic contests and the extent of Athena's help (Slatkin 2011: 104–106; Sammons 2014: 301–309). Athena's comparison is also slightly different from Agamemnon's. While Agamemnon makes a simpler comparison between the two heroes' prowess, Athena contrasts Diomedes's reluctance to fight even though she stands beside him to the conduct of his father, who was so keen to engage in contests that he found a way to confront his adversaries even after Athena had forbidden battle (Sammons 2014: 304–307). In both cases, though, the implication is clear: Diomedes is not living up to his father and should work to change that fact. From early in the poem, then, Diomedes is portrayed as the intended audience of extended paradigmatic narratives of his father's prowess designed to spur him to action in emulation of Tydeus's achievements.

DIOMEDES AS RESPONDENT

Diomedes is characterized from the start as a narratee to stories about his father, Tydeus. And he is a good audience, one who not only listens but responds appropriately to the content and intention of the stories he has been told. This characterization is apparent in book 5, where he listens respectfully to Athena's rebuke but responds by pointing out that he was only hanging back because of her earlier injunction not to attack the gods (5.815–824).

His capabilities as an audience are more clearly expressed in his response to Agamemnon's speech in book 4. Here again Diomedes listens respectfully, and this respect is all the more notable for its contrast to the fury of his companion Sthenelos's rejoinder. Whereas Diomedes responds to Agamemnon's speech by keeping silent "in awe before the majesty of the king's rebuking" (αἰδεσθεὶς βασιλῆος ἐνιπὴν αἰδοίοιο, 4.402), Sthenelos, as Christos Tsagalis notes (2012: 218–220), pointedly attacks him on several different levels (4.404–410):

Ἀτρείδη, μὴ ψεύδε' ἐπιστάμενος σάφα εἰπεῖν.
ἡμεῖς τοι πατέρων μέγ' ἀμείνονες εὐχόμεθ' εἶναι·
ἡμεῖς καὶ Θήβης ἕδος εἵλομεν ἑπταπύλοιο,
παυρότερον λαὸν ἀγαγόνθ' ὑπὸ τεῖχος ἄρειον,
πειθόμενοι τεράεσσι θεῶν καὶ Ζηνὸς ἀρωγῇ·
κεῖνοι δὲ σφετέρῃσιν ἀτασθαλίῃσιν ὄλοντο.
τῶ μή μοι πατέρας ποθ' ὁμοίῃ ἔνθεο τιμῇ.

Son of Atreus, do not lie when you know the plain truth.
We two claim to be better men by far than our fathers.
We did storm the seven-gated foundation of Thebes
though we led fewer people beneath a wall that was stronger.
We obeyed the signs of the gods and the help Zeus gave us,
while those others died of their own headlong stupidity.
Therefore, never liken our fathers to us in honor.

The contrast between the two reactions becomes even more obvious when Diomedes responds to Sthenelos's outrage by rebuking him and noting that it is Agamemnon's right as a leader to make such encouraging speeches (4.411–418).

Notably, Diomedes does not say that Agamemnon's analysis is correct, merely that it is justified (Lowenstam 1993: 80–81; Scodel 2008:

61–62), and although his response is less overtly angry than that of Sthenelos, it is no less pointed. Diomedes does not simply listen respectfully to Agamemnon's narrative: he also acts on it (see pp. 285–289) and demonstrates in book 10 that he has internalized it to the extent that he is able to tell the story himself.[3] During his preparations for departing for the night raid of the *Doloneia*, he prays to Athena to remember him as she remembered Tydeus at Thebes (10.284–291):

> κέκλυθι νῦν καὶ ἐμεῖο, Διὸς τέκος Ἀτρυτώνη.
> σπεῖό μοι, ὡς ὅτε πατρὶ ἅμ' ἕσπεο Τυδέι δίωι
> ἐς Θήβας, ὅτε τε πρὸ Ἀχαιῶν ἄγγελος ἤιει.
> τοὺς δ' ἄρ ἐπ' Ἀσωπῶι λίπε χαλκοχίτωνας Ἀχαιούς,
> αὐτὰρ ὁ μειλίχιον μῦθον φέρε Καδμείοισι
> κεῖσ'· ἀτὰρ ἂψ ἀπιὼν μάλα μέρμερα μήσατο ἔργα
> σὺν σοί, δῖα θεά, ὅτε οἱ πρόφρασσα παρέστης.
> ὣς νῦν μοι ἐθέλουσα παρίστασο καί με φύλασσε.

> Hear me also, Atrytone, daughter of great Zeus.
> Come with me now as you went with my father, brilliant Tydeus,
> into Thebes, when he went with a message before the Achaians,
> and left the bronze-armored Achaians beside Asopos
> while he carried a word of friendship to the Kadmeians
> in that place; but on his way back he was minded to grim deeds
> with your aid, divine goddess, since you stood in goodwill
>   beside him.
> So now again be willing to stand by me, and watch over me.

The prayer is an unusual one. In reaching for a narrative about Tydeus's relationship with Athena, it departs from the more normal custom of recalling an earlier relationship between the god and the hero himself: one can contrast it with Odysseus's more conventional prayer at 10.278–282 (Vergados 2014: 442–443).

It seems to be specifically Agamemnon's narrative that Diomedes is accessing at this point. He has earlier stressed his lack of personal knowledge by saying "Tydeus, though, I cannot remember" (Τυδέα δ' οὐ μέμνημαι, 6.222; cf. Christensen and Barker 2011), and the details he includes point more to a recapitulation of Agamemnon's version of the narrative than a commonly held story, given how it differs from Athena's account in book 5. Both Agamemnon's narrative and Diomedes's prayer begin their account of Tydeus's time at Thebes from the same geographic location (the river Asopos) and end by stressing Athena's aid. Even Diomedes's oblique reference to the "grim deeds" (μέρμερα . . . ἔργα, 10.289) Tydeus committed on his return specifically alludes to Agamemnon's telling of the story, rather than Athena's, which excludes the Theban ambush (Dué and Ebbott 2010: 310–311). Diomedes's rehearsal of the story of Tydeus's embassy to Thebes seems clearly intended to be taken as arising from Agamemnon's narrative, rather than originating independently of it. He does not simply listen politely to Agamemnon's story. He takes note of it and is able to tell his own version of it later in the poem.[4]

DIOMEDES AS ACTOR

Diomedes shows that he is a good audience by listening respectfully and internalizing the message of narratives about Tydeus to the extent that he can access them himself later in the poem. More than merely internalizing the message, though, he takes onboard the paradigmatic force of these narratives by attempting to emulate (and, indeed, succeeding in emulating) his father's deeds over the course of the *Iliad.* Again, it is noteworthy that he does so using the narratives he heard in books 4 and 5 as a base: he responds not just to his father's famous deeds or characteristics in myth but specifically to what his father is *described as doing* by Athena and (particularly) Agamemnon.

This description is more complex than it might at first seem. Agamemnon's primary mode of comparison is between Tydeus's excellence in battle and his son's comparative deficiency—he ends his rebuke by calling Diomedes "worse . . . at fighting" (χέρεια μάχηι, 4.400) than his father—but the story he tells in support of this comparison does not actually involve the attack on Thebes that Agamemnon seems to promise in line 378, but rather a smaller episode from the buildup to that attack. Agamemnon's tale might initially seem to be, as Martin West puts it, "less apposite" than a description of the attack itself would be (2011a: 146 at 4.372–399), but, as it turns out, Agamemnon's choice of story here allows for a more complex set of referents, each of which shapes Diomedes's behavior in the remainder of the poem.

The Tydeus of Agamemnon's story is clearly a man of war. Agamemnon's observation that he arrived at Mycenae "without war" (ἄτερ πολέμου, 4.376) suggests that *polemos*—open warfare—is Tydeus's normal mode of operation, since his approaching a city without hostile intent is so unusual as to invite comment. Still, his actions show him to be proficient, even preeminent, in two other distinct areas of competition: athletic contests and the ambush.

Agamemnon reports that, despite Tydeus's being a lone ambassador, he nevertheless challenged the Thebans to athletic contests in which, because of Athena's help, he triumphed easily (4.388–390). Meanwhile, the only martial exploit in Agamemnon's paradigm occurs in response to Tydeus's athletic victories: the Thebans are so incensed at his victory that they set up an "ambuscade of guile" (πυκινὸν λόχον, 4.392) of fifty men to attack him on his way home, the outcome of which Agamemnon narrates in three lines: "on these men Tydeus let loose a fate that was shameful. / He killed them all, except that he let one man get home again, / letting Maion go in obedience to the god's signs" (Τυδεὺς μὲν καὶ τοῖσιν ἀεικέα πότμον ἐφῆκε· / πάντας ἔπεφν', ἕνα δ' οἶον ἵει οἶκόνδε νέεσθαι· / Μαίον' ἄρα προέηκε θεῶν τεράεσσι πιθήσας, 4.396–398).

Agamemnon's paradigm shows Tydeus excelling in a number of different modes of action and thus demonstrates a more developed nexus of *comparanda* between men of the narrative's past and those of the poem's present than his introduction might have suggested. Agamemnon initially presents Tydeus as a straightforward example of a hero who distinguishes himself in open warfare, but his narrative instead shows Tydeus excelling in two other modes of competition: athletic contests and the ambush.

A similar slippage occurs in Athena's narrative, in book 5, of the same events. She starts her speech by describing Tydeus as "a fighter" (μαχητής, 5.801) and begins the paradigm by drawing attention to his disregard for her instructions concerning "fighting" (πολεμίζειν, 5.802) and "drawing of men's eyes" (ἐκπαιφάσσειν, 5.803). The narrative itself, however, contains no mention of Tydeus's martial excellence, simply repeating Agamemnon's story of his athletic prowess: "he challenged the young men of the Kadmeians, and defeated all of them / easily" (κούρους Καδμείων προκαλίζετο, πάντα δ' ἐνίκα / ῥηϊδίως, 5.807–808).

Tydeus's paradigm in both cases makes clear references to his excellence in open warfare, but moves to a more complex portrayal of success in three distinct areas (although Athena's version of the story only describes two of these): open warfare, athletic competition, and the ambush. Diomedes in turn demonstrates his successful response to narratives about Tydeus by displaying excellence in these same three areas: he is repeatedly preeminent in open warfare; he is successful in athletic competition; and he participates in the *Iliad*'s primary ambush narrative, the *Doloneia*, in book 10.

Diomedes's excellence in open warfare is well recognized (Andersen 1978: 47–94). He is said by the Trojan Helenos to be the "strongest of all the Achaians" (κάρτιστον Ἀχαιῶν, 6.98) and an even more fearsome adversary than Achilleus (6.99), and he is given the first extended *aristeia*, or period of battlefield preeminence, in the poem in books 5 and 6. Most famously, his martial endeavors in the first half of the poem are portrayed in a manner that connects him to the preeminent warrior among the Achaians, Achilleus, to the extent that he acts as something of a "substitute Achilleus" in the poem's early scenes of combat. That Diomedes functions in this fashion is a commonplace of Homeric scholarship (Andersen 1978: 9–11, 144–148; Kullmann 1984: 313–316; M. Edwards 1987b: 198–206; Louden 2006: 14–34; Dué and Ebbott 2010: 36–40), but it is nevertheless worth briefly noting some of these parallels, if only to reinforce the point that the connection between Diomedes and Achilleus is due above all to their respective fighting abilities.

Diomedes and Achilleus are the only mortals in the poem to converse directly with Athena, and they are the only mortals to attack gods: Diomedes wounds Aphrodite (5.334–346) and Ares (5.850–859), while Achilleus struggles with the river god Skamandros (21.233–271).[5] The two Achaians also fight and defeat both Aineias and Hektor (in that order) at different points in the poem, and they both see their adversaries rescued by gods. The episodes form two strikingly parallel pairs: Diomedes's attack on Aineias at 5.297–318 parallels Achilleus's at 20.259–327, and Diomedes's duel with Hektor at 11.343–367 parallels Achilleus's later confrontation at 20.419–454.

Diomedes, then, shows himself adept at Agamemnon's initial point of comparison, open warfare, throughout the poem. Joel Christensen and Elton Barker state that "Agamemnon is wrong about Diomedes's lack of martial prowess and is corrected by the narrative" (2011: 27), but perhaps another way of reading the scene is that Diomedes responds to Agamemnon's narrative by living up to his father's example, not merely listening to Agamemnon's paradigm but acting on it as well, and by so doing proves Agamemnon wrong through his own achievements.

Diomedes's abilities in open warfare are matched by his prowess in athletic competition. During the funeral games for Patroklos in book 23 he competes in two events, and, although he cannot perhaps be said to have won everything easily, as Tydeus did, he nevertheless shows a preeminence in both that seems at least to indicate an aptitude for such competitions. He competes in a duel against Aias (23.811–825), which is stopped before a clear winner has emerged, but which nevertheless seems to demonstrate Diomedes's superiority, since the Achaians stop the fight "in fear for Aias" (Αἴαντι περιδδείσαντες, 23.822), and Achilleus ends by awarding Diomedes the prize that was set aside for the victor of the contest (23.824–825).[6] Lines 824–825 were athetized by both Aristarchos and Aristophanes, on the grounds that they contradict the spirit of the previous line (schol. AT *Iliad* 23.824 [Erbse]), but such inconclusive duels do seem normally to have an obvious winner and loser, as is the case with the inconclusive duels involving Paris and Menelaos (3.340–382), Aineias and Diomedes (5.297–317), and Aineias and Achilleus (20.158–292). Earlier, Diomedes has also been victorious in the chariot race, defeating Antilochos, Menelaos, Meriones, and Eumelos (23.362–533), and although once more, this victory is complicated, this time by Athena's involvement in the race (she returns Diomedes's whip after it had been knocked from his hand by Apollo at 23.382–390, inspires *menos* in his horses at 23.390, and causes Eumelos to crash at 23.391–397), Diomedes is both given first prize for his victory (23.509–513) and presented at the race's outset as "by far the best" (ὄχ' ἄριστος, 23.357) horseman among the contestants. Again, the excellence in a particular area of competitive endeavor ascribed to Tydeus in Agamemnon's paradigm (and in Athena's) is mirrored by Diomedes's own demonstrated aptitude in that area.

Finally, Diomedes himself is shown to be outstanding in the type of ambush situation in which Tydeus was said to have defeated the fifty Thebans in Agamemnon's narrative. He is one of only two Achaians shown participating in such an episode in the *Iliad*, when he, along with Odysseus, is involved in the *Doloneia* in book 10. The episode is not described as an ambush in the poem, but it does contain many structural parallels to the named *lochos* in Agamemnon's paradigm. Moreover, these parallels can be viewed as belonging to a generalized typology of *lochoi* in the *Iliad* and the *Odyssey*, each of which exhibit many of these same features: initial planning involving the selection of two leaders from among the *aristoi*, concealment and endurance of discomfort by the ambushers, and an eventual surprise attack (A. Edwards 1985: 22–24; Dué and Ebbott 2010: 69–79). It is a less precise analogue than the two suggested earlier, since Diomedes is an attacker in the ambush in book 10, while Tydeus defends himself in Agamemnon's story. But there are some other parallels between the two, particularly since, as Adele Haft notes (1990: 52), it is Diomedes who performs all the major killings in the *Doloneia*, while Odysseus makes the majority of the plans. And the poem draws attention to this link by explicitly referring to Tydeus, both indirectly throughout the episode (where Diomedes is called *Tudeidēs* on ten occasions, and *Tudeos huios* five times), and more directly through Diomedes's prayer at the beginning of the episode (10.284–291).[7] As noted earlier, this prayer explicitly recalls Agamemnon's narrative, but omits Tydeus's victory in the athletic contests while taking note of the *mermera erga* he committed in the ambush against the Thebans (10.289), a clear prelude to Diomedes's own *mermera erga* later in book 10.

OBEDIENT DIOMEDES

Diomedes emulates his father in the three areas in which Agamemnon pronounced Tydeus superior: open warfare, athletic competition, and the ambush. But in displaying this preeminence he notably avoids the type of crimes that Tydeus is most famous for mythologically, crimes that Agamemnon omits in his book 4 narrative. A scholion reports that Tydeus committed a crime so offensive to the gods that they denied him the immortality that was planned for him (schol. AbT *Iliad* 5.126):

> φασὶν ἐν τῶι Θηβαϊκῶι πολέμωι Τυδέα τρωθέντα ὑπὸ Μελανίππου τοῦ Ἀστακοῦ σφόδρα ἀγανακτῆσαι. Ἀμφιάρεων δὲ κτείναντα τὸν Μελάνιππον δοῦναι τὴν κεφαλὴν Τυδεῖ. τὸν δὲ δίκην θηρὸς ἀναπτύξαντα ῥοφᾶν τὸν ἐγκέφαλον ἀπὸ θυμοῦ. κατ' ἐκεῖνο δὲ καιροῦ παρεῖναι Ἀθηνᾶν ἀθανασίαν αὐτῶι φέρουσαν ἐξ οὐρανοῦ καὶ διὰ τὸ μύσος ἀπεστράφθαι.
>
> They say that in the Theban war Tydeus became excessively angry after he was wounded by Melanippos the son of Astakos. And that when Amphiaraos had killed Melanippos he gave the head to Tydeus, and he, like a wild animal, uncovered and gulped down his brains from anger. And that at this time Athena gave up the immortality she was bringing him from heaven and turned back because of his defilement.

This scholion cites as its source Pherecydes (fr. 97 *EGM*), while a Geneva scholion, in paraphrasing this account, claims that it is "the narrative in the Cycle" (ἡ ἱστορία παρὰ τοῖς κυκλικοῖς, Gen. II Schol. V 126).[8] In artwork, meanwhile, the moment that Athena denies immortality to Tydeus may have been depicted on the Rosi krater, a fifth-century Attic red-figured vase (Beazley 1947), while the terracotta antepagmentum to a fifth-century Etruscan temple at Pyrgi shows, among other scenes, Tydeus engaged in eating Melanippos's brains.[9]

Agamemnon and Athena make no mention of this story and instead set their narratives before the actual attack by the Seven on Thebes, portraying Tydeus as a relatively blameless—if somewhat impetuous—figure. Nor does it seem to be a case of a post-Iliadic narrative being retrojected by the scholion onto the poem itself, since, as was noted earlier, Diomedes's companion Sthenelos responds to Agamemnon's narrative in book 4 by condemning both Tydeus and his own father Kapaneus for their *atasthaliai*, reckless or criminal behaviors (4.409).[10] Sthenelos does not name these *atasthaliai* directly, but he notes that they were enough to cause the Seven's destruction: "those others died of their own headlong stupidity" (κεῖνοι δὲ σφετέρῃσιν ἀτασθαλίῃσιν ὄλοντο, 4.409). He also draws a pointed contrast with the Epigonoi, the sons of the Seven, who "obeyed the signs of the gods" (πειθόμενοι τεράεσσι θεῶν, 4.408) and succeeded in taking Thebes where their fathers had failed.

Diomedes is a member of the Epigonoi, and his behavior in the *Iliad* suggests that there is force to Sthenelos's contrast.[11] He is "if anything, overly punctilious in his obedience to Athena's commands" (Sammons 2014: 300) and even points out to her after she rebukes him (5.800–813) that she had told him not to attack the gods and that he was hanging back from challenging Ares out of respect for her orders (5.815–824). Indeed, in an exchange with the Lykian Glaukos in the next book, he expands on this theme, providing an extended account of the *theomachos* Lykourgos, who attacked the followers of Dionysos and hit them with an ox-goad (6.132–135), frightening but not physically harming the god (6.135–137). Lykourgos's fate, at least in Diomedes's narrative, illustrates the importance of respecting the gods and heeding their commands: "but the gods who live at their ease were angered with Lykourgos, / and the son of Kronos struck him to blindness, nor did he live long / afterward, since he was hated by all the immortals" (τῷ μὲν ἔπειτ' ὀδύσαντο θεοὶ ῥεῖα ζώοντες, / καί μιν τυφλὸν ἔθηκε Κρόνου παῖς· οὐδ' ἄρ ἔτι δὴν / ἦν, ἐπεὶ ἀθανάτοισιν ἀπήχθετο πᾶσι θεοῖσιν, 6.138–140).

Maureen Alden has suggested that Diomedes does in fact emulate Tydeus in this regard outside of the *Iliad*, being driven from home and later killed on his return as a result of Aphrodite's anger (2000: 151–152). The sources for this story are an Iliadic scholion that records Diomedes's exile on his return home (schol. bT *Iliad* 5.412) and a scholion to Lycophron's *Alexandra* 610 (schol. A N m t = Mimnermos fr. 22 Gerber) according to which the Archaic elegist Mimnermos wrote that Diomedes subsequently escaped to Italy, where he was murdered by the Italian Daunos. Some Iliadic support can also be found in the goddess Dione's response to Diomedes's wounding of her daughter Aphrodite (5.330–352). Dione predicts a calamitous future for Diomedes, as for all those who attack the gods (5.405–415):

σοὶ δ' ἐπὶ τοῦτον ἀνῆκε θεὰ γλαυκῶπις Ἀθήνη·
νήπιος, οὐδὲ τὸ οἶδε κατὰ φρένα Τυδέος υἱός,
ὅττι μάλ' οὐ δηναιὸς ὃς ἀθανάτοισι μάχηται·
οὐδέ τί μιν παῖδες ποτὶ γούνασι παππάζουσιν
ἐλθόντ' ἐκ πολέμοιο καὶ αἰνῆς δηϊοτῆτος.
τῶ νῦν Τυδείδης, εἰ καὶ μάλα καρτερός ἐστι,
φραζέσθω μή τίς οἱ ἀμείνων σεῖο μάχηται·
μὴ δὴν Αἰγιάλεια περίφρων Ἀδρηστίνη
ἐξ ὕπνου γοόωσα φίλους οἰκῆας ἐγείρηι
κουρίδιον ποθέουσα πόσιν, τὸν ἄριστον Ἀχαιῶν,
ἰφθίμη ἄλοχος Διομήδεος ἱπποδάμοιο.

It was the goddess grey-eyed Athena who drove on this man
against you; poor fool, the heart of Tydeus's son knows nothing
of how that man who fights the immortals lives for no long time,
his children do not gather to his knees to welcome their father
when he returns home after the fighting and the bitter warfare.
Then, though he be very strong indeed, let the son of Tydeus
take care lest someone even better than you might fight with him,
lest for a long time Aigialeia, the wise child of Adrastos,
mourning wake out of sleep her husband's beloved companions,
longing for the best of the Achaians, her lord by marriage,
she, the strong wife of Diomedes, breaker of horses.

Dione's attitude is clear: Diomedes fights and wins with the help of Athena, as he is doing presently (5.405), but at some point soon he will be killed in battle by someone stronger than Aphrodite, presumably after first being abandoned by Athena.

The parallels between this projected fate and the fate that tradition records for Tydeus are striking. But they are not parallels that the poem seems to authorize: it nowhere suggests an ending for Diomedes at all like that of his father, or indeed the ending foretold by Dione in *Iliad* 6. Even the post-Iliadic sources for Diomedes's death suggest a different outcome from that predicted by Dione, who envisages Diomedes's wife's distress at being bereft of her husband, rather than her unfaithfulness being the cause of his demise (Gantz 1993: 699). Nor do these stories suggest Athena's abandonment of Diomedes. In fact, they claim the opposite, noting that Diomedes avoids danger in Argos by fleeing to the altar of Athena and that Athena helps Diomedes and his men escape death entirely (schol. bT *Iliad* 5.412). Athena never truly abandons Diomedes, and in at least one tradition her protection leads to his eluding death. Dione's prediction proves to be unfounded.

Diomedes's traditional fate is not at all comparable to that of his father, Tydeus, and the rest of the Seven, and in this regard he shows himself to be unlike the Tydeus of common mythological imagining.[12] He is rather very much like the Tydeus of Agamemnon's story, who himself acts "in obedience to the god's signs" (θεῶν τεράεσσι πιθήσας, 4.398) in sending home Maion to be a witness to his slaughter in the Theban ambush. Diomedes does not emulate his father so much as the version of his father that has been presented to him as the addressee to extended narratives about Tydeus. He is an audience to stories within the *Iliad*, and a good one at that.

DIOMEDES AS SPEAKER

As we have seen, Diomedes shows himself to be an ideal audience to stories about Tydeus within the *Iliad*: he listens well, internalizes the substance of the stories, and precisely follows the paradigms they present, even when they differ from other accounts of Tydeus's behavior. But Diomedes's relationship with his father is moderated through speech even more closely than might be first apparent. Diomedes himself also functions as a speaker in ways that clearly relate to Tydeus's reputed speaking abilities, and he does so in a manner that is perhaps even more complex and worthy of comment than his emulation of Tydeus's more active heroism, discussed earlier.

Tydeus is portrayed in the narratives of both Athena and (more particularly) Agamemnon not just as a man of action but as someone who engages with both sides of the Iliadic injunction on heroes presented by Phoinix at 9.443: he is a "speaker of words" (μύθων τε ῥητῆρ') as well as a "doer of deeds" (πρηκτῆρά τε ἔργων). But Agamemnon's depiction of Tydeus as a "speaker of words" is not as straightforwardly positive as his portrayal of the other deeds discussed earlier. According to Agamemnon's narrative in book 4, Tydeus participates in two separate embassies (cf. Sammons 2014: 301–302), and in each case, although his speaking abilities are not called into question, his embassy is unsuccessful, and his advice is shown to be problematic at best. His role as an ambassador to the Thebans themselves is ultimately overtaken by his challenge to and subsequent defeat of them in athletic contests (4.386–490), a sequence that may indicate a failure in his primary mission, and one brought on by his own lack of attention to his duties.[13] We are, however, briefly shown Tydeus engaging in persuasive speech in Mycenae before this embassy (4.376–381):

> ἤτοι μὲν γὰρ ἄτερ πολέμου εἰσῆλθε Μυκήνας
> ξεῖνος ἅμ᾽ ἀντιθέωι Πολυνείκεϊ λαὸν ἀγείρων.
> οἳ δὲ τότ᾽ ἐστρατόωνθ᾽ ἱερὰ πρὸς τείχεα Θήβης,
> καί ῥα μάλα λίσσοντο δόμεν κλειτοὺς ἐπικούρους.
> οἳ δ᾽ ἔθελον δόμεναι καὶ ἐπήινεον ὡς ἐκέλευον,
> ἀλλὰ Ζεὺς ἔτρεψε παραίσια σήματα φαίνων.

> Once on a time he came, but not in war, to Mycenae
> with godlike Polyneikes, a guest and a friend, assembling
> people, since these were attacking the sacred bastions of Thebes,
> and much they entreated us to grant him renowned companions.
> And our men wished to give them and were assenting to what
> they asked for,
> but Zeus turned them back, showing forth portents that
> crossed them.

As David Elmer points out (2013: 112–113), Agamemnon does his best to put a positive spin on Tydeus's speech, emphasizing its theoretically persuasive nature and the Mycenaeans' goodwill toward the speech.[14] Tydeus is a good speaker, just as he is good in competitive endeavors. But in this case Agamemnon's narrative is complicated by Tydeus's failure. Not merely unsuccessful, his speech constitutes bad advice. Zeus clearly indicates that the mission does not have divine support, and it could even be argued that the ominous *paraisia sēmata* of line 381 point to the ultimate destruction of Tydeus and the other Seven, a destruction that Sthenelos reminds us comes about through their own *atasthaliai* and the consequent disapproval of the gods (Ebbott 2014: 332–334).

There are, of course, both mythological and narrative reasons for the failure of both embassies. Mythologically, Tydeus cannot succeed in persuading the Thebans, since it would avert the war, and his unsuccessful supplication of the Mycenaeans could serve as an explanation for their nonparticipation in the later war, but in each case, the narrative emphasizes Tydeus's impetuous nature and disregard for the commands of the gods as the proximate causes of his failures. Equally, in the Iliadic context Tydeus's failure is part of Agamemnon's broader point, that whereas Diomedes is good at speaking but not fighting (4.400), his father was the opposite. Nevertheless, the portrait he paints of Tydeus in book 4 is more complex: a speaker who is talented but ultimately ineffective, one whose impetuosities are liable to get the better of him, and one whose judgment in counsel is lacking, perhaps because of this very impetuosity.

Once again, Diomedes takes up and echoes this characterization during the main narrative of the *Iliad.* He also begins his career in the *Iliad* as a broadly persuasive, even effective speaker, but one who is perhaps too impetuous to be truly excellent. This pattern starts in book 4 with Agamemnon's backhanded compliment that speech is the one area in which he is better than Tydeus (4.400) and continues through two speeches in books 7 and 9 that draw the formulaic approval of his fellow Achaians, expressed by the couplet "so he spoke, and all the Achaians shouted / acclaim for the word of Diomedes, breaker of horses" (ὣς ἔφαθ', οἳ δ' ἄρα πάντες ἐπίαχον υἷες Ἀχαιῶν / μῦθον ἀγασσάμενοι Διομήδεος ἱπποδάμοιο, 7.403–404 = 9.50–51). It is first used after Diomedes's rejection of the Trojan embassies at 7.398–402 and is repeated in response to his speech disparaging Agamemnon's suggestion that they abandon the war and return home and promising that even if the rest of the Achaians gave up he and Sthenelos would fight and sack Troy by themselves (9.32–49), a speech that overtly takes up Agamemnon's insults of book 4 and rebuts them: "I was the first of the Danaans whose valor you slighted / and said I was unwarlike and without courage" (ἀλκὴν μέν μοι πρῶτον ὀνείδισας ἐν Δαναοῖσι / φὰς ἔμεν ἀπτόλεμον καὶ ἀνάλκιδα, 9.34–35).

In both of these cases general approval is clear, but there are indications that, as was the case with Tydeus, Diomedes's speaking abilities are not as straightforwardly effective as they seem. The two-line formula itself is generally used to suggest broad approval, but perhaps not total acceptance, and it is placed third on the ascending scale of five possible levels of communal approval in the *Iliad* according to the typology laid out by Elmer (2013: 23–38). Furthermore, Nestor's response in book 9 emphasizes Diomedes's relative youth and suggests that his speaking ability is diminished because of it. He says that Diomedes is "in counsel also . . . noblest among all men of [his] own age" (βουλῇ μετὰ πάντας ὁμήλικας ἔπλευ ἄριστος, 9.54) but chides him for not reaching the *telos* of his speech (9.56) (cf. Christensen 2009; Elmer 2013: 117–119). Diomedes has not done so, Nestor suggests, simply because he is "a young man still" (ἦ μὴν καὶ νέος, 9.57), and Nestor therefore concludes his address with the line "but let me speak, since I can call myself older than you" (ἀλλ' ἄγ' ἐγών, ὃς σεῖο γεραίτερος εὔχομαι εἶναι, 9.60).

Commentators have used Nestor's critique to argue for a general deficiency in Diomedes's speaking abilities and, in particular, to suggest that this deficiency manifests itself in an impetuousness that is markedly similar to that displayed by Tydeus. Bryan Hainsworth says of the speech that "Diomedes had begun impetuously" and that it is "quite beside the point" (1993: 66 at 9.52–78), while Maurice Bowra sums up Diomedes's speechmaking in general as "impetuous and careless of restraint or compromise" (1930: 205). But these evaluations miss the progression Diomedes makes during the poem (Martin 1989: 22–26; Christensen 2009: 151–152; Elmer 2013: 123–125). Later in the same book (9.697–709) he delivers a speech deploring the failed embassy and proposing that the army sleep and be ready to fight in the morning. His proposal, crucially, wins the wholehearted approval of the *basileis*, who respond in a manner that Elmer terms "the fifth and most efficient reception formula" (2013: 34) and that stands in stark contrast to Nestor's response to him at the start of book 9: "so he spoke, and all the kings gave their approval, / acclaiming the word of Diomedes, breaker of horses" (ὣς ἔφαθ· οἳ δ' ἄρα πάντες ἐπήνησαν βασιλῆες / μῦθον ἀγασσάμενοι Διομήδεος ἱπποδάμοιο, 9.710–711).

Finally, at 14.110–132, Diomedes's increasing mastery of public speech is confirmed when he once more makes a persuasive speech that is met by the general approval of the Achaians: "so he spoke, and they listened well to him, and obeyed him" (ὣς ἔφαθ', οἳ δ' ἄρα τοῦ μάλα μὲν κλύον ἠδ' ἐπίθοντο, 14.133). Elmer does not discuss this speech, and this approval formula is not part of his typology, but its vocabulary is clearly positive, and it is elsewhere used of speeches that finish the conversation on a generally positive note and precipitate a particular course of action: the most notable in this context is Nestor's reply to Diomedes at 9.53–78, which evinces this response at 9.79, but one can also look to 7.378 (after Priam's proposal of a ceasefire to bury the dead), 14.378 (after Poseidon's suggested marshaling of Achaian troops), 15.300 (after Thoas's proposal that the *aristoi* make a stand against Hektor),[15] 23.54 (after Achilleus's suggestion that the Achaians feast and rise at dawn to burn Patroklos's body), and 23.738 (after Achilleus's speech stopping the wrestling match). As was the case in book 9, Diomedes's speech can be seen as a reply to Agamemnon's *neikos* (albeit a more oblique response than Book 9's explicit criticism). Diomedes prefaces his advice by claiming authority to speak because his "generation is of an excellent father" (πατρὸς δ' ἐξ ἀγαθοῦ καὶ ἐγὼ γένος, 14.113) and by hoping that his lineage, along with his own abilities, will preempt any criticism of his advice: "therefore you could not, saying that I was base and unwarlike / by birth, dishonor any word that I speak, if I speak well" (τῶ οὐκ ἄν με γένος γε κακὸν καὶ ἀνάλκιδα φάντες / μῦθον ἀτιμήσαιτε πεφασμένον ὅν κ' εὖ εἴπω, 14.126–127).[16]

Diomedes even serves as a successful internal taleteller in the *Iliad*. He tells Tydeus's story again at 10.284–291 (see pp. 284–285), albeit briefly as part of a prayer and to a potential audience of Athena alone, but he also presents a more extended narrative regarding the inadvisability of challenging gods as part of a battlefield flyting exchange with the Lykian Glaukos in book 6 (6.123–143). This paradigm of Lykourgos was discussed earlier (see p. 290), and it is part of a complex rhetorical exchange between Diomedes and Glaukos that demonstrates Diomedes's proficiency in this mode of heroic behavior to parallel his competence in other areas of speaking.[17] Diomedes's role as a taleteller (rather than more generally as a speaker) is understated in the *Iliad*, but he still performs it and does so successfully when the situation demands.

In speaking ability, then, Diomedes again models himself on Tydeus, but in a fashion slightly different from his previous emulation. He is once more attentive to the initial narrations by Agamemnon and Athena, for whom he formed the primary audience in books 4 and 5. This time, though, he is able to go one better. Rather than increasingly emulating his father's narrated excellence throughout the poem, here Diomedes begins by emulating Tydeus's talented but unwise and unsuccessful modes of speech, but improves from this base. He is still engaged with the paradigm of Tydeus as it is presented by Agamemnon, but he adds to Tydeus's excellence, surpassing him in the process.

CONCLUSION

In book 9, Phoinix reminds Achilleus that Peleus sent him along with Achilleus "to make you a speaker of words and one who accomplished in action" (μύθων τε ῥητῆρ' ἔμεναι πρηκτῆρά τε ἔργων, 9.443). Richard Martin sees Phoinix's phrase as the foundation of heroic expectations in the poem: the "heroic imperative" is to be both a speaker of words and a doer of deeds (1989: 26; cf. Christensen, this volume). Diomedes, this chapter has argued, is preeminent in both of those areas of heroic endeavor, but he adds a third: engagement with internal performance and conversational strategies both as a narrator and a narratee. Diomedes is not just a "speaker of words" and a "doer of deeds." He is a listener to stories, and it is this attribute that is most important to his development as a character in the poem.

NOTES

1. All quotations from the *Iliad* are from the text of van Thiel (1996). Translations come from the edition of Lattimore (1951) with some modifications to spelling.

2. *Per* van Thiel. Lattimore reads "Polyphontes" with the Oxford Classical Text (and Venetus A).

3. Analysis of this speech is complicated by the general scholarly consensus that the *Doloneia* should be seen as a later addition to the *Iliad*: note in particular the detailed discussion of objections by Danek (1988: 48–176) and the briefer summary by Hainsworth (1993: 154). Dué and Ebbott defend the book on the grounds of its general oral nature (2010: 3–29). For the purposes of this analysis, what is more important is that the episode is integrated well enough into the poem to allow a consistency of character and plot, something generally agreed upon.

4. Sammons sees this mirroring as more likely to be reflective of the *Doloneia* poet's careful reflection of the *Iliad*'s themes (2014: 309n39), but even if Sammons's interpretation is correct, such behavior would not be out of character for Diomedes.

5. Christensen and Barker suggest that the simile toward the beginning of Diomedes's *aristeia* that compares him to a river in flood (5.87–88) prefigures Achilleus's battle with Skamandros (2011: 27n1).

6. This view is shared by van der Valk (1952: 270) and N. Richardson (1993: 259 at 23.798–825), but note the suggestion by Scodel (2008: 40) that Achilleus must have added a gift for Aias as well.

7. *Tudeidēs* at 10.109, 150, 234, 249, 255, 363, 367, 489, 528, and 566; and *Tudeos huios* at 10.159, 487, 494, 509, and 516. He is called simply *Diomēdēs* seventeen times, at 10.150, 219, 227, 234, 241, 283, 340, 341, 369, 446, 476, 477, 502, 508, 536, 559, and 568. On Diomedes's naming patterns in general, see Tsirpanlis 1966: 248–253; Schnapp-Gourbeillon 1981: 95–100; Higbie 1995: 87–100; Pratt 2009: 146–150.

8. It also forms part of *Thebais* fr. 9 Bernabé, while West records the similar D scholion to *Iliad* 5.126 and adds, "*Similiter schol.* [AbT], *ubi additur* ἱστορεῖ Φερεκύδης [3 F 97]" (*Thebais* fr. 9 *GEF*).

9. *LIMC* 7, *s.v.* "Septem" 47, 730-748.

10. On the referential force of *atasthaliai* in the *Iliad*, see further O'Maley 2014: 9–24.

11. This contrast can also be applied across two different traditions, since Diomedes and Sthenelos also belong to the domain of Theban epic, where they would have naturally been portrayed differently and to which their Iliadic counterparts can be seen as a sophisticated response. I will address neither this question nor the equally interesting question of the extent to which the Tydeus of Agamemnon's and Athena's narratives is representative of the Tydeus of Theban epic, since both topics are outside the scope of this chapter, which is concerned with the Iliadic character Diomedes's response to a particularly Iliadic shaping of narratives surrounding his father.

12. Scodel points out that this pattern (modern heroes avoiding the excess that characterizes their forebears) is common in Homeric attitudes toward previous generations (2004).

13. This impetuosity becomes even more apparent in Athena's narrative, which does not discuss Tydeus's speaking ability, but does note his unwillingness "to feast at his ease" (δαίνυσθαί . . . ἕκηλον, 5.805), a lack of composure that in Agamemnon's narrative leads to the failure of his embassy.

14. Ebbott discusses the possible traditional referentiality of the term *meilichion muthon* that Tydeus is said to have brought to the Thebans (10.288), suggesting that the phrase implies a performative utterance that "would have started from a friendly stance and would have been gracious toward Eteocles and the Thebans, regardless of what happened next" (2010: 249–252, quotation from 251).

15. Christensen (this volume) points out the further connections between Diomedes and Thoas: these two, along with Odysseus and Nestor, illustrate the different stages of a Homeric speaker's development.

16. It should be noted that Diomedes is not claiming an ability to speak based on Tydeus's speaking abilities, but based on his nobility alone, as can be seen from his concern about being labeled "base and unwarlike by birth" (γένος γε κακὸν καὶ ἀνάλκιδα, 14.126).

17. On the exchange as a whole, see Alden 2000: 128–140; Grethlein 2006: 43–106. The scene's ending—in which Diomedes and Glaukos exchange unequal gifts in commemoration of their discovered ancestral guest-friendship (Glaukos's gold armor for Diomedes's bronze, nine oxen's worth for one hundred [6.232–236])—has prompted much speculation about its interpretive value for the conversation as a whole: see Donlan 1989; Martin 1989: 126–130; Scodel 1992; Alden 2000: 305–308.

CHAPTER ELEVEN

Hektor, the Marginal Hero: Performance Theory and the Homeric Monologue

LORENZO F. GARCIA JR.

RICHARD MARTIN ARGUES THAT HOMERIC CHARACters "commit themselves to a full enactment of their words before an audience that can criticize these acts; thus they accomplish 'performances' of verbal art, in a manner not different from that of poets and storytellers immersed in the performance situation" (1989: 47).

Following Martin's insight that in the epics actors enact their own character through performance and their display of verbal art (32–33, 47), I examine Hektor's monologue at *Iliad* 22.98–130 as a performance that characterizes Hektor and informs the representation of heroism in the *Iliad.* I am interested in Hektor's long monologue as a demonstration of his character as it is caught between heroism and anti-heroic escapism. Hektor's monologue itself contains elements of different genres of speech and shifts between them as he considers various options for action. Hektor explores alternate avenues before facing Achilleus in combat, but couches each of those options within different speech genres—namely, public speech and the erotically charged encounter termed "intimate exchange" (τὸ ὀαρίζειν)—as he confronts first one and then another internalized audience in his soliloquy. My analysis aims to show that in Hektor's performance he finds himself straying from the very genre of epic itself. His speech marks him as a kind of poet of the peaceful and the pastoral who is out of place in war-torn Ilium. The flights of fancy in which he indulges during his monologue are indicative of his vulnerability as a mortal hero, as set against the implacable Achilleus.

A few words are necessary to introduce Homeric monologues and to raise the issue of monologues as performances. Among the many speeches in the Homeric epics are those in which a hero speaks to himself and often directly to his own *thumos.*[1] Several of these speeches begin with the formulaic line: "Deeply troubled, he spoke to his great-hearted spirit" (ὀχθήσας δ' ἄρα εἶπε πρὸς ὃν μεγαλήτορα θυμόν: *Iliad* 11.403, 17.90, 18.5, 20.343, 21.53, 21.552, 22.98; *Odyssey* 5.298, 355, 407, 464).[2] In four of these ὀχθήσας-monologues the character's *thumos* appears to be engaged in dialogue with the character, suggesting alternatives that the character ultimately rejects: "But why indeed does my own spirit debate these things with me?" (ἀλλὰ τίη μοι ταῦτα φίλος διελέξατο θυμός: *Iliad* 11.407, 17.97, 21.562, 22.122).[3] All four of these speeches in the *Iliad* feature major characters engaged in deliberative monologues as each character, isolated and in a dangerous situation, ponders viable alternatives and decides upon a course of action (Odysseus: 11.403–410; Menelaos: 17.90–105; Agenor: 21.552–570; Hektor: 22.98–130).

The critical bibliography on character monologue in Homeric epic is extensive. Scholars have been divided as to whether to see merely a convention or dramatic technique for representing a character's inner thoughts,[4] or to take the talking *thumos* as a separate entity, an alter ego that represents a not-yet-integrated psychic whole.[5] Other scholars see the Homeric monologues as evidence of Homeric psychology in general and use them to study Homeric decision making as it prefigures later Aristotelian and Stoic theories about human rationality and motivation.[6]

Although Gregory Nagy notes, "as a performance, . . . a monologue is of course implicitly a dialogue with the audience who is being addressed" (1996b: 38), scholarship does not generally treat the question of Homeric monologues as performances. Anthropologist and folklorist Elliott Oring (2011: 365–366, citing Bauman 1992: 38–49) has defined performance as

> an act of communication that is framed and displayed for an audience. Performers assume responsibility for their communicative skills, and they are assessed on their abilities to communicate effectively and artistically. Every performance is a function of place, time, situation, and personnel. Performances emerge only within the field of dynamic interaction between these variables. Furthermore, performance is a reflexive activity. Performers must be able to see themselves not only as objects of direct contemplation, but through the eyes of their audience. Indeed, the notion of performance presumes the notion of feedback—the notion that auditory, visual, and even olfactory messages are constantly being received and shape what is being performed.

From a folklorist's perspective, it is difficult to construe soliloquies as performances because of issues of audience and responsibility: to whom is the performer attempting to communicate and to whom is he responsible in his performance? At best, one may accept the notion that "a performer's audience may on occasion only include himself, as when a magician, mime, or dancer practices a routine alone in front of a mirror" (Oring 2011: 382n3) or that a skilled performer can monitor and evaluate his own performance as an audience would (cf. Glassie 2003: 185).

From a sociological perspective, however, monologues are more readily apparent as performances, since the self as a negotiated construct of social interaction emerges and is sustained through the act of soliloquizing (Athens 1994; cf. Mead 1934: 135–226; Freeman 2010). In soliloquy, the self converses not so much with itself but with an internalized other. George Mead interpreted the social self as a negotiation between a "Me" that is "the organized set of attitudes of others which one himself assumes" (1934: 175) and an "I" that represents the urge or impulse to act and "reacts to the self which arises through the taking of the attitudes of others" (174). This negotiation takes place especially in conversation with the self. In other words, soliloquy is the act of the "I" defining itself through negotiation with the system of expectations, values, and judgments of a given community. When the "I" finds itself in a situation in which its impulses are at odds with social expectations, it deliberates through soliloquy (Athens 1994, 1995). In a nuanced discussion of Mead's importance for sociological concepts of the self, Lonnie Athens notes (1994: 525–526, emphasis in original),

> When soliloquizing we always converse with an interlocutor, even though it may deceivingly appear as if we are only speaking to ourselves. Everything that is said to us, including what we say to ourselves, some interlocutor tells us. . . . We also converse with *phantom others*, who are not present, but whose impact upon us is no less than the people who are present during our social experiences. . . . The individual phantom companions, when taken together, comprise a *phantom community*, which provides people with a multi but unified voice and sounding board for making sense of their varied social experiences.

Athens's "phantom others" and "phantom community" are precisely the internalized system of expectations, values, and judgments of a community that form our basic social identity in response to which our active and judging self decides what to do in a given situation. In soliloquizing, we look at ourselves through the eyes of the community and essentially judge our own actions based on the community's standards (Athens 1994: 527–528; cf. Mead 1934: 138; Freeman 2010: 146–147): the soliloquist, therefore, is very much a performer who is responsible to an internalized or projected audience for his decisions and actions. The sociological conception of a subject "I" and social "Me" fits well with recent work in cognitive science and conceptions of the self. George Lakoff and Mark Johnson's work uncovering the system of metaphorical conceptions that underlie "the self" demonstrates a similar view of a divided self: a subject and a multiplicity of selves that instantiate social roles associated with various conflicting values (Lakoff and Johnson 1999: 267–289; cf. Lakoff 1992; Freeman 2010: 144–145).

The Homeric soliloquist finds himself in a moment of crisis in which his sense of self comes to feel fragmented. He is "divided at heart" as he ponders his situation (cf. διάνδιχα μερμήριξεν, *Iliad* 1.189, 8.167, 13.455), and it is this precise feeling of division that is expressed in monologues to one's *thumos*. As they perform, Homer's soliloquists engage in a dialogue between their immediate impulses and communal values. When we turn to the monologues, we will find an emphasis on concepts of *aidōs* and *nemesis* and on a hero's adherence to heroic ideology and community standards.[7] It is critical to note that these ideas have been internalized. Christopher Gill speaks of Homeric monologues as representing "a society in which the participants have an *internalized* sense of the judgments (relating to shame or honour) that other members of their culture would make on their actions" (1996: 75, emphasis in original; cf. B. Williams 1993: 81–88; D. Cairns 1993: 15–18, 80–83). This internalized sense of community serves as a judging and evaluating audience before whom the soliloquists perform. The reason they soliloquize is because they are in dire straits and adherence to community values is at odds with their present circumstances. As we will see, the speakers of all four *thumos*-monologues in the *Iliad* are isolated and in dangerous circumstances (Schadewaldt 1966: 61; Gill 1996: 58, 88n206; Pelliccia 1995: 139–143); they explore nonheroic possibilities of escape and express fear of dying (Hentze 1904: 15; Arend 1933: 110; Scully 1984: 14), and their emotional state is marked by expressions of grief or agitation such as ὤ μοι ἐγών or ὢ πόποι.[8]

These monologues function for the Homeric audience as what could be called "meta-performative" moments when the poet and character effectively stand outside of the dramatic situation to comment on larger thematic issues.[9] As a moment that dramatizes narrative distance, the monologue is particularly suited for challenging and reaffirming ideological formations, including heroism, masculinity, and public identity, thereby characterizing the speaker at the very moment he must choose a course of action. In his commentaries on Homer's *Odyssey*, Eustathius noted that the poet includes such deliberative monologues largely for the purpose of depicting character (ἠθοποιία).[10] Since monologues provide a window into a character's thinking and decision-making process, they serve to externalize the interior, the "thought and other psychological processes" of a character (Gill 1996: 15; cf. Leo 1908: 5; Walsh 1990: 4). As such, the monologue is a unique genre of heroic speech performance that simultaneously recognizes personal doubt regarding the heroic ideal and engages in the fantasy that a hero outside of public scrutiny may entertain. As Stephen Scully has argued (1984: 14),

> The private thoughts of a hero question the values of heroic activity as he could never do publicly. Thus, it is the privileged domain of the soliloquy to convey the anxiety of the hero as he moves from indecision to resolution, from fear to courage, from thought to reaffirmation of heroic action. Although the soliloquy calls into question the values of society, it also serves to highlight the particular nature of heroism as conceived in the *Iliad*.

These monologues offer contemplation of nonheroic outcomes, even if only to reaffirm the heroic through rejecting alternatives.

Hektor's speech is in many ways similar to the earlier monologues by Odysseus, Menelaos, and Agenor—especially that of Agenor—but is more complex.[11] Before we look at Hektor's speech, I will examine the three other deliberative monologues of the *Iliad* in order to introduce the range and vicissitudes of Hektor's speech.

THE OTHER MONOLOGUES: ODYSSEUS, MENELAOS, AGENOR

The monologues of Odysseus, Menelaos, and Agenor share several features. In each instance, the character finds himself isolated and in a dangerous situation as hostile soldiers or named enemies advance to kill him (cf. 11.411–412, 17.106–107, 21.571). Odysseus ponders on the outcome that, if he holds his ground, he will be caught "all by himself" (μοῦνος, 11.406); Menelaos says the same thing—"I am alone" (μοῦνος ἐὼν)—and notes how many Trojans will surround him (17.94–95). Although Agenor's speech does not specify that he is alone, his situation does. As Hayden Pelliccia points out, "We are simply told Agenor's position relative to the mass of Trojans fleeing into the city; his non-participation in this flight is sufficient to isolate him" (1995: 141). Agenor's isolation is in fact necessary for the plot, for as a lone figure he draws Achilleus's attention and serves as bait to lure Achilleus from the city.

In their isolation, each figure faces a dangerous situation and expresses personal anguish: "Woe is me, what will I suffer" (ὤ μοι ἐγώ, τί πάθω, 11.404) and "Woe is me" (ὤ μοι ἐγών, 17.91, 21.553). In each instance, the speaker considers nonheroic alternatives, namely flight from battle, although the possibility of flight is measured against social expectations of heroic action. To flee from combat is "a great evil" (μέγα μὲν κακὸν), as Odysseus says, but to be caught in battle by himself is "a thing still more horrifying" (τὸ δὲ ῥίγιον, 11.404–405). Nevertheless, Odysseus decides to stand his ground (11.407–410):

> But why indeed does my own spirit debate these things with me?
> For I know that cowards [κακοὶ] withdraw from war,
> and whoever excels in battle [ὃς δέ κ' ἀριστεύῃσι μάχῃ ἔνι], that
>   man must really
> stand his ground strongly, whether he is struck or strikes another.

Odysseus decides to stay through rehearsing the difference between the coward and the brave man. Although he suffers *un momento di debolezza passeggera* ("a moment of passing weakness" [Dentice di Accadia Ammone 2012: 292]) he makes his decision based on social standards expressed in gnomic form (cf. Poseidon at *Iliad* 13.116–119; Hektor at 6.441–446).[12]

Menelaos, for his part, also considers the ramifications of running away, referring to the reproach—*nemesis*—any who see him will feel toward him (17.91–93):

> Woe is me, if I should leave behind the beautiful armor
> and Patroklos, who lies dead here for the sake of my honor;
> may no one of the Danaäns find fault with me [μή . . .
>   νεμεσήσεται], whoever sees it.

Like Odysseus, Menelaos focuses on the public dimensions of being a hero: if he abandons his post defending Patroklos's corpse, he will surely be blamed by any who see him. He consoles himself, however, with the thought that Hektor seems to be fighting with divine help, such that it would be unreasonable for anyone to blame him for fleeing (17.97–101).[13]

> But why indeed does my own spirit debate these things with me?
> Whenever a man comes, in the face of a divinity, to fight with a
>   mortal,

> whomever the god honors, swiftly a great pain rolls upon him.
> Therefore no one of the Danaäns will find fault with me [οὔ . . . νεμεσήσεται],
> whoever sees me giving way before Hektor, since he is fighting with a god's assistance.

Menelaos opts to abandon Patroklos's corpse and to seek help from Aias, calling his decision "the best among bad options" (κακῶν δέ κε φέρτατον εἴη, 17.105).

Agenor's speech is more complex than either Odysseus's or Menelaos's in that he raises three options instead of two. Whereas both Odysseus and Menelaos ponder whether to stand their ground or to give way, Agenor considers: (1) whether he should flee with the other Trojans toward the safety of the city walls (21.553–554); and (2) whether he should flee in the opposite direction, toward the plain, where he can hide (21.556–561). Once both of those options are rejected because Achilleus could catch up with him in flight and kill him (21.555, 563–566), Agenor considers a third option: (3) to stand his ground and fight Achilleus (21.567–570). Considerations of *aidōs* or *nemesis* play no role in Agenor's decision. It is not shame that holds him from flight, but the desperate hope that in hand-to-hand combat he at least stands a chance of surviving.[14] In the following narrative, Apollo magically rescues Agenor and, taking on Agenor's appearance, flees before Achilleus, leading him away from the city gates and allowing the Trojans to find safety within the city (21.595–22.13). The outcome of Agenor's speech—a decision to stand his ground and then flight—prepares us for the outcome of Hektor's own deliberative soliloquy and decision.

HEKTOR'S MONOLOGUE

Like Odysseus, Menelaos, and Agenor in their preceding monologues, Hektor stands by himself. He hesitates alone outside the Skaian Gate as other Trojans flee from Achilleus into the city, waiting as he draws nearer (22.5). Priam catches sight of Achilleus racing toward the city and Hektor standing alone outside the gates, and he begs his son to return (22.38–41)[15]:

> Hektor, my dear child, for my sake do not await that man
> alone without others [οἶος ἄνευθ' ἄλλων], lest you quickly meet up with your fate,

> conquered by Peleus's son, since, in truth, he is far stronger,
> the wretch.

Hekabe likewise addresses Hektor from the city walls and, while baring her breasts to him, she calls upon him to pity her and return to the safety of the city walls (22.82–89):

> Hektor my child, respect these [breasts] and have pity on me
> myself, if ever I offered my breast to you to forget your cares.
> Remember these things, my dear child, and ward off this murderous man
> with you being inside the city wall, and don't stand out in front to meet him,
> you stubborn man. For if he really kills you, I will no longer
> weep for you in your bed, dear scion, you whom I myself bore,
> nor will your wedded wife wooed with many gifts. But at great distance from us
> beside the ships of the Argives swift dogs will feast upon you.

Priam and Hekabe ask Hektor to come back into the city (22.56, 84–85), repeatedly addressing him as "my child" (22.38, 56, 82; cf. φίλον θάλος, 22.87). Their speeches recall Andromache's earlier plea that he, as her "father and revered mother and brother, and blossoming husband" (*Iliad* 6.429–430), stay within the city (6.407–434). Hektor is moved neither by their requests nor by their recitations of his social roles, however, and remains resolute (cf. 22.90–91), determined to face Achilleus (22.35–36).

Watching Achilleus approach, Hektor speaks in soliloquy, as if in conversation with internalized versions of his parents, his wife, his citizens, and Achilleus himself as he works through the conflicting social demands placed upon him as a son, father/husband, future king, and rival.[16] Hektor's speech is in several ways similar to the earlier monologues by Odysseus, Menelaos, and Agenor. Like Odysseus and Menelaos, Hektor is moved by consideration of *aidōs* and *nemesis*: he fears what others will think of him. Like Agenor, he considers three possibilities: fleeing to the city, approaching Achilleus in supplication, and standing his ground.[17] But unlike Agenor, Hektor does not decide to stand his ground out of a desperate hope for survival. Hektor realizes that combat is the only real option, though he fantasizes about a different possibility: peaceful surrender. In other words, instead of considering and then rejecting one or even a second alternative in a moment of indecision, Hektor's thought redoubles back on itself as he poses and explores a second alternative specifically as a way to avoid facing the necessity of his original decision to fight (Burnett 1991: 283n36; cf. Walsh 1990: 9n27).

Hektor's soliloquy, I argue, operates in three movements. First, Hektor responds to internalized audiences, demonstrating his fractured self as he is drawn in contradictory directions by social obligations in conflict with his own personal impulses. Second, Hektor realizes his desire to avoid conflict is impossible and, in a moment of despair, rejects his various social roles altogether. Third and finally, Hektor ends his speech with a brief image from the margin of war and community itself as he speaks wistfully of loss in a situation in which speech itself has lost its power to save him. He soliloquizes (22.98–130):

> Deeply troubled, he spoke to his great-hearted spirit:
> "Woe is me! [ὤ μοι ἐγών] If I go inside the gates and walls,
> Poulydamas will be the first to place reproach upon me,
> he who bid me to lead the Trojans back to the city
> that destructive night when brilliant Achilleus roused himself.
> But I didn't obey him, though in truth, it would have been far more profitable.
> But now since I destroyed the fighting men by my recklessness,
> I feel shame before the Trojans and Trojan women with their trailing robes,
> lest some other person who is less of a man than me should say,
> 'Hektor trusted in his strength and destroyed the fighting men.'
> That's what they will say. As for me, it would be far more profitable then
> to go back after having killed Achilleus in hand-to-hand combat,
> or else to be killed by him gloriously in front of the city.
> But if I lay down my shield, massive in the middle,
> and my strong helmet, and lean my spear against the city wall
> and go as I am to meet blameless Achilleus face-to-face
> and promise him Helen and her possessions along with her,
> all those many things, as many as in the hollow ships of Alexandros
> were brought to Troy, which things were the beginning of the conflict;
> to give these to Atreus's sons to take away, and at the same time for the Achaians
> to divide up other things, as much as this city has laid away,
> and afterward to take an oath among the elders on behalf of the Trojans[18]

> not to conceal anything, but to divide everything in two,
> as much property as lay enclosed within the lovely city . . .
> But why is my own heart discussing these things with me?
> Even if I approached him, he might not pity me
> and would not respect my position at all, and would kill me, naked though I am,
> just as if I were a woman, since I took off my armor.
> No, there is no way now from tree or from rock
> to converse intimately with him, the things a maid and a youth,
> a maid and a youth converse intimately with one another.
> Better to come together with him in contention as quickly as possible.
> We will see to whichever one of us the Olympian will grant glory."

As if responding to his parents and wife, Hektor raises a first possibility proposed by both parties—a return to the safety of the Trojan walls (22.99; cf. *Iliad* 6.431–434, 22.56–58, 22.84–86)—only to reject it immediately out of shame (αἰδέομαι, 22.105), a feeling of social responsibility he feels toward the Trojans.[19] Hektor now imagines an audience of Trojan men and women who will listen to the blame Poulydamas and an anonymous speaker—a lesser man than Hektor—will heap upon him for "destroying the people" (Ἕκτωρ . . . ὤλεσε λαόν, 22.107), a claim Hektor admits to himself: "I destroyed the people in my recklessness" (ὤλεσα λαὸν ἀτασθαλίῃσιν ἐμῇσιν, 22.104).[20] For a leader, traditionally figured in epic as the "shepherd of the people" (ποιμένα/ποιμένι λαῶν: cf. Haubold 2000: 17, 197), the destruction of the people indicates the failure of the heroic ideal (Taplin 1992: 50; Haubold 2000: 28–32, 198).

Had Hektor listened to Poulydamas's advice (*Iliad* 18.249–313; cf. Redfield 1975: 143–153; Schofield 1986: 18–22; Clark 2007: 94–98), "in truth, it would have been far more profitable" (ἦ τ' ἂν πολὺ κέρδιον ἦεν, 22.103). The modal particle ἄν and imperfect verb ἦεν only serve to show the present impossibility of going back to a time when following Poulydamas's advice—and thereby saving the people—was still a possibility (Chantraine 1953: 227; Rijksbaron 2002: 7, 73). The opening verses of Hektor's speech, then, are marked as a performance to parents, wife, and Trojan citizens. His duties as son, father, and husband are in conflict with those of his role as protector of the city, and his expression of *aidōs* is associated with vivid features of a public that will disapprove of his actions: he imagines speakers who will blame him (ἐλεγχείην, 22.100).[21]

Hektor's sense of shame (αἰδέομαι, 22.105; cf. *Iliad* 6.442) prevents him from any further consideration of returning to the city. The better choice—indicated with the potential optative, "it would be far more profitable for me" (ἐμοὶ δὲ τότ' ἂν πολὺ κέρδιον εἴη, 22.108)—is to return only after having defeated Achilleus in battle, or else to die gloriously at Achilleus's hands (22.109–110). But even as Hektor reaches the same decision as Odysseus does in his monologue, he immediately proposes a second alternative in a conditional sentence, as his own impulse drives him to try to preserve his own life—to paraphrase, "What if I put down my arms and approach Achilleus . . ." (22.111–114), a thought that, despite its detailed elaboration, trails off without reaching its full expression (cf. Crotty 1994: 85). He imagines approaching Achilleus and engaging in a different kind of speech situation: instead of public speech before a large audience, Hektor envisions an intimate, face-to-face encounter with Achilleus as a suppliant (ἀντίος ἔλθω, 22.113).[22] Hektor imagines approaching Achilleus and asking him to spare Hektor's life in exchange not only for Helen and all her belongings but for half of everything still held in store in the city (22.114–121). Hektor goes on for eleven verses, as if now conversing with an internalized version of Achilleus himself, as if Helen and her possessions could still be considered the *causa belli*.[23] Here, too, Hektor must negotiate between his own wish to live and his role as captain of the Trojans vis-à-vis Achilleus. But Hektor's imagined negotiations with Achilleus form an impossible possibility (cf. Fowler 1987: 22): after the death of Patroklos, after all, Achilleus is no longer fighting Hektor for Helen's sake, and there will be no cutting oaths between the parties (cf. *Iliad* 3.264–301), for Achilleus thinks of Hektor only as the murderer of his companion (*Iliad* 20.425–426, 22.331; cf. Taplin 1992: 235; Gill 1996: 86–89).

Hektor breaks off his imagined supplication in the middle of a sentence: "But if I lay down my shield . . . and go as I am to meet blameless Achilleus face-to-face and promise him . . ."; he trails off as his train of thought derails in anacoluthon: "But why is my own heart discussing these things with me" (ἀλλὰ τίη μοι ταῦτα φίλος διελέξατο θυμός, 22.122; cf. Chantraine 1953: 362–363; Janko 1992: 83–84; N. Richardson 1993: 119). The break at verse 22.122 indicates a rupture of both syntax and thought, implying Hektor's psychological stress.[24] Yet it also indicates a breakdown in his imagined intimate discourse with an internalized version of Achilleus. Hektor now expresses the impossibility of surrender in a fear clause: to paraphrase, "I fear that if I approach Achilleus as a suppliant, he will not pity me" (22.123–124; cf. Chantraine 1953: 208, 363;

de Jong 2012: 91). That is to say, he realizes the impossibility of peaceful negotiation with Achilleus and knows that his words and gestures will fail to persuade. Instead, Achilleus will slay him in spite of his nudity now that he has set aside his armor and weapons, "just as if I were a woman" (αὔτως ὥς τε γυναῖκα, 22.125).[25]

The image of Hektor as a "naked" suppliant approaching Achilleus recalls Lykaon, who likewise set down his arms (*Iliad* 21.50). But Hektor's characterization of himself as a woman in a self-applied comparison (cf. W. Scott 1974: 200; M. Edwards 1991: 29; Ready 2011: 31, 55) is surprising, especially when we consider that gendered terms are largely used in the *Iliad* to feminize one's opponent.[26] When Hektor imagines himself cut down "naked, just like a woman," he is violating the pattern of gendered speech in combat scenes: instead of feminizing his enemy, Hektor effectively feminizes himself.

It is at this point in his soliloquy that Hektor begins to despair of any possibility of reconciling his immediate impulses of seeking safety with those of his internalized feelings of shame: he cannot flee, cannot surrender, but does not want to fight. When Hektor "feminizes" himself, then, we can read it as an act of rejecting his various roles of son, husband/father, future king, and even rival of Achilleus. Instead of the defender of the city, he momentarily sees himself as one who needs to be protected, a woman and, soon after, a youth (cf. Redfield 1975: 119–127; Scully 1990: 54–68). It is especially Hektor's association with the vulnerable that creates the force of his soliloquy as a meta-performative moment in which destructive war is set against the city and its vulnerable inhabitants. Hektor, in his vulnerable state, is marginalized: he is outside of and apart from the various speech communities in which he could justify his actions to his family and fellow Trojans or even preserve his city and his life through successful supplication of his enemy.

Hektor continues to figure himself as a female in a second, even more striking simile, in which he represents his imagined conversation with Achilleus as an erotic encounter between a young woman and a young man (22.126–128):

> οὐ μέν πως νῦν ἔστιν ἀπὸ δρυὸς οὐδ' ἀπὸ πέτρης
> τῶι ὀαριζέμεναι, ἅ τε παρθένος ἠΐθεός τε
> παρθένος ἠΐθεός τ' ὀαρίζετον ἀλλήλοιιν.
>
> No, there is no way now from tree or from rock
> to converse intimately with him, the things a maid and a youth,
> a maid and a youth converse intimately with one another.

The meaning of the proverbial expression "from tree or from rock" remains obscure,[27] but it may involve themes of the origin of mankind and sexual reproduction.[28]

The idea of a sexual encounter is emphasized by Hektor's vision of a young woman and a young man: the terms παρθένος and ἠΐθεός specify "young people on the threshold of a recognized sexuality and hence marriage" (Ready 2011: 59; cf. Levaniouk 2011: 85), and the verbal and iconic juxtaposition of the terms at 22.127–128 may even suggest their coupling (Cressey 1982: 23). Moreover, Hektor's youths are imagined as "conversing intimately" with one another: ὀαριζέμεναι (22.127), ὀαρίζετον (22.128). The denominative verb ὀαρίζειν "to converse intimately" (*Iliad* 6.516, 22.127–128; cf. Mader, *LfgrE* 16 [1997]: 481 *s.v.* ὀαρίζω) derives from the noun ὄαρ "wife" (*Iliad* 5.486, 9.327; cf. Mader, *LfgrE* 16 [1997]: 480–481 *s.v.* ὄαρ) and is related to ὄαρος "intimate intercourse/conversation" (Hesiod *Theogony* 205; Pindar *Pythian* 1.98, 4.137, *Nemean* 3.11, 7.69; *Homeric Hymn to Aphrodite* [*Homeric Hymn* 5] 249; *Homeric Hymn* 23.3; Callimachus *Hymn* 5.66, fr. 403.3 [Pfeiffer]; cf. Mader, *LfgrE* 16 [1997]: 482 *s.v.* ὄαρος) and two action nouns, ὀαριστύς "intimate encounter" (*Iliad* 13.291, 14.216–217, 17.228; cf. Mader, *LfgrE* 16 [1997]: 482 *s.v.* ὀαριστύς)[29] and ὀαριστής "confidant" (*Odyssey* 19.179; Plato *Minos* 319e; cf. Mader, *LfgrE* 16 [1997]: 482 *s.v.* ὀαριστής; Levaniouk 2011: 82–92).[30] The verb ὀαρίζειν is used in early Greek poetry to denote the intimate commerce of words between lovers: Hektor and Andromache (*Iliad* 6.516), Zeus and Maia (*Homeric Hymn to Hermes* [*Homeric Hymn* 4] 58), Zeus and Themis (*Homeric Hymn* 23.3). It is telling that Hektor's own interaction with Andromache is termed "intimate conversation" (ὀάριζε γυναικί, 6.516). Even the nominal forms suggest a kind of conversation or intimate exchange: Aphrodite's magical brassiere (*Iliad* 14.216–217) features ὀαριστύς paired with πάρφασις "seductive speech" in asyndeton, functioning as a gloss implying "intimate speech" (Janko 1992: 185; Levaniouk 2011: 84n5).

Intimacy does not occur only between lovers, however. In two passages ὀαριστύς is used to refer to the "intimate encounter" between rivals in war: at *Iliad* 13.291 Idomeneus acknowledges Meriones's valor in battle, noting that he would not be wounded in the back while fleeing from battle, but would be stabbed in his chest as he advanced "through the *intimate encounter* of front-line fighters" (μετὰ προμάχων *ὀαριστύν*); and at *Iliad* 17.228 Hektor encourages the Trojan allies to fight bravely and either be victorious in combat or perish, "for this is the *intimate encounter* of war" (ἡ γὰρ πολέμου *ὀαριστύς*; cf. Vermeule 1979: 103, 157, 235n24; Mader, *LfgrE* 16 [1997]: 482). We may compare the use of the verb μίσγω "to mix it up with," which is used to describe lovers meeting face-to-face in sexual congress as well as soldiers meeting face-to-face in battle (MacCary 1982: 137–148; Monscaré 2010: 71; Mader, *LfgrE* 15 [1993]: 225–229 *s.v.* μίσγω, def. 2c–d). In other words, the face-to-face encounter between soldiers in combat can be cast in erotic terms, as a kind of back-and-forth between lovers, in which penetrating weapons become fetishized, phallic substitutes.[31]

There is more to be said about Hektor's two-line image at 22.127–128, however. It is marked by chiastic arrangement and repetition: the two verbal forms—ὀαριζέμεναι (infinitive) and ὀαρίζετον (dual indicative)—echo each other, each functioning with a dative pronoun, τῶι "with him" and ἀλλήλοιιν "with one another," itself a pronoun formed from verbal doubling (ἄλλος ἄλλωι: Wackernagel 2009: 521–522; Sihler 1995: 383–384; Levaniouk 2011: 85). Between the two verbal forms and dative pronouns is the repeated phrase "young woman and young man" (ἅ τε παρθένος ἠΐθεός τε / παρθένος ἠΐθεός τ'). The repetition of a word from a marked position (at the beginning, end, or after the bucolic diaeresis) of one verse at or near the beginning of the next came to be known by Greek grammarians primarily as *epanalepsis* (cf. Wills 1996: 124–186). A version of the trope occurs several times in early Greek poetry with a proper name, epithet, patronymic, or dependent relative clause, such as: "Andromache, daughter of great-hearted *Eëtion*, / *Eëtion* who dwelled below woody Placus" (Ἀνδρομάχη, θυγάτηρ μεγαλήτορος Ἠετίωνος / Ἠετίων, ὃς ἔναιεν ὑπὸ Πλάκωι ὑληέσσηι, *Iliad* 6.395–396).[32] The expanded version of the trope—most recently called "nested double epanalepsis" (Smitherman 2013)—as at 22.127–128 (wherein the final three metra are repeated) is very rare, however, appearing only three times in the *Iliad* (20.371–372, 22.127–128, 23.641–642), and is not found again in Greek poetry until the Alexandrian age.[33] Of the three extended passages featuring nested double epanalepsis, Hektor speaks two of them (20.371–372, 22.127–128).[34] Hektor envisions an ideal meeting of partners that allows for an equitable exchange as if he were speaking with his own wife, but also as if he were in some way Achilleus's sexual partner: in Hektor's phraseology, both "young woman" and "young man" are in the nominative case and hence both subjects, neither suffering dominance at the hands of the other (Ready 2011: 60); moreover, the dual form of the verb ὀαρίζετον (22.128) demonstrates mutual interaction (Crotty 1994: 84; Ready 2011: 60).

In conclusion, Hektor's soliloquy features verbal performances in which Hektor himself tries to negotiate between his various conflicting social roles. As a son, husband, and father, he is called upon to return to the city and save himself (*Iliad* 22.37–89, 6.405–434). As future king of the Trojans, he has an obligation to all his citizens and feels shame at shrinking from those duties (cf. Redfield 1975; Scully 1990). In the conflict between these various internalized audiences, Hektor even engages with an internalized figure of Achilleus. To Hektor's despair, however, there is no reconciliation possible now that Patroklos is dead: he is cut off from all verbal efficacy.

In such a moment of despair Hektor adopts a different kind of speech genre altogether. His verses at 22.127–128 are indicative of a refined poetic sensibility (cf. Martin 1989: 131–132, 138; H. Mackie 1996: 106–111): the repeated phrases are reminiscent of Near Eastern traditions of lamentation (Griffin 1992) and pastoral poetry (Hunter 2005b: 229). Indeed, Hektor's poetic repetitions call to mind the refrains found in Theocritus's *Idylls* (Hunter 2005b: 228–229; cf. Rosenmeyer 1969: 94–97, 118–119; Haber 1994: 18). Beyond verbal repetition, the inner metric rhythm of 22.127–128 (heavily dactylic verses with bucolic diaresis) is precisely the pattern imitated by Theocritus, as David Halperin notes: "the first seven Idylls share a tendency to emphasize certain metrical patterns already present in Greek epic poetry and to exaggerate them to the point of extreme mannerism" (1983: 259–266, quotation from 264).

It has been argued that early Greek hexameter poetry contains "reflections" of other poetic performance genres, including choral song and what various scholars have referred to as "lyric" and even "proto-pastoral." Nicholas Richardson has discussed the "reflection" of various types of song in early Greek hexameter, such as choral or monodic songs, including wedding songs, laments, paeans, and work songs (2011). Even similes, the *sine qua non* of Homeric poetry, may be considered representatives of an alternate, non-epic genre. Michel Bréal called them *morceaux évidemment déplacés, qui ont l'air d'être des emprunts à un autre genre littéraire* ("pieces apparently out of place, which have the look of borrowings from another literary genre" [1911: 107]).[35] William Scott considers the Homeric simile to be drawn from an alternate "tradition" that "must be independent from the narrative at least in conception" (1974: vii–viii, 53–54, quotation from 53). Furthermore, the shield of Achilleus makes reference to wedding hymns (*Iliad* 18.491–495; cf. N. Richardson 2011), the Linos song (18.570; cf. Stephens 2002/2003; Karanika 2014: 117–132),[36] a festival song with accompanying chorus of dancing men and women (18.590–605), and even the song two shepherds play upon a *syrinx* (δύω δ' ἅμ' ἕποντο νομῆες / τερπόμενοι σύριγξι, 18.525–526).[37] In short, in his isolation, Hektor has recourse to a non-epic mode of poetry, something closer to lyric or pastoral in its imagery, language, simplicity, and (as Andromache Karanika points out to me) almost childlike innocence.[38]

Outside of Hektor's monologue, the pairing of παρθένος and ἠΐθεος occurs twice more, both on Achilleus's shield (*Iliad* 18.567, 593), and both in idyllic scenes (cf. Segal 1971: 35n4; W. Scott 1974: 82n57; Ready 2005: 159). Charles Segal poignantly observes (1971: 35),

> Hector, so much closer than Achilles to the vulnerable, precious creations of civilization, lets his mind dwell on youths and maidens (note the repetition in 127–8) when he is about to face this lonely, implacable warrior who has just clogged Troy's "lovely streams" with corpses. Only here and on Achilles' shield, both ominous contexts, does one glimpse the happiness or gaiety of young love, at least in the human world.

Hektor's nested double epanelepsis with the simile of a young woman and man functions much as some similes seem to: it creates a world outside and apart from the moment of action, a world of peace and nature as opposed to war and death. That Hektor is caught between the two worlds is reflected in the very language of his image. Intimate conversation with Achilleus activates allusions both to Hektor's own "intimate conversation" with his wife (ὀάριζε γυναικί, *Iliad* 6.516) and to the charged encounters between rivals on the field of battle (cf. ἤ γὰρ πολέμου ὀαριστύς, *Iliad* 17.228).[39] The violent juxtaposition (D. Porter 1972; cf. Rosenmeyer 1969: 193) of the content of Hektor's simile with its context, as he awaits death at Achilleus's hands, makes a powerful argument for the value of the community Hektor strives to protect.[40]

As a self shaped by his community and enmeshed in a network of expectations and obligations, Hektor in his soliloquy is not only making public an inner dialogue. His soliloquy is a performance before various internalized audiences and their conflicting values. When his verbal skills fall short, he turns to action instead of words, although it is a choice without conviction. The final image in his speech, of youth and maid, constitutes a poetic *cri de coeur* of longing for happier times and fleeting youth. Achilleus may be a poet of *kleos* (*Iliad* 9.186–191), but Hektor, I suggest, finds his inspiration elsewhere. His expressions point to a proto-pastoral poetry that celebrates the world of peacetime activity that is only to be found at the margins in the *Iliad*: in similes, in the peaceful and pastoral scenes on Achilleus's shield, and in the poem's brief descriptions of landscapes. Hektor, with his song and his representations of a world toward which he can only feel nostalgia (cf. 22.156), offers one final violent juxtaposition when set against the brutal song of Achilleus.[41]

NOTES

Many thanks to Jonathan Ready, Christos Tsagalis, Osman Umurhan, Andromache Karanika, and Emily Kratzer for their generous suggestions and critical assessments of this piece.

1. For general discussion of Homeric monologues, see Hentze 1904; Leo 1908: 1–6, 94–96; Otter 1914: 8–21; Voigt 1934: 82–101; Schadewaldt 1926, 1965: 300–303, 1966: 61–64; Dodds 1951: 16; Fenik 1968: 96–98, 163–164, 1978 *passim*; Russo 1968: 288–294; Scully 1984; M. Edwards 1987b: 94–96; Fowler 1987: 20–23; Pelliccia 1995: 115–281; Gill 1996: 29–93; de Jong 2001: 140–141; Dentice di Accadia Ammone 2012: 287–299 (with a useful history of scholarship, 287–291). See Arend 1933: 106–115 for indirect monologues (Arend's "μερμηρίζειν-*Szenen*"). For other forms of "fictive contact" (Pelliccia's term, 1995: 48) in which one character delivers a speech to another without expecting a response, see Medda 1983: 11–57 on prayers, Petersmann 1973: 11, 14 and Pelliccia 1995: 154n87 on lament speeches to the dead, and Pelliccia 1995: 150–161 on taunting speeches "addressed to newly dead persons" (151n76).

2. There are also four speeches by gods addressed to their *thumos* that begin with the formulaic line "and moving his head he spoke to his own spirit" (κινήσας δὲ κάρη προτὶ ὃν μυθήσατο θυμόν): Zeus at *Iliad* 17.200, 442, and Poseidon at *Odyssey* 5.285, 376. See Pelliccia 1995: 181–182 for discussion. Throughout this chapter citations of Homer's *Iliad* are from T. W. Allen's 1931 edition; all translations are my own.

3. A fifth and final use of the phrase ἀλλὰ τίη μοι ταῦτα φίλος διελέξατο θυμός (*Iliad* 22.385) occurs not in monologue, but in a speech by Achilleus after the death of Hektor as he first proposes sacking Troy but stops himself with the memory that Patroklos has not yet been buried.

4. Hentze 1904: 18–20; Leo 1908: 95; Arend 1933: 114; Schadewaldt 1966: 62n1; Petersmann 1974: 128. See Pelliccia 1995: 115–120, 200–216 for discussion. Note Dodds 1951: 4–5 on the Homeric "*façon de parler.*"

5. Böhme 1929: 77–80; Snell 1930, 1931: 75–76, 82, 1953: 14–22; Voigt 1934: 73–74, 86, 90–92; Dodds 1951: 16–17; Adkins 1970: 21–27, 47, 90, 126, 196–197, 271. For discussion, see Petersmann 1974; Redfield 1975: 20–23; Schmitt 1990; Pelliccia 1995: 15–27; Gill 1996: 29–93; M. Clarke 1999: 61–126.

6. Lesky 1961; Lloyd-Jones 1983: 238–240; Sharples 1983; Gaskin 1990; Schmitt 1990; Rosenmeyer 1990: 187–195; Burnett 1991; B. Williams 1993: 1–49; Gill 1996: 41–60; Mifsud 1997, 1998.

7. On *aidōs* "shame" and *nemesis* "reproach," see Snell, *LfgrE* 2 (1956): 279–280 *s.v.* αἰδώς; Redfield 1975: 115–119; D. Cairns 1993: 52, 84–85, 98–100; Yamagata 1994: 156–175; Gill 1996: 78n166; Nordheider, *LfgrE* 16 (1997): 317–319

s.v. νέμεσις. On a character's weighing personal impulses against social imperatives, see Schein 1984: 173–179 and Schofield 1986: 22, who speaks of Hektor's monologue as "a struggle between thought and impulse, or again between the hero and his kin and community."

8. On ὤ μοι ἐγώ in monologues, see *Iliad* 17.91, 18.6, 21.553, 22.99; *Odyssey* 5.356, 6.119, 13.200; cf. ὤ μοι ἐγὼ δειλός (*Odyssey* 5.299); ὤ μοι ἐγώ, τί πάθω (*Iliad* 11.404; *Odyssey* 5.465); ὤ μοι (*Odyssey* 5.408); ὢ πόποι (*Iliad* 20.344, 21.54, 22.297; *Odyssey* 5.286, 13.209). See Hentze 1904: 14; Otter 1914: 11; Arend 1933: 113–114; Fenik 1978: 68–70; Pelliccia 1995: 121–123.

9. Pelliccia refers to these monologues as taking place in "an artificially contrived nowhere" (1995: 139n55). Tsagalis describes Homeric monologues in terms of metalepsis (defined as the "temporary collapse of the distinction between the spatiotemporal levels pertaining to the narrator and the narrated world") and its characteristic blurring or collapsing of spatial designations (2012: 34 with n33).

10. Eustathius comments on *Odyssey* 13.197 (ed. Stallbaum, II.46.17): "Because the poet *expresses character* in speech here, too, by imitating the very things that Odysseus would say when he failed to recognize where he had been let out by the Phaiakians" (Ὅτι *ἠθοποιεῖ* τὸν λόγον κἀνταῦθα ὁ ποιητής, μιμούμενος ἅ περ ἄν εἴποι Ὀδυσσεὺς ἀγνοῶν ποῦ ἐξετέθη πρὸς τῶν Φαιάκων). Schol. gen. at *Iliad* 11.404 (Nicole) similarly terms Odysseus's Iliadic monologue an exercise in ἠθοποιία. Cf. Hentze 1904: 17–18; Arend 1933: 114; M. Edwards 1987b: 94; Pelliccia 1995: 213–216; de Jong 2001: 140–141.

11. For a comparison of the speeches, see Hentze 1904: 28–29; Fenik 1978: 83; Duban 1980: 14–19; Pelliccia 1995: 209n183; Gill 1996: 78–93; Dentice di Accadia Ammone 2012: 299.

12. On Odysseus's speech, see Hentze 1904: 15–16; Schadewaldt 1966: 61–63; Lohmann 1970: 39–40; Fenik 1978: 71–77; Griffin 1980: 92; Hainsworth 1993: 269–270; Pelliccia 1995: 117–122, 144, 196, 208–211; Gill 1996: 69–80; G. Zanker 1996: 38; Dentice di Accadia Ammone 2012: 291–293. For the view that Odysseus's speech does not constitute a "decision" or an act of will but rather a reaction to a social norm, see Snell 1930: 145; Voigt 1934: 91; and perhaps Fenik 1978: 78. For arguments that Odysseus's speech does represent a "decision," see Petersmann 1974: 151; Lloyd-Jones 1983: 239–240; Gaskin 1990: 8–10; Gill 1996: 69–78; Dentice di Accadia Ammone 2012: 292n11.

13. Cf. Nestor at *Iliad* 8.139–144; Diomedes at 5.601–606; Aeneas at 20.97–98; Agamemnon at 9.17–28, 14.74–81. On Menelaos's speech, see Arend 1933: 114; Voigt 1934: 92–94; Fenik 1978: 86–89; Renehan 1987: 111; Gaskin 1990: 8–9; M. Edwards 1991: 72–73; Pelliccia 1995: 121–122, 139–140, 195, 209n183, 228–229; Gill 1996: 78–79; Dentice di Accadia Ammone 2012: 293–295.

14. On Agenor's speech, see Arend 1933: 114; Schadewaldt 1966: 62; Petersmann 1974: 154–157; Fenik 1978: 77–81; Pelliccia 1995: 121–122, 196, 209n183; Gill 1996: 80–81; Dentice di Accadia Ammone 2012: 295–297.

15. Hektor's being called οἶος ("alone") by Priam recalls his role as lone defender of the city: cf. Andromache at *Iliad* 6.403, "For Hektor alone defends Il-

ium" (οἶος γὰρ ἐρύετο Ἴλιον Ἕκτωρ) and Hekabe at 22.507, "For [Hektor] alone defended the gates and long walls for them" (οἶος γάρ σφιν ἔρυσο πύλας καὶ τείχεα μακρά). See Tsagalis 2012: 49n67.

16. On Hektor's monologue, see Hentze 1904: 26–29; Schadewaldt 1965: 300–303; Lohmann 1970: 37–38; Petersmann 1974: 154–157; Redfield 1975: 155–159; Fenik 1978: 81–85; Sharples 1983; Scully 1984: 16–18; M. Edwards 1987b: 291–292; Burnett 1991: 283–287; Taplin 1992: 230–239; Crotty 1994: 85–86; Gill 1996: 81–93; Farmer 1998; Gonzáles de Tobía 1998/1999; Clark 2007: 98–101; de Jong 2012: 80–92; Dentice di Accadia Ammone 2012: 297–299.

17. Note that both Hektor and Agenor use similar formulaic language: ἐμοὶ δέ τότ' ἂν πολὺ κέρδιον εἴη does not appear in either Menelaos's or Odysseus's speeches.

18. On the interpretation of Τρωσὶν . . . γερούσιον ὅρκον, see N. Richardson 1993: 119.

19. On Hektor and *aidōs*, cf. *Iliad* 6.441–446, and see Redfield 1975: 115–119, 157–158; Fenik 1978: 84; D. Cairns 1993: 78–83; N. Richardson 1993: 117–118. Hektor's αἰδέομαι here reads as a corrective to Hekabe's appeal that he "respect" her breast (τάδε τ' αἴδεο, *Iliad* 22.82). See further Redfield 1975: 109–127; Scully 1990: 114–127.

20. ἀτασθαλίη "wild recklessness" (3× *Iliad*, 9× *Odyssey*) and its cognates ἀτασθάλλω (2× *Odyssey*) and ἀτάσθαλος (3× *Iliad*, 15× *Odyssey*) are more common in the *Odyssey* (in which they refer chiefly to Aigisthos, the suitors, and Odysseus's own crew) than in the *Iliad*. On the meaning of the term and its connection to human error, see Nordheider, *LfgrE* 8 (1976): 1483–1485 *s.v.* ἀτασθαλίη; S. West 1988: 72; Finkelberg 1995.

21. Anticipation of blame seems to be a particular trait of Hektor's speeches: he is constantly concerned about what others will say about him (cf. *Iliad* 6.459–462, 6.479–481, 7.87–91, 7.300–302, 16.838–842). Cf. Martin 1989: 133–138; N. Richardson 1993: 118; H. Mackie 1996: 64–65.

22. On ἀντίος ἔλθω in the context of supplication, cf. *Iliad* 20.463. On Hektor's imagined encounter with Achilleus as a supplication scene, note ἵκωμαι ἰών (*Iliad* 22.123) with schol. A *Iliad* 22.123b (Erbse), Gould 1973: 75, and the excellent treatment by Ready 2011: 55–58. On "face-to-face conversation" in this scene, see H. Mackie 1996: 44–45. However, Hektor's vision of approaching Achilleus "face-to-face" remains ambiguous at best: note that ἀντίος ἔλθω is also the term for closing in combat as at *Iliad* 20.422: "[Hektor] approached Achilleus in face-to-face combat" (ἀντίος ἦλθ' Ἀχιλῆϊ); cf. ἄντην at *Iliad* 22.109, and see Chantraine 1968–1980: 91–92 and Beekes 2010: 107–109 on ἀντίος and ἄντην.

23. On Paris's theft of Helen and her possessions as the cause of the war (ἥ τ' ἔπλετο νείκεος ἀρχή, *Iliad* 22.116; cf. 3.39–94), see Roisman 2006 with citations.

24. Chantraine 1953: 362; Lohmann 1970: 38; Burnett 1991: 283–288; Farmer 1998: 24; González de Tobía 1998/1999: 118.

25. See MacCary 1982: 153–162 on the act of stripping a fallen warrior's ar-

mor—thereby rendering him naked—as a "symbolic castration" (153). By extension, Hektor feminizes himself by taking off his own armor in supplication.

26. In general, as Monscaré argues (2010: 93), to be likened to a woman was the worst sort of insult for a Homeric warrior.

27. For "tree and rock" in classical literature, cf. *Odyssey* 19.163, Hesiod *Theogony* 35; later allusions include Plato *Apology* 34d, *Phaedrus* 275b, *Republic* 544d; Lucillus *Anthologia Palatina* 11.253; Juvenal *Satires* 6.12 (conjectured); Plutarch *Morales* 1.608c; Philostratus *Imagines* 2.3.1; Palladas *Anthologia Palatina* 10.55.

28. See West 1966: 268 at Hesiod *Theogony* 35; Nagy 1990a: 181–201; C. Watkins 1995: 161–164; Lopez-Ruiz 2010: 48–83, 205–210; Levaniouk 2011: 90–91.

29. F. Cairns (2010) speaks of ὀαριστύς as signaling an ancient poetic genre of "wooing" speeches in early Greek poetry, such as Paris's conversation with Helen at *Iliad* 3.424–448, Zeus's interactions with Hera at *Iliad* 14.159–353, Aphrodite's seduction of Anchises at *Homeric Hymn to Aphrodite* 1–167, and the wooing of Neoboule's sister at Archilochus fr. 196a.

30. On the etymologies of the ὄαρ family of words, see Chantraine 1968–1980: 771; Frisk 1960–1972: II.343–344; Beekes 2010: 1042.

31. Fenik 1968: 40–41; MacCary 1982: 137–148; Ready 2005: 154–155, 2011: 58–59; Monscaré 2010: 67–87.

32. Compare *Iliad* 2.671–673, 2.837–838, 2.849–850, 2.870–871, 6.153–154, 7.137–138, 12.95–96, 21.85–86, 21.157–158; *Odyssey* 1.23–24; Hesiod *Shield* 317–319, 578–581; Pindar *Pythian* 2.49–51, *Isthmian* 5.52–53.

33. Fehling 1969: 184–185; N. Richardson 1980: 282; Macleod 1982: 50–53; M. Edwards 1991: 59–60; Wills 1996: 126–130, 178–179, 394–397; West 1997: 254–257; de Jong 2012: 91–92. See West 1997: 255–257, 2007: 106–107 for parallel uses of epanalepsis from both Indo-European and Akkadian, Ugaritic, and Hebrew poetic traditions. Griffin (1992) and Hunter (2005b) discuss *Iliad* 22.127–128 in the context of Near Eastern poetic traditions. For examples of epanalepsis in Hellenistic poetry, see Wills 1996: 128–130, 179–180, 394–397.

34. The third is spoken by Nestor in a performance of memory (*Iliad* 23.641–642). On "memory" speeches as a performance genre in the *Iliad*, see Martin 1989: 47, 77–88.

35. See also Martin 1997b; Ready 2011: 93–96.

36. Karanika argues convincingly for the appropriateness of Linos being recalled on the shield of Achilleus, since Linos, through his various mythological histories, is always figured as a young man killed prematurely, sometimes even at the hands of Apollo.

37. Alden calls the song a "rural idyll" (2000: 63). On the *syrinx* as an index of "pastoral" poetry, see Pearce 1993: 70–71; cf. Rosenmeyer 1969: 75.

38. See further Levaniouk's rich study in this volume on women's traditional discourse genres, such as lament songs and wedding hymns, and their influence upon and incorporation into epic poetry. Following Levaniouk's argument, Hektor's soliloquy not only evokes lyric and pastoral poetic performance genres but is marked by gendered idiolectal features of a female rhapsode singing songs of marriage and lament.

39. Redfield 1975: 158; Moulton 1977: 82; Fenik 1978: 85; Taplin 1992: 235; N. Richardson 1993: 120; H. Mackie 1996: 118; Farmer 1998: 23n15; Van Nortwick 2001; Ready 2011: 55–61; de Jong 2012: 11–13.

40. One may interpret the detailed description of the landscape as Hektor flees from Achilleus (*Iliad* 22.136–157) as an example of the lyric or pastoral topography being made to reflect certain aspects of Hektor's speech: the reference to the twin springs of the Skamandros and the washing tubs where Trojan wives and daughters used to wash clothes is explicitly marked as a peacetime event from before, an almost unimaginable world now—τὸ πρὶν ἐπ' εἰρήνης, πρὶν ἐλθεῖν υἷας Ἀχαιῶν (22.156). The description emphasizes the contrast between war and peace, with the effect of heightening the horror of Hektor's imminent demise through marking the precise spot where he will face Achilleus and die (*Iliad* 22.208–209; Treu 1955: 93–94; Schadewaldt 1965: 308). The description of the landscape features, although related by the Homeric narrator, is focalized through the character of Hektor (Fenik 1978: 85; de Jong 2012: 97).

41. On the nostalgic views of Troy before the war as signaled here by τὸ πρίν (*Iliad* 22.156), cf. 22.440–441, 22.500–504; for references to a time when Troy was rich, cf. 9.401–403, 18.288–289, 24.543–546; for references to a time when Priam still had many sons, cf. 24.495–497, 24.546.

CHAPTER TWELVE

Performance, Oral Texts, and Entextualization in Homeric Epic

JONATHAN L. READY

THE *ILIAD* CONTAINS THE HOMERIC EPICS' ONE REFerence to writing: Bellerophon carries "a folded tablet" (*pinaki*) on which Proitos has scratched (*grapsas*) "baneful signs" (*sēmata lugra*) (*Iliad* 6.168–169) (cf. Powell 2011).[1] Despite this occlusion of written texts, the world depicted in the epics does not lack texts or a concept of textuality. Rather, one comes across an abundance of texts in the *Iliad* and the *Odyssey* if one follows the lead of linguistic anthropologists who investigate "the constitution of oral texts" (Barber 2007: 67) through processes of entextualization. This chapter describes the model of entextualization and then applies it to the Homeric poems in order to shed light on the performances depicted in the poems and on the Homeric poet's own performance.

PERFORMANCE, ORAL TEXTS, AND ENTEXTUALIZATION

The study of oral performance made great strides in the 1970s. First, Richard Bauman offered what would prove to be an enduring definition of performance: "performance as a mode of spoken verbal communication consists in the assumption of responsibility to an audience for a display of communicative competence" (1977: 11; cf. Bauman 2004: 9).[2] Second, scholars reacted against the excision of an oral performer's words from the real-world context of their utterance. It would no longer do merely to study a written transcript of what a performer had said. As Richard Martin reviews, these researchers argued that "meaning emerges only through performance," that "it is the performance, not the text, which counts" (1989: 7; cf. Bakker 2005: 55; Finnegan 2007: 192; L. Edmunds 2016: 33).

Others have sought to clarify this second point, dubbed the "performance is king" model by Lauri Honko (2000: 13; cf. Finnegan 2007: 192). I cite the oft-quoted manifesto (Finnegan 2007: 193; Jensen 2011: 119–120) penned by the anthropologist Karin Barber (2005: 265–266, emphasis in original [= 2003: 325]):

> In oral traditions, the co-presence of performance and text is of course more difficult to see, because there is no visible, tangible document to contrast with the evanescent utterance. Nonetheless, it is clear that what happens in most oral performances is not pure instantaneity, pure evanescence, pure emergence and disappearance into the vanishing moment. The exact contrary is usually the case. There is a performance—but it is a performance *of* something. Something identifiable is understood to have pre-existed the moment of utterance. Or, alternatively, something is understood to be constituted in utterance that can be abstracted or detached from the immediate context and re-embodied in a future performance. Even if the only place this "something" can be held to exist is in people's minds or memories, still it is surely distinguishable from immediate, and immediately disappearing, actual utterance. It can be referred to. People may speak of "the story of Sunjata" or "the praises of Dingaan" rather than speaking of a particular narrator's or praise-singer's performance on a particular occasion. And this capacity to be abstracted, to transcend the moment, and to be identified independently of particular instantiations, is the whole point of oral traditions. They are "traditions" because they are known to be shared and to have been handed down; they can be shared and handed down because they have been constituted precisely in order to be detachable from the immediate context, and capable of being transmitted in time and disseminated in space. Creators and transmitters of oral genres use every resource at their disposal to consolidate utterance into quasi-autonomous texts.

Two points stand out here. First, a tale is felt to exist independently of any one enunciation (cf. Finnegan 2011: 162; Frog 2011: 10–11). Second, this phenomenon arises when oral performers craft something "that is woven together in order to attract attention and outlast the moment"

(Barber 2007: 2). Barber joins scholars from a range of disciplines in calling that something "an oral text" (2007: 1–2; cf. Doane 1991: 78; Joubert 2004: 6n5, 89–90). One need not, then, speak, as Pietro Pucci does (1987: 27, 30), of oral performers "writing" in Jacques Derrida's sense to be able to say that they produce texts. "Writing," Barber avers, "is not what confers textuality" (2007: 1). Oral performers produce oral texts. Observe that this use of the term "oral text" differs from the use of the term to refer to a written document that results from the textualization of an oral performance (Finnegan 2007: 10 with n9).

Performers impart textuality—the attributes that make a text—to a verbal act through strategies of what linguistic anthropologists call "entextualization." Entextualization is "the process of rendering a given instance of discourse a text, detachable from its local context" (Urban 1996: 21; cf. Bauman and Briggs 1990: 73; Wilce 2009: 32–33). To be clear, entextualization differs from textualization: the latter refers to the recording of the verbal component of an oral text in written form (cf. Honko 2000; Ready 2015). Although, as Barber observes (2005: 267), some scholars conflate the terms (A.-L. Siikala 2000; McCall 2011: 23), the production of an oral text merits its own label. The strategies of entextualization are numerous and variable (cf. Bauman and Briggs 1990: 74; Barber 2005: 268), but I highlight the following.

Richard Bauman stresses the formal component: entextualization requires fashioning an utterance that is "bounded off to a degree from its discursive surround (its co-text), internally cohesive (tied together by various formal devices), and coherent (semantically intelligible)" (2004: 4). Bauman and Charles Briggs note, "From a formal perspective, this line of inquiry takes us into familiar territory," and they point to the contribution of parallelism to entextualization (1990: 74; cf. Wilce 2009: 34). Take, for instance, a portion of a tale told by Howard Bush whom Bauman recorded in Nova Scotia (Bauman 2004: 121):

> He went hóme,
> he went to béd,
> and he had nó rést the whóle níght.
> He coúldn't gét asléep, he sáid.
> He was pláying cárds with the dévil all níght.
> He had nó rést at áll, he sáid.
> He was . . . like it séemed he wás in a bláze of fíre.
> "That séttled the cárd playing thére," he sáid.
> It séttled hím and it séttled it thére.

Bauman comments,

> The passage is marked, first of all, by parallel syntactic constructions in the first six lines and the last two lines of the above excerpt, making for two parallel sets. This is not the hesitant, repetitive, insecure parallelism of the earlier examples; beginning with "He went home," Bush's voice becomes louder, more forceful, and higher in pitch, and in the seventh line the quoted speech of the uncle's statement takes on a shift in voice, reenacting his emphatic delivery. Moreover, the lines display perceptible patterns of rhythmic stress, with a single beat in the first two lines and four in each of the remaining lines (in the sixth line, the four beats occur after the false start): . . . This is a breakthrough into performance, signaled, or keyed, by this confidently rendered, mutually reinforcing set of formal devices: syntactic, prosodic, and paralinguistic.

Bush breaks through into performance and moves to entextualize. As Bauman and Briggs explain, "Full performance seems to be associated with the most marked entextualization" (1990: 74). In Bush's telling, formal devices give shape to the utterance and endow it with textuality.

In her discussions of entextualization, Barber begins by finding evidence for the desire to fix words in the practice of attaching texts to objects (2007: 76):

> Oral texts in Africa are often actually attached to or secreted in material objects. The Luba *lukasa* board, Zulu bead messages, Dahomeyan *récades* or message-staffs, Asante *adinkra* symbols, gold weights and umbrella finials, and a host of other material repositories and memory-prompts operate in different ways to transcend time, to fix or trap text in a material form. Kwesi Yankah describes a system by which in certain parts of the Akan-speaking area of Ghana, newly coined sayings were "registered" by being associated with a mnemonic object which would then be hung on a string from the ceiling of a proverb-custodian's house.

Such efforts are "the most vivid indication of the desire to consolidate fleeting speech," "the most visible form of a much wider impulse to consolidate spoken words into compact formulations" (Barber 2005: 268–269).

From here, Barber draws attention to two other mechanisms of entextualization beyond the sort Bauman and Briggs study. First, casting a verbal act as a quotation positions it as a text: quotation "foreground[s] the perception that these words preexisted their present moment of utterance and could also continue to exist after it" (Barber 2005: 268; cf. 1999: 19). By introducing a statement with "As the elders say . . ." or "Listen/how this hero must be lamented," "the performer draws attention to the preexistence of the formulation, to its character as already-constituted text" (Barber 2007: 77–78). This "preexistence" implies portability and transportability; it implies that the utterance could be repeated in a different setting. This detachability is at the heart of entextualization.

Barber also discusses under the rubric of quotation moments in which performers use material from different genres in their texts and thereby endow the incorporated material with textuality (cf. Tarkka 2016: 184). She thus builds on scholarship on generic dialogue: how a text belonging to one genre can include material belonging to another genre or other genres (Tarkka 2013: 93–100). Barber writes (2007: 78–79, emphasis in original):

> Quotation also takes place *between* genres, when one genre incorporates chunks of other genres and subsumes them to its own project—but in such a way that they retain recognisable features. In this way the performer highlights them as a resource that already existed and was available for use when he/she undertook the performance. Yorùbá praise poetry—*oríkì*—incorporates divination verses, riddles and proverbs, in each case displaying them as recognisable genres while using them to redound to the honour of the person being praised. Strongly marked, immediately recognisable genre characteristics are retained. . . . The open weave of *oríkì* allows great chunks of other genres to be incorporated with their genre markers intact. . . . These strategies underline and consolidate the "text-ness" of the materials incorporated. By being recontextualised within another genre, their characteristic features are thrown into relief and their preexistence as text is affirmed.

Barber finds exegesis operating as a second mechanism of entextualization. Explication of an utterance keeps it at the forefront of one's consciousness and helps it to outlast the moment. It also suggests that the text exists on its own out in the world as an object for contemplation and analysis (cf. Barber 2007: 100). Barber observes that exegesis can take place within a text, as happens in Asante praise poetry (2007: 97):

> For example, *Okoro-man-so-fone* ("The one who goes to a town and causes everyone to [become] emaciate[d]") is elaborated with *A wo ne no twe manso wofon* ("If you have a legal battle with him, you [become] emaciate[d]"). The second line explains the context—litigation—in which the subject's devastating impact on other people is felt; without this elaboration, the praise epithet would be completely baffling. These internal expansions present and consolidate the text without fully constituting its meaning.

Exegesis can also take the form of explaining a previous utterance and doing so in a different genre. For instance (2007: 80):

> The most common form of obscurity, however, and the hallmark of African praise poetry, is the laconic formulation that can only be interpreted in the light of a narrative or a highly specific circumstance that is not implicit in the words themselves, but has to be supplied by an interpreter drawing on a separate parallel tradition. . . . The performer has to learn two repertoires, two genres, not one.

By subjecting an utterance or stretch of discourse to scrutiny—by making it "the focus of sustained attention and discussion" (2007: 77)—the exegete "reinforces its consolidation as text" (2005: 272).

Barber's analysis of exegesis dovetails with her analysis of quotation. She points out that quotation operates as a form of commentary or evaluation, be it endorsement, questioning, or dissent: "in resaying what someone else has said or even what you yourself have said on another occasion there is always an implied interpretation" (Sherzer 1983: 205, quoted in Barber 2007: 230n5). One might imagine a spectrum of response to an utterance, ranging from implicit interpretation to detailed exegesis. Whatever the response, the mere fact of response renders the utterance "an object of attention" (Barber 2007: 79) and thereby contributes to its entextualization.

To sum up: one can speak of an oral text both when a performer repeats a stretch of discourse heard elsewhere and when a performer crafts a stretch of discourse to be the object of attention, reflection, replication, or commentary (cf. Barber 2007: 33). Several discursive strategies, employed both during and after the relevant stretch of discourse, entextualize it—that is, they endow it with textuality. Scholars also highlight nondiscursive mechanisms of entextualization, such as melody and gestures (Wilce 2009: 35–40), but I will discuss those in a subsequent presentation.

The researchers who have promulgated and applied the concept of entextualization work with a variety of genres. Many of Bauman's essays look at storytellers. Barber writes a lot on praise poetry but attends as well to the ways in which "certain styles of epic narrative are best seen as open-ended assemblages of free-standing or semi-autonomous components" (2007: 214). In a book on the oral literature, ranging from proverbs to praise poems to epic ballads, of the Haya in western Tanzania, Peter Seitel deploys the concept of entextualization, defining it as "the generic finalization of style" (1999: 18). (By finalization, he means "the sense of completion achieved in an artistic work" [17], and by style, he means "concrete verbal patternings" [29].) Lotte Tarkka explores the use of entextualized proverbs in nineteeth- and early twentieth-century Kalevala-meter poetry, including some epic, from the Viena Karelian parish of Vuokkiniemi in Finland (2016). In a book devoted to the Siri epic of the Tulu people of Karnataka, in southern India, Lauri Honko speaks like those who utilize the model of entextualization, even though he criticizes one of Bauman and Briggs's discussions of entextualization (1990) for "burning the bridges to the very arena where the folkloric act is taking place and finding acclaim" (1998: 149–151, quotation from 150). Honko observes, for instance, "Without boundaries there is no text, and without coherence there is no textuality" (1998: 141), and he points to "the source of textuality: the coherence which gives interpretability to the text" (143; cf. 146). Of oral epics he writes, "Oral epics are clearly bounded even if flexibly used textual products" (143).

The performance paradigm has proven productive for scholars working with a host of genres and in a host of cultures, and Homerists have profited from it as well. So, too, has the model of entextualization, a refinement of our understanding of performance (Barber 2005: 268, 2007: 86), proven useful for scholars investigating a range of genres, including epic, in a range of cultures, and the Homerist should benefit from it as well. That colleagues in classical studies have begun to see the value of this concept further encourages this application (cf. Thomas 2012: 230; Karanika 2014: 18–19, 179).

In the next part of this chapter, I use the model of entextualization to elucidate both the representation of performance in the Homeric epics and the performance of the Homeric epics. I focus solely on discursive modes of entextualization and reserve for another occasion an analysis of nondiscursive mechanisms. I spend the bulk of my time investigating the existence and creation of oral texts in the world of the Homeric characters. I then look briefly at the narrator text and the poems *tout court* before drawing an inference about the poet's own desire to entextualize.

APPLICATION TO HOMERIC EPIC

I divide this part of the chapter into four subsections. The first subsection takes two steps in beginning to apply to the Homeric epics the work of the linguistic anthropologists cited earlier. First, I show that in the world constructed in the Homeric epics something preexists a performance and can be passed along to others, who can in turn pass it along to still others. Second, I show that utterances in that world can acquire an object-like status. That preparation allows me, in the second and third subsections, to begin querying the production of oral texts by performers in the Homeric epics and the mechanisms of entextualization they employ. In the fourth subsection, I broaden the inquiry to include the narrator text and the poems in their entirety.

The Preexistence of Oral Texts and Their Object-Like Status in Homeric Epic

In the Homeric poems, nonbardic tellers perform tales and bards and nonprofessional singers perform songs of varying lengths and genres (cf. Scodel 2002a: 73–74). Homeric characters think of these tales and songs as independently preexisting entities that performers and audience members know or know of. That is, whereas scholars have brought out the extent to which Homer alludes to other stories, be they real or imagined (Sammons 2010: 33–34, 68, 209; West 2011a: 28; Tsagalis 2014: 240–244; Currie 2016: 140–143), and whereas the characters tell many stories about the past, often for paradigmatic purposes (see pp. 346–347), I assemble here some passages that do not just refer to other stories but suggest a vision of the preexistence of tales and songs on specific subjects.

Penelope claims that Phemios has a repertoire of enchanting songs from which he can pick and choose (cf. González 2013: 193, 269). She then asks him to stop singing that (*tautēs*) particular song that always (*aiei*) makes her upset (*Odyssey* 1.337–342). In his rejoinder, Telemachos cites that song by name: "the evil fate of the Danaans" (*Odyssey* 1.350;

cf. 1.326–327 with Ford 1992: 20–21). As Jukka Siikala observes, "The names of narratives essentialise them as something, which can be lifted up from one context and replicated in another" (2003: 32). When Nestor urges Telemachos to emulate Orestes, Telemachos states, "The Achaians / will carry his glory far and wide and a song for those to come" (καὶ οἱ Ἀχαιοὶ / οἴσουσι κλέος εὐρὺ καὶ ἐσσομένοισιν ἀοιδήν, *Odyssey* 3.203–204). Tellers and singers alike will know and audiences will be able to request the story or song about Orestes. Odysseus asks Demodokos to sing "the song [*kosmon*] of the wooden horse" (*Odyssey* 8.492, trans. González 2013: 198). Kalypso evokes the story of the Argonauts' expedition when she speaks of the Argo as *pasi melousa* (*Odyssey* 12.70), which means something like "sung by all poets" or "taken up by everyone in stories" (see Dräger 1993: 14–18). Aineias refers to any number of well-known stories—"famed words" (*proklut' . . . epea*)—about Achilleus's ancestors and his own as well (*Iliad* 20.203–204). The phrase might even refer to "poetic words" (Nagy 1999a: 271). Characters point to the existence of familiar stories with the phrase "they say" (*phasi*) (cf. O'Maley forthcoming, section 1.2). Agamemnon positions his review of Tydeus's victories over the Kadmeians in games and battle as a recollection of stories told about Tydeus: "men say [*phasi*] that he was preeminent over all" (*Iliad* 4.375). Telemachos alludes to stories about Odysseus's exceptional cunning (*mētis*): "for they say [*phas'*] / you have the best mind among men for craft [*mētin*]" (*Odyssey* 23.124–125).

S. Douglas Olson traces the "network of gossip, rumor, and reputation" so prominent in the society envisioned by the *Odyssey* (1995: 1–23). Building on his discussion of the transmission of stories and information, I note that, as entities that ostensibly preexist independently, songs and tales can be passed around and down. The poet references nonheroic, occasional songs (N. Richardson 2011; cf. Karanika 2014: 22–23, 52–67, 117–132). As a group, the Achaians sing a paean (*aeidontes paiēona*) to propitiate Apollo (*Iliad* 1.472–474). Weddings take place in one of the cities depicted on Achilleus's shield, and "loud rose the bridal song [*humenaios*]" (*Iliad* 18.493; cf. Hesiod *Shield* 274). Wherever these songs fall on a spectrum ranging from "simply a matter of refrains or cries (such as ὑμὴν ὦ ὑμέναιε, ἰὴ παιῆον, etc.)" to "a more elaborate form of choral song" (N. Richardson 2011: 27), individuals will have learned these traditional standards from someone else. Just so, someone taught the Linos song to the boy (*pais*) singing it on Achilleus's shield (*Iliad* 18.569–571), and the harvesters, if they sing the song's refrain (N. Richardson 2011: 28), learned it from others.[3] Odysseus passes on to the Phaiakians a song (*aoidēn*) performed by the Sirens (*Odyssey* 12.183–192), even if it is not the song they promise to sing, the one that traps their audience (Karanika 2014: 50; Schur 2014). Achilleus sings "the glorious deeds of men" (*klea andrōn, Iliad* 9.189), songs that he presumably picked up from listening to a bard, such as Demodokos, who sings *klea andrōn* (*Odyssey* 8.73). Patroklos perhaps waits to continue the singing once Achilleus leaves off (*Iliad* 9.190–191) (Nagy 2003: 43–44; González 2013: 372–377): he has learned what to sing, too.

To be sure, "not only do poets not learn from other poets, they do not learn from anyone except the gods" (Scodel 2002a: 78). The epics famously mystify the process by which professional singers of heroic song master their craft. Yet two passages might offer a peek behind the curtain, the second even more so than the first: Telemachos defends Phemios when he sings the newest song to "circulate" (*amphipelētai, Odyssey* 1.352) and asserts that men will carry the song of Orestes far and wide (*oisousi . . . aoidēn, Odyssey* 3.204). Both statements can be read as indicating a process of transmission from singer to singer (cf. p. 9).

As for tale telling, Phoinix speaks of how "we learn the stories about men of old" (τῶν πρόσθεν ἐπευθόμεθα κλέα ἀνδρῶν, *Iliad* 9.524) (cf. Scodel 1998: 174). Telemachos speculates that Nestor or Menelaos may have heard an account (*muthon akousas*) from another traveler (*Odyssey* 3.94–95 = 4.324–325). In reporting to Telemachos on the returns of the Achaians from Troy, Nestor also points to a process of transmission: "As many things as I learn by inquiry [*peuthomai*] sitting here in my palace, / this you shall know [*daēseai*]" (*Odyssey* 3.186–187) (cf. Olson 1995: 13).

The second part of my preparation starts from Barber's assertion: "Everywhere in African orature there is evidence of a will to fix speech, to give it the compact solidity and durability of a material object" (2007: 75). This same idea—an utterance can acquire an object-like status—crops up repeatedly in Homeric epic. The utterances of performers are objectified. The noun *aoidē* "is an action noun and therefore describes poetry not as something completed and stable, but as something in progress. . . . It consequently refers to something that is closer to activity and performance than to a text or an aesthetic object" (Tsagalis 2004: 4; cf. González 2013: 190). Yet one cannot help but translate the noun as "song" (Nagy 1999a: 37–38; Ford 1992: 108; Tsagalis 2004: 3). This slippage occurs in part because the language used with the noun *aoidē* aligns it with objects. Penelope asks Phemios to cease from "this sad song" (*aoidēs / lugrēs*) (*Odyssey* 1.340–341). The adjective sums up the list "wars, throwing spears with polished hafts, and the arrows" (*Odyssey* 14.225–226) and describes the clothes (*heimata*) with which Odysseus disguises himself as a beggar (*Odyssey* 16.457). Agamemnon predicts, "The immortals will make a lovely song for prudent Penelope for earthly beings" (τεύξουσι δ' ἐπιχθονίοισιν ἀοιδὴν / ἀθάνατοι χαρίεσσαν ἐχέφρονι Πηνελοπείηι, *Odyssey* 24.197–198). The verb (*teuxousi*) places the song in the realm of craft (Ford 1992: 38; Grandolini 1996: 167 at 197): Hephaistos makes (*teuxe*) armor for Achilleus (*Iliad* 18.609–613); Arete and her maids make (*teuxe*) clothes (*Odyssey* 7.235). The adjective (*khariessan*) aligns the song with clothes (*Iliad* 5.905, 6.90, 22.511; *Odyssey* 5.231, 10.544), temples (*Iliad* 1.39), and gifts (*dōra*) (*Iliad* 8.204, 9.599), as well as with the works of a smith (*Odyssey* 6.234 = 23.161) and a weaver (*Odyssey* 10.223). The mourners at Hektor's tomb sing a "sorrowful song" (*stonoessan aoidēn*, *Iliad* 24.721). The adjective elsewhere describes spears, arrows, and other missiles hurled in battle (*Iliad* 8.159, 15.590, 17.374; *Odyssey* 21.12, 21.60, 24.180).

Going beyond *aoidē*, I cite other relevant passages. Alkinoös wants Odysseus to "rejoice in the feast and in listening to the tale [*humnon*] of the song" (*Odyssey* 8.429) (or, more technically, the "weaving" of the song [Nagy 2009a: 231]). The Homeric use of *humnos* depicts "the performance of epic song . . . as a product manufactured by tying or sewing" (González 2013: 397; cf. Nagy 2009a: 322–323) or depicts "epic song . . . as something 'bound' or 'linked' together, fitting very well . . . with the metaphorical image of οἴμη" (Duffy and Short 2016: 66).[4] Men transport stories and songs (*oisousi kleos . . . aoidēn*, *Odyssey* 3.204) just as they transport gold from a sacked city (*oisei*, *Iliad* 2.229), a sacrificial animal (*oisete . . . oisomen*, *Iliad* 3.103–104), or a lyre (*oisetō*, *Odyssey* 8.255) (cf. Olson 1995: 12n25). Antenor recollects that Odysseus and Menelaos "wove speeches" (*muthous . . . huphainon*, *Iliad* 3.212), and various characters "weave a spoken counsel," such as Nestor (*huphainein . . . mētin*, *Iliad* 7.324) and the suitors (*mētin huphainon*, *Odyssey* 4.678): Helen weaves (*huphaine*) a robe (*Iliad* 3.125) (cf. Scheid and Svenbro 1996: 112–114; González 2013: 364–365; Karanika 2014: 40). When Alkinoös declares that Odysseus's tale exhibits "a shapeliness" (*morphē*, *Odyssey* 11.367), he assigns it a degree of materiality, or at least "a visible quality" (Bassi 2016: 65; cf. 95). Alkinoös also asks Odysseus to "tell me the wondrous deeds [*theskela erga*]" (*Odyssey* 11.374), and a bit later Odysseus refers to Herakles's belt with its depictions of "wondrous deeds" (*theskela erga*, *Odyssey* 11.610): "The compositional ring . . . establishes an equivalence between Odysseus's narration and the crafted artifact" (Elmer 2005: 24–25). Eumaios speculates that the disguised Odysseus might "fashion a story" (*epos paratektēnaio*) to get a cloak (*Odyssey* 14.131): Tekton "built" (*tektēnato*) ships for Paris (*Iliad* 5.62) (cf. Worman 2002: 80). Aineias describes reproaches (*oneidea*) as a cargo that would overwhelm a ship with one hundred benches (*Iliad* 20.246–247) (cf. Martin 1989: 17).

Epos and *epea*, both used by characters and narrators alike to label the speech of characters, "have a reference not shared by muthos, to speech as utterance, as thing heard and transmitted, as an item of exchange that is at the same time a physical object, like a weapon" (Martin 1989: 30). Speeches labeled with the more precise phrase *pukinon epos*, used only by characters, are to be characterized as "enduring through time, unassailable in the way of well-constructed, solid, or dense-packed objects in the poem that are called *pukinon*" (Martin 1989: 36; cf. 18).

Andromache Karanika notes that in the *Odyssey* "female speech acts are voiced in the context of work," such as textile making, and argues that this "careful emphasis on the female setting prepares the narrative to entextualize the speech act" (2014: 30, 41; cf. 75). I have traced in a more concrete fashion how Homer—"arguably the first materialist in the West" (J. Porter 2010: 127)—depicts many utterances as object-like, akin to Pindar's aligning his poetry with objects (Steiner 1994: 91–99; Dougherty 2001: 41; J. Porter 2010: 462–463; Phillips 2016: 2). That an utterance can be like an object does not mean that it lasts forever—as Homeric characters are well aware, things decay (*Iliad* 2.135, 23.326–333) or can be broken (*Iliad* 13.507, 14.55–56, 15.469; *Odyssey* 12.409) (cf. Ford 1992: 144–145, 152, 171; Garcia 2013: 52–54, 115, 150)—but does suggest its durability: after all, characters give one another gifts as mementos of their interaction in the belief that the objects will last (*Iliad* 23.615–619; *Odyssey* 15.123–128, 21.40). I connect the objectification of utterances, then, with the fact that characters envision songs and tales as preexisting entities that can be passed around and down. Both moves suggest that certain utterances can achieve textual status. They can outlast the moment.

As I will now demonstrate, Homeric characters fashion oral texts and use the mechanisms of entextualization reviewed in the first part of this chapter to do so. I should make clear that, whereas the depiction of poets and poetry has figured prominently in the analysis so far, in the following subsections I concentrate on the nonbardic characters' performances (cf. Martin 1989). I find it helpful to quote Barber once again: "The process of entextualization is ubiquitous in everyday life. It is not reserved for the production of monumental works of art" (2007: 209; cf. Karanika 2014: 114).

Source Texts and Entextualization

My present task is to trace the representation of oral texts in the world of the characters. In that world, the most explicit flagging of the production of an oral text, an utterance intended to outlast the moment, comes when one character tells another to pass along what he says to a third party. Scholarship labels this kind of event a "mediational routine": a source generates an oral text for a mediator to relay to an audience (Bauman 2004: 132–133; cf. de Jong 2004a: 180–181, 241–243; Kelly 2007: 325–329). Two contextually distinct texts result: the source utterance or text generated by the source in a source dialogue and the target utterance or text generated by the mediator in a target dialogue. To be fair, source texts do not reveal any more of an effort to entextualize than one might find in other passages. Stylization marks all of Homeric discourse (Martin 1989: 45, 225; Karanika 2014: 24), and one could detect, for instance, efforts at cohesion in many stretches of verse from either the narrator text or the character text (cf. Friedrich 2000: 14; Graziosi and Haubold 2015: 10). But in the world of the characters source dialogues stand out as sites of entextualization because they foreground the goal of entextualization, namely "making words stick" (Barber 2007: 67).

In examining these scenes, then, one notes the source's insistence that the mediator pass on what he is about to say: (B) in what follows. That declaration indicates a desire to fashion an utterance that will "spite the power of time" (Bauman 2004: 147). One also encounters another overture to entextualization. The external narrator, and sometimes the source himself, points to the production of an entextualized oral utterance by marking the entire speech that includes the source text as a performance: (A) in what follows. For, as mentioned earlier, performers work to entextualize, and I add here Bauman and Briggs's reminder that "performance as a frame intensifies entextualization" (1990: 74). As James Wilce explains, "The very act of performing entails making oneself accountable for the very sort of structuring, coherence, and memorability we have been calling entextualization" (2009: 34). Finally, the source prepares for the reproduction of the source text—that is, of the message proper. He entextualizes his utterance by stitching it together via various formal devices: (C) in what follows. I analyze here two scenes from the *Iliad* in which Zeus generates a source text.

Zeus sends Dream to deliver a message to Agamemnon (*Iliad* 2.7–16):

> καί μιν φωνήσας ἔπεα πτερόεντα προσηύδα·
> "βάσκ' ἴθι, οὖλε Ὄνειρε, θοὰς ἐπὶ νῆας Ἀχαιῶν·
> ἐλθὼν ἐς κλισίην Ἀγαμέμνονος Ἀτρεΐδαο
> πάντα μάλ' ἀτρεκέως ἀγορευέμεν, ὡς ἐπιτέλλω.
> θωρῆξαί ἑ κέλευε κάρη κομόωντας Ἀχαιοὺς
> πανσυδίῃ· νῦν γάρ κεν ἕλοι πόλιν εὐρυάγυιαν
> Τρώων. οὐ γὰρ ἔτ' ἀμφὶς Ὀλύμπια δώματ' ἔχοντες
> ἀθάνατοι φράζονται· ἐπέγναμψεν γὰρ ἅπαντας

Ἥρη λισσομένη, Τρώεσσι δὲ κήδε᾽ ἐφῆπται."[5]
ὣς φάτο· βῆ δ᾽ ἄρ Ὄνειρος, ἐπεὶ τὸν μῦθον ἄκουσε,

And he spoke, and addressed him with winged words:
"Up, go, destructive Dream, to the swift ships of the Achaians,
and when you come to the hut of Agamemnon, son of Atreus,
tell him everything exactly as I charge you.
Tell him to arm the long-haired Achaians
with all speed, since now he may take the broad-wayed city
of the Trojans. For the immortals who have their homes on Olympus
are no longer divided in counsel, since Hera has bent the minds of all
by her entreaties, and sorrows have been fastened on the Trojans."
So he spoke, and Dream set out, when he had heard the command.

(A) Verses 7 and 16 mark Zeus's speech as a performance. Martin shows that the phrase *epea pteroenta* ("winged words") is "a synonymous phrase for muthos" (1989: 30; cf. 69), and verse 16 reminds one of that fact. In turn, the word *muthos* labels a performance (Martin 1989: 12, 47, 54, 88–89, 231) in the sense outlined by Bauman, which I quote again for ease of reference: "performance as a mode of spoken verbal communication consists in the assumption of responsibility to an audience for a display of communicative competence" (1977: 11). The phrase "winged words" also testifies to the nature of Zeus's performance: he performs a directive (Martin 1989: 31–32, 46). The content of the speech from its beginning makes clear that the directive takes the form of a command (Martin 1989: 51; cf. Minchin 2007: 196–203, 211–215), as it always does when Zeus utters "winged words" (cf. *Iliad* 4.69, 15.48, 15.157, 19.341). In turn, commands constitute one of the genres in which Homeric characters perform (Martin 1989: 47–66). So even if one disagrees with Martin's interpretation of "winged words" (cf. D. Beck 2005: 43), one can still understand Zeus to be performing a command. Zeus doubles down on performing commands insofar as his command to Dream includes a command that Dream is to pass on to Agamemnon (cf. D. Beck 2012: 15).

(B) Verse 10 signals Zeus's desire to create an oral text that will endure, but the phrase *bask' ithi* in verse 8 strongly hints in that direction: five of the six appearances of this phrase initiate a mediational routine (Kelly 2007: 61, 324–325).

(C) The repetition in sound engendered by the double consonant ξ followed by the palatals κ and χ holds the initial verse 11 together: θωρῆξαί ἑ κέλευε κάρη κομόωντας Ἀχαιοὺς. The first component of a textual package itself coheres as a textual package. The threefold repetition of *gar* points up the textuality of Zeus's entire speech (cf. Martin 1989: 51). Each sentence explains the previous one: Agamemnon should arm the Achaians *because* he will now take Troy *because* the gods have settled their dispute over the city *because* they acceded to Hera's supplication and suffering awaits the Trojans. As a result, Zeus progresses ever backward in time (epic regression): Agamemnon will in the (not-too-distant) *future* take the city because of the *current* arrangement among the gods that is due to what has recently transpired in the *past* (cf. Brügger, Stoevesandt, and Visser 2010: 14 at 11–15). The final clause—Τρώεσσι δὲ κήδε' ἐφῆπται (lit. "and on the Trojans sorrows have been fastened")—partially rehearses this sequence: that the Trojans will in the *future* suffer pains has been determined in the recent *past*. In recapitulating in shorter compass the temporal dynamic of verses 12 through the first half of 15, this final clause provides a suitable ending for this stretch of text.

Enjambment contributes to the passage's cohesion, too, with each verse of the message connecting syntactically to the previous one (Clark 1997a: 162): the adverb *pansudiēi* at the start of verse 12 modifies the infinitive *thōrēxai* of verse 11; the genitive *Trōōn* at the start of verse 13 depends on the accusative *polin* in verse 12; verse 14 provides a verb (*phrazontai*) for the nominative *ekhontes* of verse 13; in verse 15, *Hērē* specifies the subject of verse 14's *epegnampsen*. Whether or not these connections render the verses "dramatic" (Clark 1997a: 162), they knit Zeus's text together.

Later, Zeus sends Iris to deliver a message to Athena and Hera (*Iliad* 8.398–408, 412):

> Ἶριν δ' ὤτρυνε χρυσόπτερον ἀγγελέουσαν·
> "βάσκ' ἴθι, Ἶρι ταχεῖα, πάλιν τρέπε μηδ' ἔα ἄντην
> ἔρχεσθ'· οὐ γὰρ καλὰ συνοισόμεθα πτόλεμόνδε.
> ὧδε γὰρ ἐξερέω, τὸ δὲ καὶ τετελεσμένον ἔσται·
> γυιώσω μέν σφωιν ὑφ' ἅρμασιν ὠκέας ἵππους,
> αὐτὰς δ' ἐκ δίφρου βαλέω κατά θ' ἅρματα ἄξω·
> οὐδέ κεν ἐς δεκάτους περιτελλομένους ἐνιαυτοὺς
> ἕλκε' ἀπαλθήσεσθον, ἅ κεν μάρπτηισι κεραυνός·
> ὄφρ' εἰδῆι γλαυκῶπις, ὅτ' ἂν ὧι πατρὶ μάχηται.
> Ἥρηι δ' οὔ τι τόσον νεμεσίζομαι οὐδὲ χολοῦμαι·
> αἰεὶ γάρ μοι ἔωθεν ἐνικλᾶν ὅττι νοήσω."
> . . .
> . . . Διὸς δέ σφ' ἔννεπε μῦθον· 412

and he sent golden-winged Iris to carry a message:
"Up, go, swift Iris; turn them back and do not allow them to come
face to face with me, for it will be no good thing if we join in combat.
For thus I will speak and surely this thing will come to pass.
I will maim their swift horses beneath their chariot,
and themselves will I hurl from the chariot, and will break the chariot in pieces;
nor in the space of ten circling years will they be healed
of the wounds which the thunderbolt inflicts;
so that she of the flashing eyes may know what it is to fight against her own father.
But against Hera I have not such great indignation or wrath,
since she is always in the habit of thwarting me in whatever I devise."
. . .
. . . and [Iris] declared to them the command of Zeus:

(A) For Martin, verse 412 holds the key: it refers to Zeus's speech as a *muthos* and thereby characterizes it as a performance (1989: 51–54). I suggest that the earlier speech introduction (398) characterizes Zeus's speech as the performance of a command. To begin with, the verb *otrunō* readily partners with verbs meaning "to order": "since so had Nestor charged [*epetelleto*] them / when he urged [*otrunōn*] them to the battle from the black ships" (*Iliad* 17.382–383); "Telemachos then urged and ordered [*epotrunas ekeleusen*] his companions / to lay hold of the tackle, and they listened to his urging [*otrunontos*]" (*Odyssey* 2.422–423) (cf. *Iliad* 5.461–463; *Odyssey* 23.264). More important, when the verb appears in a verse introducing a speech, such as "he came to the old king's side and roused [*ōtrunen*] him" (*Iliad* 3.249), the speech includes a command (see also *Iliad* 10.158, 11.185, 15.560, 15.568, 24.143; *Odyssey* 6.254, 7.341, 10.546, 12.206; cf. *Iliad* 5.461, 13.44). Zeus twice elsewhere functions as the subject of such a verse (*Iliad* 11.185, 24.143). Similarly, when the verb appears in a verse concluding a speech, such as "so was the old man urging [*ōtrune*] them on" (*Iliad* 4.310), that speech includes a command (see also *Iliad* 12.277, 16.210; *Odyssey* 8.15). Four of Zeus's speeches conclude this way (*Iliad* 4.73, 19.349, 22.186; *Odyssey* 24.487). Finally, on two other occasions, the poet couples *otrunō* and a word from the root *aggel-*: "speed [*otrunai*] the man along to the city / to take your message [*aggeliēn*] to circumspect Penelope" (*Odyssey* 15.40–41); "or shall we send her a messenger" (*aggelon otrunōmen*) (*Odyssey* 24.405). In both cases, the sense is "order the messenger to deliver a message." These three factors would lead the tradition-oriented audience member to anticipate a command from Zeus upon hearing 398. Again, like in *Iliad* 2, Zeus's performance of a command intended for Iris includes a command that Iris is to pass on to Hera and Athena (see 412).

(B) Verse 401 highlights Zeus's wish to craft an utterance that lasts.

(C) In commenting on the "verbal texture" of Zeus's speech, Martin points to "the amplitude of his rhetoric, achieved by repetition and synonymity" (1989: 53). Additional features merit attention. Verses 402 to 408 fall into three segments: two verses, two verses, and three verses. That the final segment takes up one more verse than the others neatly rounds off the text (cf. Faraone 2013 on the "superlative cap"). The initial segment of two verses (402–403) contains three finite verbs, each in a clause shorter than the previous one (a descending tricolon). The decreasing length of the three clauses matches Zeus's plan to disable or destroy three entities one at a time: (1) I will lame (a) the swift horses pulling (b) their (c) chariot; (2) hurl (b) them from (c) the chariot; and (3) destroy (c) the chariot. Verses 402 and 403 also have the same sequence of dactyls and spondees: two spondees, three dactyls, and a spondee. The second segment (404–405) offers a memorable image of what happens when Zeus strikes a god with his lightning bolt: the wounds take more than ten years to heal. These two verses present this information only gradually, however, and thereby gain in cohesion. Zeus moves from talking about a length of time to talking about the length of time it takes to recover from wounds to talking about the length of time it takes to recover from wounds inflicted by his lightning bolt. Zeus builds the final three-verse segment (406–408) around an antithesis between Athena and Hera. In addition, the sole use in both epics of *glaukōpis* in the nominative (406) without an accompanying *Athēnē*, a combination found seventy-nine times, and the appearance of *eniklaō* (408), a word that does not recur until Hellenistic poetry, lodge the final segment in the hearer's mind.

In both these scenes, the narrator identifies Zeus as a performer and, therefore, one who will seek to entextualize. Zeus himself makes clear his intention to create an enduring stretch of discourse and then works to entextualize his utterance via formal devices. The performer's preparation of an oral text for subsequent reiteration becomes an essential concern of these scenes.

Other Mechanisms of Entextualization in the Character Text

The two speeches by Zeus illustrate the formal mechanisms of entextualization that performers deploy. This subsection continues to explore the connection between entextualization and performance by looking at the other components of entextualization discussed in the first part of this chapter: quoting, attaching a text to an object, and explicating.

I drew two initial lessons from Barber's discussion of quotation. Casting an utterance as quoted suggests that it existed prior to its present enunciation and could remain in existence afterward. Moreover, quotation implies interpretation and therefore renders the quoted material an object of attention or reflection. Keeping these points in mind, I look at Odysseus's quotation of Kalchas's prophecy during his performance (see *muthon* at *Iliad* 2.282) before the assembled Achaians in *Iliad* 2 (cf. D. Beck 2012: 42–43). While mustering at Aulis, the Achaians saw a serpent eat eight sparrows and the mother-bird too (*Iliad* 2.317–330):

> But when he had devoured the sparrow's little ones and the mother with them
> the god who had brought him to the light made him conspicuous;
> for the son of crooked-counseling Kronos turned him to stone;
> and we stood there and marveled at what had happened.
> So, when the dread portent interrupted the hecatombs of the gods,
> then immediately Kalchas prophesied, and addressed our assembly, saying:
> "Why are you silent, long-haired Achaians?
> To us has Zeus the counselor showed this great sign,
> late in coming, late in fulfillment, the fame of which shall never perish.
> Just as this serpent devoured the sparrow's little ones and the mother with them
> —all eight, and the mother that bore them was the ninth—
> so shall we war there for as many years,
> but in the tenth we shall take the broad-wayed city."
> Thus spoke Kalchas, and now all this is being brought to pass.

Gregory Nagy writes, "The quoting itself is a demonstration of the unchangeability of these poetic words" (2003: 29). I reverse that proposition. Quoting provides the utterance with "unchangeability" and entextualizes it because it suggests the preexistence and so transportability of the text. Moreover, having quoted the utterance, Odysseus explicitly makes it an object of analysis: "now all this is being brought to pass." Kalchas's prophecy, he says, was correct. This tactic, too, suggests the utterance's independent existence, its "out-there-ness" (Barber 2007: 100).

I likewise build on Nagy's discussion of Penelope's dream. Beginning an exchange of *muthoi* (*Odyssey* 19.508) with the disguised Odysseus, Penelope asks him to interpret a dream she had in which an eagle killed her twenty pet geese and then returned to explain the event (*Odyssey* 19.535, 544–551):

> But come, listen to a dream of mine and interpret it for me.
> . . .
> But he came back again and perched on the jut of the gabled
> roof. He now had a human voice and spoke aloud to me:
> "Do not fear, O daughter of far-famed Ikarios.
> This is no dream, but a blessing real as day. You will see it
> done. The geese are the suitors, and I, the eagle, have been
> a bird of portent, but now I am your own husband, come home,
> and I shall inflict shameless destruction on all the suitors."
> So he spoke; . . .

Odysseus responds (19.555–558):

> Lady, it is impossible to read this dream and avoid it
> by turning it another way, since Odysseus himself has told you
> its meaning, how it will end. The suitors' doom is evident
> for one and all. Not one will avoid his death and destruction.

Nagy interprets the passage as follows (2003: 25):

> But there is in fact one way—and only one way—to respond, namely, by repeating the words already quoted by Penelope herself in verses 546–553. For the meaning to be clarified, the quoted words would have to be quoted again, that is, performed. We see at work here the poetic mentality of unchangeability: once the words of response have been performed as a speech-act, they are ready to be quoted again as a fixed and unchangeable saying.

Nagy's reading speaks to my interest in the connection between quotation and entextualization. Whereas he sees the eagle performing a speech act that becomes "fixed and unchangeable," I suggest that, once Penelope quotes the words of the eagle, they can be quoted again because Penelope's action has enhanced their textuality. Her act of quotation implies the words' preexistence and subsequent survival. Moreover, Penelope makes another entextualizing move when she explicitly makes her quotation an object of analysis.

In Barber's model, quotation also includes the incorporation of material that belongs to a different genre. To repeat, performers incorporate material from other genres "with their genre markers intact": "these strategies underline and consolidate the 'text-ness' of the materials incorporated. By being recontextualised within another genre, their characteristic features are thrown into relief and their preexistence as text is affirmed" (Barber 2007: 78–79). Application of this notion to the Homeric epics (cf. Jensen 2011: 265) can take two forms.

One could borrow Lotte Tarkka's phrasing in her book on Karelian oral poetry and speak of a "generic insert" when the embedded passage comprises "actual" lines found in other instantiations of that genre, not simply "lines that are strongly reminiscent of" another genre (2013: 97). Homer might have incorporated into the character text preexisting material with its genre markers intact. As suggested in portions of an article by André Lardinois (2001b), Homer might have made use of preexisting proverbs. Different authors present gnomai about the same theme but word them in various ways (2001b: 95–97). Homer joins the group here, and many of the proverbs in his poetry likely would have resembled, if not been considered the exact same as (cf. Finnegan 2011: 161), proverbs his audience had heard before. For instance, while engaging in a flyting match and so performing (Martin 1989: 65–77, 141–143), both Menelaos and Achilleus state "what is done even a fool can understand" (ῥεχθὲν δέ τε νήπιος ἔγνω, *Iliad* 17.32, 20.198), a variation of the "learning brings suffering" proverb. The sentiment appears variously expressed also in Aeschylus *Agamemnon* 177 and 250, Pindar *Isthmian* 1.40b, and Hesiod *Works and Days* 218 (Lardinois 2001b: 95–96). For his part, Lardinois speculates that the proverb "had become more or less 'fixed,' at least within hexameter poetry" (2001b: 106). If Homer quotes preexisting proverbs in the character text, he not only, per Barber, affirms the textness of that quoted material but also finds another way to fill the world of his characters with oral texts as they make use of preexisting entextualized sayings.

One could also set aside the question of the preexistence of the material. Barber reviews how in three different traditions of African epic the characters and the narrator present praise poems (2007: 55–58). Just so, starting from the explorations of the various genres of speech (Martin 1989) and the various speech types or formats (Minchin 2007) that Homeric characters put to work, I observe that the characters depicted as performers in Homeric epic entextualize (portions of) what they say by speaking in a generic mode that differs from their usual mode of speaking. This generic shift sets off and renders memorable or even extractable the utterance or the relevant portion of it. To provide two concrete examples of how Homeric epic introduces discrete and distinctive generic modes in the character text, I return to Lardinois's work on proverbs and add Benjamin Sammons's research on catalogues (2010). I look to the fact that each scholar stresses how the material he reviews stands apart from the surrounding narrative.

Lardinois shows that, using a toolkit of formulae and themes, Homeric characters (re)composed proverbs (2001b: 94, 105–107). These tools "constitute a distinct language that helps the speaker to create a gnomic saying extemporaneously and the listener to identify the expression as gnomic" (98). That is, "a number of these lexical and structural features . . . mark[s] the style of these expressions as gnomic" (100; cf. Tarkka 2016: 185). Homeric characters produce recognizably proverbial statements that stand out from the surrounding narrative: for instance, "acoustic elements . . . served to make the text of the gnomai stand out from their context. Expressions displaying such acoustic elements are, as Russo says, 'the equivalent of complete little poems' [1983: 123]" (Lardinois 2001b: 102).

I build on these findings as follows, bringing in two additional points to arrive at a third. First, whether they are performing or not, characters do not speak entirely in proverbs. Second, Homeric characters use proverbs when performing, but proverbs themselves constitute a genre of performance in their own right (Lardinois 1997; Yankah 2012: esp. 20–22; cf. Martin 1989: 77, 102–104, 108). Adding these facts to Lardinois's contribution, I observe that by speaking proverbially a performer can entextualize either a portion or the entirety of his utterance.

Sammons elucidates the generic features of catalogues, "a marked and peculiar manner of speech" (2010: 3). First, the catalogue is "a non-narrative form" (8; cf. Elmer 2005: 28). Second (Sammons 2010: 9, emphasis in original),

> a catalogue is a list of *items* which are specified in discrete *entries*; its entries are formally distinct and arranged in sequence by anaphora or by a simple connective, but are not subordinated to one another, and no explicit relation is made between the items except for their shared suitability to the catalogue's specified *rubric*.

Its distinct formal features mean that a catalogue "is a marked and unusual mode relative to ordinary narrative[;] it stands out from its surroundings" (21). Odysseus's performance among the Phaiakians (Bakker 2009: esp. 131–135) includes a catalogue of women (*Odyssey* 11.235–327), for instance, that is "highly excerptable" (Sammons 2010: 76n35). Beyond always standing apart for these reasons from the surrounding co-text, a Homeric catalogue can evoke a specific genre, distinct from Homer's usual mode. Zeus's catalogue of women (*Iliad* 14.315–328), labeled a *muthos* by Hera (14.330), resembles "a genealogical poem of the Hesiodic type" (Sammons 2010: 64). This notional poem, in offering "one action with many parts"—or "a series of episodes or disparate narrative threads"—"differs, structurally and paradigmatically, from the *Iliad*" (73). Resembling (74, 79) even if "fail[ing] to take the shape of a coherent genealogical history like" the Hesiodic *Catalogue of Women* (92), Odysseus's catalogue of women departs from Homer's concern with "heroes and heroic *kleos*" (84, emphasis in original):

> The catalogue may represent the furthest remove from the kind of heroic tale Alcinous requests. This is because it has least to do with Odysseus qua hero of the Trojan War; because it reaches back to a time *before* Troy and says little about the war; because it focuses on women rather than heroes; and, perhaps, because it is non-narrative in form.

Again, I ask what the performers accomplish with this generic shift. They do not make a habit of talking in catalogues even when performing. When characters generate these catalogues, the resulting generic shift from how they usually talk helps them entextualize portions of what they say.

The entextualization of generically distinct material embedded in the speech of Homeric characters emerges in another phenomenon as well. In this case, I start from Bauman's discussion of *kraftaskáld* legends in Iceland (2004: 15–33). These tellings involve two genres: a *saga* (story) portion and a *vísa* (verse) portion (20). The story recounts how a poet, a *kraftaskáld*, responded to an adverse situation by fashioning verses that have a magical effect. Bauman asks, "*How* are genres brought into dialogue?" (29, emphasis in original)—that is, he studies "for this one dialogic form how that generic contextualization gets done." He observes that in these legends the verse portion not only can be "formally impenetrable" (23) but also can exercise "a strong formative influence on the narrative discourse that follows it; it has the capacity to shape and permeate the narrative beyond its own formal boundaries" (22).

Bauman's analysis of the interaction between an embedded, generically distinct chunk and its co-text prompts consideration of what happens to the surrounding co-text when a Homeric character switches into a distinct generic mode. I suggest that the resulting interaction can aid the entextualization of the generically distinct portion. By way of example, I investigate the catalogue of women that Zeus performs in his attempt to seduce Hera (*Iliad* 14.313–328):

Ἥρη, κεῖσε μέν ἐστι καὶ ὕστερον ὁρμηθῆναι·
νῶι δ' ἄγ' ἐν φιλότητι τραπείομεν εὐνηθέντε.
οὐ γάρ πώ ποτέ μ' ὧδε θεᾶς ἔρος οὐδὲ γυναικὸς
θυμὸν ἐνὶ στήθεσσι περιπροχυθεὶς ἐδάμασσεν,
οὐδ' ὁπότ' ἠρασάμην Ἰξιονίης ἀλόχοιο,
ἣ τέκε Πειρίθοον θεόφιν μήστωρ' ἀτάλαντον·
οὐδ' ὅτε περ Δανάης καλλισφύρου Ἀκρισιώνης,
ἣ τέκε Περσῆα πάντων ἀριδείκετον ἀνδρῶν·
οὐδ' ὅτε Φοίνικος κούρης τηλεκλειτοῖο,
ἣ τέκε μοι Μίνω τε καὶ ἀντίθεον Ῥαδάμανθυν·
οὐδ' ὅτε περ Σεμέλης οὐδ' Ἀλκμήνης ἐνὶ Θήβηι,
ἥ ῥ' Ἡρακλῆα κρατερόφρονα γείνατο παῖδα,
ἡ δὲ Διώνυσον Σεμέλη τέκε χάρμα βροτοῖσιν·
οὐδ' ὅτε Δήμητρος καλλιπλοκάμοιο ἀνάσσης,
οὐδ' ὁπότε Λητοῦς ἐρικυδέος, οὐδὲ σεῦ αὐτῆς,
ὡς σέο νῦν ἔραμαι καί με γλυκὺς ἵμερος αἱρεῖ.

Hera, you may go there later.
But for us two, come, let us take our joy bedded together in love;
for never yet has desire for goddess or mortal woman
so shed itself about me and overmastered the heart within my breast—
not even when I was seized with love of Ixion's wife,
who bore Peirithoös, the peer of the gods in counsel;
nor of Danaë of the fair ankles, Akrisios's daughter,
who bore Perseus, preeminent above all warriors;
nor of the daughter of far-famed Phoinix,
who bore me Minos and godlike Rhadamanthys;
nor of Semele, nor of Alkmene in Thebes,
and she brought forth Herakles, her son stout of heart,
and Semele bore Dionysos, the joy of mortals;
nor of Demeter, the fair-tressed queen;
nor of glorious Leto; nor yet of yourself,
as now I love you, and sweet desire lays hold of me.

Two additional passages illuminate the structure of this one. Paris wishes to sleep with Helen (*Iliad* 3.441–446):

ἀλλ' ἄγε δὴ φιλότητι τραπείομεν εὐνηθέντε·
οὐ γάρ πώ ποτέ μ' ὧδέ γ' ἔρως φρένας ἀμφεκάλυψεν,
οὐδ' ὅτε σε πρῶτον Λακεδαίμονος ἐξ ἐρατεινῆς
ἔπλεον ἁρπάξας ἐν ποντοπόροισι νέεσσι,
νήσωι δ' ἐν Κραναῆι ἐμίγην φιλότητι καὶ εὐνῆι,
ὥς σεο νῦν ἔραμαι καί με γλυκὺς ἵμερος αἱρεῖ.

But come now, let us take our joy, bedded together in love;
for never yet has desire so encompassed my mind—
not even when I first snatched you from lovely Lakedaimon
and sailed with you on my seafaring ships,
and on the isle of Kranae slept with you on the bed of love—
as now I love you, and sweet desire seizes me.

This passage has the following parts:

1. Proposal (441)
2. Unprecedented feeling of desire (442)
3. Exceeded precedent (443–445)
4. Present feeling of desire (446)

The other passage occurs a bit before Zeus's speech in *Iliad* 14. The narrator reports Zeus's reaction when he first sees Hera (14.294–296):

ὡς δ' ἴδεν, ὥς μιν ἔρως πυκινὰς φρένας ἀμφεκάλυψεν,
οἷον ὅτε πρώτιστον ἐμισγέσθην φιλότητι
εἰς εὐνὴν φοιτῶντε, φίλους λήθοντε τοκῆας.

And when he saw her, then love engulfed his shrewd mind,
just as when they first had joined in love,
going off to bed unbeknownst to their dear parents.

This shorter passage follows a similar pattern:

2. Feeling of desire (294)
3. Precedent (295–296)

Zeus's speech in *Iliad* 14 segments as follows:

1. Proposal (313–314)
2. Unprecedented feeling of desire (315–316)

3. Exceeded precedents (317–327)
4. Present feeling of desire (328)

This collation shows that, whereas parts 1 and 4 can be omitted from this topos, part 3 is the most variable of the parts and subject to expansion or contraction. In Zeus's speech in *Iliad* 14, that part takes the distinct generic form of a catalogue.

I can now delve further into Zeus's speech. Two peculiarities in its part 2 (verses 315 and 316) show that the subject matter of the catalogue (part 3) shapes part 2. First, the phrase "desire [*eros*] for goddess or mortal woman" stands out. In archaic Greek epic, the noun *eros* (or *erōs*) in the nominative case takes an objective genitive only once elsewhere: δεινὸς γάρ μιν ἔτειρεν ἔρως Πανοπηΐδος Αἴγλης ("for a terrible desire for Panopeus' daughter Aegle was wearing him down") (Hesiod fr. 298 M-W; trans. Most [2007]). The noun *himeros*, by contrast, appears several times in the nominative followed by an objective genitive (*Iliad* 11.89 and *Homeric Hymn to Apollo* 461 [*sitoio* ("food")]; *Odyssey* 16.215 [*gooio* ("lamentation")], 22.500–501 [*klauthmou kai stonakhēs* ("crying and groaning")]; Hesiod *Works and Days* 618 [*nautiliēs* ("sailing")]). In addition, nowhere else does one feel desire (*eros* or *erōs*) for a generic individual. Far more frequently (twenty-eight times), the accusative form *eron* takes an objective genitive when it appears as the object of the verb *hīēmi* in the formulaic "to send away one's desire for X" in the sense of "to have one's fill of X." X is usually food and/or drink (twenty-four times); twice it is feasting (*dais*); once, lamentation. Menelaos presents a more elaborate instance: "Of all things is there satiety, of sleep, and love [*philotētos*], / and sweet song, and the incomparable dance; / of these things [*tōn*] surely a man hopes to have his fill [*ex eron heinai*] rather than of war [*polemou*]" (*Iliad* 13.636–638). I note as well how the syntactical equivalence of "goddess" and "mortal woman"—they are both objective genitives—mirrors their equivalence in Zeus's mind: he has sex with females regardless of their ontological status. This equivalence contrasts with the conceptual opposition between the terms found elsewhere. Hera observes that a mortal woman (*gunaika*) nursed Hektor whereas a goddess (*theas*) bore Achilleus (*Iliad* 24.58–59). The goddess (*thea*) Athena assumes the form of a mortal woman (*gunaiki*) when conversing with Odysseus (*Odyssey* 13.287–288).[6] In sum, fashioning a phrase in *Iliad* 14.315 that introduces the subject matter of the catalogue—Zeus's sexual escapades—requires departures from the norm.

Second, only here in archaic Greek epic poetry does desire (*eros*) "subdue" (*edamassen*): elsewhere, the related entities *himeros* (*Iliad* 14.198) and *philotēs* (*Iliad* 14.353; *Homeric Hymn to Aphrodite* 17) "subdue"; *eros* "took" (*heilen*) Anchises (*Homeric Hymn to Aphrodite* 91) and, as just noted, "was wearing down" (*eteiren*) Theseus (Hesiod fr. 298 M-W). The subject matter of the following catalogue prompts this deviation. In archaic Greek epic, forms of the verb *damazō* primarily denote defeat on the battlefield (*Iliad* 9.118, 11.98) or rape (*Iliad* 3.301; Hesiod fr. 43a, line 55 and fr. 185, line 1 M-W). Zeus's catalogue reviews a series of rapes, two of which resulted in the birth of male children who became renowned fighters: Perseus and Herakles. The verb's appearance in verse 316 presages these themes.

Verses 315 and 316, then, are crafted with a view to the following catalogue. The same effect results from the use of the verb *eramai* in verse 328. Even though the verse seems, and most likely is, formulaic (cf. *Iliad* 3.446), the verb acts in this instance as a repetition inspired by the use of the verb at the start of the catalogue in verse 317 (*ērasamēn*).

In short, whereas the catalogue itself is, to borrow Bauman's metaphor, formally impenetrable, it shapes its co-text. This dynamic contributes to the entextualization of the catalogue. It suggests that the surrounding verses must accommodate the catalogue as a discrete, complete, unified, perhaps even ready-made, chunk.

Barber's work on the entextualizing power of quotation has inspired the analysis so far. I turn next to the linking of utterance and object. I concentrate not on the simple fact that stories attach to objects, but on what a performer gains by connecting an utterance to an object. Recall that Barber finds an "impulse" to entextualize in this practice. I suggest that this practice can itself aid entextualization. The clearest example of what happens at such moments comes in Odysseus's speech from *Iliad* 2 quoted earlier. Odysseus attaches Kalchas's prophecy about the fate of the Achaian expedition to the peculiar stone (cf. Nagy 2003: 25–27, 29). By linking speech and object, Odysseus endows the utterance with textuality twice over. First, he suggests that Kalchas's utterance comes to mind when one looks at the stone. That sequence depicts the utterance as an item that preexists any one enunciation. Second, he suggests that Kalchas's utterance will endure as long as the stone endures.

Keeping this programmatic scene in view, I assemble some other relevant passages. Character and narrators alike make clear that speakers who perform recollections about the past (cf. Martin 1989: 77–88) regularly attach utterances to objects. Poseidon fears that "men will forget the wall that I and Phoibos Apollo / toiled over making for the warrior Laomedon" (*Iliad* 7.452–453). Poseidon envisions speakers linking an utterance about his and Apollo's service to Laomedon to the wall surrounding Troy (cf. Grethlein 2008: 33). A cup that Priam includes in the ransom for Hektor's corpse (*Iliad* 24.234–235) "recalls a diplomatic exploit from Priam's past" (Sammons 2010: 108–109, quotation from 109): that is, a speaker would attach an utterance on that subject to the cup. On three occasions, an object merits the designation "a *mnēma* of X," a token of the memory of/a mechanism for remembering X. Achilleus labels the amphora he gives Nestor a *mnēma* of Patroklos's funeral (*Iliad* 23.619). Helen gives Telemachos a robe to be a *mnēma* "of the hands of Helen" (*Odyssey* 15.126). Odysseus's bow functions as a *mnēma* "of his dear friend," Iphitos (*Odyssey* 21.40). In each case, one is to envision a speaker linking his or her utterance to the object (cf. Scodel 2008: 34; Ready 2010: 138–139).

These examples have to do with utterances that take the object as a jumping off point. The utterances are not about the object so much as they are about the actors who came into contact with the object. Another class of utterances attached to objects comprises those detailing the history of the object itself. I refer the reader to Jonas Grethlein's list of the myriad objects in the Homeric poems that have a biography accompanying them, ranging from the tools of war to household items to horses and mules (2008: 36; cf. Higbie 1995: 195–203). In the case of biographies of objects, a character or the narrator presents the entirety of the relevant utterance itself or a portion of it. Otherwise—like in the scenes mentioned in the previous paragraph—a character or the narrator alludes to a performer attaching an utterance to an object. The distinction is irrelevant to this investigation. What matters is that performers repeatedly attach utterances to objects. In all the cases in which a speaker pins an utterance to an object, he achieves what Odysseus achieves in *Iliad* 2. He portrays his utterance as existing before any one presentation and implies that the utterance will endure as long as the object endures. He thereby works to entextualize his utterance.

Barber focuses as well on how exegesis enables entextualization. Homeric characters do not engage in intensive exegesis of the kind Barber investigates. They nevertheless enhance the textual status of the recollections they perform by making the story an object of analysis. Like the Asante praise poets who offer an obscure noun phrase in one line and then explain it in the next, characters perform a story and then engage in their own interpretative efforts, commenting on the relevance of the tale to the present situation. As previous scholarship makes clear the paradigmatic purposes to which characters put stories (Alden 2000; Sammons 2010: 23), I cite two examples of this well-understood phenomenon. Phoinix declares that the story he has just told about Meleagros should prompt Achilleus to return to battle (*Iliad* 9.600–605). Agamemnon finds that a story about how Atē once bested Zeus excuses his own folly (*Iliad* 19.134–136). My point is that in these cases a performer strives to entextualize a stretch of his own discourse by making it an object of reflection, attention, or commentary.

The Poet and Entextualization

I want to take a couple of more pages to illustrate how one might broaden the investigation. I have explored the oral texts that populate the world constructed in the epics and the oral texts that the characters fashion before our eyes. Of course, the narrator text also contains what come across as discrete stretches of entextualized verse. Take, for example, the catalogues that appear in the narrator text. I point again to Sammons's comments on the generic features unique to catalogues. David Elmer, too, seeks to "differentiate the Catalogue [in *Iliad* 2] and catalogic poetry from epic narrative proper" and suggests that when cataloguing "the poet speaks with the voice of inscription" (2005: 27)—that is, one sees in the *Iliad* "the conceptualization of catalogue poetry as the captioning of an implied image" (28). One factor contributing, then, to the textuality of, for instance, the famous Catalogue of Ships in *Iliad* 2 is its status as a distinct generic chunk within the larger epic narrative.

One can look beyond stretches of verse. Each poem as a whole is characterized as existing prior to its performance and as possessing an object-like status. First, through his request at the start of the poem that the Muse present the tale, the poet positions his account as "an already available" (Scodel 2002a: 67), preexisting entity that endures to be re-presented as needed. Second, in the passages depicting Andromache and Helen weaving, "the act of epic narration is figured metaphorically as an act of pattern-weaving" (Nagy 2010: 278; cf. Clader 1976: 8; Elmer 2005: 24; Karanika 2014: 25, 41–42). Numerous other objects also align the poetry with objects because they "signify poetic creation" (J. Porter 2011: 18), such as Achilleus's shield in *Iliad* 18 (Nagy 2009a: 101; J. Porter 2011: 18–19; *pace* Ford 1992: 169), Odysseus's raft in *Odyssey* 5 (Dougherty 2001: 28–37; cf. Rood 2008), and Odysseus's pin at *Odyssey* 19.226–231 (J. Porter 2011: 33). Its preexistence and its objectification suggest the poetry's ability to outlast the moment (cf. Karanika 2014: 28).

As for the strategies of entextualization that enable this persistence, I cite scholarship's continued interest in the parallelism and ring composition evident not only in portions but also across the entirety of our *Iliad* and *Odyssey* (Louden 1999, 2006; Minchin 2001: 181–202; Cook 2014; Arft 2017). The poet's use of these techniques evinces a desire to create a work that holds together and spites the power of time. I highlight as well José González's suggestion that the poet represents himself as quoting the Muse (2013: 183–186, 201, 208, 358; cf. Nagy 1990b: 26–27, 1996b: 61). On the one hand, if one understands the poet to be quoting the Muse, one can set aside the idea that the poet functions as a mouthpiece of the Muse (cf. de Jong 2004a: 46 on Lenz 1980: 27). The Muse does not possess the poet. On the other hand, the quotation model does not account for the several passages in which the narrating voice is that of a mortal: "at certain points he gives expression to his admiration for divine objects or apologizes for his human limitations" (de Jong 2004a: 49). One struggles to imagine the Muse saying, "But others were fighting in battle about the other gates, and hard would it be for me, as though I were a god [*theos hōs*], to tell the tale of all these things" (*Iliad* 12.175–176) (cf. de Jong 2004a: 47). Qualifying González's argument, one can assert that the poet sometimes represents himself as quoting the Muse. Indeed, when the poet demands of the Muse, "Sing, goddess, the wrath of Peleus's son Achilleus" (*Iliad* 1.1), he seems to imply that he will pass on precisely what the Muse herself performs. By positioning his utterance as a quotation, the poet seeks to endow it with textuality.

In Homeric epic, then, oral texts and textuality come to the fore. Based on this chapter's findings, I envision the Homeric poet fashioning an oral text through processes of entextualization each time he performed. Two other pieces of evidence point in the same direction. First, the practitioner assigns a telling label to his craft (González 2013: 417): the performer of epic is one "sewing/stitching a song" (339), that is, he is a rhapsode (416–431). Like the metaphor of weaving, "the metaphor of stitching parts into a whole" (419) points up the object-like status of what the performer generates (cf. Barber 2007: 1). Second, rhapsodes of Homeric poetry commented on passages as they performed them (González 2013: 299–304, 319–320, 328–329). When, for example, Ion of Ephesus "adorns" Homer (*kekosmēka*, Plato *Ion* 530d7), he subjects it to "exegetical scrutiny" and therefore "reinforces its consolidation as text" (Barber 2005: 272).

CONCLUSION

Barber reports from the field of linguistic anthropology (2005: 267, emphasis in original):

> We have begun to see how work goes into constituting oral genres as something capable of repetition, evaluation, and exegesis—that is, something that can be treated as the *object* of com-

> mentary by the communities that produce them, and not just by the collector or ethnographer.

This work, the work of entextualization, generates oral texts. Endorsing Barber's statement that when it comes to entextualization "the questions that arise—the things to look for—can . . . be profitably drawn from one body of material and applied to another" (2007: 74), this chapter has applied to the Homeric poems the findings of linguistic anthropologists who study entextualization in oral traditions. That exercise sheds light on the nature of Homeric performance, both the performances of the characters and of their poet himself.

Here is what I have shown. Songs and stories seem to have an independent preexistence in the world constructed in the Homeric poems and circulate from teller to teller. What is more, these and other utterances possess an object-like status. These two phenomena suggest that the Homeric poets depict a world in which oral pronouncements endure and prompt an investigation into the creation of oral texts in the poems and the strategies of entextualization represented therein. Performances meant to be repeated showcase the production of oral texts and bring out the use of formal devices in entextualization. Additional mechanisms of entextualization emerge in other performances: I investigated the practices of quoting previous utterances and introducing generically distinct segments, of attaching utterances to objects, and of explicating paradigmatic stories. Looking beyond the character text, one sees that stretches of verse in the narrator text achieve entextualization in part due to their shifting to another generic mode distinct from that of their co-text. Setting aside the distinction between character text and narrator text, one notes the positioning of the poetry as existing prior to its presentation and the objectification of the poetry: both point up its endurance. Fittingly, the poet's use of formal devices, such as parallelism and ring composition, and his positioning himself as one who quotes the Muse reflect an attempt to entextualize his utterance. The constitution of oral texts within the poem and references to the constitution of oral texts within the poem, the efforts to endow the entire poem with textuality—these moves encourage one to picture the Homeric poet as a performer aiming to entextualize, to fashion an oral text, as he performs.

NOTES

1. Translations of passages from the *Iliad* are based on those in Wyatt 1999. Translations of passages from the *Odyssey* are based on those in Lattimore 1965.

I quote from van Thiel's texts of the *Iliad* (1996) and the *Odyssey* (1991), but I do not reproduce his lunate sigmas. Except where noted all other translations are my own.

2. Bauman ventriloquizes a performer's self-description in a 2011 publication: "This is performance. I'm on! I invite you to watch and listen closely and I will impress you, entertain you, move you. I invite you as well to judge just how skillful, effective, and moving a display I can accomplish" (711).

3. Declaring, "there's no Linos-song in our passage" (2016: 296), Silva Barris argues that in *Iliad* 18.570 *linon* is the subject of the verb *aeide* and is to be translated "'lyre-string' or even 'flax.'" This reading encounters trouble when (1) in verse 571 the subject of *aeide* is said to possess a "voice," a *phōnē* (*leptaleēi phōnēi*) and (2) in verses 571 and 572 the harvesters "follow" (*heponto*). (1) In archaic Greek hexameter poetry, an object is one time said to have a *phōnē*: "clear as the trumpet's voice [*phōnē*]" (*Iliad* 18.219). Elsewhere, animate beings possess a *phōnē*—mortals (*Iliad* 3.161), pigs (*Odyssey* 10.239), birds (*Odyssey* 19.521), monsters (*Theogony* 829)—and the verb *phōneō* designates their utterances—mortals (*Odyssey* 1.122), immortals (*Iliad* 2.182). Apart from *Iliad* 18.219, the farthest one gets from animate beings is the assertion in *Works and Days* that Zeus took away the voices (*phōnēn*) from the sicknesses that stalk men (104). From this perspective, it is easier to take *pais*, as opposed to *linon*, as the subject of *aeide* at *Iliad* 18.570. (2) The harvesters "follow" the child, obviously. Still, progression (a) is easier to process than progression (b): (a) the child played the lyre and sang, and the harvesters followed the boy; (b) the child played the lyre, the string sang out, and the harvesters followed the child (not the string).

4. The Muse prompts Demodokos to sing the tale (*oimēs*) (or, more technically, the "'band,' 'cord,' or 'thread of song'" [González 2013: 393; cf. Nagy 2009a: 231, 322]) of the quarrel between Achilleus and Odysseus (*Odyssey* 8.73–74). Odysseus praises singers whom the Muse taught tales (*oimas*) (*Odyssey* 8.480–481), and Phemios claims that the god implanted "all kinds of tales [*oimas*]" in his mind (*Odyssey* 22.347–348). The word *oimē* corresponds to what the narratologist terms the "story" (the *fabula*, in de Jong's terminology [2004a]): *oimē* "constitutes a sequence of events to be followed" (Clay 2007: 249; cf. González 2013: 207n121, 368, 395, 418). Duffy and Short see in the Homeric use of *oimē* "a metaphor of the epic tradition as a kind of physical (binding or linking) structure or again as a kind of building" (2016: 66; cf. González 2013: 392–396).

5. In his 1998 edition, West opts for the second half of the verse as quoted by Aristotle: δίδομεν δέ οἱ εὖχος ἀρέσθαι ("we grant him to win glory"). See West 2001: 175 for discussion.

6. In the *Homeric Hymn to Aphrodite*, the mingling of gods (*theous*) with mortal women (*katathnētēisi gunaixi*) and of goddesses (*theas*) with mortal men (*katathnētois anthrōpois*) (50–52) serves as the poem's precipitating crisis (Clay 2006: 165–166).

CHAPTER THIRTEEN

Homer's Rivals? Internal Narrators in the Iliad

ADRIAN KELLY

The greatest trick the devil ever pulled was convincing the world he didn't exist.

KEYSER SÖZE

HOMER'S AUTHORITY IS EVERYWHERE EVIDENT IN the ancient world, from biography to history, art, and literature, yet the two poems that have come down to us under his name tell us nothing about their author. The near-contemporary poetry of Hesiod is very forthcoming about biographical details and family quarrels, but neither the *Iliad* nor the *Odyssey*—though they contain plenty of first-person pronouns referring to the poet—give us anything like that kind of detail (cf. Kelly 2008). Presumably this occlusion helped to make his later biographical tradition so rich and contested, but it poses an interesting problem for any interpreter of Homeric poetry: why, in a world in which who you are matters as much as what you say, is this absent figure granted so much authority? What is it about his poetry that makes Homer such a uniquely trusted figure in the history of ancient narrative? Though modern scholars have approached this question from a number of angles, the particular approach in this chapter has not, to my knowledge, been explored before, or at least not in this way. And that is perhaps rather fitting for the strategy with which we are concerned.

The uniqueness of the *Iliad* and the *Odyssey*, in several respects, has been clear to ancient audiences since well before Aristotle, and one element that seems to differentiate them from what remains of early Greek epic is their proportion of direct speech (cf. Griffin 1977: 49–50, 2004:

156–157). Though this can be overstated, especially given the exiguous remains of the Epic Cycle, many passages (such as Plato *Republic* 393c7–394b) show us that our impression was already current in the ancient world. Direct speech in Homer has been often studied, but the current chapter focuses on a slightly different and neglected aspect of this well-known phenomenon: how frequently the poet has his characters summarize or retell his narrative, and more specifically how this common practice adds tremendously, and largely *e silentio*, to Homer's narrative authority. It amounts to a sleight of hand, if you will, and it is one so slight that we do not notice it, all the while encountering it everywhere.

A celebrated example is the retelling of his quarrel with Agamemnon which Achilleus serves up to Thetis (*Iliad* 1.365–392), and one might also at a pinch recall Thetis's mini-*Iliad*, told to Hephaistos when she goes to him in order to obtain new armor for her son (18.444–456). But these are only the largest and best-known examples of a phenomenon that obtains throughout the *Iliad*, and on every scale.[1] Perhaps it is no surprise, natural even, that characters should speak, and often, about the events informing the contexts in which they are acting. In one sense, retelling of this sort is entirely unexceptional, and it may not seem self-evident that this adds to Homer's authority. Yet another case, this time from the *Odyssey*, can help to show how it does so: I have argued elsewhere that one of the things Homer was doing by constructing Odysseus as a quasi-bardic figure was comparing his own disinterested or distanced poetics with the interested or proximate poetics of his main character (Kelly 2008: esp. 179–181). At the heart of this comparison was the idea that the more one knows of the speaker's personality and history, and the more one knows of the tale's context, the less reason one has to trust in either. The prime example is Odysseus's retelling to her parents in book 7 of the decision Nausikaa had made in book 6 not to return home with him, when she told Odysseus to enter the city separately (*Odyssey* 6.248–296 ~ 7.290–307). She did this basically out of sexual propriety, knowing that the young Phaiakian men would take it amiss to see her out and about with an unattached man. However, under questioning from Arete and Alkinoös, and in order to remove any sense of blame toward the young Phaiakian maiden who had saved him, Odysseus took the responsibility for this plan upon himself (7.302–307).

Homer here contrasts his own version of the story with a purposed, contextualized retelling of it by one of his characters. The retelling is marked as false, or not as disinterested as the poet's own, primarily because of the context, in which Odysseus is attempting to get his benefactress out of trouble. By contrast, Homer gives us no information about himself, and so no comparable opportunity to question the truth-value of his tale. In fact, he actively discourages—or disencourages, if you will—that kind of speculation about his own story, by encouraging it with regard to his character's retelling. All our attention is focused on, or diverted to, that character and his/her context.

This strategy of having a character retell the poet's narrative bolsters the authority of the poet because it depends on the first telling (T) as the default narrative, next to which subsequent retellings (RT) are automatically and unavoidably judged. Of course, the poet also retells events in his own voice, but much more rarely and with almost no detail: "They are very brief remarks within the context of an explanation or an identification, not designed specifically to recall that earlier moment in the story but to account for something in the present scene" (S. Richardson 1990: 96). This reticence is well accounted for by the current argument: when one is trying to elide one's own role in the creation of narrative, supplementation or confirmation of that narrative is best achieved through the mouth of another.

To return to character retellings, the T may comprise either the poet's narrative or character speech or a combination of the two and will be referred to variously in this chapter, according to the context, as the poet's version, the original version, the original telling, and so on.[2] The RT, which may be of any scale, need not be entirely or even partially erroneous when measured next to the T, though such cases are the clearest examples, since the authority deriving from repetition remains: the original T is the benchmark, the means to confirm or deny the accuracy of the character's RT, with this comparative process all the while silently reinforcing the authority of the poet and his version of events. As Ruth Scodel comments, "*If we assume that the main narrative is reliable in what it actually says* (despite its occasional omissions), nearly all such 'mirror-scenes' are slightly inaccurate" (1999: 62, emphasis added).[3] This reflects perfectly the way in which modern analysis of this phenomenon has been conducted and the success of the poet's strategy: the truth of his "main narrative" has become a secondary object of attention. In effect, the argument advanced here is that one part of Homer's narrative authority is a trick of misdirection. Questions of motivation, truth, and falsehood are directed toward internal speakers, and away from the narrator.

Our first example, mentioned earlier, is Achilleus's retelling to Thetis of his quarrel with Agamemnon from book 1. In an important study, Irene de Jong called this passage a "mirror story" and related such analepses to the interplay between the different (but at points interchangeable) levels of knowledge exhibited by the poet and one of his characters

(1985, 2001), while Michael Apthorp suggested we could view episodes like this as "recapitulatory summaries" of things that have already happened (1977: 7–8).[4] In such a long poem as the *Iliad*, this can be extremely useful, and perhaps such a feature would allow for performance in parts, by giving a natural way of filling in the necessary backstory. But that is not going on here (de Jong 2001: 487), surely, since the episode has just happened, and it's difficult to imagine a performance of book 1 or its material separating the quarrel and its retelling—so something else is happening.

In order to see what that is, note the sequence of events in Achilleus's RT, especially the way in which he emphasizes his own role in bidding Agamemnon to return the girl, once Kalchas had given his instructions. His version runs as follows (1.380–392):

> χωόμενος δ' ὁ γέρων πάλιν ᾤχετο· τοῖο δ' Ἀπόλλων
> εὐξαμένου ἤκουσεν, ἐπεὶ μάλα οἱ φίλος ἦεν,
> ἧκε δ' ἐπ' Ἀργείοισι κακὸν βέλος· οἳ δέ νυ λαοὶ
> θνῆισκον ἐπασσύτεροι, τὰ δ' ἐπῴχετο κῆλα θεοῖο
> πάντηι ἀνὰ στρατὸν εὐρὺν Ἀχαιῶν· ἄμμι δὲ μάντις
> εὖ εἰδὼς ἀγόρευε θεοπροπίας Ἑκάτοιο.
> αὐτίκ' ἐγὼ πρῶτος κελόμην θεὸν ἱλάσκεσθαι·
> Ἀτρεΐωνα δ' ἔπειτα χόλος λάβεν, αἶψα δ' ἀναστὰς
> ἠπείλησεν μῦθον, ὃ δὴ τετελεσμένος ἐστίν.
> τὴν μὲν γὰρ σὺν νηῒ θοῆι ἑλίκωπες Ἀχαιοί
> ἐς Χρύσην πέμπουσιν, ἄγουσι δὲ δῶρα ἄνακτι·
> τὴν δὲ νέον κλισίηθεν ἔβαν κήρυκες ἄγοντες
> κούρην Βρισῆος τήν μοι δόσαν υἷες Ἀχαιῶν.

> And in anger the old man went back; and Apollo heard
> his prayer, since he was particularly dear to him,
> and he cast his evil weapons on the Argives; and now the
> people were dying in heaps, and the god's shafts went
> everywhere throughout the broad Achaian army; and to us did
> the seer knowing them well speak the far-worker's oracles.
> Straightaway was I the first to bid him propitiate the god;
> and then anger took Atreus's son, and standing immediately
> he threatened a word which has been brought to its end;
> for the glancing-eyed Achaians send her in a swift ship
> to Chryse, and they lead gifts for the lord [Apollo];
> and the heralds leading her are just gone from my tent,
> the maid Briseis, whom the sons of the Achaians gave me.

But this is not precisely how it unfolded in the poet's version of events (1.92–129). There Agamemnon stands and agrees to give up Chryseis *immediately* after Kalchas's speech (101–120). This does not fit Achilleus's RT, since, first, Agamemnon's agreement to give up the girl is entirely unbidden by him (ἀλλὰ καὶ ὧς ἐθέλω δόμεναι πάλιν, εἰ τό γ' ἄμεινον· / βούλομ' ἐγὼ λαὸν σόον ἔμμεναι ἢ' ἀπολέσθαι ["but even so I am willing to give her back, if that is better: / I want the people to be safe rather than perish"], 116–117) and precedes any injunction on Achilleus's part to obey Kalchas's instructions. Achilleus's claim to immediacy and priority in this process (1.386) is simply inaccurate. Second, Achilleus is also wrong to suggest that Agamemnon became angry *after* this point (1.387): Agamemnon's anger was already aroused by Kalchas's speech (92–100; cf. 103–104: μένεος δὲ μέγα φρένες ἀμφὶ μέλαιναι / πίμπλαντ', ὄσσε δέ οἱ πυρὶ λαμπετόωντι ἐΐκτην ["and his *phrenes*, black all-round, were greatly filled / with rage, and his two eyes were like gleaming fire"]); it is reignited or redirected by Achilleus's intervention, but Agamemnon was already angry. Third, Agamemnon had stood up directly after Kalchas finishes speaking (1.101–102) and not, as Achilleus says, straight after he himself had suggested propitiating the god (387); notice how Achilleus stresses the temporal progression, with clear staging markers in ἔπειτα and αἶψα. Indeed, on that last expression (in full αἶψα δ' ἀναστάς ["and standing up immediately"]) and fourth, the poet had not told us that Agamemnon had sat down after his reply to Kalchas, so Agamemnon was in all probability still standing at the point when he replied to Achilleus (130–147). There is, in short, some rather creative retelling going on here.[5]

Why does Homer have Achilleus do this? A bT scholion suggests that the Homeric poet was sufficiently interested in rhetoric (broadly defined) as to want to display the trope of backwards summary (*anakephalaiōsis*).[6] This term appears not infrequently in the scholia, and is roughly equivalent in meaning to παλλιλογία (though this can refer to repetitions of several different sorts), since both terms are deployed in the context of Aristarchus's atheteses or querying of repetitions.[7] As often in the bT scholia, this note is probably responding to a criticism of the passage, made usually by Aristarchus. Indeed, the A scholion to 1.365 suggests that the whole passage (366–392) should be athetized, since that verse (οἶσθα· τίη τοι ταῦτα ἰδυίῃ πάντ' ἀγορεύω; ["you know; why do I say these things to you when you know them all?"]), addressed to his mother, apparently means that Achilleus refuses to repeat to her the information he then goes on to repeat.[8] Modern critics too have noted the problem and addressed it in their own ways. Analysts suspected corruption or layering in the poem, and Neoanalysts allusion to a preexisting version of the story, while those with a more literary bent have speculated, much as the scholiasts do, about the character's motives: he's speaking from anger, or from a need to persuade Thetis to act on his behalf, etc.[9]

Much of this latter sort of speculation must be right, in the first instance. But consider what all these discussions, ancient and modern, are not doing: none of them is questioning *Homer's* version of the events. All the critical attention is focused on Achilleus's motivations because all the contextual information surrounds his RT, and the poet's T is already the set version in the narrative line. By retelling the event, and inaccurately, Achilleus reinforces the authority of the poet's narrative. Moreover, we—like the scholia, like Aristarchus, like all modern critics—apparently do not notice the authority of the poet's version even as we rely on it to interpret the unfolding narrative.

As we saw earlier, this very common strategy—which we shall call "character RT"—attracted some limited critical attention in the ancient world, and it has not been without study in more recent times, although most scholars subsume it within a broader discussion of cross-references across the poem.[10] This may be partly due to the fact that a typology of examples is difficult to establish, since characters' references to past events within the *Iliad* are as common and varied in their form and context as we would expect in a poem so dominated by speech, and they are usually very short. Regardless of size, however, these examples show a consistent conception behind their function within the narrative, and the possibilities they afford the poet.

Let us return to the other of our large introductory paradigms, when Thetis relates a more developed version of the quarrel and its aftermath to Hephaistos, this time with the aim of securing another set of armor for her son. After introducing her maternal woes, she launches into the story (18.444–452):

κούρην, ἣν ἄρα οἱ γέρας ἔξελον υἷες Ἀχαιῶν,
τὴν ἂψ ἐκ χειρῶν ἕλετο κρείων Ἀγαμέμνων·
ἤτοι ὃ τῆς ἀχέων φρένας ἔφθιεν, αὐτὰρ Ἀχαιοὺς
Τρῶες ἐπὶ πρύμνῃσιν ἐείλεον, οὐδὲ θύραζε
εἴων ἐξιέναι· τὸν δὲ λίσσοντο γέροντες
Ἀργείων, καὶ πολλὰ περικλυτὰ δῶρ' ὀνόμαζον.
ἔνθ' αὐτὸς μὲν ἔπειτ' ἠναίνετο λοιγὸν ἀμῦναι,
αὐτὰρ ὃ Πάτροκλον περὶ μὲν τὰ ἃ τεύχεα ἕσσε,
πέμπε δέ μιν πόλεμόνδε, πολὺν δ' ἅμα λαὸν ὄπασσεν.

the maid whom the sons of the Achaians chose for him
as his prize, her did lordly Agamemnon take from his hands.

> And he grieving for her wasted away his *phrenes*; while the Trojans whirled the Greeks to the ships' prows, nor did they let them exit from (the camp); and the elders of the Argives supplicated, and they named many glorious gifts.
> Then he himself at that stage refused to ward off disaster,
> but he clothed Patroklos about with his own armor,
> and sent him out to war, and lent him a great host.

An A scholion tells us that Aristarchus once more athetized the entire passage because he was generally suspicious of such recapitulations and felt (a) that there was no need for Thetis to summarize the poem in this context rather than explain why she had come and (b) that her narrative disagrees with Homer's on the question of precisely when and why Patroklos was sent out (18.450–451).[11] Leaving aside the predictable Analyst (von Wilamowitz-Moellendorff 1916: 172–173; Mühll 1952: 280–281; van Thiel 1982: 465) and Neoanalyst (Schoeck 1961: 45–46) responses, one might note that it's been a long time since the external audience was reminded of the basic outline of the story, so that it makes sense from a performative angle to have a recapitulation here. This would certainly work better than in the case of the mirror story from book 1, especially if Oliver Taplin is right about a tripartite performance division for the *Iliad*, in which the third day's performance would start in book 18 shortly before this point (18.353–354) (1992: 285–293).[12]

But the really interesting thing about the passage is its perspective: Thetis begins the narrative by foregrounding the motivation behind the quarrel (observe the left-dislocation of κούρην in verse 444!) but omits the request to Zeus to destroy the Greeks, noting simply that Achilleus wasted away his *phrenes* out of grief for Briseis, while the Greeks just happened to be penned against the ships (446–447). The omission of her own and her son's roles in putting the Greeks to flight is sensible, given the pro-Hellenic stance of Hephaistos and the sense of outrage she conveys in the passage. Moreover, just as Aristarchus noted, Thetis elides the narrative staging in verses 450 and 451 and apparently combines the refusal of the embassy in book 9 with the sending out of Patroklos in his stead in book 16. This seems deliberate; once more, note the temporal markers: ἔνθ' αὐτὸς . . . ἔπειτ' ("then he himself . . . then," 450), and then the resumptive αὐτὰρ ὅ ("and he," 451). Though one could try to argue that Thetis is only summarizing what is necessary for her purpose, there is a strong impression that the actual course of events is being shaped in order to provide the most favorable picture of Achilleus. As with the quarrel in book 1, the poet's original T is altered in line with the feelings and perspective of the retelling character. One does not need to accuse Thetis of lying, any more than Achilleus is lying in book 1, but it seems pretty clear that the poet has allowed one of his interested characters to give a very self-interested RT of much of the preceding poem.

The nature and effect of this self-interest in character RTs can be extremely varied. Wounded by Pandaros, Menelaos allays his brother's fears (4.184–187):

> θάρσει, μηδέ τί πω δειδίσσεο λαὸν Ἀχαιῶν.
> οὐκ ἐν καιρίωι ὀξὺ πάγη βέλος, ἀλλὰ πάροιθεν
> εἰρύσατο ζωστήρ τε παναίολος ἠδ' ὑπένερθεν
> ζῶμά τε καὶ μίτρη, τὴν χαλκῆες κάμον ἄνδρες.
>
> Be encouraged, do not yet cause fear to the host of Achaians;
> the keen shaft is not fixed in a mortal place, but before that
> the gleaming belt held it off and from beneath
> the girdle and the apron, which bronze-worker men toiled at.

Menelaos puts the credit for the arrow's failure to kill him down to his armor, and his equipment was indeed emphasized in the original scene (with the same individual items mentioned: ζωστῆρι [134], ζωστῆρος [135], μίτρης [137]), but there the poet repeatedly stressed that these items *failed* to protect him. Most important, Menelaos says nothing of Athena's role, reflecting clearly the superior levels of knowledge possessed by the privileged narrator and the external audience. In an episode like this, the audience need not reflect at any great length on the lesson, as it were, for the authority of the primary narrative to work its magic both on their understanding of this character and even more subtly on their reliance on the author's version. Similarly, in book 8 Hektor scorns the impact of the Greek wall and its ability to hold him off (177–178). Though he will breach it briefly in book 12, the audience already knows that it will survive the war, since Zeus encourages the angry Poseidon in book 7 to destroy it *after* the Greeks' departure (459–463). Hektor, of course, had no opportunity to hear that conversation, or (more generally) to know Zeus's rather delimiting intentions for his success. Somewhat similarly, Glaukos accuses Hektor of leaving Sarpedon's corpse to be claimed by the Greeks (17.150–151), when the body had actually been spirited back to Lykia by Sleep and Death, acting under Zeus's orders (16.666–683).

Yet even when gods make their intentions and views known to mortals, they are not always honest—or perhaps more accurately, they twist the truth for more direct ends. For example, Iris tells Achilleus in book 18 that Hektor is minded to put Patroklos's head on a stake (κεφαλὴν δέ ἑ θυμὸς ἄνωγεν / πῆξαι ἀνὰ σκολόπεσσι ταμόνθ' ἁπαλῆς ἀπὸ δειρῆς ["and his *thumos* drives him to stick his head / on stakes, cutting it from his gentle neck"], 176–177), and in doing so she goes a little beyond the poet's own claim, in book 17, that Hektor was raging to cut Patroklos's head off and give his corpse to the dogs (ἵν' ἀπ' ὤμοιιν κεφαλὴν τάμοι ὀξέϊ χαλκῶι, / τὸν δὲ νέκυν Τρωιῇισιν ἐρυσσάμενος κυσὶ δοίη ["in order that he might cut the head from his shoulders with the sharp bronze / and drag and give his corpse to the Trojan dogs"], 126–127). To be sure, Iris also repeats this latter detail at the end of her appeal to Achilleus (18.178–179), but, though nasty things happen to heads quite a bit in the *Iliad*, they are not elsewhere planted on stakes.[13] In adding such a vividly *untypical* detail to the common theme of corpse mutilation, Iris deepens the dire nature of the situation into which she is trying at Hera's request to send Achilleus.[14] One could compare the reasons given by Xanthos/Skamandros when requesting Achilleus to continue elsewhere the killing granted him by Zeus, viz his streams are choked and cannot reach the sea (21.216–220). Yet the river's earlier perturbation was explicitly caused by pro-Trojan feeling (21.136–138), as he immediately confirms to Apollo after the request (21.228–232).

Though perhaps with not quite so much persuasive deliberation, Hera retells to Poseidon and Athena in book 20 in a very partisan way the reasons Zeus had given for the gods to journey to the battlefield at the start of the book. In the poet's narrative, Zeus was concerned to make sure that the Trojans would be able to withstand Achilleus, even to the point of fearing a premature sack of the city (εἰ γὰρ Ἀχιλλεὺς οἶος ἐπὶ Τρώεσσι μαχεῖται, / οὐδὲ μίνυνθ' ἕξουσι ποδώκεα Πηλείωνα . . . δείδω μὴ καὶ τεῖχος ὑπέρμορον ἐξαλαπάξηι ["for if Achilleus fights alone against the Trojans / not even for a short while will they hold off swift-foot Peleus's son. . . . I fear that he will throw down the wall beyond what is fated"], 20.26–27, 30). Hera turns this into a mission statement for the pro-Greek gods, in effect, of protecting Achilleus from suffering something untoward (πάντες δ' Οὐλύμποιο κατήλθομεν ἀντιόωντες / τῆσδε μάχης, ἵνα μή τι μετὰ Τρώεσσι πάθηισιν / σήμερον· ["and we all came down from Olympos to meet / this battle, lest he suffer something among the Trojans / today"], 20.125–128). Though she happens to be speaking to two gods who were present at that earlier scene, it's quite natural that she should do this, given her implacable hatred of the Trojans and rather one-eyed support of the Greeks. Nonetheless, in the variation between Hera's and Zeus's perspectives on the reasons for divine participation we get another glimpse into the potential for strife on Olympos, and the complexities of the differences impelling the major gods.

To this case, we should compare Hektor's boast (16.837–842) that Achilleus gave a confident instruction to Patroklos when he set out in book 16, in which the younger man apparently urged his elder *therapōn* to kill Hektor himself. Achilleus, of course, had done no such thing, but sought to restrain Patroklos's sense of adventure (16.83–96). Note there how much Achilleus stressed the fact that Patroklos should fight and win honor for him (ὡς ἄν μοι τιμὴν μεγάλην καὶ κῦδος ἄρηαι / πρὸς πάντων Δαναῶν ["so you win great honor and glory for me / from all the Danaans"], 84–85), and how *he* would lose out in those terms should Patroklos attempt too much (ἀτιμότερον δέ με θήσεις ["you will make me less honored"], 90). Hektor's is not an entirely unreasonable supposition, but once more it illustrates his triumphant and tragically doomed state of mind, and his ignorance of Achilleus's personality. Predictably, the latter hero then uses the same trope, much more accurately, in his corresponding boast over the dying Hektor (22.331–335).

There is an obvious advantage to this kind of *ex post facto* wisdom, but characters do also reflect on their own earlier errors: Agamemnon admits his responsibility for the original quarrel on several occasions (2.377–378, 9.115–116, 19.88–89, 19.134–137), and Hektor his for the disaster which has overtaken the Trojan army (22.100–104). Poulydamas (18.257–260) tries a different tack, reminding Hektor of his correct decision to stay outside the walls of the city on the previous night in order to contrast that with the current circumstance (cf. Grethlein 2006: 240–245).

If characters can erroneously impute speeches to others and refer to their own previous errors in speech, it is no surprise that they also repeat others' speeches, especially when conveying instructions or commands. This kind of verbatim repetition has been well studied (cf. Kelly 2007: 325–329 [§182]; Ready, this volume, pp. 331–336), and here we see yet again the same variety in perspectives, such as at the end of the embassy in book 9, when Odysseus reports to the assembled Greek leaders Achilleus's refusal to rejoin the battle (9.677–692):

Ἀτρείδη κύδιστε, ἄναξ ἀνδρῶν Ἀγάμεμνον
κεῖνός γ' οὐκ ἐθέλει σβέσσαι χόλον, ἀλλ' ἔτι μᾶλλον
πιμπλάνεται μένεος, σὲ δ' ἀναίνεται ἠδὲ σὰ δῶρα.
αὐτόν σε φράζεσθαι ἐν Ἀργείοισιν ἄνωγεν,
ὅππως κεν νῆάς τε σαῶις καὶ λαὸν Ἀχαιῶν·
(i) αὐτὸς δ' ἠπείλησεν {ἅμ' ἠοῖ φαινομένηφιν
νῆας ἐϋσσέλμους ἅλαδ' ἑλκέμεν ἀμφιελίσσας·}
(ii) {καὶ δ' ἂν τοῖς ἄλλοισιν ἔφη παραμυθήσασθαι
οἴκαδ' ἀποπλείειν, 'ἐπεὶ οὐκέτι δήετε τέκμωρ
Ἰλίου αἰπεινῆς· μάλα γάρ ἑθεν εὐρύοπα Ζεὺς
χεῖρα ἑὴν ὑπερέσχε, τεθαρσήκασι δὲ λαοί.'}

ὣς ἔφατ'· εἰσι καὶ οἵδε τάδ' εἰπέμεν, οἵ μοι ἕποντο,
Αἴας καὶ κήρυκε δύω, πεπνυμένω ἄμφω.
(iii) {Φοῖνιξ δ' αὖθ' ὃ γέρων κατελέξατο, ὡς γὰρ ἀνώγει,
ὄφρά οἱ ἐν νήεσσι φίλην ἐς πατρίδ' ἕπηται
αὔριον, ἢν ἐθέλῃσιν· ἀνάγκῃ δ' οὔ τί μιν ἄξει.}

Son of Atreus, most honored lord of men Agamemnon,
that man is unwilling to quench his anger, but still more
he is filled with rage, and he rejects you and your gifts.
He bids you take thought among the Argives
how you will save the ships and the people of the Achaians.
(i) And he himself threatens {as soon as the dawn appears
to drag his well-benched, balanced ships down to the sea.}
(ii) {And he said he advises the others to sail away,
"since no longer will you find the proving point
of steep Ilion; for broad-seeing Zeus holds his hand
over it, and the people are encouraged."}
So he spoke; and these men who followed me are here to say
this, Aias and the two heralds, prudent men both.
(iii) {but old Phoinix has slept there, for thus he ordered,
so he should follow in the ships to his dear fatherland
in the morning, if he wills; by compulsion he will not lead him.}

Although Odysseus repeats verbatim some of Achilleus's comments to him (9.684–687 [ii] = 417–420; 691–693 [iii] = 427–429), he focuses in his report almost entirely on Achilleus's threat to leave in the morning (682–683 [i] ~ 356–361). All of this presents the direst possible picture to the other Greek leaders, but does not actually reflect the progressive relenting in Achilleus's original three speeches, in which he had moved from threatening to leave tomorrow (in his reply to Odysseus), to deciding tomorrow whether he would leave (to Phoinix) (617–619), to expressing the firm opinion that Hektor's raging would be stopped at his own ships (to Aias) (650–655). Note in particular the fact that the expression that Odysseus uses for dawn (ἅμ' ἠοῖ φαινομένηφι ["at the same time as dawn appearing"], 682) when he is reporting Achilleus's intention to leave is taken from Achilleus's reply to Phoinix (ἅμα δ' ἠοῖ φαινομένηφι, 618), but without any mention of the closing concession in the very next verse (φρασσόμεθ' ἤ κε νεώμεθ' ἐφ' ἡμέτερ' ἦ κε μένωμεν ["we will consider whether we travel to our own (land) or whether we stay"], 619). Again, we need not think Odysseus is deliberately misreporting the event, merely that the Greeks' very serious situation—and their awareness of it—is underlined by an overly pessimistic reporting of the response from their most recalcitrant figure. Even Odysseus is rattled (cf. Reichel 1994: 92, 95, 97–98).

A similar example may be seen in Patroklos's slightly erroneous reporting to Achilleus about the state of affairs in the Greek camp (16.23–29), in which he reflects the information given him by Nestor (11.658–664) and his own care for Eurypylos, but not the fact that Diomedes, Agamemnon, and Odysseus are no longer being treated for their wounds. The poet keeps track of his narrative by showing how partial and incomplete is Patroklos's view of its continuation.

Yet this view into individual perspectives is also possible when the character remembers an event that, however likely, did not happen, at least not in the poet's narrative. By this I mean not those events that may have happened before the poem's beginning, but those that could only have fallen within the framework of the *Iliad*. Sometimes these are difficult to identify, as with Apollo's mocking reference to Aineias's previous promises to face Achilleus alone in battle (20.83–85), or Ares's apparent promises to Hera and Athena to fight with the Greeks (5.832, 21.413–414), where we cannot be sure that the promises were understood as having been made within the time frame of the *Iliad* (and so they are marked with square brackets in appendix 13.1).[15] But there are plenty of cases where the internality of the reference is clear. For instance, when stirring the Myrmidons into battle, Achilleus reminds them of their habitual criticisms of his intractible anger, even going so far as to imagine a quotation (16.200–208):

Μυρμιδόνες, μή τίς μοι ἀπειλάων λελαθέσθω,
ἃς ἐπὶ νηυσὶ θοῇσιν ἀπειλεῖτε Τρώεσσιν
πάνθ' ὑπὸ μηνιθμόν, καί μ' ᾐτιάασθε ἕκαστος·
'σχέτλιε Πηλέος υἱέ, χόλωι ἄρα σ' ἔτρεφε μήτηρ,
νηλεές, ὃς παρὰ νηυσὶν ἔχεις ἀέκοντας ἑταίρους·
οἴκαδέ περ σὺν νηυσὶ νεώμεθα ποντοπόροισιν
αὖτις, ἐπεί ῥά τοι ὧδε κακὸς χόλος ἔμπεσε θυμῶι.'
ταῦτά μ' ἀγειρόμενοι θάμ' ἐβάζετε· νῦν δὲ πέφανται
φυλόπιδος μέγα ἔργον, ἕης τὸ πρίν γ' ἐράασθε.

Myrmidons, let none of you forget the threats,
which you threatened the Trojans by the swift ships
during the whole time of my anger, and each of you faulted me:
"Harsh son of Peleus, your mother raised you in anger,
pitiless, since you hold your unwilling companions by the ships;

> then let us go homewards with our sea-faring ships
> once more, since evil anger has thus fallen on your soul."
> Often did you gather and speak these things; but now the great
> work of strife has appeared, which before you desired.

This is not an implausible reaction, but the poet has not given much insight into the views of the Myrmidons before this point, confining himself to Achilleus's tent in book 9 and a description of the amusements of his *laos* as they yearned for war in book 2 (2.773–779). As a more general objection to the current project, perhaps, we may also feel that we should not limit the possibility of narrative only to the things the poet tells us. Nonetheless, there is no mention of any such threats or criticisms before this point, and it is surely revealing that Achilleus at this moment should impute these feelings to his men, implying a new or at least newly expressed awareness on his part that this anger has seemed, even to his own men, excessive. The fact that the external audience has never heard of this before surely tells us something (if indirectly) about Achilleus's growing sense of his own responsibility for the events of the poem.

Consider the same character's similarly individuated claim that he prayed to Zeus (16.236–237), when in fact Thetis conveyed his request in book 1, as Aristarchus recognized (schol. A *Iliad* 16.236a). Thetis herself later repeats this mistake (18.75), but in neither passage is the poet simply eliding the prayer's process and substance (viz, that it was, in effect, a prayer to Zeus), because it is important to the configuration of Achilleus's character at this point that he is assuming a more direct and informed relationship with Zeus than in fact he has, at the very moment when the limitations of that relationship are to be revealed, as is made clear by Zeus's immediate and ambivalent answer (16.249–252).

The same dynamic can be seen in the famous case of 1.355–356, where Achilleus claims to Thetis that Agamemnon came to his hut personally to take Briseis (αὐτὸς ἀπούρας ["himself taking (her)"]), a claim repeated by Thetis to Zeus (1.507), Thersites to the Greeks (2.240), and then Nestor to the council (9.106–107). Agamemnon did not of course come to the tent himself, and the point of these subsequent recastings is to emphasize his responsibility, since all three characters have a powerful rhetorical motivation for individuating the event in that way: Thetis's partiality is clear (as we have seen), Thersites's view is explicitly condemned in his beating, and Nestor is, however respectfully, rebuking Agamemnon for the disastrous ramifications of this action at the moment when they are about to try rectifying it.[16]

A more straightforward case is Menelaos's invocation in book 17 of his encounter with the Trojan Hyperenor from book 14. Menelaos is here facing off against Euphorbos, Hyperenor's brother, over the corpse of Patroklos, and so he mentions the earlier combat (which he had won) in order to make the point that Hyperenor—who had apparently "said that I was the least warrior / among the Danaans" (μ' ἔφατ' ἐν Δαναοῖσιν ἐλέγχιστον πολεμιστὴν / ἔμμεναι, 17.26–27)—was as unwise in his advance against Menelaos as is Euphorbos. Yet the poet's version of that encounter in book 14 had no flyting whatsoever (14.516–519), and the killing took place only once Poseidon had turned the battle and the Trojans were in headlong flight (14.506–510), which makes it difficult (though not impossible) to think of the kind of combat pause that would enable such a confrontation.[17] In the context of book 17, Euphorbos's challenge is a significant slight to Menelaos: much will be made in the ensuing narrative of his personal shortcomings as a fighter, so that the disjunction here between the character's retelling and the poet's story is surely to be linked with Menelaos's awareness of his standing and abilities, and his need to give them the lie.[18] Like Achilleus when he is speaking to the Myrmidons, in other words, Menelaos puts into the mouth of another a view of himself the import—the *truth*—of which he is keenly aware.

The examples go on, and the level and type of disjunction between the T and the character's RT are extremely varied, but behind them all lies the sanctity of the original version. Issues of context, character, and the development of the plot are all brought together to explain and contextualize the RT, whether the character is lying, wrong, or simply partisan. These cases represent a significant portion of the total, especially as they are the most elaborated and prominent examples in the poem, but they are only a portion. In fact, around 60 percent of character RT in the *Iliad* shows no such variance or individuality of perspective.[19] That does not mean that they are not reinforcing the authority of the poet's narrative, for a confirmation of the T still serves that purpose, by reifying through repetition: when, for instance, in book 1 Athena repeats to Achilleus Homer's statement in his own voice that Hera loved both Agamemnon and Achilleus (1.195–196 = 1.208–209), the T is hardly contradicted by the RT.[20] Indeed, in this case the RT relies on the T to make Athena's rhetorical point, which is that Achilleus must bear in mind Hera's love for him and Agamemnon "both alike" (ἄμφω ὁμῶς, 196 = 209), amounting to an implicit warning about her disfavor. Many cases of this sort show that, whether the RT is correct or not, the poet's story and therefore his authority gain in strength simply from the fact of repetition.[21]

A T/RT like this one, where the latter follows the former almost im-

TABLE 13.1

(1)	5.103	Pandaros boasts to the Trojans that **he has just wounded Diomedes**.
(2)	5.119–120	Diomedes prays to Athena to kill **the man who has hit him and boasted about it**.
(3)	5.184–191	Pandaros makes comments to Aineias about **his failure to kill Diomedes**.
(4)	5.206–207	Pandaros talks to Aineias about **his failure to kill Menelaos and Diomedes**.
(5)	5.244–248	Sthenelos warns Diomedes about **the approach of Aineias and Pandaros**.
(6)	5.277–278	Pandaros reminds Diomedes of **his previous failure** (and then makes a threat).
(7)	5.284–285	Pandaros boasts to Diomedes **about his most recent strike**.
(8)	5.287	Diomedes replies to Pandaros about **his failure** (and then makes a threat).

mediately, is a self-contained unit, but the poet can also deploy a developing series of such retellings, not only to point up deficiencies in the characters' understanding of the narrative or explore their motives and beliefs but also to join up and undergird the different episodes in his storyline with a running parallel commentary.[22] For instance, with regard to the combat between Pandaros and Diomedes (5.103–287), there are eight moments during the first third of book 5 in which characters—usually Pandaros or Diomedes, but once Sthenelos—refer to events in this conflict as events move to a denouement (table 13.1).

Each stage of this section is linked with each successive stage by the characters constantly reminding both the internal and the external audience about what has just happened.[23] The participants' motivations and expectations are thus constantly kept alive, as they move from one action to the next: Pandaros approaches Aineias at 5.184–191 (3) explicitly to fix the failure about which he had prematurely boasted at 103 (1) and which Diomedes had noted at the time (119–120) (2). Lest we be uncertain as to the extent to which Pandaros is trying to rectify his earlier error, he repeats the complaint at 206–207 (4). Aineias then encourages him to join him on his chariot in an attempt to rectify the earlier failure (217–228), upon which the poet switches to Diomedes's charioteer,

Sthenelos (241–250), who notes the advance of the two and suggests retreat (249–250) (5). Sthenelos's fear once more represents his own necessarily poor understanding of the situation, as the conversation between Aineias and Pandaros had hardly suggested that either of them felt great confidence in facing Diomedes (170–228, esp. 174–178, 180–187, 224–225). As the two teams approach one another, Pandaros reminds Diomedes of their earlier encounter (277–279) (6), casts his spear and then gloats—once more prematurely and erroneously: with Pandaros's claim βεβλῆαι κενεῶνα διαμπερές, οὐδέ σ' ὀίω / δηρὸν ἔτ' ἀνσχήσεσθαι ("you are hit right through the flank, and I do not think / you will endure long," 284–285) compare Diomedes's known survival of the war and the poet's immediately preceding comment that the spear was stopped by Diomedes's breastplate (281–282)—over the apparent success of the strike (284–285) (7). Diomedes denies that success (287) (8) before closing with his own, immediately fulfilled, threat.

At each point the poet takes pains to have his characters remind themselves and one another of what has happened, even as they move to rectify or address their own and others' prior actions. The parallel commentary, in other words, not only informs us about their motivations and attitudes but also reinforces the narrative line itself, anchoring subsequent acts in previous ones and even, on one occasion (4) (5.206–207), extending that line back into the wounding of Menelaos in book 4, thus making it no surprise at all when Pandaros is killed by Diomedes (5.290–296) in a manner particularly suitable for an oath-breaker (cf. Kirk 1985: 89). That there are significant misunderstandings at several stages (Sthenelos about the approach of Pandaros and Aineias, Pandaros about the uselessness of his bow,[24] and his hope in each case that he has killed Diomedes) encourages the audience to focus on those characters' perspectives, their limited understanding about what has just happened, and their hopes for what is going to happen, even as the narrative is wound together more tightly on the level of causation. Combining both speeches and third-person narrative, the T thus becomes a developing or dynamic predicate for the unfolding narrative, the stuff of the characters' conversations, mistaken inferences, hopes, and interpretations.[25]

This T/RT operates over a fairly small and discrete section of narrative, but some of the poem's most important events can be referred to some thousands of verses later, as several of the previous examples have shown. Of course, we might wonder whether this kind of recall is possible, especially when we lack answers to basic questions about textual integrity and the (source, type, and extent of the) audience's knowledge of the *Iliad*. Aside from the greater levels of memory recall possible in a largely oral culture,[26] it is not unreasonable to assume the poet's expectation that his audience would recall the earlier event, given the frequent use of T/RT over short spaces of narrative where memory resource or textual (perhaps we should call it performative?) integrity would not be at issue. The widely separated examples are simply an extension of this practice, an extension enabled by the special (if unknown) circumstances that gave rise to the fixed *Iliad* and *Odyssey*. As with other elements of Homer's orally derived compositional technique (ring composition, doublet structure, etc.), the strategies that work on a small scale are greatly expanded in order to generate monumental narrative.[27] Indeed, the need to use an enhanced and enhancing version of this strategy can help to explain the evidence of table 13.2, which shows that important events are constantly referenced at a great remove, at least partly so as to remain alive in the audience's memory.

There is almost no major event or episode in the poem that does not receive repeated RT coverage in its original context or near proximity. Neither context rules out the other, as with the case of (i), the original quarrel in book 1. RT concerning this event—its pretext and course—is obviously prominent in book 1 itself, in which a run of RT connects several events in much the same way as the Pandaros and Diomedes sequence. Once more, every stage in the motivation of the characters and their view of the quarrel as it unfolds is allowed to link each event with the last, but its serial run ends, and the quarrel becomes the defining theme of the poem, when Thetis retells it to Zeus (1.506–507), moving the RT for the first time beyond the immediate participants and onto what we might call the poem's directive plane. From that point on, having become established in the narrative, it can be easily referenced whenever the poet requires it.

Particularly interesting in this regard is the fact that the three events in the *Iliad* subject to repeated RT beyond their original setting or near proximity are (i) the original quarrel, (xv) the death of Patroklos, and (xix) the death of Hektor. Obviously the scope for RT in the case of Hektor's death is limited by the fact that it occurs so near the end of the poem, but together these three themes represent the turning points of the *Iliad*, especially when viewed from Achilleus's perspective: aside from his participation in it, the quarrel and its consequences set the precondition for the poem's events until book 16, whereupon the death of Patroklos and the struggle for his corpse replace it and render that theme effectively irrelevant. This new motivation then dominates the narrative until (in fact well after) Hektor's death in book 22, the remembrance of which closes the poem. A skeptic might remark that these are naturally

TABLE 13.2

Theme	Book	Telling (T)	Retelling (RT) and Citations
i	1	Quarrel	*Quarrel* 1.208–209, 335–336, 355–356, 365–932, 412, 506–507
ii	1	Thetis & Zeus	*Thetis & Zeus* 1.557
iii	2	Dream & test	*Dream & test* 2.26–33, 56–73, 80–81, 193–194
[i]	2		*Quarrel* 2.239–241, 377–378
iv	3	Menelaos & Paris	*Menelaos & Paris* 3.52, 88–94, 132–135, 250–258, 367–368, 439, 457, 4.12–13
v	4	Oath-breaking	*Oath-breaking* 4.155–157, 185–187, 195–197 (~ 205–207), 236
vi	5	Pandaros & Diomedes	*Pandaros & Diomedes* 5.103, 119–120, 184–191, 206–207, 244–248, 277–278, 284–285, 287
vii	5	Diomedes & gods	*Diomedes & gods* 5.361–362, 376–380, 405, 424–425, 458–459, 809–812, 818–824, 881–885
viii	6	Paris's retreat	*Paris's retreat* 6.326–329, 335–338, 518–519
ix	7	Hektor & Aias	*Hektor & Aias* 7.97–98, 109–110, 129–130, 159–160, 191, 285
[v]	7		*Oath-breaking* 7.351–352, 357–360, 385–397
x	8	Combat	*Combat* 8.39–40, 102–104, 140–142, 234–235, 294–299, 354–356, 452–453, 500–501
[ii]	8		*Thetis & Zeus* 8.370–372
xi	9	Embassy	*Embassy* 9.519–522, 680–692
[i]	9		*Quarrel* 9.106–111, 118, 262–298, 335–336, 344–345, 367–369, 375, 647–648
xii	10	*Doloneia*	*Combat* 10.391–399, 462–464, 478, 559–563
xiii	11–15	Combat	*Combat* [passim]
[i]	13		*Quarrel* 13.50, 111–114
[ii]	15		*Thetis & Zeus* 15.74–77
xiv	16	Sarpedon's death	*Sarpedon's death* 16.541–543, 558–559, 671–675
xv	16	Patroklos's death	

(*continued*)

TABLE 13.2 (*CONTINUED*)

Theme	*Book*	*Telling (T)*	*Retelling (RT) and Citations*
[i]	16		*Quarrel* 16.17–18, 55–59, 236–237, 274
[xv]	17		*Patroklos's death* 17.14–15, 92, 122, 187, 202–206, 450, 471–473, 478, 671–672, 689–690 (693)
[xiv]	17		*Sarpedon's death* 17.150–151
[xv]	18		*Patroklos's death* 18.20–21, 79, 80–84, 99–100, 130–132, 170–177, 460–461
[i]	18		*Quarrel* 18.75, 111, 444–456
[xv]	19		*Patroklos's death* 19.211–213, 403, 411–414
[i]	19		*Quarrel* 19.56–58, 88–89, 134–137, 140–141, 261–263, 270–274
xvi	20	Aineias & Achilleus	*Aineias & Achilleus* 20.83–85, 117–118, 344–346
xvii	21	combat	*combat* [*passim*]
xviii	22	Hektor & Achilleus	*Hektor & Achilleus* 22.172–173, 229–230, 250–252, 279–282, 298–299
xix	22	Hektor's death	*Hektor's death* 22.393, 436, 451, 482–483
xx	23	contests	*Contests* 23.273, 405–406, 459–472, 492–495, 536, 545–556, 570–572, 585, 592, 662–663, 782
[xv]	23		*Patroklos's death* 23.19–23 (= 179–183), 78–79, 103–107, 280–284
xxi	24	Priam's mission	*Priam's mission* 24.134–137, 175–187, 194–196, 223, 309–313, 460–461, 499–501, 556, 561–562, 593–594, 638–642
[xix]	24		*Hektor's death* 24.52–54, 151, 214–216, 241–242, 260, 384–385, 411–423, 499–501, 637–642, 725–726, 729, 754–756

the most remembered events in the *Iliad*, as they're the most important ones. Yet the notion that poetic authority is a general beneficiary of this strategy, when added to the external context in which Homer was composing, suggests a different conclusion.

Consider the fact that quarrels are a dime a dozen in early Greek epic, and the *Iliad*'s first audiences must have heard dozens if not hundreds of songs centered upon that motif (cf. Nagy 1999a: 170–171). Consider, next, that Patroklos's death is elevated in scale and importance in the *Iliad* well beyond what one might expect for a relatively minor character.[28] Consider, third, that Hektor's importance to Troy's fate is massively elevated in the *Iliad*, but played down in the rest of the early Greek tradition.[29] Here is where we find the raison d'être of this expanded T/RT strategy, of referring to the events of one's own narrative across large swathes of the poem, and especially with regard to these three themes. Oralists and Neoanalysts[30] have accustomed us to the ways in which Homer drew on and differentiated himself from his poetic tradition and bardic rivals: if Patroklos and Hektor were otherwise minor characters who were played up for the first time by Homer himself (as the Neoanalysts have contended), the facts of their deaths, and the importance of those deaths, needed to be underlined; equally, if audiences knew dozens of quarrel poems (as the Oralists have shown), then Homer had to make this one distinctive. Homer's response to these two rather different requirements was largely the same: embed the controversial event in the mouths of the characters and have them refer to it repeatedly. Repetition reifies.[31] It is a truism of Homeric narrative, at least since Norman Austin's treatment of digressions (1966),[32] that the more important a thing is, the larger it is. Turn that around a little: the more important a thing is, the more novel, contested, or contestable it is to the ears of an informed and experienced external audience, the more often and the more pointedly will Homer's characters retell it.

This argument also holds for the oath-breaking (v), which recreates within the *Iliad* the original offense for which the Trojans are doomed and is part of a sequence of such reactivations, recreations, or appropriations that include the duel of Menelaos and Paris (iv), Paris's lovemaking with Helen, and his refusal to hand her back in the Trojan assembly in book 7. The oath-breaking thus represents Homer's re-creation of the line of Trojan perfidy within his *Iliad* (cf. Allan 2006), a narrative line that is obviously derivative of the original offense and whose particular Homeric version therefore requires bolstering.

Homer is constantly using, for every development in his narrative, the same RT strategy: generate an action and then reinforce its presence and importance, the fact of its occurrence, in the mouths of the characters participating in that action and the narrative that results. The fact that many of these retellings are also marked by the speaker's individuality or limited knowledge allows the poet simultaneously to direct his audience's attention away from the novelties of his own narrative. The use of this RT strategy for the most contentious elements in the poem just takes this basic tactic to its greatest extreme, hiding Homer's most daring innovations in plain sight.[33]

There are plenty of additional avenues for further study. Not only should we extend the focus to the *Odyssey* but we should also examine character foreshadowing, and include character-retold and character-foreshadowed events beyond the parameters of both poems to see how or if they relate to the thesis advanced here. One particularly pressing case is the reverse of the phenomenon observed here: the poet retells a story first told by a character. The obvious example is the famous recapitulation at the end of the *Odyssey*, where the poet in his own voice shows us Odysseus carefully picking and choosing which of his adventures he will tell his wife (23.310–343).[34] But further discussion is beyond the scope of this avowedly preliminary chapter, whose aim is more modest.

What this chapter has tried to illustrate is one way in which Homer gets us, his external audience, to trust his story. He does it by reinforcing its events, from the incidental to the crucial, with a constant parallel and reflective commentary delivered by his characters. Because we spend so much time hearing and evaluating the individual perspective of those retelling characters, we do not notice that we're being tricked into granting authority to the poet's original version. About his version and its motives we are given no information, compared to the flood of contextual detail that dominates characters' retellings. When the RT is marked by degrees of error or difference, the priority of the poet's T becomes reinforced by an (importantly) unspoken sense of its accuracy, as the privileged external audience—scholarly or not—is lured into using it as a check text for the unprivileged characters within the story. We mentioned at the outset that Homer was unusual, in what is left of early Greek epic, for his reliance on direct speech. The argument here suggests that one reason he made so much use of direct speech was precisely because it allowed him to use a T/RT strategy to bolster the authority and believability of his narrative.

This sleight of hand, this directing of our attention away from the poetic self and the accuracy of its story, calls to mind nothing so much as the epigraph to this chapter—the final, triumphant maxim of the master criminal Keyser Söze, who channels Baudelaire's "Le Joueur généreux" (*Petits Poèmes en prose XXIX*) in the 1995 film *The Usual Suspects*: "The greatest trick the devil ever pulled was convincing the world he didn't exist."

APPENDIX 13.1: RETELLINGS IN THE *ILIAD*

1.94–97, 111–112, 208–209, 335–336, 355–356, 365–392, 412, 442, 453–454, 506–507, 557.

2.26b–33, 56–70, 80–81, 193–194, 239–241, 274–275, 377–378.

3.52, 132–135, 367–368, 439, 457.

4.12–13, 155–157, 185–187, 195–197, 236, 340–342, 269–270.

5.103, 119–120, 184–191, 206–207, 244–248, 277–278, 284–285, 287, 361–362, 376–380, 405, 424–425, 458–459, 467–468, 604, 757–761, 791, 809–812, 818–824, [832], 881–885.

6.100–101, 125–126, 255–257, 326–329, 335–338, 518–519.

7.34–35, 53, 69–70, 97–98, 109–110, 129–130, 159–160, 191, 229–230, 285, 328–330, 351–352, 357–360, 385–397, 446–450.

8.34, 39–40, 102–104, 108, 140–142, 156, 177–178, 234–235, 294–299, 354–355, 360–361, 370–372, 452–453, 465, 500–501.

9.17–22, 34–36, 106–111, 118, 232–234, 264–299, 335–336, 344–345, 349–350, 367–369, 375, 519–522, 647–648, 680–692.

10.124–126, 391–399, 462–464, 478, 559–563.

11.200–209, 288–289, 362–364, 380, 442, 451, 649–650, 658–664, 825–827, 840.

12.217–222, 236, 355–363.

13.49–50, 68–72, 111–114, 123–124, 256–258, 312–314, 414–416, 446–447, 467, 481–482, 737–739, 778–783.

14.45–48, 53–60, 65–68, 358–360, 454–457, 471–472.

15.14–16, 55–56, 66–68, 74–77, 110–112, 131, 174–183, 222–224, 248–250, 254–256, 287–293, 440, 467–470, 488–489, 506–507, 555.

16.17–18, 22–29, 55–59, 61–63, 200–207, 236–237, 274, 424–425, 517–518, 541–543, 558–559, 671–675, 745–750, 837–842, 844–846, 849–850.

17.14–15, 24–26, 35, 79–81, 92, 122, 150–151, 166–167, 174–178, 187, 202–206, 338–339, 450, 471–473, 478, 486–487, 512–513, 587–590, 671–672, 689–690, 608–609.

18.13–14, 20–21, 75, 79, 80–84, 99–100, 111, 130–132, 170–177, 184, 189–190, 257–260, 286, 357–358, 444–456, 460–461.

19.56–58, 88–89, 134–137, 140–141, 203–204, 211–213, 261–263, 270–274, 288, 344–346, 403, 411–414.

[20.83–85], 117–118, 125–127, 344–346, 426, 449–451.

21.55–56, 90–91, 96, 107, 133–135, 186, 218–220, 229–232, 394–399, [413–414], 472–473, 512.

22.15–16, 18–19, 44–48, 100–104, 172–173, 229–230, 250–252, 271–272, 279–282, 298–299, 331–332, 374, 380, 386–387, 393, 436, 451, 482–483.

23.20–21, 78–79, 103–107, 180–183, 208–211, 273, 280–284, 405–406, 459–472, 492–495, 536, 545–546, 560, 570–572 and 585, 592, 662–663, 782, 808.

24.52–54, 88, 104–105, 107–109, 134–137, 151, 175–187, 194–196, 204–205, 214–216, 223, 241–242, 260, 309–313, 384–385, 391–395, 411–423, 460–461, 499–501, 556, 561–562, 593–594, 637–642, 683–685, 725–726, 729, 754–756, 779–781.

NOTES

I would like to thank the editors for their invitation to contribute to this volume and for their comments on an earlier draft of this chapter, the anonymous press readers, and also audiences in Oxford, Swansea, and Reading, signal among whom were Bill Allan, Bernardo Ballesteros Petrella, Katherine Harloe, Peter Kruschwitz, John Morgan, Matthew Nicholls, Ian Repath, and Ian Rutherford. None of them should be assumed to agree with the thesis of this chapter, but all of them helped to improve it. I use West's Teubner text of the *Iliad* (1998, 2000), and all translations are my own.

1. See appendix 13.1 for the full list, amounting to 301 cases, though no doubt some contention over their definition (see note 10) makes it unwise to be too dogmatic. It would be a natural extension of this project, beyond the scope of this chapter, to examine this phenomenon in the *Odyssey*, such as Amphimedon's famously biased retelling of the *Odyssey* at 24.123–190; cf. my comments on Odysseus's deliberately false retelling (7.290–307) of Nausikaa's instructions (6.258–296) (p. 352).

2. No further narratological differentiation is employed here, since, aside from the fact that this chapter is not the work of a narratologist, there is already a plethora of different terms employed in the scholarship to describe this phenomenon (see note 10); our conclusions seem to be equally valid for all combinations of T/RT, regardless of the size or composition of the original T; and the variety of T/RT form and function cannot easily be captured by one terminological apparatus.

3. De Jong is more circumspect, at least in theory: "Although I take the NF_1-version as the standard to which the character-version is compared, it should not be forgotten that the NF_1-version is itself also a selection, interpretation and evaluation of the events of the (primary) fabula" (2004a: 211). On the audience's ability to remember the T when listening to the RT, see pp. 366–367.

4. In her later treatment, de Jong argues for a slightly restricted definition of the mirror story as rather closer to the phenomenon examined in this chapter: "a clear and sustained echo of something also told by the primary narrator" (2001: 478n5); see de Jong 2004a: 216–218 and my note 10. This is not a new approach: see von Wilamowitz-Moellendorff 1916: 253; Notopoulos 1951:

91–97; Eustathius 1.186 at 1.370ff.: ὁ ποιητὴς σχήματι ἀνακεφαλαιώσεως χρῆται διὰ τοῦ Ἀχιλλέως ἐπαναλαμβάνων τὰ πρὸ μικροῦ ἱστορηθέντα εἰς ἀνάμνησιν τοῦ ἀκροατοῦ ("the poet uses the figure of backwards summary [*anakephalaiōsis*] through Achilleus because he is repeating things told a little earlier to remind the listener"). On the term ἀνακεφαλαίωσις, see further note 7.

5. It entirely misses the point of this process to say that "apart from this example of *an effective arrangement of his material* I think we can say that Achilles presents a faithful picture of what has happened" (de Jong 1985: 15 = 2001: 492; emphasis added).

6. Schol. bT *Iliad* 1.366 (Erbse): ῥητορικὸς ὢν ὁ ποιητὴς καὶ τρόπον ἀνακεφαλαιώσεως βουλόμενος διδάξαι ἡμᾶς ταὐτὰ πάλιν ἐξ ἀρχῆς διηγεῖται ("the poet, being a rhetorician and wishing to teach us the trope of backwards summary, narrates the same things once more from the beginning").

7. For ἀνακεφαλαίωσις, see schol. bT *Iliad* 18.444–456b and pp. 355–356; for παλλιλογία, see schol. A *Iliad* 10.51–52a1, 15.56a, 20.205–209b2; Nünlist 2009: 45–46. The terms elsewhere refer more technically to summaries at the end of speeches (and their parts): Aristotle fr. 133 Rose (ἀνακεφαλαίωσις); [Aristotle] *Rhetoric to Alexander* 1433b29 (παλλιλογία*); Dionysius of Halicarnassus *Lysias* 19.28 (ἀνακεφαλαίωσις); Quintilian *Institutio oratoria* 6.1.1 (*repetitio et congregatio, quae Graece dicitur* ἀνακεφαλαίωσις, *a quibusdam . . . enumeratio*): Lausberg 1960: 237–238 (§434), 240 (§442). Eustathius 1.486 at 1.370ff. (cf. note 4) defined two types of these recapitulations in Homer: ἕνα μὲν τὸν αὐτὰ ἐκεῖνα ξηρὰ τὰ προλεχθέντα πάντα φράζοντα, ἕτερον δὲ τὸν ἐπιδρομάδην τοῖς καιρίοις μόνοις ἐπεξιόντα ("one that mentions all those dry things that have already been said, and the other that goes rapidly through only those opportune details"). There does not seem to have been much ancient study of this phenomenon in Homeric poetry, which Nünlist plausibly explains by reference to both its frequency and the dominance of prolepsis in critical discourse (2009: 48).

8. Schol. A *Iliad* 1.365: ὅτι παλιλλογεῖν παρῄτηται. ἀλλότριοι ἄρα οἱ ἐπιφερόμενοι στίχοι εἴκοσι ἑπτά ("because he refuses to repeat the events. So the following twenty-seven lines are foreign").

9. For an Analytical take, see Bethe 1914: 194–195; Wackernagel 1916: 232; van Thiel 1982: 123–124. For a Neoanalyst's view, see Kullmann 1960: 287–288 (though more concerned with the story of Thebes's capture). For more literary treatments, see de Jong 1985: 10–12, 2001: 487–488. Cf. Reichel 1994: 12–14, 93–98 for the ways in which such disjunctions have been interpreted and Nünlist 2009: 45–48 for a recent analysis of the scholiastic context.

10. The phenomenon has been variously termed—"Innerepische Rückverweise" (Reichel 1994: 62); "internal analepsis" (de Jong 2004a: 81–84); "actorial analepsis" (de Jong 2007: 37); Nünlist does without the epithet (2009)—*quot homines, tot sententiae*; cf. de Jong 2004a: 82–83. The two most detailed examinations, Balensiefen 1955 and Reichel 1994, cast their nets considerably wider than does the current chapter, and the former in particular is unsystem-

atic (noting only 122 Iliadic "Rückverweise") and light on discussion of actual examples. Andersen 1990 is the closest in scope, though he focuses on a relatively narrow subset, and so his conclusion is different from mine; cf. note 15. Discussion of some examples and features may be found in Notopoulos 1951 (esp. 91–97); Hellwig 1964: 46–53; Létoublon 1983; de Jong 1985, 2001; S. Richardson 1990: 95–108 (with 227n17); Scodel 1999: 62–77; de Jong 2004a: 81–90, 149–160, 210–214, 2007: 17–38; Grethlein 2006: 240–245.

11. Schol. A *Iliad* 18.444–456a (Erbse's cross-references): ἀθετοῦνται στίχοι τρεῖς καὶ δέκα, ὅτι συνήγαγέ τις τὰ διὰ πολλῶν εἰρημένα εἰς ἕνα τόπον, ὡς ἐκεῖνα 'ᾠιχόμεθ' ἐς Θήβην ἱερὴν πόλιν' [A 366], διὰ δὲ τῶν ἑξῆς [scil. Σ 457–461] ἐπιδείκνυσιν ὅτι τε ὁ Πάτροκλος τελευτήσας ἀπώλεσε τὰ ὅπλα καὶ πάρεστιν ἕτερα ληψομένη. διὰ μέντοι τούτων [scil. 444–456] οὐδὲν ἀναγκαῖον λέγεται. καὶ ψεῦδος περιέχουσιν· οὐ γὰρ ταῖς λιταῖς πεισθεὶς Ὀδυσσέως καὶ Αἴαντος ἐξέπεμψε τὸν Πάτροκλον [cf. 448–452], ἀλλ' ὕστερον ἑκουσίως ὁ Πάτροκλος, κατελεήσας τὴν φθορὰν τῶν Ἑλλήνων, ἱκέτευσε δοθῆναι αὐτῶι τοῦ Ἀχιλλέως τὰ ὅπλα ("Thirteen lines are athetized, since someone has brought together things said in many places into one passage, like the phrase 'we went to Thebes, holy city' [1.366], and in the following verses [scil. 18.457–461] he shows that Patroklos when he died lost the arms and she [Thetis] is present to take another [set of arms]. Yet in these lines [scil. 444–456] nothing necessary is said. And they contain falsehood; for not because of the supplication of Odysseus and Aias did he send out Patroklos [cf. 448–452], but it was later when the willing Patroklos, out of pity for the Greeks' destruction, begged that the arms of Achilleus be given to him").

12. For recent contributions to the never-ending debate over the authenticity of the book divisions, cf. Heiden 1998 and Jensen et al. 1999.

13. Achilleus threatens to bring Hektor's head to Patroklos's corpse (18.334–335) and chops off Deucalion's head (20.478–483). Lokrian Aias decapitates the dead Imbrios and throws the head among the Trojans (13.202–203). Euphorbos threatens to do this to Menelaos and give the head and his armor to his parents (17.38–40). Agamemnon beheads and behands Hippolochos and lets those body parts roll on the ground (11.146), and he chops off Iphidamas's head (11.261). Peneleus kills Ilioneos and holds his head up while boasting to the Trojans (14.496). Cf. Janko 1992: 72.

14. Cf. schol. A *Iliad* 18.154–155: ὅταν μὲν οὖν ὕστερον ἡ Ἶρις εἴπηι τῶι Ἀχιλλεῖ ὅτι βούλεται ὁ Ἕκτωρ τὸν Πάτροκλον αἰκίσασθαι, νοητέον μὴ τἀληθὲς <αὐτὴν> ὑποφαίνειν, ἀλλὰ παρορμῆσαι αὐτὸν εἰς τὴν κατὰ τῶν βαρβάρων ὀργήν ("so when later on Iris tells Achilleus that Hektor wants to disgrace Patroklos, it must be realized that she is not revealing the truth, but stirring him toward anger against the barbarians"). M. Edwards well compares Athena's "maliciously exaggerating Thetis's gesture of supplication to Zeus (8.371)" (1991: 167–168).

15. The most thorough treatment of discrepancies of this sort is Andersen 1990: 28–41, though I disagree with his central thesis that the poet simply makes things up to suit the immediate needs of his narrative; cf. note 10 and Scodel

1999: 62–77 for the related principle of "Homeric inattention." The T/RT strategy stretches well beyond this particular group of examples, and any account needs to take in the entirety of the material.

16. Cf. Scodel 1999: 74. Latacz proposes either exaggeration or an expression of Agamemnon's overall authority (2000: 130 at 1.356), when it is surely both, simultaneously.

17. One might consider as a situational parallel the episode in which Sarpedon turns against the flow of battle, in which his Lykians are in headlong flight, in order to face Patroklos (16.419–426).

18. And Euphorbos then reaffirms or redoubles the connection with the earlier episode (17.35), linking his own determination to win with his desire to avenge his brother. On Menelaos, cf. Willcock 2002: 224: "not a great fighter, not a strong character, but a thoughtful and responsible man who is considerate of other people, and others are considerate of him"; also Roisman 2011.

19. *Contra* Scodel 1999: 62 ("nearly all such 'mirror-scenes' are slightly inaccurate").

20. For similar cases in which characters repeat and/or modify the reason for their arrival, see 7.34–35 (Athena to Apollo), 11.649–650 (Patroklos to Nestor), 15.254–256 (Apollo to Hektor), 18.184 (Iris to Achilleus).

21. One might ask why the poet should bother with a change in perspective like this if the result is the same in terms of boosting authority. I suggest that some RTs confirm and others deny or vary their T because it is simply not believable for all the players in the epic world to be right or wrong all the time.

22. One is immediately reminded of simile runs (linked similemes [W. Scott 2009: 17–31]) performing a structural and thematic function to bind larger portions of narrative; cf. Moulton 1977: 18–116; Ready 2011: 87–101, 183–196, 211–214.

23. For the need to remind an audience over larger sections of narrative, see pp. 353–354, 357.

24. This is coupled with his erroneous inference that things would have worked out better had he only brought his chariot team with him to Troy, so superior was it to his skill in archery (5.192–216)—but he is about to die fighting on a chariot.

25. There are several other serial runs of this sort, many associated with combat narrative, helping to bind discrete episodes in the fighting, such as the back and forth between Meriones, Deiphobos, and Idomeneus (13.164–168, 247–248, 255–258, 312–314, 414–416, 446–447, 467, 481–482), or that between Teukros, Aias, and Hektor surrounding the breaking of Teukros's bow (15.440, 467–470, 488–489, 506–507, 555); de Jong 2004a: 157–159.

26. "Memory has become gravely degraded in Western culture, even more so with the escalating advances of audio-visual aids and information technology. But just because our depleted minds find it impossible to imagine such a huge and complex feat of memory without the use of scriptural aids, that does not mean it was impossible" (Taplin 1992: 36).

27. Scodel limits the "competent listener" to the "immediate context" (1999: 65), but, to my mind, this imposes an unrealistic boundary on the audience, stopping its members from importing their knowledge of other stories, or other versions of this story, into their understanding of the current text/performance.

28. A Neoanalytical staple; cf. Burgess 1999 for a recent exploration.

29. Cf. Willcock 2004, who argues that neither Hektor nor Patroklos were Homeric creations *ex nihilo*.

30. Consider in particular the range of essays in Montanari, Rengakos, and Tsagalis 2012.

31. On the enduring power of oral stories in Homeric narrative and beyond, see Ready (this volume) for a discussion of entextualization.

32. See Alden 2000 for a more recent and thorough treatment of the phenomenon.

33. J. Scott makes the same point about Homeric foreshadowing: "the simple fact that the poet . . . felt it necessary to point out in advance the course of the story . . . is a strong indication that the plot was not the gift of tradition, but the independent creation of the poet himself" (1921: 260).

34. Cf. Kelly 2008, arguing that the poet here comments slyly on his character's ambivalent relationship with truthful narrative, which would complement the thesis of this chapter, in that the poet still encourages the audience to use a comparative method to suggest problems in the RT (recapitulation) when measured next to the T (*apologoi*), though the poet is less self-effacing since he does not merely quote Odysseus's actual speech.

Works Cited

ABBREVIATIONS

ABV	J. D. Beazley, *Attic Black-Figure Vase Painters* (Oxford: Clarendon Press, 1956)
AE	*L'Année Épigraphique*
ARV^2	J. D. Beazley, *Attic Red-Figure Vase Painters*, 2nd ed. (Oxford: Clarendon Press, 1963)
BAPD	Beazley Archive Pottery Database (www.beazley.ox.ac.uk)
BCH	*Bulletin de Correspondance Hellénique*
CGL	G. Goetz, *Corpus Glossariorum Latinorum*, 2nd ed. (Amsterdam: Hakkert, 1965)
CIG	A. Boeckh, *Corpus Inscriptionum Graecarum* (Berlin: Reimer, 1828–1877)
D-K	H. Diels and W. Kranz, *Die Fragmente der Vorsokratiker*, 6th ed. (Berlin: Weidmann, 1951–1952)
EGM	R. Fowler, *Early Greek Mythography* (Oxford: Oxford University Press, 2000)
EM	T. Gaisford, *Etymologicum Magnum* (Amsterdam: Hakkert, 1967)
EO	V. Ch. Petrakos, *Οι επιγραφές του Ωρωπού* (Athens: Athens Archaeological Society, 1997)
FD	*Fouilles de Delphes* (Paris: de Boccard)
FGrH	F. Jacoby et al., *Die Fragmente der griechischen Historiker* (Leiden: Brill, 1961–1969)
FHG	K. Mühler et al., *Fragmenta Historicorum Graecorum* (Paris: Ambrosio Firmin Didot, 1848–1878)
GDI	H. Collitz et al., *Sammlung der griechischen Dialekt-Inschriften* (Göttingen: Vanderhoeck and Ruprecht, 1884–1915)

GEF	M. L. West, *Greek Epic Fragments: From the Seventh to the Fifth Centuries BC* (Cambridge, MA: Harvard University Press, 2003)
GG	G. Uhlig et al., *Grammatici Graeci* (Leipzig: Teubner, 1867–1910)
GrL	H. Keil, *Grammatici Latini* (Hildesheim: Olms, 1961)
GVI	W. Peek, *Griechische Vers-Inschriften*, I: *Grab-Epigramme* (Berlin: Akademie, 1955)
IChios	D. F. McCabe and J. V. Brownson, *Chios Inscriptions* (Princeton: Princeton University Press, 1986)
IG	*Inscriptiones Graecae*
IK	*Inschriften griechischer Städte aus Kleinasien* (Bonn: R. Habelt)
ISide	G. E. Bean, *The Inscriptions of Side* (Ankara: Türk Tarih Kurumu Basımevi, 1965)
IThesp	P. Roesch, *Les Inscriptions de Thespies*; electronic edition by G. Argoud, A. Schachter, and G. Vottéro (http://www.hisoma.mom.fr/production-scientifique/les-inscriptions-de-thespies)
Kaibel	G. Kaibel, *Epigrammata Graeca ex Lapidibus Conlecta* (Hildesheim: Olms, 1965) [First published in 1878 by G. Reimer]
LfgrE	B. Snell et al., *Lexikon des frühgriechischen Epos* (Göttingen: Vandenhoeck and Ruprecht, 1955–2010)
LIMC	*Lexicon Iconographicum Mythologiae Classicae* (Zurich: Artemis, 1981–2009)
M-W	R. Merkelbach and M. L. West, *Fragmenta Hesiodea* (Oxford: Clarendon Press, 1967), supplemented in R. Merkelbach and M. L. West, *Fragmenta selecta*, in F. Solmsen, *Hesiodi Theogonia, Opera et Dies, Scutum*, 3rd ed. (Oxford: Clarendon Press, 1990)
SEG	A. Chaniotis et al., *Supplementum Epigraphicum Graecum* (Leiden: Brill)
SIG	W. Dittenberger, *Sylloge Inscriptionum Graecarum* (Leipzig: Hirzelium, 1915–1924)
Steinepigramme II	R. Merkelbach and J. Stauber, *Steinepigramme aus dem griechischen Osten, 2: Die Nordküste Kleinasiens (Marmarameer und Pontos)* (Munich: Saur, 2001)
Stephanis	I. E. Stephanis, *Διονυσιακοὶ τεχνῖται* (Herakleion: Πανεπιστημιακές Εκδόσεις Κρήτης, 1988)
Su	A. Adler, *Suidae Lexicon*, 5 vols. (Leipzig: Teubner, 1928–1938)
TrGF	*Tragicorum Graecorum Fragmenta*

REFERENCES

Adkins, A. W. H. 1970. *From the Many to the One: A Study of Personality and Views of Human Nature in the Context of Ancient Greek Society, Values, and Beliefs*. Ithaca, NY: Cornell University Press.

Akinnaso, F. N. 1992. "Schooling, Language, and Knowledge in Literate and Nonliterate Societies." *Comparative Studies in Society and History* 34:68–109.

Akínyemí, A. 2003. "Yorùbá Oral Literature: A Source of Indigenous Education for Children." *Journal of African Cultural Studies* 16:161–179.

Alden, M. J. 2000. *Homer Beside Himself: Para-Narratives in the "Iliad."* Oxford: Oxford University Press.

Alexiou, M. 2002 [1974]. *The Ritual Lament in Greek Tradition*. 2nd ed. Ed. P. Roilos and D. Yatromanolakis. Lanham, MD: Rowman and Littlefield.

Allan, W. 2006. "Divine Justice and Cosmic Order in Early Greek Epic." *Journal of Hellenic Studies* 126:1–35.

Allen, R. E. 1996. *Plato: Ion, Hippias Minor, Laches, Protagoras*. New Haven: Yale University Press.

Allen, T. W. 1931. *Homeri Ilias*. 3 vols. Oxford: Clarendon Press.

Allen, T. W., W. R. Halliday, and E. E. Sikes. 1936. *The Homeric Hymns*. Oxford: Clarendon Press.

Aloni, A. 1986. *Tradizione arcaiche della Troade e composizione dell'Iliade*. Milan: Unicopli.

———. 1989. *L'aedo e i tiranni: Ricerche sull'Inno omerico a Apollo*. Rome: Edizioni dell'Ateneo.

———. 2010. "Esiodo a simposio: La performance delle *Opere e giorni*." In *Tra panellenismo e tradizioni locali*, ed. E. Cingano, 115–150. Alessandria: Edizioni dell'Orso.

———. 2017. "Hesiod between Performance and Written Record." In *Poetry in Fragments: Studies on the Hesiodic Corpus and Its Afterlife*, ed. C. Tsagalis, 3–28. Berlin: de Gruyter.

Andersen, Ø. 1978. *Die Diomedesgestalt in der Ilias*. Oslo: Universitetsforlaget.

———. 1990. "The Making of the Past in the *Iliad*." *Harvard Studies in Classical Philology* 93:25–45.

Andreev, N., and G. Vinogradov (Н. Андреев и Г. Виноградов). 1937. "Русские Плачи." In *Русские Плачи (причитания)*, ed. G. Vinogradov (Г. Виноградов), vi–xxxv. Moscow: Советский Писатель.

Aneziri, S. 2009. "World Travelers: The Associations of Artists of Dionysus." In Hunter and Rutherford 2009:217–236.

Apthorp, M. 1977. "The Language of *Odyssey* 5.7–20." *Classical Quarterly* 27:1–9.

Arend, W. 1933. *Die typischen Scenen bei Homer*. Berlin: Weidmann.

Arft, J. 2017. "Structure as *Sēma*: Structural and Liminal Middles in the *Odyssey*." *Yearbook of Ancient Greek Epic* 1:5–45.

Arthurs, J. 1994. "The Term *Rhetor* in Fifth- and Fourth-Century B.C. Greek Texts." *Rhetoric Society Quarterly* 23:1–10.

Astakhova, A. (А. Астахова). 1938. *Былины Севера. Том первый: Мезень и Печора*. Moscow: Издательство Академии Наук СССР.

———. 1939. "Беломорская сказительница М.С. Крюкова." *Советский Фольклор* 6:176–213.

———. 1951. *Былины Севера. Том второй: Прионежье, Пинега и Поморье*. Moscow: Издательство Академии Наук СССР.

Athanassaki, L. 2009. *Ἀείδετο πὰν τέμενος: Οι χορικές παραστάσεις και το κοινό τους στην αρχαϊκή και πρώιμη κλασική περίοδο*. Herakleion: University of Crete.

Athens, L. 1994. "The Self as Soliloquy." *Sociological Quarterly* 35:521–532.

———. 1995. "Dramatic Self Change." *Sociological Quarterly* 36:571–586.

Austin, J. L. 1962. *How to Do Things with Words*. Cambridge, MA: Harvard University Press.

Austin, N. 1966. "The Function of Digressions in the *Iliad*." *Greek, Roman, and Byzantine Studies* 7:295–312.

———. 1975. *Archery at the Dark of the Moon: Poetic Problems in Homer's "Odyssey."* Berkeley: University of California Press.

———. 1991. "The Wedding Text in Homer's *Odyssey*." *Arion* 1:227–243.

Bachvarova, M. R. 2015. "Migrations in the Anatolian Epic Tradition." In *Nostoi: Indigenous Culture, Migration, and Integration in the Aegean Islands and Western Anatolia during the Late Bronze and Early Iron Ages, March 18, 2011, Koç University, Istanbul*, ed. K. Kopanias, Ç. Maner, and N. C. Stampolidis, 117–155. Istanbul: Koç University Press.

———. 2016. *From Hittite to Homer: The Anatolian Background of Ancient Greek Epic*. Cambridge: Cambridge University Press.

Baggio, M. 2006. "*Tutius est igitur fictis contendere verbis quam pugnare manu* (Ov. *Met*. XIII, 98): Il caso della pelike H3358 al Museo Archeologico di Napoli." In *Iconografia 2005: Immagini e immaginari dall'antichità classica al mondo moderno. Atti del Convegno Internazionale (Venezia, Istituto Veneto di Scienze Lettere e Arti, 26–28 gennaio 2005)*, ed. I. Colpo, I. Favaretto, and F. Ghedini, 89–104. Rome: Quasar.

Bakker, E. J. 1997a. *Poetry in Speech: Orality and Homeric Discourse*. Ithaca, NY: Cornell University Press.

———. 1997b. "Verbal Aspect and Mimetic Description in Thucydides." In *Grammar as Interpretation: Greek Literature in Its Linguistic Contexts*, ed. E. J. Bakker, 7–54. Leiden: Brill.

———. 2005. *Pointing at the Past: From Formula to Performance in Homeric Poetics*. Washington, DC: Center for Hellenic Studies.

———. 2009. "Homer, Odysseus, and the Narratology of Performance." In *Narratology and Interpretation: The Content of Narrative Form in Ancient Literature*, ed. J. Grethlein and A. Rengakos, 117–136. Berlin: de Gruyter.

———. 2013. *The Meaning of Meat and the Structure of the "Odyssey."* New York: Cambridge University Press.

Bal, M. 1983. "The Narrating and the Focalizing: A Theory of the Agents in Narrative." *Style* 17:234–269.

Balensiefen, E. 1955. "Die Zeitgestaltung in Homers Ilias." PhD diss., Tübingen.

Banfield, A. 1982. *Unspeakable Sentences: Narration and Representation in the Language of Fiction*. Boston: Routledge and Kegan Paul.

Barber, K. 1999. "Quotation in the Constitution of Yorùbá Oral Texts." *Research in African Literatures* 30:17–41.

———. 2003. "Text and Performance in Africa." *Bulletin of the School of Oriental and African Studies* 66:324–333.

———. 2005. "Text and Performance in Africa." *Oral Tradition* 20:264–277.

———. 2007. *The Anthropology of Texts, Persons, and Publics: Oral and Written Culture in Africa and Beyond*. Cambridge: Cambridge University Press.

Barker, E. T. E. 2004. "Achilles' Last Stand: Institutionalising Dissent in Homer's *Iliad*." *Proceedings of the Cambridge Philological Society* 50:92–120.

———. 2009. *Entering the Agôn: Dissent and Authority in Homer, Historiography, and Tragedy*. Oxford: Oxford University Press.

Barker, E. T. E., and J. P. Christensen. 2015. "Odysseus' Nostos and the *Odyssey*'s Nostoi." *Philologia Antiqua* 7:87–112.

Bassett, S. E. 1938. *The Poetry of Homer*. Berkeley: University of California Press.

Bassi, K. 2016. *Traces of the Past: Classics between History and Archaeology*. Ann Arbor: University of Michigan Press.

Bauman, R. 1977. *Verbal Art as Performance*. Rowley: Newbury House.

———. 1992. "Performance." In *Folklore, Cultural Performances, and Popular Entertainments*, ed. R. Bauman, 41–49. Oxford: Oxford University Press.

———. 2004. *A World of Others' Words: Cross-Cultural Perspectives on Intertextuality*. Malden, MA: Blackwell.

———. 2011. "Commentary: Foundations in Performance." *Journal of Sociolinguistics* 15:707–720.

Bauman, R., and C. Briggs. 1990. "Poetics and Performance as Critical Perspectives on Language and Social Life." *Annual Review of Anthropology* 19: 59–88.

Baumeister, A. 1860. *Hymni Homerici*. Leipzig: Teubner.

Beaulieu, M. C. 2004. "L'héroïsation du poète Hésiode en Grèce ancienne." *Kernos* 17:103–117.

Beazley, J. D. 1947. "The Rosi Krater." *Journal of Hellenic Studies* 67:1–9.

Beck, D. 1999. "Speech Introductions and the Character Development of Telemachus." *Classical Journal* 94:121–141.

———. 2005. *Homeric Conversation*. Washington, DC: Center for Hellenic Studies.

———. 2012. *Speech Presentation in Homeric Epic*. Austin: University of Texas Press.

Beck, J.-W. 2015. "Poetae novelli." *Der Neue Pauly*. Brill Online.

Beekes, R. S. P. 2010. *Etymological Dictionary of Greek*. 2 vols. Leiden: Brill.

Beissinger, M., J. Tylus, and S. Wofford, eds. 1999. *Epic Traditions in the Contemporary World: The Poetics of Community*. Berkeley: University of California Press.

Belfiore, E. 2000. "Narratological Plots and Aristotle's Mythos." *Arethusa* 33: 37–65.

Bélis, A. 2003. "Un lyrikos de l'époque des Antonins: Mésomède de Crète." In *La poésie grecque antique. Actes du 13ème colloque de la Villa Kérylos à Beaulieu-sur-Mer les 18 et 19 octobre 2002*, 223–235. Paris: Académie des Inscriptions et Belles Lettres.

Bentz, M. 1998. *Panathenäische Preisamphoren: Eine athenische Vasengattung und ihre Funktion vom 6.–4. Jahrhundert v. Chr.* Basel: Freunde antiker Kunst.

Bergquist, B. 1990. "Sympotic Space: A Functional Aspect of Greek Dining-Rooms." In Murray 1990:37–65.

Bethe, E. 1914. *Homer: Dichtung und Sage* I: *Ilias*. Leipzig: Teubner.

Blondell, R. 2010. "'Bitch That I Am': Self-Blame and Self-Assertion in the *Iliad*." *Transactions of the American Philological Association* 140:1–32.

Boersma, J. 2000. "Peisistratos' Building Activity Reconsidered." In Sancisi-Weerdenburg 2000:49–56.

Böhme, J. 1929. *Die Seele und das Ich im homerischen Epos. Mit einem Anhang: Vergleich mit dem Glauben der Primitiven*. Leipzig: Teubner.

Bonaria, M. 1965. "Hegesias" and "Hermophantos." *Realencyclopädie der classischen Altertumswissenschaft*, Supplement Band X, cols. 244 and 321. Stuttgart: Druckenmuller.

Bonifazi, A. 2012. *Homer's Versicolored Fabric: The Evocative Power of Ancient Greek Epic Word-Making*. Washington, DC: Center for Hellenic Studies.

Bonifazi, A., A. Drummen, and M. de Kreij. 2016. *Particles in Ancient Greek Discourse: Five Volumes Exploring Particle Use across Genres*. Washington, DC: Center for Hellenic Studies. http://chs.harvard.edu/CHS/article/display/6391.

Bonnet, A. 2001. "En parcourant le Val des Muses. Remarques sur un concours musical de l'Antiquité: Les *Mouseia* de Thespies." In *Musique et poésie dans l'Antiquité*, ed. G.-J. Pinault, 53–60. Clermont-Ferrand: Presses de l'Université Blaise-Pascal.

Bowie, E. L. 1990. "Greek Poetry in the Antonine Age." In *Antonine Literature*, ed. D. A. Russell, 53–90. Oxford: Clarendon Press.

Bowra, C. M. 1930. *Tradition and Design in the "Iliad."* Oxford: Clarendon Press.

———. 1961. *Greek Lyric Poetry: From Alcman to Simonides*. Oxford: Oxford University Press.

Boyd, T. W. 1994. "Where Ion Stood, What Ion Sang." *Harvard Studies in Classical Philology* 96:109–121.

Bozzone, C. 2014. "Constructions: A New Approach to Formularity, Discourse, and Syntax in Homer." PhD diss., University of California Los Angeles.

Bréal, M. 1911. *Pour mieux connaître Homère*. 2nd ed. Paris: Hachette.

Broman, E. 2004. "Narratological Viewpoint Models—A Critical Survey." In *Essays in Fiction and Perspective*, ed. G. Rossholm, 57–89. Bern: Lang.

Brouillet, M. 2013. "Que disent les mots des dieux?" *Mètis* 11:147–182.

Brügger, C., M. Stoevesandt, and M. Visser. 2010. *Homers Ilias Gesamtkommentar*, Band II, Zweiter Gesang (B), Faszikel 2: *Kommentar*. Berlin: de Gruyter.

Bryce, T. R. 2006. *The Trojans and Their Neighbours: An Introduction*. London: Routledge.

Budelmann, F., and P. LeVen. 2014. "Timotheus' Poetics of Blending: A Cognitive Approach to the Language of the New Music." *Classical Philology* 109:191–210.

Bundrick, S. D. 2005. *Music and Image in Classical Athens*. Cambridge: Cambridge University Press.

———. 2015. "Recovering Rhapsodes: A New Vase by the Pantoxena Painter." *Classical Antiquity* 34:1–32.

Burgess, J. 1999. *The Death and Afterlife of Achilles*. Baltimore: Johns Hopkins University Press.

———. 2001. *The Tradition of the Trojan War in Homer and the Epic Cycle*. Baltimore: Johns Hopkins University Press.

———. 2004. "Performance and the Epic Cycle." *Classical Journal* 100:1–23.

Burkert, W. 1972a. *Homo Necans: Interpretationen altgriechischer Opferriten und Mythen*. Berlin: de Gruyter. [Rpt. 1997.]

———. 1972b. "Die Leistung eines Kreophylos: Kreopyleer, Homeriden und die archaische Heraklesepik." *Museum Helveticum* 29:74–85.

———. 1979. "Kynaithos, Polycrates, and the Homeric Hymn to Apollo." In *Arktouros: Hellenic Studies Presented to B. M. W. Knox*, ed. G. W. Bowersock, W. Burkert, and M. C. J. Putnam, 53–62. Berlin: de Gruyter.

———. 1987. "The Making of Homer in the Sixth Century B.C.: Rhapsodes versus Stesichoros." In *Papers on the Amasis Painter and His World*, 43–62. Malibu: J. Paul Getty Museum.

———. 1992. *The Orientalizing Revolution: Near Eastern Influence on Greek Culture in the Early Archaic Age*. Trans. M. E. Pinder and W. Burkert. Cambridge, MA: Harvard University Press.

———. 1998. "La cité d'Argos entre la tradition mycénienne, dorienne et homérique." In *Les Panthéons des cités des origines à la Périégèse de Pausanias*, ed. V. Pirenne-Delforge, 47–59. Liège: Centre international d'étude de la religion grecque antique.

Burnett, A. P. 1991. "Signals from the Unconscious in Early Greek Poetry." *Classical Philology* 86:275–300.

Burrage, D. G. 1947. "Education in the Homeric Age." *Classical Journal* 43: 147–152.

Cairns, D. L. 1993. *Aidōs: The Psychology and Ethics of Honour and Shame in Ancient Greek Literature*. Oxford: Oxford University Press.

———, ed. 2001. *Oxford Readings in Homer's "Iliad."* Oxford: Oxford University Press.

———. 2012. "*Atē* in the Homeric Poems." *Papers of the Langford Latin Seminar* 15:1–52.

Cairns, F. 2010. "The Genre '*Oaristys*.'" *Wiener Studien* 123:101–129.

Calame, C. 1996. "Montagne des Muses et *Mouseia*: La consécration des *Travaux* et l'héroïsation d'Homère." In Hurst and Schachter 1996:43–56.

Calvet, M., and P. Roesch. 1966. "Les Sarapieia de Tanagra." *Revue Archéologique* 2:297–332.

Camp, J. M. 2001. *The Archaeology of Athens*. New Haven: Yale University Press.

Capps, E. 1900. "Studies in Greek Agonistic Inscriptions." *Transactions and Proceedings of the American Philological Association* 31:112–137.

Caraveli, A. 1986. "The Bitter Wounding: Lament as a Social Protest in Rural Greece." In *Gender and Power in Rural Greece*, ed. J. Dubisch, 169–194. Princeton: Princeton University Press.

Carnes, M. C. 2014. *Minds on Fire: How Role-Immersion Games Transform College*. Cambridge, MA: Harvard University Press.

Cassio, A. 2005. "I dialetti eolici e la lingua della lirica corale." In *Dialetti e lingue letterarie nella Grecia antica. Atti della IV Giornata ghisleriana di Filologia classica*, ed. F. Bertolini and F. Gasti, 13–44. Pavia: Ibis.

Càssola, F. 1975. *Inni omerici*. Milan: Fondazione Lorenzo Valla.

Chafe, W. 1988. "Punctuation and the Prosody of Written Language." *Written Communication* 5:395–426.

Chaniotis, A. 1990. "Zur Frage der Spezialisierung im griechischen Theater des Hellenismus und der Kaiserzeit auf der Grundlage der neuen Prosopographie der dionysischen Techniten." *Ktéma* 15:89–108.

———. 2010. "'The Best of Homer': Homeric Texts, Performances, and Images in the Hellenistic World and Beyond. The Contribution of Inscriptions." In *Myths, Texts, Images: Homeric Epics and Ancient Greek Art*, ed. E. Walter-Karydi, 257–275. Ithaca, Greece: Center for Odyssean Studies.

———. Forthcoming. "The Oral Transmission of Memory in the Greek Cities of the Imperial Period." In *Orality and Greek Literature in the Roman Empire*, ed. C. Ruiz Montero.

Chantraine, P. 1953. *Grammaire homérique* II: *Syntaxe*. Paris: Klincksieck.

———. 1968–1980. *Dictionnaire étymologique de la langue grecque: Histoire des mots*. Paris: Klincksieck.

Chernyaeva, N. (Н. Черняева). 1981. *Русские эпические песни Карелии*. Petrozavodsk: Карелия.

Chicherov, V. (В. Чичеров). 1982. *Школы сказителей Заонежья*. Moscow: Наука.

Chistov, K. (К. Чистов). 1990. "Забытая статья А.И. Веселовского о Причитаниях Северного Края, собранных Е. В. Барсовым." In *Res philologica: Филологические исследования памяти академика Г.В. Степанова*, 453–459. Moscow: Наука.

Chistova, B., and K. Chistov (Б. Чистова и К. Чистов). 1997. *Причитания Северного Края собранные Е. В. Барсовым*. Saint Petersburg: Наука.

Christensen, J. P. 2009. "The End of Speeches and a Speech's End: Nestor, Diomedes, and the *Telos muthôn*." In *Reading Homer: Film and Text*, ed. K. Myrsiades, 136–162. Madison, NJ: Farleigh Dickinson University Press.

———. 2010. "First-Person Futures in Homer." *American Journal of Philology* 131: 543–571.

———. 2015a. "Trojan Politics and the Assemblies of *Iliad* 7." *Greek, Roman, and Byzantine Studies* 55:25–51.

———. 2015b. "Reconsidering 'Good' Speakers: Speech-Act Theory, Agamemnon, and the *Diapeira* of *Iliad* 2." *Gaia* 18:67–81.

Christensen, J. P., and E. T. E. Barker. 2011. "On Not Remembering Tydeus: Agamemnon, Diomedes, and the Contest for Thebes." *Materiali e Discussioni per l'Analisi dei Testi Classici* 66:9–44.

Cingano, E. 1985. "Clistene di Sicione: Erodoto e i poemi di ciclo tebano." *Quaderni Urbinati di Cultura Classica* 20: 31–40.

———. 2004. "Tradizioni epiche intorno ad Argo da Omero al VI sec. A.C." In *La città di Argo: Mito, storia, tradizioni poetiche*, ed. P. A. Bernardini, 59–78. Rome: Edizioni dell'Ateneo.

———. 2005. "A Catalogue within a Catalogue: Helen's Suitors in the Hesiodic *Catalogue of Women* (frr. 196–204)." In Hunter 2005a:118–152.

Clader, L. 1976. *Helen: The Evolution from Divine to Heroic in Greek Epic Tradition.* Leiden: Brill.

Clark, M. 1997a. *Out of Line: Homeric Composition beyond the Hexameter.* Lanham, MD: Rowman and Littlefield.

———. 1997b. "Chryses' Supplication: Speech Act and Mythological Allusion." *Classical Antiquity* 17:5–24.

———. 2007. "Poulydamas and Hektor." *College Literature* 34:85–106.

Clarke, H. 1967. *The Art of the "Odyssey."* Englewood Cliffs, NJ: Prentice Hall.

Clarke, M. 1999. *Flesh and Spirit in the Songs of Homer: A Study of Words and Myths.* Oxford: Clarendon Press.

Clay, J. S. 1983. *The Wrath of Athena: Gods and Men in the "Odyssey."* Princeton: Princeton University Press.

———. 1997. "The Homeric Hymns." In *A New Companion to Homer*, ed. I. Morris and B. Powell, 489–507. Leiden: Brill.

———. 2006. *The Politics of Olympus: Form and Meaning in the Major Homeric Hymns.* 2nd ed. London: Bristol Classical Press.

———. 2007. "Homer's Trojan Theater." *Transactions of the American Philological Association* 137:233–252.

———. 2011. *Homer's Trojan Theater: Space, Vision, and Memory in the "Iliad."* Cambridge: Cambridge University Press.

Collins, D. 2001a. "Homer and Rhapsodic Competition in Performance." *Oral Tradition* 16:129–167.

———. 2001b. "Improvisation in Rhapsodic Performance." *Helios* 28:11–27.

———. 2004. *Master of the Game: Competition and Performance in Greek Poetry.* Washington, DC: Center for Hellenic Studies.

Cook, E. F. 2009. "On the 'Importance' of *Iliad* Book 8." *Classical Philology* 104:133–161.

———. 2014. "Structure as Interpretation in the Homeric *Odyssey*." In *Defining Greek Narrative*, ed. D. Cairns and R. Scodel, 75–100. Edinburgh: Edinburgh University Press.

Cressey, J. C. 1982. "The Dogs of War." *Liverpool Classical Monthly* 7:22–24.

Crotty, K. 1994. *The Poetics of Supplication: Homer's "Iliad" and "Odyssey."* Ithaca, NY: Cornell University Press.

Crowther, N. B. 1994. "The Role of Heralds and Trumpeters at Greek Athletic Festivals." *Nikephoros* 7:135–155.

Csapo, E., and P. Wilson. 2015. "Drama outside Athens in the Fifth and Fourth Centuries BC." In *Reperformances of Drama in the Fifth and Fourth Centuries BC: Authors and Contexts*, ed. A. Lamari, 316–395. Berlin: de Gruyter.

Currie, B. 2006. "Homer and the Early Epic Tradition." In *Epic Interactions: Perspectives on Homer, Virgil, and the Epic Tradition Presented to Jasper Griffin*, ed. M. J. Clarke, B. G. F. Currie, and R. O. A. M. Lyne, 1–45. Oxford: Oxford University Press.

———. 2012. "Perspectives on Neoanalysis from the Archaic Hymns to Demeter." In *Relative Chronology in Early Greek Epic Poetry*, ed. Ö. Andersen and D. T. T. Haug, 184–209. Cambridge: Cambridge University Press.

———. 2016. *Homer's Allusive Art*. Oxford: Oxford University Press.

Dancygier, B. 2006. "What Can Blending Do for You?" *Language and Literature* 15:5–15.

———. 2008. "Personal Pronouns, Blending, and Narrative Viewpoint." In *Language in the Context of Use: Discourse and Cognitive Approaches to Language*, ed. A. Tyler, Y. Kim, and M. Takada, 167–182. Berlin: de Gruyter.

———. 2012. *The Language of Stories: A Cognitive Approach*. New York: Cambridge University Press.

Dancygier, B., and E. Sweetser. 2014. *Figurative Language*. New York: Cambridge University Press.

Danek, G. 1988. *Studien zur Dolonie*. Vienna: Österreichischen Akademie der Wissenschaften.

———. 1998. "Darstellung verdeckter Handlung bei Homer und in der südslawischen Heldenlied-Tradition." *Wiener Studien* 111:67–88.

D'Angour, A. 2013. "Plato and Play: Taking Education Seriously in Ancient Greece." *American Journal of Play* 5:293–307.

Davies, M. 2016. *The Aethiopis: Neo-Neoanalysis Reanalyzed*. Washington, DC: Center for Hellenic Studies.

Davison, J. A. 1958. "Notes on the Panathenaea." *Journal of Hellenic Studies* 78: 23–42.

———. 1962. "Addenda to 'Notes on the Panathenaea.'" *Journal of Hellenic Studies* 82:141–142.

———. 1965. "Thucydides, Homer, and the Achaean Wall." *Greek, Roman, and Byzantine Studies* 6:5–28.

Debiasi, A. 2003. "Ναυπάκτια–Ἀργοῦς ναυπηγία." *Eikasmòs* 14:91–101.

de Jong, I. J. F. 1985. "*Iliad* 1.366–92: A Mirror Story." *Arethusa* 18:5–22.

———. 1993. "Studies in Homeric Denomination." *Mnemosyne* 46:289–306.

———. 2001. *A Narratological Commentary on the "Odyssey."* Cambridge: Cambridge University Press.

———. 2004a [1987]. *Narrators and Focalizers: The Presentation of the Story in the "Iliad."* 2nd ed. London: Bristol Classical Press.

———. 2004b. "Homer." In *Narrators, Narratees, and Narratives in Ancient Greek Literature*, ed. I. J. F. de Jong, R. Nünlist, and A. Bowie, 13–24. Leiden: Brill.

———. 2007. "Homer." In *Space and Time in Ancient Greek Literature*, ed. I. J. F. de Jong and R. Nünlist, 17–38. Leiden: Brill.

———. 2009. "Metalepsis in Ancient Greek Literature." In *Narratology and Interpretation: The Content of Narrative Form in Ancient Literature*, ed. J. Grethlein and A. Rengakos, 87–115. Berlin: de Gruyter.

———. 2012. *Homer: "Iliad" Book XXII.* Cambridge: Cambridge University Press.

Dentice di Accadia Ammone, S. 2012. *Omero e i suoi oratori: Tecniche di persuasione nell'"Iliade."* Berlin: de Gruyter.

Deubner, L. 1969. *Attische Feste.* Darmstadt: Wissenschaftliche Buchgesellschaft.

de Vet, T. 2008. "Context and the Emerging Story: Improvised Performance in Oral and Literate Societies." *Oral Tradition* 23:159–179.

Dickson, K. 1995. *Nestor: Poetic Memory in Greek Epic.* New York: Garland.

Doane, A. N. 1991. "Oral Texts, Intertexts, and Intratexts: Editing Old English." In *Influence and Intertextuality in Literary History*, ed. J. Clayton and E. Rothstein, 75–113. Madison: University of Wisconsin Press.

Dodds, E. R. 1951. *The Greeks and the Irrational.* Berkeley: University of California Press.

Donlan, W. 1989. "The Unequal Exchange between Glaucus and Diomedes in Light of the Homeric Gift-Economy." *Phoenix* 43:1–15.

———. 1997. "The Relations of Power in the Pre-State and Early State Polities." In *The Development of the Polis in Archaic Greece*, ed. L. Mitchell and P. J. Rhodes, 39–48. London: Routledge.

———. 2002. "Achilles the Ally." *Arethusa* 35:155–172.

Dougherty, C. 2001. *The Raft of Odysseus: The Ethnographic Imagination of Homer's "Odyssey."* Oxford: Oxford University Press.

Dräger, P. 1993. *Argo pasimelousa: Der Argonautenmythos in der griechischen und römischen Literatur.* Stuttgart: Franz Steiner.

Duban, J. M. 1980. "Distortion as a Poetic Device in the 'Pursuit of Hektor' and Related Events." *Aevum* 54:3–22.

Duclos, G. S. 1987. "The Education of Achilles: Through a Glass Darkly." *Journal of Humanities* 1:55–64.

Dué, C. 2002. *Homeric Variations on a Lament by Briseis.* Lanham, MD: Rowman and Littlefield.

———. 2006. *The Captive Woman's Lament in Greek Tragedy.* Austin: University of Texas Press.

Dué, C., and M. Ebbott. 2010. *"Iliad" 10 and the Poetics of Ambush: A Multitext Edition with Essays and Commentary.* Washington, DC: Center for Hellenic Studies.

Duffy, W., and W. M. Short. 2016. "Metaphor as Ideology: The Greek 'Folk

Model' of the Epic Tradition." In *Oral Poetics and Cognitive Science*, ed. M. Antović and C. Pagán Cánovas, 52–78. Berlin: de Gruyter.

Ebbott, M. 2010. "Error 404: Theban Epic Not Found." *Trends in Classics* 2: 239–258.

———. 2014. "Allies in Fame: Recruiting Warriors in the Theban and Trojan Traditions." *Trends in Classics* 6:319–335.

———. Forthcoming. "Homeric Epic in Performance." In *Cambridge Homer Encyclopedia*, ed. C. Pache. Cambridge: Cambridge University Press.

Eck, W. 1983. "Jahres- und Provinzialfasten der senatorischen Statthalter von 69/70 bis 138/139. 2. Teil." *Chiron* 13:147–237.

Edelstein, L. 1945. *Asclepius: Collection and Interpretation of the Testimonies*, vol. 2. Baltimore: Johns Hopkins University Press.

Edmunds, L. 2016. *Stealing Helen: The Myth of the Abducted Wife in Comparative Perspective*. Princeton: Princeton University Press.

Edmunds, S. 1990. *Homeric Nēpios*. New York: Garland.

Edwards, A. T. 1985. *Achilles in the "Odyssey."* Königstein: Anton Hain.

Edwards, M. W. 1970. "Homeric Speech Introductions." *Harvard Studies in Classical Philology* 74:1–36.

———. 1987a. "*Topos* and Transformation in Homer." In *Homer: Beyond Oral Poetry. Recent Trends in Homeric Interpretation*, ed. J. M. Bremer, I. J. F. de Jong, and J. S. Kalff, 47–60. Amsterdam: Grüner.

———. 1987b. *Homer: Poet of the "Iliad."* Baltimore: Johns Hopkins University Press.

———. 1991. *The "Iliad": A Commentary*, vol. 5: *Books 17–20*. Cambridge: Cambridge University Press.

Elmer, D. F. 2005. "Helen *Epigrammatapoios*." *Classical Antiquity* 24:1–39.

———. 2013. *The Poetics of Consent: Collective Decision Making and the "Iliad."* Baltimore: Johns Hopkins University Press.

———. 2015. "The 'Narrow Road' and the Ethics of Language Use in the *Iliad* and the *Odyssey*." *Ramus* 44:155–183.

Emlyn-Jones, C. 1984. "The Reunion of Penelope and Odysseus." *Greece and Rome* 31:1–18.

Erbse, H. 1969, 1971, 1974, 1975, 1977. *Scholia graeca in Homeri Iliadem*, vols. 1, 2, 3, 4, 5. Berlin: de Gruyter.

———. 1994. "Milman Parry und Homer." *Hermes* 122:257–274.

Fantuzzi, M. 1988. "Introduction." In Ziegler 1988:xxv–lxxxxix.

Fantuzzi, M., and C. Tsagalis. 2015. "Introduction." In *A Companion to the Greek Epic Cycle and Its Fortune in the Ancient World*, ed. M. Fantuzzi and C. Tsagalis, 1–40. Cambridge: Cambridge University Press.

Faraone, C. A. 2013. "The Poetics of the Catalogue in the Hesiodic *Theogony*." *Transactions of the American Philological Association* 143:293–323.

———. 2016. "On the Eve of Epic: Did the Chryses Episode in *Iliad* I Begin Its Life as a Separate Homeric Hymn?" In *Persistent Forms: Explorations in Historical Poetics*, ed. B. Maslov and I. Kligers, 397–428. New York: Fordham University Press.

Farmer, M. S. 1998. "Sophocles' Ajax and Homer's Hector: Two Soliloquies." *Illinois Classical Studies* 23:19–45.

Fauconnier, G. 1994 [1985]. *Mental Spaces: Aspects of Meaning Construction in Natural Language.* Cambridge: Cambridge University Press.

Fauconnier, G., and M. Turner. 2002. *The Way We Think: Conceptual Blending and the Mind's Hidden Complexities.* New York: Basic Books.

Faulkner, A. 2008. *The Homeric Hymn to Aphrodite: Introduction, Text, and Commentary.* Oxford: Oxford University Press.

Fehling, D. 1969. *Die Wiederholungsfiguren und ihr Gebrauch bei den Griechen vor Gorgias.* Berlin: de Gruyter.

———. 1991. *Die ursprüngliche Geschichte vom Fall Trojas, oder: Interpretationen zur Troja-Geschichte.* Innsbruck: Institut für Sprachwissenschaft der Universität Innsbruck.

Fein, S. 1994. *Die Beziehungen der Kaiser Trajan und Hadrian zu den litterati.* Stuttgart: Teubner.

Felson-Rubin, N. 1994. *Regarding Penelope: From Character to Poetics.* Princeton: Princeton University Press.

Fenik, B. 1968. *Typical Battle Scenes in the "Iliad."* Wiesbaden: Franz Steiner.

———. 1978. "Stylization and Variety: Four Monologues in the *Iliad.*" In *Homer: Tradition and Invention*, ed. B. Fenik, 68–90. Leiden: Brill.

Feyel, M. 1942. *Contribution à l'épigraphie béotienne.* Le Puy: La Haute-Loire.

Finkelberg, M. 1995. "Patterns of Human Error in Homer." *Journal of Hellenic Studies* 115:15–28.

———. 1998. *The Birth of Literary Fiction in Ancient Greece.* Oxford: Clarendon Press.

———, ed. 2011. *The Homer Encyclopedia.* Malden, MA: Wiley-Blackwell. [Electronic.]

———. 2012. "Late Features in the Speeches of the *Iliad.*" In *Relative Chronology in Early Greek Epic Poetry*, ed. Ø. Andersen and D. T. T. Haug, 80–95. Cambridge: Cambridge University Press.

Finnegan, R. 2007. *The Oral and Beyond: Doing Things with Words in Africa.* Oxford: James Currey.

———. 2011. *Why Do We Quote? The Culture and History of Quotation.* Cambridge: Open Book Publishers.

Fleischman, S. 1990. *Tense and Narrativity: From Medieval Performance to Modern Fiction.* Austin: University of Texas Press.

Fletcher, K. B. 2006. Review of Hunter 2005a. *Bryn Mawr Classical Review* 2006.10.03.

Fludernik, M. 1993. *The Fictions of Language and the Languages of Fiction: The Linguistic Representation of Speech and Consciousness.* London: Routledge.

Flueckiger, J. B. 1989. "Caste and Regional Variants in an Oral Epic Tradition." In *Oral Epics in India*, ed. S. Blackburn et al., 33–54. Berkeley: University of California Press.

———. 1996. *Gender and Genre in the Folklore of Middle India.* Ithaca, NY: Cornell University Press.

Foley, H. P. 1994. *The Homeric Hymn to Demeter.* Princeton: Princeton University Press.

Foley, J. M. 1991. *Immanent Art: From Structure to Meaning in Traditional Oral Epic.* Bloomington: Indiana University Press.

———. 1995. *The Singer of Tales in Performance.* Bloomington: Indiana University Press.

———. 1999. *Homer's Traditional Art.* University Park: Pennsylvania State University Press.

———. 2002. *How to Read an Oral Poem.* Urbana: University of Illinois Press.

Ford, A. 1988. "The Classical Definition of ΡΑΨΩΙΔΙΑ." *Classical Philology* 83:300–307.

———. 1992. *Homer: The Poetry of the Past.* Ithaca, NY: Cornell University Press.

———. 1997. "The Inland Ship: Problems in the Performance and Reception of Homeric Epic." In *Written Voices, Spoken Signs: Tradition, Performance, and the Epic Text,* ed. E. Bakker and A. Kahane, 83–109. Cambridge, MA: Harvard University Press.

———. 2011. "Singers." In Finkelberg 2011.

Forrest, W. G. 1981. "A Lost Peisistratid Name." *Journal of Hellenic Studies* 101:134.

Fowler, R. L. 1987. "The Rhetoric of Desperation." *Harvard Studies in Classical Philology* 91:5–38.

Frame, D. 2009. *Hippota Nestor.* Washington, DC: Center for Hellenic Studies.

Fränkel, H. 1962. *Dichtung und Philosophie des frühen Griechentums: Eine Geschichte der griechischen Epik, Lyrik und Prosa bis zur Mitte des fünften Jahrhunderts.* 2nd ed. Munich: Beck.

Fraser, P. M., E. Matthews, M. J. Osborne et al. 1987–2000. *A Lexicon of Greek Personal Names.* 3 vols. Oxford: Clarendon Press.

Freeman, J. C. 2010. "Interrogating the Soliloquist: Does It Really Go without Saying?" *Symplokē* 18:131–154.

Frei, J. 1900. *De certaminibus thymelicis.* Basel: E. Birkhaeuser.

Friedman, R. 2001. "Divine Dissension and the Narrative of the *Iliad.*" *Helios* 28:99–118.

Friedrich, R. 2000. "Homeric Enjambement and Orality." *Hermes* 128:1–19.

———. 2002. "'Flaubertian Homer': The *Phrase Juste* in Homeric Diction." *Arion* 10:1–13.

Friis Johansen, K. 1967. *The "Iliad" in Early Greek Art.* Copenhagen: Munksgaard.

Frisk, H. 1960–1972. *Griechisches etymologisches Wörterbuch.* 3 vols. Heidelberg: Winter.

Frog. 2011. "Distinguishing Continuities: Textual Entities, Extra-Textual Entities, and Conceptual Schemes." *Retrospective Methods Network Newsletter* 2:7–15.

Gagliardi, P. 2006a. "Il lamento di Elena e il finale dell'*Iliade.*" *Seminari Romani du Cultura Greca* 9:189–217.

———. 2006b. "I lamenti di Andromaca nell'*Iliade*." *Gaia: Revue Interdisciplinaire sur la Grèce Archaïque* 10:11–46.

Gainsford, P. 2015. *Early Greek Hexameter Poetry*. Cambridge: Cambridge University Press.

Gangloff, A. 2010. "Rhapsodes et poètes épiques à l'époque impériale." *Revue des Études Grecques* 123:51–70.

Gantz, T. 1993. *Early Greek Myth: A Guide to Literary and Artistic Sources*. 2 vols. Baltimore: Johns Hopkins University Press.

Garcia, L. F., Jr. 2013. *Homeric Durability: Telling Time in the "Iliad."* Washington, DC: Center for Hellenic Studies.

Garelli-François, M.-H. 2000. "Ludions, homéristes ou pantomimes? (Sénèque, *Ep.* 117; Fronton, éd. Naber p. 158)." *Revue des Études Anciennes* 102:501–508.

Gaskin, R. 1990. "Do Homeric Heroes Make Real Decisions?" *Classical Quarterly* 40:1–15.

Gelzer, T. 1987. "Bemerkungen zu Homerische Ares-Hymnus (Hom. Hy. 8)." *Museum Helveticum* 44:150–167.

Genette, G. 1972. *Figures 3*. Paris: du Seuil.

———. 1980. *Narrative Discourse: An Essay in Method*. Ithaca, NY: Cornell University Press.

Gentili, B. 1988. *Poetry and Its Public in Ancient Greece: From Homer to the Fifth Century*. Trans. A. T. Cole. Baltimore: Johns Hopkins University Press.

Gera, D. L. 2003. *Ancient Greek Ideas on Speech, Language, and Civilization*. Oxford: Oxford University Press.

Germain, G. 1954. *Genèse de l'Odyssée*. Paris: Presses Universitaires de France.

Ghedini, F. 2009. "L'oratore fra Grecia e Roma: I gesti dell'eloquenza attraverso le immagini." In *Gesto—Immagine tra antico e moderno. Riflessioni sulla comunicazione non-verbale*, ed. M. Salvadori and M. Baggio, 47–61. Rome: Quasar.

Gilferding, A. (А. Гильфердинг). 1894–1900. *Онежские былины, записанные А. Ф. Гильфердингом*, vol. 1 (1894), vol. 2 (1896), vol. 3 (1900). Saint Petersburg: Типография Императорской Академии Наук.

Gill, C. 1996. *Personality in Greek Epic, Tragedy, and Philosophy: The Self in Dialogue*. Oxford: Oxford University Press.

Glassie, H. 2003. "Tradition." In *Eight Words for the Study of Expressive Culture*, ed. B. Feintuch, 176–197. Urbana: University of Illinois Press.

Goldman, L. 1983. *Talk Never Dies: The Language of Huli Disputes*. London: Tavistock.

González, J. M. 2013. *The Epic Rhapsode and His Craft*. Washington, DC: Center for Hellenic Studies.

González de Tobía, A. M. 1998/1999. "Un soliloquio escénico significativo: *Ilíada*, XXII, 99–130." *Praesentia* 2:109–126.

Gottesman, A. 2008. "The Pragmatics of Homeric *Kertomia*." *Classical Quarterly* 58:1–12.

Gottschall, J. 2012. *The Storytelling Animal: How Stories Make Us Human*. Boston: Mariner Books.

Gould, J. 1973. "IKETEIA." *Journal of Hellenic Studies* 93:74–103.

Grandolini, S. 1996. *Canti e aedi nei poemi omerici: Edizione e commento*. Pisa: Istituti Editoriali e Poligrafici Internazionali.

Graziosi, B. 2002. *Inventing Homer: The Early Reception of Epic*. Cambridge: Cambridge University Press.

Graziosi, B., and J. Haubold. 2005. *Homer: The Resonance of Epic*. London: Duckworth.

———. 2015. "The Homeric Text." *Ramus* 44:1–24.

Grethlein, J. 2006. *Das Geschichtsbild der Ilias: Eine Untersuchung aus phänomenologischer und narratologischer Perspektive*. Göttingen: Vandenhoeck and Ruprecht.

———. 2008. "Memory and Material Objects in the *Iliad* and the *Odyssey*." *Journal of Hellenic Studies* 128:27–51.

Griffin, J. 1977. "The Epic Cycle and the Uniqueness of Homer." *Journal of Hellenic Studies* 97:39–53.

———. 1980. *Homer on Life and Death*. Oxford: Clarendon Press.

———. 1986. "Homeric Words and Speakers." *Journal of Hellenic Studies* 106: 36–57.

———. 1992. "Theocritus, the *Iliad*, and the East." *American Journal of Philology* 113:189–211.

———. 2004. "The Speeches." In *The Cambridge Companion to Homer*, ed. R. Fowler, 156–167. Cambridge: Cambridge University Press.

Griffith, M. 1990. "Contest and Contradiction in Early Greek Poetry." In *Cabinet of the Muses: Essays on Classical and Comparative Literature in Honor of Thomas G. Rosenmeyer*, ed. M. Griffith and D. J. Mastronarde, 185–207. Atlanta: Scholars Press.

———. 2001. "Public and Private in Early Greek Systems of Education." In *Education in Greek and Roman Antiquity*, ed. Y. L. Too, 23–84. Leiden: Brill.

Grigoriev, A. (А. Григорьев). 2002. *Архангельские Былины и Исторические Песни*, vol. 1. Saint Petersburg: Тропа Троянова.

———. 2003. *Архангельские Былины и Исторические Песни*, vol. 3. Saint Petersburg: Тропа Троянова.

Groddeck, G. E. 1786. *De Hymnorum Homericorum Reliquiis*. Göttingen: J. C. Dieterich.

Grossardt, P. 2006. "Die Träume der Penelope in 19. und 20. Buch der Odyssee: Eine ethnographische Parallele aus Usbekistan." *Wiener Studien* 119:23–37.

Grote, G. 1869. *A History of Greece*. 2nd ed. Vol. 2. London: John Murray.

Guenther, M. 2006. "N//àe ('Talking'): The Oral and Rhetorical Base of San Culture." *Journal of Folklore Research* 43:241–261.

Gutsfeld, A. ed. 2013. *Der gymnische Agon in der Spätantike*. Gutenberg: Computus.

Haber, J. 1994. *Pastoral and the Poetics of Self-Contradiction: Theocritus to Marvell*. Cambridge: Cambridge University Press.

Haft, A. J. 1990. "'The City-Sacker Odysseus' in *Iliad* 2 and 10." *Transactions of the American Philological Association* 120:37–56.

Hainsworth, J. B. 1993. *The "Iliad": A Commentary*, vol. 3: *Books 9–12*. Cambridge: Cambridge University Press.

Halperin, D. M. 1983. *Before Pastoral: Theocritus and the Ancient Tradition of Bucolic Poetry.* New Haven: Yale University Press.

Hamilton, R. 1989a. *The Architecture of Hesiodic Poetry.* Baltimore: Johns Hopkins University Press.

———. 1989b. "Alkman and the Athenian Arkteia." *Hesperia* 58:449–472.

Hammer, D. 1997. "'Who Shall Readily Obey?' Authority and Politics in the *Iliad.*" *Phoenix* 51:1–24.

———. 2002. *The "Iliad" as Politics: The Performance of Political Thought.* Norman: University of Oklahoma Press.

Hatto, A. 1983. "Jantay: A Kirghiz Lament for a Chieftain, Dated 1867–1869." In *Documenta Barbarorum. Festschrift für Walther Heissig zum 70. Geburtstag,* ed. K. Sagaster and M. Weierseds, 186–195. Wiesbaden: Harrassowitz.

———. 1990. *The Manas of Wilhelm Radloff.* Wiesbaden: Harrassowitz.

Haubold, J. 2000. *Homer's People: Epic Poetry and Social Formation.* Oxford: Oxford University Press.

Heath, J. 2001. "Telemachus *PEPNUMENOS*: Growing into an Epithet." *Mnemosyne* 54:129–157.

———. 2005. *The Talking Greeks: Speech, Animals, and the Other in Homer, Aeschylus, and Plato.* Cambridge: Cambridge University Press.

Hedreen, G. 2001. *Capturing Troy: The Narrative Functions of Landscape in Archaic and Early Classical Greek Art.* Ann Arbor: University of Michigan Press.

Heger, N. 1980. "Ein Homerista in einer Inschrift aus Noricum." In *Symmicta Philologica Salisburgensia Georgio Pfligersdorffer Sexagenario Oblata,* ed. J. Dalfen, 235–239. Rome: Edizioni Ateneo.

Heiden, B. 1998. "The Placement of the Book Divisions within the *Iliad.*" *Journal of Hellenic Studies* 118:68–81.

Heitman, R. 2005. *Taking Her Seriously: Penelope and the Plot of Homer's "Odyssey."* Ann Arbor: University of Michigan Press.

Heitsch, E. 1965. *Aphroditehymnos, Aeneas und Homer.* Göttingen: Vandenhoeck and Ruprecht.

———. 1968. *Epische Kunstsprache und Homerische Chronologie.* Heidelberg: Winter.

Hellwig, B. 1964. *Raum und Zeit in homerischen Epos.* Hildesheim: Olms.

Henrichs, A. 1975. "Philodems *De pietate* als mythographische Quelle." *Cronache Ercolanesi* 5:5–38.

Hentze, C. 1904. "Die Monologe in homerischen Epen." *Philologus* 63:12–30.

Herington, J. 1985. *Poetry into Drama: Early Tragedy and the Greek Poetic Tradition.* Berkeley: University of California Press.

Herman, D. 2009. "Cognitive Approaches to Narrative Analysis." In *Cognitive Poetics: Goals, Gains, and Gaps,* ed. G. Brône and J. Vandaele, 79–118. Berlin: de Gruyter.

Hermann, K. F. 1846. *Lehrbuch der griechischen Antiquitäten.* Vol. 2. Heidelberg: J. C. B. Mohr.

Herrero de Jáuregui, M. 2011. "Priam's Catabasis: Traces of the Epic Journey to Hades in *Iliad* 24." *Transactions of the American Philological Association* 141:37–68.

Higbie, C. 1995. *Heroes' Names, Homeric Identities.* New York: Garland.

Hillgruber, M. 2000. "Homer im Dienste des Mimus: Zur künstlerischen Eigenart der Homeristen." *Zeitschrift fur Papyrologie und Epigraphik* 132:63–72.

Hogan, J. C. 1981. "Eris in Homer." *Grazer Beiträge* 10:21–58.

Högemann, P. 2000. "Zum Iliasdichter—Ein anatolischer Standpunkt." *Studia Troica* 10:183–198.

Holleaux, M. 1890. "Inscriptions du temple d'Apollon Ptoos." *Bulletin de Correspondance Hellénique* 14:1–64, 181–204.

Holst-Warhaft, G. 1992. *Dangerous Voices: Women's Laments and Greek Literature.* New York: Routledge.

Honko, L. 1998. *Textualising the Siri Epic.* Helsinki: Suomalainen Tiedeakatemia.

———. 2000. "Text as Process and Practice: The Textualization of Oral Epics." In *Textualization of Oral Epics*, ed. L. Honko, 3–54. Berlin: Mouton de Gruyter.

Horrocks, G. C. 1997. "Homer's Dialect." In *A New Companion to Homer*, ed. I. Morris and B. Powell, 193–217. Leiden: Brill.

Hubbard, T. K. 1992. "Remaking Myth and Rewriting History: Cult Tradition in Pindar's *Ninth Nemean*." *Harvard Studies in Classical Philology* 94:77–111.

Huitink, L. 2013. Review of D. Beck 2012. *Bryn Mawr Classical Review* 2013.10.57.

Hunter, R. ed. 2005a. *The Hesiodic Catalogue of Women: Constructions and Reconstructions.* Cambridge: Cambridge University Press.

———. 2005b. "'Sweet Talk': *Song of Songs* and the Traditions of Greek Poetry." In *Perspectives on the Song of Songs*, ed. A. C. Hagedorn, 228–244. Berlin: de Gruyter.

Hunter, R., and I. Rutherford, eds. 2009. *Wandering Poets in Ancient Greek Culture: Travel, Locality, and Pan-Hellenism.* Cambridge: Cambridge University Press.

Hurst, A., and A. Schachter, eds. 1996. *La montagne des Muses.* Genève: Droz.

Hurwit, J. M. 1999. *The Athenian Acropolis: History, Mythology, and Archaeology from the Neolithic Era to the Present.* Cambridge: Cambridge University Press.

Husson, G. 1993. "Les homéristes." *Journal of Juristic Papyrology* 23:93–99.

Huxley, G. L. 1969. *Greek Epic Poetry from Eumelus to Panyassis.* London.

Ilgen, C. D. 1796. *Hymni Homerici cum Reliquis Carminibus Minoribus Homero Tribui Solutis et Batrachomyomachia.* Halle: Hermerden.

Irwin, E. 2005. "Gods among Men? The Social and Political Dynamics of the Hesiodic *Catalogue of Women*." In Hunter 2005a:35–84.

Iser, W. 1974. *The Implied Reader: Patterns of Communication in Prose Fiction from Bunyan to Beckett.* Baltimore: Johns Hopkins University Press.

Jacoby, F. 1916. "Iason von Nysa." *Realencyclopädie der classischen Altertumswissenschaft*, vol. 9, col. 180. Stuttgart: Druckenmuller.

Jamison, S. W. 1994. "Draupadi from the Walls of Troy: *Iliad* 3 from an Indic Perpective." *Classical Antiquity* 13:5–16.

Jamot, P. 1895. "Fouilles de Thespies: Les jeux en l'honneur des Muses." *Bulletin de Correspondance Hellénique* 19:311–385.

Janko, R. 1982. *Homer, Hesiod, and the Hymns: Diachronic Development in Epic Diction*. Cambridge: Cambridge University Press.

———. 1992. *The "Iliad": A Commentary*, vol. 4: *Books 13–16*. Cambridge: Cambridge University Press.

Jensen, M. S. 1980. *The Homeric Question and the Oral-Formulaic Theory*. Copenhagen: Museum Tusculanum Press.

———. 2011. *Writing Homer: A Study Based on Results from Modern Fieldwork*. Copenhagen: Det Kongelige Danske Videnskabernes Selskab.

Jensen, M. S., et al. 1999. "Dividing Homer: When and How Were the *Iliad* and *Odyssey* Divided into Songs?" *Symbolae Osloenses* 74:5–91.

Johnston, S. I. 1992. "Xanthus, Hera, and the Erinyes." *Transactions of the American Philological Association* 122:85–98.

Jones, B. N. 2011a. "Relative Chronology and an 'Aeolic Phase' of Epic." In *Relative Chronology and Early Greek Epic Poetry*, ed. Ø. Andersen and D. Haug, 44–64. Cambridge: Cambridge University Press.

———. 2011b. "Relative Chronology within (an) Oral Tradition." *Classical Journal* 105:289–318.

Jörgensen, O. 1904. "Die Auftreten der Goetter in den Buechern ι–μ der Odyssee." *Hermes* 39:357–382.

Joubert, A. 2004. *The Power of Performance: Linking Past and Present in Hananwa and Lobedu Oral Literature*. Berlin: Mouton de Gruyter.

Jowett, B. 1931. *The Dialogues of Plato*. 3rd ed. Vol. 3. Oxford: Oxford University Press.

Kahane, A. 1994. *The Interpretation of Order: A Study in the Poetics of Homeric Repetition*. Oxford: Clarendon Press.

———. 1997. "The Call of the Epic: The Poetics of Proper-Name Vocative Localization in Homer." In Létoublon and Dik 1997:251–262.

Kaibel, G. 1965. *Epigrammata Graeca ex Lapidibus Conlecta*. Hildesheim: Olms. [First published in 1878 by G. Reimer.]

Karanika, A. 2013. "Wedding and Performance in Homer: A View in the 'Teichoskopia'." *Trends in Classics* 5:208–223.

———. 2014. *Voices at Work: Women, Performance, and Labor in Ancient Greece*. Baltimore: Johns Hopkins University Press.

Karataev, M. (М. Каратаев). 1968. "Аитыс XIX–начала XX в." In *Казахский фольклор*, ed. N. Smirnova (Н. Смирнова), 324–340. Alma Ata: Наука.

Karomatli, F. (Ф. Кароматли). 1999. "О музыке узбекских дастанов и особенностях ее проявления в Алпамыше." In Mirzaev, Abdurakhimov, and Mirbaldaeva 1999:50–63.

Kelly, A. 2007. *A Referential Commentary and Lexicon to Homer "Iliad" VIII*. Oxford: Oxford University Press.

———. 2008. "Performance and Rivalry: Homer, Odysseus, and Hesiod." In *Performance, Reception, Iconography: Studies in Honour of Oliver Taplin*, ed. M. Revermann and P. Wilson, 177–203. Oxford: Oxford University Press.

Kennedy, G. 1963. *The Art of Persuasion in Greece*. Princeton: Princeton University Press.

Kern, O. 1897. "Brauronia 2." In *Paulys Realencyclopädie der classischen Altertumswissenschaft*, vol. 3.1, ed. G. Wissowa, cols. 825–826. Stuttgart: Alfred Druckenmüller.

Kimmel-Clauzet, F. 2013. *Morts, tombeaux et cultes des poètes grecs: Étude de la survie des grands poètes des époques archaïque et classique en Grèce ancienne*. Bordeaux: Ausonius.

Kirk, G. S. 1962. *The Songs of Homer*. Cambridge: Cambridge University Press.

———. 1978. "The Formal Duels in Books 3 and 7 of the *Iliad*." In *Homer: Tradition and Invention*, ed. B. C. Fenik, 18–40. Leiden: Brill.

———. 1985. *The "Iliad": A Commentary*, vol. 1: *Books 1–4*. Cambridge: Cambridge University Press.

———. 1990. *The "Iliad": A Commentary*, vol. 2: *Books 5–8*. Cambridge: Cambridge University Press.

Knoepfler, D. 1988. "Sur les traces de l'Artémision d'Amarynthos près d'Érétrie." *Comptes Rendus de l'Académie des Inscriptions et Belles-Lettres* 132:382–421.

———. 1996. "La réorganisation du concours des Mouseia à l'époque hellénistique: Esquisse d'une solution nouvelle." In Hurst and Schachter 1996: 141–167.

———. 2004. "Les *Rômaia* de Thèbes: Un nouveau concours musical (et athlétique?) en Béotie." *Comptes Rendus de l'Académie des Inscriptions et Belles-Lettres* 148:1241–1279.

Knudsen, R. A. 2014. *Homeric Speech and the Origins of Rhetoric*. Baltimore: Johns Hopkins University Press.

Koning, H. H. 2010. *Hesiod: The Other Poet. Ancient Reception of a Cultural Icon*. Leiden: Brill Academic.

Kotsidu, H. 1991. *Die musischen Agone der Panathenäen in archaischer und klassischer Zeit*. Munich: Tuduv.

Kourouniotis, K. 1899. "Ἐπιγραφαὶ Χαλκίδος καὶ Ἐρετρίας." *Ἐφημερὶς Ἀρχαιολογική* 38:133–148.

Krauskopff, I. 1981. "Amphiaraos." In *LIMC* I.1, 691–713.

Kullmann, W. 1956. *Das Wirken der Götter in der Ilias: Untersuchungen zur Frage der Entstehung des homerischen "Götterapparats."* Berlin: Akademie.

———. 1960. *Die Quellen der Ilias (Troischer Siegenkreis)*. Wiesbaden: Steiner.

———. 1984. "Oral Poetry Theory and Neoanalysis in Homeric Research." *Greek, Roman, and Byzantine Studies* 25:307–323.

———. 2015. "Motif and Source Research: Neoanalysis, Homer, and Cyclic Epic." In *The Greek Epic Cycle and Its Ancient Reception: A Companion*, ed. M. Fantuzzi and C. Tsagalis, 108–125. Cambridge: Cambridge University Press.

Kurbanova, D. 2000. "The Singing Traditions of Turkmen Epic Poetry." In *The Oral Epic: Performance and Music*, ed. K. Reichl, 115–128. Berlin: Verlag für Wissenschaft und Bildung.

Lakoff, G. 1992. "Multiple Selves: The Metaphorical Models of the Self Inherent in Our Conceptual System." University of California, Berkeley, Miscellaneous Papers and Publications. http://escholarship.org/uc/item/53g1n5b2.

Lakoff, G., and M. Johnson. 1999. *Philosophy in the Flesh: The Embodied Mind and Its Challenge to Western Thought*. New York: Basic Books.

Lancy, D. F. 1975. "The Social Organization of Learning: Initiation Rituals and Public Schools." *Human Organization* 34:457–468.

———. 1980. "Becoming a Blacksmith in Gbarngasuakwelle." *Anthropology and Education Quarterly* 11:266–274.

Lang, M. L. 1995. "War Story into Wrath Story." In *The Ages of the Homer: A Tribute to Emily Townsend Vermeule*, ed. J. B. Carter and S. P. Morris, 149–162. Austin: University of Texas Press.

Langacker, R. W. 1987. *Foundations of Cognitive Grammar.* Vol. 1. Stanford: Stanford University Press.

———. 1990. "Subjectification." *Cognitive Linguistics* 1:5–38.

———. 2015. "Construal." In *Handbook of Cognitive Linguistics*, ed. E. Dabrowska and D. Divjak, 120–142. Berlin: de Gruyter.

Lardinois, A. P. M. H. 1997. "Modern Paroemiology and the Use of *Gnomai* in Homer's *Iliad*." *Classical Philology* 92:213–234.

———. 2000. "Characterization through *Gnomai* in Homer's *Iliad*." *Mnemosyne* 53:641–661.

———. 2001a. "Keening Sappho: Female Speech Genres in Sappho's Poetry." In *Making Silence Speak: Women's Voices in Greek Literature and Society*, ed. A. Lardinois and L. McClure, 75–92. Princeton: Princeton University Press.

———. 2001b. "The Wisdom and Wit of Many: The Orality of Greek Proverbial Expressions." In *Speaking Volumes: Orality and Literacy in the Greek and Roman World*, ed. J. Watson, 93–107. Leiden: Brill.

———. 2003. "The Wrath of Hesiod: Angry Homeric Speeches and the Structure of Hesiod's *Works and Days*." *Arethusa* 26:1–20.

Larson, S. 2000. "Boeotia, Athens, the Peisistratids, and the *Odyssey*'s Catalogue of Heroines." *Greek, Roman, and Byzantine Studies* 41:193–222.

———. 2014. "Boeotia, Athens, the Peisistratids, and the *Odyssey*'s Catalogue of Heroines." In *Theban Resonances in Homeric Epic*, ed. C. Tsagalis. *Trends in Classics* 6:412–427.

Latacz, J., et al. 2000. *Homers Ilias: Gesamtkommentar* Band 1, Erster Gesang, Fasz. 2: *Kommentar.* Munich: Saur.

Lateiner, D. 1995. *Sardonic Smile: Nonverbal Behavior in Homeric Epic.* Ann Arbor: University of Michigan Press.

Latte, K., et al. 1953–1966, 2005–2009. *Hesychii Alexandrini Lexicon.* 4 vols. Copenhagen: Munksgaard; Berlin: de Gruyter.

Lattimore, R. 1951. *The "Iliad" of Homer.* Chicago: University of Chicago Press.

———. 1965. *The "Odyssey" of Homer.* New York: HarperCollins.

Lauffer, S. 1959. "Ptoion." *Realencyclopädie der classischen Altertumswissenschaft* 23, cols. 1506–1578. München: Alfred Druckemuller.

Lausberg, H. 1960. *Handbuch der literarischen Rhetorik.* 2 vols. Munich: Hueber.

Leaf, W., ed. 1900. *The "Iliad,"* vol. 1: *Books I–XII.* 2nd ed. London: MacMillan and Co.

Legrand, Ph.-E. 1905. "Observations sur le *Curculio*." *Revue des Études Anciennes* 7:25–29.

Lenz, A. 1980. *Das Proöm des frühen griechischen Epos: Ein Beitrag zum poetischen Selbstverständis*. Bonn: Habelt.

Leo, F. 1908. *Der Monolog im Drama: Ein Beitrag zur griechisch-römischen Poetik*. Berlin: Weidmann.

Lérat, L. 1952. *Les Locriens de l'Ouest*. 2 vols. Paris: de Boccard.

Lesky, A. 1961. *Göttliche und menschliche Motivation im homerischen Epos*. Heidelberg: Winter.

Létoublon, F. 1983. "Le miroir et la boucle." *Poetique* 14:19–36.

———. 1999. "*Epea Pteroenta* ('Winged Words')." *Oral Tradition* 14:321–335.

Létoublon, F., and H. Dik, eds. 1997. *Hommage à Milman Parry: Le style formulaire de l'épopée homérique et la théorie de l'oralité poétique*. Amsterdam: Gieben.

Levaniouk, O. 1999. "Penelope and the Pênelops." In *Nine Essays on Homer*, ed. M. Carlisle and O. Levaniouk, 95–136. Lanham, MD: Rowman and Littlefield.

———. 2011. *Eve of the Festival: Making Myth in "Odyssey" 19*. Washington, DC: Center for Hellenic Studies.

———. Forthcoming. "The Dreams of Barchin and Penelope." In *Singers and Tales in the Twenty-First Century*, ed. D. Elmer. Washington, DC: Center for Hellenic Studies.

LeVen, P. 2014. *The Many-Headed Muse: Tradition and Innovation in Late Classical Greek Lyric Poetry*. Cambridge: Cambridge University Press.

Lloyd-Jones, H. 1983. *The Justice of Zeus*. 2nd ed. Berkeley: University of California Press.

Lohmann, D. 1970. *Die Komposition der Reden in der Ilias*. Berlin: de Gruyter.

Lopez-Ruiz, C. 2010. *When the Gods Were Born: Greek Cosmogonies and the Near East*. Cambridge, MA: Harvard University Press.

———, ed. 2017. *Gods, Heroes, and Monsters: A Sourcebook of Greek, Roman, and Near Eastern Myths*. 2nd ed. New York: Oxford University Press.

Lord, A. B. 1991. *Epic Singers and Oral Tradition*. Ithaca, NY: Cornell University Press.

———. 2000 [1960]. *The Singer of Tales*. 2nd ed. Ed. S. Mitchell and G. Nagy. Cambridge, MA: Harvard University Press.

Lord, M. L. 1994. "Withdrawal and Return: An Epic Story Pattern in the Homeric *Hymn to Demeter* and in the Homeric Poems." In *The Homeric Hymn to Demeter: Translation, Commentary, and Interpretive Essays*, ed. H. P. Foley, 181–189. Princeton: Princeton University Press.

Louden, B. 1993. "Pivotal Contrafactuals in Homeric Epic." *Classical Antiquity* 12:181–198.

———. 1999. *The "Odyssey": Structure, Narration, and Meaning*. Baltimore: Johns Hopkins University Press.

———. 2006. *The "Iliad": Structure, Myth, and Meaning*. Baltimore: Johns Hopkins University Press.

Lowe, N. J. 2000. *The Classical Plot and the Invention of Western Narrative*. Cambridge: Cambridge University Press.

Lowenstam, S. 1992. "The Use of Vase-Depictions in Homeric Studies." *Transactions of the American Philological Association* 122:165–198.

———. 1993. *The Scepter and the Spear: Studies on Forms of Repetition in the Homeric Poems*. Lanham, MD: Rowman and Littlefield.

———. 1997. "Talking Vases: The Relationship between the Homeric Poems and Archaic Representations of Epic Myth." *Transactions of the American Philological Association* 127:21–76.

———. 2008. *As Witnessed by Images: The Trojan War Tradition in Greek and Etruscan Art*. Baltimore: Johns Hopkins University Press.

MacCary, W. T. 1982. *Childlike Achilles: Ontogeny and Phylogeny in the "Iliad."* New York: Columbia University Press.

Machacek, G. 1994. "The Occasional Contextual Appropriateness of Formulaic Diction in the Homeric Poems." *American Journal of Philology* 115:321–335.

Mackie, C. J. 1999. "Scamander and the Rivers of Hades in Homer." *American Journal of Philology* 120:485–501.

Mackie, H. 1996. *Talking Trojan: Speech and Community in the "Iliad."* Lanham, MD: Rowman and Littlefield.

Macleod, C. 1982. *Homer: "Iliad" XXIV.* Cambridge: Cambridge University Press.

Manieri, A. 2009. *Agoni poetico-musicali nella Grecia antica 1: Beozia*. Pisa: Fabrizio Serra.

Marckscheffel, G. ed. 1840. *Hesiodi, Eumeli, Cinaethonis, Asii et Carminis Naupacti Fragmenta*. Leipzig: Fr. Chr. Guil Vogel.

Marek, C. 1993. *Stadt, Ära und Territorium in Pontus-Bithynia und Nord-Galatia.* Tübingen: Wasmuth.

Marks, J. 2003. "Alternative Odysseys: The Case of Thoas and Odysseus." *Transactions of the American Philological Association* 133:209–226.

———. 2008. *Zeus in the "Odyssey."* Washington, DC: Center for Hellenic Studies.

Martin, R. P. 1984. "Hesiod, Odysseus, and the Instruction of Princes." *Transactions of the American Philological Association* 114:29–48.

———. 1989. *The Language of Heroes: Speech and Performance in the "Iliad."* Ithaca, NY: Cornell University Press.

———. 1993. "Telemachus and the Last Hero Song." *Colby Quarterly* 29:222–240.

———. 1997a. "Formulas and Speeches: The Usefulness of Parry's Method." In Létoublon and Dik 1997:263–273.

———. 1997b. "Similes and Performance." In *Written Voices, Spoken Signs: Tradition, Performance, and the Epic Text*, ed. E. Bakker and A. Kahane, 138–166. Cambridge, MA: Harvard University Press.

———. 2000. "Synchronic Aspects of Homeric Performance: The Evidence of the Hymn to Apollo." In *Una nueva visión de la cultura griega antigua hacia el fin del milenio*, ed. A. M. González de Tobia, 403–432. La Plata: Editorial de la Universidad Nacional de la Plata.

———. 2008. "Keens from the Absent Chorus: Troy to Ulster." In *Lament: Studies in the Ancient Mediterranean and Beyond*, ed. A. Suter, 118–138. Oxford: Oxford University Press.

Martinus, B. 1605. *Variarum lectionum libri IV.* Paris: Petrus Chevalier.

Matthews, M. 1976. "The Expression ΥΠΕΡ ΜΟΙΡΑΝ in Homer." PhD diss., Harvard University.

Matthews, V. J. 1977. "Naupaktia and Argonautica." *Phoenix* 31:189–207.

Matthiae, A. 1800. *Animadversiones in hymnos homericos cum prolegomenis de cuiusque consilio, partibus, aetate*. Leipzig: Weidmann.

Mazon, P. 1928. *Hésiode, Théogonie, Les travaux et les jours, Le bouclier.* Paris: Les Belles Lettres.

———. 1942. *Introduction à l'Iliade.* Paris: Les Belles Lettres.

McCall, S. 2011. *First Person Plural: Aboriginal Storytelling and the Ethics of Collaborative Authorship.* Vancouver: University of British Columbia Press.

Mead, G. H. 1934. *Mind, Self, and Society: From the Standpoint of a Social Behaviorist.* Chicago: University of Chicago Press.

Medda, E. 1983. *La forma monologica: Ricerche su Omero e Sofocle.* Pisa: Scuola Normale Superiore di Pisa.

Meineke, A., ed. 1867. *Athenaei Deipnosophistae*, vol. 4: *Analecta critica continens.* Leipzig: Teubner.

Merkelbach, R. 1952. "Die pisistratische Redaktion der homerischen Gedichte." *Rheinisches Museum* 95:23–47.

Mifsud, M. L. 1997. "The Rhetoric of Deliberation in Homer." PhD diss., Pennsylvania State University.

———. 1998. "On the Idea of Reflexive Rhetoric in Homer." *Philosophy and Rhetoric* 31:41–54.

Miller, M. C. 1997. *Athens and Persia in the Fifth Century B.C.: A Study in Cultural Receptivity.* Cambridge: Cambridge University Press.

Minchin, E. 2001. *Homer and the Resources of Memory: Some Applications of Cognitive Theory to the "Iliad" and the "Odyssey."* Oxford: Oxford University Press.

———. 2007. *Homeric Voices: Discourse, Memory, Gender.* Oxford: Oxford University Press.

Minton, W. W. 1962. "Invocation and Catalogue in Hesiod and Homer." *Transactions and Proceedings of the American Philological Association* 93:188–212.

Mirzaev, T., M. Abdurakhimov, and A. Mirbaldaeva (Т. Мирзаев, М. Абдурахимов, и А. Мирбалдаева), eds. 1999. *Алпамыш: Узбекский Народный Героический Эпос.* Tashkent: Фан.

Mitchell, A. G. 2009. *Greek Vase-Painting and the Origins of Visual Humour.* Cambridge: Cambridge University Press.

Monscaré, H. 2010 [1984]. *Les larmes d'Achille: Héros, femme et souffrance chez Homère.* Repr. Paris: Kiron/Félin.

Montanari, F., A. Rengakos, and C. Tsagalis, eds. 2009. *Brill's Companion to Hesiod*. Leiden: Brill.

———. 2012. *Homeric Contexts: Neoanalysis and the Interpretation of Oral Poetry*. Berlin: de Gruyter.

Morrison, A. D. 2007. *The Narrator in Archaic Greek and Hellenistic Poetry*. Cambridge: Cambridge University Press.

Morrison, J. V. 1992. *Homeric Misdirection: False Predictions in the "Iliad."* Ann Arbor: University of Michigan Press.

Mosconi, G. 2000. "La democrazia ateniese e la 'nuova' musica: L'Odeion di Pericle." In *Synaulia: Cultura musicale in Grecia e contatti mediterranei*, ed. A. Cassio, D. Musti, and L. Rossi, 7–55. Naples: Istituto Universitario Orientale.

Most, G. W. 2006. *Hesiod: Theogony, Works and Days, Testimonia*, vol. 1. Cambridge, MA: Harvard University Press.

———. 2007. *Hesiod: The Shield, Catalogue of Women, Other Fragments*. Cambridge, MA: Harvard University Press.

Moulton, C. 1977. *Similes in the Homeric Poems*. Göttingen: Vandenhoeck and Ruprecht.

Muellner, L. 1996. *The Anger of Achilles: Mēnis in Greek Epic*. Ithaca, NY: Cornell University Press.

Mühll, P. von der. 1952. *Kritisches Hypomena zur Ilias*. Basel: F. Reinhardt.

Müller, C. 1996. "Les travaux de l'École française d'Athènes au sanctuaire du Val des Muses: Le passé et l'avenir." In Hurst and Schachter 1996:171–183.

Müller, K. O. 1875 [1841]. *Geschichte der griechischen Literatur bis auf das Zeitalters Alexander's*, vol. 1. 3rd ed. Stuttgart: Albert Heitz.

Müller, W. 1836. *Homerische Vorschule*. 2nd ed. Leipzig: F. A. Brookhaus.

Murnaghan, S. 1987. *Disguise and Recognition in the "Odyssey."* Princeton: Princeton University Press.

———. 1999. "The Poetics of Loss in Greek Epic." In Beissinger, Tylus, and Wofford 1999:203–220.

Murphy, W. P. 1980. "Secret Knowledge as Property and Power in Kpelle Society: Elder vs. Youth." *Africa* 50:193–207.

Murray, O. ed. 1990. *Sympotica: A Symposium on the Symposion*. Oxford: Clarendon Press.

———. 2008. "The *Odyssey* as Performance Poetry." In *Performance, Iconography, Reception. Studies in Honour of Oliver Taplin*, ed. M. Revermann and P. Wilson, 161–176. Oxford: Oxford University Press.

Murray, P. 1996. *Plato: On Poetry*. Cambridge: Cambridge University Press.

Musaev, S. (С. Мусаев). 1994. *Эпос Манас: научно-популярный очерк*. Bishkek: Илим.

Nachtergael, G. 1977. *Les Galates en Grèce et les Sôtéria de Delphes*. Brussels: Académie Royale de Belgique.

Nagler, M. N. 1974. *Spontaneity and Tradition: A Study in the Oral Art of Homer*. Berkeley: University of California Press.

———. 1992. "Discourse and Conflict in Hesiod: Eris and the Erides." *Ramus* 21:79–96.

Nagy, G. 1990a. *Greek Mythology and Poetics*. Ithaca, NY: Cornell University Press.

———. 1990b. *Pindar's Homer: The Lyric Possession of an Epic Past*. Baltimore: Johns Hopkins University Press.

———. 1995. "An Evolutionary Model for the Making of Homeric Poetry: Comparative Perspectives." In *The Ages of Homer: A Tribute to Emily Townsend Vermeule*, ed. J. Carter and S. Morris, 163–180. Austin: University of Texas Press.

———. 1996a. *Homeric Questions*. Austin: University of Texas Press.

———. 1996b. *Poetry as Performance: Homer and Beyond*. Cambridge: Cambridge University Press.

———. 1999a. *The Best of the Achaeans: Concepts of the Hero in Archaic Greek Poetry*. 2nd rev. ed. Baltimore: Johns Hopkins University Press.

———. 1999b. "Epic as Genre." In Beissinger, Tylus, and Wofford 1999:21–32.

———. 2001. "Homeric Poetry and Problems of Multiformity: The 'Panathenaic Bottleneck.'" *Classical Philology* 96:109–119.

———. 2002. *Plato's Rhapsody and Homer's Music: The Poetics of the Panathenaic Festival in Classical Athens*. Washington, DC: Center for Hellenic Studies.

———. 2003. *Homeric Responses*. Austin: University of Texas Press.

———. 2007. "Did Sappho and Alcaeus Ever Meet? Symmetries of Myth and Ritual in Performing the Songs of Ancient Lesbos." In *Literatur und Religion* I: *Wege zu einer mythisch-rituellen Poetik bei den Griechen*, ed. A. Bierl, R. Lämmle, and K. Wasselmann, 211–269. Berlin: de Gruyter.

———. 2009a. *Homer the Classic*. Washington, DC: Center for Hellenic Studies.

———. 2009b. "Hesiod and the Ancient Biographical Traditions." In Montanari, Rengakos, and Tsagalis 2009:271–311.

———. 2010. *Homer the Preclassic*. Berkeley: University of California Press.

———. 2011. "The Aeolic Component of Homeric Diction." In *Proceedings of the 22nd Annual UCLA Indo-European Conference*, ed. J. Jamison, H. Melcher, and B. Vine, 133–179. Bremen: Hempen.

———. 2013. *The Ancient Greek Hero in 24 Hours*. Cambridge, MA: Harvard University Press.

———. 2015. *Masterpieces of Metonymy: From Ancient Greek Times to Now*. Washington, DC: Center for Hellenic Studies. http://nrs.harvard.edu/urn-3:hul.ebook:CHS_Nagy.Masterpieces_of_Metonymy.2015.

———. 2016. "A Poetics of Sisterly Affect in the Brothers Song and in Other Songs of Sappho." In *The Newest Sappho: P. Sapph. Obbink and P. GC inv. 105, Frs. 1–4*, ed. A. Bierl and A. Lardinois, 449–492. Leiden: Brill.

Neils, J. ed. 1992a. *Goddess and Polis: The Panathenaic Festival in Ancient Athens*. Princeton: Princeton University Press.

———. 1992b. "The Panathenaia: An Introduction." In Neils 1992a:13–27.

———. 2007. "Replicating Tradition: The First Celebrations of the Greater

Panathenaia." In *The Panathenaic Games. Proceedings of an International Conference Held at the University of Athens, May 11–12, 2004*, ed. O. Palagia and A. Choremi-Spetsieris, 41–51. Oxford: Oxbow Books.

Neri, C. 2014. "A Hoped-For Festival? (Sapph. fr. 17 V. and P. GC. inv. 105 fr. 2 col. ii ll. 9–28)." *Eikasmós* 25:11–24.

Newton, N. M. 1997–1998. "Cloak and Shield in *Odyssey* 14." *Classical Journal* 93:143–156.

Nicolai, W. 1983. "Rezeptionssteuerung in der *Ilias*." *Philologus* 127:1–27.

Nilsson, M. P. 1906. *Griechische Feste von religiöser Bedeutung (mit Ausschluss der attischen)*. Leipzig: Teubner.

Nimis, S. 1999. "Ring-Composition and Linearity in Homer." In *Signs of Orality: The Oral Tradition and Its Influence in the Greek and Roman Worlds*, ed. E. A. Mackay, 65–78. Leiden: Brill.

Notopoulos, J. A. 1951. "Continuity and Interconnexion in Homeric Oral Composition." *Transactions and Proceedings of the American Philological Association* 82:81–101.

———. 1964. "Studies in Early Greek Oral Poetry." *Transactions and Proceedings of the American Philological Association* 122:1–77.

Nünlist, R. 2009. *The Ancient Critic at Work*. Cambridge: Cambridge University Press.

———. 2011. "Focalization." In Finkelberg 2011.

Nwachukwu-Agbada, J. O. J. 1994. "The Proverb in the Igbo Milieu." *Anthropos* 89:194–200.

Olson, S. D. 1995. *Blood and Iron: Stories and Storytelling in Homer's "Odyssey."* Leiden: Brill.

———. 2010. *Athenaeus: The Learned Banqueters (Books 12–13.594b)*. Cambridge, MA: Harvard University Press.

———. 2011. *Athenaeus: The Learned Banqueters (Books 13.594b–14)*. Cambridge, MA: Harvard University Press.

O'Maley, J. 2014. "Controlling the Web: Hypertextuality, the *Iliad*, and the Crimes of Previous Generations." In *Between Orality and Literacy: Communication and Adaptation in Antiquity*, ed. R. Scodel, 6–28. Leiden: Brill.

———. Forthcoming. *Storytelling and the Presentation of the Past in the "Iliad."* Oxford: Oxford University Press.

Onchukov, N. (Н. Ончуков). 1904. *Печорские былины*. Saint Petersburg: Типолитография Н. Соколова и В. Пастор.

Opelt, I. 1978. "Gefühlswörter bei Homer und in den Argonautika des Apollonius Rhodius." *Glotta* 56: 170–190.

Oring, E. 2011. "Contested Performance and Joke Aesthetics." In *The Individual and Tradition: Folkloristic Perspectives*, ed. R. Cashman, T. Mould, and P. Shukla, 365–385. Bloomington: Indiana University Press.

Otter, H. 1914. *De Soliloquiis Quae in Litteris Graecorum et Romanorum Occurrunt Observationes*. Marburg: Typis C. Schaaf.

Padgett, J. M. 1989. "The Geras Painter: An Athenian Eccentric and His Associates." PhD diss., Harvard University.

Paga, J. L. 2012. "Architectural Agency and the Construction of Athenian Democracy." PhD diss., Princeton University.

Page, D. L. 1959. *History and the Homeric "Iliad."* Berkeley: University of California Press.

Pallone, M. R. 1984. "L'epica agonale in età ellenistica." *Orpheus* 5:156–166.

Parke, H. W. 1977. *Festivals of the Athenians.* London: Thames and Hudson.

Parks, W. 1990. *Verbal Dueling in Heroic Narrative: The Homeric and Old English Narrative Traditions.* Princeton: Princeton University Press.

Parry, A., ed. 1987. *The Making of Homeric Verse: The Collected Papers of Milman Parry.* Oxford: Oxford University Press.

Pascal, R. 1977. *The Dual Voice: Free Indirect Speech and Its Functioning in the Nineteenth-Century European Novel.* Manchester: Rowman and Littlefield.

Patzer, H. 1952. "ΡΑΨΩΙΔΟΣ." *Hermes* 80:314–325.

Pearce, J. B. 1993. "Theocritus and Oral Tradition." *Oral Tradition* 8:59–86.

Pelliccia, H. 1995. *Mind, Body, and Speech in Homer and Pindar.* Göttingen: Vandenhoeck and Ruprecht.

Pellizer, E. 1990. "Outlines of a Morphology of Sympotic Entertainment." In Murray 1990:177–184.

Pernigotti, C. 2001. "Tempi del canto e pluralità di prospettive in Saffo, fr. 44 V." *Zeitschrift für Papyrologie und Epigraphik* 135:11–20.

Perrin, B. 1967. *Plutarch's Lives: Demosthenes and Cicero, Alexander and Caesar,* vol. 7. Cambridge, MA: Harvard University Press.

Pestalozzi, H. 1945. *Die Achilleis als Quelle der Ilias.* Erlangen: Rentsch.

Petersmann, G. 1973. "Die monologische Totenklage der Iliad." *Rheinisches Museum für Philologie* 116:3–16.

———. 1974. "Die Entscheidungsmonologe in den homerischen Epen." *Gräzer Beiträge* 2:147–169.

Petropoulos, J. C. B. 2011. *Kleos in a Minor Key: The Homeric Education of a Little Prince.* Washington, DC: Center for Hellenic Studies.

Phillips, T. 2016. *Pindar's Library: Performance Poetry and Material Texts.* Oxford: Oxford University Press.

Pontani, F. 2007. *Scholia Graeca in Odysseam.* 2 vols. Rome: Edizioni di Storia e Letteratura.

Porter, D. 1972. "Violent Juxtaposition in the Similes of the *Iliad.*" *Classical Journal* 68:11–21.

Porter, J. I. 2010. *The Origins of Aesthetic Thought in Ancient Greece: Matter, Sensation, and Experience.* Cambridge: Cambridge University Press.

———. 2011. "Making and Unmaking: The Achaean Wall and the Limits of Fictionality in Homeric Criticism." *Transactions of the American Philological Association* 141:1–36.

Powell, B. B. 2011. "Writing, in Homer." In Finkelberg 2011.

Power, T. 2004. "Cleisthenes and the Politics of Kitharōidia at Delphi and in Sicyon." *Aevum Antiquum* 4:415–437.

———. 2010. *The Culture of Kitharōidia.* Washington, DC: Center for Hellenic Studies.

Praetorius, N. 2009. "Intersubjectivity, Cognition, and Language." In *Handbook of Phenomenology and Cognitive Science,* ed. D. Daniel Schmicking and S. Gallagher, 301–316. Dordrecht: Springer.

Pratt, L. H. 2009. "Diomedes, the Fatherless Hero of the *Iliad.*" In *Growing Up Fatherless in Antiquity,* ed. S. R. Hübner and D. M. Ratzan, 141–161. Cambridge: Cambridge University Press.

Prinz, F. 1979. *Gründungsmythen and Sagenchronologie.* Munich: Beck.

Prior, D. 2000. *Patron, Party, Patrimony: Notes on the Cultural History of the Kirghiz Epic Tradition.* Bloomington, IN: Research Institute for Inner Asian Studies.

Pritchard, M. 2011. "Creativity and Sorrow in Kyrgyzstan." *Journal of Folklore Research* 48:167–196.

Pucci, P. 1987. *Odysseus Polutropos: Intertextual Readings in the "Odyssey" and the "Iliad."* Ithaca, NY: Cornell University Press.

Purves, A. C. 2010. *Space and Time in Ancient Greek Narrative.* New York: Cambridge University Press.

Raaflaub, K. 1993. "Homer to Solon: The Rise of the Polis. The Written Sources." In *The Ancient Greek City-State. Symposium on the Occasion of the 250th Anniversary of the Royal Danish Academy of Sciences and Letters, July, 1–4 1992,* ed. M. H. Hansen, 41–105. Copenhagen: Royal Danish Academy of Sciences and Letters.

Rabel, R. 1997. *Plot and Point of View in the "Iliad."* Ann Arbor: University of Michigan Press.

Rackham, H. 1952. *Aristotle.* Aristotle in Twenty-Three Volumes, vol. 20. Cambridge, MA: Harvard University Press.

Radloff, W. 1870. *Proben der Volkslitteratur der türkischen Stämme Süd-Sibiriens,* vol. 3: *Kirgisische Mundarten.* Saint Petersburg: Commissionäre der Kaiserlichen Akademie der Wissenschaften.

Rao, V. N. 1991. "A *Rāmāyaṇa* of Their Own: Women's Oral Tradition in Telugu." In *Many Rāmāyaṇas: The Diversity of a Narrative Tradition in South Asia,* ed. P. Richman, 114–136. Berkeley: University of California Press.

Razumova, I. (И. Разумова). 1989. "П.Н. Рыбников." In Rybnikov 1989:9–43.

Ready, J. L. 2005. "*Iliad* 22.123–128 and the Erotics of Supplication." *Classical Bulletin* 81:145–164.

———. 2010. "Why Odysseus Strings His Bow." *Greek, Roman, and Byzantine Studies* 50:133–157.

———. 2011. *Character, Narrator, and Simile in the "Iliad."* New York: Cambridge University Press.

———. 2012a. "Comparative Perspectives on the Composition of the Homeric Simile." In *Orality, Literacy, and Performance in the Ancient World,* ed. E. Minchin, 55–87. Leiden: Brill.

———. 2012b. "Zeus, Ancient Near Eastern Notions of Divine Incomparability, and Similes in the Homeric Epics." *Classical Antiquity* 31:56–91.

———. 2015. "The Textualization of Homeric Epic by Means of Dictation." *TAPA* 145:1–75.

Redfield, J. 1975. *Nature and Culture in the "Iliad": The Tragedy of Hector*. Chicago: University of Chicago Press.

———. 1994. *Nature and Culture in the "Iliad": The Tragedy of Hector*. 2nd ed. Durham, NC: Duke University Press.

Reece, S. 1994. "The Cretan Odyssey: A Lie Truer than Truth." *American Journal of Philology* 115:157–173.

Reichel, M. 1994. *Fernbeziehungen in der Ilias*. Tübingen: Gunter Narr.

Reichl, K. 1992. *Turkic Oral Epic Poetry: Traditions, Forms, Poetic Structure*. New York: Garland.

Reinhardt, K. 1961. *Die Ilias und ihr Dichter*. Göttingen: Vandenhoeck and Ruprecht.

Reisch, E. 1885. *De Musicis Graecorum Certaminibus, Capita Quattor*. Vienna: C. Gerold.

Remijsen, S. 2015. *The End of Greek Athletics in Late Antiquity*. Cambridge: Cambridge University Press.

Renehan, R. 1987. "The *Heldentod* in Homer: One Heroic Ideal." *Classical Philology* 82:99–116.

Reynolds, D. F. 1995. *Heroic Poets, Poetic Heroes: The Ethnography of Performance in the Arabic Oral Epic Tradition*. Ithaca, NY: Cornell University Press.

Richardson, N. J. 1974. *The Homeric Hymn to Demeter*. Oxford: Clarendon Press.

———. 1980. "Literary Criticism in the Exegetical Scholia to the *Iliad*: A Sketch." *Classical Quarterly* 30:265–287.

———. 1993. *The "Iliad": A Commentary*, vol. 6: *Books 21–24*. Cambridge: Cambridge University Press.

———. 2010. *Three Homeric Hymns: To Apollo, Hermes, and Aphrodite*. Cambridge: Cambridge University Press.

———. 2011. "Reflections of Choral Song in Early Hexameter Poetry." In *Archaic and Choral Song: Performance, Politics, and Dissemination*, ed. L. Athanassaki and E. L. Bowie, 15–31. Berlin: de Gruyter.

Richardson, S. 1990. *The Homeric Narrator*. Nashville: Vanderbilt University Press.

———. 2006. "The Devious Narrator of the *Odyssey*." *Classical Journal* 101: 337–359.

Riggsby, A. M. 1992. "Homeric Speech Introductions and the Theory of Homeric Composition." *Transactions of the American Philological Association* 122: 99–114.

Rijksbaron, A. 2002. *The Syntax and Semantics of the Verb in Classical Greek*. 3rd ed. Amsterdam: Gieben.

Rizzo, D. 2004. "Cratere a calice attico a figure rosse." In *Scavo nello scavo: Gli*

Etruschi non visti. Ricerche e "riscoperte" nei depositi dei musei archeologici dell'Etruria meridionale, ed. A. M. Moretti Sgubini, 259–260. Viterbo: Union.

Robert, L. 1936a. "ΑΡΧΑΙΟΛΟΓΟΣ." *Revue des Études Grecques* 49:235–254.

———. 1936b. *Collection Froehner*. Paris: Éditions des Bibliothèques nationales de France.

———. 1938. "Les Aelius Alcibiade de Nysa." In *Études épigraphiques et philologiques*, ed. L. Robert, 45–53. Paris: Champion.

———. 1943. "Voyages épigraphiques en Asie Mineure." *Revue de Philologie, de Littérature et d'Histoire Anciennes* 17:170–201.

———. 1980. "Deux poètes grecs à l'époque impériale." In *Στήλη: Τόμος εἰς μνήμην Νικολάου Κοντολέοντος*, ed. K. Schefold and J. Pouilloux, 1–20. Athens: Σωματεῖον Φίλων τοῦ Νικολάου Κοντολέοντος.

———. 1983. "Bulletin épigraphique 475." *Revue des Études Grecques* 96:182–184.

———. 1984. "Discours d'ouverture." In *Πρακτικά του Η' διεθνούς συνεδρίου ελληνικής και λατινικής επιγραφικής, Αθήνα, 3–9 Οκτωβρίου 1982*, vol. 1., ed. A. G. Kalogeropoulou, 35–45. Athens: Υπουργείο Πολιτισμού και Επιστημών.

Robertson, H. G. 1968. "Another Look at Hector." *Echos du Monde Classique* 10:6–10.

Roesch, P. 1965. *Thespies et la confédération béotienne*. Paris: de Boccard.

———. 1982. *Études béotiennes*. Paris: de Boccard.

Roisman, H. 2005. "Nestor the Good Counsellor." *Classical Quarterly* 55:17–38.

———. 2006. "Helen in the *Iliad*; *Causa Belli* and Victim of War: From Silent Weaver to Public Speaker." *American Journal of Philology* 127:1–36.

———. 2011. "Menelaos." In Finkelberg 2011.

Roller, D. W. 1989. *Tanagran Studies*. Vol. 1. Amsterdam: Gieben.

Roochnik, D. 1990. "Homeric Speech Acts: Word and Deed in the Epics." *Classical Journal* 85:289–299.

Rood, N. 2008. "Craft Similes and the Construction of Heroes in the *Iliad*." *Harvard Studies in Classical Philology* 104:19–43.

Roscher, W. H. 1884–1937. *Ausführliches Lexikon der griechischen und römischen Mythologie*. 6 vols. Leipzig: Teubner.

Rose, C. B. 2014. *The Archaeology of Greek and Roman Troy*. New York: Cambridge University Press.

Rosenmeyer, T. G. 1969. *The Green Cabinet: Theocritus and the European Pastoral*. Berkeley: University of California Press.

———. 1990. "Decision Making." In *The Poetics of Therapy: Hellenistic Ethics in Its Rhetorical and Literary Context*, ed. M. C. Nussbaum, 187–219. Edmonton: Academic.

Rösler, W. 1990. "Mnemosyne in the Symposion." In Murray 1990:230–237.

Ross, S. A. 2005. "Barbarophonos: Language and Panhellenism in the *Iliad*." *Classical Philology* 100:299–316.

Rotstein, A. 2012. "*Mousikoi Agones* and the Conceptualization of Genre in Ancient Greece." *Classical Antiquity* 31:92–127.

Roueché, C. 1993. *Performers and Partisans at Aphrodisias in the Roman and Late Roman periods*. London: Society for the Promotion of Roman Studies.

Roux, G. 1954. "La Val des Muses et les Musées chez les auteurs anciens." *Bulletin de Correspondance Hellénique* 78:22–48.

Russo, J. 1968. "Homer against His Tradition." *Arion* 7:275–295.

———. 1983. "The Poetics of the Ancient Greek Proverb." *Journal of Folklore Research* 76:121–130.

———. 1992. "Homer's Literacy." In *New York Review of Books*. http://www.nybooks.com/articles/archives/1992/jun/25/homers-literacy/?pagination=false.

———. 1997. "The Formula." In *A New Companion to Homer*, ed. I. Morris and B. Powell, 238–260. Leiden: Brill.

Rutherford, I. C. 2000. "Formulas, Voice, and Death in *Ehoie*–Poetry, the Hesiodic *Gunaikon katalogos*, and the Odysseian *Nekuia*." In *Matrices of Genre: Authors, Canons, and Society*, ed. M. Depew and D. Obbink, 81–96. Cambridge, MA: Harvard University Press.

———. 2005. "Mestra at Athens: Hes. Fr. 43 and the Poetics of Panhellenism." In Hunter 2005a:99–117.

———. 2013. *State Pilgrims and Sacred Observers in Ancient Greece: A Study of Theoria and Theoroi*. Cambridge: Cambridge University Press.

Rybnikov, P. (П. Рыбников). 1989. *Песни Собранные П.Н. Рыбниковым*, vol. 1. Petrozavodsk: Карелия.

———. 1991. *Песни Собранные П.Н. Рыбниковым*, vol. 3. Petrozavodsk: Карелия.

Saïd, S. 2011. *Homer and the "Odyssey."* Trans. R. Webb. Oxford: Oxford University Press.

Sale, W. M. 1989. "The Trojans, Statistics, and Milman Parry." *Greek, Roman, and Byzantine Studies* 30:341–410.

———. 1994. "The Government of Troy: Politics in the *Iliad*." *Greek, Roman, and Byzantine Studies* 35:5–102.

Salmond, A. 1975. "Mana Makes the Man: A Look at Maori Oratory and Politics." In *Political Language and Oratory in Traditional Society*, ed. M. Bloch, 45–64. London: Routledge.

Sammons, B. 2010. *The Art and Rhetoric of the Homeric Catalogue*. New York: Oxford University Press.

———. 2014. "A Tale of Tydeus: Exemplarity and Structure in Two Homeric Insets." *Trends in Classical Studies* 6:297–318.

Sancisi-Weerdenburg, H., ed. 2000. *Peisistratos and the Tyranny: A Reappraisal of the Evidence*. Amsterdam: Gieben.

Sanders, J., and G. Redeker. 1996. "Perspective and the Representation of Speech and Thought in Narrative Discourse." In *Spaces, Worlds, and Grammar*, ed. G. Fauconnier and E. Sweetser, 290–317. Chicago: University of Chicago Press.

Sanford, A. J., and C. Emmott. 2012. *Mind, Brain, and Narrative*. Cambridge: Cambridge University Press.

Schachter, A. 1981, 1986. *Cults of Boiotia* I, II. London: Institute of Classical Studies.

———. 2010–2011. "The Mouseia of Thespiai: Organization and Development." *Rudiae* 22–23:29–47.

Schadewaldt, W. 1926. *Monolog und Selbstgespräch: Untersuchungen zur Formgeschichte der griechischen Tragödie*. Berlin: Weidmann.

———. 1959. *Von Homers Welt und Werk: Aufsätze und Auslegungen zur homerischen Frage*. 3rd ed. Stuttgart: Koehler.

———. 1965. *Von Homers Welt und Werk: Aufsätze und Auslegungen zur homerischen Frage*. 4th ed. Stuttgart: Koehler.

———. 1966. *Iliasstudien*. 3rd ed. Darmstadt: Wissenschaftliche Buchgesellschaft.

Schauenburg, K. 1979. "Herakles Musikos." *Jahrbuch des Deutschen Archäologischen Instituts* 94:49–76.

Scheid, J., and J. Svenbro. 1996. *The Craft of Zeus: Myths of Weaving and Fabric*. Trans. C. Volk. Cambridge, MA: Harvard University Press.

Schein, S. L. 1984. *The Mortal Hero: An Introduction to Homer's "Iliad."* Berkeley: University of California Press.

Scheliha, R. von. 1943. *Patroklos: Gedanken über Homers Dichtung und Gestalten*. Basel: Schwabe.

———. 1987. *Vom Wettkampf der Dichter: Der musische Agon bei den Griechen*. Amsterdam: Castum Peregrini Presse.

Scheub, H. 2002. *The Poem in the Story: Music, Poetry, and the Narrative*. Madison: University of Wisconsin Press.

Schmitt, A. 1990. *Selbständigkeit und Abhängigkeit menschlichen Handelns bei Homer: Hermeneutische Untersuchungen zur Psychologie Homers*. Stuttgart: Steiner.

Schnapp-Gourbeillon, A. 1981. *Lions, héros, masques: Les répresentations de l'animal chez Homère*. Paris: Maspero.

Schoeck, G. 1961. *Ilias und Aithiopis: Kyklische Motive in homerischer Brechung*. Zurich: Atlantis.

Schofield, M. 1986. "*Euboulia* in the *Iliad*." *Classical Quarterly* 36:6–31.

———. 1999. *Saving the City: Philosopher Kings and Other Classical Paradigms*. London: Routledge.

Schur, D. 2014. "The Silence of Homer's Sirens." *Arethusa* 47:1–17.

Schwartz, J. 1960. *Pseudo-Hesiodeia: Recherches sur la composition, la diffusion et la disparition ancienne d'oeuvres attribuées à Hésiode*. Leiden: Brill.

Scodel, R. 1992. "The Wits of Glaucus." *Transactions of the American Philological Association* 122:73–84.

———. 1998. "Bardic Performance and Oral Tradition in Homer." *American Journal of Philology* 119:171–194.

———. 1999. *Credible Impossibilities: Conversations and Strategies of Verisimilitude in Homer and Greek Tragedy*. Stuttgart: Teubner.

———. 2002a. *Listening to Homer: Tradition, Narrative, and Audience*. Ann Arbor: University of Michigan Press.

———. 2002b. Review of de Jong 2001. *Bryn Mawr Classical Review* 2002.06.12.

———. 2004. "The Modesty of Homer." In *Oral Performance and Its Context*, ed. C. J. Mackie, 1–19. Leiden: Brill.

———. 2008. *Epic Facework: Self-Presentation and Social Interaction in Homer*. Swansea: Classical Press of Wales.

———. 2012. "ἦ and Theory of Mind in the *Iliad*." In *Homer, gedeutet durch ein großes Lexikon: Akten des Hamburger Kolloquiums vom 6.–8. Oktober 2010 zum Abschluss des Lexikons des frühgriechischen Epos*, ed. M. Meier-Brügger, 319–334. Berlin: de Gruyter.

———. 2014. "Narrative Focus and Elusive Thought in Homer." In *Defining Greek Narrative*, ed. D. Cairns and R. Scodel, 55–74. Edinburgh: Edinburgh University Press.

Scott, J. A. 1921. *The Unity of Homer*. Berkeley: University of California Press.

Scott, W. C. 1974. *The Oral Nature of the Homeric Simile*. Leiden: Brill.

———. 2009. *The Artistry of the Homeric Simile*. Hanover: University Press of New England.

Scully, S. 1984. "The Language of Achilles: The ΟΧΘΗΣΑΣ Formulas." *Transactions of the American Philological Association* 114:11–27.

———. 1990. *Homer and the Sacred City*. Ithaca, NY: Cornell University Press.

Seaford, R. 1987. "The Tragic Wedding." *Journal of Hellenic Studies* 107:106–130.

Sealey, R. 1957. "From Phemios to Ion." *Revue des Études Grecques* 70:312–355.

Searle, J. R. 1969. *Speech Acts: An Essay in the Philosophy of Language*. Cambridge: Cambridge University Press.

Segal, C. 1971. *The Theme of Mutilation of the Corpse in the "Iliad."* Leiden: Brill.

Seitel, P. 1999. *The Powers of Genre: Interpreting Haya Oral Literature*. New York: Oxford University Press.

Shapiro, H. A. 1983. "Painting, Politics, and Genealogy: Peisistratos and the Neleids." In *Ancient Greek Art and Iconography*, ed. W. G. Moon, 87–96. Madison: University of Wisconsin Press.

———. 1989. *Art and Cult under the Tyrants*. Mainz: von Zabern.

———. 1992. "*Mousikoi Agones*: Music and Poetry at the Panathenaia." In Neils 1992a:53–75.

———. 1993. "Hipparchos and the Rhapsodes." In *Cultural Poetics in Archaic Greece: Cult, Performance, Politics*, ed. C. Dougherty and L. Kurke, 92–107. Cambridge: Cambridge University Press.

Sharples, R. W. 1983. "'But Why Has My Spirit Spoken with Me Thus?': Homeric Decision-Making." *Greece and Rome* 30:1–7.

Shear, J. L. 2001. "Polis and Panathenaia." PhD diss., University of Pennsylvania.

Sherzer, J. 1983. *Kuna Ways of Speaking*. Austin: University of Texas Press.

Shive, D. 1987. *Naming Achilles*. Oxford: Oxford University Press.

Sidnell, J., N. J. Enfield, and P. Kockelman. 2014. "Interaction and Intersubjectivity." In *The Cambridge Handbook of Linguistic Anthropology*, ed. N. J. Enfield, P. Kockelman, and J. Sidnell, 343–345. Cambridge: Cambridge University Press.

Sifakis, G. M. 1967. *Studies in the History of Hellenistic Drama*. London: Athlone Press.

Sihler, A. L. 1995. *New Comparative Grammar of Greek and Latin*. Oxford: Oxford University Press.

Siikala, A.-L. 2000. "Generic Models, Entextualization, and Creativity: Epic Tradition on the Southern Cook Islands." In *Textualization of Oral Epics*, ed. L. Honko, 343–369. Berlin: Mouton de Gruyter.

Siikala, J. 2003. "'God Spoke Different Things': Oral Tradition and the Interpretative Community." In *Dynamics of Tradition: Perspectives on Oral Poetry and Folk Belief*, ed. L. Tarkka, 21–34. Helsinki: Finnish Literature Society.

Silva Barris, J. 2016. "No Linos-Song in Achilles' Shield." In *Tra lyra e aulos: Tradizioni musicali e generi poetici*, ed. L. Bravi et al., 285–296. Pisa: Fabrizio Serra.

Simon, E. 1969. *Die Götter der Griechen*. Munich: Hirmer.

———. 1983. *Festivals of Attica: An Archaeological Commentary*. Madison: University of Wisconsin Press.

Sinding, M. 2005. "*Genera Mixta*: Conceptual Blending and Mixed Genres in *Ulysses*." *New Literary History* 36:589–619.

Slater, W. 2010. "Paying the Pipers." In *L'argent dans les concours du monde grec*, ed. B. Le Guen, 249–281. Saint-Denis: Presses Universitaires de Vincennes.

Slatkin, L. M. 1991. *The Power of Thetis: Allusion and Interpretation in the "Iliad."* Berkeley: University of California Press.

———. 2011. "Theban Traces at Troy." In *The Power of Thetis and Selected Essays*, 99–119. Washington, DC: Center for Hellenic Studies.

Slings, S. R. 2000. "Literature in Athens, 566–510 BC." In *Peisistratos and the Tyranny: A Reappraisal of the Evidence*, ed. H. Sancisi-Weerdenburg, 57–77. Amsterdam: Gieben.

Smirnova, N. (Н. Смирнова). 1967. *Казахская народная поэзия*. Alma Ata: Наука.

Smitherman, V. H. 2013. "Epanelepsis." In *Encyclopedia of Ancient Greek Language and Linguistics*, ed. G. Giannakis, vol. 1, s.v. *epanalepsis*. Leiden: Brill.

Snell, B. 1930. "Das Bewusstsein von eigenen Entscheidungen im frühen Griechentum." *Philologus* 85:141–158.

———. 1931. Review of Böhme 1927. *Gnomon* 7:74–86.

———. 1953. *The Discovery of the Mind: The Greek Origins of European Thought*. Trans. T. G. Rosenmeyer. Oxford: Blackwell.

Sommerstein, A. H. 2008. *Aeschylus*, vol. 3: *Fragments*. Cambridge, MA: Harvard University Press.

Spawforth, A. J. S. 1989. "Agonistic Festivals in Roman Greece." In *The Greek Renaissance in the Roman Empire*, ed. A. Cameron and S. Walker, 193–197. London.

Spivey, N. 1994. "Psephological Heroes." In *Ritual, Finance, Politics: Athenian Democratic Accounts Presented to David Lewis*, ed. R. Osborne and S. Hornblower, 39–51. Oxford: Clarendon Press.

Stanford, W. B. 1996 [1948]. *Homer: "Odyssey."* 2 vols. London: Bristol Classical Press.

Stansbury-O'Donnell, M. D. 2006. *Vase Painting, Gender, and Social Identity in Archaic Athens*. Cambridge: Cambridge University Press.

Steiner, D. T. 1994. *The Tyrant's Writ: Myths and Images of Writing in Ancient Greece*. Princeton: Princeton University Press.

Stensgaard, J. 2003. "*Peitho* in the *Iliad*: A Matter of Trust or Obedience?" *Classica et Medievalia* 54:41–80.

Stephanis, I. E. 1988. *ΔΙΟΝΥΣΙΑΚΟΙ ΤΕΧΝΙΤΑΙ*. Herakleion: Πανεπιστημιακές εκδόσεις Κρήτης.

Stephens, S. 2002/2003. "Linus Song." *Hermathena* 173/174:13–28.

Stoevesandt, M. 2004. *Feinde–Gegner–Opfer: Zur Darstellung der Troianer in den Kampfszenen der Ilias*. Basel: Schwabe.

Strasser, J.-Y. 2002. "Choraules et pythaules d'époque impériale: À propos d'inscriptions de Delphes." *Bulletin de Correspondance Hellénique* 126:97–142.

Sultan, N. 1999. *Exile and the Poetics of Loss in Greek Tradition*. Lanham, MD: Rowman and Littlefield.

Sweetser, E. 2012. "Introduction: Viewpoint and Perspective in Language and Gesture, from the Ground Down." In *Viewpoint in Language: A Multimodal Perspective*, ed. B. Dancygier and E. Sweetser, 1–22. Cambridge: Cambridge University Press.

Swift, L. 2006. "Mixed Choruses and Marriage Songs: A New Interpretation of the Third Stasimon of *Hippolytos*." *Journal of Hellenic Studies* 126:125–140.

Sykutris, J. 1928. "Epigramm aus Kition." *Hermes* 63:110–111.

Tannen, D. 1989. *Talking Voices: Repetition, Dialogue, and Imagery in Conversational Discourse*. Cambridge: Cambridge University Press.

Taplin, O. 1992. *Homeric Soundings: The Shaping of the "Iliad."* Oxford: Clarendon Press.

Tarkka, L. 2013. *Songs of the Border People: Genre, Reflexivity, and Performance in Karelian Oral Poetry*. Helsinki: Suomalainen Tiedeakatemia.

———. 2016. "The Poetics of Quotation: Proverbial Speech, Entextualization, and the Emergence of Oral Poems." In *Genre–Text–Interpretation: Multidisciplinary Perspectives on Folklore and Beyond*, ed. K. Koski, Frog, and U. Savolainen, 175–199. Helsinki: Finnish Literature Society.

Tedeschi, G. 2002. "Lo spettacolo in età ellenistica e tardo antica nella documentazione epigrafica e papiracea." *Papyrologica Lupiensia* 11:88–149.

Thalmann, W. G. 1998. *The Swineherd and the Bow*. Ithaca, NY: Cornell University Press.

———. 2004. "The Most Divinely Approved and Political Discord." *Classical Antiquity* 23:359–399.

Thomas, R. 2012. "Pindar's 'Difficulty' and the Performance of Epinician Poetry: Some Suggestions from Ethnography." In *Reading the Victory Ode*, ed. P. Agócs, C. Carey, and R. Rawles, 224–245. Cambridge: Cambridge University Press.

Thompson, K., et al. 2006. "Kyrgyzstan's 'Manas' Epos Millennium Celebrations: Post-Colonial Resurgence of Turkic Culture and the Marketing of Cultural Tourism." In *Festivals, Tourism, and Social Change: Remaking Worlds*, ed. D. Picard and M. Robinson, 172–190. Clevedon: Channel View Publications.

Thornton, A. 1984. *Homer's "Iliad": Its Composition and the Motif of Supplication*. Göttingen: Vandenhoeck and Ruprecht.

Torres Guerra, J. B. 1995. *La Tebaida homérica como fuente de Ilíada y Odisea*. Madrid: Fundación Pastor de Estudios Clásicos.

———. 2012. "The Writing Down of the Oral *Thebaid* That Homer Knew." In Montanari, Rengakos, and Tsagalis 2012:517–530.

Trapp, M. B. 1994. *Maximus Tyrius: Dissertationes*. Stuttgart: de Gruyter.

Traugott, E. C., and R. B. Dasher. 2002. *Regularity in Semantic Change*. Cambridge: Cambridge University Press.

Travlos, I. N. 1971. *Bildlexikon zur Topographie des antiken Athen*. Tübingen: E. Wasmuth.

Treu, M. 1955. *Von Homer zur Lyrik*. Munich: Beck.

Trowbridge, M. A., and W. A. Oldfather. 1935. "Naupaktos." In *Paulys Realencyclopädie der classischen Altertumswissenschaft*, vol. 16.2, ed. G. Wissowa and W. Kroll, cols. 1979–2002. Stuttgart: Alfred Druckenmüller.

Tsagalis, C. 2004. *Epic Grief: Personal Laments in Homer's "Iliad."* Berlin: de Gruyter.

———. 2006. "Poet and Audience: From Homer to Hesiod." In *La poésie épique grecque: Métamorphoses d'un genre littéraire*, ed. F. Montanari and A. Rengakos, 79–130. Geneva: Fondation Hardt.

———. 2007. "The Metaphor of Sailing and the *Athlon* of Song: Reconsidering the 'Nautilia' in Hesiod's *Works and Days*." In *Άθλα και έπαθλα στα ομηρικά έπη*, ed. M. Paizi-Apostolopoulou, A. Rengakos, and C. Tsagalis, 269–295. Ithaca, Greece: Center for Odyssean Studies.

———. 2008. *The Oral Palimpsest: Exploring Intertextuality in the Homeric Epics*. Washington, DC: Center for Hellenic Studies.

———. 2009a. "Naming Helen." In **Ἀντιφίλησις: Studies on Classical, Byzantine, and Modern Greek Literature and Culture*, ed. E. Karamalengou and E. Makrygianni, 39–47. Stuttgart: Steiner.

———. 2009b. "Poetry and Poetics in the Hesiodic Corpus." In Montanari, Rengakos, and Tsagalis 2009:131–177.

———. 2011. "Towards an Oral, Intertextual Neoanalysis." *Trends in Classics* 3:209–244.

———. 2012. *From Listeners to Viewers: Space in the "Iliad."* Washington DC: Center for Hellenic Studies.

———. 2014. "Preface." *Trends in Classics* 6:239–246.

Tsirpanlis, E. C. 1966. "Patronymics in Homer." *Platon* 35/36:241–256.

Tsopanakis, A. 1984. "Σύμμεικτα κυπριακά." *Hellenika* 35:389–401.

Turner, M. 1996. *The Literary Mind*. New York: Oxford University Press.

———. 2015. "Blending in Language and Communication." In *Handbook of Cognitive Linguistics*, ed. E. Dabrowska and D. Divjak, 211–232. Berlin: de Gruyter.

Urban, G. 1996. "Entextualization, Replication, and Power." In *Natural Histories of Discourse*, ed. M. Silverstein and G. Urban, 21–44. Chicago: University of Chicago Press.

Vandelanotte, L. 2009. *Speech and Thought Representation in English: A Cognitive-Functional Approach*. Berlin: de Gruyter.

van der Heide, N. 2008. *Spirited Performance: The Manas Epic and Society in Kyrgyzstan*. Tilburg: Rozenberg.

———. 2015. *Spirited Performance: The Manas Epic and Society in Kyrgyzstan*. Bremen: EVH Academic Press.

van der Valk, M. H. A. L. H. 1952. "Ajax and Diomede in the *Iliad*." *Mnemosyne* 5:269–286.

Van Nortwick, T. 2001. "Like a Woman: Hector and the Boundaries of Masculinity." *Arethusa* 34:221–235.

van Thiel, H. 1982. *Iliaden und Ilias*. Basel: Schwabe.

———. 1991. *Homeri Odyssea*. Hildesheim: Olms.

———. 1996. *Homeri Ilias*. Hildesheim: Olms.

van Wees, H. 1992. *Status Warriors: War, Violence, and Society in Homer and History*. Amsterdam: Gieben.

———. 1996. "Growing Up in Early Greece: Heroic and Aristocratic Educations." In *Education in Greek Fiction*, ed. A. H. Sommerstein and C. Atherton, 1–20. Bari: Levante.

Vasi antichi. Museo Archeologico Nazionale di Napoli. 2009. Naples: Electa.

Vasiliev, N. (Н. Васильев). 1907. "Из наблюдений над отражением личности в былинах." *Известия отделения русского языка и словесности Академии Наук* 12:170–196.

Vendries, C. 1999. "Les concours musicaux dans le Péloponnèse sous le Haut-Empire: L'exemple de Corinthe." In *Le Péloponnèse: Archéologie et histoire*, ed. J. Renard, 269–285. Rennes: Presses universitaires de Rennes.

Vergados, A. 2014. "Form and Function of Some Theban References in Homer's *Iliad* and *Odyssey*." *Trends in Classics* 6:437–451.

Verhagen, A. 2005. *Constructions of Intersubjectivity: Discourse, Syntax, and Cognition*. New York: Cambridge University Press.

Vermeule, E. 1979. *Aspects of Death in Early Greek Art and Poetry*. Berkeley: University of California Press.

Veselovsky, A. 1873. "Die Russische Todtenklagen." *Russische Revue* 12:487–524.

Vidan, A. 2003. *Embroidered with Gold, Strung with Pearls: The Traditional Ballads of Bosnian Women*. Cambridge, MA: The Milman Parry Collection of Oral Literature.

Visser, E. 1988. "Formulae or Single Words? Toward a New Theory on Homeric Verse-Making." *Würzburger Jahrbücher für die Altertumswissenschaft* 14:21–37.

Voigt, C. 1934. *Überlegung und Entscheidung: Studien zur Selbstauffassung des Menschen bei Homer.* Meisenheim: Anton Hain. [Rpt. 1972.]

von der Mühll, P. 1952. *Kritisches Hypomnema zur Ilias.* Basel: Reinhardt.

von Wilamowitz-Moellendorff, U. 1916. *Die Ilias und Homer.* 2nd ed. Berlin: Weidmann.

———. 1920. *Die Ilias und Homer.* Berlin: Weidmann.

Vos, M. F. 1986. "Aulodic and Auletic Contests." In *Enthousiasmos: Essays on Greek and Related Pottery*, ed. H. Brijder, 121–130. Amsterdam: Allard Pierson Museum.

Wackernagel, J. 1916. *Sprachliche Untersuchungen zu Homer.* Göttingen: Vandenhoeck and Ruprecht.

———. 2009. *Lectures on Syntax, with Special Reference to Greek, Latin, and Germanic.* Ed. and trans. D. Langslow. Oxford: Oxford University Press.

Wade-Gery, H. T. 1952. *The Poet of the "Iliad."* Cambridge: Cambridge University Press.

Wakker, G. C. 2002. "Une première description de ἤδη chez Xénophon." *Syntaktika* 23:1–14.

Wallace, R. W. 2004. "Damon of Oa: A Political Theorist Ostracized?" In *Music and the Muses: The Culture of Mousikē in the Classical Athenian City*, ed. P. Murray and P. Wilson, 249–267. Oxford: Oxford University Press.

Walsh, G. B. 1990. "Surprised by Self: Audible Thought in Hellenistic Poetry." *Classical Philology* 85:1–21.

Warner, R. 1972. *Thucydides: The History of the Peloponnesian War.* London: Penguin Classics.

Watkins, C. 1995. *How to Kill a Dragon: Aspects of Indo-European Poetics.* Oxford: Oxford University Press.

Watkins, M. H. 1943. "The West African 'Bush' School." *American Journal of Sociology* 48:666–675.

Wentzel, G. 1895. "Aristokles." *Realencyclopädie der classischen Altertumswissenschaft* II.1, cols. 936–937. Stuttgart: Metzler.

West, M. L. 1966. *Hesiod: Theogony.* Oxford: Clarendon Press.

———. 1978. "Phocylides." *Journal of Hellenic Studies* 98:164–167.

———. 1981. "The Singing of Homer and the Modes of Early Greek Music." *Journal of Hellenic Studies* 101:113–129.

———. 1985. *The Hesiodic Catalogue of Women: Its Nature, Structure, and Origins.* Oxford: Oxford University Press.

———. 1992. *Ancient Greek Music.* Oxford: Clarendon Press.

———. 1997. *The East Face of Helicon: West Asiatic Elements in Greek Poetry and Myth.* Oxford: Oxford University Press.

———. 1998, 2000. *Homerus Ilias.* 2 vols. Stuttgart: Teubner.

———. 1999. "The Invention of Homer." *Classical Quarterly* 49:364–382.

———. 2001. *Studies in the Text and Transmission of the "Iliad."* Munich: Saur.

———. 2002a. "The View from Lesbos." In *Epea Pteroenta: Beiträge zur Homer-*

forschung. Festschrift für Wolfgang Kullmann zum 75. Geburtstag, ed. M. Reichel and A. Rengakos, 207–220. Stuttgart: Steiner.

———. 2002b. "'Eumelos': A Corinthian Epic Cycle?" *Journal of Hellenic Studies* 122:109–133.

———. 2003a. *Greek Epic Fragments from the Seventh to the Fifth Centuries BC*. Cambridge, MA: Harvard University Press.

———. 2003b. *Homeric Hymns, Homeric Apocrypha, Lives of Homer*. Cambridge, MA: Harvard University Press.

———. 2007. *Indo-European Poetry and Myth*. Oxford: Oxford University Press.

———. 2010a. "Rhapsodes at Festivals." *Zeitschrift für Papyrologie und Epigraphik* 173:1–13.

———. 2010b. "Rhapsodes at Festivals: Addenda." *Zeitschrift für Papyrologie und Epigraphik* 174:32.

———. 2011a. *The Making of the "Iliad": Disquisition and Analytical Commentary*. Oxford: Oxford University Press.

———. 2011b. "Rhapsodes." In Finkelberg 2011.

West, S. 1988. "Homer *Odyssey*: Books I–IV." In *A Commentary on Homer's "Odyssey," vol. 1: Introduction, Books I–VIII*, ed. A. Heubeck, S. West, and J. B. Hainsworth. Oxford: Clarendon Press.

———. 2012. "Some Reflections of Alpamysh." In Montanari, Rengakos, and Tsagalis 2012:531–541.

Whallon, W. 1979. "Is Hector *Androphonos*?" In *Arctouros. Hellenic Studies Presented to Bernard M. W. Knox on the Occasion of His 65th Birthday*, ed. W. G. Bowersock, W. Burkert, and C. J. Putnam, 19–24. Berlin: de Gruyter.

Whitmarsh, T. 2004. "The Cretan Lyre Paradox: Mesomedes, Hadrian, and the Poetics of Patronage." In *Paideia: The World of the Second Sophistic*, ed. B. E. Borg, 377–402. Berlin: de Gruyter.

Wilce, J. M. 2009. *Crying Shame: Metaculture, Modernity, and the Exaggerated Death of Lament*. Malden, MA: Wiley-Blackwell.

Wilhelm, A. 1905. "Zwei Denkmäler des eretrischen Dialekts." *Jahreshefte des Österreichischen Archäologischen Instituts* 8:6–17.

Willcock, M. M. 2002. "Menelaus in the *Iliad*." In *Epea Pteroenta: Beiträge zur Homerforschung. Festschrift für Wolfgang Kullmann zum 75. Geburtstag*, ed. M. Reichel and A. Rengakos, 221–229. Stuttgart: Steiner.

———. 2004. "Traditional Epithets." In *Antike Literatur in neuer Deutung. Festschrift für Joachim Latacz anlässlich seines 70. Geburtstages*, ed. A. Bierl, A. Schmitt, and A. Willi, 51–62. Munich: Saur.

Williams, B. 1993. *Shame and Necessity*. Berkeley: University of California Press.

Williams, D. 1980. "Ajax, Odysseus, and the Arms of Achilles." *Antike Kunst* 23:137–145.

Wills, J. 1996. *Repetition in Latin Poetry: Figures of Allusion*. Oxford: Clarendon Press.

Wilson, D. F. 2002. *Ransom, Revenge, and Heroic Identity in the "Iliad."* Cambridge: Cambridge University Press.

Wilson, E. O. 2002. *The Future of Life*. New York: Random House.

Wilson, P. 2009. "Thamyris the Thracian: The Archetypal Wandering Poet?" In Hunter and Rutherford 2009:46–79.

Winner, T. 1958. *The Oral Art and Literature of the Kazakhs of Russian Central Asia*. Durham, NC: Duke University Press.

Winter, N. 1993. *Greek Architectural Terracottas*. Oxford: Oxford University Press.

Wissman, J. 2009. "Athena's 'Unreasonable Advice': The Education of Telemachus in Ancient Interpretations of Homer." *Greek, Roman, and Byzantine Studies* 49:413–452.

Worman, N. 2002. *The Cast of Character: Style in Greek Literature*. Austin: University of Texas Press.

Wörrle, M. 1988. *Stadt und Fest im kaiserzeitlichen Kleinasien: Studien zu einer agonistischen Stiftung aus Oinoanda*. Munich: Beck.

Worthington, I. 2007. "Rhetoric and Politics in Classical Greece: Rise of the *Rhētores*." In *A Companion to Greek Rhetoric*, ed. I. Worthington, 255–271. Malden, MA: Blackwell.

Wyatt, W. F. 1999. *Homer "Iliad."* 2 vols. Rev. ed. Cambridge, MA: Harvard University Press.

Yamagata, N. 1994. *Homeric Morality*. Leiden: Brill.

Yankah, K. 2012. *The Proverb in the Context of Akan Rhetoric*. 2nd ed. New York: Diaspora Africa Press.

Yon, M., et al. 2004. *Kition dans les textes: Testimonia littéraires et épigraphiques et corpus des inscriptions*. Paris: Recherche sur les Civilisations.

Zanetto, G. 2006 [1988]. *Inni omerici*. 3rd ed. Milan: Bibliotheca Universale Rizzoli.

Zanker, G. 1996. *The Heart of Achilles: Characterization and Personal Ethics in the "Iliad."* Ann Arbor: University of Michigan Press.

Zanker, P. 1995. *The Mask of Socrates: The Image of the Intellectual in Antiquity*. Trans. H. A. Shapiro. Berkeley: University of California Press.

Zhirmunsky, V. (В. Жирмунский). 1962. *Народный Героический Эпос: Сравнительно-исторические очерки*. Moscow: Государственное Издательство Художественной Литературы.

Ziegler, K. 1988 (1934). *L'epos ellenistico: Un capitolo dimenticato della poesia greca*. 2nd ed. with an appendix (*Ennio poeta epico ellenistico*) by F. de Martino. Bari: Levante.

Ziehen, L. 1949. "Panathenaia." *Real-Encyclopädie der classischen Altertumswissenschaft* 18.2:457–493.

Zschietzschmann, W. 1931. "Homer und die attische Bildkunst um 560." *Jahrbuch des Deutschen Archäologischen Instituts* 46:45–60.

Notes on Contributors

MARY R. BACHVAROVA is a professor of classics at Willamette University. She is the author of *From Hittite to Homer: The Anatolian Background of Ancient Greek Epic* (2016).

DEBORAH BECK is an associate professor of classics at the University of Texas at Austin. Among the books she has published is *Speech Presentation in Homeric Epic* (2012).

ANNA BONIFAZI is a professor of linguistics at the University of Cologne. Her books include *Homer's Versicolored Fabric: The Evocative Power of Ancient Greek Epic Word-Making* (2012).

SHERAMY BUNDRICK is a professor of art history at the University of South Florida St. Petersburg. She is the author of *Music and Image in Classical Athens* (2005).

JOEL P. CHRISTENSEN is an associate professor of classical studies at Brandeis University. His most recent book is *The Homeric Battle of the Frogs and Mice* (with Erik Robinson, 2018).

ANNE GANGLOFF is a lecturer at the University of Rennes 2 and a member of the Institut Universitaire de France. She is the author of *Dion Chrysostome et les mythes: Hellénisme, communication et philosophie politique* (2006).

LORENZO F. GARCIA JR. is an associate professor of classics at the University of New Mexico. He is the author of *Homeric Durability: Telling Time in the "Iliad"* (2013).

ADRIAN KELLY is an associate professor of classical languages and literature at the University of Oxford. He is the author of *A Referential Commentary and Lexicon to Homer, "Iliad" VIII* (2007).

OLGA LEVANIOUK is an associate professor of classics at the University of Washington. She is the author of *Eve of the Festival: Making Myth in "Odyssey" 19* (2011).

JAMES O'MALEY is a lecturer in the history of ideas at Trinity College, Melbourne. His book *Storytelling and the Presentation of the Past in the "Iliad"* is currently under contract.

JONATHAN L. READY is an associate professor of classical studies at Indiana University. His books include *The Homeric Simile in Comparative Perspectives: Oral Traditions from Saudi Arabia to Indonesia* (2018).

CHRISTOS C. TSAGALIS is a professor of Greek at the Aristotle University of Thessaloniki. His most recent book is *Early Greek Epic Fragments I: Antiquarian and Genealogical Epic* (2017).

Index of Terms

Index of Passages